Lutheran Worship
History and Practice

To Sharon —

On the Occasion of the
53rd Convention
of the Texas District of
the Lutheran Church —
Missouri Synod.

June 23-26, 1994

.- Power to be his Witnesses -.

David

Lutheran Worship
History and Practice

Edited by
Fred L. Precht

Authorized by
The Commission on Worship
of
The Lutheran Church—Missouri Synod

Publishing House
St. Louis

Copyright © 1993 Concordia Publishing House
3558 S. Jefferson Avenue, St. Louis, MO 63118-3968
Manufactured in the United States of America

Library of Congress Cataloging-in-Publication Data

Lutheran worship : history and practice / James L. Brauer and Fred L. Precht, editors ;
    authorized by the Commission on Worship of the Lutheran Church—Missouri Synod.
        p.   cm.
    Includes bibliographical references (pp. 578–96) and index.
    ISBN 0-570-04255-0
    1. Lutheran Church—Missouri Synod—Liturgy. 2. Lutheran Church—Liturgy. I. Brauer, James Leonard. II. Precht, Fred L., 1916– . III. Lutheran Church—Missouri Synod. Commission on Worship. IV. Lutheran Church—Missouri Synod. Lutheran worship. Altar Book.
    BX8067.A1L82   1993
    264' .041322—dc20   93-23460

2   3   4   5   6   7   8   9   10   02   01   00   99   98   97   96   95   94

Contents

CONTENTS

CONTENTS

CONTENTS

Preface

One can imagine various first impressions when this book is opened. Some may say, "This is too much; it surely can't be this complicated." Others may say, "This doesn't provide enough help; I want something more practical." Or, "It's too parochial. Where's the big sweep of history?" Each reader will have sensed some of the frustration of being limited to one volume. Not every current topic and issue about worship could be addressed.

In this book the Commission on Worship seeks to provide sound, concise, and precise information on the history and practice of corporate worship in Word and Sacrament in The Lutheran Church—Missouri Synod. Many of the authors herein were personally involved in developing *Lutheran Worship* and its supporting volumes. While they may reveal details of their work, they perhaps do an even greater service by sharing an attitude, an understanding, and a spirit about corporate worship. This will be helpful to those who shape and lead worship, pastors, assisting ministers, church musicians, but also to seminarians, members of parish worship committees, and those interested in worship and its renewal.

As these pages demonstrate, theology and practice are intertwined. The practical interacts with, indeed, should be drawn from, the theological. When *Lutheran Worship* was first introduced, little of this supporting material was available and present readers might ask, "Why didn't you tell me this before?" Perhaps some will discover that for ten years they were using the services in this book in a way that was hardly intended. But that would be all the more reason to provide this book for worship leaders. It is more likely that many chapters will give new clarification to what is happening in our corporate worship and will reveal riches where heretofore there seemed to be none.

The "history" in this work grows from Lutheran understandings. For readers who are acquainted with the explosion of literature about liturgy in the last fifty years, there may be a desire to relate the contents of *Lutheran Worship* more strongly to the early church or to recent ecumenical trading of ideas and materials. These topics must await other volumes. What is here provides background to the materials in *Lutheran Worship* and to the theological expressions of a particular church, revealed in its official worship materials. Clearly, Luther's insights are still informing and guiding Lutherans of the late 20th century as they did Missouri Synod founders 150 years ago.

Current issues are not the focus. Challenges from individualism ("my music" and "my style") and "non-liturgical alternatives" are increasing in the 1990s. It is certainly better to address them knowing about the past than by being ignorant of the past. Especially, knowing what was intended in the published materials will help develop honest and informed responses to new situations. Thus, no excuse need be offered for telling what happened up to a certain point and what guided certain choices in the worship materials. That's enough of a contribution for one book.

While the editorial process has tried to unify the work of the various authors, the integrity of each chapter as a resource also had to permit some overlap. A lack of unanimity may still be evident here and there because fairness to each writer required caution in shaping material to fit with others. When contrasting viewpoints had to be melded, a guiding principle was this: what was intended, as well as it could be determined, when the preparers of the *Lutheran Worship* materials did their work. May this companion to *Lutheran Worship* help worship leaders serve God's people with a richness of Word and Sacrament that leads to heartfelt prayer and praise.

JAMES L. BRAUER

The Presentation of Our Lord, 1991

Contributors

James L. Brauer, S.T.M., S.M.M., Ph.D., associate professor of practical theology and chaplain at Concordia Seminary, St. Louis; faculty member of Concordia College, Bronxville, N. Y. (1965–87); member of the Special Hymnal Review Committee of The Lutheran Church—Missouri Synod (1977–78); executive director of the Commission on Worship (1987–91).

Paul G. Bunjes, Ph.D., Litt.D., associate and professor of music theory and organ (1951–83); chairman, music department (1961–77) at Concordia College, now Concordia University, River Forest, Ill.; designer of pipe organs; member of Missouri Synod's Commission on Worship and Inter-Lutheran Commission on Worship; music editor of and contributor to *Lutheran Worship*; author, composer, editor of *The Service Propers Noted, The Formulary Tones Annotated, The Praetorius Organ,* and *Musikdrucke Rhau V*; professor emeritus 1983.

Donald L. Deffner, Th.M, Ph.D., guest professor and chairman, pastoral ministry department, Concordia Theological Seminary, Ft. Wayne, Ind. (1987ff.); campus pastor, University of California-Berkeley (1947–59); professor, Concordia Seminary, St. Louis (1959–69); professor, Pacific Lutheran Theological Seminary and the Graduate Theological Union, Berkeley (1969–87); emeritus since 1990.

Charles J. Evanson, B.A., B.D., formerly of St. Matthew Lutheran Church, Stratford, Ontario, Canada; St. John's, Detroit; Christ English, Chicago; presently pastor of Redeemer Lutheran Church, Ft. Wayne, Ind.; frequent lecturer in areas of liturgy and church music; secretary of Liturgical Texts and Music Committee of the Missouri Synod's Commission on Worship in the production of *Lutheran Worship* (1979–81); secretary of the Commission on Worship (1981–90).

Alfred E. Fremder, Ph.D., associate professor practical theology, coordinator of music and cultural activities, and chaplain at Concordia Seminary, St. Louis; member of the Missouri Synod's Commission on Worship (1978–86); chairman of its Hymn Text and Music Committee (1978–82); chairman of the Commission on Worship (1980–82), the years *Lutheran Worship* was prepared for publication; professor emeritus July 1991.

David Held, D.M.A. in church music; professor of music and chairperson of the music division, Concordia College, Seward, Neb.; chairman of the Introductory Process Committee (1979–82) for *Lutheran Worship* (1982); member of the Commission on Worship of The Lutheran Church—Missouri Synod (1982–85).

F. Samuel Janzow, Ph.D., served pastorates in Minnesota and London, England (1936–54); professor of English literature at Concordia College, now Concordia University, River Forest, Ill. (1954–89); author of *Luther's Large Catechism: A Contemporary Translation with Study Questions* (1978); member of the Missouri Synod's Commission on Worship and of its Hymn Text and Music Committee in the production of *Lutheran Worship*.

Arthur A. Just, Jr., S.T.M., Ph.D., associate professor of pastoral theology at Concordia Theological Seminary, Ft. Wayne, Ind.

Edward Klammer, LL.D., manager, music department of Concordia Publishing House (1950–84); music editor of choral, organ, and instrumental publications; music director, Resurrection Lutheran Church, Sappington, Mo. (1957–81); member of the Hymn Text Committee of the Inter-Lutheran Commission on Worship in the production of *Lutheran Book of Worship* (1978); member of the Commission on Worship of the Missouri Synod (1979–80); project director of *Lutheran Worship* (1982) for Concordia Publishing House.

Norman E. Nagel, M.Div., Ph.D., professor of doctrinal theology and chairman of its department, Concordia Seminary, St. Louis; pastor of Luther-Tyndale Church, London, England (1954–57); preceptor of Westfield House, Cambridge University (1962–68); professor of theology, dean of Chapel of the Resurrection, university preacher, Valparaiso, Ind. (1968–83); member of the Missouri Synod's Commission on Worship and of its Liturgical Text and Music Committee (1978–84) in the production of *Lutheran Worship*.

CONTRIBUTORS

Roger D. Pittelko, Th.D., president of the English District of The Lutheran Church—Missouri Synod; member of the Commission on Worship (1981–89) and chairman (1982–89) in the production of *Lutheran Worship* and its companion volumes; lecturer and writer on the services and rites in *Lutheran Worship* and *Lutheran Worship: Agenda* (1984).

John T. Pless, M.Div., pastor of University Lutheran Chapel (University of Minnesota), Minneapolis; author of articles on liturgy in a variety of publications; author of "Liturgy and Adiaphora in the Lutheran Confessions" in *Let Every Tongue Confess: Essays in Honor of Norman Nagel on the Occasion of his Sixty-Fifth Birthday*; contributing editor of the *Forum Letter* and book review editor of the *Bride of Christ*.

Fred L. Precht, M.Mus., Th.D, professor of worship and music, dean of chapel (1940–68; 1972–76), Concordia Theological Seminary, Springfield, Ill.; member of Missouri Synod's Commission on Worship (1965–75) and the Inter-Lutheran Commission on Worship (1966–1976); executive secretary of Commission on Worship (1978–87) in the production of *Lutheran Worship* and its companion volumes; author of *Handbook to Lutheran Worship* (1992); retired June 1987.

Robert C. Sauer, D.D., third vice-president of The Lutheran Church—Missouri Synod; first vice-president (1981–86); fourth vice-president (1977–79); USAF chaplain in the Korean conflict; vice-president of the Synod's Missouri District (1987–89); represented the Synod's president on the Commission on Worship during the production of *Lutheran Worship*; author of *Daily Prayer* (2 vols.) for Lutheran pastors and *The Church Takes Shape*, a church history study for Lutheran high school juniors.

Carl F. Schalk, M.Mus., M.A.R., LL.D., L.H.D., professor of music, teacher of graduate and undergraduate courses in church music and liturgy at Concordia University, River Forest, Ill.; extensive writer on church music; his original hymns appear in the hymnals of most major denominations, his choral works and hymn concertatos are widely sung; *Luther on Music: Paradigms of Praise* (1988) is his most recent book.

Wayne E. Schmidt, M.S., M.Mus., Ph.D., Concordia Seminary, St. Louis, professor of practical theology, chairman of the department of practical theology, and director of graduate studies; campus pastor, Madison, Wis. (1971–75); principal of Luther High School, Onalaska, Wis. (1957–71); pastor, Lena/Oconto Falls, Wis. (1955–57); instructor, Dr. Martin Luther College, New Ulm, Minn. (1948–50).

Jaroslav J. Vajda, M.Div., Litt.D., Lutheran Church—Missouri Synod pastor (1945–63); magazine and book editor, Concordia Publishing House (1963–86); member of the Hymn Text Committee of the Synod's Commission on Worship (1960-78); member of the Hymn Text Committee of the Inter–Lutheran Commission on Worship (1967–78); author and translator of numerous hymns, conductor of hymn writing and worship workshops; pastor emeritus July 1986.

Abbreviations

AC	Augsburg Confession (1530)
AE	*Luther's Works*, American Edition
Ap	Apology of the Augsburg Confession (1531)
BSLK	*Die Bekenntnisschriften der evangelische-lutherische Kirche*
CP	*Congregational Praise* (1951)
EH	*English Hymnal* (1906)
EpH	*The Hymnal 1940*
FC Ep	Formula of Concord Epitome (1577)
FC SD	Formula of Concord Solid Declaration (1577)
GW	Wilhelm Löhe, *Gesammelte Werke* (1951–85)
HCS	*Hymnal for Colleges and Schools* (1956)
ILCW	Inter-Lutheran Commission on Worship
LBW	*Lutheran Book of Worship* (1978)
LC	Large Catechism (1529)
LW	*Lutheran Worship* (1982)
SA	Smalcald Articles (1537)
SBH	*Service Book and Hymnal* (1958)
SC	Small Catechism (1529)
SoP	*Songs of Praise* (1931)
TDNT	*Theological Dictionary of the New Testament* (1964–74)
TLH	*The Lutheran Hymnal* (1941)
Tr	Treatise on the Power and Primacy of the Pope (1537)
WA	*D. Martin Luther's Werke*, Weimar Ausgabe
WA TR	*D. Martin Luther's Werke*, Weimar Ausgabe Tischreden
WS	*Worship Supplement* (1969)

1

Liturgical Renewal
in the Parish

Arthur A. Just

A chapter on liturgical renewal suggests that liturgy is in need of renewal. Liturgical renewal is an issue these days and has been a concern of the Lutheran Church since the Reformation in the sixteenth century.[1] There would be no talk of renewal if people were satisfied with their liturgical life or were convinced that the liturgy had meaning for them.

Discussing liturgical renewal tempts one to give what people want—a panacea, a recipe, a perfect liturgy, ten steps to a contemporary, Lutheran, liturgical Church. Such an approach centers on *tactics* of renewal, another how-to manual toward relevant liturgy that, next year, would be totally irrelevant.[2] The Roman Catholic Church, with its rich and ancient liturgical heritage, the seedbed for our own Lutheran liturgy, has succumbed to liturgical trends. This is borne out by a cursory reading of the literature on the liturgical movement since Vatican II (1962–65). The search goes on for the perfect liturgy, for the secret to liturgical renewal, and thus far, no one has *the* answer. The tactical approach to liturgical renewal never satisfies. It ignores the complexity of the context in which liturgy is acted out, confusing a church that has liturgies with a liturgical church. This approach assumes that the liturgical structures need to be renewed; but what is good for one congregation may be a disaster for another.

But perhaps this is assuming too much. Perhaps what is wrong is not the liturgy but those who do the liturgy. The targets of liturgical renewal are the clergy and the congregation. The problems are less liturgical and more theological, centering more in our anthropology and ecclesiology than our liturgiology. What is wrong is not the liturgy but the culture, and thus, instead of constantly asking "What's wrong with the liturgy?" we should be asking "What's wrong with the culture?"— concentrating our attention on the renewal of the culture through liturgy, not vice versa. The goal of good liturgy is always to transform the lives of people [the transforming of culture] by the Gospel of Jesus Christ. This is hardly accomplished if the liturgy is subjected to the whimsies of culture. Culture, untransformed by liturgy, in effect destroys that liturgy. The church becomes indistinguishable from the culture and the Gospel is lost. This is the real secularization and destruction of the Gospel.[3]

Because this is true, then our approach cannot be *tactical* but must be *strategical*. Our run at renewal comes from viewing the whole life of the church through the liturgy, a holistic view that calls for strategy, not tactics. A tactical approach trivializes our life in Christ, focusing that life on today's relevancies and today's style. A strategical approach is focused more on reverence than on relevance, more on renewal of substance than on renewal of form, more on theology than on practice. If we are reverent in worship, we will be relevant; if our life in Christ is substantial, we will develop forms to support that life; if our vision is biblically theological, we will be confessionally practical.[4]

Such an approach may disappoint those looking for the once-and-for-all liturgy. A cut-and-paste approach is presumptuous and flies in the face of tradition, succumbing to the current liturgical trend of decreeing, from above, what true liturgy should be. In our changing culture, today's congregations are often too likely to subject the liturgy to the same criteria by which they judge everything else in society: if it doesn't work, fix it, change it, tinker with it until it's right. After all, this is what we do with our cars, our marriages, our lifestyles, and sadly, with our theology. Liturgy and theology should not conform to this world, but should transform the world. One of the worst results of the liturgical movement in the sixties and seventies was the notion that there must be change for the sake of change.[5] Liturgical surprises were so frequent as to be unsurprising. The faithful, who knew the liturgy from their youth, were stumbling through pages and inserts so that worship measured the dexterity of their fingers and the quickness of their minds. No one would argue against change if something needed changing. But it is a cultural assumption that it is the liturgy that needs to be changed, when, as we have already suggested, it is we who need to be changed through the liturgy, for here Jesus Christ comes to us most completely, Sunday in and Sunday out. Although there are many lay people in our congregations who are dissatisfied with our liturgies, there are many more who are very satisfied. Perhaps it is pastors who are bored with the liturgy and demand the changes. Liturgical conferences become sales promotions for the latest fads.[6] The liturgical movement must give priority to restoring the liturgy to the faithful, to recognizing that the liturgy does not belong exclusively to any one congregation, to the clergy, or to the synodical office. It belongs to the whole church as it is expressed in a congregation. With the invention of the Gutenberg press, the notion that liturgy was the text, which could be edited or rewritten or even frozen in time, gradually became dominant. Since liturgy is an expression of God's people connected to his Word, lasting liturgical change comes from below, from the congregation, and not from above, from commissions on worship.

But this view must be tempered lest we find ourselves returning to those makeshift liturgies of our very recent past. This requires a hard look at who we are as The Lutheran Church—Missouri Synod. We do have a tradition with a cultural and historical context, and that tradition is both evangelical and catholic, a tradition our forefathers attempted to shape into a very distinct Lutheran identity that mediated between our catholic and Reformation roots.[7] Luther was both catholic and evangelical. To resolve this tension, his followers decided to call themselves Lutheran. In many ways we are at a watershed in our history as our forefathers were in the 16th century. A battle is taking place for the heart and soul of our church. This battle is being waged between those who want to move toward an American form of Protestantism with Calvinistic roots and those who want to regain historical Lutheranism. At stake in liturgical renewal is nothing more and nothing less than the very ethos of our church.[8] One of the goals of Lutheran liturgical renewal is the development of a distinctly *Lutheran* ethos.

The problem today is that our congregations are generally uninstructed, not only in biblical theology and Lutheran liturgical traditions, but worse, they do not know the Lutheran tradition as a positive unfolding of the New Testament and early post-apostolic church, which in turn comes from the Old Testament as practiced by Jesus himself. They do not know what it means to be Lutheran. But people want to be Lutheran, and they accomplish this, they think, because they sing hymns that are foreign to them and listen to sermons that are without meaning for them. In the end, they mime those meaningless rituals we call liturgy. But those hymns and sermons and liturgies bind them together as Lutherans.[9] And, true to the nature of liturgy, its conservative character caters to the conservative history of our church body and helps to preserve its Lutheran identity.[10] If people lose their Lutheran identity, it will result in the irrecoverable loss of the liturgy, and the loss in each case would be a tragedy hard to imagine.

Concerned liturgical scholars are well aware of the consequences of lost liturgy and are equally aware of the sad state of biblical knowledge and traditional awareness in our congregations. They recognize that it is disastrous to leave the liturgy in the hands of people who know little of liturgy, theology, or Scripture. Thus, liturgy cannot be an exclusive enterprise from below, from congregations who are not in touch with their historical roots. We still need liturgical scholars to give us liturgy from above. The challenge for liturgical renewal today is to mediate between the two. How do we resolve the tension between the scholars and the people who actually do the liturgy? How can we incorporate the findings of liturgical studies into our tradition and make them our own? How we resolve this tension will determine whether our church remains Lutheran and retains both its Reformation and catholic foundations.

These questions can give rise to a methodology of liturgical renewal that may satisfy both the strategists and the tacticians. For as congregations see changes from the liturgical and cultural scholars sweeping over them, some criteria must be provided to enable them to judge these changes. This method of diagnosis will assist congregations and parish pastors in deciding whether or not these changes are good for them. The major question they must ask is, What needs to be renewed in our congregation? Answering the question will require them to become liturgical critics capable of analyzing liturgical structures and diagnosing liturgical diseases. Such liturgical renewal will have important side effects for theology, pastoral care, evangelism, catechesis, preaching, architecture, and language. But the real benefit is that this approach will allow congregations to do what they should be doing—developing their own liturgy within strict parameters by taking advantage of the expertise of liturgiologists who know the tradition and who are trying to be faithful to it.

The maxim of Prosper of Aquitaine bantered about in liturgical circles today ("The law of worshiping founds the law of believing") needs to be worked out in our church so that both scholars and people may be reconciled in their goals and the means to accomplish them. Our most recent tradition has in effect reversed that maxim to read: "The law of believing founds the law of worshiping." That may be true on one level in our church body, but on the congregational level, we who are so passionate about congregationalism need to recognize that if we want *orthodidaskalia* (right teaching) to be a leaven in our churches, then *orthodoxia* (right worship) must prevail and help to form *orthodidaskalia*. If this does not happen, we will continue to experience warped worship and with it warped doctrine. Only with a knowledge of Scripture and a clear head about liturgical tradition will we be able to approximate orthodoxy in the true sense of the word. Our "right worship," our "authentic orthodoxy," will be right for us because we are continually "rehearsing the faith of the fathers and then drawing its implications for today and tomorrow, playing the melody of theology and then developing variations on its ancient themes."[11]

Thus, the watchwords for our church must be *reverence*,[12] not relevance, *fidelity*, not innovation.[13] This will necessarily involve us with biblical theology, Christology, ecclesiology, eschatology, liturgical tradition, and the Reformation. For some lay people, these may be heady, irrelevant topics, let alone incomprehensible words. But when our people are at worship, regardless of whether they can pronounce the word and articulate the concept, they are engaging in all those heady topics and more. The goal of liturgical renewal in The Lutheran Church—Missouri Synod must be to give the worshiping community access to a Lutheran ethos that embraces the depth of our theology and the richness of our heritage. The parameters of this goal will be outlined here by looking at two areas of our liturgical life, which, if renewed, will influence all others: the renewal of the theology of worship and the renewal of time. On the basis of these two areas of renewal, a brief look at some practical ramifications will be considered in the renewal of space and rite.

Renewal of the Theology of Worship

An analysis of the congregation's understanding of the theology of worship is the first step toward liturgical renewal. Most congregations have never really asked what is taking place at worship. This becomes abundantly clear to many pastors when their board of elders begins to make delinquent calls and does not know how to respond to the question, Why should I go to worship? Perhaps some pastors would rather not face this question. Such a crisis comes from a less-than-adequate theology of worship and calls for a renewal of that theology. Governed by the watchwords of reverence and fidelity, this renewal involves the renewal of our belief in the real presence of Jesus Christ in worship and the renewal of our belief that Jesus Christ is present in worship to bind the church together as a community.

There appears to be no lack of reverence or fidelity to the Scriptures in our church body. Faithfulness to the scriptural witness has been the rallying cry of our church in the past two decades. Inerrancy, infallibility, and inspiration are bywords for all of us. But how do we account for the constant complaint that the Gospel is not heard enough in our sermons? How do we account for the biblical illiteracy among our congregations and their complaint about a lack of biblical preaching?[14] It appears as if biblical Christianity is almost an unknown in today's church. A possible reason for this is the absence of a biblical theology that employs real- presence hermeneutics. We say we believe in the real presence, but the question must be faced, How does it affect our faith? The presence of Jesus Christ in our worship as we assemble around Word and Sacrament is central to a Lutheran ethos. For any renewal of the theology of worship, there must first be a restoration of our belief that Jesus Christ is present and, more than that, that he is actively present to save us when we encounter him within the worshiping assembly.[15]

This is nothing more nor less than a recognition that a sacramental vision of the church must be present in our perception of the liturgy from the entrance hymn to the closing *Amen*. Worship can be nothing less than a recognition on a Sunday morning that a dynamic presence is among us. We must show that we truly believe in "the proclamation of the Word as actually moving into a man and taking hold of his whole being—pulling him inside out in conversion."[16] This is a powerful presence that is there whether it is a high church or a low church, whether the liturgy is done well or is done poorly. Our worship may be emotionally uplifting, "edifying, exciting, [and] entertaining,"[17] but unless there is an awareness of the presence of Jesus Christ in that worship and a belief that an encounter with that presence will radically change a person into one of God's very own, then worship is not everything it can, should, and *must* be.

We could go a long way toward restoring the real presence of Christ to the center of our liturgy if we would only recognize our Lord's presence with his people throughout their history. As we interpret the story of God's people in the Scripture, are we able to see the revelation of God's presence among those people in Jesus Christ as the center of that story? And are we able to see that the story of Abraham, Isaac, and Jacob, of Moses and Joshua, of David and Solomon, and the story of the Israelites is *our* story? We are also a pilgrim people making their way through the wilderness, supported and sustained on our trek by the very same presence that supported Moses and the Israelites on manna and the water from a rock. We are bound together as a community at worship by the common history that we, as the children of Adam and Eve, have for we are now one in Christ through Baptism.[18]

One of our principal responsibilities on Sunday mornings is to proclaim to each other, and to the world, that the kingdom of God in Jesus Christ is present among us. He has redeemed all of creation, recreating it in his image and restoring it by his grace. His presence has been with the world from the beginning of time with the singular purpose of accomplishing this redemption through suffering and sacrifice, through death and resurrection. Liturgy must straddle the gap of history so that all saints are joined in one worshiping assembly. For the Christian story is an eschatological one. The presence of the kingdom of God in the world's midst in Jesus Christ is the same yesterday, today, and tomorrow. We are on a historical and eschatological continuum. The liturgy helps us reinforce for one another our present position on the continuum where we have the same status in the kingdom of God as both the prophets of old and the saints in glory. In the words of Hebrews, we are surrounded by a cloud of witnesses who have gone before us. This is what our liturgy means when it says we celebrate the Lord's Supper "with angels and archangels and with all the company of heaven." The hiddenness of the kingdom in the world in no way vitiates against the present reality of that kingdom when we gather together as God's people in worship. If we are serious about liturgical renewal we must proclaim every Sunday that the kingdom of God is present among us. Liturgical renewal will only happen "when leaders of worship, faithful to the testimony, and expectant of the presence, are willing to celebrate the signs of the kingdom now at work in the world."[19] It cannot be historical repristination.

With such an eschatological view of reality that does not confine God's saving activity only to our space and time, a real-presence hermeneutics requires that we think twice about the metaphors we use in describing our worship. This leads us to our second consideration in a theology of worship: the renewal of our belief in the church as community. The metaphors we use to describe who we are and what we do reflect our theological vision. If a renewal of biblical theology allows the people of God to see themselves first and foremost as a community of saints, then they will no longer tolerate metaphors of their life that reflect the individualism of today's culture which has become pervasive in their lives. Our congregations need to bind themselves together as communities. Individualism is a chronic problem that undermines the corporate character of the Christian assembly. The tension between the individual character of society and the corporate character of the church cannot be allowed to be resolved by adapting the church to the culture. The culture must be shaped by the church. Without this victory of the church over culture, we have not overcome the world with our faith.

Liturgies catering to individuals will at times be exciting, entertaining, and edifying. Their responses will at most give immediate satisfaction. Liturgy as "education of surface memory" reduces worship to pedantry. This has been described as "the abstract character of Protestant worship today,"[20] which is the direct result of the loss of a sacramental understanding of the Bible that sees the real presence of Christ moving into the lives of people and changing them through the Gospel. Preaching and sacramental piety are separated and the Gospel is ultimately lost. When our concern is education of surface memory, then our basis for any liturgy becomes superficial, and our theology is destroyed.

Such commonplace metaphors as the "service station," the "commissary," the "distribution center of grace" will not serve our theology because they appeal to the individual who sees worship as the time to tank up intellectually and emotionally for another run at the world. Each individual, like a car pulling up for gas, receives a supply of moral imperatives for the week so that he or she can fight the battle alone in the wilderness.[21] It is fine that the individual is educated in the proper moral behavior according to prescribed spiritual laws. Certainly this view does not totally disregard the corporate nature of the church, for the distribution center where grace is dispensed is a corporate center. But unfortunately the vision is inward, the focus is on the individual, and the goal is superficial. The parishioner is apt to ask of worship, "What does this mean for me? What can I get out of this? What food for thought is there for me to take home for the week?" The subjectivism of such questions is superficial, touching the intellect and emotions, bringing satisfaction only for the moment.

This has serious ramifications not only for our liturgiology and ecclesiology, but for our missiology as well. Is it any wonder that our evangelism efforts are failing as we proceed through program after program after program? When the vision of the worshiper is inward and the goal educational, then it is almost impossible to shape an evangelical vision for the church that is outward and transforming. Our evangelism problems will not be reversed until the liturgy becomes the first priority of evangelism and the liturgiologists and missiologists begin talking with one another.

The corporate nature of the church is best served by a different approach. Some have suggested the "caravan" image, defined as "a more biblical view of the church as the pilgrim people of God under way from resurrection to parousia, from Baptism to death/resurrection."[22] Others have suggested the "faith-community" where "the passerby, or the inquirer, now comes into the community to taste its life."[23] In both descriptions, the focus is not on the individual but on the community, and the "pastoral work becomes community building, climaxed in roles of leadership in the Sunday assembly's common prayer."[24] The goal is formation of "deep memory" that gives the individual access to the "archetypal images"[25] of his eschatological destiny that are corporate, priestly, and christic. The liturgy actually involves the worshiper with Christ, and the real presence of the Sacrament permeates liturgy and preaching. This "deep memory" is reached by conversion through the Spirit, giving the individual help "to construct reality in a Christian way,"[26] a reality that is always corporate.

Christ is present throughout the service, not for himself, but for us, his community. The overarching concern is always the community. This conforms with Paul's image of the church as the body of Christ composed of individual members, but members who sacrifice their individuality for the sake of the church. They become like Christ by sacrificing themselves. There is diversity in the unity, but the dominating image is still the one body of Christ, the church:

> Make every effort to keep the unity of the Spirit through the bond of peace. There is one body and one Spirit—just as you were called to one hope when you were called—one Lord, one faith, one baptism, one God and Father of all, who is over all and through all and in all (Eph. 4:3–6).

Such a corporate model of the church is sacramental, and because it is sacramental the Gospel is glorified. The corporate life of the church is one in which the incarnated, crucified, risen, and ascended Lord is joined with the community at worship through Word and Sacrament. Through Baptism we are initiated into the Christian way of life; through the preaching of the Gospel and the Eucharist we are sustained in that life. This sustenance is not exclusively for our own benefit, for we are part of a caravan making its way through the wilderness toward the promised land. The tradition of Abraham and Israel is maintained. We are not "Lone Rangers" riding into town to stock up and then strike out to fight the battle alone. This romantic image may fit our American, western view of reality, but it hardly does justice to the biblical view of the church. The rugged individual will ultimately die a tragic death. The Old West was also made up of wagon trains that survived the onslaughts of the wilderness because they bound themselves together as a community. So also the church as caravan makes its trek, stopping by the oasis on Sunday to be refreshed; but as it sets out for another week, it sets out as community and survives as community.[27] It survives, not because of common economics or social similarities, but because it is the body of Christ and the members of this body are in Christ. This unity is not superficial. Reeducation can be helpful, but no education qualifies one to accept this position. An act of conversion forms us into Christian beings, and this conversion means a common Baptism.

The corporate model of the church and a real-presence hermeneutic will give rise to a renewal of the theology of worship. The vision of what we are about as the body of Christ gathered together for worship will fuel all other areas of liturgical renewal. For the liturgy will be seen as "the most potent, effective, and God-given weapon we have for the conversion of the world."[28] Liturgy will be an outward expression of the inward character of the hearts of the baptized who are one in Christ. Liturgy will be the outward expression of those who are coming to worship not to get something for themselves, but to give something of themselves, to serve as God's agents of renewal in the world by proclaiming to the world that Jesus Christ has redeemed that world through suffering, death, and resurrection. The achievement of this renewal requires reverence for the real presence of Christ in our midst and fidelity to the Word by which Christ is made present.

Renewal of Time

An analysis of the congregation's structuring of time is the second step toward liturgical renewal. This may sound like an obvious question to those who observe the church year, but there is increasing reluctance among our congregations to organize their time from Advent to the Sunday of the Fulfillment. The church year, however, gives to the congregation access to the life of Christ so that it may fully employ an understanding of the Bible in light of his real presence that forms it into the body of Christ. This is again a real-presence hermeneutic. Time has always been a critical commodity in the church, and the church has no other choice but to be a good steward of time.[29]

Time in the Christian sense is a servant of theology, and in this time the church has taken the incarnation and the crucifixion, the two scandals of Christianity, and raised them up to be the two great festivals of the church year, Christmas and Easter. These are the pivotal points of the liturgical year. Within sacred time, the church has harmonized the seasons of nature with the seasons of the church year. Thus, as nature experiences its yearly death in the fall and winter of the year, the church year focuses on judgment, the ultimate death of the world as we know it. The transition to Advent is a natural one, for the church now prepares for the birth of the Christ Child who tolls the death of the old world and the resurrection of the new one. When the sun reaches the point of death at the winter solstice and begins to rise again, the church celebrates the birth of the new world when "the sun of righteousness will rise with healing in its wings" (Mal. 4:2). Then Christian time goes on to coordinate the rebirth of nature in the spring and summer with images of new life through the resurrection of Jesus Christ. It is not a coincidence that Easter occurs in the spring. The themes of new birth and resurrection dominate, and Baptism becomes the reigning metaphor. The Pentecost season carries out the image of our full-grown, mature life in Christ as the summer fields become ripe with the fruits of God's creation. The church has transformed the world by its liturgy and served the Gospel's goal. The church has raised secular time to the level of the sacred. This sacred time becomes sacramental because Christ now appears in it for the benefit of his people.

A comparison between our marking of time and that of early Christians shows that we need a renewal of time. Recognition of the church year has been threatened by special interest groups who vie for the attention of the congregation. The specialization of our culture has often crept into the church year, revealing that liturgy and theology have been adapted to the culture:

> Our de facto calendar stresses human agency; that of the early
> church centered upon what God had done and continues to do

32

through the Holy Spirit. . . . Recovery of the church year can help us determine our real priorities. Keeping time with the rhythms of the early church can be a source of renewal for us today in sorting out our own priorities.[30]

If the congregation is not faithfully observing the church year, it is ignoring a premier opportunity to elevate the Gospel of him who dies and rises for the life of the world into the center of its life. *Reverence* of sacred time assists the congregation to believe that it worships a presence whose mighty deeds of salvation took place in time because that presence enfleshed itself in time and space. *Fidelity* to the historical acts of Jesus' life as marked in the church year allows the congregation to see that these past acts of salvation are now made present realities, that the future benefits of salvation are now available to the congregation sacramentally. Christian time is God's time; the church year is God bringing home his Son to the congregation year after year. The daily, weekly, yearly rhythm of commemorating the saving deeds of Jesus Christ forms the congregation into a Christian community living in time sanctified by Jesus Christ. As a restored creature of a restored creation, the Christian lives out his restored life in restored time within the framework of the church year.[31] Ordinary time has become sacred.

A life in restored time begins by restoring Sunday to its proper place as *the* holy day. A comparison between our marking of time and that of early Christians shows that we need a renewal of Sunday. For the first three hundred years of Christianity the church organized time by the week, and Sunday was the day of celebration of God's restored creation because God's Son rose from the dead on that day. It was regarded by early Christians as "the Lord's day . . . an eighth day of creation, a day beyond the Sabbath rest, 'the beginning of another world' . . . the beginning of both the first and the new creation . . .'the image of the age to come.' "[32] Reverence for Sunday as the holy day was the way early Christians gave thanks to God for the redemption of all creation in the death and resurrection of Jesus Christ, the way they petitioned him to continue to act redemptively in their midst through Word and Sacrament. Its view was eschatological, for it saw Sunday as the day in which the future blessings of the kingdom were now made present in the midst of the worshiping assembly. The celebration of the Lord's

Supper on the Lord's day demanded this eschatological view of Sunday and all of Christian worship:

> In the eucharist the church met the sacramentally present Christ, risen and bringing the new creation, risen and revealed to his disciples in the breaking of the bread. Eschatologically the meal was a participation in the end time—a foretaste of the kingdom rather than an expectation of its coming. Historically, it was a meeting with the crucified and risen Christ now present with his church rather than a recollection of the events of his career. Until the sixteenth century, we have no evidence of a significant Christian community that did not celebrate the eucharist on the Lord's day. But in the first century and the second, we have no evidence that any commemoration of a particular event ever helped shape a Lord's day celebration of the new creation. General commemorations of specific points in sacred history were not present until well into the fourth century. Until then, and for a long time after, the Lord's day simply marked the presence with his church of the resurrected Christ.[33]

The church's departure from this view of Sunday and Christian worship has affected its efforts at liturgical renewal. Although a return to pre-Constantinian Christianity is not our goal, early Christianity informs us once again that reverence and fidelity to sacred time is critical to liturgical renewal.

The role of liturgical preaching and catechesis is of vital importance in the congregation's renewal of time. Liturgical preaching and catechetics belong under the rubrics of *renewal of language*, but liturgical renewal of time will take place through liturgical preaching and catechetics. In both of them, the language and metaphors of Scripture must become the language and metaphors of our sermons and our catechesis. Scriptural language must again become the primary theological language of the congregation, a language that is rich in the stories, the images, and the people of the Bible. But today there is an expressed weariness with liturgical language in our churches. Again, the crisis is in the metaphors we use. How are kings and shepherds, priests and sacrifices relevant in our world? Changes have been tried. New metaphors have been suggested. Attempts have been made to develop a new liturgical language that has a contemporary sound to it. But the old images, though bound to a given time, are still universally understood, and

34

thus the language of Scripture is still the best vehicle for communicating the Gospel for it transcends all cultures.[34]

Those who want to modernize liturgical language devise new ways of telling the story. The goal is variety in worship, a goal that is demanded by our diverse society. This is a fair goal if all the old ways have been exhausted. But have they been tried? Variety is possible in every service if the church year is followed and the propers of the day are used.[35] Liturgical preaching recognizes the season of the year and the readings of the day, providing the hinge between the Service of the Word and the Service of Holy Communion by reflecting on how the Gospel, Old Testament Reading, Epistle, Introit, Psalm, and Collect present Christ to the people as they prepare to meet him in his Supper. Liturgical preaching assists the congregation to see how the liturgy is relevant for today.[36]

Catechesis also belongs to liturgical renewal, since it has always been understood as foundational for Baptism, the church's claim to be incorporated into Christ. Thus it is not surprising to find that catechesis is also suffering from the same malaise as preaching. A comparison with early Christian catechesis demonstrates that renewal is necessary. Catechesis was a vibrant force in the conversion of adults, shaped around the church year as the Lenten preparation for Baptism in the Easter vigil. For example, unknown to contemporary Christians is the genre of the mystagogical catechesis, a genre rich in biblical and sacramental theology. This method of catechetical instruction recreates for us a sense of the intensely practical and pastoral ambience that existed in early Christian communities. The actions of the liturgy were interpreted pastorally for the care of the souls of the newly baptized on the basis of a strong scriptural witness. These catecheses are drenched with scriptural references and allusions, for the catechumens needed to hear what the Bible had to say about the sacraments of Baptism and Eucharist, and how the liturgy was "Scripture's home rather than its stepchild, and the Hebrew and Christian Bibles were the church's first liturgical books."[37] The act of catechizing was within the context of the church year, an endeavor of uniting pastoral concerns for the catechumen's understanding of the sacraments with the biblical witness to them. Early Christian catechesis was reverent to the presence of the Holy Spirit in the act of conversion and faithful to the Word through which the Holy Spirit acted. Catechesis today must restore this reverence and fidelity if it is to serve the church in the renewal of the liturgy.

Reverence and fidelity to the church year allows congregations "to construct reality in a Christian way."[38] Through the church year, the incarnate Christ is present among them in time and speaks to them through their remembrance of the historical events of his life. The renewal of the liturgy necessitates a perception by the congregation that the church year is the primary means of ordering its life around the salvific events of Christ's life. This vision of life in Christ is sacramental and corporate in which all of time is filled by God's grace. Liturgical preaching and catechesis are the means by which this vision is shaped and sustained.

Renewal of Space and Rite

On the basis of a renewal of the theology of worship and a renewal of time, a more practical analysis of the congregation's structuring of space and rite is now possible. These two areas of renewal are intimately related because they deal with the two basic structures of Christian worship: the proclamation of the Word and the administration of Holy Communion. The way we structure our liturgical space and rites depends on our desire to make the Word of God accessible to the people in the liturgy of the Word, and the Supper of the Lord accessible to the people in the liturgy of Holy Communion. Here are the questions the church must face: Are our liturgical spaces reverent to the presence of Jesus Christ in Word and Sacrament? Are our liturgical rites faithful to Scripture and tradition that have handed down to us Word and Sacrament as the two basic synaxes of Christian worship that form Christians together as the body of Christ? These questions will make us diagnosticians of space and rite under the criteria of Word and Sacrament, criteria basic to a Lutheran and apostolic construction of theology and worship.

As diagnosticians of liturgical space, there is no single way in which to structure these spaces, but there are guidelines to follow. First, the tension between the horizontal axis (human to human) and vertical axis (God to human) needs to be resolved.[39] The foci for the liturgy of the Word and the liturgy of Holy Communion must be organized so that both human and divine communication can take place. Second, the architectural placement of pulpit, altar, and font needs to be firmly fixed. Focus on the Bible-pulpit, on the food-altar-table, and on the washing-font sends certain theological signals, all of which relate to the congregation's belief or lack of belief that Jesus Christ is present to bind them together as the body of Christ. The Gospel needs to be heard by all people when it is read and preached; the Sacrament needs to be central to the liturgical space so that the church building could be described as "a roof over an altar;"[40] Baptism, as initiatory in the life of the church, needs to be perceived as the way in which the congregation is composed of people who are the body of Christ. The space is both God's space and their space as God's people. Therefore, liturgical space is utilitarian, providing shelter and ease of movement as people shift focus from pulpit to altar to font; it is simple, allowing the Gospel to be heard, the meal to be eaten, the bodies to be washed without distraction or disruption; it is flexible, giving the community freedom to express the Gospel freely from the pulpit, around the table, and at the font; it is intimate, revealing to the congregation a presence that is incarnate to absolve, to forgive, to reconcile, to save.[41] Finally, the worship space must fulfill Augustine's maxim that "beauty is the splendor of truth."

As diagnosticians of liturgical rites, our task is really very simple, since the church has handed down to us two basic structures: Word and Sacrament. When all the accretions are cut away, all that remains is the liturgy of the Word and the liturgy of Holy Communion. Our analysis of our rites begins with an awareness of these two structures and a commitment to maintain their integrity. These structures are as ancient as the Scriptures and will not change. They reflect the basic need of human beings to meet together to talk and eat. When the early Christians were gathered together in one small room in a domestic house-church, they simply read his Word and ate his meal. Their songs and prayers were offered in light of his Word and in thanksgiving for his meal. They did not need elaborate liturgies because they did not have the space in which to act them out. Our rites must fit our spaces, for a "high church" service in a small country church is not just bad liturgy, it is bad taste.

Therefore, a congregational analysis of rite must see to it that the rites of Word and Sacrament remain central to congregational worship within the setting of that worship. The decisions of a congregation about the shape of these two structures will determine the liturgical style of that congregation, and, in turn, this style is directly related to the pattern of liturgical participation.[42] When one begins to talk about liturgical style, liturgical participation, and even liturgical rites, one is stepping on shaky ground. Each congregation must carefully decide these things for itself, with reverence to Christ's presence in his Word and in his Sacrament, and with fidelity to the Scriptures and the traditions of the church. Whatever the congregation decides, those decisions will determine the identity of that congregation and will define the nature of that community.

As promised, no recipes or panaceas for liturgical renewal have been offered here. Instead, some thoughts about liturgy were offered and some principles about renewal were suggested that may guide a congregation as it contemplates liturgical renewal. Hopefully these set some people to thinking seriously about what it is we are about at worship. The process of liturgical renewal is the responsibility of everyone in the church. We can all participate in renewal. And if that participation is reverent to his presence and faithful to his Word, then it will be right worship.

Notes

1. See Arthur Carl Piepkorn, "The Protestant Worship Revival and the Lutheran Liturgical Movement," in *The Liturgical Renewal of the Church,* ed. Massey H. Shepherd, Jr. (New York: Oxford University Press, 1960), pp. 55–97. Piepkorn writes, p. 82: "The Reformation itself, in its immediate homiletical, liturgical, ecclesiological, and sacramental goals, and in its eschatological emphasis, was a liturgical movement." For a brief and updated history of the liturgical movement from its inception in the year 1832 in the Benedictine Abbey of Solesmes see H. Ellsworth Chandlee, "The Liturgical Movement," in *The New Westminster Dictionary of Liturgy and Worship* (Philadelphia: Westminster Press, 1986), pp. 307–314.

2. See Aidan Kavanagh, "Relevance and Change in the Liturgy," *Worship* 45 (February 1971): 58–59.

3. See Aidan Kavanagh, *Elements of Rite* (New York: Pueblo Publishing Co., 1982), pp. 103–104, whose final point, states: "Adapt culture to the liturgy rather than liturgy to culture." This does not mean that we ignore the cultural context of the liturgy, but the dominating principle in renewal is to conform the world to the Gospel, not the Gospel to the world. Cf. Jaroslav Pelikan,

"Worship Between Yesterday and Tomorrow," *Worship: Good News in Action,* ed. Mandus A. Egge (Minneapolis: Augsburg Publishing House, 1973), p. 63, who comments on this very thing: "For too long, being Christian has been equated with being conventional or being safe, worship has been equated with archaic forms, and holiness has been equated with respectability. But the heritage of the people of God, as expressed in the lives of the saints, is anything but conventional. It all began, you will recall, with one who ate with publicans and prostitutes, and who was crucified because his incandescent holiness was too much for the respectable to bear."

4. Piepkorn describes the agenda for the Lutheran liturgical movement in the sixties: "The liturgical movement in the Lutheran Church is strongly confessional. It insists that Lutheran pastors and Lutheran parishes must take the Symbolical Books seriously, in the belief that such a serious acceptance of the Confessions will inevitably carry with it acceptance of the major theses of the liturgical revival: the importance of evangelical preaching and intensive Biblical study; the necessity of the sacraments for the Church and for the individual Christian; the significance of Baptism as participation in the death and resurrection of our Lord; the recognition of the need for individual Absolution and of the desirability of private Confession; the restoration of the Holy Eucharist to its historic place as the chief parochial service of the congregation; a due appreciation of the roll of the sacred ministry; and the value of fraternal admonition and counsel by all Christians." Cf. Piepkorn, pp. 91–92. One would like to think that this is still our agenda in the nineties.

5. This period of the liturgical movement gave many of us the opportunity to work some things out of our systems. This period serves as a warning to us against shallowness, and teaches us the danger of excessiveness.

6. In our individualistic society, where everyone wants to do things his own way, one of the worst things we can do in our liturgies is cater to all these individual tastes. Variety does not solve problems but creates them. The reason some people are bored with the liturgy is not because there is a lack of variety but because what takes place in the liturgy is perceived to be insignificant. Such a view suggests that God is not really present, a view that we encourage with our vapid liturgies that seek to adapt the ligurgy to the culture. In our liturgies, a fuller expressing of our Lutheran liturgical traditions would nurture a fuller recognition that a major part of Lutheran theology revolves around an encounter with God in worship.

7. Liturgical renewal is not exclusively a Lutheran and Roman Catholic phenomenon. The rest of the Protestant church is also involved in the liturgical movement. See James F. White, "A Protestant Worship Manifesto," *Christian Century* 99 (27 January 1982): 82–86 for a description of the direction in which Protestants are going.

8. See Louis Bouyer, *Liturgy and Architecture* (Notre Dame: University of Notre Dame Press, 1967), pp. 1–2, who defines "ethos" in this way: " 'Spirit' always means, for Christians, some interior reality, one which tends toward incarnation, or rather cannot even exist without being incarnate. It is not just in the rubrics that the spirit of the liturgy has to take flesh, whatever may be their use and even necessity in leading us along the right path. It is in a general behavior, in a whole atmosphere, more deeply, it is in what we call an 'ethos,' a turn of mind and heart which is to pervade all the details of the ritual, so as to

make of them all a coherant embodiment of that 'spirit' which is not just the spirit of man, but what this becomes when the Holy Spirit, the Spirit of God, is at work in man."

9. Liturgical studies in this century have been influenced by anthropologists and their work with rituals in primitive societies, particularly concerning the importance of rhythm and ritual in binding people together into a community. On a human level, their insights are helpful. These anthropologists suggest that ritual encourages the perception that the deity is present, a numinous presence that binds the worshiping community together. For further reading in the area of liturgy and ritual see Louis Bouyer, *Rite and Man: Natural Sacredness and Christian Liturgy* (Notre Dame: Univesity of Notre Dame Press, 1963); Aidan Kavanagh, "Relevance and Change in the Liturgy," pp. 58–72; Mary Douglas, *Natural Symbols: Explorations in Cosmology* (New York: Pantheon, 1970); James D. Shaughnessy, *The Roots of Ritual* (Grand Rapids: Eerdmans, 1973); Victor Turner, *The Ritual Process* (Ithaca: Cornell University Press, 1969); Victor Turner, "Passages, Margin, the Poverty: Religious Symbols of Communitas," *Worship* 56/7 (September 1982): 390–412; 46/8 (October 1972): 482–494; A. van Gennep, *The Rites of Passage* (University of Chicago Press, 1960).

10. One of the hermeneutical principles applied to liturgical texts is that they tend to be very conservative. This comes from the belief that people at worship tend to change their way of thinking and speaking about God more slowly than theologians do. This was borne out when our church body maintained the same hymnal through the turmoil of the sixties and seventies. It was not until the theological controversies had subsided that a new hymnal was offered. Some might argue that this was purely coincidence, but one should never underestimate the subtle power of the liturgy as it forms people and church bodies. If one really wants to know what a church believes, just open up their worship book and read their hymns and their liturgies. This will tell you more about their theology than any of their theological documents.

11. Pelikan, p. 59.

12. Searle first suggested "reverence" as a watchward for liturgical reform. Although he reflects on the reform of the liturgy in the Roman Catholic Church since Vatican II, his comments ring true for our church as well. He writes, "Perhaps, if there is one work that can sum up the direction in which we need to go, it is 'reverence.' Reverence is one of the things that many thought had disappeared from the liturgy after the reform. If that was so, it is time to cherish it again. But let it be a reverence that goes beyond a preoccupation with sacred things. Let it be a reverence for the word as well as the sacrament, for the world as well as the Church, for the people of God as well as for the ordained and the vowed. Let it be a reverence which shows itself in mutual service and, above all, in sensitivity and respect for the faith-life of ordinary Catholics, for the burdens they carry and for the testimony they can bear in the joys and struggles of the Christian life." Cf. Mark Searle, "Reflections on Liturgical Reform," *Worship* 56/5 (September 1982): 430.

13. See Pelikan, pp. 58–59, who insists that the watchword for liturgical renewal is "not innovation, but fidelity." Fidelity to the fathers "does not mean living in the past, but living from the past and being faithful to it in facing the present and the future."

14. Too often the sermons of today are not biblical but topical with anecdotes interspersed. The text is never really preached in light of the whole biblical witness but is used as a jumping off point for moralizing and exhortations to holy living. The power of positive thinking has replaced the Gospel as parishioners are urged to discover their potential (i.e., their spiritual gift quotient) instead of hearing the declarations of how God acted on behalf of the world through Jesus Christ from the beginning of time.

15. This deficiency in our liturgical theology has been pointed out by many people. Perhaps it was said most succinctly by Henry E. Horn in "Worship: The Gospel in Action," *Worship: Good News in Action*, p. 31, when he writes, " . . . our traditional theology, while paying lip service to the Real Presence, shows no sign of dynamism that this presence brings. . . . Forgotten by the theologian—and often by the liturgist—is the reality of *Christus praesens* (Christ making himself present) throughout the history of the church."

16. Ibid., p. 33.

17. White, "A Protestant Worship Manifesto," p. 50. These three words sum up the popular view of the content of good worship.

18. See White, p. 51, who writes: "Becoming aware of God in and through Jesus Christ does not mean receiving new information but the rediscovering what we already know and constantly forget. One could speak of it equally well as reconsideration or recollection of past memories, particulary those shared by the community. Above all, this means the commemoration of historic events that the Christian community remembers as clues to the meaning of all history. Thus the worshiping community gathers to rehearse its corporate memories of God's acts as narrated in Scripture."

19. Horn, p. 39.

20. Ibid., p. 29.

21. See Eugene Brand, "New Accents in Baptism and the Eucharist," in *Worship: Good News in Action*, p. 88, who suggested these metaphors. According to these metaphors, the eucharist becomes exclusively that of "an individual drawing upon the store of grace."

22. The caravan image comes from Vernard Eller, *In Place of Sacraments* (Grand Rapids: Eerdmans, 1972), pp. 30ff., and the description from Brand, p. 88. This view of the church further suggests the eschatological dimension of the Eucharist. Thus Brand writes on p. 87: "The eschatological accent in the Eucharist strengthens hope in the promise that the kingdom has and shall come; the Eucharist becomes a foretaste of the perfect fellowship of that kingdom."

23. The faith-community image comes from Robert Hovda, "Response to the Berakah Award," *Worship* 56/4 (July 1982): 354.

24. Ibid.

25. O. C. Edwards, *Elements of Homiletic* (New York: Pueblo Publishing House, 1984), p. 11.

26. Ibid., p. 19.

27. In his catechetical instructions, Hippolytus (c. 170–c. 235) recognizes the importance of community for the survival of the catechumenate. Under the threat of persecution and martyrdom, he recognized that the catechumens

could not sustain the madness of Christianity in a hostile world without the support of the community. The identity of the catechumen was formed from his association with the body of Christ, a body that he was to be baptized into, a body that contained all the saving realities of Christ's death and resurrection in Word and Sacrament. See Aidan Kavanagh, *The Shape of Baptism: The Rite of Christian Initiation* (New York: Pueblo Publishing Company, 1978), p. 58.

28. See John Oliver Patterson, "The Pastoral Implications of the Liturgical Renewal," *The Liturgical Renewal of the Church* (New York: Oxford University Press, 1960), p. 146.

29. See James F. White, *Introduction to Christian Worship* (Nashville: Abingdon Press, 1980), pp. 44–75. His chapter entitled "The Language of Time" is an excellent summary of the history and significance of the church year. He emphasizes the importance of the church year when he writes on p. 45: "The centrality of time in Christianity is reflected in Christian worship. This worship, like the rest of life, is structured on recurring rhythms of the week, day, and the year. Far from trying to escape time, Christian worship uses time as one of its basic structures. Our present time is used to place us in contact with God's acts in time past and future."

30. Ibid., p. 62. These two ways of organizing time are not mutually exclusive. It is possible to mention mothers on Pentecost and to incorporate Lutheran Women's Missionary League Sunday into the propers for the Eighteenth Sunday after Pentecost.

31. The church subjugates the Gospel to the world when its liturgical calendar celebrates national holidays. Do Election Day, Martin Luther King Day, or Memorial Day have any place in our worship?

32. See Paul V. Marshall, "The Little Easter and the Great Sunday," *Liturgy* 1/2 (1980): 28, who quotes the *Epistle of Barnabas* 15:8b–9, Ignatius's *Ad Magnesios* 9:1, and Basil's *De Spiritu Sancto*, 27, in support of his view. On a theology of Sunday see also White, *Introduction*, pp. 47–49, and Mark Searle, *Sunday Morning: A Time for Worship* (Collegeville: The Liturgical Press, 1982).

33. Marshall, p. 29.

34. See Daniel B. Stevick, "Renewing the Language of Worship," *Worship: Good News in Action*, pp. 119–120, who discusses the problem of kings and shepherds, priests and sacrifice. He concludes, p. 120, "Images of trains, radios, and the like, which one hears occasionally, are contrived, not discovered. Certainly the conditions of modern life provide materials in which the Christian imagination can find images of God in action, as Jesus saw them in everyday life of Palestine. But the new images are tested by a gospel which has been given in other images. The old, difficult images from a bedouin, prescientific, preindustrial, prebehavioral studies keep reasserting themselves. The old, with all their difficulties, remain the criterion for the new." See also George M. Bass, *The Renewal of Liturgical Preaching* (Minneapolis: Augsburg Publishing House, 1967), p. 20, who quotes Archbishop William Ramsay's question: "Amid all the changes of thought and language are there not Biblical and Christian images which seem to bear permanence?"

35. See White, *Introduction*, p. 66, who writes, "Variety, then, is an important characteristic of Christian worship as worship relates both to the eternal gospel

and to our ongoing daily life. One of the sharpest criticisms of Christian worship in recent years has been that of dullness. Yet this criticism is apt only when Christian worship has been unfaithful to its own nature. The surest way to avoid the boredom of constant repetition is to revel in the rich variety inherent in Christian worship. And the best way to ensure dullness is to ignore this same variety."

36. See Bass, pp. 17–19, who credits liturgical renewal with reshaping the sermon. Unfortunately, the last twenty years have not seen a movement in the direction he suggests. His observations are still pertinent and need to be repeated. He writes, "First, the liturgical renewal insists that Scripture is the basis for and the content of the sermon. The liturgical sermon is a biblical sermon. . . . The liturgical renewal also gives positive form and shape to the liturgical sermon by delineating its nature as proclamation. The liturgical sermon declares God's mighty act of salvation effective for man by Jesus Christ. . . . The Word of the sermon is addressed to people where they are. The subject of that Word is Jesus Christ, who is present himself when the Word is rightly proclaimed. Inherent in every liturgical sermon is the reality of the Christ who died on Calvary and rose from the dead on the third day. Christ, in a sense, actually does the work of preaching in the properly formed sermon. He speaks for himself, through the preacher, to man in his existential situation."

37. Kavanagh, *The Shape of Baptism*, p. xiii.

38. Edwards, p. 19.

39. See White, *Introduction*, p. 80.

40. Patterson, p. 140.

41. The four criteria just listed, "utility, simplicity, flexibility, and intimacy," come from White, *Introduction*, pp. 94–97, who gives a fuller description on how these criteria can serve as guidelines in renewal of space.

42. See Craig Douglas Erickson, "Liturgical Participation and the Renewal of the Church," *Worship* 59/3 (May 1985): 231–243, who provides an excellent discussion of this topic. He claims that the labels "high church" and "low church," formal and informal worship are misleading and reflect more the style of participation than the rites themselves. He offers even different patterns of liturgical participation, showing their strengths and weaknesses, but recommending none of them.

2

Corporate Worship of the Church

WORSHIP AND THE COMMUNITY OF FAITH

Roger D. Pittelko

Definition of Terms

Worship. That is what this book is all about. However, it is not *worship* in the usual sense of the word. The usual meaning of this word leads us astray.

Worship is usually defined as honoring or revering a supernatural being or power. This adoration is done with appropriate acts, rites, or ceremonies. In fact, the word *worship* and its formation are peculiar to the English language going back to the root words of *worth* and *ship*, that is, a being or power that has worth and merit and is to be honored and adored.[1]

There is much about this meaning of worship that is salutary. God has worth, merit. That merit or worth is to be adored and honored. However, the main thrust of the English word *worship* is from the worshiper to the worshiped. The direction is from us to God. We recognize the merit or worth of God. When we recognize the merit or worth of God, we offer appropriate acts, rites, and ceremonies of worship. The English word *worship* makes the activity ours. It is something that we do when we have recognized the greatness of God.

Such a view of worship is antithetical to the Evangelical Lutheran understanding of worship. The dictionary understanding makes worship our action or response. It turns worship into an

44

anthropocentric activity that is measured and normed by what we do, by what we understand God to be. The evangelical Lutheran understanding of worship is just the opposite. It is from God to us. It begins with God. It has its foundation and source with God. It is theocentric and, more specifically, it is Christocentric. It is the theocentric, Christocentric view of worship that forms and norms *Lutheran Worship*. The introduction to *Lutheran Worship* says it this way:

> Our Lord speaks and we listen. His Word bestows what it says. Faith that is born from what is heard acknowledges the gifts received with eager thankfulness and praise. . . . Saying back to him what he has said to us, we repeat what is most true and sure. Most true and sure is his name, which he put on us with the water of our Baptism. . . . The rhythm of our worship is from him to us, and then from us back to him. He gives his gifts, and together we receive and extol them. We build one another up as we speak to one another in psalms, hymns, and spiritual songs. Our Lord gives us his body to eat and his blood to drink. Finally his blessing moves us out into our calling, where his gifts have their fruition. How best to do this we may learn from his Word and from the way his Word has prompted his worship through the centuries.[2]

Worship is God speaking. It is our listening. Worship begins with God's Word. He is the content. Evangelical Lutheran worship begins with God giving us his Word. It comes to us and we respond in faith and devotion. It is God's action, not ours. He is the mover, the doer. Faith comes as the gift from God, not from our own doing or action.

Such an understanding of worship is quite different from the dictionary definition of the word. It is for that reason that the Evangelical Lutheran Church has shown a preference for the word *service*. The chief gathering of Christians on a Sunday morning is called the Divine Service. In the Divine Service, God serves us. He gives us his Word and sacraments. Only after we have received the Word and the gifts that he offers do we respond in our sacrifice of thanksgiving and praise. The Divine Service (liturgy) is God giving to us and our responding to him. It is theocentric and Christocentric, not the man centered activity that is usually defined as worship.

Theology of Worship in Scripture and the Lutheran Confessions

Instead of turning to the dictionary for a definition of worship, we ought to turn to the way the church has defined worship in the Athanasian Creed:

> And the Catholic faith is this, that we worship one God in three persons and three persons in one God. . . . For the right faith is that we believe and confess that our Lord Jesus Christ, the Son of God, is God and man.[3]

> This obedience toward God, this desire to receive the offered promise, is no less an act of worship than is love. God wants us to believe him and to accept blessings from him; this he declares to be true worship.[4] . . .The greatest possible comfort comes from this doctrine that the highest worship in the Gospel is the desire to receive forgiveness of sins, grace, and righteousness. About this worship Christ speaks in John 6:40, "This is the will of my Father, that everyone who sees the Son and believes in him should have eternal life." And the Father says (Matt. 17:5), "This is my beloved Son, with whom I am well pleased; listen to him."[5]

Perhaps then we could simply say that worship for the Christian is in its essence faith in God through Jesus Christ and that faith in God through Jesus Christ is worship.

To the secular world, worship must seem very strange. People are gathered according to a regular schedule to hear words read and proclaimed, to eat a bite of bread and drink a sip of wine, to apply water, to sing, and to pray. These Christians are engaged in an activity that produces no product. After it is over there is nothing that remains. There is nothing that you can see or sell. It is of no apparent value to the world since it does not produce a saleable item or add to the gross national product. Yet the event that we call worship is central to what the Christian faith means.

The Evangelical Lutheran Church views the sacred Scriptures as the source and norm of Christian faith, doctrine, and life. While it might be interesting and informative to speak of worship from the context of sociology or the anthropology of worship, worship begins and ends with the God who has revealed himself in the Word. In both the Old and New Testaments it is evident that worship is central to the sacred story.

In the Old Testament worship is a given. It is a reality that needs no explanation. Corporate worship in the opening chapters of Genesis is taken for granted. It is a given after human beings were expelled from the Garden of Eden where they had been in perfect worship and communion with God. Note that the sin born in the heart of Cain against his brother Abel happened as they were offering sacrifice to God (Gen. 4:1–16).

The only response for Noah upon landing after the flood was the offering of sacrifice to God for his protection and mercy in the act of worship. God had delivered, and now Noah and his family responded to the mercy and the grace of God (Gen. 8:20 –22). "Our Lord speaks and we listen."[6] God had spoken to Noah and had saved Noah. They listened and acknowledged "the gifts received with eager thankfulness and praise."[7]

Abraham, having been ordered to offer his only son Isaac as a sacrifice, was heavy of heart. At the very last moment his son, his only son, was spared from the sacrificial offering; the only response that was appropriate for Abraham was the offering of the sacrifice of a ram to God in worship. Note that even the ram had been supplied by the Lord (Gen. 22:1–14). God gives. We respond.

One of the foundation events of the Old Testament was the exodus as the people of Israel left slavery in Egypt. During the exodus the priesthood was instituted. Aaron was chosen by God to be the first high priest. His sons after him were to serve in the priesthood. It was a priesthood not only of the offering of sacrificial animals but also a priesthood of prayer and intercession as the priests represented the priestly and kingly people of God, the nation of Israel (Ex. 28:1–31:11; 19:6). Very careful instructions were laid down in the foundation of the priesthood regarding the actions of the priests, the vestments of the priests, and the form of sacrifice (Ex. 28 –30). Very clear instructions were given regarding the construction of the Tabernacle with exact dimensions and materials to be used in the construction of this place of worship. These details were reproduced again in the building of the temple many centuries later (1 Kings 6 –7). Note the care and the precision of the Old Testament instructions regarding the place and manner of worship. Nothing was slipshod. Nothing but the best and finest were to be used in the worship of God (1 Kings 5:17; 6:22, 30).

In the book of Psalms the Old Testament hymnal has been preserved. The Psalms are still a treasure trove of devotion, prayer, praise, comfort, and strength. They continued to be prominent in the worship of the New Testament church and in the prayer and devotional life of the Christian.

Liberal German theology of the 19th century taught that the prophet and the priest stood in opposition to each other. According to 19th-century German theology, the suppression of the priestly religion of the temple by the prophetic preaching of the prophet was the will of God. That view, while now discredited, is still popularly held by many Christians. The prophetic role of the preacher is exalted, while the priestly role of the representative of the people leading in prayer and praise is derogated and looked upon as being a perversion of true faith. The false message of 19th-century German theology needs to be unlearned. Both the prophetic and the priestly ministries of the Old Testament are properly instituted ministries of God. The call of the prophet was not to abolish the temple and its worship. The call of the prophet was for the purification and cleansing of the temple and its worship, that the holy name of God might be praised.

The centrality of worship seen in the Old Testament continues in the New Testament. There is no less interest in the New Testament in the true worship of God than in the Old Testament.

The New Testament message of the birth of the forerunner of the Christ happens in the temple. The announcement is made to a priest who is about his duty leading the people of Israel in worship of God at the time of the evening sacrifice: a child will be born who will be the son of a priest whose own mother was the daughter of a priest. John the Baptist, the last prophet before the Christ was born, is a priest (Luke 1).

When the Christ is born to Mary in Bethlehem, it is a birth announced by the angelic choir as it offers worship to the newborn Savior with the words that are used each time the church gathers in Divine Service: "Glory to God in the highest, and on earth peace to men on whom his favor rests" (Luke 2:14). Shepherds and wisemen came to worship the newborn Savior. Only one response was appropriate. The shepherds worshiped (Luke 2:15–20). The wisemen brought their gifts of gold and frankincense and myrrh to lay them before the Christ Child in worship (Matt. 2:11).

According to the fourth gospel, Jesus visited the temple at the beginning of his ministry. At the outset of his ministry, which would fulfill the Old Testament sacrificial system represented by the temple, Jesus cleansed the temple that it might be a place of proper worship. It was not to be a place of buying and selling (John 2:13–22).

The cleansing is repeated. According to the synoptic gospels, at the end of our Lord's ministry the money changers are driven from the temple. They are told that the house of the Lord was to be a house of prayer (Matt. 21:12–13; Mark 11:15–17; Luke 19: 45–46).

In the fourth chapter of John, our Lord is asked a question about worship by the woman at the well of Samaria. Where, she asks, is the true place of worship? Is it here at Mount Gerizim or is it in Jerusalem? Our Lord answers the critical question about the place of worship once and for all; it is a question that, had it not been answered, would have plagued Christianity to the present.

> Believe me, woman, a time is coming when you will worship the Father neither on this mountain nor in Jerusalem. You Samaritans worship what you do not know; we worship what we do know, for salvation is from the Jews. Yet a time is coming and has now come when the true worshipers will worship the Father in spirit and truth, for they are the kind of worshipers the Father seeks. God is spirit, and his worshipers must worship in spirit and in truth (John 4:21–24).

Our Lord is identified in the New Testament as the Lamb of God who takes away the sins of the world. At the very beginning of his ministry Jesus is so identified by St. John the Baptist (John 1:29). The picture of the Christ as the Lamb of God is unfolded in the book of Hebrews and the book of Revelation (Heb. 10:1–10; Rev. 5:12–14). The sacrificial animal of the Old Testament is completed and fulfilled in the one Lamb of God who is Jesus Christ, our Lord. However, the picture and identification of the Lamb of God who takes away the sins of the world is meaningless unless you understand the temple and the worship of the people of Israel.

To the end of his ministry our Lord continues to take part in the worship of the Old Testament people of God. He visits the temple and participates in its worship (Luke 19:47–20:8; John 7:37–39). In the day preceding his crucifixion, our Lord participates in the holy meal of Israel, the Passover. In the context of the Passover meal he institutes the sacrament of his body and blood for the forgiveness of sins (Matt. 26:26–29; Mark 14:22–25; Luke 22:14–23).

It comes as a surprise to many that even after the resurrection of the Lord and his ascension, the apostles continue to attend the temple and join in the worship of prayer, praise, exposition of the Word and sacrifice (Acts 3–4; 21:26–30). It is at the temple that the apostles gave a mighty witness to the resurrection of the Lamb of God who takes away the sins of the world (Acts 4:1–4).

The apostolic church gathered regularly for "doctrine, fellowship, breaking of bread and prayer" (Acts 2:42). Teaching, prayer, fellowship, and the holy meal comprehended what the church did when it gathered. It gathered for worship.

The book of Hebrews expounds the meaning of the priesthood and the Old Testament sacrifices. Priesthood and sacrifice as Israel's form of worship were pointing beyond themselves to the real priest of God, Jesus Christ (Heb. 7–11). The sacrificial lambs were but representations of the real sacrifice for sins, the real Lamb of God, Jesus Christ (Heb. 10:1–18). The identification made by the book of Hebrews of our Lord as the priest and the lamb is beautifully drawn together in the words of the early Latin eucharistic hymn, "Himself the victim and himself the priest" (LW 240, st. 1).

The book of Revelation unfolds the picture of heaven and the eternal worship of the Lamb who was slain and has been raised from the dead. When all the important tasks of the church (education, evangelism, stewardship, acts of mercy) have come to an end, there will be only one thing of importance and meaning: the worship of God, the worship of the Lamb who was slain, as the saints of God gather about his eternal throne (Rev. 5:12–14; 19:1–10). Worship, finally, the last book of the Bible tells us, is all that there is. In the end all that matters and counts is God himself. In his presence all that we can do is but worship him.

The Evangelical Lutheran Church is committed to the theological view that the *Book of Concord* of 1580 is the correct exposition and exhibition of the Holy Scriptures. All of the teaching of the Evangelical Lutheran Church is to be in conformity with the Confessions. What the *Book of Concord* has to say about worship is of vital importance to the Lutheran Christian.

The Confessions of the Evangelical Lutheran Church understand that there can be no real worship of God except by Christians. It may not be polite or politic in pluralistic America to admit to such a teaching. "On the other hand," the Large Catechism does teach, "you can easily judge how the world practices nothing but false worship and idolatry."[8] "All who are outside the Christian church, whether heathen, Turks, Jews, or false Christians and hypocrites, even though they believe in and worship only the one, true God, nevertheless do not know what his attitude is toward them. They cannot be confident of his love and blessing."[9] The Apology says, "We steadfastly maintain that those who believe otherwise do not belong to the church of Christ but are idolaters and blasphemers."[10]

While the true worship of God is faith in Jesus Christ, the Confessions teach that the worship of God includes both faith and signs or exercises of that faith. "The worship of the New Testament is spiritual; it is the righteousness of faith in the heart and the fruits of faith."[11]

According to the Confessions, worship is not restricted to religious services (Sunday Divine Service). The Confessions describe ceremonies, pilgrimages, fasts, prayer, vows, giving of alms, observance of traditions, and other kinds of spiritual exercises. Worship then includes the cultus, that is, the acts of worship.

While affirming the importance of ceremonies, the Confessions emphasize that external ceremonies are instituted by men and are not worship in the strict sense of the term. The Formula of Concord says, "To settle this controversy we believe, teach, and confess unanimously that the ceremonies or church usages which are neither commanded nor forbidden in the Word of God, but which have been introduced solely for the sake of good order and the general welfare, are in and for themselves no divine worship or even a part of it."[12] Having affirmed the human institution of some rites and ceremonies, the Confessions teach that in a time of persecution a rite or ceremony that is indifferent and external might become a matter of confession. "We believe, teach, and confess that in time of persecution, when a clear-cut confession of faith is demanded of us, we dare not yield to the enemies in such indifferent things."[13] To accept or to drop, in time of persecution, a ceremony that might be indifferent in itself, might be sin. Nevertheless, external human ceremonies are a necessary condition to corporate worship. Human beings are flesh and blood with bodies. Human beings are affected by the physical world. They are not pure spirit. The Large Catechism says,

> Any conduct or work done apart from God's Word is unholy in the sight of God, no matter how splendid and brilliant it may appear. . . . Other trades and occupations are not properly called holy work unless the doer himself is first holy. But here a work must be performed by which the doer himself is made holy; this, as we have heard, takes place only through God's Word. Places, times, persons, and the entire outward order of worship are therefore instituted and appointed in order that God's Word may exert its power publicly.[14]

"It is an ungodly error to maintain that we merit the forgiveness of sins by these observances."[15] The Augsburg Confession, or Augustana, says that "traditions instituted by men for the purpose of propitiating God and earning grace are contrary to the Gospel and the teaching about faith in Christ. Accordingly, monastic vows and other traditions concerning distinctions of foods, days, etc., by which it is intended to earn grace and make satisfaction for sin, are useless and contrary to the Gospel."[16] "We teach that the sacrificial death of Christ on the cross was sufficient for the sins of the whole world and that there is no need for additional sacrifices as though this were not sufficient for our sins. Men are not justified, therefore, because of any other sacrifices, but because of this one sacrifice of Christ if they believe that it has redeemed them."[17]

In Christ, Christian worship is a sacrifice of praise and thanksgiving, that is, a eucharistic sacrifice. The Apology says, "a sacrifice is a ceremony or act which we render to God to honor him."[18] The Apology points out that there are two kinds of sacrifice. The first sacrifice is propitiatory, that is, a sacrifice that reconciles God and merits forgiveness. Such a sacrifice is beyond human ability and was offered once and for all by our Lord Jesus Christ. "The other type is the eucharistic sacrifice; this does not merit the forgiveness of sins or reconciliation, but by it those who have been reconciled give thanks or show their gratitude for the forgiveness of sins and other blessings received."[19] "There has really been only one propitiatory sacrifice in the world, the death of Christ, as the Epistle to the Hebrews teaches" (10:4).[20]

The Confessions teach that there is a close connection between the means of grace and worship. "Among the praises of God or sacrifices of praise we include the proclamation of the Word. In the same way, the reception of the Lord's Supper itself can be praise or thanksgiving."[21] The Augustana says that the corporate reception of the Sacrament of the Altar "increases the reverence and devotion of public worship. . . . Such worship pleases God, and such use of the sacrament nourishes devotion to God."[22] The Apology puts it most boldly, "This use of the sacrament, when faith gives life to terrified hearts, is the worship of the New Testament."[23]

On the North American continent, where Reformed theology has set the theological agenda for Protestants, the remembering of the saints is considered inappropriate if not idolatrous. The Confessions of the Evangelical Lutheran Church, however, teach that the recollection of the saints is salutary. "Our Confession approves giving honor to the saints. This honor is threefold. The first is thanksgiving. . . . The second honor is the strengthening of our faith. . . . The third honor is the imitation, first of their faith and then of their own virtues, which each should imitate in accordance with his calling."[24] If this is true of the saints in general, it is especially true of the virgin Mary whom the Symbolical Books, or the Confessions, call the mother of God and that most "blessed Mary, . . . worthy of the highest honors."[25] The Symbolical Books also take for granted that the saints and angels intercede for the church: "We also grant that the saints in heaven pray for the church in general, as they prayed for the church universal while they were on earth."[26] The authority for regulating the external ceremonies of public worship is vested in the church. The Formula says,

> The community of God in every place and at every time has the right, authority, and power to change, to reduce, or to increase ceremonies according to its circumstances, as long as it does so without frivolity and offense but in an orderly and appropriate way, as at any time may seem to be most profitable, beneficial,

and salutary for good order, Christian discipline, evangelical decorum, and the edification of the church."[27]

In establishment of human ceremonies "it is not necessary for the true unity of the Christian church that ceremonies, instituted by men, should be observed uniformly in all places."[28] From time to time revisions of ceremonies will be necessary. The Augustana teaches that "a certain few abuses . . . have crept into the churches without proper authority."[29] "Perhaps there were acceptable reasons for these ordinances when they were introduced, but they are not adapted to later times. It is also apparent that some were adopted out of misunderstanding."[30]

The authority to change ceremonies given to the church is exercised by those who have oversight in the church, that is, the pastors. The Apology teaches,

> It is lawful for bishops or pastors to make regulations so that things in the church may be done in good order, but not that by means of these we make satisfaction for sins, nor that consciences are bound so as to regard these as necessary services. . . . It is proper that the churches comply with such ordinances for the sake of love and tranquility and that they keep them, insofar as one does not offend another, so that everything in the churches may be done in order and without confusion. However, consciences should not be burdened by suggesting that they are necessary for salvation. . . . Of the same sort is the observance of Sunday, Easter, Pentecost, and similar festivals and rites.[31]

However, as the pastors exercise that authority, "bishops do not have power to institute anything contrary to the Gospel."[32] Any changes should be made carefully and circumspectly. "But in this matter all frivolity and offenses are to be avoided, and particularly the weak in faith are to be spared."[33] "Therefore we reject and condemn as false and contrary to God's Word . . . when . . . external ceremonies and indifferent things are abolished in a way which suggests that the community of God does not have the liberty to avail itself of one or more such ceremonies according to its circumstances and as it may be most beneficial to the church."[34]

No church should criticize another because it has a greater or a smaller number of ceremonies. The Formula teaches, "We believe, teach, and confess that no church should condemn another because it has fewer or more external ceremonies not commanded by God, as long as there is mutual agreement in doctrine and in all its articles as well as in the right use of the holy sacraments."[35] This does not mean that external ceremonies are without value. The use of external ceremonies teaches. The use of ceremonies contributes to external decency and order. The use of ceremonies helps to identify the external society of the church. The use of ceremonies is a means for private and corporate devotion. "The purpose of observing ceremonies is that men may learn the Scriptures and that those who have been touched by the Word may receive faith and fear and so may also pray."[36] "After all, the chief purpose of all ceremonies is to teach the people what they need to know about Christ."[37] "The holy Fathers did not institute any traditions for the purpose of meriting the forgiveness of sins or righteousness. They instituted them for the sake of good order and tranquillity in the church."[38] "The church is not merely an association of outward ties and rites like other civic governments, however, but it is mainly an association of faith and of the Holy Spirit in men's hearts. To make it recognizable, this association has outward marks, the pure teaching of the Gospel and the administration of the sacraments in harmony with the Gospel of Christ."[39]

To have value, ceremonies must be explained and understood. The Confessions teach that this is the responsibility of the Christian family, the church, and the Christian school. "No one has ever written or suggested that men benefit from hearing lessons they do not understand, or from ceremonies that do not teach or admonish, simply *ex opere operato,* by the mere doing or observing. Out with such pharisaic ideas!"[40]

The Reformers taught that the traditional rites and ceremonies of worship were to be retained if they could be used without sin. The Evangelical Lutheran Church has lived with that principle from the time of the Reformation to the present. "Our churches teach that those rites should be observed which can be observed without sin and which contribute to peace and good order in the church."[41] "This is the simple way to interpret traditions. We should know that they are not necessary acts of worship, and yet we should observe them in their place and without superstition, in order to avoid offenses."[42] "This subject of traditions involves many difficult and controversial questions, and we know from actual experience that traditions are real snares for consciences. When they are required as necessary, they bring exquisite torture to a conscience that has omitted some observance. On the other hand, their abrogation involves its own difficulties and problems."[43]

During the Reformation era the iconoclasts tried to rid the church of all past worship practices and forms. In the face of that pressure the Lutheran Reformers followed a conservative liturgical principle. The Apology says, "The holy Fathers . . . observed these human rites because they were profitable for good order, because they gave the people a set time to assemble, because they provided an example of how all things could be done decently and in order in the churches, and finally because they helped instruct the common folk."[44] The Conclusion of the Augustana states it most clearly: "It may be understood that nothing has been received among us, in doctrine or in ceremonies, that is contrary to Scripture or to the church catholic."[45]

The Confessions also make suggestions regarding private worship and devotion. The best known of these suggestions is the private rite of prayer for morning and evening in the Small Catechism. Upon rising and going to bed the Christian is instructed to bless himself with the sign of the holy cross and to say the invocation, the Creed, and the Lord's Prayer with a prayer of blessing, morning and evening.[46] The Large Catechism expands on the meaning of private acts of devotion:

> For this purpose it also helps to form the habit of commending ourselves each day to God—our soul and body, wife, children, servants, and all that we have—for his protection against every conceivable need. Thus has originated and continued among us the custom of saying grace and returning thanks at meals and saying other prayers for both morning and evening. From the same source came the custom of children who cross themselves when they see or hear anything monstrous or fearful and exclaim, "Lord God, save us!" "Help, dear Lord Christ!" etc. Thus, too, if anyone meets with unexpected good fortune, however trivial, he may say, "God be praised and thanked!"[47]

Importance of Worship in the Life of the Church

Scripture and the Confessions teach that worship is vital to the life of the Christian. Worship is not an option for a Christian or for the church. It is the very substance, the essence of the Christian faith and life. Communion with God through his Word and holy sacraments is essential to the Christian and the entire people of God.

The ancient rule of prayer and worship is true: *Lex orandi, lex credendi.* The rule of praying or worship is the rule of believing. This maxim was first enunciated by theologian Prosper of Aquitaine in the fifth century. It constituted an important principle in the early church and continues to be an important principle of worship and faith in the Evangelical Lutheran Church of the 20th century. As we worship, we will believe. As we believe, we will worship. The two are bound together and cannot be separated. If you worship as a Muslim, you will ultimately believe as a Muslim. If you believe as a Muslim, you will worship that way. Conversely, if you worship in the liturgical order of the Evangelical Lutheran Church with its scriptural theology, you will believe as a member of that church. If you believe in the biblical theology of the Evangelical Lutheran Church, you will worship in the liturgical forms that express the belief of that church. The worship of the Evangelical Lutheran Church is a celebration of the victory of our Lord Jesus Christ. The saving action of God through the death and resurrection of Jesus Christ is proclaimed to us through the Word of God. In and through that Word we celebrate our Lord opening the gates of heaven for us through his life, death, and resurrection. The church does not gather in worship to commemorate the "late departed" Jesus of Nazareth, but to witness to the resurrection of our Lord by proclamation, preaching, prayer, thanksgiving, and the sacraments celebrated and administered. Jesus Christ is present in our midst according to his promise. He is with his church to the end of the age.

LITURGY AND EVANGELISM

Kurt Marquart

A thousand years ago Grand Duke Vladimir of Kiev sent envoys to various cultural centers to find the religion best suited to his infant Russian nation. Vladimir's delegates were duly impressed with Islam and with Rome, but it was Constantinople that won their hearts. Such was the solemn splendor of the divine liturgy there that the visiting Russians found themselves wondering whether they were in heaven or on earth!

One is tempted to rush to instant applications. One might conclude, for example, that public worship ought to be elaborate, ceremonious, highly ritualistic. However, the cultural relativist will be quick to counter, "Yes, that may have been impressive to primitive Russians. But modern Americans prefer casual, informal arrangements, and therefore require relatively unstructured, nonliturgical worship." There is no defense on purely pragmatic grounds against the MacDisneyland Mass. It is not at all self-evident, really, just what lessons are to be drawn from historical examples of "attractive" worship. It is certain, however, that Christ and his apostles did not set out, moist fingers in the wind, to see what sort of worship practices might be culturally most palatable to the Graeco-Roman *oekoumene*. The true secret and significance of evangelistically attractive worship lies beyond the reach of a shallow, psychologizing and trivializing pragmatism. This part of the chapter will attempt to suggest some parameters relevant to Lutherans in modern America.

Liturgy as Content

The word *liturgy* itself is a good conversation starter. It seems to be taken by many as a collective term for everything that is not important in a service: *Liturgy* means the fillers to round things out, the icing on the cake, or, even more bluntly, the window-dressing for the proper stage-managing of sermons and collections. And so we have "opening" and "closing" liturgies, but the meat of the sandwich is somewhere else. If liturgy is simply decorative, it is of course basically trivial. Since, in this view, it has no theological substance of its own, it naturally becomes the plaything of psychology, sociology, "cultural" this and that, and of course "the arts."

How different is the understanding of *liturgy* in Article XXIV of the Apology of the Augsburg Confession:

> But let us talk about the term "liturgy." It does not really mean a sacrifice but a public service. Thus it squares well with our position that a minister who consecrates shows forth the body and blood of Christ to the people, just as a minister who preaches shows forth the Gospel to the people, as Paul says (I Cor. 4:1), "This is how one should regard us, as ministers of Christ and dispensers of the sacraments of God," that is, of the Word and sacraments.[48]

Clearly, *liturgy* here is first of all theological content, not ritual form. In itself the word means simply and generically "public service." (The expression *divine liturgy* should therefore raise eyebrows as little or as much as *divine service,* of which it is the exact equivalent.) More concretely, the church's *liturgy* means its whole cycle of ordered services, including the daily offices like Matins and Vespers, and other "minor" services, which grew out of New Testament adaptations of Old Testament forms and practices (see Acts 2:15; 3:1; 10:9; 12:12). The Apology, however, uses the term *liturgy* in a more special sense here. Following the custom of the Eastern Church, the Apology equates *liturgy* with what had come to be called the Mass in the Western Church of the Middle Ages. In other words, not any sort of service in general is meant, but quite concretely the rite of the Lord's Supper as the matrix and content of regular Gospel proclamation. This bifocal liturgical structure of sermon and sacrament forms the heart and core of "the whole worship of the New Testament,"[49] and is therefore the vital center or gathering point of the church's public assemblies (1 Cor. 10:17; 11:20, 33). The German of the Apology says that the ceremony of the Holy Supper was "instituted for the sake of preaching, as Paul says: 'As often as you eat the bread and drink the cup, you are to proclaim the Lord's death.' "[50] It is this concrete Word-and-Sacrament liturgy that, according to the Augsburg Confession, "is preserved among us in its proper use, the use which was formerly observed in the church and which can be proved by St. Paul's statement in I Cor. 11:20ff. and by many statements of the Fathers."[51] The church, in this view, meets in solemn public assembly not to conduct pep rallies for worthy causes, or to boost a religious talk with publicity stunts, but to transact the awesome and life-giving "mysteries of God" (1 Cor. 4:1). God and his gifts are all-decisive, not man and his moods. The "eternal life" which God has given us and which "is in his Son" (1 John 5:11) reaches us needy sinners not through our own religious chatter, but through God's own appointed witnesses: "For there are three that testify: the Spirit, the water, and the blood; and the three are in agreement" (1 John 5:7–8). For Luther it was self-evident that these three witnesses are the Gospel itself, or absolution (see John 6:63), Holy Baptism, and the blood of the New Testament in the Sacrament of the Altar.

What is at stake here is the centrality of the means of grace. Consider the Augsburg Confession's unique and laser-like concentration on the Gospel as the very essence of the public ministry: "To obtain such faith God instituted the office of the ministry [*Predigtamt*, or preaching office], that is, provided the Gospel and the sacraments. Through these, as through means, he gives the Holy Spirit, who works faith, when and where he pleases, in those who hear the Gospel."[52] There is no interest here in hierarchical chains of command, or in successions, whether broken or unbroken, of properly qualified hands. Nor is there any suggestion that ministers are the custodians of public morals or the heralds of social and political reforms. On the contrary, the public ministry is there simply for the Gospel, which means, primarily for the public service, the *liturgy* of Word and Sacrament:

> This power of keys or of bishops is used and exercised only by teaching and preaching the Word of God and by administering the sacraments. . . . In this way are imparted not bodily but eternal things and gifts, namely, eternal righteousness, the Holy Spirit, and eternal life. These gifts cannot be obtained except through the office of preaching and of administering the holy sacraments, for St. Paul says, "The gospel is the power of God for salvation for everyone who has faith" [Rom. 1:16].[53]

Two comments will round out the picture. First, it must never be forgotten that good preaching, that is "practical and clear sermons,"[54] constitutes the church's strongest missionary attraction. This major element of the liturgy is the minister's most demanding task. He may not escape from it—for instance by exchanging the role of shepherd, who feeds and defends the flock, for that of sheep dog, harassing sheep brigades to "do the real work" themselves.[55]

The second point is about the Holy Supper. Since it is rude even in ordinary life to receive gifts without saying thank you, it goes without saying that God's great gifts are to be received with thanksgiving. Therefore, in this secondary sense, "the ceremony [of the Lord's Supper] becomes a sacrifice of praise."[56] Its primary and basic nature and purpose, however, is that of pure gift or Gospel: forgiveness, life, and salvation are freely granted to penitent sinners in the very body and blood of the Lamb, by which these gifts were won. More is the pity that much "liturgical" fashion today again turns the sacrament into a sacrifice, contrary to Luther's great evangelical breakthrough. Impressive ceremonial edifices can then be erected on such faulty foundations, but the more such structures gain in cultic, symbolic weight of their own, the more they can do without the real New Testament Holy of Holies, the really present body and blood of the God-Man. The sacramental presence may or may not be affirmed in such schemes—it is simply no longer central or crucial.[57] By way of contrast, the vital meaning of the Sacrament as pure gift (1 Cor. 10:16–17) is confessed in Krauth's splendid pronouncement: "The Sacramental Presence is the necessary sequel, the crowning glory of the Incarnation and Atonement. . . . The glory and mystery of the Incarnation combine there as they combine nowhere else."[58]

Liturgy, then, is much more than forms and ceremonies, which are in themselves indifferent. It is first and foremost a firm theological content, namely, the holy Gospel and sacraments of God. Taken in this nontrivial sense, liturgy cannot be in competition with evangelism. After all, the "Spirit, the water, and the blood" of the liturgy are the very agents ("witnesses") of world evangelization! "Make disciples of all nations" and "This do in remembrance of me" go hand in hand. Ultimately, of course, the worship of God is its own end, while evangelism is a means to that end. The highest worship of God on earth is faith itself—and "the catholic faith is this, that we *worship* one God in three persons and three persons in one God" (Athanasian Creed). There will come a time, however, when the complete will replace the incomplete, and the caterpillar of faith will turn into the glorious butterfly of beatific sight (1 Cor. 13:8–12). Death itself will then be swallowed up in victory (1 Cor. 15:54), and all mission work or evangelism will cease. But the New Jerusalem will make the new heavens and the new earth resound forever with the worship of God, the Lamb, and the Spirit (Rev. 19–22).

Deep Structure and Surface Form

It is a very hallmark of our evangelical confession that "it is not necessary for the true unity of the Christian church that ceremonies, instituted by men, should be observed uniformly in all places,"[59] and that "the community of God in every place and at every time has the right, authority, and power to change, to reduce, or to increase ceremonies," but, of course, "without frivolity and offense."[60]

Today this is often misunderstood as liturgical *carte blanche*, and cited in support of license and chaos. The founding fathers of the Missouri Synod evidently understood the matter quite differently. The original synodical constitution made it a part of the "Business of Synod" to "strive after the greatest possible uniformity in ceremonies." This "desired uniformity in the ceremonies [was] to be brought about especially by the adoption of sound Lutheran agendas (church books)." All this grew out of serious theological concerns:

> Furthermore Synod deems it necessary for the purification of the Lutheran Church in America, that the emptiness and the poverty in the externals of the service be opposed, which, having been introduced here by the false spirit of the Reformed, is now rampant.

> All pastors and congregations that wish to be recognized as orthodox by Synod are prohibited from adopting or retaining any ceremony which might weaken the confession of the truth or condone or strengthen a heresy.[61]

In other words, so-called "indifferent" matters, or adiaphora, are not absolutely but only relatively indifferent. They are indifferent in the sense that the New Testament has no divinely instituted ritual law, like the Levitical. The external divine institutions —Baptism, the Holy Supper, and the preaching ministry within the one priestly and royal people of God—require that many particular decisions about time, place, and manner be taken in Christian wisdom and love. The fact that such decisions are not divinely prescribed does not make them unimportant. Already the Formula of Concord insisted that even "indifferent" matters could, in certain situations, have strong doctrinal implications, in which case they were no longer indifferent.[62]

Yet such clear-cut "cases of confession" are in the nature of the case the exception, not the rule in adiaphora. A more general principle is needed for the vast majority of cases requiring guidance about what is desirable or preferable rather than about what is commanded or forbidden. McLuhan's jingle, "the medium is the message," is a modern reminder of the important truth that *how* something is said is an integral part of *what* is said. Educators, too, have long known that indirect education—the whole ethos, atmosphere, and unspoken assumptions of a situation—conveys more powerful messages than what is expressly verbalized in direct education. This has enormous implications for the *how* of the liturgy.

One of the prime requirements of evangelical liturgical form is that it cultivate reverence. Luther says,

> Today we have in the churches an altar because of the communion of the Eucharist; we have platforms or pulpits for the purpose of teaching the people. This has been done, not only for the sake of necessity but also for the sake of solemnity.[63]

The Augsburg Confession itself says that "nothing contributes so much to the maintenance of dignity in public worship and the cultivation of reverence and devotion among the people as the proper observance of ceremonies in the churches."[64] And since "good order is very becoming in the church," reasons the Apology, it "is therefore necessary."[65] Slovenly irreverence must be called to repentance, lest priceless evangelical pearls be trampled underfoot by swine (Matt. 78:6).

Connected with good order is the matter of the stability of liturgical form. There are two aspects to this stability. One is the principle of continuity with the ancient church. The church of the evangelical Reformation wishes to be neither a new-fangled sect nor a biblicistic one which imagines that it can bypass the whole intervening history of the church. Wanting to be simply a faithful continuation of the orthodox church of the ages, it makes a point of having "introduced nothing, either in doctrine or in ceremonies, that is contrary to Holy Scripture or the universal Christian church."[66] Article XXIV in both the Augsburg Confession and the Apology repeatedly refers to the church fathers and to the Greek liturgy, by way of precedent. Luther's Large Catechism says, "Since from ancient times Sunday has been appointed for this purpose, we should not change it. In this way a common order will prevail and no one will create disorder by unnecessary innovation."[67] Behind this respect for genuine tradition—Chesterton called it "the democracy of the dead"—stands what might be called the principle of ecclesial humility: "Did the word of God originate with you? Or are you the only people it has reached?" (1 Cor. 14:36).

The second aspect concerns the pedagogical value of stability. In his preface to the Small Catechism Luther strongly urged the teachers of the Catechism to "adopt one form, adhere to it, and use it repeatedly year after year," and not to "alter a single syllable or recite the catechism differently from year to year," so as not to confuse the simple.[68] What holds for catechetics holds perhaps even more for liturgics, even though Luther's early writings seem to encourage a *laissez-faire* attitude. After his encounter with the flutter-spirits of emotional fanaticism, Luther grew more cautious, and the various Lutheran church orders of that time are decidedly conservative.[69]

A point made by C. S. Lewis is worth repeating here. Deploring the "liturgical fidget," Lewis saw the itch of novelty as an obstacle to worship, indeed as a confusion of worship with entertainment. A service, he said, "is a structure of acts and words through which we receive a sacrament, or repent, or supplicate, or adore." As in dancing so in worship, Lewis suggested, one needs to be thoroughly at home with the form in order to concentrate on the content without distraction: "As long as you notice, and have to count the steps, you are not yet dancing, but only learning to dance." The ideal service, he said, "would be one we were almost unaware of; our attention would have been on God. But every novelty prevents this. It fixes our attention on the service itself; and thinking about worship is a different thing from worshiping." Concluding with "an entreaty for permanence and uniformity," he said he could make do with almost any kind of service whatever if only it [would] stay put. But if each form is snatched away just when I am beginning to feel at home in it, then I can never make any progress in the art of worship.[70]

A certain healthy variety is of course built into the liturgy itself by way of the church year. So it is a wrong kind of variety, not variety itself, which ought to be criticized. In his 1523 *Formula Missae* (Form of the Mass) Luther, with characteristic bluntness, expressed his hesitancy about changing accustomed forms,

and more so because of the fickle and fastidious spirits who rush in like unclean swine without faith or reason, and who delight only in novelty and tire of it as quickly, when it has worn off. Such people are a nuisance even in other affairs, but in spiritual matters, they are absolutely unbearable.[71]

In his German Mass of 1526 he deplored "the great variety of new masses, for everyone makes his own order of service." The implication is that not everyone can do it equally well. A certain variety in rites has always existed, said Luther, but "it would be well if the service in every principality would be held in the same manner and if the order observed in a given city would also be followed by the surrounding towns and villages." "As far as possible we should observe the same rites and ceremonies, just as all Christians have the same baptism and the same sacrament [of the altar] and no one has received a special one of his own from God."[72]

The longer one examines the whole topic of liturgical form, the more it seems to take on the aspect of a paradox: On the one hand, adiaphora lie in the realm of Christian liberty, yet on the other hand, severe constraints operate to limit the hypothetical freedom of choice. Apart from the obvious fact that Christian liberty may never be equated with carnal license, is it possible to explain the paradox systematically? Perhaps an analogy from modern linguistics can help. Noam Chomsky suggests that children acquire linguistic competence much more quickly than a mechanical trial and error method would allow. Their brains seem to be "pre-wired" for language. Instead of sticking words together into a haphazard "string," or repeating set phrases in parrot fashion, children soon use syntactic structure to produce quite original turns of phrase. Language works, says Chomsky, not by mechanical rearrangements of the "surface" sentences, but by highly orderly transformations from the underlying "deep structures."

Let us now imagine a "liturgical grammar." The idea would be that although many "surface" forms are theoretically possible, only those are acceptable that are consistent with the theologically determined "deep structure"—for instance, the holistic understanding of *liturgy* in Article XXIV of the Apology of the Augsburg Confession previously alluded to. It would follow that different surface forms are appropriate to different deep structures ("Baptist forms for Baptist theology"). Apparently innocent surface changes, therefore, could signal serious mischief deeper down. Since orthodoxy, or the pure Gospel, is not the only possible theological "deep structure," and since, unlike language, the right "liturgical grammar" is far from inborn, the whole thing will take some careful sorting out. Even liturgical form, then, requires sound theological judgment. Artistic talent, though a great gift, is not enough.

Now, in the case of the words of a liturgical rite, it is fairly obvious how they can express or fail to express a given theological "deep structure." This is less clear in the case of music or of other "body language" generally. Indeed, many seem to assume that so long as the words are orthodox, the music is simply a matter of taste, and is theologically neither here nor there. A moment's reflection will show that this is not the case at all.

The new discipline of *sentics* claims with all due scientific rigor that much more than subjective taste is involved in music. It is possible to show, apparently, that different kinds of music have quite different effects, which are objectively, physiologically measurable.[73] This supports Luther's strong convictions about the power of music for good or ill.[74]

Of course music is not a means of grace. And while it obviously cannot of itself communicate cognitive content, it does affect the psyche at deep levels and in ways that are not well understood, but which may be described as *modal*. That is to say, *modes* like reverence, fear, eroticism, mirth, and the like are clearly distinguishable attitudinal states, which presumably are not reducible to propositions, although they can, of course, be discussed by means of propositions.

Whatever may be the rights and wrongs of *sentics,* however, it is sufficient for our purposes to go with a weaker form of the argument, to the effect that much of the impact of music depends on association. For example, Strauss waltzes evoke one kind of mental picture, polkas quite another, and marches a different one again. The stronger and the more specific these associations are in nonchurchly directions, the less suitable the corresponding music is for congregational worship. This is easily verified by means of a thought experiment. Imagine a "Sousa Mass," with churchified lyrics like "From the halls of Pontius Pilate, To the shores of New Guinea." (This is no worse than what one often has to endure for "special events.") Clearly, the "orthodox" lyrics do not save the day. The music's associational impact is too strong in the wrong direction. The whole thing is incongruous and grotesque. The same would be true of a "Waltz Mass" or a "Polka Mass," no matter how orthodox or traditional the words. Taste, be it noted, has nothing to do with these judgments. The present writer happens to be very fond of marches, waltzes, and polkas—in their places. Nor is there anything wrong with the implied "values" of patriotism, military valor, or romantic enchantment. If, as seems likely, most people would agree with the general argument so far, it is difficult to understand why all this good common sense should wilt into abject diffidence before the impudent vulgarities of the "Rock Mass," which ape the howling savages of soft drink commercials or worse. Such associations should be the least acceptable in the sanctuary of the Most High.

What we have considered here under the unassuming name of musical "associations" usually goes by the more pompous title of "culture." The conventional wisdom on that topic seems to flow fairly uncritically along some such syllogistic pathway as the following: (1) all adiaphora should be arranged for their maximal evangelistic impact; (2) cultural differences are theologically neutral, adiaphorous; (3) ergo, evangelistic faithfulness demands a liturgy in the "cultural idiom" of the "target audience."

That may well be a good formula for selling soap or cigarettes, but it will not do either as evangelism or as liturgics. To be sure, the Gospel can and must be proclaimed in the freewheeling atmosphere of the public square and the university (Acts 17:16ff.). But

St. Paul did not celebrate the liturgy there! The observance of the Holy Supper requires a setting which simply rules out any notion of liturgy as publicity stunting. The contrary argument seems convincing only when couched in intimidating generalities about "culture." But "culture," as Larry Vogel pointed out in an incisive essay, "is not a biblical term. To do a truly biblical theology of culture, the components of culture must be considered from a biblical perspective. The Bible says nothing about culture, per se, but it says much about the dimensions of culture."[75]

Broadening the previous conclusion, it may be said that the various components of culture must submit to the discipline of a sound "liturgical grammar" to be of service in the worship of the church. The application of such a discipline will probably mean that "local culture" is to be absorbed by the liturgy in small doses rather than big chunks, and gradually, preferably in the course of centuries. "Small dosage" coloration is virtually unavoidable, if for no other reason than that every translation is to some extent a cultural adaptation. But just as it would be grotesque to "enrich" the human anatomy with implants of pieces of pork, beef, or celery—as distinct from absorption by natural metabolism at the minute, molecular level—so it would be equally absurd to insert into the Christian liturgy, undigested as it were, large chunks of alien cultural matter. The culture is to pay homage to the liturgy, not the other way around. It is a great mistake to think that the traditional forms of the Lutheran liturgy represent 16th-century Saxon (or Swedish, or Norwegian, etc.) culture, and must now be Americanized, Africanized, or what have you. The liturgy is already transcultural, or crosscultural. It did not originate in Wittenberg, or in Uppsala, or for that matter in Rome. Whenever the orthodox church is planted in a new country or culture, its liturgy must not arise "from scratch," or by happenstance, but it is to be lovingly adapted to confess the new church's continuity with the "deep structures" of the pure Gospel throughout space/time.

Image and Integrity

What if Vladimir's emissaries had notified the Constantinople authorities in advance of their visit and had found the service for the occasion deliberately designed to appeal to them—perhaps with ancient cossack break-dancing thrown in for effect? They might have "liked" it, but they could hardly have respected such a performance. Modern Americans are of course quite sophisticated about manipulation. We are surrounded by it, take it for granted, and discount almost everything with the (usually silent) question, "What's his percentage?" In the case of religious huckstering, both question and answer seem to be getting louder. A careful reading of James Turner's *Without God, Without Creed: The Origins of Unbelief in America* does not support the view that the churches lost out because they failed to adjust quickly enough to the changing times. If anything, they adjusted too readily and too cravenly. Instead of meeting the cultural challenges with the necessary care and character, the churches largely capitulated to populist moods and expectations, with consequent loss of public respect.[76] In evangelism as in liturgy honesty is the best policy.

Evangelistic and liturgical honesty requires that the outward forms really correspond to and inculcate the intended theology. Attempting to disguise Lutheran content with sectarian and quasi-Pentecostal ways in hymns and worship "format" (a tacky term, but very expressive of a certain approach), is both dishonest and ultimately self-defeating. It is intellectualistic self-deception to imagine that as long as a few overly heterodox sentences are weeded out, no alien deep structures are being imported with alien surface forms. Once a taste arises for sectarian forms—including "gospel hymns" which often are neither—it will be found that a whole ethos comes with them, which will in the long term assert itself also theologically. Liturgical forms, with their deep structure implications and "subliminal" appeal, are Trojan horses, whose cargo is not obvious at first sight.

Not to beat about the bush, what is at stake today is not this or that detail, but the liturgical, churchly spirit as a whole. Will orthodox Lutheranism in America retain (or return to) its historic character as one of the three liturgical churches of Western Christendom, or can all this be safely left behind as Old World cultural baggage, to be replaced with freewheeling, cheery popfests of snappy tunes and upbeat chitchat?

The orthodox fathers of the Lutheran Church believed that the confession of the church was at stake in its liturgy. They therefore resisted Pietism's persistent nibbling away at the liturgy by degrees.[77] Yet Pietism largely won out and, completely contrary to its own intentions and expectations, paved the way for the dogmatic and liturgical devastations of Rationalism. In the Leipzig of Bach's day, for example, the flourishing church-life was systematically destroyed, beginning with Superintendent Rosenmueller's seemingly minor "reforms," like free texts instead of standard Gospels, public rather than private confession; the elimination of exorcism in Baptism, of chasubles, litanies, the sign of the cross, chanting, and of ceremonies emphasizing the real presence. All these changes were meant to make the worship more meaningful, attractive, and contemporary. The actual result, however, was that church and communion attendance declined catastrophically.[78]

In the New World too, a pietistically "softened-up" Lutheranism was soon casting longing glances at the seemingly greener grass of popular revivalism. Pastor J. Nicum, the centenary chronicler of the New York Ministerium, reports with deep sorrow how the emotional "conversion" technology gripped his church body like a fever.[79] The irony was that the very "new measures" which were so eagerly embraced for the sake of better evangelism, of involving the laity, and of keeping the youth with the church, had in the long term the very opposite effect. Congregations that had seemingly flourished as a result of revivals were nonexistent a few years later, and others were brought to the very brink of extinction. The youth went on to various sects which could do it all even better. This is not to say, of course, that revivalism cannot be "successful"—within the framework of revivalistic theology. It is difficult, however, to imagine a more self-defeating schizophrenia than that of the pastor who "on one Sunday morning examined, consecrated, and admitted his confirmands to the Holy Supper, but in the evening dragged them to the anxious bench, in order to convert them there."[80] The founders of the Missouri Synod also were told to abandon their "sacramental religion" and turn to the "new measures" instead, if they wished to be a living and growing church. C. F. W. Walther answered one such attack by the *Lutheran Observer*:

The reason why the Lutherans of the old school hold so firmly to the means of grace is not that they would save men without repentance and faith . . . but because they firmly hold that a poor sinner is justified before God and saved solely by faith, without works, without his merit, by grace, that is, that his salvation is due not to what he does, works, merits, but to God alone, who offers him full salvation in the means of grace. In that sense we are, indeed, "sacramentalists."[81]

The historical experience of their church body ought to warn modern Lutherans to be slow in bartering their liturgical treasures for illusory promises of huge evangelistic successes. The modern assault on liturgical worship is aimed not simply at a few old-fashioned customs or adiaphora, but at the whole liturgical, churchly spirit itself, which necessarily goes with a serious doctrine of the means of grace. One of the most significant books of our time, Marilyn Ferguson's *The Aquarian Conspiracy*, tells us in no uncertain terms that there is a massive cultural "shift from a religion mediated by authorities to one of direct spiritual experience."[82] The church of the "external Word and Sacrament" should be the last to yield to that carnal spiritualizing which is "the source, strength, and power of all heresy."[83] And Carter Lindberg has shown the deep inner connections between the fanatics of Luther's day, the Pietism that followed, and our modern Pentecostalist/Charismatic "renewals."[84] If the means of grace are to rule, and not just to reign ceremonially, then they cannot be combined with all sorts of incompatible, anti-liturgical bric-a-brac like the "Spiritual Gifts" scheme.[85] One must choose either the one or the other, the liturgy or the "new measures," the Gospel or enthusiasm.

The church's historic liturgical ways, however, are not, as it were, a necessary evil, an evangelistic liability, to be endured for the sake of orthodoxy. Quite the contrary, the "liturgical mode" is actually a great missionary advantage, because it is the best, most natural setting for the priceless jewels of the means of grace. It is deeply moving to observe among the spiritual heirs of Zwingli, Calvin, and Finney the sort of yearning for sacramental and liturgical fullness expressed by The Chicago Call of 1977.[86] A decade later some 1,800 of these "evangelicals" as a body joined the Antiochene Orthodox Church.[87] But why did these seekers have to wander as far away from the Reformation as exotic Damascus? Why did they not see in contemporary Wittenberg[88] a credible bearer of historic Christianity, in content as well as form?

In sum, the argument of this writing is not a plea for an unthinking, rigid traditionalism. It is rather an appeal for spiritual, churchly consistency. Let Lutheran practice be determined by Lutheran theology, and then it will be accorded the kind of respect which is the best possible basis for genuine missionary attraction. Integrity, not image or cheap verbiage, must draw men to the Gospel (1 Pet. 3:1–2), and the Gospel itself converts and confirms. No one can doubt the Good Shepherd's missionary zeal and compassion for his sheep. Yet he draws them with a quiet dignity that is entirely free of that breathless pestering and pandering which is mere salesmanship. When multitudes turn from him in fickle disenchantment, he does not run after them, shouting, "Wait! Just a moment! You've misunderstood my words about flesh and blood. All this can be put differently, too! Let me make it clear to you in cultural forms you will find more congenial!" None of that. Sadly but serenely he turns to his disciples: "You do not want to leave, too, do you?" Peter replies for them and for the church of all ages, "Lord, to whom shall we go? You have the words of eternal life" (John 6:67–68).

Notes

1. *Oxford Universal Dictionary*, 3d rev. ed. (Oxford: Oxford University Press, 1955), p. 2453.
2. LW, p. 6.
3. Ibid., pp. 134–135.
4. Ap IV, 228.
5. Ap IV, 310.
6. LW, p. 6.
7. Ibid.
8. LC I, 17.
9. LC II, 66.
10. Ap I, 2.
11. Ap XXIV, 27.
12. FC Ep X, 3; see also X, 8 –9.
13. FC Ep X, 6; see also X, 11.
14. LC I, 93 –94.
15. Ap XV, 11.
16. AC XV, 3, 4.

17. Ap XIII, 8.
18. Ap XXIV, 18.
19. Ap XXIV, 19.
20. Ap XXIV, 22.
21. Ap XXIV, 33–34.
22. AC XXIV, 5, 8.
23. Ap XXIV, 71.
24. Ap XXI, 4–6.
25. Ap XXI, 27.
26. Ap XXI, 9.
27. FC SD X, 9.
28. AC VII, 3.
29. AC XXI, 2.
30. AC XXVIII, 73–74.
31. AC XXVIII, 53–57.
32. AC XXVIII, 34.
33. FC Ep X, 5.
34. FC Ep X, 8, 12.
35. FC Ep X, 7.
36. Ap XXIV, 3.
37. AC XXIV, 3 (German).
38. Ap XV, 13.
39. Ap VII and VIII, 5.
40. Ap XXIV, 5.
41. AC XV, 1.
42. Ap XXVIII, 17.
43. Ap XV, 49.
44. Ap XV, 20–21.
45. AC Conclusion, 5.
46. SC VII.
47. LC I, 73–74.
48. Ap XXIV, 80.
49. Ap XXIV, 36.
50. Ap XXIV, 35.
51. AC XXIV, 35
52. AC V, 1–2.
53. AC XXVIII, 8–9.
54. Ap XXIV, 50.
55. For a defense of the Authorized Version's translation, "for the perfecting of the saints" (Eph. 4:12), against the modern "equipping," see H. P. Hamann, "Church and Ministry: An Exegesis of Ephesians 4:1–16," *Lutheran Theological Journal* (Australia) 16/3 (December 1982): 121–128.

56. Ap XXIV, 74.

57. Note the strange Roman Catholic/Presbyterian convergence in Christopher Kiesling and Ross Mackenzie, "The Eucharist as Sacrifice: A Roman Catholic–Reformed Dialogue," *Journal of Ecumenical Studies* 15/3 (Summer 1978): 415–440. The Lutheran authors of the 1983 U.S. Lutheran/Reformed union formula, which gives equal rights to both confessions, note, "But the structure of the eucharistic liturgies of the Presbyterian Church (U.S.A.) and the Reformed Church in America are identical to that of the *Lutheran Book of Worship.*" They also quote from the Lutheran/Episcopal Dialogue: "In most contemporary exegesis the words 'body' and `blood' are interpreted increasingly not as substances but as saving event." See James E. Andrews and Joseph A. Burgess, eds., *An Invitation to Action* (Philadelphia: Fortress Press, 1984), pp. 116, 123.

For a general orientation see Charles Evanson, "Worship and Sacrifice," *Concordia Theological Quarterly* 42/4 (October 1978): 347–377; John Pless, "Implications of Recent Exegetical Studies for the Doctrine of the Lord's Supper: A Survey of the Literature," *Concordia Theological Quarterly* 48/2–3 (April–July 1984): 203–220; and John R. Stephenson, "The Holy Eucharist: at the Center or Periphery of the Church's Life in Luther's Thinking?" in Kurt Marquart, John R. Stephenson, and Bjarne W. Teigen, eds., *A Lively Legacy: Essays in Honor of Robert Preus* (Fort Wayne: Concordia Theological Seminary, 1985), pp. 154–163.

58. C. P. Krauth, *The Conservative Reformation and Its Theology* (Minneapolis: Augsburg Publishing House, 1963), pp. 650, 655.

59. AC VII, 3.

60. FC SD X, 9.

61. *Concordia Historical Institute Quarterly* 19/3 (October 1946): 5, 12. In 1979 the synodical Constitution's Article III, Par. 5 ("The endeavor to bring about the largest possible uniformity in church practice, church customs, and, in general, in congregational affairs") was changed to a new Par. 7: "Encourage congregations to strive for uniformity in church practice, but also to develop an appreciation of a variety of responsible practices and customs which are in harmony with our common profession of faith" (see 1977 *Handbook*, p. 16, and 1979 *Handbook*, p. 253).

62. FC Ep X.

63. Quoted in W. Elert, *The Structure of Lutheranism* (St. Louis: Concordia Publishing House, 1962), p. 338. See WA 42: 72.

64. "Articles About Matters of Dispute . . .," par. 6, after AC XXI.

65. Ap XV, 22.

66. AC Conclusion, 5.

67. LC I, 85.

68. LC Preface, 7–8.

69. Luther D. Reed, *The Lutheran Liturgy*, rev. ed. (Philadelphia: Muhlenberg Press, 1959), p. 78 and passim.

70. C. S. Lewis, *Letters to Malcolm: Chiefly on Prayer* (New York: Harcourt, Brace, and World, 1964), pp. 4–5.

71. AE 53: 19.

72. Ibid., pp. 61–62.

73. Daniel Reuning, "Luther and Music," *Concordia Theological Quarterly* 48/1 (January 1984): 18.

74. A doctoral dissertation on "Music as Pastoral Care in the Theology of Martin Luther" is now being written by Pastor Richard Gudgeon and may appear in print upon completion.

75. Larry M. Vogel, "Mission Across Cultures and Traditional Lutheran Cultus," *Concordia Journal* 12/3 (May 1986): 88.

76. One specific dimension of the churches' accommodation to the prevailing culture is treated in Ann Douglas, *The Feminization of American Culture* (New York: Alred Knopf, 1977).

77. Friedrich Kalb, *Theology of Worship in 17th Century Lutheranism* (St. Louis: Concordia Publishing House, 1965), p. xi.

78. Guenther Stiller, *Johann Sebastian Bach and Liturgical Life in Leipzig* (St. Louis: Concordia Publishing House, 1984), pp. 158–167.

79. J. Nicum, *Geschichte des evangelisch-lutherischen Ministeriums vom Staate New York und angrenzenden Staaten und Laendern* (Verlag des New York-Ministeriums, 1888), pp. 124–139. Of great interest are the 13 theological objections to the "new measures" recorded by Charles Porterfield Krauth in testimony before the court in Allentown, Pennsylvania (pp. 138–139, note).

80. Ibid., p. 133.

81. Cited in Francis Pieper, *Christian Dogmatics*, 3 vols. (St. Louis: Concordia Publishing House, 1951), 2: 523, n. 38.

82. Marilyn Ferguson, *The Aquarian Conspiracy: Personal and Social Transformation in the 1980s* (Los Angeles: J. P. Tarcher, 1980), p. 369.

83. SA III, VIII, 9.

84. Carter Lindberg, *The Third Reformation?* (Philadelphia: Fortress Press, 1983).

85. C. Peter Wagner praises the "*Congregatio Crista*" because it "believes so much in their body life that they refused to hire pastors for their churches." The members are so well supplied by "properly using gifts" that "a professional minister is simply excess baggage. . . . The only man the church hires is a bookkeeper." *What Are We Missing?* (Carol Stream, Ill.: Creation House, 1973), p. 79. Lutherans trying to graft this scheme onto the means of grace tend to make it sound as if the latter were inert and ineffective until activated by the "enzymes" of the "gifts." And to invent a "gift of evangelism" ("to share the Gospel with unbelievers in such a way that the unbeliever becomes a disciple of the Lord Jesus") is to attribute conversion to that gift rather than to the means of grace. It also implies that the Savior himself lacked that gift in John 6:66, 8:59, and elsewhere! For broad implications of the "gifts" scheme, see H. A. Snyder and D. V. Runyon, *Foresight: 10 Major Trends That Will Dramatically Affect the Future of Christians and the Church* (New York: Thomas Nelson, 1986), pp. 81–94. For a radical antidote see "On the Doctrine of the Holy Spirit" in H. Sasse, *We Confess the Church* (St. Louis: Concordia Publishing House, 1986), pp. 17–39.

86. Robert Webber and Donald Bloesch, eds., *The Orthodox Evangelicals* (New York: Thomas Nelson, 1978).

87. Religious News Service Dispatch, *Christian News*, November 17, 1986.

88. Leading spirits of The Chicago Call had Lutheran connections. Webber and Bloesch, p. 20, and *Religious News Service Dispatch,* November 5, 1986.

3

Worship Resources in Missouri Synod's History

Fred L. Precht

General European Background

Lutheran Orthodoxy

The period of Lutheran Orthodoxy is commonly taken to have begun with the issuance of the Formula of Concord in 1577. Critics of this period describe it as one of fixed dogmatic interpretation; they posit and exaggerate its intellectual conformity and thus charge it with losing sight of the vital relationship of the believer with his God. Such criticism has produced the label of *dead orthodoxy*.[1] Granted that the 17th century was an age of polemics—polemics not only against Rome, but also against the Reformed communion as a result of the ecclesiastico-political situation—a more balanced evaluation reveals that the term *dead orthodoxy* is a caricature and recognizes that the influential authors in this era of orthodoxy were also almost without exception profoundly interested in the maintenance of a living spirituality.[2] This was the period of some of the great Lutheran dogmaticians: Martin Chemnitz (1522–86), John Gerhard (1582–1637), Nicholas Hunnius (1585–1623), and Jasman Rasmussen Brochmond (1585–1652). Their works inspired men entering the public ministry with a clear conception of biblical truth. Granted that there were situations that justly evoked criticism, these should not be allowed to become the basis for grossly exaggerated generalizations.[3]

Thirty Years' War

The bitter theological debates, first between Romanists and Protestants and later between Lutherans and Calvinists, which followed the publication of the Book of Concord in 1580, containing the Lutheran symbols, finally resulted in the Thirty Years' War (1618–48), a religious-political war, fought at different times and in various places, a war that ended in compromise, that left untold destruction and disrupted church life.[4] New political structures—Germany was divided into more than three hundred territories, or states, each governed by a separate prince or ruler—caused church and state to become so united that the state controlled the church, and pastors became officials of the state. Generally, a ruler, who could decide whether his territory would be Lutheran[5] or Reformed, exercised authority over the church through the consistory, the members of which were appointed by and responsible to him. Congregations were subject to the rule of their ministers, who often acted more as state officials than as pastors. Class distinctions were rigidly observed, at the bottom of which were workers and peasants. Since the upper classes (professional people and wealthy burghers) often wanted their baptisms, weddings, funerals, and Communion in private (in church or at home), it was mostly for the common people that such acts were performed in the church. Clergy, trained at the universities in their respective theology through the medium of Latin and expounded in the light of current controversies, had trouble edifying their hearers with their long sermons. Hence sleeping during the sermon became common.[6] Despite this, people attended church; they received Holy Communion when it was offered—customarily not too often in the course of the year. Lacking, however, was the vital spirit that characterized the faith and worship in the 16th century.

Pietism

Against this backdrop Pietism arose, a movement that began in the Lutheran Church,[7] but which was to exert influence far beyond such theological boundaries, spreading through Germany, Scandinavia, and Switzerland. While its exact origins are somewhat obscure, Philip Jacob Spener (1635–1705), senior pastor at Frankfort am

Main, later court preacher at Dresden, gave it direction and momentum in the Lutheran Church. In 1675 he published his *Pia Desideria* (Heartfelt Desire), which appeared originally as the preface to John Arndt's (1555–1621) "Church Postil," a series of sermons. In this work, after giving an overview of the corrupt conditions in the Lutheran Church, Spener made various proposals to correct matters and bring about a second Reformation of the church that was, so to speak, stranded in orthodoxy. Herein were set forth all the basic ideas and aspirations of what later was called Pietism. Primitive Christianity was the pattern for the rebirth of the church. Reflective of the mystical spiritualism of John Tauler (1300–61) and others, regeneration (a biological image) became the central subject instead of the Word of God and justification (a forensic image), so highly stressed by the reformers and orthodox theologians. Hence expressions such as *rebirth, new man, inner man, illumination,* and *edification* became common parlance and were given inordinate attention. As a result, Pietism modified the concept *church.* No longer the community of those called by Word and Sacrament, it was more an association of the reborn, of those who "want to be Christians in earnest."[8] Although Spener, in the *Pia Desideria,* gave only passing attention to the *collegia pietatis* (private study and conventicles, devotional assemblies in his house), he gradually attached so much importance to such gatherings of true Christians—intended as leaven to the whole lump—that they spread and developed into little churches within the church (*ecclesiolae in ecclesia*).

Famous pietist concepts and slogans were *life versus doctrine, Holy Spirit versus the office of the ministry,* and *reality versus the appearance of godliness* (cf. 2 Tim. 3:5). Faith, so important to the 16th-century reformers, was now more clearly defined as *living faith,* evidence of which was demonstrated by the *fruits of faith* (Matt. 7:16ff; John 7:17; Gal. 5:22; Rom. 6:22), namely, in the sanctified life, above all in the exercise of love. On the positive side, this emphasis on love resulted in various social welfare activities and, more important, in inner and foreign mission endeavors—in which, for example, August Hermann Francke (1663–1727), son-in-law and avid colaborer of Spener, distinguished himself by organizing and establishing various charitable institutions. The stature and influence of Francke also made the University at Halle in Germany become the headquarters of Pietism, a school that educated many of the sons of the nobility as pastors, who then spread Pietism far and wide. Granted there were other positive contributions of Pietism to Christianity: awakening the established church from coldness and institutionalism; emphasis on exemplary personal character of both clergy and laity; encouragement of Bible reading, Bible distribution, personal devotion, and prayer; and involvement of laity in church and mission endeavors. But the negative aspects, particularly in the matters of corporate worship, dare not be overlooked. The pietists understood the Christian faith as being largely ontological (i.e., concerned with the true nature of things, with the *being of God*), so that the Word of God as address and promise, Law and Gospel, man's response in faith, and justification as a real life event—the dynamic categories so emphasized by Luther—were pushed into the background and minimized. The pietistic striving for personal consciousness of regeneration led to an underevaluation of the means of grace, namely, the Word of God and the sacraments, the very core of corporate worship. Moreover, little importance was attached to the ministry of Word and Sacrament. The pastor was more the accountable representative, witness, and example of the spiritual life of godliness. Preaching stressed the personal, revivalistic, admonitory elements in preference to sound doctrine. Stories of exemplary living and dying, the devotion of twice-born people played a prominent role. Where the sermon was based on the traditional pericopes, it was invariably supplemented with a Bible study. Moreover, the thoroughly regenerated, Pietists thought, did not need such crutches as the formal liturgy, the observance of the church year and Christian customs. Formal prayers gave way to extempore utterances by ministers as well as laity. Hymns based on the objective facts of God's redemptive love in Jesus Christ were discarded for hymns of human experience. The subjective and emotional held sway in corporate worship.

In regarding itself as an international and interconfessional movement, Pietism diluted and dissolved the confessional consciousness of orthodoxy from within. Spener, for instance, with his emphasis on subjective faith (*fides qua creditur*) over against objective faith (*fides quae creditur*), played down the difference between Lutheran and Reformed, though he bemoaned the Calvinistic doctrine of predestination. Pietists often felt more close to "fellow believers" in other churches than to their own church members. This attitude gave rise to a false ecumenicity, foreshadowing a certain transdenominationalism current today.

The aforementioned tendencies of Pietism quite naturally involved it in a long and oftentimes venomous controversy with orthodox church authorities and theologians, a struggle that orthodoxy was little able to win before the onset of Rationalism or the Enlightenment, as it was known in Germany.

Rationalism

Rationalism occupied a period in history from the early 17th century to the late 18th century, when philosophers emphasized the use of reason as the best method of learning truth. Its leaders included the French Rene Descartes, Denis Diderot, Jean Jacques Rousseau, Voltaire, and the English philosopher John Locke. Relying heavily on the scientific method, with its emphasis on experimentation and careful observation, the movement produced many important advances in such fields as anatomy, astronomy, chemistry, mathematics, and physics. Moreover, in their formulation of ideals of human dignity and worth, the thinkers of this period greatly influenced the leaders of the French Revolution as well as the American Revolution.

Set within the worldwide tendency to Rationalism is what is called the Enlightenment (German: *Aufklärung*), a movement of thought that appeared especially in clear cut form in 18th-century Germany. Its direct bearing on corporate worship prompts the focus of this discussion on this more restrictive movement.

The Enlightenment, in its focus on reason and religion, sought to release man from the coercion of the church's dogma by establishing man's reason as the ultimate authority in place of divine revelation. In its concern with the practical side of Christianity, the rationalists "discovered" a nondogmatic natural religion in the Scriptures and they separated what they considered to be the reasonable and original Gospel from what was to them perverted, institutionalized Christianity. This view, of course, led to biblical criticism on a philosophical basis, the most radical of which is found in the writings of Hermann S. Reimarus (1694–1798), professor at the University of Hamburg. In his *Wolfenbüttel Fragments*, for instance, published after his death by Gotthold E. Lessing (1729–81), critic and dramatist, Reimarus, influenced by the English Deists, completely rejected supernatural, biblical revelation, charging the authors with deliberate deception. Lessing himself held that man had developed beyond the need for Christianity (*Education of the Human Race*, 1780). Moreover, in his best-known work, *Nathan the Wise* (1779), he argued that truth is found in Christianity, Islam, and Judaism, and thus religious toleration is imperative. With Immanuel Kant's "Have the courage to make use of your own understanding" as the watchword of the Enlightenment (*Religion Within the Bounds of Reason Only*, 1793), it is understandable that, while Pietism rejected the historical church's liturgy as being too objective and sacramental, thus rejecting its fixed forms, Rationalism rejected both forms and content. Similar to later Pietism, Rationalism could not tolerate the fixed and recurring elements in the liturgy. It was ever striving for something new, to the confusion of the congregation and the unimaginable destruction of the liturgy. The ancient and beautiful Introits, Kyries, Glorias, and Creeds, for instance, were frequently discarded. The brief, terse, laconic ancient collects and prayers were exchanged for verbose, sentimental emotings. The church year with its major and minor festivals and their unfolding of the great events of God in Jesus Christ for the redemption of sinful mankind held little meaning to those who denied the resurrection. In fact, the Enlightenment not only rejected supernatural revelation but also man's sinfulness. Moreover, to the Rationalists, an ideal of happiness was substituted for the divine plan of redemption. With the church considered more as a lecture hall, and the pastor more as a moral instructor than preacher of the Gospel, sermons emphasized the practice of virtue and civil service as cherished ideals. The Sacrament, bereft of its biblical and confessional essence, the result of Genevan influence, was infrequently observed in the Reformed tradition. The Words of Institution, as well as the words at the distribution, were frequently recast to reflect the intellectual nuances of Rationalism. The stream of notable hymns by such authors as Tobias Clausnitzer, Simon Dach, Paul Gerhardt, and Johann Rist, albeit produced during the subjective and emotional era of Pietism, dried up. The earlier, strong, confessional hymns, if used, were often altered beyond recognition, to make them conform to the new theology. As for the occasional rites, these were modified in moralizing fashion as deemed necessary for the occasion or borrowed from the privately produced agendas or liturgical forms that appeared and supplanted the historic rites.[9]

Efforts Toward Recovery

The cumulative effects of the Thirty Years' War, Pietism, and Rationalism, spanning almost two centuries, left worship and the life of the churches of the Reformation at a low ebb at the opening of the 19th century. Removed from the sound theology of the Reformers and the Lutheran symbols, there occurred, as someone has said, a depopulation of the congregations. Worship was manward instead of Godward; moral perfection was exalted above the grace of God in Christ Jesus. Freedom in matters of worship, coupled with the desire for relevance to the *Zeitgeist*, resulted in rare celebrations of Holy Communion—considered to be an appendage—with the sermon, or address, given chief emphasis. Congregational participation was limited to listening to the sermon and to highly verbose homiletical prayers. The church year, except for the observance of a few high festivals, lost its meaning. Areas in which there was still some semblance of retaining the historic service with its theology and customs—for instance in parts of Saxony, Mecklenburg, and Nürnberg—were the exception. It is to be noted that it was in this period of the church's history that the large migrations of confessional Lutherans to America took place.

The time for change had arrived; and it was in, what is referred to as the confessional revival of the 19th century that a reaction to the deteriorated situation occurred.

In 1817 Claus Harms (1778–1855) archdeacon of St. Nikolai Church at Kiel—a man who had turned from Rationalism to Lutheranism—reissued Luther's Ninety-Five Theses together with his own in which he tried strenuously to arouse German Lutherans to the dangers of the "papacy of reason."[10] Revised liturgies and hymnals based on earlier models began to appear in some of the Lutheran territorial churches. What is known as the Saxon Agenda

appeared in 1812, a book that will be discussed below. The Prussian Agenda of Fredrick William III, introduced in the cathedral
church in Berlin in 1822, was part of the effort to unite the Lutheran
and Reformed churches. Despite its equivocating language relative
to the Lutheran view of the real presence, from the standpoint of
form—based as it was on historic 16th-century models—it was not
only a step in the right direction, but it also gave impulse to the
movement of liturgical study and worship renewal.

Of special note is the *Agende für Christliche Gemeinden* (1844),
prepared by Wilhelm Löhe,[11] pastor in Neuendettelsau, Bavaria, the
founder of the Synod's Concordia Theological Seminary, since 1976
located in Fort Wayne, Indiana. In the foreword, directed to pastor
Friedrich Conrad Wyneken (1810–76), a missionary who came to
America in 1838 and who began serving Lutheran congregations at
Friedheim and Fort Wayne, Indiana, Löhe says that he looked
through 200 old agendas in order to arrive at a consensus of best
usage. The liturgical completeness of the *Hauptgottesdienst* (Chief
Service) contained therein can readily be seen from the following
outline:

Hymn	Offertory Sentence (4)
Confiteor	General Prayer
Absolution	Hymn
Introit	Preface
Kyrie	Sanctus
Gloria	Verba
Salutation and Response	Agnus Dei
Collect	Lord's Prayer
Epistle	Pax Domini
Hallelujah	Distribution
Hymn (in lieu of historic	
Graduals)	Nunc Dimittis
Salutation and Response	Salutation and Response
Gloria tibi	Thanksgiving Collect (3)
Gospel	Salutation and Response
Laus tibi	Benedicamus
Credo	Aaronic Benediction
Sermon	

In addition to the above service, the agenda includes Matins and Vespers, Lauds, Prime, Compline, the Litany, General Prayers, rites of Installation of a Pastor, Baptism, Confirmation, Marriage, and Communion of the Sick. Prepared especially for Lutherans in America, this book was used largely by congregations in Michigan, Ohio, and Indiana, until it was gradually supplanted by the official agenda of the Synod, published twelve years later. Luther D. Reed asserts that Löhe's agenda was one of the most important works in the 19th-century movement toward the recovery of the liturgy.[12]

There were other notable contributions toward the confessional-liturgical revival of the 19th century. Theodore Kliefoth (1810–95), Lutheran theologian and cathedral preacher at Schwerin, produced *Die ursprüngliche Gottesdienst-Ordnung in den deutschen Kirchen lutherischen Bekenntnisses* (1847) and *Liturgische Abhandlungen* (1854–61), both erudite works, the latter consisting of eight volumes. Ludwig Schöberlein, professor at Heidelberg and later at Göttingen, issued his *Schatz des Liturgischen Chor und Gemeindegesangs* (1865–72) in three volumes, which explored the musical and liturgical treasures of the 16th century. Johannes Zahn (1817–95), prominent hymnologist and church musician, published *Die Melodien der deutschen evangelischen Kirchenlieder*, a monumental work in six volumes. Georg Rietschel, professor of practical theology at the University of Leipzig, issued his two-volume *Lehrbuch der Liturgik* (1899–1908). Friedrich Spitta (1852–1924) and Julius Smend (1857–1930), professors at the University of Strasbourg, founded the *Monatschrift für Gottesdienst und Kirchliche Kunst* in 1896. Of inestimable value for the student of early Lutheran liturgies is the work of the Erlangen University professor, Emil Sehling, *Die evangelischen Kirchenordnungen des XVI. Jahrhunderts*, begun prior to World War I and completed after World War II.

The Saxons in Missouri: Early Beginnings

In 1839 the followers of Martin Stephan, pastor in Dresden, having banded together into an emigration society, left Germany and came to St. Louis and Perry County, Missouri—some 600 people in four ships (one ship with about 57 people was lost at sea). While the political and economic conditions existing in Saxony left much to be desired, it was the religious factor, especially the spirit of Rationalism, that exerted the more direct influence on their coming to America. On April 26, 1847, the German Evangelical Lutheran Synod of Missouri, Ohio, and Other States was organized at Chicago, and C. F. W. Walther was elected as its first president.

Kirchenbuch (1812)

It was the *Kirchenbuch für den evangelischen Gottesdienst der Königlich Sächsischen Lande*,[13] commonly referred to as the Saxon Agenda (1812), that the Saxons brought with them to America. Walther occasionally refers to this book in his *Pastoraltheologie*.[14] Although the agendas of Herzog Heinrich (1539) and Kursachsen (Electorate of Saxony, 1580) still had official status, they were accorded little authority as a result of Pietism and Rationalism. Hence the 1812 Agenda was a service book more in line with the spirit of the day. The disastrous effects of the foregoing on the liturgy are clearly in evidence, for the book does not even include an outline of the *Hauptgottesdienst* (Chief Service). This was not specifically issued until 1842.[15] In contrast to many liturgies at the time, in which the opening hymn simply afforded the congregation opportunity to assemble for the sermon, this agenda retained the Salutation, the Collect, and the reading of the Epistle and Gospel before the sermon. As for the Communion, the Words of Institution and the Lord's Prayer remained,[16] together with a versicle and response, Post-Communion Prayer, and Blessing.[17] The book leaned heavily on G. F. Seiler (1733–1807), a German theologian of Erlangen with supranaturalistic views.

The following translation represents an overview of this agenda's contents:

Part I

Epistles and Gospels for the customary Sundays and Festivals
Epistles and Gospels for Various Festival and Days of Apostles
History of the Suffering and Death of Jesus
History of the Resurrection of Jesus
History of the Ascension on Jesus
History of the Destruction of Jerusalem

86

Part II

Intonations and Collects
  On Sundays and Ferial Days
  On Festivals and at Festival Occasions
  On Penitential Days and at Penitential Admonitions
  Concerning the Chief Articles of the Christian Faith
  At Special Occasions
General Prayers for Sundays
Performance of Holy Baptism (five forms)
Performance of Confirmation
Celebration of the Lord's Supper
Marriage Ceremony (five forms)
Performance of Ordination of a Minister
Benedictions (four forms)

In briefly assessing the contents, it appears as though the church year is adhered to more generally than by most agendas of this period. The Hebrew Hallelujah is always transcribed into the German "Gelobet sei er" or "Gelobet sei Gott," for it was felt that Jewish elements do not belong in the Christian service.[18] Many of the ancient collects, having come from the Gelasian, Gregorian, and Leonine sacramentaries, are considerably altered. The most striking influences of Rationalism appear in the rites of Baptism, largely viewed as a ceremony of consecration, initiation, or inauguration. The term *Einweihung* (consecration, initiation) occurs *ad nauseam*, as, for example: "Durch die heilige Taufe werden wir eingeweiht zum Bekenntnisse und zur Befolgung der Religion, deren Stifter Jesus Christus ist."[19] The admonitions to Baptism are inordinately long, and the language verbose and homiletical. The sign of the cross upon the forehead and upon the breast is retained. Of these baptismal forms Steffens says: "Of the five forms for Baptism . . ., but one was in some measure endurable."[20]

The confession of sins, listed under the General Prayers for Sundays (thus harking back to the practice in *Offene Schuld*), is the form from the Saxony church order of 1581, as included in Divine Service I, left column (LW, pp. 136–137). This is followed by a declarative absolution (Saxon Agenda, Part II, 147–148).

The Holy Communion contains no Preface. Instead, the pastor reads what is called "Anrede an die Communicanten vor der Communion" (Address to the Communicants before the Communion). Toward the conclusion of this address the communicants are encouraged to approach the Lord's Table with joyful hearts as they celebrate the "Remembrance of the Love of Christ"—admittedly a rather pleasant note in contrast to the often doleful, downcast, unworthy attitude assumed by the pietists.

Pastors' chants for the Lord's Prayer and Verba Testamenti are provided at the end of the agenda. This is considered good usage and should not fall into disuse. In addition to the traditional chants, alternative melodies are offered. The sign of the cross is employed with the Verba in the chant settings. Typical nineteenth century music designations appear: *Divotamente, Con Divozione, Langsam, Etwas Geschwinder, Feierlich, Ernsthaft und Choralmässig.*

Of interest is Steffen's remark,

> The rationalistic Book of Forms [*Agende*], the rationalistic hymnal, and the rationalistic schoolbooks were enough in themselves to burden any Lutheran-believing conscience without further prodding.[21]

Kirchengesangbuch (1847)

While the Saxon Agenda left much to be desired, both theologically and liturgically, the more immediate concern of the Saxon immigrants was the matter of a good, confessionally sound hymnal for use in corporate worship. Coming as they did from different parts of Germany, each with its own hymnal, the hymnals they brought with them were numerous and varied, both as to texts and tunes. Moreover, the orthodox texts of many of the sixteenth- and seventeenth-century hymns had been altered to suit the spirit of Pietism and Rationalism. One can readily imagine the confusion in worship that such diversity would create. The solution was to publish a new hymnal.

As early as November 1845, the need for producing a new hymnal for the confessional groups of Lutherans was presented to Trinity congregation (*Gesamtgemeinde*: federated congregation) in St. Louis by C. F. W. Walther, its pastor. After giving its ready approval, the congregation soon proceeded to appoint a committee to implement the project.[22] In August 1847 the hymnal apppeared with the title *Kirchengesangbuch für Evangelisch-Lutherische Gemeinden ungeänderter Augsburgischer Confession,*[23] the work of "several Lutheran pastors in Missouri," with Walther undoubtedly as the leading figure.[24] Simply a text edition, it included 437 hymns, prayers, antiphons, Luther's Small Catechism (*Enchiridion*), and the Augsburg Confession.

The committee's concern for quality hymns is exhibited in the criteria for selection that appeared in *Der Lutheraner,* announcing the appearance of the hymnal:

> In the selection of the adopted hymns the chief consideration was that they be pure in doctrine; that they have found almost universal acceptance within the Orthodox German Lutheran Church and have thus received the almost unanimous testimony; that they had come forth from the true spirit [of Lutheranism]; that they express not so much the changing circumstances of individual persons but rather contain the language of the whole church, because the book is to be used primarily in public worship; and finally that they, though bearing the imprint of Christian simplicity, be not merely rhymed prose but the creations of a truly Christian poetry.[25]

As for the hymn tunes, besides supplying a helpful index in the hymnal, the committee envisioned publishing shortly a book of tunes, tunes reflecting their concern for "the proper preservation of the wonderful rich treasury of . . . church melodies."[26] Thus this hymnal constituted an important contribution to the confessional-liturgical revival of the 19th century begun in Germany. This hymnal remained in use until the Synod's gradual transition from German worship services to English with these changes in three editions: the addition of the Epistle and the Gospel pericopes and the history of the Destruction of Jerusalem in 1848; six hymns in 1857; and 41 additional hymns in 1917.

The Polyrhythmic Chorale

The "wonderful rich treasury of . . . church melodies" about which the hymnal committee was intent on preserving, has reference to the chorales in their polyrhythmic, or rhythmic, form, a form that originated and was prevalent in Reformation times. Various influences, not the least of which were Pietism and Rationalism, had

turned the free, pliable, irregular rhythmic flow of the early German chorale and Genevan psalter tunes into the isometric form,
where all the notes are of more equal value, arranged in strict measures of 3/4 or 4/4 meter, often prefixed with a time, or meter, signature, thus depriving the sturdy chorale tunes of their original
rhythmic vitality, of their natural flow and freedom. This "flattened
out" form of the chorale, less musically interesting and less exciting to sing, resulted in a slow, dragging singing on the part of the
congregation, a custom which the immigrants coming to America
had experienced in their fatherland. An article appearing in a church
paper in Germany in 1847 describes what must have been a rather
horrendous experience:

> Each syllable is sung without distinction for a period of about four
> beats; on the last syllable of each line or at the end of the melodic
> phrase there follows a long fermata lasting 8–12 beats, the last part
> of which is incorporated in a more or less intricate organ inter-
> lude. So all the melodies follow one line after the other in this rep-
> etitious manner, whether sad or joyous, mournful or exultant, all
> performed in a creeping, dragging fashion. The hymns of Luther
> have had their wings clipped and have put on the straightjacket of
> 4/4 time. And so it came about that the more inflexible the singing
> of the chorale was, the more solemn it was thought to be.[27]

In reversing this situation, no small credit is due Friedrich Layriz
(1808–59) for his efforts in behalf of the polyrhythmic form of the
chorale in Bavaria, with the guidance and encouragement of Wilhelm Löhe. Educated at Erlangen and Leipzig, Layriz became a pastor, serving parishes successively at Hirschlag, St. Georgen (near
Bayreuth), and Schwaningen (near Ansbach). Disappointed with the
1811 hymnal for Bavarian Lutherans, a book—he strongly insisted—
that contained wretched products of Rationalism, hymns that neither
exhibited faith nor love, and that were decidedly at odds with the
fundamental doctrines of Lutheranism,[28] prompted him to publish, in
1839, the year the Saxons left Germany, a collection of 117 chorales
in their rhythmic form.[29] This was followed by two more collections for school and home, in 1848 and 1850.[30] However, it was his
Kern des deutschen Kirchengesangs,[31] his *magnum opus*, appearing
from 1844–55, that had the greatest impact on the course of the
polyrhythmic chorale, as well as on the movement to recapture the

Kernlieder, the splendid normative core of Reformation hymnody. It made him one of the most influential musicians not only in Bavaria,[32] but also in the history of the Synod.

Appreciating the original rhythmic form of the chorales, Walther wasted no time training his congregation in their performance. As early as 1849 his congregation resolved to hold weekly practice sessions.[33] Gradually the enthusiasm for this form of the chorale spread to other congregations. Not all congregations, however, became so enamored with the form, and a certain amount of opposition developed to the point that the Altenburg congregation asked the 1852 convention of the Synod "to publish a sound opinion (*Gutachten*) about the rhythmic chorale, not only giving a historical presentation of the matter, but also taking into consideration the various objections to the introduction of the same."[34] The synod instructed Pastor Gustav Schaller to respond with an article in *Der Lutheraner*. About nine months later the article appeared with the title *"Was ist's mit den rhythmischen Chorälen?"*[35] A few lines from this sound, convincing article, which both defends and extols the rhythmic chorale, deserve mention.

For those who think the rhythmic chorale is something new, Schaller asserts,

> This dragging method of singing, which is unnatural, is the mode of singing which has come into fashion through laziness and degeneration, a product of that disastrous time when spiritual death settled over the provinces of Germany. . . . The rhythmic form . . . is the old, original true form and is alone the most natural way to sing.[36]

For those who consider switching to the rhythmic form an unnecessary change, he argues

> As with the text—where we want what not simply is old but rather the original and uncorrupted—so with the music. . . . This change is from inferior to something better, and no one should be too old for that! It is a sign of spiritual senility to be so opposed to change as no longer to accept the best or to lay aside the inferior.[37]

The encouraging and evangelical words with which Schaller concludes the article undoubtedly contributed as much as anything else to furthering the rhythmic chorale to the point that by the early 1860s it became the normative usage in the Synod:

A good thing develops slowly. Let it grow! The strength and beauty of the old songs in their original dress will make their own way as they have already made their way in many congregations of this land where people will once again sing the old rhythmic chorales with heartfelt joy and devotion and, in addition to the blessed possession of the pure and uncorrupted doctrine, of the heart-warming old songs, also delight in the moving and beautiful old melodies of the church.[38]

Cultivation of the polyrhythmic chorale and its popular acceptance by congregations in the Synod would hardly have been possible without the availability of good chorale books (*Choralbücher*), containing the tunes and harmonizations for the organists.[39] Here the efforts of the Bavarian musician Friedrich Layriz must be recognized, both in Germany and in America. In brief, it was the second edition (1849) of his *Kern des deutschen Kirchengesangs* that became the chief source for such helpful publications that became known as the "Volkening *Choralbuch*" (1863),[40] the "Hoelter *Choralbuch*" (1886),[41] and the "Brauer *Choralbuch*" (1888).[42]

Kirchen-Agende (1856)

The hymnal problem having been solved with the *Kirchengesangbuch* of 1847, the Synod turned its attention to the production of an agenda to supplant the Saxon Agenda of 1812 that the immigrants had brought with them. As early as 1853 the St. Louis Conference was instructed by the Synod to examine this book and to suggest revisions. When the Synod met in 1854, this committee came with a preliminary scriptural recension. Various items were discussed; certain alterations moved by the convention were considered and discussed, and the committee was instructed to carry out the matter.[43] In 1856 the result of this committee's work appeared in the *Kirchen-Agende*, the first official agenda issued by the Synod.[44] Derived from the old true Saxon agendas—evidently the Herzog Heinrich (1539) and Kursachsen (1580)—as was also, for that matter, the Saxon Agenda (1812)—it eschewed the pietistic and rationalistic elements of the latter and was broader in its overall contents, as here given:

A. Sacred Acts
  - Baptism of Children
  - Emergency Baptism
  - Baptism of Adults
  - Confirmation
  - Marriage
  - The Communion of the Sick
B. Order of Services
  - The Chief Service
  - Afternoon and Weekday Service with Sermon
  - Examination in the Catechism
  - Prayer Services
  - The Preparatory Service
  - Early Communion
  - Burial
  - Day of Repentance
C. Antiphons and Collects
  - Antiphons
  - General Antiphons and Collects
  - Collects for Festivals
  - Collects in Sundry Needs
  - Collects for the Chief Parts of the Catechism
D. Church Prayers
  - Festival Prayers
  - Special Prayers
Appendix
  - Ordination

Of more immediate concern is the Chief Service (*Hauptgottes-dienst*) in this book, the outline of which is here transcribed into English:

Kyrie
The congregation sings "Kyrie, God Father in heaven above" (LW 209 or TLH 6).

Gloria
The pastor chants the intonation "Glory to God in the highest." The congregation sings all four stanzas of "All Glory be to God on high" (LW 215 *or* TLH 237).

Salutation and Response

Antiphon
Responsively chanted by pastor and congregation.

Collect of the Day

The Epistle
The congregation stands.

Hymn of the Day (*Hauptlied*)

Gospel
The congregation stands.

Creed
The congregation sings "We all believe in one true God, Maker" (LW 213 *or* TLH 251).

Sermon

Confession (from pulpit)

Absolution (from pulpit)

General Prayers with special intercessions (from pulpit)

Announcements (from pulpit)

Lord's Prayer (from pulpit)

Votum (from pulpit)

Offertory
Congregation sings "Create in me a clean heart, O God" (LW p. 143 *or* TLH p. 22), during which the pastor prepares the elements.

Preface and Proper Preface
Chanted by the pastor.

Sanctus
The congregation sings "Holy, holy, holy Lord, God of Sabaoth" (TLH p. 26 *or* LW pp. 148–49).

Lord's Prayer
Chanted by the pastor; the congregation sings "For thine is the kingdom . . ."

Words of Institution
Chanted by the pastor.

Angus Dei
The congregations sings "O Christ the Lamb of God" (LW Canticle 7) *or* "O Christ, Thou Lamb of God" (TLH p. 28).

Distribution of the Elements

Post-Communion Antiphon and Collect

Benediction

Hymn
The congregation sings "O Lord, we praise you" (LW 238 *or* TLH 313) *or* some other appropriate closing stanza.

Silent Lord's Prayer

When there is no Communion, the rubrics state that after the Votum the congregation sings a short hymn. Then follows an Antiphon and Collect, Benediction, Closing Hymn Verse, and Silent Lord's Prayer.

A listing such as the foregoing, as well as in other instances, may at first glance appear somewhat meaningless, unless patiently and thoughtfully assessed. Regrettably, space does not permit the inclusion of the actual texts of the various liturgical pieces indicated. Still, this overview can afford a glimpse of the connection between the Christian faith and its expression in language and sign, for it is in ritual in the broad sense, that is, in rite and ceremony, that the faith-expression of the Christian congregation becomes visible, audible, and perceptible. It is in such external forms that one can often also discover the theological rationale for a liturgical practice as well as note the piety and the profession of faith that is exemplified in both texts and actions.

As for the Chief Service in this 1856 agenda, this constituted a great improvement, both theologically and liturgically, over that represented in the 1812 Saxon Agenda, and it became the norm in congregations of the Synod, even for the Bavarian congregations in Michigan that had been using the more complete Löhe service.[45] With but slight changes, this agenda appeared in six more editions—1865, 1876, 1880, 1890, 1896, and 1902, the last two with the addition of some liturgical music. The custom in this agenda of singing hymns (metrical paraphrases) for certain parts of the Ordinary was reflective of Luther's *Deutsche Messe* (1526). The eventual introduction and use of a Chief Service reflective of the richer traditions of the 16th century would have to wait until the transition to the English language.

Transition to the English Language

Expressions of fear that sound biblical, and confessional Lutheran doctrine would become corrupted and that the German culture of the immigrants would gradually be lost did not deter the Synod from proceeding to the use of the English language. As early as 1857 the Synod encouraged congregations to become involved in establishing English-speaking congregations.[46] Already in 1850 St. Peter's Lutheran Church in Baltimore established the first English congregation in the Synod. In those early years individual pastors began mission work among English-speaking people on their own initiative; their interest and zeal resulted in the English Evangelical Lutheran Conference of Missouri, organized in 1872. In 1891 this became the English Evangelical Synod of Missouri, Ohio, and Other States.

English Agendas

In the transition to English corporate worship, pastors had to resort either to translating liturgical pieces from the German books or to borrowing from existing English materials, procedures that quite naturally resulted in a lack of uniformity, thus lacking a defined order of regular expectations so necessary in a participated activity. The pastors of the English Synod influenced the Missouri Synod to produce the *Liturgy and Agenda*, a book designed to serve pastors both as an altar book for corporate worship and as a common ritual for the various sacred acts of the congregation. Eventually appearing in three editions—1917, 1921, and 1936—and published by Concordia Publishing House, this became the predecessor to *The Lutheran Agenda* (1948), authorized by the synods constituting the

Evangelical Lutheran Synodical Conference of North America. As such, this work was the companion to *The Lutheran Hymnal* (1941).

English Hymnals

The English hymnals used in establishing English congregations antedate any such official hymnals published by the Synod itself. One such hymnal appeared in 1879 entitled *Hymn Book for Use of Evangelical Lutheran Schools and Congregations*. Published by the Lutheran Publishing House, Decorah, Iowa, an arm of the Norwegian Lutherans, it was edited by and contained translations of August Crull (1845–1923), Lutheran pastor and professor at the Synod's Concordia College, Fort Wayne, IN.[47]

Lutheran Hymns, For the Use of English Lutheran Missions, a small book of 18 familiar hymns with tunes, appeared in 1882, translations of which were done by Martin Günther (1831–93), pastor and later professor at Concordia Seminary, St. Louis, and by C. Janzow.

Another hymnal, published by Concordia Publishing House in 1886 and entitled *Hymns of the Evangelical Lutheran Church, For the Use of English Lutheran Missions*, a tune-text edition of 33 hymns, was undoubtedly used extensively, for it saw a number of printings. Collected and edited by August Crull, professor of German at Concordia College, Fort Wayne, it drew high praise from C. F. W. Walther for its choice of the *Kernlieder*, that is, hymns considered to be the normative, choice core of Lutheran hymnody, and their rhythmic tunes.[48] Subsequent editions appeared in 1896 and 1901.

The noteworthy influence of both August Crull and the English Lutheran Conference of Missouri in behalf of English hymnody for the Synod is especially seen in the appearance of the *Evangelical Lutheran Hymn-Book*, published at Baltimore in 1889 by the Lutheran Publication Board. Prepared by Crull, it was a text edition of 400 hymns plus the three ecumenical creeds, the Augsburg Confession, an order for morning service, and one for evening service, the latter prepared by a committee previously elected by the conference. This became known as the "Baltimore hymnal." When the English conference constituted itself as the English Evangelical

Lutheran Synod in 1891, it ordered a new edition of this book, expanded to include more hymns, the Common Service, Matins, and Vespers. Permission to include these three services was granted by the General Synod, the General Council, and United Synod of the South, a joint commission of which had previously prepared them. This new hymnal, also a text edition, appeared in 1892, published in Baltimore. When this hymnal was published in Pittsburgh a short time later, it became known as the "Pittsburgh Hymnal." Two more editions appeared, both published in Chicago, the first in 1895, containing additional liturgical material and a number of psalms; the second in 1905, with an abridged liturgical section. English worship was advanced very much and enhanced by these editions.

Concordia Seminary's interest in English worship prompted Friedrich Bente (1858–1930), one of its professors in St. Louis, to edit a hymnal. Entitled *Hymnal for Evangelical Lutheran Missions*, it contained 199 hymns without music, a communion service, three doxologies and some antiphons, or versicles, and was published by Concordia Publishing House in 1905. This became commonly known as the "Grey Hymnal" from the color of its cover.

As early as 1891 the English Evangelical Lutheran Synod of Missouri, Ohio, and Other States, recognizing both the importance and convenience of supplying a hymnal with appropriate tunes, appointed a committee to prepare such an edition of its *Evangelical Lutheran Hymn-Book*.[49] When in 1911, at St. Louis, this English Synod became the English District of the Evangelical Lutheran Synod of Missouri, Ohio, and Other States, it presented to the convention the manuscripts of this tune-text *Evangelical Lutheran Hymn-Book* that were ready for publication by Concordia Publishing House. The book, when it appeared on the market in 1912, constituted the first official English hymnal of the Synod.[50] The fullness of its liturgical section—inclusion, for example, of the Common Service, Matins (text only), Vespers, Introits and Collects—together with 567 hymns, clearly indicated that it was both a service book and a hymnal.

This hymnal could hardly have appeared at a more propitious time, for in 1914 World War I confronted the Synod with serious challenges. In some parts of the nation, for instance, it was assumed that German Lutherans were pro-German. Occasional acts of mob violence against congregations broke out.[51] With German haters in abundance, it took some doing to demonstrate the difference between being a Lutheran and being unpatriotic.[52] The impact of the war, however, hastened the switch to the English language in many localities, a process that was eased by the ready availability of the new *Evangelical Lutheran Hymn-Book.* Thus, what had first appeared as a foreboding aspect of the war, became a blessing in disguise as English worship attendance as well as church membership gradually increased. Indeed, the time had come to reach out to the unchurched neighbors, irrespective of their ethnic background.

The desire, among other things, for better translations of some German heritage hymns, for the inclusion of other German hymns of merit, as well as treasures from Scandinavia, Bohemia, France, and other countries, prompted the 1929 Synod assembled at River Forest, IL, to authorize the "ultimate publication of a new hymnal" in cooperation with the sister synods of the Synodical Conference of North America.[53] Thus, the Intersynodical Committee on Hymnology and Liturgics was organized in Milwaukee, January 3, 1930, with W. G. Polack, professor at Concordia Seminary, St. Louis, as chairman, and Bernard Schumacher, teacher and musician, as secretary. The result of this committee's painstaking work appeared in 1941 with the title *The Lutheran Hymnal.*[54] In comparison to its predecessor, its expanded liturgical section (167 pages against 112) as well as its hymn section (660 against 567) offered congregations a considerably greater liturgical and hymnological spread. The addition of chorales from 16th- and 17th-century Germany, as well as treasures from England, Slovakia, and Scandinavia, greatly enriched the hymn corpus. Hymn text contributions came from no less than 15 different denominations, some necessarily altered theologically to make them suitable for Lutheran worship. What is particularly noteworthy is the concern of this hymnal and its immediate predecessor for orthodox texts rooted in sound, biblical, confessional theology and the retention of the rhythmic form of the chorale.[55]

The Common Service

The inclusion of the Common Service in the *Evangelical Lutheran Hymn-Book* (1912) and *The Lutheran Hymnal* (1941) demands an explanation.

Lutheran groups from various countries of northern and central Europe that had preceded the Saxons to America also brought with them the liturgical books, hymnals, and customs with which they had been familiar. This, plus their coming at different periods, created vast diversity in worship practices.

The first liturgy produced in America was part of the *Kirchen-Agende* prepared for the Pennsylvania Ministerium by Henry Melchior Muhlenberg (1711–87), with the assistance of Peter Brunnholtz (d. 1757) and Johann Friedrich Handschuh (1714–64). These three men were clergy who had been educated in Europe and who, after emigrating to America, were instrumental in organizing the Pennsylvania Ministerium in 1748. In fact, this liturgy was adopted by the Ministerium in its first organizational meeting. Not only that, members of the Ministerium considered the matter so important, they pledged to use no other form for corporate worship in their respective parishes. The arrangement of this liturgy was as follows:

Hymn of Invocation
Confession of Sins
Gloria in Excelsis (metrical form)
Collect preceded by Salutation and Response
Epistle
Hymn
Gospel
Creed (Luther's metrical version)
Hymn
Sermon
General Prayer or Litany
Lord's Prayer
Announcements
Votum
Hymn
Offering
Collect, preceded by Salutation and Response

Benediction
Closing Hymn Verse

The Communion section included:
Preface (no Benedictus in the Sanctus)
Exhortation to Communicants and
Lord's Prayer in paraphrase
Lord's Prayer
Consecration
Invitation
Distribution
Benedicamus
Thanksgiving Collect
Benediction with trinitarian conclusion

In the German language and, based as it was on the liturgies contained in the conservative church orders of Saxony and North Germany, this liturgy was significant in establishing a certain fullness, reflective of Luther's reform of the Latin Mass in his *Formula Missae* of 1523. The substitution of metrical paraphrases for the prose versions of the Gloria in Excelsis and the Creed represented, of course, the custom in Luther's *Deutsche Messe* of 1526. Though never printed, this liturgy was circulated in handwritten copies.

The previously mentioned *Kirchen-Agende*, later translated into English by Charles W. Schaeffer (1813–96), pastor and professor, contained five parts: (1) Concerning Public Worship, (2) Concerning Baptism, (3) Proclaiming the Bans and Marriage, (4) Concerning Confession and Holy Communion, (5) Burial.

In 1786 a revised form of this *Agende*, with its liturgy, was published in which the influences of Rationalism were clearly in evidence.

Credit must be given the Ministerium of New York for publishing the first English liturgy in 1795, a translation of the 1786 printed form of the Muhlenberg liturgy. Sad to state, as the Lutheran churches gradually began worshiping in English, the Lutheran liturgical forms suffered erosion, and congregational participation waned to the point that many congregations became almost indistinguishable from their Reformed neighbors. The low point was reached in 1817 when Fredrick H. Quitman prepared an English liturgy for the New York Synod, a work thoroughly poisoned by

Rationalism. And it was not until the middle of the 19th century with its great waves of immigration that the influence of the Lutheran confessional-liturgical revival in Germany became apparent in America. The *Liturgie und Agende* (1855), prepared by the Pennsylvania Ministerium and the New York Synod, clearly exhibited the effects of liturgical reform in Germany. In 1860, when an English version of this liturgy was published, the influence of Wilhelm Löhe, pastor in Neuendettelsau, was very evident. When the General Council was organized in 1867, it adopted this 1860 liturgy and included it, with further improvements, in its *Church Book* of 1868. The edition of 1870 involved the expertise of Beale M. Schmucker (1827–88), Charles Porterfield Krauth (1823–83) (whom C. F. W. Walther described "as the most eminent man in the English Lutheran Church . . . devoted to pure doctrine"), and Joseph A. Seiss (1823–1904). It included additional translations of the historic Introits and Collects. To meet the needs of German congregations, the General Council instructed a committee to prepare a German version of the *Church Book*, which appeared as the *Kirchenbuch* in 1877, a book that restored full Matins and Vespers to American Lutheranism.

The spirit of Rationalism persisted the longest among the synods comprising the General Synod that was organized in 1820, but here, too, the forces of confessional and liturgical renewal began to prevail, as witnessed by that synod's acceptance in 1869 of what became known as the "Washington Service," a service that approximated an historical order. Also, the time had come when voices were raised for greater uniformity in the corporate worship of English-speaking synods.

Thus it came about that the General Synod[56] and the General Council[57] accepted the invitation of the General Synod South[58] to cooperate in the production of one book containing the same hymns and the same orders of services. Work was begun on what became known as the Common Service. Following a preliminary meeting of several representative leaders in 1884, in May of 1885 the Joint Committee met in Philadelphia. Three of these leaders, namely, Beale M. Schmucker (GC), chairman; Edward T. Horn (1850–1915, GSS), secretary; and George U. Wenner (1844–1934, GS) constituted the subcommittee that drafted most of the texts and rubrics. Their work, after approval by the Joint Committee, was presented to the constituent parent bodies for comment and evaluation. Work on this liturgy, confined only to the text, was completed in 1888. Musical settings would in time be supplied by the use of historical melodies as well as other chant forms.

The rule governing the work to produce the Common Service, as suggested by the General Council, was agreed to be

> the common consent of the pure Lutheran liturgies of the sixteenth century, and when there is not an entire agreement among them, the consent of the largest number of the greatest weight.[59]

The laudable aim of the Joint Committee was expressed in a letter from Beale M. Schmucker to Edward Trail Horn (Oct. 23, 1885):

> If the coming generations of Lutherans have put into their mouths and hearts the pure, strong, moving words of our church's Service from week to week and year to year, they will be brought up in the pure teaching of the church, and the church of the future will be a genuine Lutheran Church.[60]

In supplying texts for the Common Service, the Joint Committee not only incorporated the language of the then prevalent King James Version, it also took over directly from the Anglican/Episcopal *Book of Common Prayer* the wording of such traditional liturgical pieces as the Kyrie, Gloria in Excelsis, the Creeds, Prefaces, Lord's Prayer, Collects, as well as other items. Where but in this book could the committee find better English translations of the texts contained in the German, Swedish, and other vernacular Lutheran liturgies of the 16th century? Subsequent English service books and hymnals incorporating the Common Service would also see a wholesale borrowing of the Anglican chants to which the liturgical pieces had been set by the Anglican/Episcopal Church.[61] Moreover, the traditional pre-Reformation series of Introits, Epistles, and Gospels were likewise provided for every Sunday and for certain festivals in the church year.

A contribution of the Joint Committee that appears to be generally forgotten is that it also supplied English Lutheranism in America with the historic forms of Matins and Vespers, together with the necessary Invitatories, Antiphons, Responsories, and Versicles appropriate to the church year.

The appearance of the Common Service in 1888 (even in three slightly variant versions) marked a momentous occasion with respect to corporate worship in American Lutheranism. In the estimation of Luther D. Reed, eminent liturgiologist, this service rose

> above the provincialism and nationalism that characterized developments in Europe. It provided a liturgy . . . of universal scope and influence . . . more fully representative of Lutheranism in its best estate than any other order of service that could be named.[62]

Representative of sound, biblical, confessional theology, small wonder that the Common Service soon became accepted by an ever broadening circle of Lutherans who worshiped in the English language.

Inter-Lutheran Commission on Worship

Genesis

As previously mentioned, *The Lutheran Hymnal*, produced by the Intersynodical Committee on Hymnology and Liturgics for the Synodical Conference of North America, appeared in 1941. In due course companion volumes made their appearance: *The Lutheran Liturgy* (1943), the altar book for pastors; *Music for the Liturgies of The Lutheran Hymnal* (1944); *The Lutheran Lectionary* (1945), a book that provided the appointed Epistles and Gospels of the Old Standard pericopic series plus 93 selected psalms and various tables helpful to the pastor; *The Lutheran Agenda* (1948), containing the necessary rites, or occcasional services, in the life of the Christian congregation; and *The Pastor's Companion* (1950), a small, pocket-size book containing rites for the more personal ministrations of pastors, all prepared by the Inter-Synodical Committee on Hymnology and Liturgics, as authorized by the synods constituting the Evangelical Lutheran Synodical Conference in North America and published by Concordia Publishing House.

As early as 1956, in its report to the Synod's convention in St. Paul, MN, the Committee on Hymnology recommended that a revised edition of *The Lutheran Hymnal* "should be prepared within the near future and the pocket-size edition [the tune-text edition requested by the 1953 convention[63]] should be prepared simultaneously, so that the two versions will be in perfect agreement with each other."[64] The point was made that this was to be a revised and improved edition, not a new hymnal. Among the reasons advanced for such a revision was that certain hymn tunes and some liturgical pieces should be transposed to lower keys for more vital singing; the key signature of certain hymns with too many sharps or flats should be changed to make accompanying easier for the less advanced musician; if possible, another musical setting or two of the liturgy or parts of the liturgy should be provided.[65]

In response to this report the Synod resolved that the Committee on Hymnology and Liturgics

> initiate a thorough study of the problems arising from the present edition and connected with any possible revision of *The Lutheran Hymnal*, including a reasonable testing of the results.[66]

Three years later, at the 1959 convention in San Francisco, the committee reported that it had carried out the 1956 assignment and as a result had learned that an overwhelming percentage of congregations were not desirous of a thoroughly revised edition at that time. While many criticized the hymnal rather severely, the majority appeared to treasure it highly. Insisting that the "musicological workmanship" in the hymnal was obsolete, the committee, including the members of the sister synods, felt that a thoroughly revised edition should appear in approximately ten to twelve years. Noting that the less experienced organists were having great difficulty playing many of the hymns, especially on a pipe organ, the committee had decided that Paul G. Bunjes, professor at Concordia, River Forest, should prepare an organist's edition of *The Lutheran Hymnal*. Moreover, numerous requests from pastors insisting that a thoroughly revised and expanded edition of *The Lutheran Agenda* (1948) was necessary to meet the needs of the time, prompted the committee to assign this task to a subcommittee under the supervision of David Schuller, professor at the St. Louis seminary.[67] In response to a memorial to modernize the language and another to simplify and make more meaningful to the average worshiper certain parts of the liturgy, the Synod resolved

> that the Commission on Worship, Liturgics, and Hymnology[68] be encouraged to keep these matters in mind in the contemplated revision of *The Lutheran Hymnal* and the new *Lutheran Agenda*.[69]

In its report to the 1962 synodical convention in Cleveland the Commission on Worship, among other things, mentioned that notable progress had been made jointly with the members of the Committee on Hymnology and Liturgics of the Synodical Conference toward the eventual revision of both *The Lutheran Hymnal* and *The Lutheran Agenda*; that responses and suggestions from the field had been very supportive, encouraging, and helpful.[70] The convention in turn encouraged the commission to heed the suggestion of Memorial 711[71] "to include hymns which express the relationship of the church to contemporary society, such hymns being doctrinally sound and exalting our Lord Jesus Christ"[72] and "to continue as speedily as possible the work of the hymnal revision as outlined in Report 705."[73]

In its report to the 1965 convention of the Synod in Detroit the Commission on Worship, Liturgics, and Hymnology laid out its elaborate plans for the new and revised editions of *The Lutheran Hymnal* and *The Lutheran Agenda*; it sketched the progress to date of the various committees—Liturgical Texts, Hymn Texts, Liturgical Music, and Music for the Hymns—involving some 25 individuals, including commission members and supplementary committee members.[74] Setting 1970 as the target date for the completion of the task, the commission envisioned that this thoroughly revised edition of *The Lutheran Hymnal* would constitute a major contribution toward the eventual production of one hymnal for all American Lutheran churches, possibly within the present century. At the time this report was written—toward the end of 1964—little did the Commission on Worship envision the strong feelings of the Synod in support of a common hymnal for all Lutherans in America, a fact attested by the 16 (plus four unpublished) resolutions from congregations as well as pastoral conferences and districts favoring such a hymnal that appeared in the *Workbook* in April 1965 for that summer's Detroit convention.

Asigned to Committee 13, after open hearings and considerable discussion with concerned groups and individuals, this committee formulated and presented the following resolution to the convention, a resolution that said in part:

> WHEREAS, There is a desire in various Lutheran bodies in America to express the faith which they hold in common through more

uniform texts and musical settings in both liturgy and hymnody; and

WHEREAS, The Commission on Worship, Liturgics, and Hymnology indicates that it is desirable to cooperate with other groups in developing hymnological and liturgical materials; . . . therefore be it . . .

RESOLVED, That we authorize the President in conjunction with the Vice-Presidents to appoint representatives to pursue a cooperative venture with other Lutheran bodies as soon as possible in working toward, under single cover:

a) a common liturgical section in rite, rubric, and music;
b) a common core of hymn texts and musical settings; and
c) a variant selection of hymns if necessary; and be it further
. . .

RESOLVED, That we pledge our joy, willingness, and confidence to the other Lutheran bodies as work in this cooperative project begins; and be it finally

RESOLVED, That a progress report on these cooperative efforts be made to the next regularly scheduled convention.[75]

In the discussion of this resolution by the delegates, an amendment to have the commission produce the hymnal on which it had been working failed to carry. Time having run out, the above resolution was presented again the next day and forthwith adopted.[76] History attests that this resolution had far reaching effects—immediately for the Commission on Worship of the Synod as well as its counterparts in the Lutheran Church in America and the American Lutheran Church; eventually for practically all congregations in American Lutheranism.

In due time Oliver Harms, president of The Lutheran Church—Missouri Synod, sent invitations to the presidents of the various Lutheran bodies in America. Thus on February 10–11, 1966, representatives and observers from six such bodies gathered in Chicago to participate in what was called the Inter-Lutheran Consultation on Worship.[77] Convened by Oliver Harms, the various presentations by previously selected persons representing the American Lutheran Church, the Lutheran Church in America, and the Missouri Synod surveyed the past and assessed the present, thus to begin to appreciate the task ahead and to conceptualize a *modus operandi*.[78] Thus was born the Inter-Lutheran Commission on Worship (ILCW), a representative group that eventually included eight people from the Lutheran Church in America; seven from the American Lutheran Church; seven from The Lutheran Church—Missouri Synod; one from the Synod of Evangelical Lutheran Churches (Slovak Synod); and one from the Evangelical Lutheran Church of Canada.[79] Four standing committees were established which, shortly after the first meeting of the ILCW in November 1966,[80] began to chart and plan their work. These committees met frequently; all their work had to be approved by the the the plenary ILCW, which met no less than twice a year.

Contemporary Worship Series

In its desire to involve congregations in the decision-making process regarding the contents of the joint hymnal, the Inter-Lutheran Commission on Worship encouraged the Commission on Worship, Liturgics and Hymnology of the Synod to proceed with its earlier plan to publish a supplement to *The Lutheran Hymnal* that would contain some of the hymns and liturgical materials (some quite experimental!) that the Commission on Worship had envisioned for a revised edition of *The Lutheran Hymnal*. Further impetus was given this venture by Resolution 2–08 of the 1967 New York convention of the Synod, which instructed the Commission on Worship[81] to prepare for publication such a supplement.[82] This *Worship Supplement* appeared in 1969, in time for use at that summer's convention of the Synod in Denver.[83] The influence of this little volume, especially its hymn section, on the eventual ILCW hymnal would be significant.

To that same end, the Inter-Lutheran Commission on Worship itself began the publication of the *Contemporary Worship* series, booklets in liturgy and hymnody "designed to broaden the scope of currently available hymnic and liturgical resources," for review by the congregations of the participating churches. Published through the cooperative efforts of Augsburg, Concordia, and Fortress, their importance in the review process bears a listing of these issues:

Contemporary Worship 01: The Great Thanksgiving (1975). Introductory essays plus eight eucharistic prayers.

Contemporary Worship 1: Hymns (1969). Twenty-one in all, mostly new and contemporary; five hymns from *Worship Supplement* (1969).

Contemporary Worship 2: The Holy Communion (1970). Four new music settings of the proposed liturgical text, each in a different idiom—contemporary, hymnic, chant, folk.

Contemporary Worship 3: The Marriage Service (1972). Within the Holy Communion or as a rite standing alone.

Contemporary Worship 4: Hymns for Baptism and Holy Communion (1972). Thirty in all, new and old; four are from *Worship Supplement* (1969), one of which had appeared in *Contemporary Worship 1.*

Contemporary Worship 5: Services of the Word (1972). Four seasonal —Advent, Christmas-Epiphany, Lent, Easter; two general.

Contemporary Worship 6: The Church Year, Calendar and Lectionary (1973). A notable volume, still useful today especially for its introductions, pp. 5-30.

Contemporary Worship 7: Holy Baptism (1974). Two forms are for the festive use with the Holy Communion; one for other services.

Contemporary Worship 8: Affirmation of the Baptismal Covenant (1975). The term "Affirmation" here replaces the term "confirmation." This fascicle contains two forms, one when Baptism is celebrated; the other within the rite of Baptism.

Contemporary Worship 9: Daily Prayer of the Church (1976). Morning Prayer, Prayer at the Close of the

Day, Responsive Prayer, and the Litany (classic Western form).

Contemporary Worship 10: Burial of the Dead (1976). The service with Holy Communion as an option, plus the committal.

Responses to these, as well as to a listing of hymn texts and tunes being considered for inclusion in the hymnal, were reviewed and considered by the Inter-Lutheran Commission on Worship. Formal testing procedures and schedules were initiated with the cooperation of certain parishes chosen on a random basis. Contact was maintained with leadership people in the participating churches, especially with official review committees that had been appointed carefully to examine the commission's proposals. Changes and revisions in both the liturgical and hymnic materials were made in the light of such reviews, responses, and comments.

By late summer 1977, the American Lutheran Church, the Evangelical Lutheran Church of Canada, and the Lutheran Church in America had approved the proposals of the Inter-Lutheran Commission on Worship and authorized the publication of the *Lutheran Book of Worship*—a title, as well as its color and size, that had been selected by said commission already in 1976. There remained the approval of The Lutheran Church—Missouri Synod.

Notes

1. Theodore G. Tappert, "Orthodoxism, Pietism and Rationalism," *The Lutheran Heritage, Christian Social Responsibility*, ed. Harold C. Letts (Philadelphia: Muhlenberg Press, 1957), II: 38–39.

2. Cf. Hans Leube, *Die Reformideen in der deutschen lutherischen Kirche zur Zeit der Orthodoxie* (Leipzig: Verlag von Dörfling und Francke, 1924). "It must also be borne in mind that one's judgment is easily clouded by later controversialists who have either bitterly assailed or ardently defended the orthodoxists." Tappert, p. 37.

3. Cf. Leube, pp. 21ff. Andrew L. Drummond, *German Protestantism Since Luther* (London: Epworth Press, 1951), adopts the negative view. Drummond's analysis should be read against Manfred P. Fleischer, ed., *The Harvest of Humanism in Central Europe* (St. Louis: Concordia Publishing House, 1992). These 13 essays in honor of Lewis W. Spitz of Stanford University show that the Lutheran reformers after Luther continued a lively interest in the humanities, language, literature, and philosophy—all topics vital not only to the narrower study of theology but to living a well-rounded life. Such topics were integrated into Reformation's education efforts early and continued to draw attention as

the evangelical movement's influence expanded during the 16th century. For a brief and concise overview see *Die Religion in Geschichte und Gegenwart*, s.v., "Orthodoxie."

4. But cf. Robert Ergang, *The Myth of the All-Destructive Fury of the Thirty Years' War* (Pocono Pines, Pennsylvania: The Craftsmen, 1956); also S. H. Steinberg, "The Thirty Years' War: A New Interpretation," in *The Making of Modern Europe*, ed. Herman Ausubel (New York: The Macmillan Co., 1951), I: 207–221. For the traditional view see C. V. Wedgwood, *The Thirty Years' War* (Garden City: Doubleday, 1961).

5. The term "Evangelical" to designate the Lutheran faith seems to have become customary at this time, prompting the distinctive locution "Evangelical and Reformed."

6. At his funeral John Gerhard, "arch theologian" of the Lutheran Church, was praised for never having slept in church. Paul Grünberg, *Philipp Jacob Spener*, 3 vols. (Göttingen, 1893–1906), I: 27. Cited in *Pia Desideria*, trans. and ed. Theodore G. Tappert (Philadelphia: Fortress Press, 1964), p. 9, n. 7.

7. English Puritanism is frequently considered both as a forerunner of Pietism and as its contemporary phenomenon. In his youth Spener read a number of devotional books, such as John Arndt's *True Christianity* (c. 1607), as well as books by Puritans, who were critical of conventional Christianity.

8. Cf. Luther, Preface to German Mass, WA 19: 75, 5; AE 53: 64. Here Luther encourages people to meet "in a house somewhere to pray, read, to baptize, to receive the sacrament, and do other Christian works." When, however, he became aware that such a procedure undermined the doctrine of the ministry and the church, he eschewed such gatherings.

9. For some wretched and disturbing examples of liturgical texts see J. F. Ohl, "The Liturgical Deterioration of the Seventeenth and Eighteenth Centuries," *Memoirs of the Lutheran Liturgical Association*, ed. Luther D. Reed, 7 vols. in 1 (Pittsburgh: The Association, 1906), IV: 73–78. Georg Rietschel in his *Lehrbuch der Liturgik*, 2 vols. (Berlin: Reuther and Reichard, 1900, 1909), I: 446, n. 5 and n. 6, gives authors and titles of some privately produced agendas, a development that contributed to the disaster of pastors "doing their own thing" rather than following their church's official texts and practices.

10. For Luther's theses see AE 31: 25–33.

11. Wilhelm Löhe, *Agende für Christliche Gemeinden lutherischen Bekenntnisses* (1844), in *Gesammelte Werke*, ed. Klaus Ganzert, 7 vols. (Neuendettelsau: Freimund Verlag, 1951–1985), VII.

12. Luther D. Reed, *The Lutheran Liturgy*, rev. ed. (Philadelphia: Muhlenberg Press, 1959), p. 153.

13. This two-part agenda, from the very library of C. F. W. Walther, is available on loan from the Pritzlaff Memorial Library, Concordia Seminary, St. Louis. The complete data: *Kirchenbuch für den evangelischen Gottesdienst der Königlich Sächsischen Lande* (Dresden: in der Königlichen Hofbuchdruckerei, 1812), hereafter "Saxon Agenda."

14. Carl Ferdinand Wilhelm Walther, *Americanisch-Lutherische Pastoraltheologie*, 5th ed. (St. Louis: Concordia Publishing House, 1906), p. 133.

15. Rietschel, I: 454.

16. Ibid., I: 446.

17. Saxon Agenda, Part II, pp. 122–123; and Part II, pp. 355–356.

18. Paul Graff, *Geschichte der Auflösung der alten gottesdiestlichen Formen in der evangelischen Kirche Deutschlands*, 2 vols. (Göttingen: Vandenhoeck & Ruprecht, 1939), pp. 115–116.

19. Saxon Agenda, Part II, p. 181.

20. D. H. Steffens, *Doctor Carl Ferdinand Wilhelm Walther* (Philadelphia: Lutheran Publication Society, 1917), p. 83.

21. Ibid., p. 88.

22. For details see O. A. Dorn, "Early Printing in the Missouri Synod," *Concordia Historical Institute Quarterly* XXIV (April 1951): 6.

23. Complete citation: *Kirchengesangbuch für Evangelisch- Lutherische Gemeinden ungeänderter Augsburgischer Confession darin des seligen D. Martin Luthers und andere geistreichen Lehrer gebräuchlichste Kirchen-Lieder enthalten sind* (New York: *Gedruckt für die Herausgeber bei H. Ludwig. In Verlag der deutschen evang. luth. Gemeinde A.C. in St. Louis, Mo., 1847*).

24. The book contained no preface. An announcement in *Der Lutheraner* shortly before the book's appearance described the contents. Cf. *Der Lutheraner* III (June 15, 1847): 84. For a translation of this announcement see Carl S. Meyer, ed., *Moving Frontiers: Readings in the History of the Lutheran Church—Missouri Synod* (St. Louis: Concordia Publishing House, 1964), pp. 182–183.

25. Meyer, p. 182.

26. Ibid., p. 183.

27. *Evang. Kirchenzeitung*, 1847, No. 84. Quoted in Johann Daniel von der Heyt, *Geschichte der Evangelischen Kirchenmusik in Deutschland* (Berlin: Trowitsch & Son, 1926), p. 195. The author is indebted to Carl Schalk for this quotation, contained in his notable monograph, *The Roots of Hymnody in The Lutheran Church—Missouri Synod* (St. Louis: Concordia Publishing House, 1965), p. 25. For more specific and detailed information on hymnody than presented in this chapter, the reader is encouraged to read Schalk's work.

28. Eduard Emil Koch, *Geschichte des Kirchenlieds und Kirchengesangs der christlichen insbesondere der deutschen evangelischen Kirche*, 8 vols. (Stuttgart: Druck und Verlag der Chr. Belser'chen Verlagshandlung, 1866–71), 7: 60.

29. *CXVII Geistliche Melodien meist aus dem 16. und 17. Jahr. in ihren ursprünglichen Rhythmen zweistimmig gesetzt von Dr. Friedrich Layriz* (Erlangen: Theodor Bläsing, 1839).

30. *Geistliche Melodien meist aus den 16. und 17. Jahr. in ihren ursprünglichen Tönen Rhythmen zum Gebrauche für Schule und Haus zweistimmig gesetzt von Dr. Friedr. Layriz*. Erstes Hundert, 2d rev. ed. (Erlangen: 1848) and *Geistliche Melodien . . .* Zweites hundert, 2d ed. (Erlangen: Theodor Bläsing, 1850).

31. Friedrich Layriz, *Kern des deutschen Kirchengesangs*. Eine Sammlung von CC. Chorälen, meist aus dem 16. und 17. Jahrhundert in ihren ursprünglichen Tönen und Rhythmen mit alterthümlicher Harmonie, vierstimmig zum Gebrauch in Kirche und Haus, 4 vols. (Nördlingen: C. H. Beck'sche Buchhandlung, 1853).

32. Of note are his liturgical settings for pastor and congregation in the second edition of Wilhelm Löhe, *Agende für christliche Gemeinden des Lutherischen Bekenntnisses* (Nördlingen: C. H. Beck'sche Buchhandlung, 1853).

33. Minutes of Trinity Congregation, St. Louis, MO, January 8, 1849; transcript at Concordia Historical Institute, campus of Concordia Seminary, St. Louis.

34. *Synodal-Bericht* 1852, 2d ed., 1876, p. 220.

35. *Der Lutheraner* IX (May 10, 1853): 122–124.

36. Ibid., p. 123.

37. Ibid., p. 124.

38. Ibid. Not all Lutherans in America became acquainted with and accustomed to the polyrhythmic, or rhythmic, form. The inclusion of such tunes in *Lutheran Book of Worship* (1978), largely due to the influence of Missouri Synod members on the Inter-Lutheran Commission on Worship, evoked considerable negative response in some quarters of Lutheranism. And today, for example, the isometric form of "A Mighty Fortress" (LBW 229; LW 298) is still preferred over the rhythmic form (LBW 228; LW 298) by many congregations in the Evangelical Lutheran Church in America.

39. For a detailed overview of chorale books see Schalk, pp. 31–38.

40. *Evangelisch-Lutherisches Choralbuch für Kirche und Haus*, Sammlung der gebräuchlichsten Choräle der lutherischen Kirche ausgezogen und unverändert abgedruckt aus "Kern des deutschen Kirchengesangs von Dr. Fr. Layriz" (St. Louis: Verlag von L. Volkening, 1863).

41. H. F. Hoelter, ed., *Choralbuch, Eine Sammlung der gangbarsten Choräle der evang.-lutherischen Kirche, meist Dr. Fr. Layriz, nebst den wichtigsten Sätzen* (St. Louis: Lutherischer Concordia Verlag, 1886).

42. *Mehrstimmiges Choralbuch zu dem "Kirchengesangbuch für Evangelisch-Lutherische Gemeinden Ungeänderter Augsburgischer Confession,"* ed. Karl Brauer (St. Louis: Concordia Publishing House, 1888).

43. *Achter Synodal-Bericht der deutschen Ev. Luth. Synode von Missouri, Ohio u. a. Staaten vom Jahre 1854*, 2d ed. (St. Louis: Druckerei der Synode von Missouri, Ohio und andern Staaten, 1876), p. 286.

44. Complete citation: *Kirchen-Agende für Evangelisch-Lutherische Gemeinden ungeänderter Augsburgischer Confession, Zusammengestellt aus den alten rechtgläubigen Sächsischen Kirchenagenden und herausgegeben von der allgemeinen deutschen Evangel.-Lutherischen Synode von Missouri, Ohio und anderen Staaten* (St. Louis: Druckerei der deutschen Ev.-Luth. Synode v. Missouri, Ohio und anderen Staaten, 1856).

45. A translated and transcribed version of the service in the *Kirchen- Agende* (1856) was issued for congregational use by the Lutheran Heritage Anniversary Committee (1987). As The Order of Morning Service (Second Form), this service appears in English dress in *Liturgy and Agenda*, abr. ed. (St. Louis: Concordia Publishing House, 1918), a book intended as a pocket edition for pastors.

46. *Synodal-Bericht* 1857, 2d. ed., 1876, pp. 354–355.

47. C. F. W. Walther praised this hymnal, both for its exemplary selection of hymns (130 in all) and its doctrinal purity. Cf. *Der Lutheraner* XXXV (July 1, 1879): 104.

48. *Der Lutheraner* XLII (1 April 1886): 56.

49. Slow progress on the project resulted in the appointment of a number of subsequent committee members, among whom was H. B. Hemmeter, who in 1936 became president of Concordia Theological Seminary, Springfield, IL. Beginning in 1940, this author was privileged to serve on his faculty and, when Hemmeter retired in 1945, the author became the fortunate possessor of his three-volume *Schatz des liturgischen Chor- und Gemeindegesangs* by Wilhelm Schoeberlein (Göttingen: Vanderhoeck & Ruprecht's Verlag, 1565–72) for the paltry sum of six dollars, important volumes that Hemmeter had used as a committee member.

50. An article announcing this hymnal appeared in *The Lutheran Witness* XXXI (May 9, 1912): 79–80.

51. This author recalls his now long-sainted father relating to him that members of several congregations in Minnesota were greeted by yellow church doors on Sunday morning, painted the night before by angry mob leaders. It was such demonstrations of antipathy to German Lutherans that prompted some congregations to display the American flag in the nave, a symbol to prove their patriotism. Such practice now appears anachronistic.

52. See Geo. M. Stephenson, "Are Lutherans Un-American?" reprinted from the *Lutheran Companion* in *The Lutheran Witness* XXXV (25 July 1916): 224–225. Also Theodore Graebner, "Unjustified Aspersions" (editorial), *The Lutheran Witness* XXXVIII (28 May 1918): 168–169.

53. Cf. Missouri Synod, *Proceedings*, 1929, pp. 131, 133. The Evangelical Lutheran Synodical Conference, organized in 1872, was a federation of American Lutheran synods, the charter members of which were the Missouri, the Ohio, Wisconsin, Norwegian, Illinois, and Minnesota synods. Doctrinal disagreements finally led to the dissolution of this federation in 1967.

54. *The Lutheran Hymnal*, authorized by the synods constituting the Evangelical Lutheran Synodical Conference of North America (St. Louis: Concordia Publishing House, 1941).

55. Schalk, pp. 46–47. For additional information about English hymnals in the Synod, the reader is encouraged to consult the preface and introduction in W. G. Polack, *The Handbook to the Lutheran Hymnal* (St. Louis: Concordia Publishing House, 1942), pp. V-XII.

56. In 1888 the General Synod was a federation of the Maryland, W. Virginia, Hartwick (NY), E. Ohio, Allegheny (PA), Miami (OH), Wittenberg (OH), Olive Branch (IN), Pittsburgh, N. Illinois, Central Pennsylvania, N. Indiana, Iowa, S. Illinois, Franckean (NY), Nebraska, Wartburg (German), Middle Tennessee, Susquehanna (PA), Kansas, Central Illinois, and New York-New Jersey synods.

57. The General Council included the Pennsylvania Ministerium, New York Ministerium, the District Synod of Ohio, and the Pittsburgh, Canada, Augustana (Swedish), Texas, Indiana, and Northwest (N. Minnesota, North Dakota, Wisconsin) synods.

58. The General Synod South was organized in 1863, the result of the disruption of the General Synod caused by the Civil War (1861–65). By 1888 it included the synods of N. Carolina, S. Carolina, Virginia, S.W. Virginia, Georgia, Mississippi, Tennessee, and the Holston (Va.) Synod.

59. Henry Eyster Jacobs, *A History of the Evangelical Lutheran Church in the United States* (New York: Christian Literature Co. 1893), p. 506. It is the Central Saxo-Lutheran group of church orders that is considered to have the "greatest weight," in which are included Luther's *Formula Missae* (1523) and *Deutsche Messe* (1526), Brandenburg-Nürnberg (1533), Saxony (1539), and Mecklenburg (1540, 1552).

60. Quoted from Luther D. Reed, "The Common Service in the Life of the Church," *The Lutheran Quarterly* 12 (1939): 9–10.

61. Such borrowing from the *Book of Common Prayer* should not be construed as vitiating against the Lutheran, confessional stance of the Common Service, nor should it abet the mistaken notion that the Common Service simply took over the Anglican/Episcopal liturgy. Although the Common Service and the *Book of Common Prayer* (1549)—in which Lutheran influence is not lacking—stem from the same tree, namely, the historic Latin Mass of the Western Church, there are still differences, both theological and liturgical.

62. Reed, *The Lutheran Liturgy*, pp. 194–195.

63. Missouri Synod, *Proceedings*, 1953, p. 605.

64. Missouri Synod, *Reports and Memorials*, 1956, p. 610.

65. Missouri Synod, *Proceedings*, 1956, pp. 610–611.

66. Ibid., p. 615.

67. Subsequent developments prevented the completion of this project as well as the previously mentioned organist's edition of *The Lutheran Hymnal* and its tune-text edition. For the report to the San Francisco convention see Missouri Synod, *Reports and Memorials*, 1959, pp. 558–562.

68. The new name granted the committee by the 1959 synodical convention.

69. Missouri Synod, *Proceedings*, 1959, p. 280.

70. Missouri Synod, *Reports and Memorials*, 1962, pp. 304–305.

71. Ibid., p. 308.

72. Missouri Synod, *Proceedings*, 1962, Resolution 9–01, p. 144.

73. Ibid., Resolution 9–02, p. 144.

74. Misouri Synod, *Workbook*, 1965, pp. 389. Commission members were Walter Buszin, Herbert Lindemann, Martin Seltz, Fred Precht, David Appelt, Jaroslav Vajda, Stephen Tuhy, Herbert Garske, and Arthur Amt. Supplementary committee members were Theodore DeLaney, Hilton Oswald, Edgar Reinke, Richard Hillert, Jan Bender, Paul Manz, Theodore Beck, Hugo Gehrke, Robert Bergt, Louis Nuechterlein, Ernest Koenker, Arthur C. Piepkorn, George Hoyer, Carl Schalk, Edward Klammer, and Herbert Nuechterlein.

75. Missouri Synod, *Proceedings*, 1965, Resolution 13–01, pp. 185–186. It was also this convention that adopted Resolution 13–02, authorizing the Board of Directors of the Synod to establish the full-time position of executive director for the Commission on Worship. The first call was extended to and declined by the editor of this volume, who at the time was professor of worship at Concordia Theological Seminary, Springfield, Illinois. Subsequently the call was extended to and accepted by Theodore DeLaney, pastor in California.

76. Ibid., Minutes, p. 70.

77. Participants were from the American Lutheran Church, Mandus Egge, Paul Ensrud, Edward Hansen, Hans Knauer, Theodore Liefeld, Alf Romstad, Herbert Nottbohm; from the Lutheran Church in America, Conrad Bergendoff, Edgar Brown, Crosby Deaton, Edward Horn III, Ulrich Leupold, William Seaman; from The Lutheran Church—Missouri Synod, Oliver Harms, convener, Paul Bunjes, Walter Buszin, Herbert Kahler, Adalbert Kretzmann, Herbert Lindemann, Martin Seltz, Fred Precht, David Appelt; from the Synod of Evangelical Lutheran Churches, Stephen Tuhy, Jaroslav Vajda; from the Wisconsin Evangelical Lutheran Synod, Martin Albrecht, Kurt Eggert; from the Evangelical Lutheran Synod, Julian Anderson, Stanley Ubgebretson, Eivind Unseth.

78. The presentations together with the resolutions adopted are contained in *Liturgical Reconaissance*, ed. Edgar S. Brown, Jr. (Philadelphia: Fortress Press, 1968).

79. Members of the Commission on Worship, appointed by the Synod's president, served as representatives of the Missouri Synod together with their executive secretary.

80. In attendance at the first meeting were Walter Buszin, Paul Bunjes, Herbert Kahler, A. R. Kretzmann, Herbert Lindemann, Fred Precht, Martin Seltz, Jaroslav Vajda, E. Theodore DeLaney, Krister Stendahl, Daniel Moe, Mandus Egge, Ulrich Leupold, Edward Hansen, Edward Horn III, L. Likness, Theodore Liefeld, Eugene Brand, John Arthur, Leland Sateren, Edgar Brown, Crosby Deaton, Paul Ensrud.

81. This was the new title given the commission by the New York convention. See Missouri Synod, *Proceedings*, 1967, p. 90.

82. Ibid.

83. *Worship Supplement*, authorized by the Commission on Worship, The Lutheran Church—Missouri Synod and Synod of Evangelical Lutheran Churches (St. Louis: Concordia Publishing House, 1969). This soft-cover book appeared in two editions: a tune-text (both in the liturgy and hymn sections) for the congregation and an edition for the organist. The latter contained two settings for each hymn, the first in genuine organ idiom; the second playable on the organ, with or without pedals, as well as on the piano for the player of rather limited ability.

4

Lutheran Worship (1982)

THE SPECIAL HYMNAL REVIEW COMMITTEE

Robert Sauer

No subject was debated at greater length than the proposed *Lutheran Book of Worship* during the 52nd Regular Convention of The Lutheran Church—Missouri Synod held in Dallas, TX, July 1977.[1] Almost one hundred overtures from congregations and other entities of the Synod questioned further involvement in the pan-Lutheran effort.[2] Very few indicated support for the project that had been initiated by the Synod in convention at Detroit in 1965.[3] At Detroit, after the issue was brought to the floor a second time, the resolution "To Accept Reports of Commission on Worship, Liturgics, and Hymnology, and to Set Guidelines for Production of a Hymnal" was passed. The president of the Synod was authorized to invite the other Lutheran church bodies in North America to work with the Synod in the preparation of common worship materials.[4] Moreover, the Synod in convention at Milwaukee in 1971 urged the speedy completion of this project.[5]

When debate was finally terminated at Dallas, Resolution 3–04A ("To Deal with the Proposed *Lutheran Book of Worship*") was adopted. It called for the appointment of a blue-ribbon committee which, after study and review, would recommend to the next convention one of three options: adopt the final draft of the LBW, adopt the LBW with specified modifications, or reject the LBW and propose that an alternative new hymnal be developed. Further to ensure the doctrinal purity of synodical worship materials, a new bylaw that called for convention approval of all such books ("which are to be accepted as official service books and hymnals") was also adopted.[6]

The primary "whereas" of Resolution 3–04A reads, "Theological questions have been raised by agencies and members of the LCMS (*e.g.*, CTCR [Commission on Theology and Church Relations], faculty members of the two seminaries, worship material reviewers) concerning the proposed LBW (*e.g.*, commemorations, eucharistic prayer forms, adequacy of expressions, optional use of 'he descended to the dead' in the Apostles' Creed, theological implications of the hymn text alterations, confirmation promise, fellowship implications)."[7]

Immediately after the convention, seven persons were appointed to the so-called Special Hymnal Review Committee: Henry Abram was appointed by the Commission on Worship; James Brauer and Jane Schatkin Hettrick were appointed by President J. A. O. Preus; Eugene Klug was appointed by the president of Concordia Theological Seminary, Fort Wayne; Robert C. Sauer was chosen by the synodical praesidium; Norman Troyke was chosen from among the members of the Commission on Theology and Church Relations; and Lorenz Wunderlich was selected from the faculty of Concordia Seminary, St. Louis, by the president of that institution.[8] Meetings were held in August, September, October, November, and December of 1977. At the August meeting Robert Sauer was elected by the committee members to be the chairman, and Lorenz Wunderlich was elected to serve as secretary. After the September meeting a communication was directed to the Inter-Lutheran Commission on Worship in which the committee requested information as to what modifications could yet be made in the *Lutheran Book of Worship*. A letter dated September 26, 1977, to Robert Sauer read in part,

> In the opinion of the publisher's representative (who advises us on these matters), it will already be too late by the time of the next meeting of the Special Hymnal Review Committee (SHRC) to make any changes that would require the shifting of space requirements. Such changes would be the deletion of a hymn or of entire stanzas of hymns, the addition of a paragraph to a service, etc. By mid-October the dummy of the liturgy will be completed; the hymnal dummy is complete already.[9]

After the October meeting, Henry Abram resigned from the committee. Willis Wright of the Commission on Worship took his place. Subsequently, five of the remaining six members of the commission also resigned.[10]

Following a December meeting, the Special Hymnal Review Committee recommended that the Synod consider using a revised edition of the *Lutheran Book of Worship* and that a detailed report be sent to all congregations in 1978. The December announcement called attention to theological problems in both the liturgical section and the hymnody.[11] Among these were sentences in the Marriage, Burial, and Baptism rites which, the committee stated, had no scriptural basis. "Missing in these orders are clear scriptural teachings on original sin, for example, and the empowering Word in Baptism. Universalistic concepts are evident in the burial service prayers."[12] Among approximately 63 hymns the committee found objectionable was "At the cross her station keeping," a hymn describing the Virgin Mary "as sharing Christ's suffering in a manner not compatible with Lutheran theology."[13]

The committee further commented,

> Though there is much useful material in the book, the proposed LBW . . . is quite a departure from all former Lutheran service books, not only from the Missouri Synod standpoint. There seemed to be an ecumenical effort to make this hymnal acceptable not only to a Lutheran constituency, but to an even broader, wider constituency. As a result, the Lutheran confessional position, as delineated in former hymnals of all Lutherans, including those still involved in the project, has been watered down.[14]

The 43-page report of the Special Hymnal Review Committee was mailed to congregations and pastors of the Synod in May 1978. In the introduction, the committee stated, "It is not a pleasant task to point out aberrations and ambiguities in materials gathered together by fellow Christians. We pray that those who were a part of the project do not receive our report as a judgment against them."[15] But aberrations and ambiguities there were. In the initial report, the committee questioned the listing of less than orthodox theologians and mystics in the calendar: George Fox, Toyohiko Kagawa, Soren Kierkegaard, Nathan Söderblom, and Albert Schweitzer. Several prayers pertaining to the doctrine of the church blurred the distinction between *unitas* (oneness) and *concordia* (harmony). The prayer for pastors and bishops implied that women could serve as pastors, a position clearly regarded as unscriptural. In at least 20 psalms, "they" and "their" replaced "he" and "his." The translation of Psalm 51:6, a basic proof text for the doctrine of original sin, clearly sidestepped the identification of a person's sinful nature even from conception. As stated above, the order of Baptism made no reference to original sin. A "Brief Order for Confession and Forgiveness" substituted "We are in bondage to sin" for the traditional "We are by nature sinful and unclean." Article II of the Apology of the Augsburg Confession, which includes the significant statement that "recognition of original sin is a necessity," and Article I of the Formula of Concord were totally bypassed throughout the entire *Lutheran Book of Worship*.

Special problems were identified in the proposed orders for Holy Baptism, Affirmation of Baptism, the Marriage Service, and the Burial of the Dead. They were so extensive that the committee recommended deleting all four. The report stated,

> What is usually called the "exhortation" reads as follows:

> In Holy Baptism, our gracious heavenly Father liberates us from sin and death by joining us to the death and resurrection of our Lord Jesus Christ. We are born children of a fallen humanity; in the waters of baptism, we are reborn children of and inheritors of eternal life. By water and the Holy Spirit, we are made members of the Church, which is the body of Christ. As we live with him and with his people, we grow in faith, love, and obedience to the will of God.

> The phrase "children of a fallen humanity" is too vague. Eastern Orthodoxy could employ the same phrase and mean something entirely different, namely, that man has fallen from a state of undeveloped simplicity and that original guilt must be rejected. The Mormons could even employ this phrase. In the rite of Baptism there ought to be the clear teaching of man's sin and guilt and damnation, unless delivered by our Lord Jesus Christ.

> In his statement to the sponsors, the minister asks various questions of them but strangely enough does not ask the sponsors if they will pray for those about to be baptized. In the address of the minister to the baptismal group and the congregation, the following question is asked: "I ask you to profess your faith in Christ

Jesus, reject sin, and confess the faith of the church, the faith in which we baptize." Do we baptize "in the name" or "in the faith"? We "are baptized into the faith," but is it "the faith in which we baptize"?

The question is then asked, "Do you renounce all the forces of evil, the devil, and all his empty promises?" This is indeed ambiguous. What is meant by "forces of evil"? The traditional form leaves no doubt: "Do you renounce the devil and all his works and all his ways?" After the questions, the Creed is recited. Then alternate forms are presented for Baptism. They read as follows: "(name), I baptize you in the name of the Father . . . ." or "(name) is baptized in the name of the Father . . . ." No reasons seems [sic] to exist for the presence of this option.

After the Baptism, the rubric states: "The minister lays both hands upon the head of each of the baptized and prays for the Holy Spirit." The prayer reads as follows:

God, the Father of our Lord Jesus Christ, we give you thanks for freeing your sons and daughters from the power of sin and for raising them up to a new life through this holy sacrament. Pour your Holy Spirit upon (name): the spirit of wisdom and understanding, the spirit of counsel and might, the spirit of knowledge and the fear of the Lord, the spirit of joy in your presence.

Both the rubric and the prayer imply that the Spirit comes after (apart from?) the new life through this sacrament. One wonders why the traditional prayer with its clear connection of water and the Spirit was dropped for this doubtful one.

The next rubric reads: "The minister marks the sign of the cross on the forehead of each of the baptized. Oil prepared for this purpose may be used. As the sign of the cross is made, the minister says: '(name), child of God, you have been sealed by the Holy Spirit and marked with the cross of Christ forever.' " But the anointing and sealing of the Spirit happened in *Baptism*, through the washing of the water with the Word. The introduction of oil obscures the means our Lord commanded, namely, water. Especially in our neo-pentecostal era, we ought to glory in our water baptism and stress that then and there we received the Spirit.

121

The Eastern Orthodox baptismal rite includes the anointing of oil immediately after baptism.

Missing in this entire order is explicit reference to the Word and faith in that Word of God. The answer to the question "How can water do such great things?" in the Small Catechism reads: "It is not the water indeed that does them, but the Word of God which is in and with the water, and faith, which trusts such Word of God in the water. For without the Word of God the water is simple water and no Baptism."

Regarding the Affirmation of Baptism, reference was made to the rubrics title "Reception Into Membership," which read:

Christians from other denominations become members of the Lutheran Church through reception into the local congregation. In Baptism they were made Christians; now they become members of the Lutheran Church. The following rubric states, "A representative of the congregation presents the candidates to the ministry: These persons have come to us from other churches and desire to make public affirmation of their Baptism."

There is nothing in this order that would lead us to believe that instruction in the Word of God has been given to those who come from other denominations.

The report on the Marriage Service read, in part:

The couple is instructed: "The Lord in his goodness created us male and female, and by the gift of marriage founded human community in a joy that begins now and is brought to perfection in the life to come." It is not true that marriage results in a joy in the life to come. No such view is taught in Scripture regarding marriage. The obvious human joy of two heathen in marriage certainly does not result in eternal perfection.

The officiant says: "If it is your intention to share with each other your joys and sorrows and all that the years will bring, with your promises bind yourselves to each other as husband and wife." While this does not contradict Scripture, it omits God's action in the lives of the bride and the groom. The proposed vow reads: "I take you to be my wife/husband from this day forward, to join with you and share all that is to come, and I promise to be faithful to you until death parts us." The Scriptural relation between husband and wife in this "charge" is inadequately represented. It is quite obvious that the term "obey" is an option. This is not in accord with Scripture.

The Preface and the Post-Communion Prayer appointed for use when Holy Communion is given in connection with marriage contain statements that cannot be supported by Scripture. In the Preface, the statement is made, "You gave us the gift of marriage which embodies your love and which, even where your name is not known, proclaims your love for the whole human family." The Post-Communion Prayer opens with the words, "Lord Jesus Christ, as you freely give yourself to your bride, the Church, grant that the mystery of the union of man and woman in marriage may reveal to the world the self-giving love you have for your Church, and to you, with the Father and the Holy Spirit be glory and honor now and forever."

We do not know God's love apart from Jesus Christ. That God grants His blessings to just and unjust is Scriptural (Matt. 5:45) but His love is another matter. Marriage may proclaim God's providence and His goodness but not His love, except that for Christians there is the connection between Christ's love for the church and the marriage relationship (Eph. 5:21–33).

In the Post-Communion Prayer, it is not correct to say that Christ gave Himself up to the church. Nor does "the mystery of the union of man and woman in marriage," whatever that means, "reveals [sic] the self-giving love of Christ to the world." The mystery that is spoken of in the Ephesians passage is the union between Christ and the church.

A December 1977 news release had already called attention to unscriptural concepts evident in the burial service prayers. The committee commented,

> The first prayer in this rite reads:
>
> O God of grace and glory, we remember before you today our *brother/sister* (name). We thank you for giving *him/her* to us to know and to love as a companion in our pilgrimage on earth. In your boundless compassion, console us who mourn. Give us your aid so we may see in death the gate to eternal life, that we may continue our course on earth in confidence until, by your call,

we are reunited with those who have gone before us; through your Son, Jesus Christ our Lord.

The phrase "We are reunited with those who have gone before us" as it stands cannot be supported by Scripture. In burial services, it should be clearly stated that only those who die in the saving faith, namely confidence in Jesus Christ as Redeemer, enter heaven. Many people who are not Christian attend such services and to give any indication that everyone will finally reach eternal life is indeed doing them a great disservice. Similarly, the expression in a later prayer, "We may be gathered to our ancestors," is certainly not Scriptural language.

The prayer included for "the burial of a child" reads:

O God, our Father, your beloved Son took children into his arms and blessed them. Give us grace, we pray, that we may entrust (name) to your never failing care and love and bring us all to your heavenly kingdom; through your Son, Jesus Christ our Lord.

Perhaps the prayer is designed for those who have been baptized and also for those who have not. In any event, a Christian should be comforted when a child dies to know that because of his Baptism this child is indeed among the company of the blessed.

One of the prayers in this order reads: "Receive him/her into the arms of your mercy, and remember him/her according to the favor you bear for your people." Another prayer reads: "Receive him/her into the arms of your mercy, into the blessed rest of everlasting peace, and into the glorious company of the saints in light." Still another prayer reads: "We commend our brother/sister to the Lord: May the Lord receive him/her into his peace and raise him/her up on the last day." These petitions are misleading and inappropriate, as the deceased is already enjoying eternal life, the joys of heaven, in fellowing with all saints.

The report indicated disagreement with new wordings of the creeds, the Lord's Prayer, and the Verba. One of the most hotly debated issues at the time were the proposed LBW eucharistic prayers, titled "The Great Thanksgiving." The committee reported,

There is much disagreement among Lutherans in all the major bodies in our country about adding a prayer which includes the

Words of Institution in the Holy Communion service. Some take the position that by including these words in a prayer the impression is given that the Lord's Supper is something we do. In other words, a prayer is an offering to God. The Words of Institution are proclamation. They are to be proclaimed to the people and not prayed to God. It is further argued that the chief thing in the sacrament, "besides the bodily eating and drinking," is "the words here written, 'given and shed for you for the remission of sins.' " This is the way we learned it in Luther's Catechism. The emphasis now seems to be on our thanksgiving.

There are problems in the text of the proposed Thanksgiving Prayers. One has to do with calling upon the Holy Spirit in connection with the Lord's Supper. A few of the prayers include the petition: "Send now, we pray, your Holy Spirit, the Spirit of our Lord and of his resurrection, that we who receive the Lord's Body and Blood may live to the praise of your glory and receive our inheritance with all your saints in light." But where is the Spirit to be sent? Another prayer includes this petition: "Send now, we pray, your Holy Spirit that we and all who share in this bread and cup may be united in the fellowship of the Holy Spirit, may enter the fullness of the kingdom of heaven, and may receive our inheritance with all your saints in light." But aren't all Christians already united in one body (Eph. 4:4–6)?

Another prayer is more explicit about the work of the Holy Spirit. It reads: "Send your Spirit upon these gifts of your Church, gather into one all who share this bread and wine; fill us with your Holy Spirit to establish our faith in truth, that we may praise and glorify you through your Son, Jesus Christ." Why should the Holy Spirit be sent upon the bread and wine? To do what? The Eastern Orthodox Church holds that the invocation of the Holy Spirit upon the elements is necessary for the consecration of the elements, a teaching not upheld by Scripture and the Lutheran Confessions.

One of the canticles, the Beatitudes, was singled out as a poor translation of Scripture ("How blest are those who hunger and thirst to see right prevail"). In addition to the above named Hymn of the Virgin Mary, especially the following hymns were deemed to be theologically deficient,

Break Now the Bread of Life
Breathe on Me, Breath of God

Christ Is Alive! Let Christians Sing
Father Eternal, Ruler of Creation
Look, Now He Stands
Lord Christ, When First You Came to Earth
Lord, Who the Night You Were Betrayed
O God, Empower Us
Praise the Lord, Rise Up Rejoicing
The Church of Christ, In Ev'ry Age
There's A Wideness In God's Mercy
We Know That Christ Is Raised
We Who Once Were Dead
Your Kingdom Come

Others were recommended to be retained if changes were made in the wording of certain stanzas. It was also noted that in the proposed hymns on the ministry, the pastor was called a "herald." Any reference to the pastor as being male was missing.

Perhaps the most difficult decision was the selection of a suitable translation of the Psalms. The 1977 version of the Psalter, contained in the Episcopalian *Standard Book of Common Prayer*, was used in the *Lutheran Book of Worship*. The newly appointed Commission on Worship requested permission to make certain changes, as reflected above, but to maintain the remainder. Permission was not granted. After studying the existing translations, the commission recommended the New International Version.

In the second and final report of the SHRC,[16] it was pointed out that

> The *Lutheran Book of Worship* contains many fine materials, in both the liturgical and the hymnic sections. Furthermore, as an example of graphic art, it is outstanding. When therefore the . . . Committee's (initial) report recommends a revision of the LBW, it does so recognizing that on the one hand, there are many good, positive features, and that on the other hand there are a number of serious theological defects that make it unsuitable for use in its present form by congregations in our Synod. These are primarily matters of sound doctrine in accord with Scriptures and the Lutheran Confessions. Suitability for use in our churches is grounded in this.

Many objected to the LBW's changes in the wording of the creeds. One concern was the variant translations "catholic" and "Christian" of the word *catholica*. Both are acceptable. *Catholic*, as the more ancient rendering, is preferred for linguistic/historical reasons. *Christian* is preferred for pastoral reasons, but it is also justifiable historically. Significantly, the Tappert tanslation of the *Book of Concord* (p. 18) employs *Christian* rather than *catholic* in the creeds and adds the footnote: "It has been customary since the fifteenth century to translate *catholica* with *christlich*." In the (German) Small Catechism, Luther uses *christlich* (Christian) throughout. In the Smalcald Articles he employs the two words interchangeably (XII). The committee recognizes a pastoral need to use the word *Christian* in the Apostles' and Nicene Creeds, but it also believes that the word *catholic* should not be completely lost. Therefore it is recommended that *catholic* be retained in the Athanasian Creed.

Unlike the Dallas convention, the July 1979 St. Louis convention quickly adopted a proposed hymnal (Resolution 3–01, "To Adopt *Lutheran Worship* as an Official Hymnal of the LCMS").[17]

The general contents of the liturgical service listed in the resolution were:

1. The Calendar
   a) The Sundays of the Church Year and the Principal Festivals.
   b) The Lesser Festivals arranged according to the church year rather than the calendar year, thus beginning with St. Andrew (November 30). The commemorations in *Lutheran Book of Worship* (LBW) are dropped.
2. The three-year Lectionary from LBW plus the revised Old Standard series.
3. Psalms for Daily Prayer from LBW.
4. The Order of Morning Service (pp. 5ff.) and the Holy Communion (pp. 15ff.) from *The Lutheran Hymnal* (TLH) will be structured into one service with text updated, music preserved in melody but improved in notation and harmony.
5. Holy Communion, Settings I and II, from LBW. The music will be intact, but the texts will be altered to conform to the recommendations of the Special Hymnal Review Committee's

report, chiefly with regard to the Confession and the Great Thanksgiving.

6. Matins and Vespers from TLH with updated texts and improved musical settings largely based on present settings.

7. The Litany with revisions.

8. Morning Prayer from LBW with slight alterations.

9. Evening Prayer from LBW with slight alterations.

10. Compline from LBW with slight alterations.

11. Propers for Daily Prayer from LBW with alterations.

12. Choral Service of Holy Communion from LBW with slight revisions.

13. Responsive Prayer I and II from LBW with some textual changes.

14. Updated Morning and Evening Suffrages from TLH, to be called Responsive Prayer III and IV respectively, to be used as alternates to Responsive Prayers I and II.

15. The Psalms (or Psalter) from NIV [New International Version] will be included, but the number largely restricted to those appointed for use in the Lectionary during the church year. In addition the Commission on Worship is providing a series of Introits pointed to melodic formulae devised by the Liturgical Texts and Music Committee of the commission.

16. The Canticles from LBW with the exception of No. 17 (the Beatitudes).

17. A series of traditional, updated Collects for the Day to replace those in LBW.

18. The inclusion of the Six Chief Parts and the Christian Questions and Answers of *Luther's Small Catechism* (1943 version).

Hymn titles were also listed, totalling 508. Selection was in part based on a hymn-usage survey report published August 2, 1975, received from 1,500 congregations. The resolution was passed with the understanding that the hymn list could be expanded if sufficient requests were received for including hymns that were not listed.

In retrospect, the action on the hymnal reflects the mood among Lutherans in America. In the sixties they seem to have favored the gathering of all the major Lutheran Church bodies in America into a single denomination. The wording of the first whereas of Resolution 13–01 of the 1965 convention, calling for a common Lutheran hymnal, is significant: "There is a desire in various Lutheran bodies in America to express the faith which they hold in common through more uniform texts and musical settings in both liturgy and hymnody."[18] The LCMS doctrinal controversy that raged through the seventies may well have contributed to the theological awareness that precipitated the Dallas concerns.

The early eighties witnessed what Bishop James Crumley of the Lutheran Church in America called "diverging courses" between the Missouri Synod and his church body.[19] The final publication of two hymnals, similar yet different in content, is truly evidence of changes among Lutherans in America during that decade.

COMMISSION ON WORSHIP

Fred L. Precht

The resignation in December 1977 of the Commission on Worship, except for one member, namely, Willis Wright,[20] left the Synod without the services of such a commission until the appointment of a new one by President J. A. O. Preus in the summer of 1978.[21] Although this new commission had no way of knowing what the decision of the Synod in the 1979 convention might be, it decided to proceed on the assumption that the Synod would approve, at least in principle, the recommendation of the Special Hymnal Review Committee that *Lutheran Book of Worship* be revised and entitled *Lutheran Worship*. Encouraged by the praesidium to proceed with all haste, it organized committees and made assignments with a view to study and assess thoroughly the *Lutheran Book of Worship*, the Report and Recommendations of the Special Hymnal Review Committee, as well as the criticisms and suggestions that had been received, thus gradually and tentatively to circumscribe the contents of such a revised hymnal. With the untiring and cooperative efforts of the commission and its committees,[22] by the end of May 1979 the Commission on Worship was able to transmit to Floor Committee 3 of the convention the general contents of both the liturgical and hymnological sections of the proposed *Lutheran Worship* to be appended to that committee's Resolution 3–01 for action by that summer's convention.

With the convention's adoption of the above resolution, the commission now had its work cut out for it. Assisted by its adjunct committees, it forged ahead to formulate, refine, and finalize the manuscripts for *Lutheran Worship*. Numerous meetings were held, and the knowledgeable individuals who were given certain assignments worked untiringly to carry out the resolution. The commission seriously considered the many suggestions for the contents of the book that came to its office from concerned lay people, teachers, musicians, and pastors, following the 1979 synodical convention. It bent every effort to do its very best to produce a hymnal and service book strongly reflecting Lutheranism's great heritage in liturgy and hymnody, a book clear in its doctrinal expression while also artistically and liturgically satisfying.[23]

Synodwide Introductory Process

Early in 1981 the Commission on Worship began to make plans for the synodwide introduction of *Lutheran Worship* by appointing a special committee to establish the process and to prepare the necessary materials.[24] On Saturdays during October and November of that year approximately 400 congregational cluster workshops, each lasting seven hours, were conducted by three individuals (a pastor, a musician, and an educator) selected by their respective district presidents and previously trained by the commission in two-day sessions during June and July at Concordia Seminary, St. Louis; and at the synodical colleges at Bronxville, NY; Seward, NE; River Forest, IL; St. Paul, MN; and Portland, OR. At each training event six or seven representatives (pastor, organist, choir director, worship committee personnel, elder, education leader) from each of the fifteen to eighteen area congregations were invited to participate at a specified location. The purpose was to acquaint these representatives with the general contents of *Lutheran Worship* and to assist them in turn to introduce the hymnal effectively to their respective congregations. The cost of these successful introductory events and the accompanying materials was borne by a generous grant of $175,000 from Lutheran Brotherhood, a fraternal benefit society in Minneapolis, MN.

Appearance of *Lutheran Worship*

The first copies of the new hymnal from Concordia Publishing House were received with great joy and satisfaction by the Commission on Worship on December 20, 1981, a book on which the commission and its committees had tirelessly labored for more than three years.

William M. Taylor (1829–95), the Presbyterian divine, was not far wrong when he stated that a "hymnal reflects the history of the church, embodies the doctrine of the church, expresses the devotional life of the church, and demonstrates the unity of the church."

If, as Arthur Schlesinger, Jr. has said, "history is to the nation what memory is to the individual; without memory an individual would be absolutely rudderless," then without memory a church, too, is rudderless. A church that forgets and dissociates itself from its past will become confused about its identity and uncertain of its message. So, too, in worship. The past is not only important in itself, it has a very real effect on the present. Those who do not remember the past are not only condemned to repeat it, they are also condemned to a rootless, shallow practice. Memories can enrich and enable congregations to understand how they came to be where they are. Their worship experience ought to teach them how to value the past without becoming stuck there, to treasure their roots precisely because such roots enable them to grow in the present.

Preservation of Heritage and Change

A hymnal will contain both old and new elements, representing preservation of the heritage as well as change. In its desire to meet congregations "where they are," the Commission on Worship retained, among other things, the familiar Common Service (The Holy Communion) in *The Lutheran Hymnal*, Matins and Vespers, the Church Year, the Bidding Prayer, the Litany, as well as numerous hymns (approximately 375) dear to the people, albeit in revised and updated form where considered necessary and/or desirable.

As for new things, the emphasis of the Lutheran symbols on corporate worship in Word and Sacrament—God's way of calling people into his church and identifying the church where these are present—prompted the Commission on Worship to omit the Order of Morning Service Without Communion contained in *The Lutheran Hymnal*, thus reflecting a greater emphasis on the unity of Word and Sacrament in Divine Service I while at the same time according increased importance to the Lord's Supper in the life of the congregation. Moreover, the full rite of Holy Baptism was included as well as listed immediately after the Divine Services in the hymnal's table of contents (*The Lutheran Hymnal* contained only a short form for emergencies) in part to indicate the importance also of this sacrament.

To continue with the new, Divine Service II (offered with two different music settings) is structurally not far removed from Divine Service I or from the shape of the Common Service, although it contains a new and fresh Preparation (Confession and Absolution or Declaration of Grace). The two music settings for Divine Service II, by two contemporary composers,[25] interpret the liturgical texts in a musical idiom to meet today's taste, while also incorporating elements that still continue to communicate. New settings are also encountered in such minor services as Matins, Morning Prayer, and Evening Prayer.

Most noticeable is the change to contemporary language in the liturgies and in most hymns, a procedure followed in the numerous Bible translations produced in recent decades and employed by many denominations in their new service books and hymnals. This naturally followed when the commission decided to use the New International Version of the Bible for the Psalms and scriptural quotations in the hymnal, because of its concern for dignified language with simplicity, clarity, and singability, a language with which the people, both young and old, could identify and which they could readily understand. For example, how could the average reader know that "I prevented the dawning of the morning, and cried" (Ps. 119:147), in the King James Version, means "I rise before dawn and cry for help," as the New International Version has it? In the long history of Christianity, many changes in language have occurred. In the case of the Synod, the change from German to English in corporate worship was made during the first half of the 20th century, a change hastened by World War I. And what a traumatic experience that was for congregations in New Ulm, New Germany, and Hamburg, MN! Families became divided; friendships were severed; church attendance suffered. In this process of change the English of the 16th century, the Elizabethan-Jacobean language of the King James Bible, was adopted. And now, in the 20th century another change has been made, a change not nearly as extreme and unnerving as the change from Greek to Latin in early Christendom or from German to English. But a change it is.

The change, of course, is most noticeable in the use of the personal pronouns.

In Elizabethan English, God is addressed with "thee" and "thou." Quite naturally everyone came to believe that these are reverential terms of address reserved for God. Actually, that is exactly the opposite of what was intended. In Elizabethan English "thee" and "thou" were intimate and familiar forms of address. Within the family, members were addressed with "thee" and "thou." Outside the home and with close friends the form of address was "you." Today, "you," once a formal form of address, has become the familiar and everyday form. There is in fact no formal form of address in the English language. Thus, the noticeable change from "thee" and "thou" in *Lutheran Worship* is not meant to be disrespectful of God. It is rather to capture the original, familiar meaning.[26] Moreover, the use of contemporary language in worship may help Christians to see better the relationship between liturgy and daily life.

It is interesting and instructive to note that when Martin Luther translated the Bible into German, he used the familiar form of the pronoun *du* to address God, not the polite or reverential *Sie*. In German-speaking Christendom Luther's example is followed to this day.

A few changes were made in the church year: Following the lead of the Roman Catholic and the Episcopal churches, the pre-Lenten Sundays of Septuagesima, Sexagesima, and Quinquagesima have been dropped, thus avoiding a seemingly unnecessary prolongation of an already long Lenten season. Hence the Epiphany season now extends to Ash Wednesday. Sunday of the Passion, previously the Sunday before Palm Sunday, has been merged with Palm Sunday; the last Sunday of the church year, with appropriate readings, is called Sunday of the Fulfillment, although the readings for the observance of Christ the King are given as an option; the Sundays of the non-festival half, or Time of the Church, are numbered "after Pentecost" instead of "after Trinity." This change has evoked some questions.

Actually, in the gradual development of the church year, the Sundays after Trinity were originally known as the Sundays after Pentecost until the introduction of the festival of the Holy Trinity in the 14th century by Pope John XXII. In using the designation Sundays after Pentecost, *Lutheran Worship*, together with the new service books of other denominations of Christendom, is simply reflecting earlier custom. In no way is this to downgrade the important doctrine of the Trinity. In fact, the liturgies and hymns in worship invariably acclaim the Trinity every time Christians gather for worship. Moreover, the fact is worth noting that the Lutheran liturgy does not use the term *Pentecost* to refer essentially to the Old Testament "fiftieth day" ("Pentecost") that followed the Passover, the day when the first fruits of the harvest were presented (Deut. 16:9) and, in later times, when the giving of the Law by Moses was commemorated. Granted, it was on this festival day that the Lord, in his wisdom, ten days after his ascension into heaven, poured out his Spirit in a special manner to those assembled in Jerusalem so that this Gospel witness might yield a rich harvest of souls for the kingdom. The term Pentecost is used by the New Testament Church to refer to that fiftieth day after Christ's Resurrection when the great harvesting began.

Notably in evidence in *Lutheran Worship* is the ready availability and increased use of the Old Testament Psalter, so dear in history to both Jews and Christians in their devotional life as well as in corporate worship. There comes to mind Luther's laudatory statement:

> The Psalter ought to be a precious and beloved book, if for no other reason than this: it promises Christ's death and Resurrection so clearly—and pictures his kingdom and the condition and nature of all Christendom—that it might well be called a little

Bible. In it is comprehended most beautifully and briefly everything that is in the entire Bible. . . . Let us then receive them and
use them diligently and carefully, exercising ourselves in them to
the praise and honor of God.[27]

Thus, psalms have been designated in the series of readings
for use as the rubrics in various services call for or suggest; 60 select
psalms have been included in the service section of the hymnal,
each appointed for chanting to the prefixed psalm tune (all 150
psalms are included in *Lutheran Worship: Altar Book* [1982]); the
historic Introits, containing but one or two psalm verses, have been
amplified or supplanted with newer and longer sections of
psalmody; and new seasonal Graduals of psalmody have been provided, pointed for use with the psalm tones.

One new feature in *Lutheran Worship* that stands out perhaps
more than others is the emphasis on shared leadership in corporate worship, a procedure exemplified in the early church in which
deliberate effort appears to have been made to distribute the various
leadership functions among as many people as possible. Without
specifically delineating and detailing the development of the following orders and their functions, suffice it to state that there was
the bishop, or overseer (1 Tim. 3:1; Phil. 1:1) and his assistants:
presbyter, or elder (1 Tim. 5:17; James 5:14); and deacon (Phil. 1:1).
These were individuals who resided in each so-called church and,
besides being involved in corporate worship, were responsible for
the church's daily activities.[28] Later, place was given to subdeacon,
exorcist, reader, acolytes, doorkeepers, chanters, and choir. Nor
were the worshipers overlooked: They had their share in the offering and presentation at the altar of bread and wine and, at times,
other gifts for charitable purposes, as well as their share in the kiss
of peace and in the Communion itself.

It is not too many years ago that the typical Lutheran pastor,
unless he had an assistant or associate, acted as the sole leader in
worship. He "conducted the liturgy," he preached, he administered
the sacraments. Normally he was in the chancel only for his liturgical and homiletical acts. While the congregation sang its assigned
hymns, he sat in the sacristy.

If, as the Greek word *leitourgia*, from which the word liturgy is
derived, is understood by the church basically to mean "one per-

son performing an act of public service on behalf of others," then it is right to assume that, as the people of God, the congregation has its service, its liturgy, its offering of prayer, praise, and thanksgiving to do. It is of utmost importance, however, to understand that such activity is in response to God's initiative in the Divine Service, for liturgy is first of all God at work through Word and Sacrament—the means of grace—as administered by the divinely instituted office of the holy ministry. *Lutheran Worship* envisions laypeople serving as assisting ministers, as such representing the congregation as they lead in prayer, assist in the reading of the Word of God and in the distribution of the chalice at the Communion. Serving as cantor might also be considered as an assisting minister role. Such service is a visible picture of the priesthood of believers sharing a common response to God's truth.

On the other hand it is the pastor, the one ordained to the public ministry in the Church[29] who presides at the Holy Communion in the congregation. As such he has his liturgy, or service, to render. He is called to preach the Gospel, absolve, and celebrate the sacraments.[30] His ministry is from God himself, and when he offers the Word of Christ or the sacraments, he does so in Christ's place and stead.[31] His role is thus one of great responsibility. Since he has control over the general character and style of the service, it is important that he have a thorough understanding of the form and content of the liturgy established by his church.

Since most congregations have only one ordained minister, the role of assisting minister(s) is necessarily assumed by laypeople. They should not be confused with assistant or associate pastors, men who are ordained. In multiple ministry situations the assistant pastor might at times be the presiding minister in the Divine Service, with the head pastor serving as assisting minister. The respective liturgical roles of presiding and assisting ministers are designated by the symbols [P], Presiding minister (ordained); [A], Assisting minister (ordained or not); [L] Leader, (ordained or not).

Important as the service-book section of a new hymnal is for corporate worship—the new elements in *Lutheran Worship* which the preceeding paragraphs have attempted to highlight—it is the hymn section of a hymnal that appears to be of greatest concern to the laity, the section that looms as the most challenging and difficult, if not well-nigh impossible task for the compilers. In this respect *Lutheran Worship* was no exception. The multitude of hymns from which to choose and the fact that each person has his or her favorite hymn that must be included in the book create a problem of seemingly enormous proportions. Compounding the problem—in reality a blessing—is the importance that Christians have come to attach to hymnody, a fact forcefully demonstrated in this instance by the 1,700 letters that came to the office of the Commission on Worship, each pleading for the inclusion of anywhere from 1 to 100 favorite hymns. Interestingly, early in the Christian era the discovery was made that popular religion was molded by the thoughts expressed in hymns. Sermons may fly over the heads of people at times; prayers may fail to capture hearts and minds; but religious songs sink into the memory, color thought, and fashion theology, perhaps more than deliberate instruction. This fact did not escape Luther, as witnessed by his hymn output and that of his followers. Rightly did Lorenz Blankenbuehler, at one time professor of English at Concordia College, St. Paul, state,

> Of all the books written by man, with the exception perhaps of the Catechism, no book is so universally used in the church as the hymnal, and some would not even except the Catechism . . . since next to the Bible and our Catechism, there is perhaps no spiritual tool so valuable as the hymnal for the furtherance of God's kingdom on Earth and for the heightening of spirituality.[32]

It is thus no small wonder that the Commission on Worship, together with its Hymn Texts and Music Committee took this matter seriously. It heeded comments from the field; it carefully examined and weighed each hymn in *The Lutheran Hymnal* (1941), *Worship Supplement* (1969), and *Lutheran Book of Worship* (1978), plus a host of hymns in other hymnals. In the course of the selection process some hymn texts were revised for doctrinal or other reasons and/or updated, some were considerably recast in places, and occasionally some texts were coupled to a different tune. Some tunes were reharmonized, some pitched lower or higher, better to accommodate the human voice range. Of the total of 509 hymns and spiritual songs (excluding the eleven canticles) 23 texts do not appear in any one of the aforementioned hymnals. In the hymn selection process the commission conscientiously sought to establish and include a body of hymns and spiritual songs in *Lutheran Worship* that would effectively and adequately meet the needs of the church year as well as church occasions, to the praise and honor of God and Jesus Christ and the edification of the people of God.

With respect to the ecumenical character of the texts of the hymns and spiritual songs in *Lutheran Worship*, it is interesting to note that 131 texts are included in the list prepared by the Consultation on Ecumenical Hymnody from a common core of 227 hymns appearing in 26 hymnals of various denominations.[33]

The overarching concern of the commission was that the contents of the new hymnal, whether liturgical or hymnological, reflect sound, biblical and confessional theology.

Traditional Versus Contemporary

Today one occasionally hears pastors using the terms traditional liturgy and contemporary liturgy as though the former is the very antithesis of something creative, resourceful, and imaginative. More accurately—in the opinion of this writer—to worship "within a tradition" is to do so while being acutely conscious of the church's past as well as of its eschatological future in Jesus Christ. This is not to be confused with traditionalism, which, as described by historian Jaroslav Pelikan, is "the dead faith of the living." Rather, it is, so he states, "the living faith of the dead,"[34] a tradition that has the capacity to develop while still maintaining its identity and continuity; that serves as a way of relating to the present through contact with both past practice and future hope; that develops the Christian's sense of belongong to a continuing fellowship that stretches through time and space. Moreover, such tradition does not stifle the imagination nor lack creativity or resourcefulness. Quite the contrary. It passes on the received, life-giving, and sustaining Gospel, relating it to present life and future glory.

As for corporate worship, it is cogent to recall the statement of theologian Prosper of Aquitaine (d. 463?), *Lex orandi, lex credendi* (the rule of praying [i.e., worshiping] is the rule of believing), in which he appealed to the worship tradition of the early church to defend Augustine's (354–430) theology about human nature, the fall, and original sin over against his critics. Here is a reference to apostolic tradition in the church's liturgical form, in its liturgy—the fruit of faith and obedience. It is by such worship (*leitourgia*) in Word and Sacrament (not a religious program for the approbation of the worshipers; not a worship in which Word and Sacrament are either supplanted by or supplemented with certain principles of the church growth movement, so corrosive of confessional Lutheran theology) that the church lives; it is there that its heart beats. And it is from this worship that Christians are motivated and empowered to carry out, what are considered to be, the functions of the local congregation: evangelism (*marturia*), education (*didaskalia*), social ministry (*diakonia*), and fellowship (*koinonia*)—activities that not only spring from worship but, in turn, nourish and support it. In brief, such are the broader dimensions of corporate worship in Word and Sacrament.

As for the Divine Service as contained in *Lutheran Worship*, this historic liturgy needs, of course, careful planning and preparation to achieve its full effectiveness as a celebration in memory and in hope of Christ's paschal mystery. This planning will necessarily examine, assess, and use the various options available and considered appropriate in that liturgy in a creative, resourceful, and imaginative way, not only with reference to the verbal elements but also the nonverbal: the Christ encounter communicated through signs, symbols, and gestures, as well as through music, art, and the activity of the celebrating congregation. The language of the Divine Service is contemporary; its form is both natural and dignified and readily understood by all. Although liturgical music is provided, other music idioms, if so desired, can be used, as long as they express the liturgical texts and eschew secular connotations.

Part of the problem of contemporary, do-it-yourself liturgies promoted by the church growth movement in the hope of increasing church membership is the emphasis on technique and methodology and its program/entertainment aspect rather than relying on the power of the Gospel in Word and Sacrament (*verbum audibile et visibile*). When such homemade efforts grab attention, the ministry team is invariably challenged to outdo the worship effects of the week before. Moreover, because such services often lack substance and continuity, they have little sustaining value for worshipers. Pastors would do well to ponder the fact that the Christian liturgy, the Divine Service in Word and Sacrament, in its whole economy posesses inestimable formative and expressive power over human imagination, emotion, thought, and will. Here Christ's church appears for what it is, namely, according to Article VII of the Augsburg Confession, an assembly of *believers*, the faithful, "among whom the Gospel is preached . . . and the holy sacraments administered." Such worship is the very purpose of the church's existence; it is essentially what the church does. Thus the church is not identified by the character of its members but by the character of the assembly, that is, by the preaching of the Gospel. This is not to deny the conscious and urgent concern for reaching out to the unchurched visitors, particularly in the proclamation of the Word of God, the Word read and preached. The broader process of making disciples, however, involves the sending out of the faithful to spread the Word, to invite and encourage the unchurched to the church's instructional and spiritual formation program (traditionally called the catechumenate) so that these neophytes, in turn, become worshipers of the triune God through the blessed Gospel of Jesus Christ, wherein alone they will find purpose and meaning in this life and eternal salvation in the next.

Companion Volumes to *Lutheran Worship*

A new service book and hymnal such as *Lutheran Worship* (1982) invariably calls for a number of companion volumes, both to facilitate and to complement its use. Thus two volumes appeared simultaneously with the hymnal, namely, *Lutheran Worship: Accompaniment for the Liturgy* [35] and *Lutheran Worship: Accompaniment for the Hymns*, both with spiral binding for ease of use on the music rack. In July of that same year *Lutheran Worship: Altar Book* appeared, a book specially designed by the Commission on Worship to aid pastors and assisting ministers in conducting corporate worship. In contrast to the hymnal, or "Pew Edition"—intended and prepared for use in church, school, and home—the *Altar Book* includes only those liturgical items considered helpful or necessary for leading corporate worship. Certain items from the hymnal are necessarily expanded and the rubrics altered accordingly. Thus, Proper, or seasonal, Invitatories with chant have been inserted in

Matins, as well as seasonal Prefaces and the Words of Institution with chant in the Divine Services. The section entitled Petitions, Intercessions, and Thanksgivings in the "Pew Edition" has been considerably expanded. Moreover, whereas the "Pew Edition" contains 60 psalms, the *Altar Book* contains the entire Psalter, each with a select psalm tone.

Additions include a Table of Psalms for Daily Prayer and Readings for Daily Prayer, especially for pastors desiring to pursue personally a disciplined order of daily prayer. The following helpful indexes are added: Alternate Hymn Tunes, Scripture References in Hymns and Spiritual Songs, Hymns and Spiritual Songs with Scripture References, Index to One-Year Lectionary, Index to Three-Year Lectionary, Psalm Index, and Topical Index of Collects and Prayers. The addition of the rather extensive Notes on the Liturgy should prove of significant value in pointing out historical, theological, and practical aspects of the respective services and rites.[36]

As early as July 1981, the synod, assembled in convention in St. Louis, recognizing the need for a new agenda to supplant *The Lutheran Agenda* (1948), authorized the Commission on Worship to prepare a new edition, one that would "include new and updated forms, rites, and occasional services."[37] In November 1982 the first draft was sent to pastors, teachers, professors, missionaries, and deaconesses of the Synod, inviting reactions and comments. This resulted in a number of significant emendations. Subsequently the 1983 convention of the Synod approved and accepted the draft as revised by the commission,[38] declaring it to be an official service book entitled *Lutheran Worship: Agenda*.[39] The book appeared on the market in late 1984.

This new book is considerably larger than its predecessor. It is greatly enhanced by the addition of a number of new rites and the revision and the enrichment of the rites retained from the former agenda. Moreover, the new agenda does not restrict itself to rites (forms and ceremonies inserted within a formal service), but in response to requests and to meet contemporary needs it includes some liturgies, or services—largely relating to Lent and Holy Week—not included in former agendas of the Synod.[40]

As a successor to *The Pastor's Companion* (1950), a small handbook for the more personal ministrations of the pastor, the Commission on Worship prepared *Lutheran Worship: Little Agenda* (1985).[41] With the exception of the Brief Service of the Word and the designated Collects of the Day and Readings for the church year (the latter included as an aid to relating the ministrations to the ongoing church year) the rites in this small book of 172 pages are from the larger *Lutheran Worship: Agenda* (1984). Holy Baptism Short Form was included only for emergency situations, since baptisms should preferably take place in the congregation assembled for corporate worship.

Recognizing the validity of numerous requests for appropriate liturgical and hymnic resources as well as certain installation rites to be made available for use at various conferences and conventions, the Commission on Worship developed such a booklet. Consisting largely of excerpts from *Lutheran Worship* ("Pew Edition"), *Lutheran Worship: Agenda*, and *Lutheran Worship: Little Agenda*, the 144-page booklet appeared in Spring 1986 entitled *Lutheran Worship: Conference and Convention Edition*.[42]

Two more companion volumes, although not prepared by the Commission on Worship, were prepared, published, and issued by Concordia Publishing House, namely, *Lutheran Worship Lectionary* (1983), containing the appointed readings of the three-year lectionary series in the New International Version of the Bible; and *Lutheran Worship: Large Print Edition* (1985), Vol. 1: Hymns; Vol. 2: Liturgy. Both contained the respective texts.[43]

Notes

1. Missouri Synod, *Proceedings*, 1977, pp. 37, 46, 50, 51.
2. Missouri Synod, *Workbook*, 1977, pp. 39–40, 125–130.
3. Ibid., pp. 59–61, 131–132.
4. *Proceedings*, 1965, pp. 185–186.
5. *Proceedings*, 1971, pp. 113–114.
6. *Proceedings*, 1977, pp. 128–129.
7. Ibid., pp. 127–128.
8. *Report and Recommendations of the Special Hymnal Review Committee* (The Lutheran Church—Missouri Synod, 500 North Broadway, Saint Louis, Missouri, May, 1978), p. 3.
9. Ibid., p. 3.
10. "Committee completing study of new hymnal," *The Lutheran Witness* 96/16 (December 18, 1977): 22.

11. Ibid.

12. Ibid.

13. Ibid.

14. Missouri Synod, Department of Public Relations News Release, Nov. 21, 1977.

15. *Workbook*, 1979, pp. 273–283.

16. *Workbook*, 1979, pp. 89–90.

17. *Proceedings*, 1979, pp. 113–117.

18. *Proceedings*, 1965, pp. 185–186.

19. *Partners*, "The magazine for professional church leaders of The Lutheran Church in America" (August 1983), p. 5.

20. Members of the Commission on Worship at the time of the Dallas convention: Paul Foelber, chairman; Carlos Messerli, secretary; Henry C. Abram, Paul Peterson, Jaroslav Vajda, and Willis Wright.

21. Appointed were: Alfred Fremder, professor of composition and piano at Texas Wesleyan College, Fort Worth, TX; F. Samuel Janzow, professor of English literature at Concordia College, River Forest, IL; Robert Koeppen, pastor of Zion Lutheran Church, Hinsdale, IL; Leonard Laetsch, pastor of Zion Lutheran Church, Carlinville, IL; Norman Nagel, dean of chapel at Valparaiso University, Valparaiso, IN; Ralph Schultz, president of Concordia College, Bronxville, NY; and Willis Wright, president of Concordia College, Selma, AL. Robert Sauer, first vice-president of the Synod was appointed to serve in an advisory capacity. At its first meeting August 29–30, 1978, Robert Koeppen was elected chairman and Leonard Laetsch secretary. When, several months later, Laetsch accepted a call to a congregation in the Evangelical Lutheran Church in England, the commission elected Ralph Schultz secretary. Also, at this first meeting the appointment to serve as acting executive secretary of the commission—until such time as the Synod's established process for the appointment of such executive positions could be followed—was extended to Fred L. Precht. The Synodwide call for nominations and his subsequent election by the commission resulted in his being officially installed as executive secretary on October 22, 1979, by the chairman of the commission.

22. The Liturgical Text and Music Committee was comprised of Norman Nagel (chairman), Charles Evanson (secretary), Paul Bunjes, M. Alfred Bichsel, and Ralph Schultz; the Hymn Text and Music Committee consisted of Alfred Fremder (chairman), Henry Lettermann (secretary), Hugo Gehrke, F. Samuel Janzow, Edward Klammer, and Jaroslav Vajda.

23. Toward the end of this biennium, extenuating circumstances caused three members of the commission to resign, namely, Robert Koeppen, F. Samuel Janzow, and Edward Klammer. The latter, who had earlier assumed F. Samuel Janzow's place, was asked to resign by Ralph Reinke, president and chief executive officer of Concordia Publishing House, publisher of the new hymnal, thus to obviate any conflict of interest when that executive appointed Klammer to become its in-house coordinator for the hymnal. To fill the above vacancies, President J. A. O. Preus, after consultation with the vice-presidents of the Synod, appointed Henry Lettermann, Roger Pittelko, and Norman Troyke.

24. David Held, professor of music at Concordia College, Seward, NE, provided leadership for a a two-section committee: Introductory Process Committee and Introductory Materials Committee. Members of the former were Dr. David Held, chairman, Dr. Hugo J. Gehrke, Mr. Walter Gresens, Mr. Fredric W. Kamprath and Rev. Thomas J. Windsor. Members of the latter were Dr. Roger Pittelko, chairman, Dr. Dennis Janko, Rev. Charles McClean and Rev. Martin Taddey.

25. The First Setting is the work of Richard Hillert, music professor at Concordia University, River Forest, IL; the Second Setting is by Ronald Nelson, organist and composer at Westwood Lutheran Church, St. Louis Park, MN.

26. Notice that these pronouns, when referring to the Christian deity, are not capitalized even in the King James Version of the Bible, nor do most contemporary versions do so. Apropos is the statement in the preface of the New International Version (p. viii), representing the consensus of the more than hundred scholars engaged in this translation:

> As for the traditional pronouns "thou," "thee" and "thine" in reference to the Deity, the translators judged that to use these archaisms (along with the old verb forms such as "doest," "wouldest" and "hadst") would violate accuracy in translation. Neither Hebrew, Aramaic nor Greek uses special pronouns for the persons of the Godhead. A present-day translation is not enhanced by forms that in the time of the King James Version were used in everyday speech, whether referring to God or man.

27. Martin Luther, Preface to the Psalter (1528), AE 35: 254, 257.

28. It is to be noted that the terms elder and bishop are used interchangeably in Acts 20:17 and Acts 20:28, as also in Titus 1:5 and 7. Eph. 4:11–12 speaks of "shepherds [pastors] and teachers," evidently the same person in different functions. In the Lutheran symbols the shepherd/elder/bishop supervision is considered a supervision of the teaching/preaching of the Word and the administration of the sacraments. AC V.

29. Apology XIII, 12.

30. AC XIV; Ap XIII, 7–9.

31. Ap VII, 28.

32. L. Blankenbuehler, "The Christian Hymn: A Glorious Treasure" (Ogden, Iowa: Ogden Reporter Print, 1940), essay presented by him at the convention of the Iowa District West of the Missouri Synod in Sioux City, IA, August 26–30, 1940, on the eve of the appearance of *The Lutheran Hymnal* (1941). Blankenbuehler, professor of English at Concordia College, St. Paul, MN, was a member of the Intersynodical Committee which produced that hymnal.

33. Represented in this consultation (1971 and 1976) were the following denominations: Disciples of Christ, Protestant Episcopal Church, Evangelical Covenant Church of North America, The Lutheran Church—Missouri Synod, the American Lutheran Church, Lutheran Church in America, United Methodist Church, Moravian Church, United Presbyterian Church U.S.A., Presbyterian Church in the United States, Roman Catholic Church, United Church of Christ, and United Church of Canada.

34. Jaroslav Pelikan, *The Vindication of Tradition* (New Haven and London: Yale University Press, 1984), p. 65.

35. In the first edition of the *Accompaniment for the Liturgy* the page-turns occurring at very inopportune points in the music—the work of an outside jobber engaged by Concordia Publishing House—evoked severe criticism. In 1987 Concordia issued a new, greatly improved edition.

36. Notes on the Liturgy, Scripture References in Hymns and Spiritual Songs, and Hymns and Spiritual Songs with Scripture References are available in a handy, separate offprint fascicle from Concordia Publishing House, St. Louis, MO.

37. See Missouri Synod, *Proceedings*, 1981, Resolution 3–13, p. 159.

38. This draft appeared in Appendix IV, Missouri Synod, *Convention Workbook*, 1983, pp. 351–451.

39. Missouri Synod, *Proceedings*, 1983, Resolution 2–07A, pp. 145–146.

40. For a more complete overview of the contents of *Lutheran Worship: Agenda* see Fred L. Precht, "Lutheran Worship Agenda," *Lutheran Worship Notes* (Summer 1984): 3–5.

41. Although this *Little Agenda* contains a 1985 copyright date, difficulties with the job printer engaged by Concordia Publishing House prevented the book's appearance until June 1986.

42. This edition was extensively and effectively used for the first time by Herbert Mueller, chaplain at the July 1986 synodical convention in Indianapolis, IN.

43. All companion volumes here cited were published by and are available from Concordia Publishing House, St. Louis, MO.

5

The Church Year

James L. Brauer

Every family is shaped by the holidays it keeps together. Each society is identified in part by its common celebrations. So the church has a calendar that revolves around Jesus Christ. By its observance faith is shaped and nourished.

Obviously, this annual cycle is not commanded in the New Testament. In many ways though, it is a Christian replacement for the calendar of the Old Testament. God gave Israel feasts and celebrations to keep. Through them, God's involvement in Israel's history and in the lives of its people was to be regularly remembered. Many practices of Old Testament priests and worshipers were no longer possible after the temple was destroyed. Thus, only the Jewish synagogue worship has survived.

In contrast, the Christian calendar is not focused on a single place of celebration like the temple in Jerusalem. It is meant to fit over a secular year. Indeed, it has been moved from one culture to another. When its pattern is kept, the Christian is helped to remember God's words and actions. It gives regular occasion to recall God's love in sending Jesus to be the Savior of the world and of Jesus' sending the Holy Spirit to call, gather, enlighten, and sanctify the Church. It is a tool to keep the church "with Jesus Christ in the one true faith."[1]

The components of the Christian year include Sundays, Major Festivals, Minor Festivals, special Occasions, the use of customs and colors, and readings from the Bible that mark each event along the way.

Time

Time in our daily lives is marked by cycles. The minute hand and the hour hand advance around the face of a clock. The days accumulate into months, months into years, decades into centuries. Our days involve patterns of meals, work, and rest. Our years are measured by holidays, special weekends and vacation times. Newspapers, magazines, and television programs amplify these cycles.

Without some anchor of meaning these are empty cycles. Self-interest, career, or family or national interests fill the void. For Christians the pivot is obvious: all of life hinges on Jesus Christ. He came from heaven. He was born in Bethlehem (Christmas). He revealed the Father's love through his miracles and his teachings. But, most especially, Christians acknowledge his death and resurrection (Good Friday and Easter) as the saving acts that made eternal life possible for all who believe. With the ancient church and with believers today, Christians remember this daily, weekly, and yearly. They want worship to focus on Jesus who gives meaning to everything in life. Let the weekly gathering for worship reflect this priority.

Thus, the rhythm of daily life is interwoven with the story of salvation through Christ. That helps give significance to the flow of time. The earthly cycles of season, phase of the moon, and alternation of day and night are combined with incidents in the life of Christ and events in the history of the Christian Church. Though this Christian calendar is of human origin it is valid for its purpose.

Sunday

Why do Christians worship on Sunday? The Old Testament called for God's people to rest on the Sabbath (Exod. 20:8–11), now called Saturday. On the seventh day no work was to be done by master, slave, or animal. The day, reckoned from evening to evening, was to be kept holy by resting. The Jewish pattern was seven days in a week and four weeks in a lunar phase. The Greek and Roman calendar also had seven days but this system associated a planet with a particular day. Arranged in distance from the earth the planets are Saturn, Jupiter, Mars, Sun, Venus, Mercury, Moon, but the weekly sequence from which our terminology comes had this pattern: Saturn, Sun, Moon, Mars, Mercury, Jupiter, Venus.[2] The Christian calendar has roots in the Jewish calendar and in the Greek and Roman calendars.

Sunday is the first day of the week. It is associated with our Lord's resurrection. "After the Sabbath, at dawn *on the first day of the week*, Mary Magdalene and the other Mary went to look at the tomb. . . . The angel said to the women, . . . 'He is not here; he has risen, just as he said' " (Matt. 28:1–6). On the same day Jesus appeared to the women (Matt. 28:9), to the disciples on the road to Emmaus, and to the eleven (Luke 24:13–49). It was a week later, on the first day of the week, that Jesus appeared to them again and to Thomas (John 20:19–31).

There are only a few New Testament references to the first day of the week in the early Christian Church but they do relate to worship. On his third missionary journey Paul met with Christians at Troas on a Sunday. As Luke reports it, "On the first day of the week we came together to break bread" (Acts 20:7). Perhaps it is because they gather on Sunday that Paul urges the Corinthians "on the first day of every week" to set aside a sum of money for the collection (1 Cor. 16:2).

Even more interesting is the phrase "on the Lord's Day" in Rev. 1:10. It is a clear reference to Sunday. This reveals the special name that the early church had for the first day of the week. It was the Lord's Day. This led to the Latin *dominica dies* (the Lord's Day) from which the noun (*dies*) was dropped. *Dominica* then passed into French and Spanish as terms for Sunday (*dimanche, domingo*).

The early church fathers had various terms for Sunday: *First Day, Sun's Day, Eighth Day,* and *Lord's Day*.[3] It is important to note that the term Sabbath was generally avoided. The Lord's Day had a different authority and a different purpose from the Old Testament day of rest. The Sabbath observance was commanded in the Jewish ceremonial law, but the *Lord's Day* drew attention to the resurrection of Jesus Christ and the truth of the Gospel. "By observing Sunday and disregarding Saturday, Christians were confessing their faith in the Gospel, they were declaring the very nature of their religion."[4] The first day of the week is likewise associated with the sending of the Holy Spirit (Pentecost) and with creation. In A.D. 321 Constantine caused the laws of the Roman Empire to make Sunday a day of rest so that people could honor either the sun-god or Christ, whichever they followed. Thus, by the time of Council of Nicea in A.D. 325 Sunday was the day for Christians to rest and to gather for the Word of God and the Lord's Supper. And, above all other accents, Sunday was the day of the resurrection and the coming of a new creation.[5] It was a day of joy.

Major Festivals

The major festivals in the Christian year are The Nativity of Our Lord (December 25); The Epiphany of Our Lord (January 6); Ash Wednesday; Palm Sunday; Monday; Tuesday; and Wednesday of Holy Week; Maundy Thursday and Good Friday; The Resurrection of Our Lord; The Ascension of Our Lord; The Day of Pentecost; and The Holy Trinity. Major festivals "always have precedence over any other day or observance."[6] In general and taken together, they are a representation of the life of Christ. The Christmas cycle and the Easter cycle are the principal centers. Between Pentecost and the beginning of the Christmas cycle are the Sundays after Pentecost, formerly called Sundays after Trinity Sunday. This period forms a post-Easter season that awaits the return of Jesus. It is sometimes called *The Time of the Church* because "in the pilgrim state in which the church lives and exercises its ministry, it is the Spirit of God who leads and accompanies into all truth."[7] We explore the festivals in more detail after discussing the Scripture readings appointed for the various occasions of the church year.

Three-Year Lectionary

Though there were some problems with the traditional one-year cycle of readings, for centuries it seemed too ancient and too venerated ever to be replaced. In fact, from 1570, with the issuance of the *Missale Romanum,* until November 30, 1969, the Roman Catholic Church used a one-year lectionary that seemed set in stone. During those centuries Lutherans were, no doubt, aware of this "permanence," for they honored a version of the same lectionary that stemmed from Reformation times. In 1971 Herbert Lindemann had pointed to some of the problems in the Christian calendar in *The Lutheran Hymnal.* He pointed to the long Trinity season with "little order in it" except that there was some sense near the end when several Sundays dealt with the last judgment.[8] The Gospels for the first three Sundays of Lent reflected some customs and practices once associated with new converts but now no longer in use. For example, it was hard to reconcile the references to the devil that had significance with the exorcism catechumens of old underwent during this part of Lent.[9]

Source

Such complaints, however, were not the main catalyst for moving from a one-year series to a three-year cycle of Scripture readings. It did help that the Church of Sweden's three-year cycle offered a Protestant precedent. The primary impetus was the revised lectionary for the Mass published by the Roman Catholic Church in 1969, the *Ordo Lectionum Missae*. Though the list looked new, it was not a radical alteration of the liturgical year.

> Rather the criterion for its revision was that the elements making up the individual parts of each liturgical season would give clearer expression to the truth that Christ's paschal mystery is the center of all liturgical worship.[10]

This accent grew out of the theology of the liturgy and of the liturgical movement which led to Vatican Council II (1962–65). Worship was not seen as escapism where one takes refuge in contemplation or as some retreat from present chaos. The thrust was to regard "the liturgy as the summit and source of the church's activity."[11] In it the saving mysteries of Christ were made present—and part of the "presence" was a renewed emphasis on the Word, which led to a fresh vision for the readings from Scripture in the Roman Mass.

The new Roman Catholic three-year pattern was soon adapted by others. The Presbyterians and the Episcopalians in the United States began using their own versions of it in 1970. The Inter-Lutheran Commission on Worship (ILCW) followed suit in 1973 with a variation for trial use in *Contemporary Worship 6: The Church Year, Calendar and Lectionary*.[12] Some of their changes were "dictated by the orientation of Lutheran theology, liturgy, and needs of the congregations."[13]

How closely does the Inter-Lutheran Commission on Worship follow the Roman Catholic model? The commission answers this when it points out that about half the time the selections agree with the *Ordo*. And the Lutheran version

> makes minor changes, adjusting the beginning or stopping points or including or omitting verses between these points. . . . In about one-sixth of the readings a totally different passage is substituted for that of the *Ordo*, often in the same book, but sometimes from a different one (e.g., where the Apocrypha is involved, the Second Sunday in Lent, etc.).[14]

The commission's adaptation was included in the *Lutheran Book of Worship* (1978). The preparers of *Lutheran Worship* did little to alter the Old Testament, Epistle, and Gospel selections. Where there are changes, they are usually tiny adjustments in where to start or end. The appointed psalms are a different matter. In the *Lutheran Book of Worship* entire psalms were designated for each occasion in the three-year calendar and the old shortened psalms of the Introit were abandoned. Because it was not possible at the last minute to include the whole Psalter in *Lutheran Worship*, substitutes had to be found for about 45 of the psalms. Nevertheless, along the way many of the appointed psalms in *Lutheran Book of Worship* had become the material for the Introits in *Lutheran Worship*, appointed for use with the one-year cycle or the three-year cycle.

Advantages

The quick acceptance among Lutherans of the three-year cycle of Scripture readings was in part due to advantages that were claimed for the three-year cycle:

- It widens the range of Scripture heard by congregations.
- It increases scope, comprehensiveness, and variety of Scripture.
- It promotes historical knowledge of the Bible.
- It offers opportunity for treating larger units, even entire books in their historical setting.
- It expresses "solidarity with church bodies close at hand rather than to share a less immediate fellowship with European Lutherans in the cycle of readings"[15]
- It enriches the church's worship and preaching.

Not the least among the selling points was the greater number of texts on which to preach. Liturgical preaching now had nine texts in the course of three years from which to choose instead of only the two texts that came up every year. Under the new system if sermons were based only on the Gospels, it would take three years before a text would come around again. It is significant that Old Testament selections were now provided for every occasion in the calendar. The tradition of *The Lutheran Hymnal* had required only an Epistle and a Gospel.[16] Whether all the advantages looked for in the three-year lectionary will ultimately bear fruit is difficult to judge and may be clear only after a few more decades of use. At this point there are only a few who have clung to the one-year pattern.

Readings

What principles guided the ILCW selections? The readings were intended to be used in the chief service (Word and Sacrament of the Lord's Supper). Here the sequence was to be as follows: first reading, psalm, second reading, alleluia verse, gospel, and sermon. For lesser festivals and for some of the major festivals, the passages strongly identified with the occasion were to be repeated every year. Also, some traditional passages were "so good in terms of message and grandeur that they must appear" in the revised list.[17] Various cycles of readings were examined, including revisions in Germany and Scandinavia, a two-year system of the Church of England Liturgical Commission, and the *Ordo Lectionum Missae*—along with revisions of it by American church bodies.[18] For the ILCW these principles guided the selecting:

- Congruity with the Gospel, the good news of salvation.
- Preachability and balance between the indicative and imperative elements.
- Readability in public worship.
- Classic topics for the Christian faith.
- Consonance or interlocking of lessons on a day.[19]

Thus, in the new three-year system some sequences reflected a biblical book approach, some sections were treated thematically, and some passages were chosen because they had greater opportunity for the interlocking of two readings.[20]

Gospel

The primary focus in the readings is the words of our Lord from the four gospels. The other readings, from the letters in the New Testament or from books of the Old Testament, are secondary though still important. The gospel sets the "theme" for the day. In some cases, longer readings are provided, even entire chapters. Where the length would be counterproductive, there are optional abbreviations. But some long passages are retained for the dramatic sweep, as with the Fifth Sunday in Lent A (John 11:1–53).

Each of the three years in the cycle, labeled A, B, and C, employ one of the four gospels for the narrative material. While it is true that the hearers won't often notice differences from year to year, preachers can explore the unique accents of Matthew, Mark, Luke, and John. What might some of these differences be?

Year A uses Matthew. In his gospel Jesus is seen as a rabbi, a new Moses and a new Israel. He fulfills the law and the prophets. The Son of God and the Son of David is Lord of the law. He gives the commandment of love. The sweep is majestic and the tone is serious.

Year B follows Mark's account. Here the mystery of the Messiah unfolds. There is an emphasis on miracles and on true discipleship. It shows a gradual recognition of the Messiah as a suffering servant. The ministry of Jesus is the revelation of his function in the kingdom. The style is candid.

Year C employs Luke's Gospel. Jesus is the prophet who announces that God's kingdom is one of universal salvation. The Gentiles must be included. Luke makes clear that God's mercy takes in the lost, the poor, and the insignificant. The presentation has joy, wonder, and admiration.[21]

John's Gospel is not overlooked. Since Mark is shorter and has less teaching material, Year B draws material from John to fill around Mark's narrative. John contributes at other places too, particularly during the Easter season.

Epistles

Many of the second readings are of a semi-continuous type. They are not woodenly continuous portions of a letter but are selective

and may last from three to sixteen weeks. By assigning semi-conti-
nous readings to the Epiphany and Pentecost seasons, in particular, it was possible to include material from many of the New Testament books. Year A draws from 1 Corinthians, 1 Peter, Romans,
Philippians, 1 Thessalonians; Year B from 1 Corinthians, 1 John, 2
Corinthians, Ephesians, James, Hebrews; Year C from Galatians,
Colossians, 1 and 2 Timothy, Philemon, 2 Thessalonians, Revelation,
1 Corinthians, Hebrews. Thus, there are not just ethical topics but "a
more balanced selection of doctrinal and kerygmatic portions as
well as ethical sections."[22] When preachers take advantage of this
pattern, they will have considerable opportunity for expository
treatment of these pericopes.

Old Testament

More precisely, this is the "First Reading," since not all selections are
from the Old Testament. The Sundays of Easter draw from Acts in
order to relate to the Gospel or to the second reading. The Old
Testament books most used are Isaiah, Jeremiah, Deuteronomy,
Genesis, Exodus, Kings, Ezekiel, Numbers, Daniel, and Proverbs.
Readings from the Apocrypha were excluded for pastoral, not confessional reasons.[23]

It must be emphasized that the Old Testament selections are
meant to relate to the Gospel! They rarely fit both Gospel and Epistle. The passage may allude to, support, or contrast with the Gospel.
Occasionally, however, the Old Testament selection stands on its
own. Thus, where only two readings are used, it is best to omit the
second reading so that the two that blend and relate to each other
are presented.

This three-year list of readings was rather quickly accepted.
Despite all the revising, one old criticism of the Pentecost season
(*Trinity* in the old calendar) may still be voiced. The hope that this
"endless season" could be reorganized was not directly addressed.
One reviewer suggested that "three broad topics which exemplify
the church in action" should be used to divide the 28 Sundays into
sections.[24] In practice it seems that the Labor Day weekend and the
start of the new school year makes one break—provided by the secular world. Then, at the end of October many pastors like to trans-

fer Reformation and All Saints' Day to Sundays in order to provide a festival or two where none may occur.

One-Year Lectionary

In *Lutheran Worship* the One-Year Series is provided alongside the Three-Year Series for each occasion in the church year.[25] The Inter-Lutheran Commission on Worship had worked out a new version of the ancient one-year system with a better balance in the use of the biblical books and better selections from within a book. In general, it tried to retain the traditional Gospel and most of the old Epistle choices.[26] One of the readings, Old Testament or Epistle, is always interlocked with the Gospel for the day.[27] A reviewer of the ILCW's list pointed out that of the 240 readings in the one-year lectionary "over two-thirds of them are new to the day on which they are assigned (i.e., when compared to the lectionary in the *Service Book and Hymnal*)."[28] Thus, it was a revision, not a reprinting, of the old list.

Table 1

COMPARISON

THE CALENDAR (*The Lutheran Hymnal*)	Date	THE CHURCH YEAR (*Lutheran Worship*)			Color
		TIME	SEASON	OCCASION	
		THE TIME OF CHRISTMAS			
Advent Sunday			Advent Season		
The Advent Season—four weeks				First Sunday in Advent	P/B
				Second Sunday in Advent	P/B
				Third Sunday in Advent	P/B
				Fourth Sunday in Advent	P/B
St. Thomas—Apostle	Dec 21			St. Thomas, Apostle	R
			Christmas Season		
CHRISTMAS DAY—The Feast of the Nativity of Our Lord	Dec 25			THE NATIVITY OF OUR LORD	W
				Christmas Eve	
				Christmas Dawn	
				Christmas Day	
				First Sunday after Christmas	W
				Second Sunday after Christmas	W
St. Stephen—Martyr	Dec 26			St. Stephen, The First Martyr	R

	Date		Color
St. John—Apostle, Evangelist	Dec 27	St. John, Apostle and Evangelist	W
The Holy Innocents	Dec 28	The Holy Innocents, Martyrs	R
	Dec 31	New Year's Eve	W
		Eve of the Name of Jesus	
The Circumcision and the Name of Jesus (New Year's Day)	Jan 1	New Year's Day	W
		The Circumcision of Our Lord	
		Epiphany Season	
The Epiphany of Our Lord	Jan 6	The Epiphany of Our Lord	W
The Epiphany Season—one to six weeks		The Baptism of Our Lord	W
		First Sunday after the Epiphany	
		Second Sunday after the Epiphany	G
		Third Sunday after the Epiphany	G
		Fourth Sunday after the Epiphany	G
		Fifth Sunday after the Epiphany	G
		Sixth Sunday after the Epiphany	G
		Seventh Sunday after the Epiphany	G
		Eighth Sunday after the Epiphany	G
The Transfiguration of Our Lord			
Septuagesima Sunday			
Sexagesima Sunday			
Quinquagesima Sunday			

157

	Date	
The Transfiguration of Our Lord		W
Last Sunday after the Epiphany		
The Confession of St. Peter	Jan 18	W
St. Timothy, Pastor and Confessor	Jan 24	W
The Conversion of St. Paul	Jan 25	W
St. Titus, Pastor and Confessor	Jan 26	W
The Presentation of Our Lord	Feb 2	W
Martin Luther, Doctor and Confessor	Feb 18	W
St. Matthias, Apostle	Feb 24	R

THE TIME OF EASTER

Lenten Season

Ash Wednesday		BK/P
First Sunday in Lent		P
Second Sunday in Lent		P
Third Sunday in Lent		P
Fourth Sunday in Lent		P
Fifth Sunday in Lent		P

The Conversion of St. Paul

The Presentation of Our Lord and
The Purification of Mary

St. Matthias—Apostle

Ash Wednesday—the First Day of Lent

The Lententide—forty-six days

Invocavit—First Sunday in Lent

Reminiscere—Second Sunday in Lent

Oculi—Third Sunday in Lent

Laetare—Fourth Sunday in Lent

Judica—Passion Sunday—

Fifth Sunday in Lent

Holy Week

Palmarum—Sixth Sunday in Lent		PALM SUNDAY / *Sunday of the Passion*	S/P
Monday of Holy Week		Monday in Holy Week	S/P
Tuesday of Holy Week		Tuesday in Holy Week	S/P
Wednesday of Holy Week		Wednesday in Holy Week	S/P
Maundy Thursday		Maundy Thursday	S/P
Good Friday		GOOD FRIDAY	BK
Holy Saturday—Easter Eve			

Easter Season

EASTER DAY—The Feast of the Resurrection of Our Lord		THE RESURRECTION OF OUR LORD	
		Easter Eve	W
		Easter Day	W/GO
		Easter Evening	W/GO
The Easter Season—forty days			
Easter Monday			
Easter Tuesday			
The Annunciation	Mar 25	The Annunciation of Our Lord	W
Quasimodogeniti—First Sunday after Easter		Second Sunday of Easter	W
Misericordias Domini—Second Sunday after Easter		Third Sunday of Easter	W
Jubilate—Third Sunday after Easter		Fourth Sunday of Easter	W
Cantate—Fourth Sunday after Easter		Fifth Sunday of Easter	W

			Color
Rogate—Fifth Sunday after Easter		Sixth Sunday of Easter	W
The Ascension of Our Lord		The Ascension of Our Lord	W
Exaudi—The Sunday after the Ascension		Seventh Sunday of Easter	W
St. Mark—Evangelist	Apr 25	St. Mark, Evangelist	R
St. Philip and St. James—Apostles	May 1	St. Philip and St. James, Apostles	R
	May 7	C. F. W. Walther, Doctor	W
WHITSUNDAY—The Feast of Pentecost		PENTECOST	
		Pentecost Eve	
		The Day of Pentecost	
		Pentecost Evening	
Monday of Whitsun Week			
Tuesday of Whitsun Week			
		THE TIME OF THE CHURCH	
		The Season after Pentecost	
The Feast of the Holy Trinity		The Holy Trinity	W
The Trinity Season—		*The First Sunday after Pentecost*	
from twenty-two to twenty-seven weeks			
		Second through Twenty-seventh	
		Sunday after Pentecost	G
	May 31	The Visitation	W
	Jun 11	St. Barnabas, Apostle	R
The Nativity of St. John the Baptist	Jun 24	The Nativity of St. John the Baptist	W

Date		Color
Jun 25	Presentation of the Augsburg Confession	W
Jun 29	St. Peter and St. Paul, Apostles	R
Jul 2	The Visitation	
Jul 22	St. Mary Magdalene	W
Jul 25	St. James the Elder, Apostle	R
Aug 10	St. Laurence, Martyr	R
Aug 15	St. Mary, Mother of Our Lord	W
Aug 24	St. Bartholomew, Apostle	R
Sep 14	Holy Cross Day	R
Sep 21	St. Matthew, Apostle and Evangelist	R
Sep 29	St. Michael and All Angels	W
Oct 18	St. Luke, Evangelist	R
Oct 28	St. Simon and St. Jude, Apostles	R
Oct 31	Reformation Day	R
Nov 1	All Saints' Day	W
Nov 2	Commemoration of the Faithful Departed	W
Nov 30	St. Andrew, Apostle	R
	Sunday of the Fulfillment	
	Last Sunday after Pentecost	G

St. Peter and St. Paul—Apostles
The Visitation
St. Mary Magdalene
St. James the Elder—Apostle

St. Bartholomew—Apostle

St. Matthew—Apostle, Evangelist
St. Michael and All Angels
St. Luke—Evangelist
St. Simon and St. Jude—Apostles
The Festival of the Reformation
All Saints' Day

St. Andrew—Apostle

Calendar

The lectionary is intended to be used according to a liturgical calendar. A comparison of the old and the new calendars is presented in the above table. The year is organized to keep the church focused on Christ; it is not shaped by national holidays or particular causes (e.g., Labor Day, Mother's Day, stewardship). The new version is much like the old but there are significant changes.

The new church year is organized into three periods: the Time of Christmas, the Time of Easter, and the Time of the Church (often called *Ordinary Time* in other church bodies).

Time of Christmas

This period is subdivided into an Advent season, a Christmas season, and an Epiphany season. The revised Epiphany section commemorates our Lord's baptism on the first Sunday after the Epiphany. The former "gesima" Sundays, which followed the Transfiguration of our Lord, are gone. The Transfiguration now concludes the Epiphany Season, and additional Sundays "after the Epiphany" are provided to fill the gap.

Time of Easter

This period includes the Lenten season, Holy Week, and the Easter season, which begins on Easter Eve and ends with Pentecost. There are small changes to Lent. The Latin introit-names for the Sundays have disappeared but there are still five Sundays in Lent. The accent in the readings on these Sundays is on the renewal of Baptism. Passion Sunday is no longer on the fifth Sunday of Lent but is moved to the sixth Sunday, also called Palm Sunday. The intention is to have a Palm Sunday procession before the service (enacting the Hosanna "on the road") and then set the facts of the Gospel narrative before the worshipers. The procession communicates an outburst of joy; the long Scripture account focuses on the goal of the triumphal entry. The other days of Holy Week help relive the events of our Lord's preparation for death and his saving work in the crucifixion. The Sunday of Easter begins already with Easter Eve.

Where the old calendar had an Easter Monday and an Easter Tuesday, often difficult to observe in modern schedules, the new one has an Easter eve, an Easter Day, and an Easter evening. The ancient Easter Vigil, during the hours of darkness before the dawn, was revived and has proven to be a powerful liturgical expression of the victory over death.[29] The terminology "Sunday of Easter" for the second through seventh that follow is deliberate, since "The Lord has risen" continues to be the theme through these "fifty days." Pentecost, also a major festival, has an eve, a day, and an evening set of pericopes, replacing the old Monday and Tuesday celebrations.

Time of the Church

This period covers half of the year, the Sundays after Pentecost. Then the cycle starts again with Advent. The season after Pentecost begins with Trinity Sunday, which celebrates the mystery of God. The new designation "after Pentecost" is simply a return to an earlier terminology and meant to emphasize the work of the Holy Spirit. The season concludes with the Sunday of the Fulfillment, which looks forward to the time when all things in heaven and earth will be together under one head, Jesus Christ. One can also observe this Sunday as "Christ the King." Pope Pius XI had established this feast in 1925 and assigned it to the Sunday before All Saints, the last Sunday in October. In 1970 Roman Catholic revisers moved it to the end of the church year "to emphasize more the cosmic and eschatological character of Christ's kingship." They changed the proper name of the feast to "Christ, King of the Universe."[30] It thus fits into the eschatological context of looking toward the end of history when Jesus will reign eternally (Eph. 1:10).

The readings for both accents, Sunday of the Fulfillment and Christ the King, are provided for in *Lutheran Worship*.

The centerpiece of this yearly pattern is the Time of Easter with the Resurrection of Our Lord right in the middle. The new terminology of *Time* and *Season* helps make these basic subdivisions clearer. Each is assisted by seasonal colors that make these changes visible.

Liturgical Colors

The liturgical colors are both a teaching device and a way of marking days and seasons. They evolved among Christians without conscious planning and have existed since the Middle Ages. Some colors were adjusted in the revised church year. Most notably, there is a new option for Advent: blue—to distinguish Advent from Lent. Here are the colors used for altar and lectern paraments, pastor's stole and chasuble, and banners or hangings:

White Symbolizes joy, celebration, gladness, light, purity, innocence. Used for Christmas, Epiphany, and Easter and their seasons. Associated with festivals of Christ and of saints who presumably died a natural death. (White is the color of the ancient baptismal garment and is the preferred color of worship leaders' garments like the alb—from *alba*, the Latin word for white.)

Green The color of growth, leaves, foliage, fruit, and life, suggesting a time of spiritual growth. It is used for the season after Pentecost and for the Sundays during the Epiphany season.

Red Symbolizes fire, blood. For Pentecost and for days commemorating martyrs. Also appropriate for festivals of renewal in the Spirit like Reformation, church dedications, anniversary of a congregation, and ordinations.

Purple The royal color, the most costly with primitive dyes. For Lent—and as an alternate color for Advent. It symbolizes penitence and self-discipline and therefore also fits a Day of Supplication and Prayer.

Blue Represents hope, anticipation. Often associated with festivals of Mary, Mother of Our Lord. From a Swedish Lutheran tradition and from the ancient Mozarabic (Spanish) liturgy. Helps distinguish Lent and Advent.

Black Color of mourning, death, ashes. Now reserved for Good Friday; an alternate for Ash Wednesday.

Scarlet A favored color for royalty (deep scarlet or maroon) and a variant of red and purple. For the Passion of Our Lord, preferred for Holy Week (Sunday through Thursday) suggesting deeper intensity, triumph, and victory.

Gold Associated with riches and kingly attire. Reserved for Easter Day and Evening, the greatest of festivals.

Classes of Festivals

There are Major Festivals, Sundays, Minor Festivals and Occasions.[31] To locate the correct pericopes it is necessary to understand the relationship among the classes. The following principles apply.

1. The Major festivals take precedence over any other day or observance (on such days one should use their readings, prayers, psalms, etc.). They are as follows: Christmas Day, Epiphany, Ash Wednesday, Palm Sunday, Monday, Tuesday and Wednesday of Holy Week, Maundy Thursday and Good Friday, Easter Day, Ascension, Pentecost and Holy Trinity.

2. When a Minor Festival (see the list in LW, pp. 94ff.) occurs on a Sunday, the Collect of the Day for the Minor Festival may be used following the Collect of the Day appointed for the Sunday. The Sunday propers have precedence over a Minor Festival, since Sundays are weekly celebrations of our Lord's resurrection.

3. Circumstances may dictate the occasional transfer of a Minor Festival to a Sunday, when the observance of the fixed date is not possible. However, the importance of and the precedence given to Sundays should limit such practice. When transferred, the propers of the Minor Festival replace the Sunday propers.

4. Occasions, for example, Dedication of a Church or a Mission Festival, may be observed at any time except on Major Festivals. In such cases, the propers of the Occasion replace the Sunday's propers.

New Aspects of the Time of Easter

Lutheran Worship envisions a renewed accent on the resurrection of our Lord on each Sunday. Along the same lines, several new elements appear in the worship materials for Lent, Holy Week, and

Easter celebrations. Some congregations already employ them with great benefit; others have yet to discover or to make use of them. They therefore deserve special attention here.

Lenten Season

Ash Wednesday begins the Lenten Season, which lasts for 40 days excluding Sundays. Thus, the Sundays are "in" Lent but not "of" it. Lent is "a time to reflect upon baptism, a time for rebirth and renewal in preparation for the celebration of Easter."[32] To mark the season the color is purple. Other customs may be used to set Lent apart. If the items are not removable, plain, unbleached linen veils can be hung over crosses, pictures and statues during Lent. This neutral shade removes the furnishings from sight, and the resulting austerity reminds worshipers to be about something special—spiritual cleansing and deepening of devotional life.[33] It is a time for the discipline of learning and growing in faith, for repentance and for prayer, even for fasting to practice self-control and to heighten one's awareness of Christ. It is intended that the special consideration of Christ's suffering and death, so emphasized in Lenten practices before the calendar revisions, will be concentrated in the week of Palm Sunday to Easter. In fact, Holy Week now begins with the reading of the Passion history.

Ash Wednesday

Special material for an Ash Wednesday service is provided in *Lutheran Worship: Agenda* (pp. 15–18). The service begins with an Introit drawn from Psalm 51; then a short exhortation calls the congregation to prayerful and penitential reflection. Silence is kept for meditation and self-examination. A litany is provided after which the Scripture readings continue the service.

Other customs may be used, particularly the imposition of ashes on those who wish it. This ancient act is a gesture of repentence and a powerful reminder about the meaning of the day. Ashes can symbolize dust-to-dustness and remind worshipers of the need for cleansing, scrubbing and purifying. If they are applied during an act of kneeling, the very posture of defeat and submission expresses humility before God. Organ sounds may be limited to accompanying the congregation.

Weekday Services in Lent

Weekday services in Lent should focus on the deepening of faith, refreshment for the spirit and on the striving for the obedience of discipleship. It is a good time to use the special order for corporate confession (see LW, pp. 308f.) and to offer members opportunity for individual confession (see LW, pp. 310f.). When the group is small or when a way can be devised for people to come forward in a continuous fashion, the absolution can be imparted individually as each kneels near the altar or at a chancel rail. It is also a good time to use Evening Prayer, which has some of the most beautiful service music in the hymnal and lends itself to moments of quiet meditation and prayer. The Service of Light, which begins this liturgy, sets it apart from other services and would be most appropriate except during Holy Week.

Palm Sunday

Palm Sunday brings worshipers to the events of Jesus' Passion. But the day is both somber and joyful. A procession with palms (or other branches) and hosannas to commemorate our Lord's entry into Jerusalem begins the service. Versicles, responses, a prayer and the Gospel account are provided in the *Lutheran Worship: Agenda* (pp. 35ff.). The traditional hymn is "All glory, laud, and honor" (LW 102). An entrance rite like this that begins outdoors gives a festive flair and a public statement of our Lord's kingship.

A second feature is the reading of the entire passion account as presented by Matthew or Mark or Luke. John is reserved for Good Friday. As a way of assisting the dramatic aspect, several readers might be rehearsed to take the voices of the different characters. During the reading, people sit, perhaps rising only for the last paragraphs. Silence may follow the sentence describing Jesus' death.[34] Since the Gospel is long, in effect two chapters, the sermon might be a brief devotional comment on what has just been heard.

Triduum

Three sacred days—Maundy Thursday, Good Friday, and Holy Saturday—(the *Triduum*) commemorate the central events of the Christian faith.

Maundy Thursday. On this night Jesus instituted "a memorial" of his Passion in the Lord's Supper. When the Divine Service finishes, in preparation for Good Friday, the altar is stripped and the chancel is cleared. Psalm 22 may be sung by the choir (see *Lutheran Worship: Agenda*, pp. 39ff.) while the congregation watches the actions. This should be accomplished in an orderly, deliberate and unhurried fashion by the presider, assisting ministers, and servers. No further words are spoken; all leave silently.

Good Friday. The *Lutheran Worship: Agenda* provides three services for use on Good Friday. Generally, Holy Communion is not celebrated on this day, though rubrics and pericopes are given should they be required. Instrumental music may be limited to support of the singing.

At Noonday. The *Lutheran Worship: Agenda* gives a brief service with sentences and collects, a hymn, Scripture readings, sermon, hymn, a special group of prayers, and a blessing.

Good Friday I. This order has a reflective and intercessory character. Everyone enters in silence. After the Collect, the Old Testament Reading, and a hymn, the Gospel is read. A sermon is optional. Then the Bidding Prayer, traditional on Good Friday from ancient times, is led by an assisting minister with the petitions said by the presider. For this unique prayer it is good to use two different reading desks; the second, for the presiding minister, may be the pulpit if necessary. The concluding part of the service uses a rough-hewn cross. It may be carried in procession and placed in front of the altar during which time the sentence and response are said three times. Then the Reproaches, by the presiding minister, are answered by the congregation or choir singing the appointed hymn. Silence for meditation follows. A hymn and closing sentences end the service.

Good Friday II. This simple form may be used with or without Holy Communion. After the Epistle the Reproaches are chanted or said and the congregation or choir responds with an appointed hymn stanza. The Gospel, John chapters 18 and 19, is interspersed with the seven appointed hymn stanzas. After the Sermon and Offering the Bidding Prayer is said. When there is no communion, the service closes with the Benediction.

Easter Vigil. The Triduum (Great Three Days) combines accents from the Passover and the resurrection of Christ. The *Pascha*, as it is sometimes called, is seen as one festival celebrated on these successive days. On these days the accent is on freedom out of slavery, life out of death, light out of darkness, and speech out of silence. Forgiveness and the eschatological banquet are also emphasized. Pivotal in this celebration is the Easter Vigil. The 50 days of resurrection celebration (lasting until Pentecost) were preceded already in the third century by "a strict fast lasting one, two, or more days and followed by a nocturnal assembly for prayer, which closes with the Eucharist,"[35] after sundown preceding Easter Sunday. This ancient vigil service, reintroduced in the 20th century, is provided in *Lutheran Worship: Agenda.*[36]

After A.D. 313 the Easter Vigil was the prime time for baptisms of adults who had been instructed during Lent. It also ushered in the resurrection celebration. The Vigil thus focused on the saving power of Christ's death and resurrection (Rom. 6:3–5). By 400 in Africa and Northern Italy there was also a solemn celebration of light, since all lamps were customarily extinguished on Holy Thursday evening.[37] The modern adaptation of this ancient service remembers the Exodus from Egypt, celebrates the death and resurrection of Christ, includes the sacrament of Baptism, looks forward to Jesus' return, and may conclude with the Lord's Supper. A description of the service will be helpful to those who are not acquainted with it.

It begins with the Service of Light. The congregation gathers outside the church after sunset. A fire is kindled. The pastor explains the significance of the service. A paschal candle has the cross and the Greek letters Alpha and Omega traced on it along with the year. Five wax nails are put into it. It gets its flame from the fire. Then all light their candles from the paschal candle. They follow the bearer of the paschal candle into the darkened church, pausing to chant, "The light of Christ./Thanks be to God." When this candle is on its stand and the assisting minister is at the baptismal font, the Easter Proclamation (*Exsultet*) is sung.

The Service of Readings follows. There are several portions of Holy Scripture; the most important tells about crossing the Red Sea on dry land. The sequence of readings can include these subjects from the Old Testament: the creation, the flood, Abraham's sacrifice of Isaac, Israel's deliverance at the Red Sea, salvation offered freely to all, a new heart and a new spirit, faith strained but victorious, and the gathering of God's people. After each there is a collect. The canticle "All you works of the Lord" (LW 9, *Benedicite Omnia Opera*) may conclude the service of readings.

The Service of Holy Baptism begins with an address from the pastor. During a hymn, candidates for Baptism come forward. In the baptismal rite the congregation joins in the renunciation and in the profession of faith as a remembrance of their Baptism. (When there is no Holy Communion, the service concludes with the Easter Gospel, a Collect, and the Blessing.)

The Service of Holy Communion begins with the responsive greeting "Alleluia. Christ is risen./The Lord is risen indeed. Alleluia." This marks the dramatic transition from dark to light. The "Glory to God in the highest" and the Collect of the Day lead to the reading of the Epistle and the Easter Gospel. The vigil Communion should remain simple, reserving the more elaborate features for the Divine Service on Easter Day.

On paper this service may look lengthy and ineffective. In practice the sense of keeping watch and praying is strong. The element of praise balances the meditative. The symbols of light and darkness assist the action and words. God's power in Baptism is strongly connected with remembrance of his saving acts and promises in the Old Testament. The people of the New Covenant await Jesus' return. Easter joy is about to be fully expressed—in just a few hours. This is a powerful combination for the worshipers—not to be overlooked as a high point in a parish's worship life. The Vigil of Easter is unique.

Easter

The word *Easter* has no special Christian derivation since it comes from *Ostern* (Middle English), meaning the direction from which the sun rises. More typical among early Christians was the word *Pascha* derived from *Pesach*, the Hebrew word for Passover.

Easter was first celebrated in the early second century and, by the third century, was followed by a period of 50 days focusing on resurrection. The day of Easter was calculated two ways until Pope Victor (c. 190). In Asia Minor Christians celebrated on the Jewish Passover, the 14th of Nisan—no matter what day of the week. Others used the Sunday following the Passover. After A.D. 325 Easter was to be "on the Sunday that followed the first full moon after the spring equinox" which occurs between March 22 and April 25.[38] Today the date of Easter for the Orthodox churches, which calculate by the Julian calendar, still differs from Western churches, which use the Gregorian calendar. As a result, the Eastern date is usually one to four weeks later than that in the Western church.

Minor Festivals

Among the Minor Festivals are Commemorations of the Apostles of Our Lord, of the Evangelists, of Pastors and Confessors, of Doctors of the Church, and of Martyrs.[39] There are also days to recall events in the New Testament, like the Visitation or the Conversion of St. Paul, and to make other celebrations like Holy Cross Day, Reformation or All Saints' Day. The list of saints days has never stayed firm for long.

The practice of an annual commemoration of local martyrs began already by the middle of the second century. The celebrations were often at the place of burial and not at other towns or in other countries. When the Lutheran reformers tried to reduce the overloaded calendar which they inherited, they retained feasts of our Lord, the days of apostles and evangelists, St. Stephen the first martyr, Holy Innocents, St. John the Baptist, St. Michael the Archangel, and All Saints.[40] In a similar way in 1568 Pius V reduced the calendar of saints to 150—but in the next 400 years the number doubled again. Thus, the present trend is toward universal persons and for a more geographic and chronological representation. A central problem is that saints days tend to take over the regular cycle.[41] For this reason Pius X in 1911 gave Sundays precedence over minor feasts to help protect the basic liturgical year readings.[42]

171

In revising the calendar this question comes up: Why only New Testament events, why not include men and women of faith from various centuries? Would not such a list help cultivate a more universal consciousness of the church?[43] But to find the right criteria is difficult. The Inter- Lutheran Commission on Worship gave the following criterion for its more inclusive list: "The people suggested for commemoration have distinguished themselves by conspicuous service within the Christian tradition, broadly understood. So for example, Hammarskjöld is included, but Gandhi is not."[44] In contrast, *Lutheran Worship* chose to continue the more restrictive tradition, as shown in Table 1.

Some Minor Festivals in *Lutheran Worship* are new to the calendar: New Year's Eve, Martin Luther, C. F. W. Walther, Presentation of the Augsburg Confession, St. Laurence, St. Mary, Holy Cross, Commemoration of the Faithful Departed. And, to the category Occasions (where there is no fixed date in the list) have been added propers for the Anniversary of a Congregation.

Notes

1. Dr. Martin Luther's Small Catechism, in *Lutheran Worship*, pp. 300–307.

2. Willy Rordorf, *Sunday: The History of the Day of Rest and Worship in the Earliest Centuries of the Christian Church* (Philadelphia: Westminster Press, 1968), p. 25.

3. Harry Boone Porter, *The Biblical & Liturgical Meaning of Sunday: The Day of Light* (Washington, D.C.: Pastoral Press, 1987), pp. 9–11.

4. Ibid., p. 10.

5. P. Jounel, "Sunday and the Week," in *The Liturgy and Time*, vol. IV of *The Church at Prayer: An Introduction to the Liturgy*, new ed., ed. Aimi Georges Mortimort, trans. Matthew J. O'Connell (Collegeville: Liturgical Press, 1986), p. 19.

6. *Lutheran Worship: Altar Book*, prepared by the Commission on Worship of The Lutheran Church—Missouri Synod (St. Louis: Concordia Publishing House, 1982), p. 12.

7. *Contemporary Worship 6: The Church Year: Calendar and Lectionary*, prepared by the Inter-Lutheran Commission on Worship (Minneapolis: Augsburg Publishing House; Philadelphia: Board of Publication, Lutheran Church in America; St. Louis: Concordia Publishing House, 1973), p. 10.

8. Herbert Lindemann, *The New Mood in Lutheran Worship* (Minneapolis: Augsburg Publishing House, 1971), p. 91.

9. Ibid., p. 88.

10. Pope Paul VI, Apostolic Letter, *Mysterii paschalis*, quoted in James Empereur, *Worship: Exploring the Sacred* (Washington, D.C.: Pastoral Press, 1987), p. 185.

11. Adrian Nocent, *The Liturgical Year*, 4 vols., trans. Matthew J. O'Connell (Collegeville: Liturgical Press, 1977), I: 3.

12. *Contemporary Worship 6*, p. 14. The Roman Catholic 1969 lectionary and its organization is admirably described from a later perspective in Claude Wiener, "The Roman Catholic Eucharistic Lectionary," *Studia Liturgica* 21/1 (1991): 2–13. In the same issue see also: Horace T. Allen, Jr., "*Common Lectionary*: Origins, Assumptions, and Issues," pp. 14–30; Donald Gray, "The Contribution of the Joint Liturgical Group to the Search for an Ecumenical Lectionary," pp. 31–36; Karl-Heinrich Bieritz, "The Order of Readings and Sermon Texts for the German Lutheran Church," pp. 37–51.

13. Ibid., p. 19.

14. Ibid., p. 20.

15. Philip H. Pfatteicher and Carlos R. Messerli, *Manual on the Liturgy—Lutheran Book of Worship* (Minneapolis: Augsburg Publishing House, 1979), p. 30.

16. On this point it should be kept in mind that pages 159f. in *The Lutheran Hymnal* (1941) gave Old Testament readings and alternate Epistles and Gospels that could serve congregations which felt too restricted by the regular, one-year lectionary.

17. *Contemporary Worship 6*, p. 22.

18. Ibid., p. 16.

19. Ibid., pp. 16f.

20. Ibid., p. 20.

21. Characterizations are based on comments in Empereur, p. 204, and are meant only as samples of what biblical scholarship might reveal to homiletical interpreters.

22. Pfatteicher, p. 31.

23. *Contemporary Worship 6*, p. 23.

24. Wesley W. Isenberg, "Review—*Contemporary Worship 6: The Church Year, Calendar and Lectionary*," *Church Music* 74–1 (1974): 54.

25. The pew edition of the *Lutheran Book of Worship* does not contain the one-year cycle. It can be found in the *Ministers Desk Edition—Lutheran Book of Worship* (Minneapolis: Augsburg Publishing House; Philadelphia: Board of Publication, Lutheran Church in America, 1973), pp. 192–194.

26. *Contemporary Worship 6*, p. 17.

27. Ibid., p. 18.

28. Isenberg, p. 53.

29. *Lutheran Worship: Agenda*, prepared by the Commission on Worship of The Lutheran Church—Missouri Synod (St. Louis: Concordia Publishing House, 1984), pp. 73ff.

30. Jounel, pp. 107ff.

31. See the list in *Lutheran Worship: Agenda*, pp. 11f.

32. *Contemporary Worship 6*, pp. 8f.

33. Ibid., p. 9.

34. Paul Bosch, *Church Year Guide* (Minneapolis: Augsburg Publishing House, 1987), pp. 68f.

35. Jounel, p. 35.

36. See pp. 73–90. Give careful attention to the notes on page 90. An offprint for the congregation is available separately. Other books, as background and practical advice, are helpful toward planning for the Easter Vigil. Two titles are given here: Gabe Huck, *The Three Days: Parish Prayer in the Paschal Triduum* (Chicago: Liturgical Training Publications, 1981), and Reupert Berger and Hans Hjollerweger, *Celebrating the Easter Vigil*, trans. Matthew J. O'Connell (New York: Pueblo Publishing Company, 1983).

37. Jounel, p. 37.

38. Ibid., p. 34.

39. See the complete list in *Lutheran Worship: Agenda*, p. 12, and the list in Table 1 of this chapter.

40. Marion J. Hatchett, *Commentary on the American Prayer Book* (New York: Seabury Press, 1980), p. 41.

41. Empereur, p. 187.

42. R. Kevin Seasoltz, *New Liturgy, New Laws* (Collegeville: Liturgical Press, 1980), p. 151. Vatican Council II brought further results in this direction. Precedence over the regular Sunday, or Lord's Day, celebrations are limited to the Sundays of the seasons of Advent, Lent, and Easter; the feast of the Holy Family (Sunday within the octave of Christmas); the Baptism of the Lord (Sunday following January 6); the Holy Trinity (Sunday after Pentecost); and Christ the King (last Sunday in Ordinary Time). Cf. "General Norms for the Liturgical Year and Calendar," in *The Liturgy Documents: A Parish Resource*, rev. ed., ed. Mary Ann Simcoe (Chicago: Liturgy Training Publications, 1985), p. 184.

43. Lindeman, p. 100.

44. *Contemporary Worship 6*, pp. 11f.

The Setting of the Liturgy and the Decorum of Its Leaders

THE PLACE OF WORSHIP

Wayne E. Schmidt

Corporate Worship and Private Devotion

The devotional life of the people of God takes place in two quite different settings. Both have ample biblical precedent to recommend them, and both offer rich rewards. Jesus spoke of the one setting in his well-known Sermon on the Mount: "When you pray, go into your room, close the door and pray to your Father . . . . who sees what is done in secret" (Matt. 6:6). Christians are urged, in other words, to practice their devotional life in private.

On the other hand, the same Lord who himself retreated to private moments of prayer (Matt. 14:23) and who exhorted his followers to do the same spoke of the assembly of the people of God and promised, "Where two or three are gathered together in my name, there am I in the midst of them" (Matt. 18:20 KJV). With such a promise of the Lord, the exhortation of the writer of the letter to the Hebrews comes as no surprise: "Let us not give up meeting together, as some are in the habit of doing, but let us encourage one another—and all the more as you see the Day approaching" (Heb. 10:25). Christians commune with God not only individually and in private but in groups and community as well. A treatise on the setting of the liturgy is a study of the place where corporate worship occurs and the furnishings appointed for use in such a place.

It is an error, of course, to think that the activities of private and corporate worship are totally different from each other. Such is not the case because even in a group an individual does not lose his personal identity. Private prayers are surely offered in corporate worship since personal meditation does not cease when the individual worshiper joins a group. In fact, some people find their private devotion considerably enhanced in the place of public worship because of the unique physical environment created there. Church buildings and chapels that are open daily—a practice Lutherans in America might consider cultivating a bit more—are clear invitations to use those buildings for private prayer and meditation. The time of gathering in a church before a service of corporate worship, moreover, also provides refreshing moments for personal meditation and spiritual reflection. Thus the sanctuary in which public worship takes place becomes the setting also for individual worship, for corporate and private devotion blend together.

While it is common for individuals to use Christianity's public meeting places for private devotion, the blending of the corporate and personal does not occur in quite the same way in the private devotional setting. To a certain extent, however, a complementary relationship still exists, for both household and individual devotions may well employ parts or all of the service orders, prayers, or hymns that are designed for use in public worship. In this case it is not architectural space and furnishings that are held in common but rather the worship materials employed in both settings. It becomes apparent, therefore, that no strict dichotomy exists between all aspects of corporate worship and private devotion, for even in the private setting the individual may use materials also employed in group worship.

It becomes apparent that Christians exercise their devotional life in two separate settings, private and public. A discussion of the setting of the liturgy concerns itself with the place where the congregation assembles, the building that the congregation uses for worship—in other words, the furnishings in that building. It is not just group needs, however, that are accommodated in the place where the assembly gathers. The building also contributes to private devotion; for corporate worship, although affording individuals the opportunity to do things in concert, provides at the same time an inspiring channel for intensely personal meditation and prayer. A church building with its liturgical furnishings serves group worship needs and speaks to the individual as well.

Assembly in the Christian Life

The role of assembly in the Christian life calls for a certain amount of investigation. Holy Scripture makes it clear that group passports to heaven do not exist and that mere association with the faithful does not guarantee a right individual relationship with God. John the Baptist sternly declared to those in his day who harbor mistaken notions on this subject: "Do not begin to say to yourselves, 'We have Abraham as our Father'; for I tell you, God is able from these stones to raise up children to Abraham" (Luke 3:8 RSV). Saving faith in Jesus Christ is an individual matter. No one can believe for another. Although believers come together in groups to pray and hear the Word of God and gather in congregations to receive the blessings of the Lord's Supper and express their common faith in Christ and his work, the Lord still looks on the individual heart. In matters of salvation the singular of Luke 7:50 comes into sharp focus: "*Thy* faith hath saved *thee*; go in peace" (KJV). Outward affiliation with a group of Christians does not assure salvation. All will gather before the judgment seat of God, but verdicts will be spoken to every person individually (2 Cor. 5:10).

Since individual faith is of paramount importance in the Christian religion, it is reasonable to ask why Christians throughout the centuries have continued to lay such a heavy emphasis upon group worship. Church bells have summoned the faithful of the past and continue to ring an invitation today. Towering church structures in metropolitan centers have not ceased to send their spires upward and to open their huge doors to countless generations. Village and country parish churches, although not matching the monumental design of Christendom's great buildings, still carry the same message: the people of God in Christ meet here. Weekly and at times more than weekly meetings of Christians for corporate worship have been a regular pattern in Christendom for centuries.

The custom of the people of God to meet for worship can be seen already in the life of the church of the Old Testament. The psalmist expressed his pleasure in that activity when he declared, "I was glad when they said unto me, 'Let us go into the house of the Lord' " (Ps. 122:1). The Old Testament faithful made their annual pilgrimages to the holy city for the major religious festivals. This was a group activity and is especially well remembered because of the incident in the life of Jesus when as a twelve-year-old he went to Jerusalem with his parents, relatives, and acquaintances. Group prayer was not limited, moreover, to the major Jewish festivals, as becomes apparent, for example, from the episode in the life of the father of John the Baptist. When the angel Gabriel announced the impending birth of John to Zacharias, his father, the latter was performing the daily duty of burning incense in the Holy Place. At the very time of his sacrifice "the whole multitude of the people were praying outside" (Luke 1:10 RSV). The people of God under the Old Covenant had regular occasions for coming together.

The assembly activity seems to take on a new kind of significance, however, after the resurrection of Christ. Observing this, Peter Brunner in his book *Worship in the Name of Jesus* asserts that "the New Testament shows us that . . . congregational meetings for worship were the focal point for the Christian's every thought and act."[1] The apostles themselves provided a pattern for assembly by their own actions after the Lord's resurrection. One could expect, of course, that the faithful would have gathered on the day of the resurrection. Not only were they afraid, but the news of the day had left them puzzled and astonished. They met as a group so that they might order the events of the day and put the pieces together.

One week later, however, those same disciples were together again as Jesus appeared to them in the presence of Thomas (John 20:26). One might legitimately ask whether that meeting a week after the resurrection was the beginning already of the weekly observance of our Lord's triumph over death. Concrete evidence for this is not available, but it can be reported that on the day of Pentecost several weeks later the apostles were again "all together in one place" (Acts 2:1 RSV). The first day of the week seemed to be a customary meeting time also for the Christians at Troas whom Paul addressed in assembly (Acts 20:7). And when the apostle was exhorting the Christians at Corinth to gather contributions for the saints in Jerusalem, he directed his Corinthian readers to do what he told the churches in Galatia to do, namely, "on the first day of every week . . . put something aside and store it up" (1 Cor. 16:2 RSV). Coming together was a central activity in the life of the church of the New Testament era and seems to have taken place on the first day of the week.

The very nature of the Pauline corpus in the New Testament Scriptures provides further evidence of the prominent role of the assembly in the life of the early church. The bulk of Paul's epistles is addressed to churches, to groups of believers who congregate regularly. The letters that are not so addressed assume a congregational life and provide specific instructions for it. In the concluding greetings of his letters, Paul regularly takes the opportunity to send good wishes to the various house churches, which were apparently quite well known. He concluded his epistle to the Romans, for example, by sending personal greetings to the church that met at the house of Aquila and Priscilla (Rom. 16:5). When Paul wrote to the Corinthians he closed that letter with hearty greetings to those Christians from the church that met not in the Roman but in the Ephesian residence of Aquila and Priscilla (1 Cor. 16:19). Similarly, his epistle to the Colossians contains concluding greetings, among them Paul's good wishes to Nympha and the church that met at her house (Col. 4:15). Add to that the fact that the apostle's letter to Philemon is addressed as well to the church that met at his house (Philemon 2) and it becomes unmistakably clear that the coming together of Christians was not limited to the events immediately following the outpouring of the Holy Spirit on Pentecost (Acts 2:44–46) but remained the focal point of the Christian life and activity described in the New Testament.

Because of this New Testament emphasis, Peter Brunner, when searching for a term he feels would best comprehend what we today call worship, suggests the word *synaxis*, a Greek word that means bringing together, congregation, or assembly. Such a term, Brunner argues, "is the designation for the church's worship which not only is most closely related to the language of the New Testament but also conspicuously does justice to the novelty of character of the Christian worship, inasmuch as it stresses no other special content beyond that of the assembling of the people."[2] Commenting further, Brunner remarks: "Worship[3] in the sense of the assembly of the Christian congregation in the name of Jesus is virtually the dominant mode of the manifestation of the church on earth. In such an assembly the epiphany of the church takes place. The church is such an assembly in the name of Jesus, and such an assembly in the name of Jesus is church."[4] The fact of assembly in New Testament piety and practice and the importance of Christians coming together both very likely prompted the writer of the letter to the Hebrews to issue the admonition referred to previously: "Let us not give up meeting together, as some are in the habit of doing" (Heb. 10:25).

The assembly activity so evident in the life and thought of New Testament Christianity is a very natural thing for believers in Christ. Jesus informed his disciples upon one occasion that both he and his Father will come to make their home within the person who loves Jesus and keeps his word (John 14:23). The apostle Paul sounds the same note when he says to the Corinthians, "We are the temple of the living God" (2 Cor. 6:16 RSV), and "You are God's temple and . . . God's Spirit dwells in you (1 Cor. 3:16 RSV). The triune God dwells not only among his people but within them. It is to be expected that those who share this marvelous indwelling will want to come together to strengthen and celebrate the fact.

What the New Testament says about the nature of the church provides another insight into an understanding of the assembly phenomenon in Christianity. The apostle Paul says that the church is the body of Christ. Magnifying Christ in the Epistle to the Colossians, Paul declares: "He is the head of the body, the church" (Col. 1:18 RSV). When speaking in Ephesians about the exaltation of Christ, the apostle adds that God made Christ "the head over all things for the church, which is his body, the fulness of him who fills all in all" (Eph. 1:22–23 RSV). This is more than a metaphor; it is a spiritual reality. The members of the body are a unity and have an intimate spiritual relationship with one another, so that though they are many, nevertheless, they are "one body in Christ, and individually members one of another" (Rom. 12:5 RSV).

As it is in the very nature of a healthy body to have its parts joined together in order to function, so also is it essential that the members of Christ's church be in communion with one another, since they together comprise the Lord's body. The intimate rela-

180

tionship among the individual members of the body of Christ and their mutual dependence upon each other is convincingly described by Paul in both Romans (12:3–8) and 1 Corinthians (12:12–28). The bond assumes an edifying of one another, as becomes apparent from Paul's description of corporate worship in 1 Corinthians 14 and his concise exhortation to the Colossians: "Let the peace of God rule in your hearts, to which you were called in the one body; and be thankful. Let the word of Christ dwell in you richly in all wisdom, teaching and admonishing one another in psalms and hymns and spiritual songs" (Col. 3:15–16 RSV). Coming together for worship is natural for Christians because they have a oneness. Christians are the body of Christ.

A Place to Gather

Since assembly is of paramount importance in the practice of Christianity, it is obvious that meeting space must be provided for the gathering of the people. No biblical mandate exists for any particular style of worship building or type of meeting place. The Lord himself was comfortable proclaiming the good news in a synagogue, at a home, on a hillside, or by the seashore. After his ascension into heaven Jesus' followers met for prayer in an upper room (Acts 1:12–14) and gathered at the temple as well (Acts 1:46). The apostle Paul regularly went to synagogues on his missionary journeys, but he also visited a place for community prayer at a riverside (Acts 16:13). Reference has already been made to the house churches from and to which greetings were extended in Paul's epistles, the private home having become a rather common meeting place for early Christians. Conditions might not always have been ideal in the meeting rooms, as in Troas, for example, where Eutychus fell asleep while Paul was preaching in a room well lighted but apparently suffering from a lack of oxygen. Even under less than ideal conditions, however, Christ's followers of apostolic times recognized the benefits of coming together and found for their community worship life such gathering places as time and circumstances made available.

The use of houses for worship purposes continued for several centuries in early Christianity. The reasons for this are obvious.

Since Christianity remained an illegal religion in the Roman Empire until A.D. 313, it was often impossible for Christians to erect structures specifically designed for worship. In addition, the illegal status of Christianity limited the number of people who wanted to align themselves publicly with the Christian confession, with the result that large meeting places were often not necessary. It was not that Christianity was constantly persecuted in every quarter of the empire at all times. The possibility of open persecution did exist, however. Christians may not have been unwilling to confess their faith publicly, but the relatively small number within the Christian community in many places and the expediency of maintaining something of a low profile very likely made the construction of separate places of worship unnecessary or inadvisable. As a consequence, little is known about the places for worship in Christianity's early centuries.

After the Christian religion became legal in A.D. 313 and eventually the religion of the state within the Roman Empire, things changed considerably. Now it was fashionable, if nothing else, to be a Christian, the result being that large numbers of people began to affiliate with the church. Residences were no longer adequate for the meetings of the Christian community, and the need to keep worship private and under cover had vanished. With the establishment in 321 of Sunday as a civil day of rest, a convenient time for corporate worship was also supplied. Emperor Constantine's energetic support of Christianity made buildings available and encouraged the development of more elaborate worship practices. The history of a specific architecture for Christian worship had now begun. Each age has made its own contribution to interior and exterior church building design, with theological accents, climate, culture, and economic conditions all leaving their imprint upon the buildings, both small and large.

Although churches vary greatly in size and appearance, two basic considerations regularly confront Christian congregations when they undertake the task of designing and constructing worship facilities. A building obviously has to be able to accommodate the worshiping group physically. Space, heating, lighting, and numerous other essentials for physical comfort and convenience must be provided. A second issue that must be addressed, however, is far more philosophical in nature. To what extent, for example, should a church building say more than that it is a place for meeting? Should the structure give some sort of testimony with its architectural design to the purpose of the meetings held within the building? Is it possible for brick, wood, steel, and stone to make a theological statement architecturally? It must be admitted that here decision making shifts from the purely functional to the less tangible, to the aesthetic and the symbolic. Since additional cost factors often become involved in the creation of buildings that speak to the eye, the temptation frequently is to ignore or minimize the importance of the visual message that ecclesiastical buildings give.

That Christians must be concerned about responsible stewardship when it comes to spending for the erection of places of worship is not a matter for debate. The New Testament does not portray a building but a proclaiming and outreach church, activities that are totally consistent with the Lord's commission to his disciples. This does not mean, however, that the Lord disapproves of testimony apart from words. Jesus' commendation of Mary after she had anointed her Savior with costly perfume (John 12:1–7) shows that the opposite is true. Mary's was a beautiful and expensive act, but one that provoked the criticism of Jesus' disciples (Matt. 26:8–9), Judas apparently being the most outspoken critic. The Lord's acceptance of Mary's devotion is no mandate to erect extravagant houses of worship, of course, but his praise of her does demonstrate that properly motivated acts of love done solely for the purpose of honoring the Lord are laudable and pleasing to him, even when such acts necessitate a significant outlay of money. In addition, Jesus' rebuke of his disciples' argument that the perfume could have been sold and the proceeds given to the poor exposes the error of putting forward a set of false alternatives. In the kingdom of God the doing of one thing does not necessarily exclude the performance of another, for the Lord is quite able to provide his people with the opportunity and means to perform multiple tasks. It is quite possible, moreover, for one activity to assist and complement another. The Christian community does indeed have a clear call to reach far and wide with the Gospel proclamation, but such a mandate does not necessarily preclude the construction of church buildings which with their very design honor the Lord and say something about the people who worship him. The process of establishing priorities in the business of the church creates, admittedly, a tension between doing this or doing that. Such a tension is not unwholesome, however, for it compels a congregation to examine its mission of the moment, to think through practices of responsible Christian stewardship, and in the case of architectural decision making to reflect upon the role of the artistic and symbolic in Christian worship.

Theology, Temple, and Tabernacle

That a worship structure can give a message is apparent from the two major worship facilities which the people of Israel used in Old Testament times. The plan of the tabernacle and Solomon's temple were essentially the same, the later being larger, of course, a permanent structure, and more elaborate. The design and construction of the tabernacle were directed by God (Exod. 25:8–9). Although the Lord did not request or command the building of the temple, his approval for it was there, as Solomon indicates when he observes that the Lord said that David had done well to conceive of the idea (1 Kings 8:18). The fact, moreover, that God informed David that his son would build a house for the name of the Lord attests that the Lord had no objections to the construction of a building for the worship of his name. Finally, when the temple was dedicated, the Lord expressed his sanction of the whole project by filling the house with a cloud and the glory of the Lord (2 Chron. 5:13–14). This building like its predecessor, the tabernacle, was to be a place where the Lord and his people would meet in a special way. The structures, designed for the performance of specific functions, in their very shape and appearance spoke to the purpose of the buildings and the nature of worship among the people who used these worship centers. It is not surprising, therefore, that Jesus took seriously his own relationship with the temple of his day. He himself went there and wanted the place to be adorned with the spiritual dignity of which it was worthy (John 2:13–17). Not to be overlooked, of course, is the typological significance and relationship of Jesus Christ to the tabernacle and its furnishings, a topic treated rather thoroughly by the writer of the letter to the Hebrews (Hebrews 8 and 9).

A few comments about the basic design of the tabernacle, a design later incorporated into the temple, might be in place at this point to demonstrate the message the outward features of the structure gave. Although the worship facility was movable and only a tent, by God's direction it was still expensively done. Precious metals, quality fabrics, and well-crafted materials joined to say that this place was important in the community of Israel. When Israel was permanently settled, King David observed that his own house was far more ornate than the tent house of the Lord, but that observation should not be misconstrued to suggest that the tabernacle had been shabbily fashioned. For a people on the move and not permanently settled, the tabernacle was both striking and artistic.

The central feature of the tabernacle was the ark. Located in the most holy place in the tabernacle, the ark was symbolic of the presence of the Lord among his people as well as of his holiness and served as the place where the Lord met the representative of his people. A curtain with figures of cherubim separated the Holy of Holies from the Holy Place, which was itself closed off from the courtyard with another curtain. The very structure said something. God's holiness requires that he veil himself from sinners lest they be consumed by his presence. Sinners have no right of their own to step before God, but access will be given, access in the Old Testament through a mediating priesthood, which in itself was prophetic of the office of Jesus Christ, the great high priest through whom we have access to the Father (Eph. 2:18; Heb. 7:26–27).

In the open courtyard of the tabernacle stood the altar of burnt offering. Here all offerings were to be made, not the least of which would be those offerings that included the shedding of blood. The presence of that altar, the outpouring of blood upon it, and the sprinkling of that blood in such situations as the high priest's annual entry into the Holy of Holies (Lev. 16:2, 12–17) were powerful testimonies to the truth that without the shedding of blood there is no forgiveness of sins (Heb. 9:22; Lev. 17:11). What the people of the Old Testament heard with their ears was dramatically reinforced with what they saw with their eyes and were aware of when they visited tabernacle or temple. Religious buildings and their furnishings can speak theologically. To do this, of course, they have to be designed with an obvious and easily understood correlation between the spoken word and the visual symbol. That was quite clearly the case with the format and structures that God mandated for Old Testament worship.

Theology and Outside Architecture

Divine imperatives for building and ritual are strikingly absent for the church of the New Testament. God's people in Christ are to assemble, they are to use both Word and sacraments, they are to pray, praise, and give thanks. Each age, each culture, each group of Christians has the freedom, however, to exercise its sanctified judgment in some of the hows and wheres, as Lutheranism's Formula of Concord has acknowledged: "We believe, teach, and confess that the congregation of God of every place and every time has the power, according to its circumstances, to change . . . ceremonies in such manner as may be most useful and edifying to the congregation of God."[5] Although this is stated specifically with respect to ceremonies or church rites within the church, inasmuch as the concern is with matters "neither commanded nor forbidden in God's Word,"[6] the statement is equally applicable to buildings designed for worship. A right or a wrong architecture does not exist in and of itself, providing that what is used accommodates appropriately the congregation's needs and can be employed in a manner that allows for spiritual edification.

However, such an affirmation for freedom does not remove the obligation to establish principles on the basis of which to shape ecclesiastical architecture and guide architectural decision making. A regard for edification assumes that congregations of any age and place will investigate seriously what their buildings say and how theology informs church design. Reflecting on this idea, a non-Lutheran writer has said:

> A church is a place where God's people gather together to worship him, and how they worship, as well as what they believe, is either reinforced or undermined by the architecture. Church architecture is therefore first and foremost a matter of theology rather than a matter of style.[7]

Western Christianity has not failed in its history to give a powerful visual testimony to its theology through the medium of architecture. Large church buildings dedicated to Christian worship say something about both God and people. A massive structure with a towering spire or two directs the worshipers' eyes upward and reinforces the song of the psalmist, "O Lord, our Lord, how majestic is thy name in all the earth" (Ps. 8:1 RSV). Durable materials in a church building can be a reminder of the Lord's word about himself, "I the Lord do not change" (Mal. 3:6 RSV), and the very proportions of many church buildings, both large and small, suggest that in them is a place of refuge. Mute stone and wood can be combined into designs that speak a message.

Admittedly, some churches may have been built to glorify the planners and builders, but in most cases the structures rose because of the spiritual commitment and desires of the people who intended to use such places of worship. Rural America provides abundant evidence of the inclination of Lutheran Christians to want and to provide for themselves appropriate sanctuaries within which to worship their God. Carving out homes and farms for themselves on one frontier after the other, immigrants to the United States located within their communities modest church buildings. Sometimes these buildings stood unsurrounded on a vast prairie; sometimes they were perched on the top of a hill; and sometimes they were nestled in a tranquil valley. But wherever situated, these churches had a comment to make about the settlers who erected the structures. These people recognized that life was not just food and drink. The life of the spirit was important too, and the assembly of Christians was not to be overlooked in the daily and often arduous routine of life. Not just any building for meeting would do, for buildings say things. The buildings were expected to have a distinctiveness that marked them as church, as places where human beings could meet their God in a special way, as symbols of the peace and rest that come to the people of God in Christ Jesus. The buildings said something about those who erected the structures and about one of the priorities that such people had.

E. A. Sovik has argued for a return to non-church, that is, for a style of ecclesiastical architecture markedly different in its statement from what buildings of the past have said.[8] There is merit to some of Sovik's argument, but it would be regrettable if church architecture were to lose a number of those special characteristics that throughout the centuries have marked church buildings as places where God in Word and Sacrament comes to us in assembly and where we as a congregation gathered in the name of Jesus meet him. This is an architectural testimony worth keeping.

None of what has been said indicates precisely, of course, how churches should look or of what materials houses of worship should be made. Both areas allow for a large and pleasing variety and are dependent upon numerous legitimate factors. The size of the worshiping community and the resources available to it dictate some aspects of style and design. The part of the country or world in which a church is erected, as well as the specific site chosen for a building, must be considered when determining the outward appearance of a place for worship. A call for a building that is distinctively church is not a plea for worship structures that are out of harmony with their surroundings. The use of local construction materials is not only appropriate but often to be desired in order to create a building that is harmonious with its environment.

Church buildings should be compatible with the cultures that they serve and be in step as well with the general economic conditions prevailing among the people who worship in such churches. To argue for churchly buildings is not to demand a specific style of architecture or to ignore a host of conditions unique to this or that situation. It is a plea rather for buildings that say something about what the church stands for to those who visit the structures and, to the extent possible, to those who just pass by on the outside. Regardless of style, church buildings of any given time or place should articulate something about theology. Store-front churches are appropriate under given circumstances. The erection of a gymnasium-type building as the first unit in a multiple-stage construction plan may be advisable and expedient. In most of North America, however, both types of buildings have limitations as worship sanctuaries, not because they cannot accommodate people but because these buildings do not convey a theologically convincing message to the eye. The outward appearance of the places where Christians worship is able to take many different shapes and forms, but that does not mean that there are no criteria on the basis of which to design church buildings, for buildings do speak. Ralph W. Emerson (1803–82), reflecting upon the song of a bird and the natural surroundings in which the bird sang, stated the case well when he penned the line: "He sang to my ear, —they sang to my eye" ("Each and All"). The outward appearance of a church sings to the eye and should sing something of a theological song.

Mention has already been made that certain styles of arhitecturecan suggest something about the greatness, the majesty, and the awesomeness of God. That is one kind of testimony which the outward design of a building dedicated to worship can give, but it is not the only song which the exterior features of a church may sing, nor is it required that every church building sing the same melody. Other accents may be struck with equal validity. Jesus, for example, issued a most comforting invitation to the weary and troubled, regardless of the cause of their affliction, when he said: "Come unto me, all ye that labor and are heavy laden, and I will give you rest" (Matt. 11:28 KJV). If the stately Statue of Liberty with its immortal inscription, "Give me your tired, your poor, your huddled masses yearning to breathe free," has been able to inspire hope in countless numbers of immigrants, should it not be possible also for a church building to have an outward appearance that is warm and inviting and that, by that very appearance, persuades people to want to enter to find the rest offered within? Human beings have an emotional side that often responds to symbols. Church architects have the challenge to address that aspect of the human spirit with exterior designs that are inviting and winsome.

The heart of the message of the Christian church is Jesus Christ, for there is no other name given among men by which the human race can be saved (Acts 4:12). For that reason, church exteriors should, if at all possible, give testimony to this central truth of Holy Scripture. The apostle Paul acknowledges that he was determined to know nothing among those to whom he ministered except Jesus Christ and him crucified (1 Cor. 2:2). That same apostle confessed that he was not ashamed of the Gospel of Christ because it was the power of God unto salvation (Rom. 1:16). In Christ Jesus there is forgiveness of sins and there is hope for eternity, for he is the resurrection and the life (John 11:25–26). There should be no reluctance to let the exterior of a building give witness to this message, if it is possible to do so in a reverent and dignified way. A simple cross, of course, is the commonest and easiest way to convey the

Christian message symbolically, but it is not the only way. Striking sculptures are able to do the task too, and some buildings lend themselves well to an effective chiseling in stone of a Christocentric Bible passage. Various possibilities exist for the exterior of a church building to say something about Christian truth. These possibilities should be explored, for a church building is a reminder of many things to those who regularly gather there for worship and a persistent but loving invitation to the forgetful and unchurched who pass by.

Critics of church designs that seem to be otherworldly have argued that such architecture gives the impression that the church is removed from the real issues of life. Criticism of this sort may come from those who advocate more extensive ecclesiastical involvement in the critical social issues of the day. The church, of course, has no call to be oblivious to the general needs of society, for Holy Scripture makes clear that deeds of love are part of the Christian life. The same Lord, however, who incites his people to deeds of human love and kindness, is also quick to point out that his kingdom is not of this world (John 18:36). Christ came to repair a fractured relationship between God and man. This is what the church has to tell about. The church is tending to its business when the message and the activity of the church are directed primarily to the spiritual needs of the human race. The church has a mandate from the Lord to issue a clear and earnest proclamation dealing with sin and grace. That is real life for the church and the real life of the church. From that point of view, the church is indeed otherworldly, because in Christ it focuses primarily upon the restored relationship between heaven and earth, between God and man. An architectural style, therefore, that is distinctive and strikingly ecclesiastical is quite appropriate for church buildings, for the church of Jesus Christ has a unique mission in the world.

Theology and Inside Architecture

The outside of a church building has rather general things to say about the message of a church and the people who make up any given congregation. The inside of a church building, on the other hand, becomes more specific with its architectural communication.

Statuary, icons, and the subjects of paintings or stained glass windows sometimes furnish information about the denominational affiliation of a church. Placement and design of pulpit, altar, and baptismal furniture vary from denomination to denomination and speak to the person who enters a worship center. Even the arrangement and design of pews can make a statement about what a congregation wants to affirm theologically when it constructs or renovates a place of worship. It is possible, therefore, to speak about interior architectural design that is Eastern Orthodox, Roman Catholic, Baptist, Reformed, or Lutheran, because the theology or theological emphases of these various groups are expressed in bold or subtle ways by the way the churches of these worshiping communities look inside. In order to become more aware of how this is expected to take place, it may be helpful to note what non-Lutherans have said about ecclesiastical architecture.

In Roman Catholicism the sacrifice of the Mass is at the center of worship. Josef Jungmann observes that the Mass is an expiatory sacrifice.[9] Since sacrifices are offered at altars, it is certainly fitting within the context of Roman Catholic theology to call the piece of liturgical furniture upon which the priest offers the sacrifice of the Mass an altar. Because the sacrifice of the Mass is central in Roman Catholic worship, it also follows that the altar should be the central and focal point in Roman Catholic church architecture. One writer has put it this way:

> Since the Eucharistic Sacrifice is the centre of the Catholic Liturgy, it follows that the altar of sacrifice is the central and culminating point of the edifice, and its position and form should be so designed as to give expression to this prominence.[10]

Another writer concurs, but with a bit more emphasis:

> A Catholic church is built primarily to house an altar; a church cannot exist without an altar, nor may it be consecrated unless an altar . . . is dedicated at the same time. The church is, as it were, built about its high altar. This altar is the optical and architectural centre of the church—as it is the spiritual centre of its liturgical life. . . . "The altar is, so to speak, the very soul of the church and its *raison d'etre*. It is the culminating spot in the entire edifice, and in a well-designed church all matters of proportion, design, furnishing and decoration are subordinate to the altar, towards

191

which the soul of the worshippers is directed through eye and mind by means of the lines in the building. . . . Upon the altar, as the stage whereon are daily enacted the sacred mysteries of the last Supper and Calvary, all attention must be focused."

It follows that in planning a church the high altar must be clearly visible—if at all possible—from every point of the building. It should dominate the church, stand out unmistakably by its position, structure, ornamentation and lighting.[11]

These statements, it must be granted, were made before Vatican II (1962–65), as well as before some of the major changes in building design that have taken place since that time. Nevertheless, the comments do reflect how architecture was intended to reflect Roman Catholic theology. Inasmuch as the eucharistic sacrifice is still at the heart of Roman worship, it is to be expected that the altar, of whatever design, will continue to be given central place in Roman Catholic churches.[12]

A different view of the altar emerges in Protestant worship traditions. Rejecting Rome's teaching of the propitiatory nature of the Mass, some Protestant groups prefer to remove the term altar from their liturgical vocabulary or at least to modify the term. James White, for example, consistently uses the term altar-table rather than altar when referring to the place at which prayers and acts of praise are offered and from which the Lord's Supper is distributed.[13] Writing from the perspective of the Reformed Church in America, authors Donald Bruggink and Carl Droppers not only speak regularly of the table as a liturgical furnishing, they argue pointedly against even the use of the term altar. Observing that the design of altars in Roman Catholic churches has been changing in recent times, but that some heirs of the Reformation still build altars that would seem to be especially appropriate for the "Roman doctrine of the Mass as a re-sacrifice of Christ," Bruggink and Droppers assert,

There is no need for an altar. An altar in fact is either totally incongruous, or a denial of the sufficiency of Christ's once-for-all sacrifice. Calvin succinctly sums up the matter by observing that Christ has "given us a Table at which to feast, not an altar upon which to offer a victim; he has not consecrated priests to offer sacrifice, but ministers to distribute the sacred banquet." If any architectural criterion is to be stated with regard to the Sacrament of the

Lord's Supper, the very minimum statement would be thus: [FOR THE CELEBRATION OF THE LORD'S SUPPER, THE TABLE SHOULD LOOK LIKE A TABLE!][14]

Bruggink and Droppers are obviously presenting a case for more than just an alternate name for a piece of liturgical furniture. They want something in the sanctuary that is, looks like, and is called a table because they see this appointment solely as a place from which to accommodate the distribution of the meal known as the Lord's Supper. With this presupposition and in the light of Roman Catholic teaching on the Eucharist, the designation altar is for these writers anathema.

The Presbyterian/Reformed *Christ and Architecture* does not limit itself, however, merely to a discussion of table and altar. The authors of the book attach their theology to other elements of liturgical design. Thus, recognition of the preeminence of proclamation in the biblical witness leads Bruggink and Droppers to recommend interior church designs that give the pulpit extraordinary prominence. Numerous excellent photographs of center-placement and, at times, overpowering pulpits demonstrate quite clearly that the authors see these types of design as models of what it means to wed theology and architecture. The baptismal font, of course, is not overlooked and is expected to be placed where it can be seen. Like the table for the Supper, however, the font is obviously also not to have a position or shape that would make it more visible than the pulpit. Bruggink and Droppers summarize how they view the importance and relationship of pulpit, font, and table within the framework of Reformed theology in the following two theses:

> To set forth the God-ordained means by which Christ comes to his people, the Reformed must give visual expression to the importance of both word and sacraments. Because the word is indispensable, the pulpit, as the architectural manifestation of the word, must make its indispensability architecturally clear.[15]

Lutherans and the Liturgical Arts

The Lutheran approach to liturgical art and furnishings has not been the same as that of other Protestant groups who trace their roots back to the 16th-century Reformation. The difference in matters ceremonial between Lutherans and other reforming groups became apparent early in the Reformation era. Luther himself took the lead to promote an understanding that avoided radicalism in liturgical matters. While others advocated tearing down altars, discarding vestments, dismantling organs, and replacing liturgies, Luther viewed these externals as secondary, concentrating his dispute with Rome on the theology of the Mass. Where Mass theology was unbiblical, Luther spoke in no uncertain terms, but in other matters he was cautious and willing to be patient. In the *Formula Missae* (1523), his Latin service, he argued that certain externals which might be done away with could be tolerated temporarily and that all things should be proved and the good held fast.[16] In his German service, the *Deutsche Messe* (1526), Luther expressed his preference for a freestanding altar but was unwilling to force the issue and quite content to bide his time:

> Here we retain the vestments, altar, and candles until they are used up or we are pleased to make a change. But we do not oppose anyone who would do otherwise. In the true mass, however, of real Christians, the altar should not remain where it is, and the priest should always face the people as Christ doubtlessly did in the Last Supper. But let that await its own time.[17]

What was enunciated here was the principle later articulated in Article X of the Formula of Concord, namely, that in church rites and ceremonies where God has not made laws the church is not to make any either. Early Lutherans, therefore, did not demand the kind of liturgical and architectural transformation that some other reforming groups insisted on; they chose rather to reflect on the merits of existing forms and structures to determine what deserved to be kept, what should be discarded, and what could be interpreted profitably and appropriately within the context of Lutheran biblical theology.

Lutherans, like other groups in the Protestant Reformation of the 16th century, inherited buildings from the Roman Catholic Church, but chancels stayed in Lutheran churches, altars remained, and names for churches did not always experience change. In the course of time, little experiments to rearrange things were tried here and there—such as locating the pulpit behind and above the altar— but for the most part, Lutheran church buildings throughout history, except for certain kinds of art work, continued to resemble their Roman Catholic counterparts. Chancels in Lutheran churches may not have been so expansive or deep, pulpits may at times have been more predominant, and altars may have been less ostentatious, but chancels and altars did remain, with the altar regularly occupying a center position.

In recent decades pews have been set in a variety of arrangements in all denominations, but until the latter part of the 20th century, Lutherans continued to sit in pews fixed traditionally in a position parallel to the altar in the chancel, a common arrangement also in Roman Catholic churches. Moreover, even though that position has been criticized by many as being more consistent with the spectator view of the Mass and not as symbolic as it might be of the assembly as the gathering of believers who are "members one of another" (Rom. 12:5 RSV), Lutherans have still not abandoned, even in new church buildings, a pew arrangement that some have seen as more fitting for medieval Catholicism's view of the Mass than for a church body that emphasizes the doctrine of the universal priesthood of all believers. Generally speaking, Lutherans have not been at the forefront in undoing traditional designs in worship facilities.

It would be a misinterpretation, however, to conclude that, because of apathy or a disinterest in matters of this sort, thoughtful Lutheranism has not initiated many changes in the design or arrangement of liturgical furnishings. A commitment to the principle that rites and ceremonies in and of themselves are not worship will contribute quite naturally to an acceptance of things as they are, unless there is a convincing demand for something new or different. Historically, Lutheranism's focus in worship has been on orthodox teaching and preaching and on the right use of the sacraments. In these things lies the essence of worship. Symbols, when intelligible and properly understood, can communicate and reinforce a theological message, but a certain amount of subjectivity is involved in the interpretation of the symbolic. In addition, symbols can at times be interpreted in more than one way or even reinterpreted to provide more acceptable meanings. Lutherans have not failed to appreciate the symbolic in church buildings and are quite able to interpret the ecclesiastical arts in terms of Lutheran theology.

Altar and Chancel in Lutheran Churches

The pulpit, the baptismal font, and the altar are the three major pieces of liturgical furniture in Lutheran churches. These three effectively symbolize the importance of the Word of God, Baptism, and the Lord's Supper in Lutheran theology, although it is important to note that the altar in Lutheran worship is used not only as a place for the preparation and distribution of the Lord's Supper but also as the symbol of God's presence among his people and the place where prayers and offerings of praise and thanksgiving are brought to God. These three major furnishings obviously cannot occupy the same position, and attempts to arrange them in some sort of artificial clustering produces an aesthetically displeasing and contrived appearance, as early efforts to put pulpits in Lutheran churches above altars have demonstrated. Lutheran proclivity not to make changes where they did not have to be made kept altars where high altars had always been in medieval Roman Catholicism. Lutherans did not remove altars and, when more churches had to be built, these churches were constructed along traditional lines.

There is good reason to keep the altar in a center position in a Lutheran church. This placement is not an architectural statement that the Lord's Supper, which is prepared on the altar, is a sacrifice. The Supper is not that. The center placement of the altar is also not a statement that participation in the Lord's Supper is the high point or climax of Lutheran worship. The Lord does not rank his means of grace; he invites us to use them. A liturgical furnishing, however, called an altar and even designed to look like one is appropriate in a Christian church because of the centrality of sacrifice in God's plan of salvation for the human race. For centuries blood was spilled profusely on Old Testament altars for the purifying of the people of God, for "under the law almost everything is purified with blood, and without the shedding of blood there is no forgiveness of sins" (Heb. 9:22 RSV). This outpouring of sacrificial blood was not without its significance for God's New Testament revelation in Jesus Christ, for the shedding of blood in the Old Testament was done in anticipation of the supreme sacrifice of blood given upon the cross of Calvary by the Son of God and Son of Man, who offered himself as the perfect Lamb of God to redeem those who were under the law (Gal. 4:4–5). "In him," the apostle Paul says, "we have redemption through his blood, the forgivensss of our trespasses, according to the riches of his grace" (Eph. 1:7 RSV). Christ "is the head of the body, the church; he is the beginning, the first-born from the dead, that in everything he might be preeminent. For in him all the fulness of God was pleased to dwell, and through him to reconcile to himself all things, whether on earth or in heaven, making peace by the blood of his cross" (Col. 1:18–20 RSV). The altar in a center position in a Lutheran church is a visual testimony that the Gospel proclamation of the church centers in the Christ who gave his life for the sheep and reclaimed it that those who were once far from God might be brought near in the blood of his Son (Eph. 2:13). The altar is a symbol of Christ and his perfect sacrifice for sin.

But the altar makes another statement. The altar is the place to which the pastor regularly goes in his conduct of the Lutheran worship service. Sometimes the pastor faces the altar; sometimes he turns away from it to face the people. Liturgically, the first position is called sacrificial; the second, sacramental. In both cases, however, the altar is now taking on a function different from that described above. When the pastor assumes the sacrificial position, he is speaking to God; when the pastor faces the people, except for several short dialogues with the people such as "The Lord be with you," the pastor is bringing a message from God. When employed as a place to go in order to speak to God in prayer or to relay a message from him, as in absolution, the altar becomes the symbol of God's presence among us. It is a most appropriate symbol, too, in terms of what was said before about the altar and its symbolic relationship to the redemptive work of Christ, for it is only in Christ that we have access to the Father (Eph. 2:18). Altars in Lutheran churches intend to convey the message that the Lord is present in Word and Sacrament among his worshiping people and that the approach to him is mediated through Jesus Christ, the crucified and risen Savior.

A third use of the altar still needs to be addressed, for initially it was noted that the alar also gives witness to the use of the Lord's Supper as an essential in the corporate worship life of a Christian community. The altar is the place upon which the communion vessels with bread and wine in them are set and from where the Lord's Supper is ordinarily distributed. The altar thus takes on the very practical function of a table. It is a unique table, of course, because the meal is not an ordinary one but the Supper which the Lord himself instituted and in which, with the bread and wine, he gives to his people his very body and blood.

Reformed theology generally prefers to call the liturgical furnishing from which the Lord's Supper is served a table or altar-table rather than an altar. The reluctance to use the term altar stems from a legitimate objection to the Roman Catholic view that the elements in the Lord's Supper are employed as an unbloody sacrifice in the Mass as well as for distribution to communicants. Certain Reformed groups avoid the term altar, therefore, to help make clear that the Supper is not a sacrifice to God in behalf of people, living or dead.

Lutherans reject the Roman error of the sacrifice of the Mass with as much vigor as do the Reformed. The Lord's Supper is God's gift to us, not our offering of an unbloody sacrifice to him. It remains a fact, however, that in the Supper the communicants do receive the very body and blood of their Lord. The bread and wine are not mere symbols of Christ's body and blood, and his presence is not just a spiritual presence. Lutheranism's Formula of Concord declares, "In the Holy Supper the body and blood of Christ are truly and essentially present and are truly distributed and received with the bread and wine" and "the words of the testament of Christ are to be understood in no other way than in their literal sense, and not as though the bread symbolized the absent body and the wine the absent blood of Christ, but that because of the sacramental union they are truly the body and blood of Christ."[18] Since the Lutheran Church teaches and confesses that with the bread and wine in the Supper the body and blood of Christ are truly received—that very body and blood which were offered in vicarious atonement on the cross—Lutherans do not consider it inappropriate to call the liturgical furnishing from which the bread and wine are distributed an altar. The Lord's Supper is done in remembrance of him who sacrificed himself. The Supper conveys to the believing communicant the blessings of forgiveness that were obtained by Christ's sacrifice. Since the Supper is a spiritual banquet, it is also not improper, of course, to speak of the place from which the Supper is distributed as a table. But since the Supper of the Lord is so intimately bound together with his sacrifice of body and blood, Lutherans continued after the Reformation to call the place from which the Supper was served an altar. Lutherans reject the Roman Catholic doctrine of transubstantiation and do not speak of body and blood upon the altar. The Lutheran teaching of the *real presence* in the Supper, however, affirms the biblical doctrine that the body and blood of Christ are present in the Sacrament for the communicant to eat and to drink with the bread and the wine. Within that context and understanding Lutherans have not hesitated to refer to the central furnishing in their chancels as the altar.

A summary is in place. Lutherans neither dismantled altars in Roman Catholic churches that were taken over for Lutheran worship at the time of the Reformation nor did Lutherans cease in the centuries that followed to furnish churches with liturgical altars. An examination of Lutheran liturgical practice suggests that Lutherans perceived the altar as serving a threefold purpose. First, the altar was an ever-present reminder that God redeemed the world through the sacrifice of his only Son, the Lamb of God whose offering of himself, typified by the many Old Testament sacrifices, was completed on the altar of the cross. To assign a central position to an altar and to make it the focal point in a church building is to call attention to the centrality of the vicarious atonement in God's revelation to man and in Lutheran theology. Secondly, the common practice in Lutheran worship of using the altar in both communion and noncommunion services as the place at which to offer prayers and praise to the Lord of heaven and earth marks the altar as the symbol of God's presence among his people in Christ Jesus. Thirdly, to call a piece of liturgical furniture an altar and then to use it as the place upon which to put the elements employed in a sacramental meal, moreover, as the liturgical furnishing at which to speak the Words of Institution and as the center from which to distribute the Supper is to employ the altar as a table as well as to say that the Sacrament of the Altar is a unique meal in which, according to Christ's institution, his body and blood sacrificed for sin are physically present with the bread and wine in the Sacrament.

Since the liturgically furnished altar has a significant theological statement to make in Lutheran church buildings, special attention should be given to the design of the altar. It need not be extravagantly ornate, but since it portrays the presence of God, its appearance and setting should have an aura of dignity and honor about it and should evoke feelings of reverence and respect. Admittedly, the almighty and omnipresent God cannot be confined to bounded space, nor is an altar an icon to be worshiped. This does not mean, however, that the visual centers that aid finite human beings in their devotions and that suggest the presence of the Redeemer God should be clothed in ordinariness. There is a sense in which we may say of our earthly sanctuaries, "The Lord is in his holy temple; let all the earth keep silence before him" (Hab. 2:20 KJV). Altars in Lutheran churches have issued this statement and call. To be sure, the altar also has a table function for the sacramental meal and for that reason assumes a shape and dimensions to accommodate that purpose. If an altar takes on only a simple table form, however, the broader concept of the altar as a symbol also of the presence of a holy God is less easily conveyed. It is wise, therefore, to have the altar itself or the setting in which it is placed communicate something of the greatness of the eternal God. Some of the highly ornamented altars of the past may have gone to extremes in this respect, but an age that has learned to like the plain and streamlined is well advised not to overlook the desirability of creating liturgical space and furnishings that inspire feelings of awe, reverence, and respect. Altars with appropriate settings can do this in modest as well as in ornate church buildings.

The Freestanding Altar

Lutherans have continued to retain altars in the centuries-old position against what is commonly referred to as the east wall of the church. Martin Luther, as noted earlier,[19] recommended that the altar be moved forward from the wall, but not until recent times has that in fact happened. The freestanding altar has much to recommend it liturgically, but it needs to be located and used with care if it is to serve its threefold purpose as symbol of the presence of God in Christ, as indicator of the centrality of the sacrifice of Christ in Christian theology, and as the table from which the meal of Christ is served. Some contemporary arrangements for freestanding altars seem to suggest an exclusively table or community meal use of the altar. Although one is free to attach only a Lord's Supper use and significance to the liturgical altar, it must be admitted that Lutherans in their history have consistently employed the altar in a broader dimension. Lutheran pastors have regularly used altars in both communion and noncommunion services as the place for prayer. The freestanding altar of recent times is more consistent with historic Lutheranism if such an altar accomodates the several uses that have been attributed to it in traditional Lutheran practice. The kind of freestanding altar that favors this multiple function and purpose is brought forward sufficiently far from the wall of a chancel or altar space to provide easy movement from behind the altar, but not so far forward that the space in front lacks grace or makes use of the altar from that position appear incorrect or awkward. More floor space in front of the altar than behind often does much to create the right setting. A cross on a wall or dossal, or some other symbol or appointment in the vicinity of the altar to represent the Redeemer God of Holy Scripture, further indicates that an altar in a Lutheran church performs a symbolic service that extends beyond the altar's use as the table from which to celebrate the Lord's Supper.

What has been said about the placement of a freestanding altar suggests already how to use it effectively in the conduct of services. Unless, of course, the congregation requires the use of sign language, it is desirable to use the freestanding altar from both the front and the back. This preserves in an effective way the traditional Lutheran distinction between sacramental and sacrificial liturgical acts, and enables the pastor by his position to communicate the nature and flow of the liturgy.

Acts in Lutheran worship such as the confession of sins, the Kyrie, the Gloria in Excelsis, and versicles like "O Lord, open my lips" should be done facing a freestanding altar, thus preserving the view of the altar as a symbol of God's presence among us, the place toward which we turn when we speak to him. When the pastor speaks for God, as in the absolution or the declaration of grace, or when he engages in certain kinds of reciprocal dialogue with the people, as in the versicle "The Lord be with you," he will face the people. If Holy Scripture is read from the horns of the altar instead of from a lectern, the pastor will again face the congregation. In fact, the entire liturgy of the Word together with the preparatory confession should be done in front of a freestanding altar so that the pastor can turn both toward and away from it. In that way liturgical positions assist in the communication of the message of the liturgy. When the service moves to the celebration of the Lord's Supper, a position behind the freestanding altar becomes appropriate, for now the altar will be functioning primarily as the Supper table. That function of the altar is highlighted when both it and the elements upon it come into full view of the assembled congregation. The communion liturgy has sacrificial as well as sacramental liturgical acts, for the Lord's Supper liturgy includes prayers and a doxological and eucharistic "Holy, Holy, Holy." The Supper itself, however, is God's gift to us, and although the Words of Institution relate to the bread and wine upon the altar, the Words are a Gospel proclamation to the congregation and should be spoken by the pastor in a position facing the people. The historic wall-altar, which usually left the pastor with his back toward the people when the Words of Institution were spoken, has always been most unfortunate because the sacramental and declaratory nature of the Words is easily lost when the presiding minister has his back toward the people. It is precisely at this point in the liturgy that the freestanding altar performs its noblest service. The worshiping congregation has the opportunity to see the vessels containing bread and wine and to hear the pastor, in a position facing the assembly, declare how the Lord Christ will use these elements to give to his people his own body and blood and with them the spiritual gifts which he has placed in his Supper. It is for the Words of Institution that freestanding altars came into Lutheran churches.

At this point one might comment that The Order of Holy Communion in *The Lutheran Hymnal* (1941) permits the pastor to stay in front of a freestanding altar all the way to the doxology of the Lord's Prayer. Since that doxology is sung by the assembled worshipers, the pastor has ample opportunity during the singing to step behind the altar to be in position to speak or chant the sacramental Words. That kind of positioning and movement enables the pastor to do the sacrifical Proper Preface, the Sanctus, and the Lord's Prayer in a position facing the altar. The common practice, however, is to move behind the altar during the Offertory or at the Preface which begins the communion liturgy, the latter point for position change being almost mandatory in *The Lutheran Hymnal* service because the

Offertory comes before the very long General Prayer, a major sacrificial act. After the distribution, of course, it is quite in place to return to the front of a freestanding altar. This can be done conveniently during the Post-Communion Canticle so that the celebrant is able to speak the closing collect in a sacrificial position.

The Lord's Supper services in *Lutheran Worship* and the *Lutheran Book of Worship* have a design that recommends going behind a freestanding altar at the Offertory, a liturgical piece that looks forward to the Supper. Although going behind the altar at the Offertory does not permit the celebrant to maintain the usual sacrificial position for the sacrificial acts of the Preface to the Holy Communion, the liturgical position behind the altar can be justified from the point of view that the liturgy of the meal has begun and that the attention of the worshipers is now on the Supper and the elements to be used in it. When the pastor engages in the sacrificial acts of the communion liturgy, he would assume a prayer posture rather than looking at the congregation, as he would do when speaking to them and will, of course, do when he speaks or chants the Words of Institution. Using the freestanding altar in the ways described permits the use of the altar in communion as well as in noncommunion services and preserves an altar symbolism that is easily understood, meaningful, and consonant with long-standing and commonly practiced liturgical customs in the Lutheran church.

The altar has customarily found its place in a Lutheran church in that part of the building which is known as the chancel. The chancel and nave design of a church building is not unique to Lutheranism, and some have at times argued that it would be advisable to do away with that type of church architecture because, it is alleged, such a design suggests a distinction between clergy and laity which is untenable. As a result, architects of more recent decades have often designed buildings so that the worship centers reflect more of a family or community setting. In such an arrangement chancels disappear or become less prominent. The desire to remove chancels has sometimes been so strong that they have been abandoned in existing buildings. A freestanding altar is then placed among the people in the nave while the old chancel stands as a gaping hole or, if its furnishings are left intact, as some sort of museum to display relics from the past. The results of such renovation are not at all pleasant to the eye, although attempts to redesign old buildings in this way are silent testimony that people feel architectural design in churches does say something theological. The altar among the people instead of a distance from them is thought to depict better the nature of Christ's church.

A Lutheran congregation is free, of course, to choose how it wants to arrange its liturgical furniture. Appropriate symbolic interpretation can be given to more than one kind of arrangement. Since it is usually not possible in a single building or setting to portray all that one wishes to say, choices often have to be made. Such choices should be made thoughtfully and after due consideration of what church furnishings and their arrangements are able to say.

The traditional chancel setting for an altar and as the place from which to lead worship in a Lutheran church is not without its significance. On the basis of 1 Peter 2:9 the doctrine of the universal priesthood of all believers has been clearly taught throughout the history of Lutheranism.[20] On the other hand, the Lutheran Church, on the basis of passages such as 1 Tim. 3:1–5 and Heb. 13:17, has also upheld the doctrine of the public ministry in the church.[21] Although it has sometimes been argued that a chancel and nave arrangement preserves the doctrine of the priesthood as taught in Roman Catholicism, that is not the only symbol which need be attached to such architectural design. The pastor leads a congregation in worship functions because he occupies the office of the public ministry. He has been called to be the shepherd and overseer (Acts 20:28) of the flock gathered around Word and Sacrament in that place. There is no doubt that a chancel does effect a certain separation between the pastor or pastors in the chancel and the people in the pews. This is not altogether undesirable, however, for in addition to creating a position from which to lead corporate worship effectively, this architectural arrangement also makes a statement about the office of the public ministry within the priesthood of all believers. All are priests before God, but one person is chosen to exercise a public office among the priests and is charged with the responsibilities of spiritual oversight and leadership. The chancel and nave arrangement effectively portrays this relationship between pastor and people.

Not uncommon for the altar setting of a Lutheran church is a communion rail. Like chancels, this furnishing is sometimes objected to because it is viewed as a divider between pastor and people or as an indicator that worshipers may not approach God, whose presence is symbolized by the altar, without a human mediator. Since it is totally inconsistent with Lutheran theology to suggest some kind of Levitical priesthood in the New Testament church or limitations of access to God for those who are in Christ Jesus, such an interpretation for the communion rail is obviously erroneous. What the communion rail has provided, however, is a convenient place at which to distribute the Lord's Supper. Granted, a rail at which people kneel to receive the body and blood of their Lord with the bread and wine has limitations to depict the table setting within which Christ instituted his Supper. The communion rail, does, however, make it easy for worshipers to gather together in small groups to receive the Supper and with that intimate kind of arrangement to bring to mind the community and horizontal aspects of the Supper in which the Lord communicates the forgiveness of sins to those who come to him. Communion rails are not necessary for an efficient distribution of the Lord's Supper, but they have been common in Lutheran churches. Since an incorrect symbolic interpretation could be attached to a rail which separates the altar from a worshiping congregation, it is advisable to design altar rails so that there is an openness about them and the settings in which these rails are placed. In that way misconceptions are minimized and the functional intent of the communion rail is more readily apparent.

When Protestants inherited churches from Roman Catholicism, the buildings were equipped with high altars, chancels, and separating altar rails. Some Reformers moved quickly to undo those elements of church architecture that seemed too closely bound to some of the Roman Catholic doctrines that were being challenged. Lutherans exercised caution in these matters and continued to employ long-established ecclesiastical forms of architecture. Only that which was totally unacceptable was done away with. Architectural symbols that could be reinterpreted were kept and were assigned meanings consistent with Lutheran theology. The altar and the setting in which it was placed stands in this category.

The Pulpit and the Centrality of Preaching

The pulpit as a liturgical furnishing is quite different from an altar and is by no means unique to just one or only a few branches of Christianity. Styles and designs of pulpits have varied from age to age, but the purposes of pulpits have remained the same. The pulpit is the place from which the Word of God is proclaimed, and so it assumes both a practical and a symbolic function. To the worshiper who enters a church the pulpit says, "You can expect to hear a sermon here." And when the preacher is ready to deliver his sermon, it is customary for him to do so from the pulpit.

Preaching has received a major emphasis in Lutheranism since the days of the Reformation. Preaching at the funeral of the Elector Duke John of Saxony, in 1532, Luther himself commented, "You know that the greatest divine service is the preaching [of the Word of God], and not only the greatest divine service (worship), but also the best we can have in every situation."[22] Nine years earlier in a short treatise on worship he had expressed a similar sentiment:

> Know first of all that a Christian congregation should never gather together without the preaching of God's Word and prayer, no matter how briefly, as Psalm 102 says, "When the kings and people assemble to serve the Lord, they shall declare the name and the praise of God." And Paul in 1 Corinthians 14 says that when they come together, there should be prophesying, teaching and admonition. Therefore, when God's Word is not preached, one had better neither sing nor read, or even come together.[23]

Addressing the same subject, the Apology of the Augsburg Confession did not hesitate to include in its German text "There is nothing which more effectively keeps people with the church than good preaching."[24] Such a view was not restricted, moreover, to the 16th century. American Lutheranism's C. F. W. Walther spoke pointedly to his students on the awesome responsibility of preaching in the church when he said,

> A student of theology ought to make proper preaching his highest aim. For if he is unable to preach, he does not belong in the ministry. . . . The worth of a true minister of the church lies exclusively in his ability to preach properly. . . . Preaching is the central element of every divine service.[25]

The pulpit has occupied a prominent place in Lutheran church architecture because Lutherans have established preaching as a central feature in public worship.

The priority of proclamation is totally in keeping with the emphases that Holy Scripture places on this activity. Whether the prophet was Isaiah, Jeremiah, or Hosea, "Hear the word of the Lord" was the prophetic call (Isa. 1:10; Jer. 2:4; Hos. 4:1 KJV), and not even a reluctant Jonah could escape the directive of the Lord who said, "Go to Nineveh, that great city, and proclaim to it the message that I tell you" (Jonah 3:2 RSV). The Old Testament prophetic ministry was one of proclamation.

That the New Testament should abound with directives to proclaim is to be expected from the very nature of that part of God's revelation. The good news is that the Word has become flesh, the very name assigned to the Son of God, indicating that verbal communication is central to the Gospel. Christ's own ministry abounded in proclamation as he went from one place to the next with his message from the Father. Finally, with his vicarious suffering, death, and resurrection from the dead he established the Gospel for the salvation of the human race and with the gift of the Holy Spirit he empowered his disciples to be witnesses "in all Judea and Samaria and to the end of the earth" (Acts 1:8 RSV). Proclamation is intrinsic to the revelation of the New Testament, both because sinful humanity is unable by itself to discover how to come into a right relationship with God and because the essence of the New Testament is the Word Incarnate.

Christ's directives to his church are clear and plain. "Go into all the world and preach the Gospel" was his parting command to his small group of followers (Mark 16:15 RSV). Of the apostle Paul the Lord said, "He is a chosen instrument of mine to carry my name before the Gentiles and kings and the sons of Israel" (Acts 9:15 RSV). So clearly did Paul understand his call that he later declared, "Woe to me if I do not preach the gospel" (1 Cor. 9:16 RSV), and when reflecting on the absolute necessity of preaching and preachers he observed,

> "Every one who calls upon the name of the Lord will be saved."
> . . . . And how are they to believe in him of whom they have never heard. And how are they to hear without a preacher? And how

can men preach unless they are sent? As it is written, "How beautiful are the feet of those who preach good news!" .... So faith comes from what is heard, and what is heard comes by the preaching of Christ (Rom. 10:13–17 RSV).

A Christian community that is mindful of what Holy Scripture has said about proclamation will accord preaching an honored position in public worship. For that reason Lutherans have regularly placed pulpits in prominent positions in church buildings and by both the usage and the symbol of the pulpit have given unmistakable testimony that the Lutheran Church is a church of the Word.

Pulpits in Lutheran churches have by no means had a single design. Some have been massive and towering; others modest and only slightly elevated. Balcony structures sometimes demanded a high-reaching pulpit so that the preacher could be seen by worshipers seated in the balconies. Acoustics may also have prompted the construction of lofty pulpits. In some cases, however, pulpits may have been designed on a grand scale just to give testimony to the importance of preaching in Lutheran worship, a symbolic function worthy of consideration in building design. In any case, pulpits in Lutheran churches have been located near the altar, thus bringing together in Lutheran worship the previously discussed functions of the altar and preaching. Altar and pulpit cannot occupy the same position, of course, and if they are placed too close to one another the result is clutter rather than harmonious testimony to the unity between pulpit and altar. Lutheran worship is not mystical contemplation. It is rather an activity in which God through Word and Sacrament comes to his assembled people in Christ Jesus, an activity in which these redeemed people approach their gracious God in prayer and praise. Pulpit and altar unite in the front of Lutheran churches to say this about Lutheran worship.

Closely related to the pulpit is the lectern, the place from which Holy Scripture is read without exposition. Although lecterns have become common in large and small American Lutheran churches, this type of liturgical furnishing is not absolutely necessary. It does provide a convenient place at which to have ready the appointed readings for the day. In all too many churches, however, this additional piece of furniture creates crowding in the chancel area. Sometimes the lectern must even be moved at the time of the Lord's Supper to accommodate the efficient gathering of communicants. In cases where the lectern and pulpit have been designed to look much alike, the impact created by one clearly identifiable place of proclamation is lost, a cogent reason for making sure that pulpit and lectern are sufficiently distinguishable from each other. If space does not permit a lectern or if such a furnishing is deemed unnecessary, the reading of the Scriptures takes place from the horns, that is from the ends of the altar or, as some have suggested, from the same place from which the sermon is delivered. When the readings are read from the altar, the first and second would be read on the liturgical south, the Gospel on the north end of the altar. Although it may be too dogmatic to insist that "today there is no theological or liturgical reason to have [lecterns],"[26] it should nevertheless be said that lecterns are dispensable. If they are provided, they should be assigned permanent locations and be designed and placed with careful thought.

Design and Location of the Baptismal Font

The baptismal font joins the pulpit and the altar as the third major liturgical furnishing in a Lutheran church. Both the location of the font and its design have been the subject of much discussion in recent times, not only among Lutherans but within other communions of western Christendom as well. That Baptism is a major event in the life of any Christian is not a subject for debate, for it is evident from the New Testament that Baptism is Christianity's entrance rite. The Pentecost throngs, cut to the heart by the sermon of Peter, inquired earnestly, "What shall we do?" Peter's answer was, "Repent, and be baptised every one of you in the name of Jesus Christ for the forgiveness of your sins; and you shall receive the gift of the Holy Spirit" (Acts 2:38 RSV). The distraught jailer of Philippi, having been taught the word of the Lord, was baptized together with his instructed household (Acts 16:32–33). Christ himself commanded Baptism and in his conversation with Nicodemus confirmed that entry into the kingdom of God requires being born again of water and the Spirit (John 3:5). Charged to baptize, Christian communities have made provision in their church buildings for the rite of Holy Baptism.

Lutheran churches have generally had modest baptismal fonts suitable for sprinkling or pouring water and located in the vicinity of the chancel. The location of the font in the front of the church where pulpit and altar are situated calls attention to Baptism as a means of grace together with the Gospel and the Sacrament of the Altar. Although the font is usually small in comparison with the pulpit and the altar, the font's position in the front of the congregation is a regular reminder of Baptism and permits the congregation to witness baptisms.

It must be admitted, however, that Lutheran sensitivity to the significance of the font may need sharpening. The small size of this liturgical furnishing has made it an easily movable piece of furniture. If space is needed in the front of the church for a Christmas tree or some other purpose, for example, there is usually little hesitation about relocating the baptismal font or even removing it completely from congregational view. Such cavalier treatment of the baptismal font causes it to lose its symbolic value and gives the impression that it is a piece of furniture of no more significance than a folding chair. Since fonts are frequently not too large, some have questioned whether smallness in itself has diminished the effectiveness of the font as a theological symbol. Symbols, admittedly, do not have to be large to be meaningful, but when the font of regeneration joins an imposing pulpit and altar for a symbolic message, the font's design should be such that it assures that the liturgical place and symbol for baptism does not fade into the woodwork.

Fonts have not always had casual treatment. Larger and more elaborate fonts have been used in the past, and in some periods of history fonts were located in separate baptisteries. Contemporary suggestions for giving more visible testimony to the importance of Baptism as Christianity's entrance rite have included several ideas—for example, that the font be placed at the entrance to the nave so that worshipers have a striking reminder of baptism when they enter and leave the worship setting. The placement is not new, having been employed already in medieval times. The arrangement, however, is not without some problems. First, pews must be very carefully arranged so that the assembly may comfortably turn to witness the baptisms. Secondly, the congregation loses the advantage, when gathered for worship, of having all three major pieces of liturgical furniture in view simultaneously.

Another proposal is to construct large-scale basins that hold water permanently. Fonts of this type may stand quite alone at either the front or the back of the church and by their separateness be readily identified as the place for Baptism. Some have even suggested that a larger receptacle of water for baptismal use could double as a decorative fountain within the building. One questions, however, whether that makes an effective statement about Baptism. Decorative fountains abound in buildings of all sorts. To have a baptismal font that blends into the general decor makes the font a rather empty symbol. Modern proposals to improve and enhance the significance of baptismal fonts in Lutheran churches deserve attention but need to be examined with a critical eye to make sure that suggested changes in design or placement are genuine improvements and not just passing fads.

Options on matters of this sort will vary, but there should really be no argument about the importance of the baptismal font in the Lutheran worship setting. Baptism unites us with Christ, as Paul says in Gal. 3:27. It is a means of grace, for it is the washing of regeneration and renewal in the Holy Spirit (Titus 3:5). This suggests that the baptismal font and baptismal space in churches should be prominent, adequate, and clearly defined. It is consistent with Lutheran theology to have the baptismal font join altar and pulpit as an architectural focal point inside a Lutheran church.

Appropriate Liturgical Adornments

The use of altar, pulpit, and baptismal font as places from which to perform actions is taken for granted. The pastor preaches in the pulpit, prays, speaks, and serves the Lord's Supper from the altar, and performs baptisms at the font. Because of what is done from or at these liturgical centers, they also take on symbolic significance. The symbolic functions are not always served as well as they might be because of some imprudent additions that occasionally make their way into chancels or the general areas occupied by pulpit, font, and altar. Restraint should be exercised so that these permanent liturgical furnishings not lose their symbolic value. They are powerful testimonies in and of themselves and should not be over-shadowed by a variety of decorations or religious art that may have more appropriate usage elsewhere in the building.

Since no one comes to the Father except through the Son (John 14:6) and since the Supper is that of the crucified and risen Christ, all would agree that it is fitting to invest Christian altar areas with clearly visible symbols of Christ. A cross or crucifix is certainly a suitable appointment for an altar. Stained-glass windows do not have to be absent from a chancel area either, although examples exist in which too much was done, making it difficult not only for worshipers to look toward the liturgical focal points in the church but also causing those very centers to be lost in their backgrounds. A reredos, dossal, or gradine on wall altars have provided natural space for statuary, crosses, crucifixes, and paintings, although it is salutary again to remember that altar, pulpit, and font areas are not religious art galleries. Freestanding altars do not accommodate the same kinds of appointments that may be added tastefully to wall altars, but the freestanding altar and the surrounding area can be appropriately highlighted by appointments and symbols that bear testimony to the centrality of Christ in Lutheran worship. Both kinds of altars and the pulpit lend themselves well to the use of para-ments, for example, which with their liturgical colors and art work seek to relate the proclamation of the Christian Gospel to the eye and so mark the regular rhythm of the church's year. Such visual communicators make a positive contribution to the message of the altar and the pulpit. Candlesticks, candelabra, and a paschal candle are dignified and symbolically meaningful for a liturgical center. The amount of available space determines how much may be included, with simplicity rather than ornateness being the rule to follow when striving to enhance the symbolic function of pulpit, altar, and font.

The practice of placing flowers on or in the altar area of Lutheran churches has been common and need not be condemned. Cut flowers and plants in churches are symbols of God's creation, carved representations of which were also included in the art work of Solomon's temple (1 Kings 6:29–36). Christ himself testified to the beauty of natural creation when he invited his hearers to consider the flowers and plants of the field and to observe that "even Solomon in all his glory was not arrayed like one of these" (Matt.

6:29 RSV). With their freshness and beauty, flowers and plants suggest the life that God gives; they create a quiet but uplifting spirit of joy and confidence. It is not inappropriate to place such creations from the finger of God in churches.

This does not mean, however, that anything goes. The beauty of the house of the Lord is God's saving message in Christ Jesus communicated in Word and Sacrament. The permanent liturgical furnishings of altar, pulpit, and baptismal font direct our attention to this beauty. Flowers and plants should by their size or quantity neither detract from the symbolic function of the central furnishings nor interfere with the free use of them. The altar and baptismal font are not floral display stands, and clutter is surely out of place. The advice, "It is better to err on the side of simplicity than to overdecorate"[27] is sound. Altar, pulpit, and baptismal font areas that look the same week after week, except for those meaningful changes in the color of paraments proper to the church year, make a statement about the centrality of the Gospel of Jesus Christ in public worship and about the church's determination always to proclaim him who "is the same yesterday and today and forever" (Heb. 13:8). Flowers and plants placed in full view of a worshiping congregation should be but gentle accents to the unchanging message of the chancel. The penchant to decorate must be discouraged in order to preserve the effectiveness of altar, pulpit, and baptismal font as gospel-centered symbols.

Flags and Banners

To maintain the integrity of the major symbols in a church building other things should not be placed in the vicinity of altars, pulpits, and fonts that draw attention away from them or diminish their symbolic impact. Flags and banners, for example, are adornments that should be located with care because they interfere with the symbolic functions of the liturgical furnishings. National flags, denominational flags, or the Christian flag do not belong in the vicinity of altar, pulpit, and font. The latter, as one writer has put it, "all point to Christ."[28] National flags, on the other hand, "speak not of Christ, but of the nation."[29] "The Christian loves his country, not only for its bounty, but also for the freedom it has given him to worship

213

God."[30] But to place a national flag "with the means of grace, Word, and Sacraments, is to invite confusion."[31] A national flag is an appropriate symbol in a building, but the flag does symbolize something quite different from what liturgical furnishings symbolize. The flag, by its very nature, intends to draw attention to itself. If it is placed in the vicinity of the liturgical furnishings, it is bound to diminish the theological impact which they are intended to make.

Although one might argue that the Christian flag has as its purpose to direct worshipers to Christ, it is worthy of note that since the Christian flag is of rather recent origin, it lacks catholicity and is more of a rallying symbol than a communicator of what God has done for us in Christ. The main liturgical furnishings with their long-standing and well-ingrained universal traditions point more directly to the divinely ordained means of grace, are more powerful symbols than the Christian flag, and should thus not have attention diverted away from themselves.

Much of what has been said about national flags and the Christian flag applies to denominational flags as well. Denominational awareness is not unimportant, and worshipers deserve to know what kind of church they have entered. That information is best communicated outside the church building. When, however, it is communicated inside, this should not be done in the vicinity of the chancel, for if there is one place where the church should emphasize that there is "one Lord, one faith, one baptism" (Eph. 4:5 RSV), it is there where the liturgical symbols direct our attention to Christ, his Word, and his sacraments. We often are deeply indebted to the Christian denomination that schooled us in the faith, but we would not want that gratitude to develop into a denominational loyalty that blurs the doctrine of the Holy Christian Church. For that reason, denominational flags, too, do not belong in full view of the worshiping congregation.

Altar, font, pulpit, and lectern, if it is used, should be the focal point of a worship center. While flags, of whatever kind, are not inappropriate in church buildings, they should not be placed in positions that make them adornments to the major liturgical furnishings, or that suggest that they have a symbolic value of equal importance with that of altar, pulpit, and font, or that cause them to become competitors with the liturgical furnishings for the attention of worshipers. Fellowship halls, classrooms, or entrances that have been designed to include space for effective display are better places for flags. Flags deserve proper treatment, too; they should not be set on stands just anywhere so as to satisfy some kind of feeling of obligation that this or that kind of flag must be on the church premises. The symbolic function of flags in churches is different from that of pulpit, altar, and font. The differences inherent in these two types of symbols require that the two not be given common locations but be separated from each other. In that way each is able to serve its purpose more effectively.

While banners of various kinds serve purposes different from that of flags, they should be located in church buildings according to some of the same principles that guide flag placement. The chancel area, therefore, is not the best place for banners. The reason becomes obvious when one considers that banners by their very nature are intended to draw special attention to themselves. They are to be striking and prominent within their appointed settings. If banners are hung or placed on stands too close to altar, pulpit, or font, the symbolic impact of the latter will be significantly reduced. In fact, even when a banner is used for only a very specific occasion or limited period of time, such as for a congregation's anniversary, the banner should not be placed so as to supersede the symbolic function of the major liturgical furnishings. To let banners do that is to alter what should always be the focal point of attention in a Christian church.

Banners, of course, serve a variety of purposes. Some, as has just been mentioned, highlight local events. Others bear a biblical message appropriate for a particular time of year or for worship generally. Some rather quietly mark the rhythmic changes of the liturgical calendar and complement the message of the liturgical paraments. In any case, however, banners are not to be the focal center in Christian worship. This means that they are to be placed out of the vicinity of the altar, lectern, pulpit, or font. The latter are not in need of excessive supplemental adornments. Banners become that when placed near the major furnishings. For that reason, banners should have noncentral positions. Side walls and entrances are good locations for this kind of art work. In fact, such placement will make them more effective communicators, since the worshiping community will be discriminatingly surrounded rather than bombarded by the visual messages in the church building.

Acoustics to Assist Pastor, Musician, and Congregation

What we see in a Lutheran church is not inconsequential but does take a secondary position to what we hear, since oral proclamation is at the heart and core of Lutheran worship. This means that acoustics in a worship center are deserving of the most expert attention that modern technology can supply. Engineers and preachers both do well to remember that there is little point in coming to church if what is said cannot be heard. In addition, it is easier to listen to a speaker if he can be seen. Differences in the design and size of ecclesiastical structures require individual treatment of each situation, and care should always be excercised so that, regardless of the shape or size of a building, worshipers need not strain to hear or see the preacher or ministers. The expertise of acoustical consultants should be sought, therefore, when buildings are constructed, remodeled, or renovated; and since sight contributes positively to listening, clear visibility of the place from which worship is led must be incorporated with good acoustical design.

Worship includes corporate speaking and singing. That can be more inspiring and encouraging if a building's acoustics make group singing sound rich and full to the individual who is participating with the congregation. Besides its vertical dimension, worship has a horizontal dimension. This suggests that the worship setting be designed to encourage the feeling of corporateness among the worshipers. If a worshiper, speaking or singing with the group, gets the feeling that he or she is doing a solo, something of the horizontal dimension is lost, and the worshiper will tend to participate less enthusiastically. If, on the other hand, the group singing and speaking well up in a mighty chorus, the experience then becomes one of genuine encouragement for all who have gathered to confess Christ. Skillful planning of acoustics can help make that possible.

Effective acoustics are important also for the instrument that accompanies the congregational singing of the Lutheran liturgy and hymns. Organs, pipe or electronic, are the usual accompaniment medium in Lutheran churches. Proper consideration has not always been given to the placement of the organ. In fact, the impression is sometimes given that adequate space for and location of the organ are secondary considerations in the design of a building. An electronic organ, since it utilizes speakers and requires less space than a pipe organ, can often be placed more easily than a pipe organ, although examples surely exist in which electronic speakers are set rather inartistically in places hardly designed to accommodate such speakers. It is better if space is planned for speakers at the time when the building is constructed.

The location of a pipe organ requires much more attention than an electronic instrument, for the pipes and their mechanism require more space and, when once installed, are not as movable as electronic instruments and speakers. If a pipe organ is to speak clearly, it should not be crowded into a corner or, what is worse, around a corner. The rear gallery of a church still remains one of the choicest locations for the pipes of an organ as well as for the console. Adequate and appropriate space should also be provided in the balcony for the choir and other instrumentalists so that they, too, can assume positions that contribute positively to good musical performance. In addition, acoustically reflective building materials on walls and ceilings will reinforce the sound of music and do much to enhance both choir and congregational song. It is amazing how powerful and effective an even relatively small pipe organ can be to accompany congregational singing and to provide independent liturgical music if that organ is placed in the rear balcony of an acoustically well-designed church building. In fact, a smaller organ reinforced by good acoustics can be more exciting than a larger instrument without that advantage. Since such is the case, providing proper space for an organ should never be an afterthought but an integral part of the total design of a church.

It has been argued from time to time that the organ and choir should be located in the front of the church so that the assembly can see the musicians as they add their contributions to corporate worship. One can understand that argument for a concert of sacred music in the church. However, the ordinary use of organ, choir, and other instruments in worship is not concert performance, but the means for supporting and amplifying congregational worship as meaningfully and unobtrusively as possible. An organist at a console in easy view of a worshiping assembly can draw attention to himseslf or herself. Some shuffling of music is unavoidable; some movement is necessary for performance. The same is the case with a choir, vocal soloists, or other instrumentalists. A location in the back of the church is, therefore, the most suitable place for the musicians who lead a congregation in worship. Since pipe organs can also be designed to be impressive visual works of art, their location in rear balconies is capable of leaving departing worshipers with a significant message. The exhortation of the psalmist, well symbolized by a rear gallery organ, is particularly fitting for those who have met Christ in worship:

> O sing to the Lord a new song,
> for He has done marvelous things!
> Sing praises to the Lord with the lyre,
> with the lyre and the sound of melody!
> With trumpets and the sound of the horn
> make a joyful noise before the King, the Lord!

(Ps. 98:1a, 5–6 RSV)

Summary

Obedient to the Lord's command and following the clear example of apostolic Christianity, Lutherans assemble regularly for worship. Consistent with their Reformation heritage, Lutherans are not content narrowly to define worship as an activity in which baptized believers gather only to express reverence to God in prayer, praise, and thanksgiving. Lutheran churches recognize that the objective proclamation of God's grace in Christ Jesus must be the starting point and center of true worship. Word and Sacrament are central, therefore, in Lutheran worship. Through these means of grace the Holy Spirit works to create and sustain faith and to effect in those who have assembled in the name of Jesus a confidence to come to the Almighty in prayer and to thank and praise him in his Son. Lutheran worship is trinitarian, christological, and biblically based. It is a balanced pattern of activities in which believers join with each other to hear God speak and to speak to him. The coming together is a public confession of faith and an occasion for encouraging one another in the faith.

Lutheran worship is not entertainment. It is a serious encounter with God that deserves a setting designed to invite and encourage hope, joy, and a spirit of genuine devotion. The place where believers gather for worship must be able to accommodate the physical needs of the assembly as well as assist the individual worshiper to concentrate on things spiritual. The place of worship should, to the extent that available resources make it possible, be a sanctuary where the spirit of reverence prevails and where nothing of what is seen or done detracts from that spirit of reverence. Although the ultimate quality of corporate worship is not determined by the room in which the assembly meets, well-appointed worship space helps thoughtful worshipers reflect and say, "We have been in the house of God today."

THE LEADERS OF WORSHIP

John T. Pless

Vestments for Ministers

The use of ceremonial vestments in Christian worship is derived neither from prescribed dress of the Old Testament priesthood (see Exod. 28:1–43, for example) nor from the ritual garments of the Greek mystery religions.[32] Rather, liturgical vestments developed out of ordinary civilian dress of the late Roman empire. Between the fourth and ninth centuries these items of clothing became ecclesiastical garments invested with specific liturgical meaning.

Liturgical attire developed from two basic types of Roman clothing: an indoor tunic and an outdoor cloak. The indoor tunic survived as the alb, while the outdoor cloak became the chasuble, and, eventually, the cope. In addition to these two basic forms, other accessories such as the amice, cincture, maniple, and stole were maintained in churchly usage long after they had become archaic as items of dress. Only after the clothing of Roman antiquity was in regular use in the church's liturgy was theological meaning assigned to the various garments. More often than not, this meaning was derived allegorically, a trend that can be seen in the many prayers that were prescribed to be prayed while the priest was vesting. Some of this symbolism has survived to this day as indicated by a sacristy prayer from the Church of Sweden:

> Take from me, O Lord, the old man and his sinful ways and clothe me with the new man in holiness and righteousness and truth. . . . O Lord, who saidst "my yoke is easy and my burden light": make me so to bear it that I may attain unto thy grace. . . . Gird me, O Lord, with the truth and make my way blameless. . . . Clothe me, O Lord, as thy chosen one with hearty mercy, goodness, humility, meakness and patience.[33]

The most basic liturgical vestment is the alb. Originally the alb (*tunica alba*) existed in both short and long forms. The short form was something like a knee-length shirt (*chitron*), while the long form (*chitron poderes*, see Rev. 1:13) was a garment of ankle length. This long white tunic was typically worn as standard dress of professional people in the Roman empire. Around the beginning of the fifth century it became a specifically Christian vestment. Like its secular antecedents, the alb used by the clergy was sometimes decorated with stripes of colored material placed over the seams.

The alb itself was collarless. A piece of cloth, known as an amice (Latin *amictus* from *amicio*, meaning "to wrap around"), was placed around the neck as a collar to protect the alb from sweat. The amice became a regular part of eucharistic vesture by the eighth century. Allegorically, it was interpreted as "the helmet of salvation" (Eph. 6:17).

The *tunica alba* of classical times was held in place by a girdle made of cloth or by a cincture. This girdle or cincture was a utilitarian device which, with the alb, was eventually adopted for ecclesiastical use. In medieval times the girdle was said to symbolize clerical chastity as well as spiritual vigilance (Luke 12:35–38).

The maniple was originally a handkerchief that served as an emblem of office for the Roman consul. Since clothing from this period lacked pockets, the maniple was carried in the hand. By the sixth century, the maniple was in use as a liturgical vestment attached to the priest's left forearm. It was used as a towel to clean the priest's hands as well as the communion vessels.

Like the maniple, the stole was most likely a type of handkerchief used as an ensign of rank among Roman officials. Under Roman law (Codex Theodosian in the late fourth century), senators and consuls were directed to wear a colored scarf over the alb as a badge of office. Gilbert Cope suggests that the stole was adopted as an insignia of office for the clergy.[34]

As the alb was the indoor tunic in the Roman empire, so the chasuble was the outdoor cloak. The chasuble (from the Latin *casula*, "little house") was a poncho-shaped garment with a slit for the head. The garment was used in the Graeco-Roman world by all social classes and both sexes. This is the garment mentioned by the apostle Paul in 2 Tim. 4:13, where he requests that Timothy bring along his cloak (*phailones*). This outer garment became the primary eucharistic vestment in both the East and the West. Other Roman garments adapted for churchly usage would include the cope (an outdoor cloak) and the dalmatic and tunicle (variants of the *tunica alba*).

The surplice is actually a variant form of the alb. Piepkorn writes that the surplice differed from the alb "in design because it was made to go over (*super*) fur-clothing (*pelliceae*, from *pellis*)—hence the Latin name *superpelliceum*."[35] Unlike the alb, the surplice had a wider opening for the head and fuller sleeves. By the 11th century the surplice was used for non-eucharistic offices while the alb was reserved for use at the Mass.

As the Middle Ages progressed, ecclesiastical vestments became more elaborate in design and reflective of the wealth and prestige of the clergy. The question of vestments had to be faced by the Reformers. The Anabaptists and the Reformed rejected vestments as detestable reminders of the papal church. For Luther, vestments belonged within the realm of Christian liberty. In his *Formula Missae* of 1523 he commented, "We permit them [vestments] to be used in freedom, as long as people refrain from ostentation and pomp.

For you are not more acceptable for consecrating in vestments. Nor are you less acceptable for consecrating without them."[36] Luther's colleague and pastor, Johannes Bugenhagen, expressed a similar view in a letter written to a certain M. Goerlitz on September 30, 1530: "There is a twofold doctrine on chasubles . . . one is the truth, namely that chasubles can be used; this does not give scandal to those who are accustomed to hearing the Gospel. The other is a Satanic lie out of the doctrines of the devils, namely, that it is never lawful to use chasubles; this gives scandal to the people where they hear and believe such lies from the ministers."[37] Article XXIV of the Apology states that the Church of the Augsburg Confession has not abolished the Mass but celebrates it every Sunday and on other festivals and maintains "traditional liturgical forms, such as the order of lessons, prayers, vestments, etc."[38] The research of Günther Stiller[39] and Arthur Carl Piepkorn[40] demonstrates that the historic vestments (alb, chasuble, and stole) continued to be used in many places within the Lutheran Church well into the 18th century. For the most part these vestments were rejected by the proponents of Calvinism, Pietism, and Rationalism.[41] It was under these alien influences that the black gown of the academy entered into liturgical usage in the Lutheran Church.

The use of vestments in American Lutheranism varied widely. Some Scandinavian immigrant churches used full eucharistic vestments for many years. Other immigrant groups used the black gown or no vestments at all. Piepkorn notes, "In 1839, while waiting to move to Perry County, the clergymen of the Saxon Lutheran immigrant party ministered at the Lutheran Services held in Christ Church Cathedral (Protestant Episcopal), St. Louis, in albs. . . . Prior to their departure from Germany, the Saxon immigrants supplied themselves with sketches from Roman Catholic vestments used in Dresden."[42] The combination of cassock, surplice, and stole as standard clerical vestments for American Lutheran clergymen is a 20th-century development which was encouraged by Luther Reed[43] and others with a taste for things Anglican.

The Lutheran Church—Missouri Synod has wisely sought to follow the directive of Article XXIV of the Apology that vestments are retained in the church's liturgy. The continued use of vestments in the Church of the Augsburg Confession is important for at least two reasons: First, vestments are used as ensigns of the office of the holy ministry. These liturgical garments cover the man, reminding the congregation that their pastor speaks to them not simply as a fellow Christian, but as "a called and ordained servant of the Word." The vestments are clothes of a servant. In this sense we may agree with Frank Senn that "vestments are a liturgical language."[44] Secondly, vestments are a visual reminder of the continuity of the church's worship throughout history. Grisbrooke writes, "An essential element in the nature of Christian worship is its witness to the unchanging and abiding value and power of God's mighty works in Christ, and it follows that the vestments should reflect the continuity of Christian worship, rather than the discontinuities which at times have afflicted it."[45] The use of the historic vestments signals our linkage with the church catholic in confession and life. Thus in the Evangelical Lutheran Church vestments are not merely aesthetic decorations, but are symbols of the historic continuity of our church with prophets, apostles, martyrs, and confessors of all times and places.

The Notes on the Liturgy in *Lutheran Worship: Altar Book* do not legislate liturgical vesture. Suggestions are made, however, for the use of vestments appropriate to the particular service. Historically, there are two forms of vestments: eucharistic vestments and non-eucharistic vestments. For the Divine Service it is appropriate that the pastor be vested in an alb and a stole in the liturgical color of the season. The Notes on the Liturgy state that the presiding minister "may wear a chasuble over the alb and stole at the Holy Communion."[46] Like the stole, the color of the chasuble is dictated by the liturgical color of the day or season. Like the stole, the chasuble is an emblem of the office of the holy ministry. Under no circumstances is either the stole or the chasuble to be worn by non-ordained assisting ministers. The chasuble is never worn at non-eucharistic services.

While the alb, stole, and chasuble are the primary eucharistic vestments of the Church of the Augsburg Confession, the cassock and surplice are the standard vestments for non-eucharistic services. The cassock was originally used as an ankle-length coat for daily use by the clergy. It appears to have come into common usage among priests in the West in the sixth century. The surplice or alb would be worn over the cassock. In this sense, the cassock is the forerunner of the contemporary clerical shirt. Since the 11th century the surplice has been associated with non-eucharistic services, while the alb has been associated with the Eucharist. Like the alb, the surplice should extend to the ankles.

For the daily prayer services (without sermon) the cassock and surplice are used without the stole. When the service includes a sermon or other specific pastoral acts (Baptism), the stole is worn. Cassock, surplice, and stole are appropriate for services of marriage, burial, installation, and ordination, as well as for individual confession and absolution. The Notes on the Liturgy make provision for the use of a "cope, the historic vestment for daily prayer services."[47]

While the use of a stole and chasuble is reserved for ordained clergymen, lay people who assist in the service may properly be vested in alb or surplice. If the pastor wears an alb, lay assistants would properly be vested in albs. If the pastor wears a surplice, lay assistants would wear surplices. The cope may be worn by lay people as well as clergymen.

The Ceremonies of the Liturgy

While the word *rite* (or ritual) refers to the texts of the liturgy, *ceremony* refers to the actions of the liturgy that accompany the texts. A variety of ceremonies may legitimately exist in the Church of the Augsburg Confession. Article VII of that Confession states, "It is not necessary for the true unity of the Christian church that ceremonies, instituted by men, should be observed uniformly in all places."[48] Likewise, Article X of the Formula of Concord Solid Declaration maintains that

> churches will not condemn each other because of a difference in ceremonies, when in Christian liberty one uses fewer or more of them, as long as they are otherwise agreed in doctrine and in all its articles and are agreed concerning the right use of the holy sacraments, according to the well-known axiom, "Disagreement in fasting should not destroy agreement in faith."[49]

Even though ceremonies may differ from one historic period to another, and from one locale to another, ceremonies may never be completely discarded. Commenting on this, Werner Elert writes,

No matter how strongly he [Luther] emphasizes Christian freedom in connection with the form of this rite [the Sacrament of
the Altar], no matter how much he deviates from the form handed
down at the end of the Middle Ages, no matter how earnestly he
warns against the belief that external customs could commend us
to God, still there are certain ceremonial elements that he, too,
regards as indispensable.[50]

Since there is no such thing as an "informal" service, that is, a
service without form, the question of ceremonies can be ignored
only to the detriment of the pure preaching of the Gospel and the
right administration of the blessed sacraments. Thus, many of the
ceremonies of the ancient church were purified of superstition and
retained in the Lutheran Church. Article XXIV of the Apology confesses:

To begin with, we must repeat the prefatory statement that we
do not abolish the Mass but religiously keep and defend it. In
our churches Mass is celebrated every Sunday and on other festivals, when the sacrament is offered to those who wish for it after
they have been examined and absolved. We keep traditional liturgical forms, such as the order of the lessons, prayers, vestments,
etc.[51]

This proper use of ceremony is evident in Luther's instructions
regarding prayer in the Small Catechism. Here Luther directs the
head of the family to teach those in his household to use such customs as the sign of the holy cross, kneeling, standing, and the folding of hands.[52]

What, then, is the purpose of ceremonies in the liturgy of the
Evangelical Lutheran Church? Ceremonies necessarily exist to teach
the faith.[53] As the true worship of the triune God is always anchored
in the Christian's fear, love, and trust in this one God above all
things, so proper ceremonies have a didactic function in the Christian congregation. This is the intention of Article XXIV of the Apology: "The purpose of observing ceremonies is that men may learn
the Scriptures and that those who have been touched by the Word
may receive faith and fear and so may also pray."[54]

Although the function of ceremonies is never less than pedagogical, ceremonies are more than visual aids to faith. Since worship

in the name of Jesus is never without form or structure, ceremonies serve to maintain good order in the worshiping congregation.

> We gladly keep the old traditions set up in the church because they are useful and promote tranquility, and we interpret them in an evangelical way, excluding the opinion which holds that they justify. Our enemies falsely accuse us of abolishing good ordinances and church discipline. We can truthfully claim that in our churches the public liturgy is more decent than in theirs, and if you look at it correctly we are more faithful to the canons than our opponents are.[55]

As God is not a God of chaos and confusion (1 Cor. 14:33), so his divine service to the congregation is both ordered and orderly. Evangelical ceremonies reflect this order as they point to the gracious gifts of forgiveness, life, and salvation which our Lord bestows through Word and Sacrament. Even as these ceremonies point to the giver and donor, they also assist the recipient to embrace the gift in faith and reverence.

The ceremonies of the liturgy will be reflective of the church's confession of faith. Ceremonies may indeed be vehicles for the confession or denial of scriptural truths. One need only recall the so-called Adiaphoristic Controversy,[56] occasioned by the adoption of the Augsburg and Leipzig Interims of 1548, which led to the formulation of Article X of the Formula of Concord. Under the circumstances of persecution, indifferent ceremonies become a matter of confession. When the Prussian Union was consummated on Reformation Day 1817 in the Garrison Church at Potsdam, it was the ceremonial action of the fraction (breaking of the bread) that was used in effect to renounce the clear teaching of the Lutheran Confessions regarding the presence of the body and blood of Christ in the Holy Supper.

Although ceremonies are not part of the Divine Service per se,[57] they nevertheless bear witness to what the congregation actually believes regarding the means of grace. The posture and movement of the congregation during the service (i.e., standing for the reading of the Holy Gospel, or kneeling for the reception of the Lord's body and blood), the manner in which the remaining consecrated elements are treated after the Communion, and the custom of reverencing the altar are examples of ceremonies that point to the congregation's confessional position.

Some ceremonies are bound to exist in even the most "non-liturgical" congregations. Even the so-called free churches have developed ceremonies that may not be rejected or altered. The ceremonial form of Holy Baptism (i.e., immersion) is quite firmly fixed in the Baptist churches, for example. The question is never, Will there be ceremony? But rather, How are ceremonies to be evaluated in the church?

Obviously the *sola scriptura* principle eliminates the ceremonies that are in conflict with the teachings of the prophetic and apostolic scriptures. Yet, this does not lead to the reductionistic approach of the Reformed party, which purges the church of all ceremonies not explicitly commanded in Holy Scripture. Friedrich Kalb writes,

> Rites running counter to the Word of God must be abolished. . . . To judge ceremonies by this standard is not altogether easy, to be sure. The critical principle becomes operative only after a violation. As long as ceremonies are as they should be, they are in a sphere that does not trouble faith. The Reformed Church made the task easier. It also knows of the one criterion for the scripturalness of the ceremonies, viz., that they can be traced back directly to Christ. It does not recognize a province outside of the ceremonies instituted by Christ that nevertheless does not contradict the Word of God. Thus there can be no indifferent ceremonies. Yet it is in the nature of these ceremonies "not to be instituted by Christ"; for otherwise they would indeed be required of us.[58]

The Lutheran Confessions do not understand the Holy Scriptures to be a handbook of ceremonial rules and regulations (see Col. 2:16–17). Even directives given by the apostles to specific congregations (such as the practice of women covering their heads in the church services) are not binding according to the Confessions.[59] Therefore, ceremonies are not to be evaluated by citing a biblical text that determines whether or not a particular ceremony was practiced in New Testament times. Rather, ceremonies are to be judged in relationship to the Gospel of justification by grace through faith for Jesus' sake. Ceremonies that contradict or obscure this doctrine are not to be tolerated in the church.[60] Thus the Lutheran Confessions understand the key criterion for the use of ceremonies to be a doctrinal criterion and not an aesthetic principle.

Ceremonies must be viewed in light of their integral relationship to the doctrine of worship (*Gottesdienst*). This immediately exposes the conflict that exists between the theology of worship held by Luther and confessed in the Lutheran Confessions and that theology articulated by the many adherents of the contemporary Liturgical Movement.[61] A number of voices within the recent history of American Lutheranism have called for a liturgical theology that not only supersedes the position of Luther and the Lutheran Confessions but stands in contradiction to them. While the Lutheran Confessions take great pains to distinguish man's actions from God's action in the liturgy,[62] a key spokesman for contemporary liturgical scholarship within American Lutheranism writes,

> Liturgical renewal among Lutherans shares goals similar to those of other communions: restoration of significant practices of mainstream Western Catholicism, expressing the interrelation of worship and mission, recovering the spirit of joy and celebration in the eucharist, *grasping the mystery that God's work and man's work are indistinguishable* [emphasis added].[63]

This seems to have ritual expression in the *Lutheran Book of Worship* where, in the Sacrament of the Altar, the Words of Institution become part of the prayers of the gathered congregation. The actions of the congregation cannot be easily distinguished from the testamental Word of the Lord who is himself host at this supper. The Lutheran emphasis on the receptivity of faith is masked by the action of the believer as the presiding minister prays, "Therefore, gracious Father, with this bread and cup we remember the life our Lord offered for us."[64]

Having a premise that the liturgy is the church's action, the formulators of the *Lutheran Book of Worship*, not surprisingly, reinstituted two ceremonies specifically rejected by Luther and the Lutheran Confessions: an offertory procession[65] where the bread and wine are ritually offered at the altar, and a Prayer of Great Thanksgiving[66] which incorporates the Verba. Luther insisted that the sacrament be distinguished from the prayers of the liturgy:

> We must therefore sharply distinguish the testament and sacrament itself from the prayers which we offer at the same time. Not only this, but we must also bear in mind that the prayers avail utterly nothing, either to him who offers them or to those for

228

whom they are offered, unless the testament is first received in faith, so that it will be faith that offers the prayers; for faith alone is heard, as James teaches in his first chapter (James 1:6). There is therefore a great difference between prayer and the mass. Prayer may be extended to as many persons as one desires, while the mass is received only by the person who believes for himself, and only to the extent that he believes. It cannot be given either to God or to men. Rather it is God alone who through the ministration of the priest gives it to men, and men receive it by faith alone without any works or merits. Nor would anyone dare to be so foolish as to assert that a ragged beggar does a good work when he comes to receive a gift from a rich man. But the mass (as I have said) is the gift of divine promise, proffered to all men by the hand of the priest.[67]

The church's liturgical practice should not obscure the gift character of God's Word and sacraments. These are not the pious actions of men, but the very gifts of God that give and bestow the forgiveness won at Calvary. Thus confessional Lutherans will reject the anthropological understanding of ceremonial that sees the liturgy as a ritual reenactment, representation, or remembrance of "salvation history." Jesus Christ is our servant and liturgist in the Divine Service as he bestows the fruits of his death and resurrection by means of Word and Sacrament. Faith, not participation in ritual action, is the key to a proper understanding of the place of ceremonies in the liturgy. Ceremonies serve the rite (i.e., the liturgical texts)[68] in tutoring the worshiper in a faith that is reverent and receptive in the presence of the Lord, who is in the midst of the congregation as its servant.

The Language of the Liturgy

Without the Word of God there can be no worship of God. Faith is created through the hearing of the Word of Christ (Rom. 10:17) and not by the liturgical activity of the congregation. The language of the liturgy thus serves the *evangel* of our Lord by keeping the worship of the church securely grounded in "the pattern of sound words" so that the faith-creating Gospel may indeed be heard in all of its divine fullness and that God's people may respond to him in song

and prayer using the words God himself has given in the Holy
Scriptures.

Olof Herrlin has stated, "The liturgy of the church, like its
preaching, is the assertion of Scripture as God's Word."[69] If the
liturgy is the divine service of God to the congregation, the primary question does not have to do with the debate over *traditional*
or *contemporary* language. Rather, the crucial question must always
be, "Is the grammar of *sola gratia* preserved in the language of the
worshiping congregation?" Important as the question concerning
vernacular language in public worship is, it can never take priority
over the question of the content. Luther was willing to allow the
Mass to be conducted in Latin until such a time as the people might
be prepared to hear the service in their native tongue. He was
unwilling to allow unevangelical texts to remain in the liturgy even
for a short time.

The heart of the evangelical liturgy is the Gospel itself. The
words of men are distinguished from the Word of the living God.
Bonhoeffer has commented that "the richness of the Word of God
ought to determine our prayer, not the poverty of our heart."[70] The
same must be said for worship. It is the richness of God's Word
and not the poverty of the human heart that must determine our
worship. If the language of worship is measured by the standards of
human sincerity, creativity, or piety rather than the canon of *sola
gratia*, the congregation is threatened by bondage to subjectivism
and works righteousness. Thus Kenneth Korby writes on the utter
and absolute necessity of making the distinction between the Word
of God and the word of man:

> Prayer that is this kind of conversation must distinguish between
> God's Word and man's word. To confuse those words mistakes
> the desires, longings, and aspiration of religion's "I" with the Word
> of God. Such confusion leads to an acoustical illusion: what we
> hear is the echo of our own utterances. What happens, for exam-
> ple, to the great emphasis that Holy Communion, Eucharist, is
> our prayer and offering to God? We may be only victims of impre-
> cise language. If the entire worship service, in which the Lord's
> Body and Blood are received, is meant, that service includes
> proclamation, the word of forgiveness of sins, as well as praise,
> thanksgiving, prayer and intercession. But what of the heart of that
> service, the words of our Lord's final will and testament, the heart

of the Good News, where our living Lord gives us his very Body and Blood for the forgiveness of sins? Is that the word of the faithful to God? Real confusion has been inserted if the cry of the faithful to the Lord cannot be distinguished from the faithful promises of the Lord to us. Our prayer life is in trouble if we cannot make that distinction.[71]

The language of the liturgy must make a careful and clear distinction between God's words of promise and testament and man's words of thanksgiving and praise. When man's *sacrificium* and God's *beneficium* are confused, the Gospel is transformed into law and faith into a work. It was for this reason that Luther insisted that the Words of Institution be chanted or read audibly to the congregation as Christ's own proclamation, not as a prayer of thanksgiving to God. Luther's insistence on this use of the Verba was a deliberate theological move that was firmly rooted in the doctrine of justification and not a bungled piece of liturgical surgery.[72] In Divine Service I and Divine Service II in *Lutheran Worship*, Christ's Words of Institution stand separate from prayer so that there may be no confusion as to who is speaker and who is auditor.

Four general principles shape the use of language in the liturgy. The first is the doctrinal principle. The language of worship is the language of confession. The congregation's worship must be a *homologeo*, a "speaking of the same thing" with the God who has spoken to us in his Word. Sasse notes that it is characteristic of "the confession of faith that it belongs in the liturgy, in the divine service, in which the church appears as the hearing, praying, and confessing congregation."[73] It is in the divine service that the believer listens to the very speech of God who through his Word is active to vivify and bless. Thus language, no matter how artful or sincere, if it falsifies or obscures God's speaking, transforms the divine service into a human service where God is not glorified, nor his people edified, regardless of the number of times his name is mentioned. The second of the Ten Commandments and the second petition of the Our Father are the touchstones for evaluating liturgical language.

"The language of a people is its fate," says Amos Wilder.[74] So it is with the liturgical language of the church. Changes in the language of worship can and do affect changes in dogma. The shift to so-called nonsexist language in the liturgies of many English-speaking Christians is a case in point. What may be at stake in these sometimes subtle changes is not merely the adoption of a more modern text, but a changed doctrine of the very person and work of God.

A second principle is faithfulness to the original texts. "The liturgy, like the Bible, has a language of its own."[75] Failure to understand the nature of liturgical language has resulted in a number of translations (or, actually, paraphrases) of ancient liturgical texts that are flawed from both a theological and literary perspective.[76] Some liturgical language cannot escape being archaic, since the liturgy is itself rooted in God's revelation of himself within a particular history. Certain words in both the Bible and liturgy remain untranslatable. Words such as *amen, hosanna, gloria,* and *kyrie* defy translation. Faithfulness to the original texts dictates that they remain untranslated, part of the church's song. The advice of Wilhelm Löhe is indeed sound:

> Yet we must beware of misusing our liturgical freedom to produce new liturgies. One should rather use the old forms and learn to understand and have a feeling for them before one feels oneself competent to create something new and better. He who has not tested the old cannot create something new. It is a shame when everybody presumes to form his own opinions about hymns and the liturgy without having thoroughly looked into the matter. Let a man first learn in silence and not act as if it were a matter of course that he understands everything! Once a man has first learned from the old he can profitably use the developments of recent times (in language and methods of speech) for the benefit of the liturgy.[77]

The third principle may be called the principle of perspicuity. Article XXIV of the Augsburg Confession echoes Luther's concern for liturgical orders in the language of the people: "Paul prescribed that in church a language should be used which is understood by the people"[78] (1 Cor. 14:2–9). As the liturgy serves the Word of God, it is to communicate that Word clearly into the ears of the hearers. The words of the liturgy carry with them the solid objectivity of the words of Scripture. This means that the liturgical texts are not the private property of the pastor or the congregation, to be mutilated by deletions and embellishments in attempts to make them "more meaningful and relevant." The Word of God carries with it God's own authority; it is not made relevant or authentic by human effort.

So the liturgical texts of the liturgy reflect the clarity of Scripture itself.

A final principle is the pastoral principle. A constant changing of texts is not advisable. Luther recognized this in his preface to the Small Catechism:

> In the first place, the preacher should take the utmost care to avoid changes or variations in the text and wording of the Ten Commandments, the Creed, the Lord's Prayer, the sacraments, etc. On the contrary, he should adopt one form, adhere to it, and use it repeatedly year after year. Young and inexperienced people must be instructed on the basis of a uniform, fixed text and form. They are easily confused if a teacher employs one form now and another form—perhaps with the intention of making improvements—later on. In this way all the time and labor will be lost.[79]

Luther was aware of the need for a common text to be consistently used in church, classroom, and home. If a multiplicity of texts is used, memorization becomes an impossible task, and the link between the liturgy and catechesis is severed.

On this point, there appears to be a potential problem with *Lutheran Worship* as texts of the International Consultation on English Texts (ICET), for instance, the preface dialog, the Lord's Prayer, "Glory to God in the highest," "Holy, holy, holy Lord," "Lamb of God," "Lord, now let your servant go in peace," "You are God, we praise you," and "My soul proclaims the greatness of the Lord," as well as texts (some updated) from *The Lutheran Hymnal* are used. Admittedly, in the light of numerous requests from congregations essentially to keep the texts of the Common Service, Matins, and Vespers contained in *The Lutheran Hymnal* and, on the other hand, to heed more numerous requests to incorporate the ICET texts from the *Lutheran Book of Worship*, the Commission on Worship undoubtedly felt constrained to honor both urgent requests. Doing so was not to deny the desideratum of keeping the variability of the congregation's parts to a minimum. It was perhaps opined that most congregations would choose the services with the new texts and tunes. Moreover, with desktop printing on the horizon, it was felt that the text(s) of choice could readily be reproduced for inclusion in the worship folder.

The rubrics of *Lutheran Worship* envision that the pastor will prepare the intercessions and thanksgivings to be included in the Prayer of the Church (Divine Service I) and The Prayers (Divine Service II). This task calls for a very thoughtful and careful use of language so that the prayers may fulfill the apostolic aim of 1 Tim. 2:1–4. The scope of the Prayer of the Church, or The Prayers, includes the whole church, the local congregation, those in need, and particular concerns dictated by local circumstances. The pastor will avoid using these prayers as an opportunity to instruct God or to make announcements to the congregation. Like the rest of the liturgy, the language of these petitions and thanksgivings should flow out of the Word of God. The petitions should be concise (Matt. 6:7–8) and constructed with the clarity that allows the congregation to add its *Amen* (1 Cor. 14:16).

Leadership in the Liturgy

"Our churches teach that nobody should preach publicly in the church or administer the sacraments unless he is regularly called." So reads Article XIV of the Augsburg Confession. The pastor is called and ordained to serve the Word and sacraments. The Apology states that the pastor serves as Christ's representative in the midst of the Christian congregation:

> For they do not represent their own persons but the person of Christ, because of the church's call, as Christ testifies (Luke 10:16), "He who hears you hears me." When they offer the Word of Christ or the sacraments, they do so in Christ's place and stead.[80]

On the basis of these confessional statements, only the called and ordained pastor is to serve as presiding minister in the Divine Service. Under no circumstances is this work to be assigned to one who is not ordained, even on a temporary basis.

The presiding minister is the servant of the Word (*minister verbi divini*). In the liturgy, his primary responsibilities are to speak the Lord's absolution, preach God's Law and Gospel in the sermon, and, as Christ's spokesman, speak the words of consecration. Since it is the pastor who exercises the Office of the Keys within the congregation, he is the one who distributes Christ's body in the Lord's Supper:

Since the administration of the Lord's body is the decisive act of admission to the Sacrament, the presiding minister, as the responsible minister of the Sacrament, distributes the body of the Lord. The assisting minister(s) may distribute the blood.[81]

According to the Lutheran Confessions, pastors have the responsibility to regulate the external ceremonies used in the public liturgy:

What are we to say, then, about Sunday and other similar church ordinances and ceremonies? To this our teachers reply that bishops or pastors may make regulations so that everything is done in good order, but not as a means of obtaining God's grace or making satisfaction for sins, nor in order to bind men's consciences by considering these things necessary services of God and counting it a sin to omit their observance even when this is done without offense. . . . It is proper of the Christian assembly to keep such ordinances for the sake of love and peace, to be obedient to the bishops and parish ministers in such matters, and to observe the regulations in such a way that one does not give offence to another and so that there may be no disorder or unbecoming conduct in the church.[82]

The rubrics of *Lutheran Worship* also make provisions for the use of an assisting minister. The Notes on the Liturgy explain the role of the assisting minister:

The liturgy is the celebration of all who gather. Together with the pastor who presides, the entire congregation is involved. It is appropriate, therefore, that where it is considered necessary or desirable or both, lay persons fulfill certain functions within the service.[83]

The rationale for using laymen[84] in this way is, in one sense, to restore the ancient office of deacon to the liturgy. The deacons of the New Testament period served as assistants to the bishops (1 Tim. 3:8–13) with primary responsibility for the care of the needy in the Christian community (Acts 6:1–7). There is no evidence before the second century to indicate that deacons had any specific liturgical responsibilities in the church.[85] As the office of deacon developed in post-New Testament times, several functions were attached to this office, including the reading of Scripture, certain prayers in the liturgy, and the distribution of the cup in the Holy

Communion. Thus, the office of deacon represented the link between the altar and the world. In *Lutheran Worship*, the role of the assisting minister is a continuation of this tradition.

Notes

1. Peter Brunner, *Worship in the Name of Jesus*, trans. M. H. Bertram (St. Louis: Concordia Publishing House, 1968), p. 17.

2. Ibid., p. 18.

3. In Brunner's native German the word for worship is *Gottesdienst*, that is, the service of God. The term for worship in German pictures worship as a two-way street, namely, God serving his people, and his people serving him.

4. Brunner, pp. 18–19.

5. FC Ep X, 2; this translation is from *Concordia Triglotta: Die symbolischen Bücher der evangelisch-lutherischen Kirche* (St. Louis: Concordia Publishing House, 1921), p. 829.

6. Ibid., X, 1.

7. Donald J. Bruggink and Carl H. Droppers, *Christ and Architecture* (Grand Rapids: William B. Eerdmans, 1965), p. 6.

8. E. A. Sovik, *Architecture for Worship* (Minneapolis: Augsburg Publishing House, 1973), p. 39.

9. Josef A. Jungmann, *The Mass* (Collegeville, MN: The Liturgical Press, 1976), pp. 143–145, 147–148.

10. Geoffry Webb, *The Liturgical Altar* (Westminster, MD.: The Newman Press, 1949), pp. 22–23.

11. J. B. O'Connell, *Church Building and Furnishing: The Church's Way* (Notre Dame: University of Notre Dame Press, 1955), pp. 23–24.

12. Judgment regarding the altar, as well as regarding other matters germane to the subject under discussion, are, since Vatican II, expressed in *Environment and Art in Catholic Worship*, the work of the United States Bishops' Committee on the Liturgy. Published in 1978, it is recognized as a landmark among the conciliar documents. See Mary Ann Simcoe, ed. *The Liturgy Documents: A Parish Resource*, rev. ed. (Chicago: Liturgy Training Publications, 1985), pp. 283–284 et passim.

13. James White, *Protestant Worship and Church Architecture* (New York: Oxford University Press, 1964), pp. 34, 40–43.

14. Bruggink and Droppers, pp. 211–212.

15. Ibid., p. 666.

16. AE 53: 22.

17. Ibid., p. 69.

18. FC Ep VII.

19. See note 16.

20. See Tr 67–70; also Francis Pieper, *Christian Dogmatics*, 3 vols. (St. Louis: Concordia Publishing House, 1951), 3: 440–442.

21. Ibid., 3: 442–443.

22. AE 51: 232.

23. AE 53: 11.

24. Ap XXIV, 51. Translated from German.

25. C. F. W. Walther, *The Proper Distinction Between Law and Gospel*, trans. W. H. T. Dau (St. Louis: Concordia Publishing Hosue, [1928]), p. 248.

26. Walter C. Huffmann and S. Anita Stauffer, *Where We Worship* (St. Louis: Concordia Publishing House, 1987), p. 23.

27. Paul Lang, *What an Altar Guild Should Know* (St. Louis: Concordia Publishing House, 1964), p. 108.

28. Bruggink and Droppers, p. 450.

29. Ibid.

30. Ibid., p. 452.

31. Ibid.

32. "In case one is tempted to regard this development as due to the influence of pagan usage, it is worth noting that one of the charges leveled by the Emperor Julian the Apostate against the Christians was that they dressed up in special clothes to worship God." W. Jardine Grisbrooke, "Vestments," in *The Study of Liturgy*, ed. Cheslyn Jones, Geoffrey Wainwright, and Edward Yarnold (New York: Oxford University Press, 1978), p. 489.

33. Olof Herrlin, *Divine Service: Liturgy in Perspective*, trans. Gene Lund (Philadelphia: Fortress Press, 1966), p. 148. On the subject of the symbolism of the vestments, note Grisbrooke: "During the Middle Ages the origins of these vestments were lost sight of, and so an ecclesiastical rationale was found for them in terms of a more or less complicated system of symbolism. . . . In the west three basic strands of this symbolism may be traced. First, there is the tendency, especially evident among the liturgists of the earlier Middle Ages, to try to find a biblical rationale for almost all the externals of Christian worship, and in particular to find types of the impedimenta of the Christian cultus in the cultus of the Old Covenant. Certain modifications and additions to the vestments were made under the influence of this school of thought, almost all of which have since disappeared. Second, there is the tendency, especially marked in the later Middle Ages, to interpret almost everything connected with the liturgy, and especially the Eucharist, in terms of the details of the passion. . . . Third, there is the tendency, pronounced through most of the medieval centuries, to moralism, which led to the interpretation of vestments in terms of a symbolism of virtues and graces, an interpretation which survived until 1969 in the vesting prayers of the Roman rite, one of the many sets of such prayers which originated in the Middle Ages all over Christendom." Jones, pp. 489–490.

34. Gilbert Cope, "Vestments," in *The Westminster Dictionary of Worship*, ed. J. G. Davies (Philadelphia: Westminster Press, 1972), p. 368.

35. Arthur Carl Piepkorn, *The Survival of the Historic Vestments in the Lutheran Church after 1555* (St. Louis: Concordia Seminary, 1956), p. 2.

36. AE 53: 31.

37. Piepkorn, p. 9.

38. Ap XXIV, 1.

39. Günther Stiller, *Johann Sebastian Bach and the Liturgical Life in Leipzig*, trans. Herbert J. A. Bouman, Daniel Poellot, and Hilton C. Oswald (St. Louis: Concordia Publishing House, 1984), pp. 107–108.

40. "Thus we find that the alb, the cincture, the surplice, and the chasuble have never passed wholly out of use in the Church of the Augsburg Confession. . . . The carefully cultivated and propagated conviction of Pietism, of the Enlightenment, and of contemporary Protestantizing Lutherans that vestments are the inheritance of the Interims and that authentic Lutheranism always rejected them is shown to be without historic foundation. If anything, the reverse is often true; the historic service vestments tended to survive precisely in the areas of the Church where the Interims had never been in force, and they numbered among their doughtiest defenders some of the most impeccably orthodox doctors of the Church of the Augsburg Confession." Piepkorn, pp. 119–120.

41. Note the extended description of the "Protestantizing" of the liturgy in Werner Elert, *The Structure of Lutheranism*, trans. Walter A. Hansen (St. Louis: Concordia Publishing House, 1962), pp. 334–339.

42. Piepkorn, p. 90.

43. Luther D. Reed, *Worship*, rev. ed. (Philadelphia: Muhlenberg Press, 1959), p. 65.

44. Frank C. Senn, *Christian Worship and Its Cultural Setting* (Philadelphia: Fortress Press, 1983), p. 65.

45. Jones, p. 491.

46. *Lutheran Worship: Altar Book* (St. Louis: Concordia Publishing House, 1982), p. 26.

47. Ibid., p. 13.

48. AC VII, 3.

49. FC SD X, 31. Note the comment of Kurt Marquart on Article X: "It would be wrong to infer from it, for instance, that ceremonies and liturgical forms simply don't matter, and may be left to proliferate—or stagnate!—like weeds or Topsy! The technical term 'indifferent things' for *adiaphora* was never meant to suggest 'indifference' in the popular sense of boredom, contempt, or carelessness. The Formula of Concord nowhere retracts the Augsburg Confession's considered judgment that 'nothing contributes so much to the maintenance of dignity in public worship and the cultivation of reverence among the people as the proper observance of ceremonies in the churches' " (Of Abuses, introduction, 6; Tappert, p. 49). "The a-liturgical orientation of our modern Reformed-pietistic environment moreover jumps only too easily to the conclusion that Article X simply consigns everything liturgical to the realm of *adiaphora*, so that as long as Word and Sacrament still come to expression somehow, all outward arrangements are free and 'indifferent.' That too would be a grave misunderstanding." Kurt Marquart, "Confession and Ceremonies," in *A Contemporary Look at the Formula of Concord*, ed. Robert Preus and Wilbert Rosin (St. Louis: Concordia Publishing House, 1978), pp. 263–264.

50. Elert, p. 325.

51. Ap XXIV, 1. See Elert, *The Structure of Lutheranism*, pp. 326–329, for a very useful discussion of the "form" of evangelical worship.

52. SC VII.

53. AC XXIV, 3.

54. Ap XXIV, 3.

55. Ap XV, 38–39. Also note LC I, 94.

56. For historical background on the Adiaphoristic Controversy see F. Bente, *Historical Introductions to the Book of Concord* (St. Louis: Concordia Publishing House, 1965), pp. 107–111, and Oliver Olson, "Politics, Liturgics, and *Integritas Sacramenti*," in *Discord, Dialogue, and Concord*, ed. Lewis Spitz and Wenzel Lohff (Philadelphia: Fortress Press, 1977), pp. 74–85.

57. See FC Ep X, 3.

58. Friedrich Kalb, *Theology of Worship in 17th Century Lutheranism*, trans. Henry P. A. Hamann (St. Louis: Concordia Publishing House, 1965), p. 113.

59. "What are we to say, then, about Sunday and other similar church ordinances and ceremonies? To this our teachers reply that bishops or pastors may make regulations so that everything in the churches is done in good order, but not as a means of obtaining God's grace or making satisfaction for sins, nor in order to bind men's consciences by considering these things necessary services of God and counting it a sin to omit their observance even when this is done without offense. So St. Paul directed in 1 Cor. 11:5 that women should cover their heads in the assembly. He also directed that in the assembly preachers should not all speak at once, but one after another, in order.

"It is proper for the Christian assembly to keep such ordinances for the sake of love and peace, to be obedient to the bishops and parish ministers in such matters, and to observe the regulations in such a way that one does not give offense to another and so that there may be no disorder or unbecoming conduct in the church. However, consciences should not be burdened by contending that such things are necessary to salvation or that it is a sin to omit them, even when no offense is given to others, just as no one would say that a woman commits a sin if without offense to others she goes out with uncovered head." AC XXVIII, 53–56; also see Ap VII and VIII, 38–44.

60. Note the Apology, "From this point of view there is no difference between our traditions and the ceremonies of Moses. Paul condemns the ceremonies of Moses as well as the traditions because they were thought of as works meriting righteousness before God and therefore they obscured the work of Christ and the righteousness of faith. With the removal of the law and of the traditions, he therefore contends that the forgiveness of sins has been promised, not because of our works but freely because of Christ, provided that we accept it by faith; for only faith can accept a promise. Since it is by faith that we accept the forgiveness of sins and by faith that we have a gracious God for Christ's sake, it is an ungodly error to maintain that we merit the forgiveness of sins by these observances." Ap XV, 10–11; also see Ap XV, 4, and SA Part III, XV, 1.

61. For examples of this theology within American Lutheranism, see Eugene Brand, *The Rite Thing* (Minneapolis: Augsburg Publishing House, 1970), and Frank Senn, *The Pastor as Worship Leader* (Minneapolis: Augsburg Publishing House, 1977). For a well-argued critique see Oliver Olson, "Contemporary Trends in Liturgy Viewed from the Perspective of Classical Lutheran Theology," *The Lutheran Quarterly* XXVI/2 (May 1974): 110–157.

62. "The woman came, believing that she should seek the forgiveness of sins from Christ. This is the highest way of worshiping Christ. Nothing greater could she ascribe to him. By looking for the forgiveness of sins from him, she truly acknowledged him as Messiah. Truly to believe means to think of Christ in this way, and in this way to worship and take hold of him." Ap IV, 154. In the same article of the Apology, Melanchthon continues, "Thus the service and worship of the Gospel is to receive good things from God, while the worship of the law is to offer and present our good to God. We cannot offer anything to God unless we have first been reconciled and reborn. The greatest possible comfort comes from this doctrine that the highest worship in the Gospel is the desire to receive forgiveness of sins, grace, and righteousness." Ap IV, 310. The Apology is consistent with Luther's understanding of *Gottesdienst* expressed in his treatise of 1530, "Admonition Concerning the Sacrament," in which he writes, "Now if you want to engage in a marvelous, great worship of God and honor Christ's passion rightly, then remember to participate in the sacrament; in it, as you hear, there is remembrance of him, that is, he is praised and glorified. If you practice or assist in practicing this same remembrance with diligence, then you will assuredly forget about self-chosen forms of worship, for as has been said, you cannot praise and thank God too often or too much for his grace received in Christ. . . . For this is the true God who gives and does not receive, who helps and does not let himself be helped, who teaches and does not let himself be taught or ruled. In short, he does all things freely out of pure grace without merit, for the unworthy and undeserving, yes, for the damned and lost. This kind of a remembrance, confession, and glory he desires to have." AE 38: 106–107. On the Formula of Concord's use of *actio* see Bjarne Wollan Teigen, *The Lord's Supper in the Theology of Martin Chemnitz* (Brewster, MA: Trinity Lutheran Press, 1986), pp. 182–184.

63. Eugene Brand, "Lutheran Worship" in *The Westminster Dictionary of Worship*, p. 251. This is apparent in Brand's earlier book, *The Rite Thing*, p. 66: "Where the celebration is seen as a meal in common for the remembrance of the saving work of Jesus, however, the motivation (of the worshiper) enlarges significantly. The personal value of participation does not diminish but is brought into proper balance with the corporate action. Now the question is not just 'what do I receive?', but also 'how am I involved?' "

64. LBW, p. 70.

65. For the pagan roots of this ceremony see Theodor Klausner, *A Short History of the Western Liturgy*, trans. John Halliburton (New York: Oxford University Press, 1969), p. 8. Also see Olson, "Contemporary Trends in Liturgy Viewed from the Perspective of Classical Lutheran Theology," pp. 135–137.

66. On the Great Thanksgiving see Gottfried G. Krodel, "The Great Thanksgiving of the Inter-Lutheran Commission on Worship: It is the Christians' Supper and not the Lord's Supper," *The Cresset: Occasional Paper 1* (Valparaiso, IN: Valparaiso University Press, 1977), and Carl Wisloff, *The Gifts of Communion*, trans. Joseph Shaw (Minneapolis: Augsburg Publishing House, 1964).

67. AE 36: 50–51.

68. See Paul Rorem, "Toward Liturgical Hermeneutics: Some Byzantine Examples," *Currents in Theology and Mission* 13 (December 1986): 346–353 for a careful discussion of the relationship of ceremony to rite in Byzantine liturgical history.

69. Herrlin, p. 3.

70. Dietrich Bonhoeffer, *Psalms: The Prayerbook of the Bible* (Minneapolis: Augsburg Publishing House, 1970), p. 15

71. Kenneth Korby, "Prayer: Pre-Reformation to the Present," in *Christians at Prayer*, ed. John Galen (Notre Dame University Press, 1977), p. 132.

72. Eugene Brand, "Luther's Liturgical Surgery" in *Interpreting Luther's Legacy*, ed. Fred W. Meuser and Stanley D. Schneider (Minneapolis: Augsburg Publishing House, 1969), pp. 108–119. For an opposing evaluation of Luther's liturgical work see Paul Rorem, "Luther's Objection to a Eucharistic Prayer," *The Cresset* 35 (March 1975): 12–16.

73. Hermann Sasse, *We Confess Jesus Christ*, trans. Norman E. Nagel (St. Louis: Concordia Publishing House, 1984), p. 11.

74. Quoted in Paul Waitman Hoon, *The Integrity of Worship* (Nashville: Abingdon Press, 1971), p. 222.

75. Ernest Koenker, *Worship in Word and Sacrament* (St. Louis: Concordia Publishing House, 1959), p. 85.

76. "At the specifically linguistic level, translation is always a hazardous exercise, especially when texts of literary merit are involved. A hymn like "Of the Father's love begotten" (LW 36) can never be more than a good paraphrase of the original "Corde natus ex parentis;" the most we can realistically hope for is that the spirit of Prudentius' composition will be substantially retained, even if the words are not . . . . If we look at modern services in this light, their deficiencies are immediately apparent. What kind of response is "and also with you"? Why has this pseudo-colloquial form replaced "and with thy spirit"? Is it that we no longer believe that man has a spirit, and that the level of our discourse is primarily spiritual? We do not go to church just to chat or to wish each other well." G. L. Bray, "Language and Liturgy,"in *Latimer Studies 16: Language and Liturgy*, ed. Robin A. Leaver (Oxford: Latimer House, 1984), p. 10. Also see James Hitchcock, *Recovery of the Sacred* (New York: Seabury Press, 1974).

77. Wilhelm Löhe, *Three Books About the Church,* trans. and ed. James Schaaf (Philadelphia: Fortress Press, 1969), p. 178.

78. AC XXIV, 4.

79. SC, Preface, 7.

80. Ap VII and VIII, 28. Also note AC XXVIII, 5.

81. *Lutheran Worship: Altar Book,* p. 25.

82. AC XVIII 53–55.

83. *Lutheran Worship: Altar Book,* p. 25.

84. "While some might argue that assisting the presiding minister in the distribution of the elements is not necessarily a distinctive function of the pastoral office, the Synod's Commission on Theology and Church Relations strongly recommends that, to avoid confusion regarding the office of the public ministry and to avoid giving offense to the church, such assistance be limited to men." *The Theology and Practice of the Lord's Supper* (St. Louis: The Lutheran Church—Missouri Synod, 1983), p. 30. Also see the commission's *Women in the Church: Scriptural Principles and Ecclesial Practice* (St. Louis: The Lutheran Church—Missouri Synod, 1985), p. 45.

85. Bernard Cooke, *Ministry to Word and Sacraments: History and Theology* (Philadelphia: Fortress Press, 1976), p. 348.

7

Music and the Liturgy
The Lutheran Tradition

Carl Schalk

Wherever and whenever Christians gather to worship and praise God, they sing songs—songs of confidence and faith, songs of confession and contrition, songs of exile and rebirth, songs of sin and salvation. The music of Christian worship is a great *cantus firmus* extolling God's glory, praising him for his mighty acts in rescuing his people, and proclaiming the great central act of God in Jesus Christ, the victory over sin and death that is celebrated with special joy and intensity each paschal season.

Christians are a people who sing because they have a song to sing. The theme of their song has been clear and constant: it is the theme of thanksgiving for victory and salvation through the death and resurrection of their Lord Jesus Christ. Psalm 118, appointed for the festival of the Resurrection, reflects that theme in clear and unmistakable terms:

> Give thanks to the Lord, for he is good;
>> his love endures forever.
> Let Israel say:
>> "His love endures forever."
> Let the house of Aaron say:
>> "His love endures forever."
> Let those who fear the Lord say:
>> "His love endures forever."
> "The Lord's right hand has done mighty things!
>> The Lord's right hand is lifted high;
>> the Lord's right hand has done mighty things!"
> I will not die but live,
>> and will proclaim what the Lord has done.

I will give you thanks, for you answered me;
    you have become my salvation.
The stone the builders rejected
    has become the capstone;
the Lord has done this,
    and it is marvelous in our eyes.
This is the day the Lord has made;
    let us rejoice and be glad in it.

(Ps. 118:1–4, 15b, 16–17, 21–24)

Singing to the praise and glory of God has always held a place of great importance in the Lutheran tradition. It is understandable, therefore, that Christian song in the Lutheran tradition has served as a vehicle of prayer and praise pervading the entire life of the believer. Whether in the home, where the family learned the great hymns of faith and sang them regularly at their daily devotions; at work, where the songs of faith leavened every aspect of daily life; or in the liturgical assembly where the congregation lifted its voice in supplication, prayer, and praise, Christian song was the vehicle by which young and old, educated and uneducated, could join together in the prayer life of the church. As Christians join in that song, they are doing no more than that which they are enjoined to do by the psalmist, "Let all who take refuge in you be glad; let them ever sing for joy" (Ps. 5:11a).

But while Christian song inevitably permeates the entire life of the Christian, it is the liturgical assembly—the regular gathering of God's people about Word and Sacrament—that is the central and principal locus where God's people sing their songs of praise, adoration, and thanksgiving for all that he has done for them. It is in the liturgical assembly, called together by God to hear his Word and celebrate his sacred meal, that this old, yet ever new, story is told and retold, sung and sung again, with unique and special focus.

The liturgy of the church, that is, the totality of the rites and ceremonies with which Christians in the Lutheran tradition hear his Word, share his meal, and celebrate his goodness to all the world, is replete with music, abounding and overflowing with psalms and hymns and spiritual songs. And it is here in the liturgy that Lutherans, together with the whole church, find their chief vehicle and principal opportunity to offer their sacrifice of praise and thanksgiving to the Lord who is both their strength and song (Exod. 15:2a).

244

MUSIC AND THE LITURGY: THE LUTHERAN TRADITION

The general importance of song in the liturgical assembly is obvious to all. As this simple fact comes into sharper focus, however, it becomes clearer that, as music is united to liturgical texts, it forms, for all practical purposes, a necessary and integral part of the celebration of the liturgy. It is quite impossible to conceive of the regular gathering of Christians for worship without the presence of music; many of the liturgical texts virtually cry out to be sung. And the practice of the church at worship throughout its history confirms this simple fact: Christian song is an inherent part of and fundamental to the normal celebration of the liturgy.[1]

From one perspective Christian song, both within and without the liturgical assembly, is a human activity. After all, *we* sing, *we* offer our melodies of praise and thanksgiving. Yet, understood more clearly and deeply, Christian song is God's good gift to his people to be used in his praise and in the proclamation of his Word. In his preface to Georg Rhau's *Symphoniae iucundae* Luther makes this abundantly clear: "I would certainly like to praise music with all my heart as the excellent gift of God which it is and to commend it to everyone. . . . Use the gift of music to praise God and him alone, since he has given us this gift."[2]

As it was for Luther, both in the liturgical assembly and in the total life of the believer, Christian song is the inevitable eruption of joyful praise in the heart of the redeemed. For the believer to refuse to sing and speak about the faith that is within him or her is to demonstrate that he or she does not believe. In contrast to the Old Covenant, Luther says

> There is now in the New Testament a better service of God, of which the Psalm [96:1] here says: "Sing to the Lord a new song. Sing to the Lord all the earth." For God has cheered our hearts and minds through his dear Son, whom he gave for us to redeem us from sin, death, and the devil. He who believes this earnestly cannot be quiet about it. But he must gladly and willingly sing and speak about it. And whoever does not want to sing and speak it shows that he does not believe and that he does not belong under the new and joyful testament.[3]

Christian song in the liturgical assembly is both the duty and the delight of the whole gathered congregation. In the Lutheran tradition it is characterized by such terms as doxological, scriptural, liturgical (in the sense of reflecting the church's desire for ordered eucharistic worship within the rhythms of the church year, and the regular praying of the office within the rhythm of the day), traditional (in the sense of building on the best of the past), eclectic (in the sense of absorbing whatever styles, techniques, or practices may serve it best), creative, participatory, and aspiring to excellence in both conception and execution.[4] It is offered by all participants in worship according to their ability and according to their particular role in the worshiping assembly.

Liturgical song involves the entire assembly in one way or another, whether it is the song of the congregation, the song of presiding and assisting ministers, the song of the choir, the song of the organ, the song of soloists or instrumentalists. It is to a discussion of these varying roles in the gathered assembly that attention is now directed.

The Music of the Congregation

It is a commonplace to observe that one of the chief contributions of the Lutheran Reformation was the restoration of congregational song to the people and its establishment as a vital ingredient in corporate worship. Not that congregations had been completely silent prior to the 16th century Reformation. The singing of popular religious songs was indeed a part of the piety of the Middle Ages; singing by the people had even been tolerated, on certain occasions, in the medieval church, but only within prescribed bounds. It was the Reformation, however, that was to open the floodgates of popular religious song and establish it as an indispensable part of Lutheran worship ever since.

For Lutherans today liturgical song encompasses a wide variety of psalmody, hymnody, liturgical responses, canticles, and spiritual songs. The chief liturgical assignment of the congregation, however, is the singing of the ordinary of the Eucharist. As such, every congregation should be well acquainted with at least one musical setting of the liturgy, and should certainly strive to learn additional settings in the interest of variety and as a means of focusing attention on the changing character of the various seasons of the church year.

MUSIC AND THE LITURGY: THE LUTHERAN TRADITION

It is helpful to recall from our perspective some 400 years later that, for 16th-century Lutherans, the people's involvement in the liturgy was centered in the singing of the Lutheran chorale. The Lutheran chorale is that unique body of texts and melodies that took shape during the early years of the Reformation and that spread to those countries where the Lutheran Reformation took root. Drawn from a variety of sources—from the chants of the medieval church, from the popular pre-Reformation "Kyrie songs," from non-liturgical Latin and Latin-German songs of pre-Reformation times, from secular melodies to which sacred texts were added, and from newly written texts and melodies by Luther and his followers—the chorale achieved a remarkable popularity. Its texts spoke clearly of sin and salvation, of death and resurrection. They recounted the biblical account of man's fall into sin and his rescue won through Christ's victory over death and the devil. The chorale's melodies, sung by the congregation in unison and without accompaniment, were vigorous and rhythmic.

Ulrich Leupold's reminder concerning Luther's hymns might well be extended to all the early chorales. They were "meant not to create a mood, but to convey a message. They were a confession of faith, not of personal feelings. . . . They were written not to be read but to be sung by a whole congregation."[5]

Even a cursory examination of the use of the chorale in early Lutheran worship clearly reflects the concern that congregational involvement in worship was to be involvement in the liturgy; and the vehicle for that involvement was to be liturgical hymnody, namely the chorale.

It is important to point out that from the very first, Luther, Lutherans, and Lutheran congregations saw hymnody as a way of participating in the liturgy. The chorale was in no way considered to be, as in much of contemporary Christendom, simply a general Christian song loosely attached to worship. Neither was it simply a way of providing an occasional opportunity for involving the people in worship. Rather, the chorale was a means of involving the gathered assembly specifically in the historic liturgy of the Western Church.

The five great "hymns" of the ordinary of the Mass had their counterpart in five popular chorales of the early Lutheran Reformation, which were sung alongside their Gregorian counterparts, sometimes substituting for them.[6] It is interesting to note that Luther's own involvement in writing original hymns and translating and correcting older hymns dealt almost exclusively with those hymns that would be useful liturgically; hymns of the ordinary of the service, psalm hymns, hymns for the offices, sacramental hymns, hymns of the church year. Such concern that hymns be liturgically useful was not Luther's alone. It was and continues to be the concern of Lutheran worship where the spirit of Luther prevails.

Of unique importance to the Reformation period was the development of a series of *de tempore* hymns (or Hymns of the Day) that were closely tied to the appointed readings for the particular Sunday or festival, especially the Gospel (see chapter 17). These hymns are a special treasure of Lutheran hymnody and are an example of how hymnody should be employed liturgically. The Hymn of the Day has once again found its rightful place as an integral part of the celebration of Holy Communion, and a contemporary adaptation of the consensus of the early listings of *de tempore* hymns is available in *Lutheran Worship*.

Together with the rise of the Lutheran chorale, there also developed the uniquely Lutheran custom of singing hymns in alternation between congregation, choir, and also occasionally the organ. Alternating stanza for stanza throughout the entire hymn, this manner of singing not only brought a degree of variety to the congregational singing of the chorale, many of which by modern standards consisted of a large number of stanzas, but it also provided opportunity for meditation on the words of the hymn in a way not possible in any other manner. Each musical entity in the worshiping assembly—the congregation, the choir, the organ—had its turn in the singing of the chorale; at the heart and center of this music-making, however, was the congregation.

Luther himself led the way in encouraging the creation of new texts and melodies through which the congregation could give voice to its prayer and praise in corporate song. The result has been the incorporation into Lutheran worship of a large body of hymnody reflecting a wide variety of textual concerns and musical styles.

In more recent history, Lutherans have been encouraged to sing many of the other great "hymns" of the liturgy. In the Divine Service it may be the Hymn of Praise ("Glory to God in the highest" or "This is the feast of victory"), the Sanctus, the Agnus Dei, the Post-Communion Canticle ("Thank the Lord and sing his praise"). In Morning Prayer it may be such great "hymns" and canticles as the Venite ("Oh, come, let us sing to the Lord"), the Benedictus ("Blessed be the Lord"), the Te Deum ("You are God; we praise you"). In Evening Prayer it may be the candlelighting hymn "Joyous light of glory," Psalm 141 ("Let my prayer rise before you as incense"), and the Magnificat ("My soul proclaims the greatness of the Lord"). Many of the musical settings of these songs are new to the present generation of Lutherans. They need, therefore, to be carefully taught and well learned so that congregations can sing them with confidence.

Another aspect of congregational song that has received great emphasis in more recent years has been congregational involvement in the singing of psalms. A variety of musical systems is available, enabling the assembly to participate in antiphonal (one group alternating with another group) or responsorial psalmody (a single voice alternating with a group). In some systems the congregation sings a simple refrain, repeated several times throughout a psalm; in other systems the congregation sings the text of the psalm itself.

One must also include here the many short responses that congregations sing throughout the liturgy, such as the Gospel acclamations, the responses to the bids in the Kyrie, the responses in the Litany (the shorter version in Evening Prayer as well as in the classic Western Litany), and the responses to the Benedicamus, the Prayers, and the Benediction.

All these belong in a special and unique way to the congregation, the gathered assembly, which brings its sacrifice of praise and song in melodies that are uniquely its own. Whatever may be the characteristics of true congregational song, it works within the musical limitations of largely amateur singers, yet has a musical integrity and character distinctly its own. True congregational song is neither simplistic melody whose only purpose is functional, nor essentially choir music simplified for the purposes of undistinguished group singing.

True congregational song is song that unites the gathered assembly in common praise and prayer. It is a song that draws the assembly together rather than song that fragments and divides. Above all it is a song that gathers the individual voices into one grand choir of praise as these respond to God's Word, acclaim the Gospel, and sing of their salvation in Christ.

The Music of Presiding and Assisting Ministers

The corporate worship of Lutheran Christians has traditionally been sung. This is true not only of the congregation whose song was freed by the Reformation to take its rightful place in the liturgy, but it is equally true of the song of those who exercise particular roles of leadership in worship, namely, the presiding and assisting ministers.

Not only is the action of the liturgy given a more noble form when solemnized in song, the singing of the liturgy as it is shared by pastor, assisting ministers, and the congregation adds a beauty and intensity not possible in any other way, "enlarging and elevating the adoration of our giver God."[7] The singing of the liturgy by presiding and assisting ministers, as provided for in *Lutheran Worship* (1982), raises the doing of the liturgy to a plane beyond the overly personalistic and idiosyncratic—so common in much worship today—to that of truly corporate song.

In Luther's view, those who were to lead in the public worship of the church needed to be well-trained in music to meet those responsibilities. "Before a youth is ordained into the ministry, he should practice music in school."[8] He was especially scornful of those "who want to be theologians when they cannot even sing."[9] For presiding and assisting ministers to neglect their respective roles in the singing of the liturgy is to abandon the traditional practice of the Lutheran Church, often replacing it with an approach that is highly individualistic, overly personal, and inappropriately informal, and thereby depriving congregations of the ennobling experience of a sung liturgy that is rightfully theirs.

Leadership in worship at the time of the Reformation presumed sung prayer. Such was certainly the case in Luther's Latin Mass ("An Order of Mass and Communion for the Church at Wittenberg," 1523) as well as his German Mass ("The German Mass and Order of Service," 1526).[10] Both orders made specific provisions for and presumed, at the least, sung prayers, sung readings, and the singing of the Words of Institution by the presiding minister. In his German Mass Luther went so far as to give rather detailed instructions together with numerous musical examples for chanting the Collect, the Epistle, and the Gospel, as well as setting out a complete melody for the Words of Institution. It is clear that even in this rather simplified service, the sung liturgy was the norm Luther held up for emulation.

Lutheran Worship continues to reflect the importance of a liturgy sung by all participants. The delineation of roles between presiding and assisting ministers makes a sung liturgy more readily achievable by dividing the responsibility for singing those parts of the service assigned to worship leaders among several people.

The principal role of the presiding minister, an ordained clergyman, is to pronounce absolution, preach, and preside at the celebration of the sacrament. Other functions in worship such as the leading of the bids in the Kyrie, intoning the Hymn of Praise, reading the Old Testament and Epistle pericopes, providing leadership in singing the psalms, leading the prayers of the congregation, assisting in the distribution of Holy Communion, and certain other functions designated in the liturgy may be assumed by one or more assisting ministers. Assisting ministers may be non-ordained lay people with the gift of leadership in worship. Since certain of these functions involve modest amounts of singing or chanting, some musical ability is desirable. Where such musical ability is not readily apparent, the church musician should be engaged to help pastors and assisting ministers learn to sing their respective parts until they are at ease and completely comfortable with them.

The music of presiding and assisting ministers falls into two general categories: liturgical dialog and monolog. Liturgical dialog between a leader and the congregation is exemplified by such familiar exchanges as "The Lord be with you/And also with you," "Lift up your hearts/We lift them to the Lord," "Let us give thanks to the Lord our God/It is right to give him thanks and praise." Such dialog occurs frequently in the various orders of worship. When it occurs, the most natural and desirable practice is that both portions of the dialog be sung.[11]

Examples of monolog in *Lutheran Worship* include such parts of the liturgy as the Collect, the Proper Preface, and the Words of Institution, portions of the liturgy that are usually sung on one note with simple inflections. Luther himself took care to provide simple recitation formulas for them, and musical settings of the liturgy, like those in *Lutheran Worship*, provide such simple formulas.

Many pastors already sing certain parts of the liturgy—a commendable practice indeed. Presiding and assisting ministers should be encouraged by their congregations, wherever they may be hesitant, to assume their fuller role in the singing of the complete liturgical service whenever the rest of the service is sung by the congregation and choir.

The Music of the Choir

In the Lutheran tradition the choir functions liturgically as a helper and servant of the gathered assembly, assisting, enlivening, and enriching the worship of the entire congregation. Without the leadership of a choir, the liturgies and hymns are often sung indifferently, in a manner lacking vitality, and without enthusiasm. Where a choir is present and effectively leading in worship, congregational singing is usually more confident, assured, vital, and vigorous.

The choir as liturgical leader functions in three basic ways: First, the choir supports and enriches the congregation's singing of the liturgy and hymns. It does this, in part, as it devotes time in its regular rehearsals to practicing and preparing the liturgy so that the choir can effectively lead the congregation; by first learning and then teaching and introducing to the congregation those portions of the liturgy that have not yet been learned, or learned only incompletely; and by helping the congregation expand the dimensions of its participation in the liturgy by learning new musical settings of the liturgy or portions of the liturgy as may be appropriate.

By helping the congregation—of which the choir is a part—sing more effectively the services that it already knows, and by introducing over a period of time several musical settings of the liturgy that the congregation can use with the changing moods of the church year, the choir will be assuming more fully its role of leader and facilitator in the liturgical worship of the congregation.

The choir supports and enriches the congregational singing of hymns by regularly devoting time in rehearsals to practicing the hymns to be sung in the various services, thus establishing a nucleus of singers confidently able to lead the singing; by helping to enlarge the congregation's repertoire through learning new hymns of worth and introducing them in an appropriate manner to the congregation; and especially by participating in the regular presentation of the Hymn of the Day in the Divine Service. As the chief hymn in the Divine Service, the Hymn of the Day quite naturally calls for special musical treatment. Here the choir can play a most important role, whether in singing stanzas in parts in alternation with the congregation, singing a descant on a final stanza, or simply singing alternate stanzas in unison with alternate organ harmonizations. Many other ways of presenting the Hymn of the Day are available to the creative and resourceful choir director.[12]

Secondly, the choir brings richness and variety to the worship of the assembly by singing those portions of the liturgy especially designated to be sung by the choir. Certain texts in the liturgy, because of their unique appropriateness to the particular Sunday, festival, or season of the church year, change from week to week. These proper texts (proper in the sense of being uniquely appropriate to the occasion) are usually more suited to singing by a group that meets regularly for rehearsal. In the history of the church's worship these texts have changed from time to time, or in some cases they have been assigned to different participants in worship. Their use is crucially important, however, for they provide much of the variety that is inherent in liturgical worship.

In the Divine Service, the proper texts assigned to the choir or allowed by the rubrics include the Entrance psalmody, the Gradual psalmody, the Verse, and the Offertory.

The Entrance psalmody may be the complete Psalm appointed for the day, or another psalm appropriately chosen for the particular Sunday or festival, or the appointed Introit, which normally consists of a selected portion of a psalm. While under certain circumstances the congregation may also play a role in the Entrance psalmody, it is more normally the case that it be sung by the choir.

253

The Gradual psalmody, which occurs in the liturgy between the Old Testament Reading and the Epistle, consists either of a complete psalm or large portion of the psalm appointed for the day, or the appointed Gradual. Depending on the particular musical system employed for singing the psalmody, circumstances may suggest congregational involvement in either of these options. In any case the choir will certainly play a large role in modeling and leading the singing.

The Verse is the changeable text that serves to introduce the Gospel. It may be sung to any one of several newly composed sets of choral settings available. It may also be sung by the choir or a cantor to the tones provided for the psalms in *Lutheran Worship*. The Verse is one of the important new choral propers that is the specific responsibility of the choir.

The Offertory is the song sung while the gifts are presented. While *Lutheran Worship* includes two common offertories that may be sung by the congregation, the Notes on the Liturgy also provide for the possibility of using appropriate choral settings of the classic offertory texts sung by the choir.

In the services at which Holy Communion is not celebrated, chiefly Matins and Vespers, Morning Prayer and Evening Prayer, or other services centered on the Word, the major variable texts are the Psalms, the Antiphons, the Responsory, and the Canticles.

The Psalms are one of the chief components of the daily offices. The rubrics provide that in addition to those psalms that are always sung (in Matins and Morning Prayer it is the Venite; in Evening Prayer Psalm 141), additional psalms may also be sung. These additional psalms may be sung—either by a cantor, choir, congregation, or by a combination of these three—to any of the several systems of psalms available, including the tones provided in *Lutheran Worship*, or they may be sung in settings for choir from the rich treasury of psalm-based choral literature. The same applies to the antiphons to the psalms found in the Propers for Morning and Evening Prayer in the "Pew Edition" of *Lutheran Worship*. A resourceful choir director will have no difficulty in seeing that variety is achieved in the singing of the psalms.

The Responsory, a distinct form of psalmody as response to the Readings, provides another opportunity for choral participation. Several common and proper responsories for the offices are provided in *Lutheran Worship*. Appropriate selections from the large body of choral literature may also be employed as responses to the Readings.

The rich treasury of canticles provides another opportunity for involvement of the choir. Where certain canticles indicate an alternating performance between congregation and other groups (designated with I and II), the men and/or women of the choir may take those parts. In some circumstances choral settings of canticles from the historic choral literature may on occasion be substituted for the congregational singing of the canticles.

This rich selection of proper texts provides a fruitful basis for the participation of the choir in those portions of the liturgy that change from Sunday to Sunday or season to season, a participation for which the choir is uniquely suited, and through which it can make a contribution of major significance. These remain the basic texts the choir must address as it prepares for its participation in the various liturgies of the church.

Thirdly, the choir enriches the congregation's worship by presenting attendant music as appropriate as possible. The term attendant music— music that attends or serves the liturgy—refers to that entire spectrum of motets, anthems, Passions, cantatas, and other music not covered in the preceding discussions. As attendant music is planned for inclusion in worship, three factors should be given primary emphasis: (1) attendant music should be liturgically appropriate to the Sunday, festival, or season of the church year; (2) attendant music should be appropriately placed in the liturgy, giving, among other things, special consideration to the traditional Lutheran practice of music *sub communione*, that is, music sung or played during the distribution of Holy Communion; and (3) attendant music should always be within the musical ability of the choir. Certainly, care must always be exercised that the time and effort involved in preparing and rehearsing attendant music not displace preparation for those other functions of the choir that have prior claim in liturgical worship.

The choir has a unique and significant role in Lutheran worship. It can fulfill that role with music ranging from the simplest to the most complex. But complexity is never a criterion of liturgical suitability. What is important is that singers and choir director, together with pastor and congregation, develop an understanding of the proper function and priorities of the choir in liturgical worship. Then, understanding those priorities and the proper function of the choir, they work together to carry them out in an interesting, effective, and meaningful way that will contribute to the worship of the whole gathered assembly.

The Music of the Organ

The organ has played a significant role in Lutheran worship since Reformation times, although it is a relative latecomer to Christian worship. While Luther seemed not to recognize the organ as capable of making any significant contribution to the music of worship, it is clear that the organ was indeed used in Lutheran worship in the 16th century, although in ways quite different from today.

At the time of the Reformation the organ was used primarily to intone the hymns sung by the choir in polyphonic settings or sung in unison by the congregation without accompaniment; its role was also to play versets—brief compositions usually based on chant melodies—which would alternate with the singing by the choir of portions of the liturgy such as the Introit, Kyrie, Gloria in Excelsis, psalms, and sequence hymns in the Mass, and responsories and canticles in the offices. Its role in the singing of the chorale, which was sung unaccompanied and in unison by the congregation, was to substitute occasionally for the singing of a stanza as it played a composition based on the chorale melody while the congregation would follow along, meditating on the words "sung" by the organ.[13]

Today its role has been greatly expanded, not only accompanying the congregational singing of the liturgy and hymns, but playing preludes and postludes, frequently also serving as an accompaniment for choral music, and participating in music for organ and a variety of other instruments. But whatever the particulars of its involvement in worship, the chief role of the organ in liturgical worship is to serve the congregation as it offers its sacrifice of praise and thanksgiving. Although the organ may occasionally be heard independently in the service, the organist's role is first and foremost that of serving the gathered assembly as it sings its liturgy. In this way the organ, too, is the "living voice of the Gospel," and its proper use in Lutheran worship has amply demonstrated that possibility.

The organist in Lutheran worship is a liturgical organist. This means that the way in which the organ is used is determined first and foremost by the movement and requirements of the liturgical action. It is not the function of the organist in Lutheran worship to entertain, to provide meaningless meanderings at the keyboard, or to fill up silent moments with music. It is the function of the liturgical organist to lead the congregation in the singing of the hymns and chorales, to accompany, as appropriate, those portions of the liturgy sung by the congregation or choir, and to present other liturgical and attendant music as may be fitting and possible.

The most important function of the liturgical organist is that of effectively introducing and leading the congregational singing of the liturgy and the hymns. Effective leadership here can do much to make worship the exciting adventure it is at its best. Through the use of effective intonations or introductions, carefully chosen tempi, rhythmic playing, appropriately chosen registration, judicious use of varied accompaniments, the occasional singing of a stanza without accompaniment, and especially the careful use of alternation between congregation, choir, and organ in both liturgy and hymnody, the organist sets, to a very great degree, the spirit of worship and carries its momentum from beginning to end.

The organist should lead the singing with a vigor and forthrightness appropriate to the circumstances of the liturgy. An organist dare never be content with simply providing a bland and lifeless accompaniment.

It is customary in many places that the organ play at the beginning of worship, during the gathering of the gifts, and as the congregation disperses at the close of worship. It is most helpful and meaningful if the organ music heard at these times is based on the hymns and chorales sung in the service. At the least such music should clearly reflect the spirit and mood of the particular celebration.

In general, the liturgical organist plays less rather than more. When the liturgical organist does play, such playing should serve the goals of the liturgy and be functionally and practically to the point. When there is no particular liturgical function for the organ, it should remain silent. While on the one hand the liturgical organist seeks to avoid flamboyance and pretension in playing, at the same time he or she seeks to use all his or her skills in highlighting and underscoring the inherent drama of the liturgical celebration.

The Music of Instruments

The Lutheran Church, at its best, has always welcomed a variety of musical instruments as a particularly festive way of expressing the celebrative aspects of Christian worship. Indeed, in the early years of the Lutheran Church it was brass and wind instruments that were usually heard more often than the organ. Luther encouraged all Christian musicians to "let their singing and playing to the praise of the Father of all grace sound forth with joy from their organs and whatever other beloved musical instruments there are."[14] The subsequent history of the use of instruments in Lutheran worship bears eloquent testimony to the fact that Luther's advice was heeded.

While the organ has had a place of special prominence in Lutheran worship over many centuries, Lutherans have also used a great variety of instruments in praise and prayer. Brass instruments, stringed instruments, bells, woodwind instruments, percussion—all these and more have been used in Lutheran worship, at times even preferred over the organ.

A rich treasury of music for various instruments and instrumental ensembles has developed in the centuries following the Reformation. This music includes much that is useful as preludes, postludes, chorale-based music for organ and solo instruments, and large- and small-scale works for instruments and voices together.

In more recent times there has been an outpouring of music for instruments alone, for various instruments with organ, as well as music for instruments with choir, music that is particularly suitable for smaller parishes with more modest musical resources or instrumentalists of more modest ability. The availability and use of such instrumental music has brought a new dimension to the worship of many parishes.

Instruments can play an important role in corporate worship as they help worshipers express and experience more fully the changing moods of Christian worship, from the spareness and leanness of Advent and Lent to the exuberance of Easter. Instruments can help worshipers sing and dance their faith, can help foster communion with God and with fellow worshipers; they can serve as an extension of the human voice in sounding the special joy in the heart of each Christian as through faith he or she affirms the totality of God's creation.

The Pastor and the Church Musician

More than any other persons, the pastor and the church musician together shape the worship life and the church music practice in most congregations. Many others, hopefully, are also involved in the planning, preparation, and conduct of congregational worship in the local parish. Yet it is the breadth of vision and the knowledge of the history and practice of worship and church music in the Lutheran tradition—or the lack thereof—which, for the most part, are the decisive factors affecting congregational worship today.

Both pastor and church musician need to demonstrate the understanding that worship is not a peripheral activity of the congregation, but the central act of God's people. Both need to have a firsthand knowledge of and an intimate acquaintance with the wealth of liturgical materials to be found in the Lutheran tradition and made available in *Lutheran Worship*. The pastor, especially, needs to develop an awareness of the resource of the liturgy as a powerful tool in the pastoral care of God's people of whom he is the servant.

On another level, the pastor must have the desire to facilitate the worship of the congregation by obtaining the services of the most competent musician(s) available. Most competent need not necessarily imply the most highly skilled musician, although that is certainly an important consideration, but rather one who understands and loves the liturgy, who knows liturgical music and understands the proper role of all the participants in worship, one who is skilled in leading each participant—congregation, presiding and assisting ministers, choir, organist, and instrumentalists—to a fuller expression of his or her roles.

To accomplish this end, pastor, church musician, and people must work together so that a living and vital parish worship may result. Regular planning sessions are crucial, sessions devoted not only to the practical details of parish worship, but sessions in which all the leaders in worship can develop a common vision of what worship can be in a particular parish.

Regular planning must not be viewed by either pastor or church musician as an impertinent or intimidating encroachment on the domain of the other; for the same note of faithful proclamation and praise needs to be heard from both pulpit and choir loft. Doxology is surely the name of the game, and as A. R. Kretzmann has reminded us, "If we [pastors and church musicians alike] are to rise to the heights of a constant doxology, we must rise together."

There is a final concern that should be uppermost in the minds of all concerned with the worship of God's people:

> The church has always struggled to maintain the connection between two terms which signify what pastors and church musicians, among others, are all about: the *dogma* or teaching, and the *doxa* or praise. Perhaps all of us need to remind each other that *orthodoxy* first of all means "right praise," and that the dogma and the doxa are best held together when the Church sees itself first of all as a worshipping community.[15]

To realize this ever more faithfully and effectively in parish worship may mean a realignment of priorities on the part of all concerned: pastors, church musicians, and congregations. When that begins to happen, then, and only then, will worship become the exciting, enriching, nourishing, and life-sustaining focus of God's people, gathered to hear his Word and share his meal, that all of us know it can and should be.

Notes

1. See also the Constitution on the Sacred Liturgy (1963), par. 112, in *The Liturgy Documents: A Parish Resource*, ed. Mary Ann Simcoe, rev. ed. (Chicago: Liturgy Training Publications, 1985), p. 29.

2. Preface to Georg Rhau's *Symphoniae iucundae* (1538), AE 53: 321–324.

3. Preface to the Babst Hymnal (1545), AE 53: 333.

4. See Philip H. Pfatteicher and Carlos R. Messerli, *Manual on the Liturgy-Lutheran Book of Worship* (Minneapolis: Augsburg Publishing House, 1979), pp. 78–79.

5. AE 53: 197.
6. "Kyrie, God Father" (LW 209); "All Glory Be to God on High" (LW 215); "We All Believe in One True God, Maker" (LW 213); "Isaiah, Mighty Seer, in Spirit Soared" (LW 214); and "O Christ, the Lamb of God" (LW 7).
7. See Introduction in LW, p. 6.
8. Ewald M. Plass, *What Luther Says: An Anthology*, 3 vols. (St. Louis: Concordia Publishing House, 1959), p. 980.
9. AE 29: 35.
10. AE 53: 19–40; 61–90.
11. The long-standing habit of the pastor *speaking* the first portion of such dialog with the congregation *singing* the second half has unfortunately dulled the ears to the curiousness of this practice.
12. See Carl Schalk, *The Hymn of the Day and Its Use in Lutheran Worship*, Church Music Pamphlet Series (St. Louis: Concordia Publishing House, 1983).
13. See Herbert Gotsch, "The Organ in the Lutheran Service of the 16th Century," *Church Music* 67–1 (1967): 7–12.
14. Plass, p. 982.
15. Carl Schalk, *The Pastor and the Church Musician: Thoughts on Aspects of a Common Ministry*, Church Music Pamphlet Series (St. Louis: Concordia Publishing House, 1984), p. 11.

8

Holy Baptism

Norman E. Nagel

In the Name

P *In the name of the Father and of the + Son and of the Holy Spirit.*

The Lord's triune name comes first in Holy Baptism. If he had not given us his name we would still be making up our own gods. His is the initiative; the action is from him to us. "In the name" means—along with much more—at his bidding, by his authority, his mandate.

If there is no name, there is no baptism. This is the name that was put on us with the water at our Baptism. Gathered in the name of God are those who rejoice in their Baptism as they look forward to another person's Baptism by the Lord.

The Mandate

First our Lord speaks his words of Baptism. We may not have our say first, and then fit or squash what our Lord says into our words. In Matthew 28 we are told of the attempt to suppress the report of Christ's resurrection, and then

> The eleven disciples went to Galilee, to the mountain where Jesus told them to go. When they saw him, they worshiped him; but some doubted. Then Jesus came to them and [spoke to them saying], "All authority in heaven and on earth has been given to me. Therefore go and make disciples of all nations, baptizing them in the name of the Father and of the Son and of the Holy Spirit, and teaching them to obey everything I have commanded you. And surely I will be with you always, to the very end of the age." (Matt. 28:16–20)

Here from our Lord is the mandate for Baptism, the words of institution.[1] What is Baptism?—that which our Lord says and gives.

He speaks to the Eleven, that is, the Twelve minus Judas, whose place was later filled by Matthias. The Lord has his Israel. The mountain is where he has his Israel. The mountain is in Galilee, also called "Galilee of the nations" (Is. 9:1). "They worshiped him, but some doubted." There is no ground of confidence in them (Mark 16:14). "Jesus came to them," not they to him. He speaks. His words are introduced with emphasis: "He spoke to them, saying." Thus a direct quotation is introduced. The first word is the gift, a passive verb, the divine passive. God is the giver. What he has given to Jesus is "all authority." Authority means something is given to do for what there is no higher reference that can countermand it. There is no higher reference than God. What is given Jesus to do has no restriction. It runs as far as God's own doing: "All authority in heaven and on earth." This is also expressed in the next word. Here it is a participle (aorist), not a main verb; it indicates a completed action. This is obscured when it is translated as imperative. Then comes the main verb, "make disciples." How this is to be done is given by two participles: "baptizing" and "teaching." Not one or the other, but both make up our Lord's bidding to "make disciples." We may not choose to do the one and not the other. Doing the one is always aimed toward doing the other. When both are done we may celebrate that the Lord's bidding has been done, as we do at Confirmation.

No line may be drawn across our Lord's mandate: "*all* nations." His mandate runs as far as his authority. No line may be drawn excluding some because they are Gentiles, Jews, male, female, infants or slaves.[2]

Water: Death to Life

Baptizing is done with water. There were various washings commanded through the Law of Moses for various kinds of uncleanness. Uncleanness put one outside the congregation of Israel. Restoration was achieved by way of washing and sacrifice. There was a washing at the anointing of a priest and again before each time he offered sacrifice. All of these washings one did to oneself. If one counts on them as one's own doing, they may seem not enough; hence the Pharisees did additional washings that might make up any shortfall in their doing (Mark 7:3).

John was called the Baptist because he did the baptizing. His baptism was something done to you, and it was for sinners. It incensed the scribes and Pharisees for them to be included in a call to baptism for sinners. Such a baptism would surely be appropriate for others, but not for them. They were already clean. Jesus was baptized with the baptism of all sinners. Such solidarity with all sinners John did not understand. Jesus answered him:

> "Let it be so now; it is proper for us to do this to fulfill all right-eousness." Then John consented. As soon as Jesus was baptized he went up out of the water. At that moment heaven was opened, and he saw the Spirit of God descending like a dove and lighting on him. And a voice from heaven said, "This is my Son, whom I love; with him I am well pleased." (Matt. 3:15–17)

Where there is a Son, there is a Father. Where there is the dove, there is the Spirit. The words that name Jesus Son or Servant echo Psalm 2 and Isaiah 42: Davidic king and suffering servant. With the name come the identity and the task. The cross is laid on Christ at Baptism. This is the baptism with which he is baptized (Mark 10:38). And with it we are baptized, when we received the Baptism that the risen Lord gives the Eleven to do. Water does to death and brings to life—here, both: Christ's and, by baptism, ours. His death for sin is our death for sin; his life, our life, indestructible (Rom. 6:3–11); for always and every day: "The old Adam in us, together with all sins and evil lusts, should be drowned by daily sorrow and repentance and be put to death, and that the new man should come forth daily and rise up, cleansed and righteous, to live forever in God's pres-ence."[3] Only from Jesus comes such a baptism. Only from Jesus is there a baptism "in the name of the Father and of the Son and of the Holy Spirit." All of this is in his name as Son, Servant, and Savior; all of this is his life's task given with his name, all in the cross. All is given with Baptism. "Baptism now saves you" (1 Pet. 3;21; 1 Peter was probably used for baptismal teaching).

P *We also learn from the Word of God that we all are conceived and born sinful and so are in need of forgiveness. We would be lost for-ever unless delivered from sin, death, and everlasting condemna-*

tion. But the Father of all mercy and grace has sent his Son Jesus Christ, who atoned for the sin of the whole world that whoever believes in him shall not perish but have eternal life.

What kind of Savior he is, is extolled from the witness of the Word of God. There is no life for sinners unless there is forgiveness. Here again there are no distinctions: no big sinners, no little sinners. All sins were covered by his atoning death in the place of all sinners. There are no sins that are not covered: total sinner, total forgiveness. "Where there is forgiveness of sins there is also life and salvation." "Let the sacrament remain whole."[4]

The Cross

P *Receive the sign of the holy cross both upon your forehead + and upon your heart + to mark you as one redeemed by Christ the crucified.*

Those to be baptized are identified as those who receive the gifts of Baptism won for them by the cross. The mark of the cross is put upon them. "Receive" is a gifting word (John 20:22; Matt. 26:26). Here is something we have not been mandated to do. Here is something that extols what Baptism gives, and identifies the one to whom it is given.

A seal, as a mark evidencing to whom someone or something belongs, has a long history. Circumcision was such a mark (Rom. 4:11), and also the blood of the lamb on the doorposts and lintel (Exod. 12:13). In Ezekiel 9, before the wrath of God falls upon the city, secretaries with their equipment were to go through the city and put the last letter of the alphabet on the foreheads of those who grieve over the sins of the city. The letter *Taw* was then written x or +. Those thus marked were spared in the judgment (Rev. 7:1–4; 9:4; 14:1). In the secretariat or archives in Jerusalem, burned in 586, seals have been found that make the mark "in the name of so and so" (*leshem* cf. *beshem*).

When the Lord puts his name on something, he marks it as his own. The Aaronic benediction put his name on Israel (Num. 6:27). Where his name is located, he is committed by that name to see to its good. Such good the benediction draws out of his name and bestows. In the prayer at the dedication of the temple Solomon lays hold of the name:

> You said, "My Name shall be there," so that you will hear the prayer your servant prays toward this place. . . . and when you hear, forgive. (1 Kings 8:29b–30)

Where God locates his name, there he is bound to be. He cannot evacuate his name. What and whom he puts his name on are his. Where his name is, there is prayer welling up out of it, inexhaustibly. How inexhaustibly, the history of the liturgy of Baptism shows abundantly.

Water and Spirit

Our Lord's words came early to be included in a prayer with regard to the water. In the form of Jewish prayer, God was blessed in thanks and praise for his gifts, for his dealing with them as his people, for his words, and bidding; then followed the petition that with this water he give the gifts he promised to give with it. When, some centuries later, a sacrament was defined as the conjunction of the words and the water, this conjunction came to be regarded as performed by such a prayer.

What was extolled and asked in prayer was acknowledged as God's doing. In Baptism, his doing is with the water. Thus the water was made holy to his use. Making holy is the work of the Holy Spirit, and Jesus had spoken of the conjunction of water and Spirit. Jesus' words are alive with the Spirit (John 6:63), and no words are more surely so than his name. Where the name is, there is the Spirit. Where the name and the water exist, there exists the Spirit. The Spirit is the one who makes what is dead alive (2 Cor. 3:6; Rom. 8:2; John 6:63). Regeneration is then done by "water and the Spirit." One thus made alive is brought into the kingdom of God. Neither Nicodemus nor any other can lay an explanation on this. It is simply by God's initiative, by his gifting by water and the Spirit according to his name and words. This all runs together. Damage is done when things are separated which he has joined together.

What our Lord mandated was done. Those baptized knew that what they were taught from the apostles and prophets was true of them. Peter brought his Pentecost sermon to its goal with "Repent, and be baptized every one of you in the name of Jesus Christ so that your sins may be forgiven. And you will receive the gift of the Holy Spirit. The promise is for you and your children, and for all who are far off—for all whom the Lord our God will call" (Acts 2:38–39). Heeding the Lord's call, the apostolic words, meant baptism. They were baptized. They were numbered with the church and continued there; that is where the means of grace were going on (Acts 2:14, 38–42). "Christ loved the church and gave himself up for her to make her holy, cleansing her by the washing with water through the word" (Eph. 5:25–26).

Of rites of Baptism we know very little until the beginning of the third century. In the *Didache* (c. 160) we learn of instruction and confession before Baptism. There is a preference for running water, but that is not essential. What is essential is to "pour water thrice upon the head, in the name of the Father and Son and Holy Spirit." Baptism leads to the Lord's Supper: "But let no one eat or drink of your eucharist but such as have been baptized in the name of the Lord."[5] The *First Apology* of Justin Martyr of 50 years earlier does not tell much more. The baptized are called "enlightened." While it is possible to construct somewhat of a rite of Baptism from the writings of Tertullian, greater credit is due him for having written the earliest treatise on the subject, about A.D. 200, the *De Baptismo*. What begins as extolling all the wondrous gifts of baptism, goes on to begin to separate them and assign them into the sequence of points at which the separated gifts are actually given, rather than extolled. Thus Tertullian asserts, "It is not in the water that we receive the Holy Spirit."[6] The bestowal of the Holy Spirit is removed from the water and assigned to the subsequent imposition of the baptizer's hand. Here is a beginning of the breaking up of Baptism into a sequence of things we do. A reference to the church in Tertullian grew later into the church being regarded as the guarantor of Baptism, rather than the reverse. In Tertullian, however, what we mostly find is an irrepressible impulse to extol the gifts and wonders of grace. He gambols through the Old Testament rejoicing in the waters, and does get a bit carried away. He rejoices in the water, and so overthrows the Gnostics who scorn water as something too earthly and simple for the bestowing of such gifts:

We are little fishes according to our great fish, Jesus Christ. We are born in water and continue to live healthily only as we remain in the water. She [a Gnostic] therefore knew very well how to kill the little fish—that utter abnormality, a woman who had authority to teach even if it had been sound doctrine—by drawing out of the water.[7]

Fish lured out of the water perish. They live only in the water. This is enormous devotional and polemical fun in Tertullian, but already in him we see some of the separations that may become pieces that acquire a role inherent in themselves. In contrast with the frightfully impressive washings done in the mystery religions, Tertullian glories in the lowly, unimpressive, simple water and few words of Baptism. But then he later goes on to outbid the mystery religions. What infiltrates from them is nothing but baneful for Baptism.

The Catechumenate

We have already delved into the history of Baptism; we must go further before we can see the way in which the Scripture readings (and other things) were placed. We have seen the primary passage put at the blessing of the water, and the gift of the Holy Spirit removed to the post-baptismal laying on of hands. Here John 3:5 ("Unless a man is born of water and the Spirit, he cannot enter the kingdom of God") has been split apart. Baptism is on its way to becoming a series of things, and each of these has some Scripture used with it; this extends also to the preparation for Baptism.

What Scripture says of Baptism is naturally a part of "teaching them to obey everything I have commanded." In the case of adults this teaching came before Baptism. What was included in such teaching is indicated in Hebrews:

Therefore let us leave the elementary teachings about Christ and go on to maturity, not laying again the foundation of repentance from acts that lead to death, and of faith in God, instruction about baptisms, the laying on of hands, the resurrection of the dead, and eternal judgment. And God permitting, we will do so (Heb. 6:1–3).

Doing this was immensely important in missionary situations. So it was at the beginning. Those ordained to the ministry were to be "apt to teach." One of their designations was "teacher" (1 Tim. 3:2; 2:7). There was inheritance of the ways of the rabbis, and adoption of the ways of the philosophical schools as in Alexandria. Church teaching, school teaching, and teaching in church schools, was in some places the sequence, and still today indicates the location of strengths, weaknesses, and tensions in fulfilling our Lord's mandate to teach the baptized and to teach toward Baptism. There is always the danger of the dominically mandated baptizing and teaching being obscured or displaced by things added by human beings (generic term), especially when these draw attention away from Christ and his words, and direct attention to man, to what is proceeding in man's transformation or as things man does to qualify him for Baptism.

In some places we see a rigorous catechumenate emerging. In Jerusalem in the fourth century the schooling went on for three years. There were stages, and these came to expression in the liturgy. Each stage registered an advancement and with this came the dangers of quantification, with first so much, then more and then later more. This additive benefit was to be evidenced in the holier lives of the catechumens. The system had danger of fractionalizing the gifts of Baptism and spreading them separately over a process of sanctification, with Baptism at the end doing the remainder.

When Baptism is a culminating part, and not the whole, then there may also be succeeding parts that "complete" Baptism. When Baptism is not the entire gift, then man may have his parts to do; and when man does the doing, there is never enough. "To be baptized in God's name is to be baptized not by man but by God himself. Although it is performed by men's hands, it is nevertheless truly God's own act. . . . Here the devil sets to work to blind us with false appearances and lead us away from God's work to our own."[8]

When Baptism came to be regarded as partial—an initiation, part of a process, a beginning with subsequent quantitative stages and accompanying gifts that brought one to final perfection, and so to fitness to be loved by God—then grace, gifts, and Holy Spirit were quantified and fractionalized. Then the whole lot is not given in Baptism. The Gospel is the whole lot; the Law measures and quantifies.

Apostolic Tradition of Hippolytus

Important in the history of Baptism is the account of it in Hippolytus' *Apostolic Tradition*. Written a little after A.D. 200, it is our first fuller account of the various parts that had variously developed. It was widely used and served to diminish diversity. Hippolytus was conservative and not prone to novelties.

The catechumenate lasted ordinarily three years.[9] We are told of no rite of reception into the catechumenate; witnesses vouched for the candidate. A century later there is evidence of reception into the catechumenate with the laying on of hands and the signing of the cross upon the forehead and chest. In Hippolytus the sign of the cross upon the forehead came after Baptism, an anointing all over (customary in the baths) and a laying on of hands. Then came the kiss of peace (the Pax) and the Eucharist. Only those given the Pax are thereby welcomed to the Lord's Table.

During the week before Baptism (Holy Week was regarded as particularly suitable), much was done with those chosen for Baptism (*electi, competentes*; in the East, "the enlightened"): examination, witnesses, daily laying on of hands, and exorcism. At the last of these the bishop breathed into their faces ("exsufflation"; blowing on someone was a sign of derision) and signed their foreheads, ears, and noses.[10]

So many exorcisms suggest the question of how much is enough, and with that the danger of quantification and anthropocentricity. From Tertullian we hear of the renunciation but nothing of exorcisms. It may have seemed natural that those who had been worshiping idols should be exorcised (1 Cor. 10:20; 2 Cor. 6:16; Rev. 9:20). The connection between sin and devil is broken by Clement of Alexandria: "It is not that demons are driven out of us, but that the sins are forgiven."[11] He became head of the Catechetical School in Alexandria in A.D. 190. In him we can observe the infiltration of Greek philosophy, where ignorance is the great evil and illumination the great good. Sin is diminished to voluntary deeds. Sin and devil are certainly taken more seriously by the exorcisms. No idol or devil is more dangerous than one not recognized. "No one can serve two masters" (Matt. 6:24). Where Jesus is Lord there can be no others. Where his Spirit dwells, there is room for no other spirits, and certainly not the spirit who tempts us to imagine that we belong to ourselves (1 Cor. 6:19; Col. 1:13).

We return to Hippolytus for Baptism itself, and so, an indication of whose we are. "When they come to the water," first infants are baptized, then men and women. "They shall baptize the little children first. And if they can answer for themselves, let them answer. But if they cannot, let their parents answer or someone from their family."[12] The renunciation follows ("I renounce you, Satan, and all your service and all your works"), then an exorcism with the "oil of exorcism." Standing in the water, those to be baptized are asked to confess the name. After each article of the Creed they answer, "I believe," and are thereupon baptized. Then comes an anointing with the "oil of thanksgiving." When they have dried themselves they come together in the assembly before the bishop, who lays his hands on them and prays:

> Lord God, just as you have made them worthy to receive the forgiveness of sins for all time to come, make them worthy also to be filled of your Holy Spirit, and send upon them your grace, that they may serve you according to your will.[13]

To serve is the verb of the baptismal service, the opposite of what has been renounced. The baptized are now welcomed into the whole worship service; hence the Pax and the Eucharist following. Such a prayer becomes the post-baptismal blessing:

> **P** *Almighty God, the Father of our Lord Jesus Christ, who has given you the new birth of water and of the Spirit and has forgiven you all your sins, strengthen you with his grace to life everlasting. Peace be with you. (rubric 14 in Lutheran Worship)*

Infants were answered for and baptized in the same rite that was shaped by the catechumenate. In the seventh century we have the first evidence of the inclusion of Mark 10:13–16, and from the tenth century the first record of Matthew 19:13–15 as a reading. Those baptized had for a very long time been mostly infants, yet the rite of Baptism that had come to be shaped by the catechumenate was simply continued. It continued through the Reformation. We may note a distinction made by Aquinas:

> In Baptism certain things are done which are necessary for the sacrament and certain things which pertain to the solemnity of the

sacrament . . . to arouse the devotion of the faithful and reverence of the sacrament . . . to instruct . . . to check the devil's power.[14]

This distinction, as always, is exemplified by emergency baptism.

Luther: *Little Book of Baptism*

In Luther's day almost the only baptisms were of infants, and yet the form of the catechumenate continued in the liturgy. He praises God that there has been Baptism.[15] So that people might be incited the more to faith and devotion, and the priests might have greater concern for their hearers,[16] Luther translated the order of Baptism then in use (*Agenda Communis*) in his *Little Book of Baptism* (*Das tauffbuchlin verdeutscht*) in 1523. This is the same Baptism as always was and will be to the consummation. Luther's dominant concern is the fundamental certainty of one's Baptism. No one should be prompted to suppose that a new or different Baptism is being introduced, or that anyone should doubt that he or she was in fact baptized. So he distinguishes between Baptism itself and those things that men have added. Nothing depends on these, and so he is free to carry them forward so long as they run with God's words and accordant faith and prayer. The changes he makes are mostly for abbreviation, and in his revision of 1526 there are more.

Because the lineage of our liturgy of Baptism comes to us by way of the *Little Book of Baptism*, we need to look at it more closely. The order proceeds in ways of the catechumenate. Things that were done in the fifth century with days—even weeks or years—between them, here come one after another, much as they did since Carolingian times and from the Frankish Gelasian sacramentary of the eighth century and the *Pontificale Romano-Germanicum* of the tenth. Forms of the catechumenate remained, although the substance of the stages they expressed was mostly gone. With the disappearance of adult baptism, the baptismal rite underwent a drastic alteration, many of the ceremonies properly belonging to the catechumenate being squeezed into the service of baptism.[17] We may observe a long and slow decatechumenatizing movement. Luther made little change in the customary rite, but he expounded it from Christ, his words, and what they say and bestow with the water. Change may not be imposed in the way of the Law. "The Word must do this thing, and not we poor sinners."[18]

Best of the catechumenate was its fulfillment of our Lord's bidding to teach. This was obscured when the stages were seen as stages in a process of progressively evidenced sanctification. Improvements in man are then the way to Baptism, as if some level of cleanness or purification was a necessary preliminary or qualification for Baptism, as if God loved us because we are lovable. How then could Luther use material from the old catechumenate? The proper distinction between Law and Gospel is the key to understanding the *Little Book of Baptism*.

Luther had great freedom with anything that might extol Baptism. Prayers had multiplied; exorcisms had multiplied; he was free to use them to extol the Gospel of Baptism in the confidence of what our Lord has given and gives with his words and the water. Words and water make the Baptism, not the things that have been added. To make too much of the latter would bring the danger of turning them into Law, into a "must" or "must not."[19] His complaint is that the rite he translates does not sufficiently glorify Baptism.

The *Little Book of Baptism* begins abruptly with the exsufflation. Anything preceding is not taken into account. Entry into the catechumenate, or later into its final stage, was done with exsufflication and the marking with the cross. The rubrics that derive from the practice of the catechumenate Luther omits; he simply begins with the exsufflation:

> The officiant shall blow three times under the child's eyes and shall say: "Depart thou unclean spirit, and give room to the Holy Spirit." Then he shall sign him with a cross on his forehead and breast and shall say: "Receive the sign of the holy cross on both thy forehead and thy breast."[20]

Here is the first exorcism. By Baptism the Lord saves and makes us his own. The only alternative to belonging to him is belonging to the devil. Hence Satan must be banished and renounced. This is done with the words of God and prayer. This is Jesus' work (Matt. 8:16; 12:28) and is done in his name (Mark 9:38). The dominion of Satan is the dominion of sin. Baptism frees us from this. In the history of the liturgy we see the danger of this being peeled off from Baptism.

The term *exorcism* has no Christian usage in the New Testament. It is never said of Baptism. This may also be observed of *sealing* and *illumination,* which also became a part of baptismal terminology, as did *sacrament.* Each has its proper use in extolling what is given in Baptism. Baptismal sealing may indeed be evoked by Eph. 1:13 and 2 Tim. 2:19. *Anointed* or *Christed* is also found in 2 Cor. 1:22. Hence we have *christening* and the use of oil. The seal was the name of Christ, concentrated in the cross (Rev. 14:1).

Then come two prayers in the *Little Book of Baptism,* imploring the gifts of Baptism for those to be baptized. In Luther's 1526 revision of this rite these two prayers are made into one prayer. Omitted in this revision is an exorcism with salt, where, in the *Little Book,* salt is put into the mouth of the child with the words, "Receive the salt of wisdom. May it aid thee to eternal life. Amen. Peace be with thee."[21] In Luther's German, *wisdom* is the antecedent of *which*; in the Latin the reference is to the salt.

Then comes the so-called Flood Prayer (*Sintflutgebet*),[22] which gathers a number of things together that are not original with Luther, although the combination of them may well be. The matrix of this prayer are the blessing of the water and the readings contained in the Easter vigil. Cut off from these, the prayer is difficult to use with understanding, as witness the many efforts to rework it. Some of these efforts were prompted by embarrassment at its radical statement of sin. Such efforts were resisted by insistence on using the prayer, as was also the case with the exorcisms. The Flood Prayer, and exorcisms more so, were then a touchstone of sound doctrine.[23] This was not the case between Lutheran churches, some of which had these, while others did not, but rather over against Calvinism. Calvin taught that infants (of Christian parents) were already part of God's covenant, and so did not by Baptism become children of God. "They already belong to the body of Christ; they are received into the Church with this solemn sign."[24] To such a view, exorcisms and renunciations are worse than nonsense and must disappear, as well as emergency baptisms.[25] Instead of them there is then more emphasis on covenant and entry into the church. The sound doctrine expressed by the Flood Prayer and the exorcisms is confessed in the renunciation, vicariously confessed by the sponsors.[26] At the heart of the matter is the Gospel understanding of faith—all God's gifts and doing, "as the Word and promise of God declare."[27] Hence the simple "Yes" in the *Little Book of Baptism* to the creedal questions instead of "I believe," and the "I wish it" in answer to "Wilt thou be baptized?" The latter archaism, no longer usable, is a literal translation of the German in the *Little Book of Baptism*. "Do you wish to be baptized?" may draw attention away from the only solid reference, and so may prompt uncertainty. Hence it does not follow the Creed. Baptism is not "primarily concerned whether the baptized person believes or not, for in the latter case Baptism does not become invalid. Everything depends on the Word and commandment of God. . . . For my faith does not constitute Baptism but receives it."[28] When faith speaks, it speaks of gifts given and to be given. Hence the sponsors speak true when they speak the infant's faith, its being given the gifts.

After the Flood Prayer came three exorcisms, one fewer than before. In 1526 there are only two exorcisms. The prayer that comes next is also omitted in 1526, as are the versicle and response, "The Lord be with you/And with your spirit." Their function of introducing the next part is obsolete. Mark 10:13–16 is read. "Then the priest shall lay his hand on the head of the child and pray the Our Father together with the sponsors kneeling."[29] Christ's hands are here the priest's hands. The blessing bestowed is that of being drawn by Jesus into the company of those who, with and because of him, call God *Abba,* baby talk for *Father,* which no one ever dared do before Jesus.

Luther omits the Creed here, a place in the scrutinies of the catechumenate where the faith taught was said back (*redittio symboli*). The omission abbreviates by removing repetition; he has the Creed commonly at its native place. In his rite they are in the form of creedal questions,[30] as such, older than almost anything else in the rite, words that gave birth to the baptismal creed—the Apostles'—all born of the name.

The *Agenda Communis* then has the priest adjure the sponsors in German, on pain of their souls' salvation, to instruct the child when it comes to its "years of reason" in the true faith—the Lord's Prayer, the Ave Maria, the Creed—and to bear witness that it has received the holy Christian Baptism. Then comes an exorcism prayer. Both of these parts are omitted by Luther. Later at this place come the admonition and pledge of sponsors, in *Lutheran Worship* appearing under rubric 6 in the rite of Holy Baptism.

Then the baptizer puts spit on his finger, touches the right ear with it and says, "Ephphatha, that is, be thou opened." Then the nose and left ear are touched, with the priest saying, "But thou, devil, flee; for God's judgment cometh speedily." Thereupon the infant is brought into the church; the priest says, "The Lord preserve thy coming in and thy going out now and for evermore."[31]

This done, the priest has the child renounce the devil through its sponsors. "*Name*, dost thou renounce the devil?" The sponsors answer "Yes." The same answer is given to "And all his works? And all his ways?" and thereafter to each article of the Apostles' Creed. Then the priest anoints the child with oil on the chest and between the shoulders while saying, "And I anoint thee with the oil of salvation in Jesus Christ our Lord." After the affirmative response to "Wilt thou be baptized?" the priest takes the child and dips it in the font, saying, "And I baptize thee in the name of the Father and of the Son and of the Holy Ghost."[32]

While the sponsors hold the infant in the font (i.e., over the font), the priest makes the sign of the cross with holy oil upon its head, and says, "The almighty God and Father of our Lord Jesus Christ, who hath regenerated you through water and the Holy Ghost, and hath forgiven you all your sins, anoint thee with the salutary oil of eternal life. Amen" (*votum postbaptismale*).[33]

"Peace be with you/And with your spirit." While the sponsors still hold the child in the font, the priest puts on it the christening hood while saying, "Receive the white, holy and spotless robe which thou shalt bring before the judgment seat of Christ so as to receive eternal life. Peace be with you."[34]

Then the child is lifted from the font and the priest puts a candle into its hand saying, "Receive this burning torch and preserve thy baptism blameless, so that when the Lord cometh to the wedding thou mayest go to meet him with the saints into the heavenly mansion and receive eternal life. Amen."[35]

The 1526 version of the *Little Book of Baptism* omits the exsufflation and the salt. Only two exorcisms remain, and they are trimmed down. The Ephphatha is omitted with its exorcism. After the Lord's Prayer the infant is brought to the font, and the priest says, "The Lord preserve thy coming in and going out now and for evermore." After the baptizing the sign of the cross with oil is omitted. There is no reference to the christening robe in the post-baptismal blessing (*votum postbaptismale*). The candle is omitted. An ending is added (restored): "Peace be with thee. Amen."

Table 2

Comparison of Rites

Little Book of Baptism (1523)	**Holy Baptism** (LW 1982)
1.	(Hymn)
2. Exsufflation/Exorcism	Invocation/Admonition from Scripture
3. Sign of the Cross	Sign of the Cross
4. Prayers	
5. Giving of Salt	
6. Prayer (Flood Prayer)	
7. Exorcism	
8. Prayer	
9. Salutation and Response	
10. Gospel	Gospel
11.	Promises of Sponsors
12. Our Father and Laying on of Hands	Our Father/Laying on of Hands/Blessing
13. Ephphatha	
14. Renunciation/Profession of Faith	Renunciation/Profession of Faith
15. Anointing with Oil	
16. Declaration of Intent	Declaration of Intent/Naming
17. Baptism	Baptism
18. Prayer/Anointing/Sign of the Cross	Blessing and Laying on of Hands
19. Peace	
20. Presentation of White Robe	(Presentation of White Garment)

21. Presentation of Baptismal Candle	(Presentation of Baptismal Candle)
22.	Prayers
23.	(Reception as Member and Blessing)

Admonitions

After 1529 the *Little Book of Baptism* was printed with the Catechism and was formative for subsequent baptismal usage, but not to uniformity. Admonitions were early included at different places: at the beginning, after the Gospel, after the Lord's Prayer, and at the end. There was provision for emergency baptism. Already by 1544 there were warnings against too many admonitions and too many designing questions being put to the sponsors. Matthew 28 moves from the blessing of the font to a place serving as words of institution.

In the admonitions the Lord's mandate to make disciples of all nations by baptizing and teaching enjoys prominence. Only when both have been done has the mandate to make disciples been done. By baptizing—the other part of the mandate—the teaching is undertaken, and the teaching is done toward the baptizing. What our Lord gives to be done may not be partly accepted and partly refused. In the case of infants, God's deputies, those to whom he has entrusted the child, the parents, commit themselves to the whole mandate, both the baptizing and the teaching. They are joined in this by the sponsors who pledge themselves also to the whole mandate, especially if the child should lose its parents. They do this as themselves baptized, and so as members of the church and as also representative of it.

All of this derives from the mandate in the rite, under rubric 2 in *Lutheran Worship*, and is done after the Gospel reading(s) beginning with "It is your task as sponsors . . ." and the questions to the parents, "Who brings this child to be baptized?" under rubric 11. Teaching represented a great need in the early church as "the word of the Lord spread widely and grew in power" (Acts 19:20; 15:35; 18:11). Later such teaching was necessary also for the people who overran the Roman Empire, and again in Carolingian times. To these times can be traced some things in the *Agenda Communis*, which

Luther translated in the *Little Book of Baptism*. Luther served the need to teach mostly by preaching. Subsequently this need produced the admonitions, which tended to grow and grow, and also to the reform of schools and the establishment of church schools.

The impulse to glorify Baptism, as seen already in Tertullian, produced overgrowth that from time to time called for pruning. In the *Little Book of Baptism* of 1523 there was a little pruning, more in the 1526 revision. The criterion, "the glory of Baptism," produced admonitions and questionings, which led to the danger of again too much, obscuring Baptism itself. The Reformation gave rise to many admonitions. The people simply could not contain their glory in Baptism. As representative of such admonitions, those in the church order of Albertine Saxony (1539, 1540, and 1555) show the common factors. The rite therein, faithful to the *Little Book of Baptism* of 1526, was widely influential. Its opening admonition is contained in the *Kirchen-Agende* (1856), the first official agenda produced by the Missouri Synod.[36] Translated into English in 1881, the admonition therein reads:

> Dearly Beloved in Christ! We hear every day from the Word of God, perceive it, also, by our own experience in life and death, that we from Adam's fall are all conceived and born in sins, wherein we would necessarily be condemned and lost forever under the wrath of God, had we not been delivered from them by the only Son of God, our dear Lord Jesus Christ.[37]

The rite of Baptism in the Synod's 1922 *Kirchen-Agende* begins with the triune name (the Invocation); then comes the admonition, similar to the 1856 *Kirchen-Agenda* and that in the Albertine Saxony (1539). The Synod's 1916 *Liturgy and Agende* put the admonition in brackets and so offers the option of beginning with the mandate. What remains of this admonition comes after the Invocation and mandate in *Lutheran Worship* (1982), the second paragraph under rubric 2. It is of interest to note that the 1916 *Liturgy and Agenda*, with slight and optional changes, continued in use until the appearance of *Lutheran Worship* (1982). In this hymnal, Baptism without sponsors disappears; adult and infant Baptism are brought back into one rite. Interestingly, the rite for adult Baptism grew out of rites for the Baptism of a Jew. An exorcism[38] given in a footnote as optional following the Flood Prayer, in the 1856 *Kirchen-Agende*, disappeared in 1916.

The Saxons and the Missouri Synod

The Saxons who came to Missouri did not further the admonitions in use in their native Saxony. By reaching back to the old Saxon orders they avoided (as was characteristic of the 19th-century confessional revival) the anthropocentricities and rationalism of the Enlightenment that had intruded the admonitions. In the Saxon Agenda of 1812, which they brought with them, admonitions abound in five different rites for infant Baptism—something to suit everyone's taste. Moreover, there is an order for the baptizing of a Jew and an order for emergency baptism. In all that is said in this last rite, there is no reading, no mandate, no mention of sin (except in the Lord's Prayer), forgiveness, regeneration, Calvary, or the imparting of the Holy Spirit. When he became a pastor, this agenda gave Walther much grief. He speaks of Baptism and Absolution. For holy absolution he reached back to the old Saxon order and was persecuted for doing so. Then came the *Kirchen-Agende* of 1856, prepared by the St. Louis Conference. Subsequently some good things it lacked have been restored, and some things no longer serviceable have been omitted.

In following the history of the admonitions, which come as a result of the Reformation, we may observe the nearer lineage of the rite of Holy Baptism in *Lutheran Worship*. It runs through the *Little book of Baptism*, the old Saxon order, and the *Kirchen-Agende* of 1856. In this lineage one may spot a Teutonically talkative Ruth, and, subsequently, a Rahab who knows only the language of Canaan.

A pruned-down form of the old admonition is put in brackets in the Synod's 1948 *Agenda*; thus our Lord's mandate is given greater prominence. In *Lutheran Worship* (1982) anything that might deflect attention to us and away from the fact that it is all the Lord's doing is gone. The essentials of the admonition follow the Lord's mandate and promise: "We also learn from the Word of God . . ."

Within the variety of usage, the actual Baptism itself was always constant. While the addition of human traditions frequently extol the gifts of Baptism and enliven devotion and reverence, the danger is that the things thus added tend to draw attention to themselves and away from the Baptism itself which these things are there to extol; they may reach the point of themselves being regarded as bestowing the gifts of Baptism. When this distinction is blurred, Baptism itself, the actual baptizing, may come to be regarded as one of the number of things we do, and itself be seen as a similar symbolic action, one that is *our* doing and not the Lord's. Here the Lord's mandate is decisive.

The triune name and the water have always been Baptism. Where there is Baptism, there is the church, for Baptism is as sure as the words, name, and promises of God are sure. Luther lamented how sin had been divided up, and so then also forgiveness, as if Baptism's forgiveness was not entire. "One Baptism for the remission of sins."

In *Lutheran Worship* the admonition to the sponsors is pared down to essentials. Improvising pastors may still be found who make didactic or sentimental additions, or they may add questions with hooks which have more of the Law than of the Gospel about them. On the other hand, the gifts of Baptism instill an irrepressible impulse to extol. This has produced lengthening of the rite, which from time to time has called for trimming. That there is always more to be extolled is seen in the preaching and teaching toward and after Baptism itself, where the words, name, and promise of God do it all. Acceptance of what the Lord gives is expressed with a simple receptive *Yes* followed by the blessing of the Lord's enablement. The acknowledgement of our inability is followed by prayer, the Lord's Prayer with the laying on of hands.

In the *Little Book of Baptism*, following the final words of the Gospel, "He took them up in his arms, put his hands upon them and blessed them," there comes the laying on of hands with the Lord's Prayer. The latter two actions represent also the sequence in *Lutheran Worship* in accord with rubric 7. This is then what happens in Baptism, "Christ's baptism."[39] The Lord's Prayer was given by our Lord to his disciples. Only to disciples is it given, to those who, with and because of Jesus, may call God "Abba." The blessings of being brought into his family, into discipleship, are here confessed as the gift of Baptism. The laying on of hands leaves no doubt to whom the gift is given. The one upon whom the hands were laid is being brought into the company of all those who are Christ's disciples, to whom alone this prayer is given.

The Baptizing

Here ends the preliminary phase marked by the entrance blessing and the movement to the font. Here is were Baptism occurs. In our Lord's mandate Baptism is linked with teaching; hence now the questions, first regarding the renunciation and then the creedal questions (see rubric 10 in *Lutheran Worship*). Such questions are the oldest parts of the liturgy of Baptism, next to the triune name and the water, of which we have evidence. From the answers to these questions grew the Apostles' Creed, which is always the creed at Baptism. It draws out and confesses the name. To confess is to say back to God what he has said and given (*homologein*). Here, in Baptism, he gives his name, put upon the one baptized with the water. With his name God commits himself with all that is in his name. That God does this is what faith confesses. That God gives his gifts to an infant is infant faith, for faith is being at the receiving end of God's giving. This fact, this faith, is confessed for an infant by the parents and sponsors along with the church, the baptized.

First a negative faith is confessed. In our first birth we are born sinful, flesh born of flesh. We must be born again of water and the Spirit (John 3:5). Where the water is, there is the Spirit. Where his name is, there is he doing and bestowing what is his to do and bestow: regeneration. For the one baptized God is Abba (Gal. 4:6). In Baptism the Spirit is given the one baptized, who is then a temple of the Spirit. The Holy Spirit does not cohabit with the evil spirit. In Baptism the latter is banished. This is confessed with the thoroughgoing renunciation of the devil. This fact is true of the baptized infant, and this fact is confessed for the infant. Sin is denial of belonging to God, of receiving everything as a gift from his hands. If one does not belong to God, the only other alternative is belonging to sin and Satan. Satan's delusion is that we might by way of sin belong to ourselves and have the say-so (Gen. 3:5). "One Lord, one faith, one Baptism" (Eph. 4:5). "He has delivered us from the dominion of darkness and transferred us to the kingdom of his beloved Son, in whom we have redemption, and forgiveness of sins" (Col. 1:13; Mark 1:11).

Those to whom a child has been entrusted, those who are God's deputies for this child, confess this fact in answering the question, "Who brings this child to be baptized?" (see rubric 11 in *Lutheran Worship*). What has been given them to do by God may not be usurped by anyone else. With their answer they embrace all that comes with their child's being baptized. The gifts of Baptism they will nurture. They undertake the teaching which with the baptizing is the mandate of our Lord. The office of parent is expressed with all that is involved in naming a child.

The Name-Giving

The name-giving (*nomendatio*) is evidenced in the West in the fourth century. It came at the beginning of the second phase of the catechumenate, the first phase having by then fallen into decline. The name was written down when one became a candidate for Baptism in the last phase before the Baptism itself (Rev. 21:27). In the fourth and fifth centuries we see this happening at the beginning of Lent, in the Middle Ages on the First Sunday in Lent (*Invocabit*). The reason for its absence from the *Little Book of Baptism* is the same, then, as for the absence there of the *mandatum Christi*. When the teaching was revitalized at the Reformation, things that were spread out in the progressive phases of the catechumenate came gradually together in the rite of Baptism: Christ's mandate, the marking with the cross, the name-giving. The name question was put at various places: at the beginning (Brandenburg–Nürenberg 1533); after the opening admonition (Albertine Saxony 1540, 1555; Lüneberg, 1619); after the admonition to the sponsors (Hesse, 1574); immediately before the Baptism itself (Augsburg, 1537 and 1555). Walther extols it in his *Pastoraltheologie*.[40]

Name and identity go together. So we have the designation of a particular person by name, and upon that particular person the triune name of God is put with the water in the very act of baptizing. Through all the variations of liturgy this has always been there. Who and whose we are is given with the name and water.

The post-baptismal blessing (rubric 14 in *Lutheran Worship*) leaves no doubt, with the laying on of hands, to whom the gifts of Baptism have been given. The gifts are those Tertullian mentioned as confessed by every Christian: the forgiveness of sins, deliverance from death, being born again, and the bestowal of the Holy Spirit.[41]

So great was the certainty of forgiveness that it prompted consideration of the benefit of delay. Constantine (c. 280–337) delayed Baptism until his deathbed. The following is the first and, until the 16th century, the only reason urged for delaying Baptism: "The opposition to infant baptism was based upon this feeling, strengthened by the conviction that the guilt of sin after baptism was peculiarly great. . . rather than from any notion of the child's incapacity to receive the benefit of the sacrament."[42] When Tertullian singularly urges the case against infant baptism,[43] such baptizing was naturally going on. Origen (c. 195–c. 254) calls it apostolic.[44] What is apostolic is no novelty. If it were a novelty, much would have had to be said by its protagonists. The question is not whether an infant (or anyone) has the capacity to receive benefit, but rather, whether God gives what his words, name, and promises say and bestow. There was talk of "age of innocence" and "age of reason," but not thoroughgoingly, as witness the practice of emergency baptism.

The certainty of forgiveness is given in Acts 2:35, 22:16, Rom. 6:6, and Titus 3:3–7. With the forgiveness of sins comes every other gift, for, as Luther declares, "Where there is forgiveness of sins, there are also life and salvation."[45] Moreover, Baptism, he says, "effects forgiveness of sins, delivers from death and the devil, and grants eternal salvation to all who believe, as the Word and promise of God declare."[46] Not to be overlooked are these significant words of Luther:

> In Baptism, therefore, every Christian has enough to study and to practice all his life. He always has enough to do to believe firmly what Baptism promises and brings—victory over death and the devil, forgiveness of sin, God's grace, the entire Christ, and the Holy Spirit with his gifts. . . . To appreciate and use Baptism aright, we must draw strength and comfort from it when our sins or conscience oppress us, and we must retort, "But I am baptized!"[47]

"Peace be with you." With this Pax the Saxon order of 1539 ended, and so also the *Kirchen-Agende* of 1856. The Pax was the embrace and welcome to the Lord's Table of Hippolytus, and it is still with those for whom the whole mandate of Christ has been done, as we celebrate at Confirmation.

Prayers and Blessing

In the *Liturgy and Agenda* of 1916 a prayer extolling Baptism's gift to the church was added after the Pax, taken from the Württemberg (1553) church order. It appears also in the Baptism of an Adult in the *Kirchen-Agende* of 1856, as well as in *Lutheran Worship* (under rubric 17). This prayer cannot be prayed by those who regard Baptism as only an individual or private matter—"just Jesus and me." To live in one's Baptism is to live in the church as a "member of your [God's] Son, our Lord Jesus Christ." Incorporated in Christ we are incorporated into the rag, tag, and bobtail of his church, where sinners are forgiven and where they "may faithfully grow" by "teaching them to obey everything I have commanded you" (Matt. 28:20). The Pax reminds us that our Baptism is geared toward the eating and drinking of the body and blood of our Lord "for the forgiveness of sins." Only non-sinners need not heed this. The conclusion of this prayer—"and finally with all your saints obtain the promised inheritance in heaven"—clearly points to the fact that Baptism carries us all the way through to heaven and our "heavenly birthday." We die baptized. His name holds!

There is always more to extol. Württemberg followed this prayer of thanksgiving with a lengthy admonition (its fifth). The impulse to extol and teach is evidenced in *Lutheran Worship* (rubrics 15 and 16) by the optional addition of the white christening garment and the candle, ceremonies from Luther's *Little Book of Baptism* (1523). In his 1526 revision, the candle is omitted and the white garment is put on with the post-baptismal blessing, in which the "anoint thee with salutary oil" is replaced with "strengthen thee with his grace." The text in *Lutheran Worship* relative to the white garment (rubric 15) begins as in the *Little Book of Baptism*, and from there the text goes on to direct attention to Christ, imputed righteousness and faith alive. The use of "to show" expresses the distinction between what extols and what does Baptism, between Baptism itself and what has been added (Luther), between what extols and signifies and what effects (Gerhard), between what is essential and what is accidental (J. K. Dietrich).

This distinction is most clearly exemplified by the rites for emergency baptism, as witness the Lutheran church orders of the 16th century and since. That such a rite might be readily available, it is given in *Lutheran Worship* (p. 312), a procedure followed in the Synod's preceding hymnals. Granted, the triune name and water makes the Baptism; nothing more is essential. Noticeable even in this rite for emergency baptism is the addition of a brief prayer plus the Lord's Prayer—again, indicative of the tendency to extol the fact and gifts of Baptism.

Already in the second century there is evidence of the practice of emergency baptism, borne out by the inscriptions on the graves of those thus baptized. Certainty of Baptism is certainty of salvation. Failure to do emergency baptism, says Tertullian, can result in being guilty of someone's damnation.[48] Salvation/Christ is not given conditionally or by fractions. So it is with Baptism. Concerning the one who died after emergency baptism, there was no doubt. For the one who lived on, there was the need that no doubt exist that he or she was indeed baptized. Hence the custom of having the emergency baptism (done in private) publicly vouched for, recognized, and received by the church. For this procedure, the rite, Recognition by the Church of an Emergency Baptism, is provided in *Lutheran Worship: Agenda*,[49] a rite derived from the Saxony (1539) church order via the Synod's *Kirchen-Agende* of 1856.

The words in the rite of Holy Baptism in *Lutheran Worship* that go with the giving of the candle, while reflecting those in the *Little Book of Baptism* of 1523, focus more on Christ, the scriptural and the eschatological references are made clearer, and "with joy" is added. The prayer for parents and declaration of reception are further optional additions. These follow the example of the *Lutheran Book of Worship* (1978). Baptism ripples over parents and congregation, and they rejoice in the gifts that come with the birthing water of Baptism.

The final blessing of the baptized in the rite (under rubric 19) is from the "Churching of the Mother." From time to time in the history of the liturgy there happens such a perfection as this, for when there is no "Churching of the Mother," a prayer is provided. A related prayer is for a woman after childbirth, a prayer that reaches toward Baptism. In this final blessing it is the child who is spoken to. (It may be bawling its head off!) The blessing is given in the confidence of the gifts given by our Lord's words, promises, and triune name with the water. The prayers have rejoiced in his giving his gifts, and have pleaded that the gifts may live and grow. They may be rejected. Grounds for uncertainty may be located in the infant, parents, godparents, pastor, and congregation. But, with Luther we declare, "On this I build, that it is thy Word and command."[50] If we look elsewhere, the problems we may suspect are ours, not God's. He can only be true to his words, promises, and name with the water. His gifts and his authority are not subject to our diminishing measurements. And so we have in the blessing, "in all your ways from this time forth and even forevermore." Even when we stray, he remains faithful to his name, ever recalling us to himself, to his name put on us at "this time" of Baptism.

Each generation trims a little, adds a little (extolling is never finished); but always the actual Baptism itself remains the same: "one Lord, one faith, one baptism" (Eph. 4:5).

Notes

1. SA III, 5, 1.
2. Gal. 3:27; Ap IX.
3. SC IV, 12.
4. WA 30': 55, 19. Cf. Joachim Jeremias, *The Origins of Infant Baptism*, trans. Dorothea M. Barton (London: SCM Press, 1963), p. 84: "the wholeness (*Ganzheitsdenken*) of the New Testament theology about baptism." Also Edmund Schlink, *The Doctrine of Baptism*, trans. Herbert J. A. Bouman (St. Louis, London: Concordia Publishing House, 1972), pp. 199–205.
5. *Didache* 7, 1–3; 9, 5.
6. Tertullian, *De Baptismo* 6.
7. Ibid., 1.
8. LC IV, 10–11.
9. Hippolytus 17.
10. Ibid., 20, 8.
11. *Stromata* 2, 117, 3.
12. Hippolytus 21, 4.
13. Ibid., 22, 1.

14. St. Thomas Aquinas' *Summa Theologica*, trans. Fathers of the English Dominican Province (New York: Benziger Bros., 1948), III, 66, 10, 4. See also Johann Gerhard, *Ausführliche schriftmäszige Erklärung der beiden Artikel von der heiligen Taufe und dem heiligen Abendmahl* (Jena: Tobias Steinmann, 1610; Berlin: Gustav Schlawitz, 1868), pp. 153f.

15. AE 36: 57; 40: 241.

16. AE 53: 101.

17. J. N. D. Kelly, *Early Christian Creeds*, 3d ed. (New York: Longman, 1972), p. 40.

18. AE 51: 77.

19. Ibid., 70–100.

20. AE 53: 96. The extolling addition in the Missouri Synod's *Liturgy and Agenda* of 1916, "in token that thou has been redeemed by Christ the Crucified," is derived from the Cologne (1534) and Pomerania (1569) church orders.

21. AE 53: 97.

22. Ibid.

23. *In statu confessionis*, FC SD X, 10.

24. *Institutes* 4, 15, 22.

25. Ibid., 4, 15, 20.

26. AE 53: 99.

27. SC IV, 6.

28. LC IV, 52–53.

29. AE 53: 99, 108.

30. Ibid.

31. Ibid., 99.

32. Ibid., 99–100.

33. Ibid., 100.

34. Ibid., 101.

35. Ibid.

36. Complete citation: *Kirchen-Agende für Evangelische Gemeinden ungeänderter Augsburgischer Confession*. Zusammengestellt aus den alten rechtgläubigen Sächsischen Kirchenagenden und herausgegeben von der Allgemeinen deutschen Evangel.-Lutherischen Synode von Missouri, Ohio und anderen Staaten (St. Louis; Druckerei der deutschen Ev.-Luth. Synode v. Missouri, Ohio und anderen Staaten, 1856).

37. Baptism of Infants, in *Church Liturgy for Evangelical Lutheran Congregations of the Unaltered Augsburg Confession* (St. Louis: Concordia Publishing House, 1881), p. 3.

38. See *Kirchen-Agende* (1856), p. 3.

39. LC IV, 22, 35.

40. C. F. W. Walther, *Americanisch-Lutherische Pastoraltheologie*, 4th ed. (St. Louis: Concordia Publishing House, 1897), p. 131.

41. Tertullian, *Adversus Marcionem* 1, 28, 2.

42. J. F. Bethune-Baker, *An Introduction to the Early History of Christian Doctrine to the Time of the Council of Chalcedon* (London: Methuen, 1903), pp. 379f.

43. Tertullian, *De Baptismo* 18, 4–5.

44. Origen, *Commentary on Romans* 9, 5.

45. SC VI, 6.

46. Ibid., IV, 6.

47. LC IV, 41, 44.

48. *De Baptismo* 17, 3.

49. *Lutheran Worship: Agenda*, prepared by the Commission on Worship of The Lutheran Church—Missouri Synod (St. Louis: Concordia Publishing House, 1984), p. 105.

50. LC IV, 56. Cf. AC VIII.

9

Holy Communion

Norman E. Nagel

The Preface

"The Lord be with you." Similar to the beginning of the Divine Service itself, the first word spoken to begin the Communion is the name of the Lord. "It is the Lord's Supper, in name and reality, not the supper of Christians."[1] The Lord is host, the head of the family; it is the Lord who serves (Luke 22:27), hence the name *Divine Service* (from *Gottesdienst*, a subjective genitive). The Lord is serving, giving out his gifts. His gifts are given with the words that carry and bestow what they say. That is the way of his words. They are alive with his Spirit, who with the gifts thus worded to us creates and nourishes faith. There is no passage that speaks of the Holy Spirit in connection with the Lord's Supper. That is not strange, for his work is to point to Jesus and bring home to us him and his gifts. Where Jesus' words are going on, there is also the Spirit (John 6:63). Any spirit apart from Jesus is not the Holy Spirit (John 16:15). The Holy Spirit is most pleased when we speak of Jesus and not of him. He gives only Jesus gifts. The receiving of these gifts is faith. Faith speaks only of what it is given. It speaks sure when it says back the words that have been spoken to it, and so speaks of the gifts the words bestow. When we say back to him the words he has said to us, they are as indestructible as his. We confess them. *Confess* is from the Latin for *homologein*, to say the same thing. At the beginning of the Divine Service the name he put upon us with the water of Baptism is said back to him. Then we say the same thing back to him that he has said to us. Law: We are sinners. Then Gospel: You are forgiven. His words are spoken by the man put there ("called and ordained") to speak his words that bestow forgiveness. Forgiveness received, faith says, Amen. "This is most certainly true." Gift given, gift received. The way of versicle and response is the heartbeat of the liturgy: diastole, systole; breath in, breath out. Actually we are breathed into (the kiss of life), the breath of the Spirit speaking the words into our ears, the organ of faith (Rom. 10:17; 8:2; John 6:63; 20:22; Gen. 2:7). What goes on in the Divine Service is that "Our dear Lord himself [speaks] to us through his holy Word and we respond to him through prayer and praise."[2] "The woman came, believing that she should seek forgiveness of sins from Christ. This is the highest way of worshiping Christ. Nothing greater could she ascribe to him." Moreover, "It is by faith that God wants to be worshiped, namely, that we receive [German: that we are given to receiving gifts] from him what he promises and offers."[3]

There is little that is older in the liturgy than the versicles and responses, the dialogue of the Preface. "The Lord be with you" is spoken by the presiding minister, the man put there as the instrument for the Lord's speaking of his words. The words themselves come from Scripture (Judg. 6:12; Ruth 2:4; Ps. 129:8; Luke 1:28), where they speak a blessing in greeting. They appear at the presiding minister's entry here into the Service of Holy Communion. A variation was "Peace be with you," our risen Lord's words to the Eleven (Luke 24:36, John 20:19, 21, 26). In the *Didache* (c. 150), which gives us some of our earliest evidences of the liturgy, we find, "Grace come and this world go by." The Coptic version reads, "The Lord came and this world go by."[4] The response in the *Didache* to "Grace (the Lord) come and this world pass away" is Amen and "Hosanna to the son of David." On Palm Sunday these words acclaimed our lowly Lord. Nothing of the world's power and pomp was for him; everything was against him except this welcoming cry, "Hosanna to the son of David. Blessed is he who comes in the name of the Lord."

Through Holy Week he gave them many words, and then to the Last Supper, to his coronation on Calvary (INRI) and on Easter day to Emmaus where he acted as if their house was his, he the host and they his family, for he again took the bread, said the blessing and broke it and gave it to them. They rushed back to Jerusalem to the Eleven (Luke 24:30–33).

The one who was crucified (his hands, his feet, his side—the five crosses cut into the altar, where therefore no more sacrifice is done) is risen; he sends the apostles to deliver forgiveness, absolve and retain sins, to preach repentance and forgiveness of sins in his name to all nations because he has suffered and risen from the dead according to the Scriptures. He will send them his Spirit (Luke 24:45–49). To all nations he sends them to make disciples of them by baptizing them in the name of the Father and of the Son and of the Holy Spirit and by teaching them all his words. Where he puts his name with the water there is he, there his temple, there are his. "You are my disciples." "I am with you always, to the very end of the age" (Matt. 28:20). So then also they are sent to do what he gives them to do at the Last Supper.

All of this comes flooding in with "The Lord be with you/And with your Spirit." In the *Didache* the Hosanna is followed by, "If any be holy let him come; if any be not, let him repent." Nothing of the world outside belongs here, nothing that would deny the Lord, his gifts and his words, his forgiveness by which alone we are holy and his. Any denial or diminution of our Lord, his gifts, his words, and his forgiveness is excluded. Then in the *Didache* comes *Maranatha*, the Aramaic word meaning "Come, O Lord," which ends the first epistle to the church at Corinth (1 Cor. 16:22). With apostolic authority Paul pronounces anathema on anyone who does not love the Lord, then says *Maranatha*. Heiler has pointed to *Maranatha* as probably the oldest epiclesis.[5] While "The Lord be with you" has variations, the response, "And with your spirit," does not.[6] Similar to "The Lord be with you," the response extends this back together with its own special freight. Addressed to the presiding minister, it recognizes him as the Lord's man to do what has been given him to do (apostolic ministry, "called and ordained"). "Your spirit" evokes his Spirit; where the Lord, there his Spirit. His Spirit is with your spirit (John 20:22).[7] So carry on with what you have been given to do. The Lord is with your spirit with his Spirit.[8]

There is no certainty where or when the *Didache* was written. According to Jasper it was probably written about A.D. 60.[9] Stählin calls it a catechism for the laity rather than an agenda; neither is it quite clear to what services things belong.[10] It does not have the next versicle and response; these appear in the *Apostolic Tradition* of Hippolytus (c. 215). He was conservative and not prone to novelty. What is represented in this work had wide usage in the East.

Ideas derived from the Old Testament which come in later "are here entirely absent."[11] Here, after the opening, welcoming, blessing versicle and response, comes "Up with your hearts" (*Sursum corda*), and the response, "We have [them] up/at/toward/with the Lord" (*Habemus ad dominum*). No one knows the origin of this versicle and response (Lam. 3:41). *Sursum* is the translation of Col. 3:1, "where Christ is seated at the right hand of God." To be born is to be born of God, and that is by water and the Spirit (John 3:3, 5). *Sursum* hearts are therefore hearts where God is, which is expressed in the parallel response, "We lift them up to the Lord."[12] God is present in the Lord Jesus Christ with us, and hearts exult in glad welcome toward him. *Maranatha* is fulfilled, and for such boon there is nothing to do but give him thanks.

"Let us give thanks to the Lord our God." This comes by way of Jewish prayer, as is indicated also by the way God is named: *Adonai Elohenu* as in the Shema (Deut. 6:4; Mark 12:29). *Adonai* translated *Kyrios* stands in place of the unutterable *Yahweh*. "Ask ye, Who is this? Jesus Christ it is, of sabaoth Lord, and there's none other God" (LW 298, st. 2). He is present, welcomed, acclaimed, and to him we are bidden to give thanks. In Jewish prayers this invitation was used for a table prayer that blessed God for his gifts.

The invitation to give thanks to the Lord our God is embraced with "It is truly good and right so to do." This was said as equivalent to Amen in the Shema of morning prayer. Translations vary, but all acknowledge that to give thanks to the Lord our God is the only fitting thing to do when he comes among us.[13]

The invitation to table prayer has been embraced and applauded by the response, which is then taken up as transition into such a prayer. All the liturgies have such a prayer, although there is much variation in its length, content, and place. In Jewish meals there could be a prayer for each course. It is hard to set bounds to such a blessing God, as the history of the liturgy bears abundant testimony. Early it ran into much extemporizing. In the *Didache* we find, "Let the prophets give thanks as much as they wish." Hippolytus amplifies this: "When giving thanks to God, let each [bishop] pray according to his ability. . . . Only let his prayer be correct and orthodox."[14] All this was done without a book and so was prone to considerable variation and length. "No extant sacramentary is earlier than the fourth century. Service books were unknown in the early church."[15] From time to time there was need to trim such abundance. From this abundance we have eleven proper prefaces that swing into the Sanctus, which joins us in with the song of the angels in the presence of the Lord of Hosts, and with those acclaiming him as he enters upon his Passion, him to whom we look for salvation. Hosanna: "Save now."[16] Holy Baptism has put us with the family of those who pray Our Father; and so praying the Our Father here we are of that family and have here our place. "We say the prayer which the Savior gave to those of his family (household), his disciples."[17] To such then the Lord himself speaks and gives us the gifts he says he gives us.

The giving of these gifts is unduly delayed, or even overshadowed, if we keep on and on giving thanks and praying. Worse still when it is forgotten that "it is not the priest alone who does the thanksgiving, but the people with him."[18] There was a time when prayers were used that belonged solely to the priest, and this tended to remove the Preface from the people. The responses were given to the choir of clerics, and in private masses there was only the priest and no congregation at all. This takeover by the priest may be seen when our Lord's words to us are taken into a prayer which the priest says to God; when these prayers are whispered the congregation is further deprived. The congregation becomes an audience to what the priest is doing with God. Engendering of this development was the notion that the Lord's Supper is something we do and offer to God, even to an unbloody propitiatory sacrifice for the sins of the living and the dead.[19] A sure symptom of Enthusiasm [*Schwärmerei*] is the notion that the Lord's Supper is something we do.[20]

When there is no temple and so no sacrifices, as in the exile or diaspora, the confession of the *Shema* and the prayers were regarded as sacrifices.[21] "The Talmud states that the prayers (*Tefillot*) were instituted 'so as to correspond to the daily sacrifices.' "[22] As the only Christian sacrifice consists in prayer and thanksgiving for all that the Lord has given us, so that also the prayers/sacrifice might be honest, confession of sin should first be made. This admonition to repentance and prayer/sacrifice was supported by quotation of Mal. 1:11, 14.[23] With the isolation of the priest and what he did with the body and blood of Christ toward God, the notion of sacrifice was preempted to this and to him. The people were distanced to attendance upon what the priest was doing toward God, indeed propitiating God.

These developments have a long history. Most obviously at the Reformation the multiplicity of the prayers was reduced, particularly the prayers belonging to the priest. His whispering and gestures of sacrificial reenactment were abolished.[24] The elevation of the elements fell out of use in Wittenberg by 1539. That this took so long was out of deference to Luther's insistence that it might not be legalistically abolished or the people distracted.[25] The Verba were to be sung "with voice raised most high" and in the Gospel tone, the tone used for chanting the Passion.[26]

The people heard again the words of our Lord which he speaks to them. Most profoundly it is the Lord's Supper. Here he is present among us; he speaks, and with his words he does and bestows what they say. Of this then the liturgy is homology. It is the Lord's Day, the Lord's Table, where the Lord serves us his gifts, gifts that engender in and from us his praise. We are then in company again with John and the churches of Asia Minor and all the company of heaven, extolling the Lamb who once was slain, who sits upon the throne, and who gathers his people to his table to give them his body and his blood to eat and to drink for the forgiveness of their sins.

Luther and Liturgical Reform

What Luther did in liturgical reform did not spring from some liturgical theory or busy assortment of liturgical data,[27] but from the Lord's Supper itself, that is, pure Gospel, gift of his giving his body and his blood just as he says to us. So profound was Luther's Gospel recognition, his fear that it might be infringed on or intruded by the Law kept him for years from doing anything in the way of reforming the Roman Mass. Karlstadt's eagerness to reform had made things into Law.[28] Luther insisted that changes not be imposed, but that they come only in the way of God's words.[29]

In 1523, at the urging of Nicholas Hausmann, pastor in Zwickau, Luther produced the *Formula Missae*.[30] Attempts to put the Latin

Mass into German were at this time regarded by him as only doing the job halfway. Sensitive genius of language that he was,[31] this Mass was in Latin. He disavowed innovation, or the notion that this was a new sacrament seen for the first time, or now licked into shape according to some exemplary model at some time in the history of the liturgy. Return to some Golden Age was the way of the Humanists, not that of Luther. He did his work in the particularities of the place where he was put to serve in the continuity of the one holy catholic and apostolic church.[32] So he carried forward everything that did not deny or deflect from the fact that it is the Lord's Supper—Gospel, gift *for you*.

The complaints soon came pouring in that the *Formula Missae* was a job only half done. Services in German of varying worth were already being produced in a goodly number of places. So, in 1526, Luther published the *Deutsche Messe*, a Mass reflecting much greater care for the people and their need for instruction in the Gospel way of the Lord's Supper, and he looked forward to a congregation feeling at home in its use.[33] The emergence of such congregations is recognized in the various church orders that came later and that included their respective Masses. Luther disavowed his work as the final word; he tended to abbreviate rather than innovate. Gabriel Biel (c. 1420–95), whose *Exposition* had been Luther's textbook on the Mass, regarded a number of prayers in the Roman Mass as optional.[34] Wolfgang Franz (1564–1628) has shown the flux in the orders of worship at the time in his *Die Messe im deutschen Mittelalter*.[35] Luther's work was then neither novel nor so drastic as some have asserted.[36] What simply had to disappear was anything contrary to the Gospel, and that was quite a lot. So, because it is the Lord's Supper, not the Christians' supper nor the priest's, the priest's prayers disappear or became the prayers of all; in the *Deutsche Messe*, prayers of the priest which incorporated the Verba Christi disappeared,[37] and our Lord's words to us are heard as his words to us. These matter more than any praying we may do.

The *Formula Missae* and the *Deutsche Messe* exercised wide influence. What was done in Wittenberg is seen in its *Kirchen-Ordnung* of 1533.[38] With no great change, this order of worship (along with other related orders) is what is contained in the Synod's *Kirchen-Agende* of 1856 (derived from the old, orthodox Saxon church orders) and also in *Lutheran Worship* of 1982. The *Formula Missae* and *Deutsche Messe* were in a sense provisional. Luther looked beyond the *Deutsche Messe* to a time when such a didactic way would no longer be necessary. The Lord's Prayer, put as table prayer before the consecration and as prayer for worthy reception, grew to paraphrase and admonition, and in certain areas replaced the Preface. Here also, as quite especially in the matter of the holy ministry, call and ordination, we may not regard the ways appropriate to the transitional and emergency situation of the 1520s as final; Luther did not. This is borne out by the Wittenberg church order of 1533 and those which followed, as also Luther's rite for Ordination of Ministers of the Word of 1539.[39]

Prayer of Thanks

The prayer that follows the Sanctus in the *Deutsche Messe* begins in the way of Jewish table prayers to praise God as Lord of heaven and earth. He created everything. He created man and woman, and yet more to be extolled is his mercy on those whom he created when they turned away from him, from whom alone their true life comes. Sin separates from God and means utter death; nevertheless, he had mercy and sent his only-begotten Son into our flesh to bear our sin and be our Savior from sin, sin's death, hell. Repentance confesses the fact that we are sinners, those for whom Christ died. He suffered our sin's hell for us. What he did counts as ours, and therefore we can rejoice in a salvation that is only his doing and ours only as gift.[40] This is a salvation accomplished by his sacrifice; where body and blood are separated there is sacrifice. It is his sacrifice, his body and blood, and so only his doing in our stead. It happened on the cross. Here are not ideas, concepts or theories, but a deed, a fact, that happened "under Pontius Pilate." "It is finished." The deed is done.

The body and blood are about to be given us to eat and to drink. This is to be done remembering him. We are beggars who live only by what he gives.[41] He gives us to eat and to drink his body and blood as he says, and we pray that we may receive them—for all they are and have achieved and bring, as nothing but gifts—faithfully. Faith is worked by the Holy Spirit with the words of the Lord.

Where his words, there is the Spirit active in them to bestow what they say. Apart from his words we cannot speak of the activity of the Spirit. His words, our Lord's bidding, gather us here. By his name we have been made his when his name was put upon us with the water of Baptism. We do not really come. He comes; we are gathered. Everything he does is sure; any insertion of our doing is fraught with uncertainty. Best praying, then, is praying the words he has given us to pray. Our praying is in the way Jesus taught when it is "Abba praying" in childlike faith as from one who can only receive.

Very early in history we find a prayer just before the Words of Institution that prays for the Holy Spirit to do his work in those about to eat and drink the body and blood of Christ.[42] This is prayed for the communicants. To this was added a reference to the bread and wine, that the Holy Spirit would do its work with them also, for Christ's words go with them. The Holy Spirit works with the external, earthly things of words, water, bread and wine. In this prayer, the secondary reference (bread and wine) follows naturally the first (the communicants) when held within such wholeness of the Holy Spirit's use of the means of grace (*externum verbum*, "Word and Spirit"). The history of this prayer shows the displacement of the first reference by the second, and the development of the notion that an immediate descent of the Holy Spirit upon the elements at this point effects the change of the bread into the body of Christ and the wine into the blood of Christ. This has regrettably come to be called the *epiclesis*. This development grew in the East, not in the West, where we usually find here a prayer for worthy reception. In the *Deutsche Messe* the Our Father is moved from after the consecration to serve as such a prayer. Our praying the family's prayer is preliminary and reaches toward what our Lord says, does, and gives.

To continue with the communion section in the Divine Service, everything so far has been in expectation of what comes next. From "The Lord be with you," everything has been rejoicing in the fact that it is the Lord's Supper. He is with us (Matt. 18:20; Num. 6:27). He comes, and so there is no more distance between him and us. Our hearts are bidden to exult. There is nothing to do but thank and praise him. Each season of the year evokes particular praise (the

Proper Preface) in celebration of what he has done for our salvation. Not just *our* praise, for when he is with us, then we are together with all who are his: "with angels and archangels and with all the company of heaven." Our praise is carried with theirs: nearer with him, nearer with one another. We acclaim his coming among us with "Hosanna in the highest"—Palm Sunday. Echoing the song of the heavenly host at his birth, he goes to the sacrifice to end all sacrifices for sin, the sacrifice of his body and blood. "It is finished." Then Easter and "Peace be with you" (John 20:26b). The one crucified has risen and is among us.

Words of Institution

And now come the Words of Institution, beginning with "Our Lord Jesus Christ." Lord is *Kyrios, Yahweh,* who makes a covenant and so makes Israel his people, once at Sinai, and now again. Jesus quotes Ex. 24:8: "This is the blood of the covenant." Also ringing in are Zech. 9:11 and Jer. 31:31–34. What is now new is the Jesus' *proprium,* "*my* blood." At Sinai the Lord had made himself a people, his Israel, his Twelve. With his words and the blood of the sacrifice he made and gave them his covenant: book of the covenant, blood of the covenant. The blood was toward God (altar, *coram Deo*) and upon the people becovenanting them. Representative Israel, led by Moses, Aaron, Nadab and Abihu, then ate and drank with God on the mountain and were not destroyed.

The Hebrew *berith* went into Greek as διαθήκη (not συνθήκη). The Latin for this is *testamentum,* giving us the "Old Testament" and the "New Testament." Chrysostom expounded testament in the way of Hebrews 9, and Luther followed him in his first account of the Lord's Supper, an account that swells with the Gospel.[43] Testament continued as a vehicle of the Gospel better able to extol the fact that everything depends on and is fulfilled by the sacrifice of Calvary. "For whenever you eat this bread and drink this cup, you proclaim the Lord's death until he comes" (1 Cor. 11:26). It is possible to have a covenant without a death, but not a testament. Luther read the fulfillment back into the promise, confessing more than is carried by *berith. Berith* is fulfilled and burst by Jesus the Messiah, the Lord. Lev. 26:12 is the *berith* formula: "I will . . . be your God, and you will be my people." We are the ones to whom our Lord is speaking: "for many," "for you." It is only from him, his body and blood which he gave and shed for us. The words of Christ to us, they say and do and bestow what follows.

The Words of Institution are a conflation of all four biblical accounts of the Last Supper. If, in the way of the Law and our having the say-so, we would measure a quantity, then one account would be enough. We are given four, and in the way of faith we would be given everything he gives. For the same reason we would not lose what is particular in each account, but in the liturgy all four could hardly be read, and so we have their conflation, which is based on the oldest (c. A.D. 55) and fullest text in 1 Corinthians 11.[44]

The Gospel is always more than we can measure or draw a line or limit to. So when our Lord speaks his words, it is as he says it is, whether we can fit them into our measurements, categories, and definitions, or not. "Let Christ himself be responsible for them."[45] If we imagine it too difficult, even impossible for him to deliver what he says, and if we attempt to help him with our explanations and definitions that would bring him into what we would think is possible or appropriate for him to do, then it would be our supper and not the Lord's. It is the Lord's Supper, and all false doctrine here is an infringement on or denial of that fact. It is only when what the Lord said is regarded as impossible or absurd that a range of varying explanations and alternatives are produced.[46] This did not really happen for the first thousand years. It has never happened for Eastern Catholics.[47] In the West in the 11th century Berengar of Tours (c. 998–1088) laid the measurements of his reason on the matter and said *est* must be *significat*. Previously theologians had pondered and even speculated; Augustine worked his two levels *signum* theory with similitudes, but at the altar the true body and the true blood was confessed. Opposition to Berengar promoted the idea of transubstantiation.[48] To Wycliffe, Zwingli, and Calvin, transubstantiation was the great perversion. For Luther it was the denial of the fact that the Lord is here giving his gifts: "They have come to ascribe to the sacrament what belongs to the prayers, and to offer to God what should be received as a benefit [*beneficium* not *officium*]. We must therefore sharply distinguish the testament and sacrament itself from the prayers which we offer at the same time."[49] "The Mass, or the promise of God, is not fulfilled by praying, but only by believing."[50] Gift, faith, promise, testament are from him to us, not from us to him as a sacrifice or work which we do. Luther says:

> We must turn our eyes and hearts simply to the institution of Christ and this alone, and set nothing before us but the very word of Christ by which he instituted the sacrament, made it perfect, and committed it to us. For in that word, and in that word alone, reside the power, the nature, and the whole substance of the Mass. All the rest is the work of man added to the word of Christ.[51]

All such Gospel recognitions had liturgical consequences, profound rather than superficial. Much praying must go. The *Verba Christi* must stand alone—his words, from him to us, gifting us. Thus, in Luther's *Deutsche Messe*, gone are the additions and omissions of the Roman Mass. The *Verba* are stated as simple fact. A fact is a fact for us only as it has a place and a time. It is hubris to think of our transcending these, and so departing from where he is there for us.[52] We are told quite circumstantially of the place and the time.[53] The time reference, "the night when he was betrayed," points toward Calvary (John 6:64).

At first things go on as at an ordinary meal, or an ordinary special meal. Whose family and household it is, is shown by who takes the bread, says grace, and breaks the bread. Those at table with him belong to him. They are Twelve, the number of Israel. There are main verbs and attendant participles. The big thing cannot be a participle. Took, broke, gave and said are main verbs. The participle of the word that gives us *eulogy* is what we have in Mark and Matthew; in Luke and Paul the participle gives us *eucharist*. *Eucharistein* does not appear in the Septuagint. Eulogy is closer to the Hebrew way, eucharist to the Greek. Eulogy did not become a title; eucharist, however, did with the help from Philo of Alexandria (d.c. A.D. 50) and the word's susceptibility to notions of sacrifice beyond praise—this despite the fact that at first the word eucharist referred to what was eaten and drunk.[54] So, "having said the blessing" is really, more specifically, "having blessed God." It was the way of table prayers to bless God, extolling his gifts; the object of the verb is God, not the gifts. "Blessed be you, O Lord our God, ruler of the universe, you have brought forth bread from the earth." For different courses another prayer: "Blessed be you, O Lord our God, you who have created the fruit of the vine." "Having given thanks" is not so clear in Luke and Paul. The paterfamilias breaks the bread and gives out the pieces; having blessed God, he gives out the cup. All of this was going on in hundreds of other households in Jerusalem on that night (or another night—varying calendars were then observed.) We are told that our Lord was celebrating the Passover. From the Words of Institution we would hardly know this, and what is not clearly and fully stated here cannot be the main thing. So although it was a Passover, it was one such as there had never been before, a Passover to end all Passovers. What is unique is Jesus' uniqueness, what is there which could not have been there except for him. That is what is given by what he says.

In the celebration of Passover the paterfamilias expounded particular things recalling the Lord's deliverance of his people from Egypt. Those whom he delivered were his people, his Israel, his Twelve. To celebrate Passover was to rejoice in his deliverance, in being his delivered people and in the final deliverance. In the first Passover there were a yearling lamb or goat, male and without blemish, the unleavened bread, and the bitter herbs (Exod. 12:3–14). The lamb or goat was roasted, and no bones were broken (John 19:36). At the first Passover the blood of the lamb was put on the doorposts and lintel—only once, the first time. Later other things were added and some dropped. We hear of wine first in the latter half of the second century B.C.[55] We learn then also what the paterfamilias was to say of the lamb, the unleavened bread, and the bitter herbs.[56] We do not know the details of Jesus' Passover, nor which of the passover orders then in use he may have followed. The apostles who were there and bidden to "Do this" are not concerned to tell us. Nor is Paul when he quotes the account which he had received and was passing on. He does say it went back to the Lord (1 Cor. 11:23–26). In his account there is the least hint or echo of Passover. After Jesus' days, the Passover celebration shows further development. It is quite misleading to do a contemporary Seder and to imagine that is just what Jesus must have done. The uniqueness of his Passover is shown also by the fact that while the Passover was a family occasion, at his Passover even his own mother was not there, only the Twelve, the apostles who were to go

302

on doing what had never been done before. Jesus deals with the Passover as if it belongs to him, as he had done with the Sabbath (Mark 3:1–6). Only he can act as Lord of the Sabbath who gave it. In the way in which the Pharisees thought of Sabbath and Passover, Jesus was guilty of breaking them both; he fulfilled and burst them both. What the Messiah does and bestows cannot be held within the old wine skins.

What the Words of Institution are most concerned to tell us is what never happened before, what happened only because of Jesus, the Christ, the Lord, and what is given with his words. No one but he could ever have said such words.

"Take and eat." Here *take* is the same word which Jesus said in ordaining his apostles: "Receive the Holy Spirit" (John 20:22). It is a gifting word, a faith word, and so does not permit an intrusion of our doing. Here the verbs are in the imperative. Here is the first of what we are given to do. This is gift. One cannot eat without what one is given to eat. What that is, our Lord tells us: "This is my body." We have been told that he took bread and broke it just as was done by every paterfamilias. So what is the *this* if not bread? Yet the word *this* is not in grammatical agreement with bread (masculine) but with body (neuter). So it is not so much a bread word as a body word. The dominant fact is the body; it draws the demonstrative *this* into agreement with itself. It is our Lord who speaks of the bread and says that it is his body, of the wine that it is his blood. These he gives us to eat and to drink, that is, into our mouths. The statement does not dislocate from the bread; it draws us to the fact stated of the bread that it is his body. The bread is not left behind; it is bread of which our Lord says it is his body, of this bread, and not any other, and so may not be received as any other bread (1 Cor. 11:27–32). *Worthy* says according to what it is, and so not as anything less or other than it is. The primary reference of the word is to something outside ourselves, here to what is given us, that is, the true body and the true blood. What is done to the bread is done to the body of the Lord, to the wine the blood of the Lord. The presiding minister expresses the designation of the *this* when he takes hold of the paten and extends it toward the communicants, and similarly the cup. There is also the usage of specifying of which bread and wine our Lord says, "This is my body, which is given for

303

you" and "This is my blood, which is shed for you," when the presiding minister makes the sign of the cross over the bread and the wine as he says our Lord's words. This action appears first in the Lutheran church order of Coburg (1626).

In the history of the liturgy we see that the simple *took* became a laying on of hands, and that this action, since the eighth century, was displaced by the signing.[57] Signing multiplied, and actions expressive of the words were disconnected from them and assumed meanings and indeed a work of their own. Elevation of the elements was then toward God and not toward the people ("for you"), and a fraction was done after the words. Both of these were then expressive of the priest's doing a sacrifice. Luther observed that our Lord broke the bread so that there would be pieces for distribution.[58] Why we are told that Jesus took bread and cup is to identify him as the paterfamilias of his Twelve, his Israel, he the Lord, "Our Lord Jesus Christ." The signing with the cross expresses better the *given* and *shed*; the taking and extending toward the communicants expresses better the *for you*. The Calvary reference indicates the where of the sacrifice, and so, whence the body and blood. Yet Calvary without bestowal does not avail for us. Hence, when we are gathered to the Lord's table where he gives us his body to eat and his blood to drink, this is where everything is at for us and given us. Here we gladly stay; we do not think to go elsewhere: up to heaven or back to Calvary, to make ourselves contemporary with the Last Supper or Calvary or it with us, or to participate in his sacrifice or to represent it.[59] This seems to suggest that we are doing something. Hence the danger of speaking of a number of actions that we do as constitutive of the Lord's Supper. Then also, the Verba Christi can be spoken of as narrative, words that present history, but words that do and impart what they say.[60] When actions take on a role of their own (symbolical, cultical or mystical), the words may be pulled to that level also. Against this subjugation and reversal we can only cry out, "It all depends on the words." The words are the first thing.[61]

The Lord's Supper is surely what it is when it is the Lord's doing. He has done Calvary. "The passion of Christ occurred but once on the cross. But whom would it benefit if it were not distributed, applied and put to use?"[62] If you want your sins forgiven you do not go to Calvary, but to the Lord's Supper. At Calvary it was achieved but not given out. Here it is not achieved but it is given you.[63] As the Small Catechism confesses, the two chief things are the bodily eating and drinking of the body and blood of Christ and the words *for you*. Into mouth and into faith; unfaith can repudiate the gift, but it cannot make our Lord's words untrue. It can profane his body and blood to mortal consequence (1 Cor. 11:27–32).

The communicants may not be left in any doubt that what is given them is that of which our Lord has said it is his body and his blood:[64] hence the presiding minister's designating which bread and which wine; hence also the consecration of any bread and wine that may be brought to the altar because of an underestimate of the number of communicants. Spener thought this unnecessary since he regarded the Verba as prayer.[65] In the case of an overestimate, the bread and wine of which our Lord has had such use are consumed or reverently kept for further use.

At One with Christ and Each Other

We are told that what our Lord did at the Last Supper he did "while they were eating." There was a meal going on. He gave them his body to eat. Then after the meal he gave them his blood to drink. There may have been half an hour in between. Whether, where, and for how long such a meal was continued we do not know. We know there was a meal in the church at Corinth that occasioned the fearful failure to distinguish the meal's eating and drinking from the eating and drinking of our Lord's body and blood. The participants were denying the Lord's body and blood when they treated one another as if the Lord had not given them his body to eat and his blood to drink. To scorn someone into whom the Lord has given his body and blood is to scorn the Lord's body and blood. He bodies and bloods us with his own body and blood.[66] Hence we are in consequence called his body. The terms used to say this clearly are "true body" and "true blood" (*corpus verum, sanguis verus*), which are given us to eat and to drink, and "mystical body" (*corpus mysticum*), those who eat and drink, those bodied together by the "true body," and so then also all believers, the church, the baptized (1 Cor. 10:17; 12:12ff.). In 1 Corinthians 12 the apostle Paul draws out the consequences of their being the *corpus mysticumm*, as in chapter 11 he drew out the consequences of the *corpus meum*. The body and blood of Christ are not dead things, but living gifts that enliven, shape, and have their way with us.[67] We live with one another as those into whom Christ has given his body and blood. There were those in Corinth who were denying this to their peril. It is bad to scorn a man; it is fearful to scorn the body and blood of Christ in a man. Denial of *corpus verum* is denial of *corpus mysticum* and vice versa. So they are not alternatives to be played off against each other. The eating and drinking of the body and blood of Christ are not just individual "me and Jesus." When he bodies and bloods himself with me, he bodies and bloods me with all those whom he bodies and bloods with himself. Hence the apostle's urgent pastoral care, the opposite of which would be to leave each individual to himself and not care whether he is discerning the Lord's body or not; hence pastoral care, preaching, teaching, catechism, confirmation, closed communion.[68] "Let no one who has a quarrel with his companion join with you until they have been reconciled."[69] Matt. 5:23f. has early a place in the liturgies. In his commentary on Matt. 7:6 Chrysostom says, "He gives his holy things to his holy ones." Those not to be given the body and blood of Christ were to depart. The deacon cried, "The holy things for the holy ones." The "holy things" are the body and blood of Christ. They are given into each communicant. They are then common in each one and so make the communion.[70] We are never more at one with Christ and so at one with each other. Not included here then are those who do not receive the "holy things," the body and blood of Christ. The deepest communion then evidences a division. In Corinth they were divided who ate and drank as if it were ordinary bread and wine; in the early liturgies, they who were not yet baptized and had not yet made confession of the faith or been absolved were set apart. This division is evidenced in the *Deutsche Messe* by the communicants gathering around the altar, while others remain in their places.

The Peace

In the early liturgies all who received and gave the kiss of peace (Pax) received the "holy things," the body and blood of Christ. The kiss of peace then came after the dismissal of the catechumens, prior to the communion section of the service and so-called Service of Holy Communion in Divine Service I. That it comes after the consecration and before the distribution is a consequence of the Roman usage, which, along with much else, included the Lord's Prayer at this point. Then the Pax echoed "as we forgive" in the Lord's Prayer when coming to the altar (Matt. 5:23) as well as pointing up the "holy things" and "holy ones"—and so Holy Communion.[71]

Pope Innocent I (d. 417), defended placement of the Pax after the consecration—a departure from catholic (and apostolic?) usage—in the interest of the Mass as sacrifice. He also advocated putting the prayers in closest proximity to the sacrifice because, by its expiatory and meritorious power, it opens the way for their acceptance.[72] Thus the prayers after the sermon were subsumed into the sacrifice of the Mass. The prayers, which were at first the only sacrifice, were swallowed up into the Mass, now thought of as itself "a true and complete sacrifice offered to God."[73] So the putting of the Pax after the consecration had occurred by the fourth century. This is where it remains for us by way of the *Formula Missae* and the Brandenburg-Nürenberg family of church orders.

The fact that the kiss of peace appears in the conclusion of 1 and 2 Corinthians, 1 and 2 Thessalonians, Romans and 1 Peter has suggested that the epistle was read as sermon, and that the Pax indicates the transition to the Holy Communion. Only those who receive and give the kiss of peace are welcomed to the Lord's Table.[74] The *Didascalia*, (early third century) evokes the vivid scene of the kiss of peace, which comes from the altar, coming to a sudden halt as it is being given and received all the way round. The presiding minister leaves the altar and goes to where the kiss of peace is blocked. Only after he has worked reconciliation (*pacem facere inter eos* [Matt. 5:24; 6:15; 7:6]) does the kiss of peace continue on its way all the way round, and only then does the liturgy proceed.[75] We may regret the loss of the actual kiss of peace. Yet whether by kiss or handshake or words, the Pax is given and received. It comes from the Lord and we receive and embrace it together with our Amen. It is his gift, not something we set going. Lamentable is the disintegration of the liturgy at this point into lots of separate heartinesses. The one so-called Pax, from the Lord, was beautifully expressed by the usage with a piece of wood, metal, or ivory upon which a Calvary was carved. It came from the altar and was kissed by the presiding minister, and then in turn by all the communicants. How little chance for such a usage among us time-pressured people is shown by those instances when even parts of the Holy Communion are lopped off—and this at times for the sake of some cozy pleasantries or program promotions.

Meal and Passover

Where there was a meal, it disappears. This may have been when the Lord's Supper was moved from evening (meal time) to morning, to Sunday morning, the Lord's Day (Rev. 1:10). Another prompting was likely the fact of private homes becoming too small. Clearly the meal was not integral to the Lord's Supper. The apostle had said it were better to have their meal at home before they came together (1 Cor. 11:22, 34). Neither the mealness nor the Passover-ness was integral. Christ is once called "our Passover lamb" (1 Cor. 5:7), but that not in the context of the Lord's Supper. The Passover point made here is the ethical cleansing out of the old leaven.

Passover was an annual occasion. It seems there were Passover's bitter herbs at the Last Supper (Mark 14:20), but we never hear of these at any Eucharist (oil, cheese, olives, milk, honey, water—but never bitter herbs). All of the Last Supper was not repeated in the liturgies. Zwingli said we should use wooden dishes, because Jesus did. Over against Andreas Karlstadt (c. 1480–1541), who insisted on the strict observance of the details at Christ's institution, Luther ridiculed such reasoning because of its sad consequence:

> Since we do not know and the text does not state whether red or white wine was used, whether wheat rolls or barley bread were used, we must by reason of doubt at this point refrain from observing the Last Supper.[76]

If Jesus bade his apostles to go on doing, what did he mandate? We look for the verbs in the imperative. If we gather these, we find they are "Take and eat" and "Drink." The only other imperative is the one at the end, "This do, as often as you drink it, in remembrance of me." They are bidden to drink, and this is to be done remembering him (adverbial relationship to the main verb, the imperative). We are not bidden to pray, sit, kneel, stand, have a meal, have a Passover or a memorial. We are bidden to eat and to drink the body and blood of Christ. What goes with this cannot be done without our Lord's words and that there be bread and wine of which he says they are his body and blood which he bids us to eat and to drink.[77] But how could we not pray, or ponder the Passover to end all Passovers, or rejoice when our Lord has us together with him at his table now, and so at the feast of the Lamb who was slain with all his saints? There are biblical promptings for these. There are also devotional promptings that ponder how many grains are made into one bread, and many grapes into one cup.[78] This can make some fine preaching, but, as Luther observed, such pious reflections on similitudes and signs do not hold against temptation, devil or death; the words and the body and blood of Christ do.[79]

The aspect of meal and Passover have, as we observed, almost disappeared from the Words of Institution. In the accounts of Mark and Matthew, our Lord's giving his blood to drink follows directly upon his giving his body to be eaten. When the *Deutsche Messe* has the consecration of the bread and the distribution of the body of Christ before the consecration of the wine and the distribution of the blood of Christ, this is not a repristination of the space between them as indicated in 1 Cor. 11:25 and Luke 22:20. It is rather a part of the centrality of the words of Christ. The distribution comes immediately upon their being spoken in consecration, and this closeness renders then a formula of distribution unnecessary. While subsequent church orders mostly maintained the closeness of the distribution to the words of Christ by not having prayers in between, they have the consecration of the wine follow immediately the consecration of the bread.

The Distribution

Some orders have no formula at the distribution. The more general practice was to have one, one which either followed that in the priest's prayer at his communion ("May the body/blood of the Lord Jesus Christ keep my soul to eternal life"), or one that said Christ's words in a statement of fact way with the addition of the more personal "for you." This latter became the general practice with the inclusion of "true." The Nördlingen church order has this already in 1522, when the factors that are usually suggested as prompting its inclusion were absent. As a translation it says with added clarity what had long been said when the body of Christ was given to be eaten, namely, "the body of Christ," that is, the *corpus verum*. Support for its use may later be found in the Small Catechism and in the confessional need. In 1579 Wittenberg formally approved the use of "true" in the communion of the sick.[80] It came into use where there was no Crypto-Calvinist trouble or official confession of the Formula of Concord. In 1717, in Hanover, "true" was replaced by "precious."[81] "True" did not appear in the Saxon *Kirchenbuch* (1812), commonly referred to as the Saxon Agenda, the book the Saxons brought with them to America.[82] There was confessional need, however, when the Prussian King Frederick William III in his agendas of 1821 and 1822 had a referential formula of distribution reporting what Christ said. This troubled many Lutherans. They kept to the traditional Lutheran formula as contained in the *Kirchen-Agende* of 1856 and in all subsequent liturgies. Here is no place for improvisation. There are some things we need to be able to rely on hearing.[83]

Among the Reformed there was the usage of 1 Cor. 10:16 as a formula of distribution, or some other text thought to be appropriate to the individual communicant. This practice prospered in Pietism (it became a prayer and "something touching"). In the Enlightenment, deferential forms were devised for the aristocracy with use of their individual names and titles. Hamburg in 1806 had 90 variations. Against all this the Saxons who came to Missouri in 1839 kept the traditional Lutheran form, using the same for every communicant. The alternative form in *Lutheran Worship* uses "very," literal translation of *verum*. This strengthens the understanding of "true," the opposite of which is not "false"; and so it serves to confess that the body and blood are our Lord's own, which he gives us to eat and to drink as he says.[84] The fact confessed by "true" is then not passed over, ignored, or decried, as is done by those who are unwilling to confess the true body and blood, those who confess only that Christ himself is present, sharing himself with us and so making us his body (*corpus mysticum*, the Church). We are indeed made members of his body by Baptism and also are so enlivened in the Lord's Supper; but here this occurs uniquely with his true body and his true blood which he gives us to eat and to drink. And by these he bodies and bloods us with himself. We may not say less than what our Lord says. Hence the formula of distribution which says what our Lord says in direct statement to each and to all communicants. His bidding, "Take, eat" and "Take, drink," confesses that the eating and drinking are what he bids us do, and this happens as he gives into our mouths his body and his blood, without which there is no eating or drinking. Into our mouths he gives his body and blood, into our ears his words. Thus into both he gives us gifts. They may be repudiated to a person's ruin, but they are given, as our Lord says. His words are not a nothing, nor are his body and blood.[85] Hence the formula of distribution which is his words spoken "for you."

The usage was continued through the Reformation of the pastor giving the body of Christ into the mouth of the communicant. This is done by the *pastor loci* or presiding minister, since to him is given the responsibility toward the Lord and the church for the giving of the body of Christ, that it suffer no denial or contradiction in doctrine and life, no insult of unrepented sin.[86] This responsibility toward *corpus verum* and *corpus mysticum* he may not eschew.[87] He is the servant of the body of Christ, and those who may assist him of the blood of Christ, which is given to those who have been given the body of Christ.

The passive, childlike acceptance of the body of Christ, the stance of faith, is the consideration that accompanies the body of Christ simply being given into our mouths. Karlstadt insisted that it be given into the hand of the communicant. His propensity was to speak of bread rather than the body of Christ, to diminish the awesomeness, and legalistically to repristinate (cf. Zwingli's wooden dishes), as also to suggest that we have some action to perform. In our day, promotion of hand communion has come from different understanding of the Eucharist, some sort of "co-participation." The Lord's Supper is not our doing, nor is the presiding minister here anything but our Lord's instrumentality for his giving out his gifts. Any deflection of attention from his doing to ours is hardly faith's or the Gospel's way. Here is not something to make a law about, but something to ponder. The hand communion introduced by Karlstadt was cancelled by Luther in the fifth Invocavit sermon because of the offense this had given.[88] As long as leavened bread was used, hand communion seems to have been the practice[89] and it came to be invested with symbolic significance. With the use of unleavened bread came mouth communion in the ninth century.

From the 11th to the 16th century, kneeling replaced standing except for the presiding minister and bishop. The pope sat. Our Lord and his apostles reclined.[90] Kneeling or standing is surely preferable to the conveyor belt of a queue. Here is no place for the hurrying factory efficiencies of time and motion experts.

Where there is a formula of distribution in the Lutheran orders of the 16th century, the ancient usage is usually restored of saying Amen to the body and blood of Christ and his words, "This is so. Gift received." What were words of the priest's prayer became words of blessing of the communicants. These were then part of the formula of distribution. They appear in *Lutheran Worship* in the dismissal blessing: "The body and blood of our Lord strengthen and preserve you steadfast in the true faith to life everlasting. Go in peace."

The words are no longer words of the priest's prayer at his communion. Both formulas of distribution in *Lutheran Worship* are staightforward statements of fact, "for you." The fact is as sure as the Lord and his words, and is not dependent on or undone by unbelieving denial (*manducatio infidelium*) of the body and the blood of Christ or of the "for you." The Augsburg Confession has it: "The true body and blood of Christ . . . are there distributed and received."[91] No subjunctive belongs here: we do not pray that we may receive the body and blood of Christ. These are given us whether we believe it or not. We pray that we may receive them faithfully, that is, as all the gift that they are.[92] "Where there is forgiveness of sins, there is also life and salvation."[93]

Agnus Dei

The congregation's Amen to the presiding minister's "The Peace of the Lord be with you always" in Divine Service I, as also the sharing of the Peace with one another in Divine Service II, is followed by the Agnus Dei, a canticle that found its way into the liturgy as early as the eighth century. Our Lord has just said to us that he is giving us his blood to drink. It is his blood. It is the blood of the new covenant or testament. It is the blood shed for the forgiveness of sins. Blood shed is blood of a sacrifice, and here explicitly "for the forgiveness of sins." Isaiah prophesied of a lamb to be slaughtered, a lamb bearing the sins of many, stricken for the transgressions of the people, a sacrifice for sin—the Suffering Servant (*Ebed Yahweh*). Jesus was thus divinely named and acclaimed at his baptism (Ps. 2:7; Is. 42:1): Son, Servant. He is the Messiah. Jesus thus sums up his work: "For even the Son of Man did not come to be served, but to serve, and to give his life as a ransom for many" (Mark 10:45). "Many" echoes Is. 53:11 (cf. also Mark 14:24; Matt. 26:28; Heb. 9:28). He is ransomer, redeemer, deliverer. To give his life (*nephesh*, soul) is to give himself, is to pour out his blood.[94] Atonement, propitiation, expiation are the Lord's doing and gift by way of the sacrifice, the blood. Life for life: life, soul, blood, himself. "He poured out his life unto death" (Is. 53:12).[95] Those who are gathered by the Lamb who once was slain into the celebration of his kingdom are those whose robes have been washed white in the blood of the Lamb (Rev. 7:14). Following Jesus' baptism he is acclaimed by John the Baptist as the "Lamb of God who takes away the sin of the world" (John 1:36). All of the above echoes in the Agnus Dei sung by those at Messiah's table, the feast of the Lamb. Three times, twice "have mercy on us," and finally "grant us (your) peace"—*Shalom*: exuberantly alive and rejoicing as our Lord would have us be. The risen Lord's "Peace be with you" to his disciples, and showing them his hands and his side (John 20:19–20), is anamnesis. It has been anamnesis all the way through and particularly, as our Lord bids us, in eating and drinking his body and blood.[96] Indeed, "Whenever you eat this bread and drink this cup, you proclaim the Lord's death until he comes" (1 Cor. 11:26). "The anamnesis is Gospel, not prayer."[97] An understanding of anamnesis different from that given here seeped in later: a way for us to transcend time.

Thanksgiving

Then comes prayer, thanksgiving for gifts received,[98] the rejoicing, and already now, "to celebrate with all the faithful the marriage feast of the Lamb in his kingdom which has no end." Those whose names are written "in the book of life of the Lamb" (book of the covenant, blood of the lamb) cry out, "You are worthy to take the scroll and to open its seals, because you were slain, and with your blood you purchased men for God from every tribe and language and people and nation. You have made them to be a kingdom and priests to serve our God, and they will reign on earth" (Rev. 5:9–10).

The thrust of the gifts is on and out. We are on our way to present our bodies as a living sacrifice. Now one body in Christ, and so members of one another, having gifts, let us use them. With sober judgment there are things to be done in our calling at home and in the world (Rom. 12).

The chief reason for holding mass . . . is the word of God, which no one can do without. It must be used and inculcated daily, not only because Christians are born, baptized, and trained every day, but because we live in the midst of the world, the flesh, and the devil, who do not cease to assail us and drive us into sin. Against these the most powerful weapon is the word of God . . . This is shown by the fact that the Lord when he instituted the mass, said, "Do this in remembrance of me" [1 Cor. 11:24–25], as if he were saying, "As often as you use this sacrament and testament you shall be preaching of me." As St. Paul says in 1 Cor. 11:26, "As often as you eat this bread and drink this cup you preach and proclaim the Lord's death until he comes"; and Psalm 111:4–5 says, "He has caused his wonderful works to be remembered in that he has provided food for all those who fear him."[99]

Thanksgiving also continues. There is thanksgiving at the Lord's Supper, although not essential to it, in our lives with the sacrifice of prayer, praise, thanksgiving, and in giving ourselves, sacrifice too for serving the needy.[100] We can't wait to put his words into practice, and so comes the Nunc Dimittis.

Canticles and Benediction

The first trace of this canticle in the liturgy appears in the fourth-century *Apostolic Constitutions* where the dismissal consists of the bidding "Depart in peace." [101] It was part of the presiding minister's concluding prayers in the liturgy of St. John Chrysostom (c. 345–407). Although appointed at this place in the ancient Mozarabic (Spanish) liturgy, Luther, however, made no mention of it in his orders. It was the Nürnberg (1525) and Strasbourg (1525) church orders and the Swedish (1531) liturgy that early included it. First settled in Compline, it was incorporated into Lutheran Vespers, the result of Luther's reform of the canonical hours as prayed by the clergy. It first appeared in the Communion service in the Synod's *Liturgy and Agenda* of 1917.[102] The placement of the Nunc Dimittis here may be due to the influence of Wilhelm Löhe, who has it at this place in his *Agende* of 1844. As precedent for this, Löhe claims (a little mistakenly) "the oldest liturgies of the Lutheran church." There is indeed a catholicity, a communion of faith, expressed in participation in liturgies that have carried the Lord's gifts to his people and then their thanks and praise to him through the centuries. But no liturgy is "from the Lord" in the sense the apostle says of the Lord's Supper (1 Cor. 11:23); and the final ground for a particular usage is not in its being used at a particular place or at a particular time, but how serviceable it is (has proven to be) in the Divine Service where our Lord serves out his gifts with his words, with the water, and with the bread and the wine. Where this happens, there is Divine Service; it is the Lord's Day, the Lord's table, already now and hereafter. If we weigh the theological and liturgical import and fitness of the Nunc Dimittis at this place, we can only rejoice that it is here in the swift conclusion of the service.

Divine Service II provides an alternate to the Nunc Dimittis in the canticle, "Thank the Lord and sing his praise," with its text, based on select verses of Psalm 105, by John Arthur, a member of the Inter-Lutheran Commission on Worship that prepared the *Lutheran Book of Worship* (1978). The personal encounter with Christ and his gifts in the Lord's Supper leads indeed to joyful service to "tell everyone what he has done." (The concluding alleluias preclude the use of this canticle during Lent.) The gifts of the Lord have been given, and it remains only to give thanks with one of the two post-communion prayers and to pray that the gifts given into us may have their way with us. There follows the Aaronic Benediction in which the Lord recognizes us as his people, his Israel, putting his name upon us—as at the beginning of our life as his in Holy Baptism, as at the beginning of the Divine Service, as at its end, and so through all our days to the fulfillment of all his promises in his name (Num. 6:24–27; Matt. 28:19–20).

Notes

1. AE 37: 142; 1 Cor. 11:20; 10:21.
2. Sermon at the Dedication of the Castle Church in Torgau, WA 49: 588, n.16; AE 51: 333.
3. Ap IV, 154 and 49.
4. The terms Lord, grace, and peace are all interchangeable, and yet not equitable. Each says the same, and something more that is its special freight. "Peace be with you" confesses the risen Lord as the one who is among us. "Grace" tells of God's favor where Jesus is welcomed and confessed as Lord. "This world passes away" echoes Matt. 24:35, "Heaven and earth will pass away, but my words will never pass away."
5. Friedrich Heiler, *Die Ostkirchen* (Munich & Basel: Ernst Reinhardt Verlag, 1971), p. 166.
6. According to Jungmann, this is a "genuinely Hebraic" expression. Josef A. Jungmann, *The Mass of the Roman Rite*, trans. Francis A. Brunner, 2 vols. (New York: Benziger Brothers, 1951, 1955), I: 19.
7. *The Liturgical Homilies of Narsai*, trans. R. H. Connolly (Cambridge: Cambridge University Press, 1909), p. 8: "They [the people] call 'spirit,' not that soul which is in the priest, but the Spirit which the priest has received by the laying on of hands." Robert Cabie, *The Eucharist*, vol. 2 of *The Church at Prayer*, ed. Aimi Georges Mortimort (Collegeville: The Liturgical Press, 1986), p. 92.
8. The presiding minister, as the Lord's and his people's instrument, indicates which function he is filling by his positioning at the altar. When for the liturgy the presiding minister goes behind a freestanding altar and faces the people, he is most clearly functioning "in the stead and by the command of my Lord Jesus Christ," AE 37: 187. Any eccentricities or improvisations that draw attention to him as Jack or George run counter to this fact, and we are grateful for the vestments that cover him, as well as for their liturgical statement.
9. R. C. D. Jasper and G. J. Cuming, eds., *Prayers of the Eucharist: Early and Reformed*, 3d rev. ed. (New York: Pueblo Publishing Co., 1987), p. 20. Willy Rordorf, *The Eucharist of the Early Christians* (New York: Pueblo Publishing Co., 1978), pp. 1f.
10. *Leiturgia: Handbuch des evangelischen Gottesdienstes*, ed. Karl Ferdinand Müller and Walter Blankenburg, 3 vols. (Kassel: Johannes Stauda Verlag, 1954–1956), I: 16.
11. Jungmann, I: 31.

12. Where the Lord is, is *sursum*; he is here, and as now here he is acclaimed and joyfully welcomed. The scriptural usage gives no ground for a notion of two separate worlds or levels. The call in Phil. 3:14 is God's call in Christ Jesus here and now. The background of Old Testament usage indicates the parallelism; what is happening on earth is happening in heaven also. See TDNT 1: 376ff.

13. The words "true and firm" occur in the reciting of the *Shema*, the Jewish confession of faith. See David Hedegard, *Seder R. Amram Gaon*, Part I (Lund: A.-B. PH. Lindstedts Universitets-bokhandel, 1951), p. 65. Ἄξιον καὶ δίκαιον are the words in the *Apostolic Constitutions* 8, 12; *dignum et iustum* in the *Apostolic Tradition* 4, 3. Cf. TDNT 1: 379f.

14. Justin Martyr, *First Apology* 65, 1: "at some length," Jasper, *Prayers*, p. 28.

15. C. W. Dugmore, *The Influence of the Synagogue upon the Divine Office*, rev. ed. (Westminster: Faith Press, 1964), p. 112.

16. See Ps. 118:25; Is. 6:3, expressions of Scripture in the *Shema*. Hedegard, p. 48.

17. Cyril of Jerusalem, *Mystagogical Catecheses* 23, 11. Formal introductions to the Lord's Prayer, connoting confidence and assurance ("we make bold to say"), made their way into the liturgies of both East and West. Joachim Jeremias, *The Lord's Prayer*, trans. John Reumann (Philadelphia: Fortress Press, 1964), pp. 4f.

18. Chrysostom, *Homily on 2 Cor. 18*.

19. Trent XXII, 2, 1743, 1753. *Enchiridion Symbolorum: Definitionum et Declarationum de Rebus Fidei et Morum*, ed. Henricus Denzinger and Adolfus Schönmetzer, 22d ed. (Rome: Herder, 1965). Cf. AC XXIV, 30: "for the sacrifice has already taken place" with Heb. 9:25–29.

20. LC V, 7.

21. Justin Martyr, *Trypho* 117, 2.

22. Hedegard, p. XXXVII, n. 7.

23. *Didache* 14; Jasper, *Prayers*, p. 24.

24. For a discussion of the Mass as mystery see Theodor F. D. Kliefoth, *Liturgische Abhandlungen*, 8 vols. (Schwerin: Stiller, 1854–1861), V: 7.

25. AE, 35: 87, 96; 38: 319.

26. WA 6: 362, 29; AE 35: 90; 53: 59.

27. "Faddism" of the Enthusiasts. See AE 53: 19, 61.

28. Even reforms that the Gospel called for were put by Karlstadt as Law at Christmas in 1521. Luther's Invocavit Sermons in 1522 put things back where they had been.

29. AE 51: 70–100. Cf. also Bryan Spinks, *Luther's Liturgical Criteria and His Reform of the Canon of the Mass* (Bramcote, Notts.: Grove Books, 1982), pp. 18–25.

30. To examine this work, in reality an expurgated version of the Latin Mass, see AE 53: 19–40.

31. Cf. Heinz Blum, *Martin Luther Creative Translator* (St. Louis: Concordia Publishing House, 1965).

32. Cf. AC VII.

33. AE 53: 61–90.

34. *Expositio* 83.

35. See Leonhard Fendt, *Der lutherische Gottesdienst des 16. Jahrhunderts; Sein Werden und Sein Wachsen* (München: Reinhardt, 1923), p. 123.

36. Rendtorff refers to Luther's work as "some remaining pieces of rubble without any connections." Franz M. Rendtorff, *Die Geschichte des christlichen Gottesdienstes unter dem Gesichtspunct der liturgischen Erbfolge* (Giessen: Töpelmann, 1914), p. 42. Cf. also Bryan Spinks, *Luther's Liturgical Criteria*, pp. 7–14.

37. *Leiturgia*, I: 59.

38. Likewise in the Braunschweig (1528) and Saxony (1539). See Aemilius L. Richter, ed., *Die evangelischen Kirchenordnungen des sechszehnten Jahrhunderts*, 2 vols. (Weimar: Landindustriecomptoir, 1846), I: 220, 106, 307.

39. AE 53: 124. Fendt says of this ordination rite: "Not a Wittenberg rite put beside the Roman rite, but the Roman rite become Gospel." *Der lutherische Gottesdienst*, p. 189.

40. Our Lord has put repentance and joy together. There is no solid joy except by way of repentance, the joy of sins forgiven. See Luke 24:47; 15:7, 10; Matt. 18:13; Mark 1:15.

41. Matt. 5:3. Cf. Martin H. Franzmann, *Follow Me: Discipleship According to Saint Matthew* (St. Louis: Concordia Publishing House, 1961), pp. 36, 196–202.

42. Arthur Vööbus, *Liturgical Traditions in the Didache* (Stockholm: Estonian Theological Society in Exile, 1968), pp. 96–99. See also Christhard Mahrenholz, *Kompendium der Liturgik* (Kassel: Johannes Stauda Verlag, 1963), p. 105; Hippolytus, *The Apostolic Tradition*, Jasper, *Prayers*, p. 35.

43. AE 29: 213f.

44. Cf. Herman Sasse, *We Confess the Sacraments*, trans. Norman Nagel (St. Louis: Concordia Publishing House, 1985), pp. 83f.

45. AE 37: 181. FC SD VII, 76.

46. Zwingli: "Another meaning must underlie them." Letter to Matthew Alber Concerning the Lord's Supper, Nov. 1524, in *Huldrych Zwingli: Writings*, trans. H. W. Pipkin, 2 vols. (Allison Park, Pennsylvania: Pickwick, 1984), II: 138. AE 36: 279; LC V, 12–14; C. Richardson, ed., *Library of Christian Classics* (Philadelphia: Westminster Press, 1953–1966), 24: 188ff.

47. Ap X, 2.

48. Lateran Council IV (1215). Cf. Herman Sasse, *This is My Body* (Minneapolis: Augsburg Publishing House, 1959), pp. 10ff.; also Sasse, *We Confess the Sacraments*, pp. 71, 105.

49. AE 36: 50.

50. Ibid.

51. Ibid., 36; AE 35: 97.

52. AE 37: 68. See also Werner Elert, *The Structure of Lutheranism*, trans. Walter A. Hansen (St. Louis: Concordia Publishing House, 1972), p. 234.

53. Joachim Jeremias, *The Eucharistic Words of Jesus*, trans. Norman Perrin (New York: Charles Scribner's Sons, 1966), pp. 42–46.

54. *Didache* 9, 5. Justin Martyr, *First Apology* 66, 1. TDNT 9: 405f. The contrast between the Syro-Byzantine way and that of Rome is pointed out by Bryan Spinks, "Berakah, Anaphoral Theory amd Luther," *Lutheran Quarterly* III/3 (Autumn 1989): 278.

55. *Jubilees* 49, 6. *The Apocryphal Old Testament*, ed. H. F. D. Sparks (Oxford: Oxford University Press, 1984), p. 135.

56. *Pesachim* 10, 4. *The Mishnah*, ed. H. Danby (London: Oxford University Press, 1933), p. 150. See also Exod. 12:26; 13:8.

57. *Apostolic Tradition of Hippolytus* 4, 2; Jungmann, II: 146.

58. AE 37: 265ff.; 332f.

59. *Representaretur*, Trent 22, 1, Denzinger 1740, 1644. Zwingli in *Library of Christian Classics*, 24: 234. Jungmann, I: 184. Odo Casel, *The Mystery of Christian Worship*, ed. Burkhard Neunheuser (London: Darton, Longman and Todd, 1962), pp. 72, 101, 154: "our co-participation." Peter Brunner, *Worship in the Name of Jesus*, trans. M. H. Bertram (St. Louis: Concordia Publishing House, 1968), pp. 168–171. Sasse, *We Confess the Sacraments*, p. 127.

60. AE 37: 182–187.

61. Ibid., 338; AE 35: 82.

62. AE 37: 183.

63. AE 40: 214.

64. FC SD VII, 75.

65. Philip J. Spener, *Theologische Bedencken*, 4 vols. (Halle: Verlegung des Waysenhauses, 1712–1717), II: 188. Cf. Luther D. Reed, *The Lutheran Liturgy*, rev. ed. (Philadelphia: Muhlenberg Press, 1959), p. 361.

66. Σύσσωμος καὶ σύναιμος, Werner Elert, *Eucharist and Church Fellowship in the First Four Centuries*, trans. N. E. Nagel (St. Louis: Concordia Publishing House, 1966), p. 23f.

67. LC V, 29f.; AE 35: 86.

68. LC V, 2, 85–87. There comes to mind the deacon's cry, "The holy things for the holy ones," in the *Apostolic Constitutions* VIII, 13, a compilation of earlier pieces such as the *Didache*, *Didascalia*, and the *Apostolic Tradition*. It is perhaps the first (c. 375) complete liturgy extant. Evidence that it was actually used is, however, lacking. Cf. Elert, *Eucharist and Church Fellowship*, p. 223, n. 13.

69. *Didache* 14, 2.

70 Τὸ κοίνον makes the κοινωνία; *das Gemeine* makes the *Gemeinschaft*. Cf. AE 40: 178.

71. Jungmann, *Mass of the Roman Rite*, II: 321. For a brief history of the Pax and an overview of the literature see Robert F. Taft, *The Great Entrance* (Rome: Institutum Studiorum Orientalium, 1975), pp. 375–78.

72. Cf. Augustine, *Epistola* 149, 16.

73. Cyprian, *Epistola* 63, 4. Cyprian, bishop of Carthage, who has been called the father of the sacrifice theory, was martyred A.D. 258 in the Valerian persecution.

74. See "Letters of Fellowship" in Elert, *Eucharist and Church Fellowship*, pp. 151–52.

75. *Didascalia* II, 54.

76. AE 40: 133. C. F. W. Walther, *Americanische-Lutherische Pastoraltheologie*, 5th ed. (St. Louis: Concordia Publishing House, 1906), pp. 168f.

77. AE 37: 182: "embraced and embodied in command-words." FC SD VII, 78.

78. *Didache* 9, 4.

79. WA 30: 55, 37.

80. Consilia Witebergensia, III, 50, cited in "Der lutherische Distributionsformel bei Administrirung des heiligen Abendmahles," *Lehre und Wehre* 1/12 (December 1855): 374.

81. Thus, "more to the feelings than to the faith." See Friedrich Krüger, "Geschichte der Spendeformel in der Feier des heiligen Abendmahls in der deutschen evangelischen Kirchen," *Monatschrift für Gottesdienst und kirchliche Kunst* 16 (1911): 201.

82. For an overview of the contents of this agenda see pp. 93–95.

83. Walther, *Pastoraltheologie*, p. 183f.

84. Tertullian, *Adversus Marcionem* 1, 14. Cf. Ignatius, *Trallians* 9, 1f.; SC VI, 2; AE 36: 350.

85. LC V, 29.

86. All the evidence shows that closed (or close) communion was the usage from the church's beginning. Cf. Elert, *Eucharist*, pp. 75–81.

87. LC V, 2.

88. AE 51: 89–91.

89. Cyril of Jerusalem (4th century), *Mystagogical Catechesis* 5, 21, in Jasper, *Prayers*, p. 87.

90. Jungman, II: 376ff.; Jeremias, *Eucharistic Words*, p. 48.

91. AC X, 1.

92. Cf. the word translated "unworthily" in 1 Cor. 11:27. LC V, 57 and 61; SC VI, 10: "He is truly worthy and well prepared who believes these words: '*for you*' and '*for the forgiveness of sins.*' "

93. SC VI, 6.

94. Lev. 17:11b: "It is the blood that makes atonement for one's life." Heb. 9:22.

95. Cf. Gen. 9:4; Phil. 2:7 with its ἐκένωσεν, TDNT 5: 711; Matt., Mark, Luke: ἐκχυννόμενον.

96. LC V, 42.

97. Ernst Volk, "Evangelical Accents in the Understanding of the Holy Communion," *Lutheran Quarterly* 1/2 (Summer 1987): 195. Similarly Leonhard Goppelt, ibid., p. 203, n. 29.

98. Ap XXIV, 19.

99. AE 35: 105; Ap XXIV, 72–77; LC V, 27.

100. AE 35: 96–99; 38: 126, 133; Justin Martyr, *First Apology* 67,7; Ap XXIV, 19.

101. *Apostolic Constitutions* VIII, 15. The entire text appeared as part of an evening prayer in this early work; VII, 48.

102. The sacred ministerial acts and the orders of Divine Service contained in the *Kirchen-Agende* of 1856 (plus a greatly reduced number of antiphons and collects) were first translated into English 25 years later with the title *Church*

Liturgy for Evangelical Lutheran Congregations of the Unaltered Augsburg Confession (St. Louis: Concordia Publishing House, 1881). Some wanted things more or better than this and had been inserting things from here and there. There were good things in the several editions of the *Church Book* of 1888 (cf. Reed, *The Lutheran Liturgy*, p. 190). The Synod's *Liturgy and Agenda* of 1917 was to keep everybody together in the traditional liturgy without, on the one hand, slipping into legalism or, on the other, into the chaos of do-it-yourself liturgies.

10

Confession and Absolution: Sin and Forgiveness

Fred L. Precht

Penance

Penance, both as a procedure and as an institution, is of a very complex character, a fact due largely to the sparseness and obscurity of the earliest source materials and the conflicting interpretations in the course of its varied and intricate development. To reconstruct how the church dealt with individuals whose baptismal repentance had faded to the point of betrayal requires one to depend largely on anecdotal comments, homiletic exhortations, and the passing references of polemecists. Limitations of space will unfortunately only permit sketching in very broad strokes this history from New Testament times to the Reformation.[1]

As for the meaning of the word *penance,* it is to be regretted that the term has become distorted by its association with assigned penances in the history of the Western Church. Derived from the Latin *paenitentia*, it is the equivalent of the Greek *metanoia*. Both words, whether Greek or Latin, express what is meant by the terms *conversion* and *penance*. The latter is basically a shorter form of *repentance, a turning from sin.*

Biblical Foundations

The gospels clearly indicate that repentance and the forgiveness of sins constitute the very core of Jesus' preaching. He entered upon his work with the appeal to people to "repent and believe the good news!" (Mark 1:15) and he left this world with the charge that "repentance and forgiveness of sins will be preached in his name to all nations" (Luke 24:47). Furthermore, the divine willingness to forgive the penitent knows no bounds (Luke 15:20ff.). Forgiveness is excluded only when the sinner hardens his heart against God through persistent, blasphemous, and final impenitence, thus committing "the blasphemy against the Spirit," commonly known as the sin against the Holy Spirit (Matt. 12:31–32; cf. Heb. 6:4–6). Moreover, if the Father in heaven will forgive people's sins in the same measure as they are ready to grant repeated forgiveness to their brothers and sisters (Matt. 18:22, 35), then repeated acts of divine forgiveness are obviously presupposed.

Forgiveness is not a matter that is simply concluded between God and man; it comes from the mediation of the church of which a Christian has become a member by Baptism. In John 20:21–23; Matt. 16:19; and Matt. 18:17–20 Jesus bestows upon his disciples, namely, the church, what has aptly been called the *power of the keys*. This is more than the general proclamation of the Gospel. The disciples are personally and directly to deal with individual souls.[2] While Roman Catholics customarily have thought of these directives as referring to their Sacrament of Penance, the fathers of the church as referring to Baptism, this power and authority, including also Paul's command regarding the incestuous Corinthian (1 Cor. 5:1–13), transcends both Baptism and penance. The three authors clearly affirm that the Christian *ekklesia* is God's gathering of a community of salvation, that the individuals' response to this community affects their relationship to God, and that leaders of the community have authority over sin and can spell out conditions of membership.[3]

Both the Matthaean and Johannine communities thus knew that they had the power to set people free from their sin. They had it because the Spirit had come upon them (Acts 1:8); and so, like Jesus before them, they forgave sins by welcoming sinners into their gatherings (cf. Mark 16:15–16; Luke 24:47–48) as he himself had brought them into his company. Theirs were reconciling communities of salvation where old lines of distinction had been erased (Gal. 3:27–28). Entrance into this community, of course, was for the post-resurrection church, through Baptism, which incorporated men, women, and children into Christ's death and resurrection. In time, these communities continued in "the breaking of bread" (Acts 2:42), thus proclaiming God's deeds in Christ "also for the forgiveness of sins" (Matt. 26:28).

Penance plays an important part in the epistles of Paul, although he only occasionally employs the word *metanoia* (repentance). Like Christ, he insists on a thorough-going conversion (1 Cor. 5:7ff.; Rom. 8:5–13; Gal. 2:19ff.) and he speaks repeated warnings against sin (Rom. 6:12ff.; 13:14; 1 Cor. 6:18ff.; Col. 3:10). At times he expressly reproves concrete lapses in the Christian communities, such as dissensions, uncharitableness (1 Cor. 3:3ff.; 11:18ff.), idleness (2 Thess. 3:6ff.), "impurity, sexual sin and debauchery" (2 Cor. 12:21). Yet not even such backsliding Christians are necessarily lost, for "Godly sorrow brings repentance that leads to salvation and leaves no regret" (2 Cor. 7:10). But it is Christ who died and rose from the dead; it is he who intercedes for sinners, thus assuring them of forgiveness (Rom. 8:34).

According to Paul, it is sin, and consequently penance, that is also the concern of the church. Fraternal love imposes both the duty of admonishing one who errs (Gal. 6:1ff.; 2 Tim. 4:2; 2:25) and, in the case of gross immorality, of admonishing and ultimately excommunicating the offender. The classic example is that of the incestuous Corinthian previously alluded to. Here Paul instructs the Corinthian congregation, when assembled "in the name of . . . the Lord Jesus," to sever relations with the evildoer and to "hand this man over to Satan, so that the sinful nature may be destroyed and his spirit saved on the day of the Lord" (2 Cor. 5:5). As time goes on the fathers interpreted this to mean that the church does so in the hope of bringing him to a better mind. They see this interpretation confirmed by St. Paul's own action towards an excommunicate in his second letter to the Corinthians (2 Cor. 2:5–11).[4]

Only extreme cases called for such action, reserved for the assembled community (1 Cor. 5:4; cf. Matt. 18:17) when all else failed: when the offender ignored private warning, refused the correction of the small group, and turned a deaf ear to the whole community (Matt. 18:15–17). Such a sinner was not only to be treated as a pagan (1 Cor. 5:10–11; cf. Matt. 18:17) but shunned completely.

Paul reminds the Corinthians that the reconciliation of the world accomplished in Christ has been entrusted to the church's ministry:

> All this [Christ's suffering, death, and resurrection] is from God, who reconciled us to himself through Christ and gave us the ministry of reconciliation: that God was reconciling the world to himself in Christ, not counting men's sins against them. And he has committed to us the message of reconciliation. We are therefore Christ's ambassadors, as though God were making his appeal through us. We implore you on Christ's behalf: Be reconciled to God (2 Cor. 5:18–20).

As the prophets of the Old Testament had proclaimed God's law and promises to the people and the whole world, so Paul, with the other apostles, announces the message of reconciliation already accomplished through the cross of Christ. Simultaneously this message is also a request and an invitation to enter into this event of reconciliation. Paul's message, "Be reconciled to God," is substantially the post-Easter version of Jesus' call to conversion: "Repent, for the kingdom of heaven is near" (Matt. 4:17). The church is comprised of those people who have heard this call, who have been converted by the Holy Spirit, and who have accepted by faith God's active reconciliation. The church is thereby the space in which God's reign is recognized and has already begun.

The catholic epistles also refer to this subject. For John in his war against the heretic Cerinthus and his followers, who denied sin and the need of forgiveness,[5] the recognition of the universality of sin constitutes an essential point of faith. "If we claim to be without sin, we deceive ourselves and the truth is not in us" (1 John 1:8). But even the gravest sinner can count on forgiveness (James 1:21; 5:19–20), for, according to John, Christ "is the atoning sacrifice . . . for the sins of the whole world" (1 John 2:2). Neither is the universality of forgiveness abrogated by the distinction, so important in the later history of penance, between the "mortal sin" (NIV: "sin that leads to death") and the sin that is "not mortal,"[6] with reference to which John promises that intercessory prayer for a brother whose sin in not mortal will be heard (1 John 5:16). James is even more explicit in connection with the anointing of the sick: "Therefore confess your sins to each other and pray for each other so that you may be healed. The prayer of a righteous man is powerful and effective" (James 5:16).

Both here and in John (1 John 1:9) the emphasis on confession is a new element. In the Johannine context the confession is contrasted with the heretical teachers who "claim to be without sin" (1 John 1:8). When, however, "the truth is . . . in us," then sins will be confessed, admitted, and acknowledged to God.[7] Neither does John say anything about how, when, and where such confession is to be made.[8]

In contrast to James 5:16, 1 John 1:9 does not restrict the act of confessing to presbyters. In all probability the Christian brother or sister is implied.[9] Moreover, James sets no limits to possible forgiveness (1:21; 5:19–20), and 2 Peter 3:9 reflects a similar understanding of the Lord's mercy. Revelation sets no limits in calling to repentance churches as well as individuals in them (2:5, 14–16, 20–22; 3:1–5, 15–19). From the foregoing it is clearly evident that the apostolic Church had a substantial understanding of the way of life taught by Christ and his disciples. Among other things, Christians were aware that if anyone sinned, he or she could be forgiven through the ministry of the church and thus restored to the eucharistic assembly and admitted to the sacrament of the unity, namely, the Holy Communion. The New Testament, however, furnishes no evidence of a rite connected with this pardon or restoration.

Canonical Penance

The writings of the post-apostolic age, up to the second half of the third century, furnish only scanty information as to how the church dealt with sinners, although there are numerous exhortations to repentance. Perhaps in these early days, when Christianity was confined to zealous and selective communities, there was less need for a readily available ritual or process for restoring sinners. The persecutions of the third century, however, occurring after a long period of tranquility, came as a shock to the Christian communities in the Mediterranean world. Although martyrs and confessors were not lacking, those who through fear of torture denied their faith were perhaps more numerous. They had to be dealt with. Later, the growth of the church through the peace of Constantine in the fourth century also contributed to the need for a definite system or ritual for restoring sinners.

Against this backdrop what is known as canonical penance gradually took shape, developing into a rather full-blown discipline, especially from the fourth through the sixth centuries. Although practices differed from one place to another, there evolved a fairly uniform procedure—resembling somewhat the process of Christian initiation—that was followed in the Mediterranean territory as well as on the European continent.

In this procedure the characteristic public acts are excommunication and reconciliation. Having made confession of sin to the bishop, the penitent was admitted into the order of penitents (*ordo paenitentium*)—in reality a third class of Christians, distinct from the catechumens and the faithful, who were assigned a special place in the church (*locus paenitentium*). The excommunication consisted in the penitent being excluded from the Prayer of the Faithful, Offertory, and the Eucharist. The bishop decided on the amount of penance, usually according to the rule, the greater the guilt, the greater the penance, or satisfaction, required. Among the penitential exercises that had to be done in private were fasting, almsgiving, and prayer, designed to help the penitent reform his or her life. In the ongoing penitential procedure the worship service included a special rite for penitents, consisting of prayer and the laying on of hands by the bishop. Once the satisfaction was completed, the penitent was reconciled by the bishop with supplications and the laying on of hands—in the West on Maundy Thursday, in the East on Good Friday. But this, unfortunately, did not end the matter, for there were attached lifelong disabilities: the penitent could not be admitted to the clerical state; could not hold public office nor engage in military service; could not marry or have marital relations if already married. In other words, the penitent had to renounce the life of the world, to a degree not much different from that of the religious state. Moreover, such canonical penance could be experienced only once. Should the sinner fail again, no reconciliation was available until at death, and even then some would deny the sinner the laying on of hands, the symbol of reconciliation.

One wonders what sins might prompt such drastic penance, or satisfaction. Rules certainly varied. In some of the larger churches lists of varying length were drawn up, specifying sins for which the bishop could admit someone to the order of penitents. All lists included such major offences as apostasy, murder, and adultery, a fact, however, which should not be taken to imply a definite distinction between venial and mortal sins at this time. Often sins of a general character were listed, such as harming one's neighbor or being greedy or jealous. It was the responsibility of the bishop to judge the gravity of each case and accordingly assign the satisfaction.

The heavy obligations and the nonrepeatable character of canonical penance precluded the acceptance of young people into the order of penitents. Similarly, clerics, as well as the religious, presumably to protect them from the infamy of public penance, were not permitted to become penitents. Sinful clerics were treated as lapsed penitents and allowed to do private penance but without reconciliation; the religious could be expelled from the monastery.

That people flocked to undergo this severe discipline appears unlikely. Actually it was perhaps a small fraction of the Christian community that did so. And forced entry into the order of penitents was rather frowned on than encouraged. On the other hand, that Christians still had a strong awareness of their sinfulness is attested by a perusal of the prayers in the early liturgies, prayers replete with confession of sinfulness and petitions for God's mercy. In addition, these Christians gave alms, they fasted, and above all they implored God's mercy and received his forgiveness through Christ in the Eucharist.

Toward the close of the sixth century canonical penance had well nigh come to a dead end. The lifelong obligations and heavy disabilities often imposed on penitents gradually caused the procedure, if resorted to at all, to become largely a means of preparing for death. Moreover, from the standpoint of Christian growth, the restoration, having become an entity in itself, was now as inaccessible and useless for human life as the Eucharist to which it was to restore one. Obviously, the removal of the once-only stipulation would help to remedy the situation.

Tariff Penance

It was private penance, as developed by the Celtic churches in Britain and Ireland, a second major form of penance that had begun its triumphant migration to the European mainland, that did just that. Born in the monasteries of the Celtic church, this private, repeatable process of penance filled the gap of canonical penance in that it became a procedure for the living and not simply for the dying. There was no order of penitents, the penitent was not segregated nor, so to speak, excommunicated from the community, nor was he or she required to do penance in public. The confession—to priest or abbot, to bishop only in the case of peculiarly offensive actions—as well as the satisfaction was done in private. The confession, not considered to be of the essence of the rite, was the necessary means to assess and arrive at the proper amount of penance. To guide the confessor in calculating the penance, penitential books were developed that provided precisely determined penance for an unimaginable range of sins, with the only distinguishing features being the duration and extent of the penance itself.[10] Thus the term *tariff penance*. Pardon was available for all sins, whether great or small. Confession could be made as often as deemed necessary, without regard to age, sex, or social position.

In evaluating the penitentials with their heavy, oftentimes revolting, curious, and extreme penalties, cognizance must be taken of the fact that they were designed to wage war on the vice, savagery, and paganism of the day. Reflecting and representing also to a great extent secular penal law, they evidently played a civilizing and humanizing role of no small importance.

While the Irish, or Celtic, procedure of penance was less rigid in certain respects and more adaptable to the needs of the Christian community in the context of spiritual direction and growth, it also had its drawbacks. The separation of what was now private reconciliation from the eucharistic assembly fostered the idea that penance restored one to the possibility of Eucharist and not to the Eucharist itself. Moreover, the role of the Eucharist in spiritual growth was diminished.

Since the severe tariff penance often led to totals of astronomical proportions, equivalents to or substitute penalties, so-called commutations (*arrea*), generally easier and more lenient, were permitted; for instance, shorter but more intensive fasts, repeated prayers, kneeling on stones, keeping arms outstretched during prayer, and the like.[11] Their use (and abuse) helped provoke the strong ninth-century continental reaction to the penitential books. The commutations are also, incidentally, the origin of indulgences, the authoritative remission of temporal punishment—considered valid before God—which the Roman church grants outside the Sacrament after the guilt of sin has already been forgiven.

Medieval Compromise

As the Irish priests, both as missionaries and pilgrims, crossed over to the European continent, they introduced the Irish system together with the penitential books. Since the rigorous canonical public penance in vogue there had begun to wane, the new system readily took its place. With the rising popularity of the Irish system in the eighth and ninth centuries, external conflict became inevitable. Church officials reacted against the Irish innovation; Carolingian reform counsels—Tours and Rheims (813), Paris (829), Mainz (847)—attempted to revive canonical penance and to outlaw the penitential books, but to no avail. Out of the conflict a new balance emerged in the form of, in a sense, an enduring yet precarious compromise: penance according to the traditional, canonical system was to be done for grave sins publicly known, while private penance sufficed for grave sins not publicly known. Here now was the first official recognition of private penance as an ordinary form of ecclesiastical penance, as official and canonical as public penance.

In this compromise it appears that penitents, whether in the canonical or private system, were expected to be present for the solemn reconciliation in Holy Week. Because of the pastoral difficulty, however, of getting those accustomed to the private procedure to return for reconciliation, an occasion that to them seemed superfluous (they had not been excommunicated in the first place), confession and reconciliation eventually came to be joined. The primary purpose of confession, namely, assigning appropriate penitential practices to expiate and make satisfaction for sins, was initially, however, unchanged. But as time went on the amount of penance decreased while the importance of the confession increased. Frequently also, adding up the required penances for the numerous sins confessed made their performance in one lifetime prohibitive. Confessors were therefore advised to consider the penitent's abilities and not to impose too much penance, or to make simpler substitutions. Thus by the 12th century the confession itself, once the means of assigning the penance that expiated sin, became the essence of expiation, with absolution immediately following. Moreover, the immediacy of absolution, that is, prior to the penance, or satisfaction, brought the interior disposition of the penitent—the quality of sorrow or contrition—to the fore as warrant for such absolution. Theologians of the 12th and 13th centuries heightened the value of contrition, looking upon confession as an exterior sign of contrition and emphasizing the absolution as an essential element of penance.

Looking back to the Carolingian compromise, one might say that the private penance that eventually won out was spiritually in the tradition of Celtic monasticism but ritually related to canonical penance.

The Fourth Lateran Council (1215) not only introduced the duty of annual confession and Communion, it also acknowledged the validity of the private penance that originated in Ireland, at the same time ratifying the disappearance of canonical penance. Thus the latter became so rare as to have no place in the life of the church, even though still reflected in the liturgical books. The season with which it was associated, however, began to become increasingly important. Already in the tenth century, Lent—its original connection with the catechumenate and Baptism having been lost—constituted a time for all Christians to become penitents. Ceremonially enrolled on Ash Wednesday by the imposition of ashes, they fasted throughout the period, thus to purify themselves in preparation for the customary (and later obligatory) Easter Communion.

Council of Trent

In response to the Protestant Reformation, the Roman Catholic Church in the Council of Trent (1545–63) issued 15 canons on, what was by then called, the Sacrament of Penance. Limitations of space will only permit mention of a few salient points.[12]

Canons 1 to 3 emphasize the sacramental character of penance and its distinction from Baptism. John 20:22ff. is to be understood as the power of remitting and retaining sins in the sacrament and is not to be distorted to signify the authority of preaching the Gospel (pp. 101–102). Canon 4 defines the matter of penance as consisting in contribution, confession, and satisfaction, acts on the part of the penitent required "for the integrity of the sacrament and for the full and complete remission of sins." Condemned are those who maintain that "faith and the terrors of conscience are parts of penance" (chap. 3, pp. 90–91; Canon 4, p. 102). The declaratory, or declarative, significance of absolution is definitely repudiated (Canon 9, p. 103). Because of various attacks by the Reformers the council deemed it necessary to define in greater detail the nature of contrition and attrition. Contrition is "a sorrow of mind and a detestation for sin committed with the purpose of not sinning in the future." It is necessary "for obtaining the forgiveness of sins and thus indeed it prepares one who has fallen after Baptism for the remission of sins if it is united with confidence in the divine mercy and with the desire to receive this sacrament in a proper manner." Imperfect contrition, or attrition, on the other hand, arising from the "consideration of the heinousness of sin or from the fear of hell and of punishment," if it "renounces the desire for sin and hopes for pardon . . . is a gift of God and an impulse of the Holy Ghost." And although without the sacrament it cannot justify the sinner, yet it "disposes him to obtain the grace of God in the sacrament of penance" (chap. 4, pp. 91–92, passim). Left open by the council was the disputed question whether attrition is in itself sufficient, or whether contrition must first be produced through the grace of absolution.

The necessity of confession and its divine institution are proved from the power of the keys that constitute the priest as judge. All mortal sins, including those which are secret, must be confessed, along with their circumstances. Venial sins can be expiated by other means, even though confession for them is also salutary (chap. 5, pp. 92–93).

Chapter VI and Canons 9 and 10 are concerned with the minister of the sacrament and with absolution. In accordance with Matt.

18:18 and John 20:23, only bishops and priests are bearers of the power of the keys. Absolution is a judicial act, not a mere ministry of pronouncing and declaring that sins are remitted, provided the penitent believes that he or she is absolved (pp. 97ff., 103ff.). Fundamental to the teaching on satisfaction, it is asserted, the entire temporal punishment is not always remitted along with the guilt as is the case in Baptism. Besides its retributory purpose, satisfaction has at the same time an educative and medicinal value. Deriving all its power from Christ, satisfaction does not injure faith in his redemptive work. Priests are required to impose penance corresponding to the gravity of sin. Binding as well as loosing belongs to the power of the keys (chaps. 8 and 9, pp. 97–98; Canon 15, p. 104).

In its final session on December 4, 1563, the council instructed the pope to provide the necessary liturgical reforms. While the *Breviarum Romanum* and the *Missale Romanum* appeared in 1568 and 1570, respectively, it was not until 1614 that the *Rituale Romanum*, which contained the rite of penance, was completed and promulgated. From then on there was virtually no structural change in the rite until the Second Vatican Council (1962–65) when, in view of the decline in participation by the laity, it was felt that some changes were needed if the sacrament were to continue to serve the people's true needs.

Eve of the Reformation

At the start of the Reformation there were in practice—except for reconciliation in special circumstances—three types of confession: (1) private, or individual, confession, the so-called sacramental confession, followed by the indicative-operative absolution *Ego te absolvo a peccatis tuis* ("I absolve you from your sins"); (2) general confession (*Offene Schuld*), usually conducted in the vernacular after the sermon with an optative (expressing wish or desire) or declarative absolution; and (3) the *confiteor* form with an optative absolution, said at the beginning of the Mass. The exact validity of the latter two was undecided. In providing worship materials for *Lutheran Worship* (1982) the Commission on Worship was concerned about distinguishing these three forms.

Individual Confession and Absolution

Luther and the Lutheran Symbols

Luther's concern for the gracious forgiveness of sins in Christ has prompted the view that, essentially speaking, the Lutheran Reformation was precipitated by attention to the doctrine of penance as then constituted. Melanchthon, for instance, in his "Defense of Doctor Luther against the Parisian Opinion" ("Schutzrede wider das . . . Parisiche Urteil für D. Luther") expresses the thought that the greatest contribution of Luther to the church was his correct teaching and proper use of the sacrament of penance.[13] In this concern Luther's attention was directed especially to private confession and absolution. Cognizant of its importance in the life of the Christian, he set out to free the prevalent practice from misuse and false implications and to base it again on sound, biblical foundations.

Luther's thoughts on the specific act of confession must be viewed in the light of his theology of sin. In his commentary on Psalm 51 he equates the sinner and the act of sin.[14] Not only is the actual deed a sin, but the human being in his entire essence is a sinner. Therefore, confession dare not be restricted simply to individual sins but must refer also to the sinner's sinful nature as such.

In the Leipzig disputation (1519) Luther not only points up the extent of human depravity but also touches on Rome's distinction between venial and mortal sins:

> To deny that a person sins even when doing good; that venial sin is pardonable, not according to its nature, but by the mercy of God; or that sin remains in the child after baptism; that is equivalent to crushing Paul and Christ underfoot.[15]

Luther doubts that, humankind being what it is, it is possible to distinguish between venial and mortal sins. If a sin is venial, he says in his sermon on the sacrament of penance (1519), it is only by God's grace that it is considered as such.[16] In the same sermon he states that no teacher has been "learned enough to give us a dependable rule for distinguishing venial from mortal sins, except in such obvious offenses . . . as adultery, murder, theft, falsehood, slander, betrayal, hatred and the like."[17] And in the Smalcald Articles (1537) he says, "There is nothing in us that is not sinful."[18] Luther placed great stress on the conscience.[19] Confession, he says, need not embrace all sins, but only those that oppress the conscience.[20]

Should a person forget to confess certain mortal sins, he should not become troubled. These can be privately confessed to God or they can be confessed and absolved in the general absolution in the public service before the Holy Eucharist.[21] In the Small Catechism (1529), under the heading, "How Christians Should Be Taught to Confess," he says,

> Before God we should plead guilty of all sins, even those we are not aware of, as we do in the Lord's Prayer; but before the pastor we should confess only those sins which we know and feel in our hearts.[22]

In this catechism he speaks of confession as embracing two parts—confession and absolution.[23] Boehme amplifies this to include faith as the third part.[24] Indeed, note the emphasis on faith in the catechism: "a confessor will know additional passages with which to comfort and strengthen the faith of those who have great burdens of conscience or are sorrowful and distressed."[25] Thus Luther as confessor does not examine and probe into the degree of contrition or the strength or will to lead a better life. The questions addressed to the penitent simply concern themselves with faith. Contrition is naturally involved in a proper confession. On the basis of the doctrine of justification,[26] Luther and his colaborers—in contrast to the scholastic division of penance, or repentance, into contrition, confession, and satisfaction[27]—divide repentance into contrition ("terror smiting the conscience through the knowledge of sin") and faith ("born of the Gospel of absolution") that for Christ's sake sins are forgiven.[28] Contrition and faith, however, are the work of God alone through Law and Gospel, and in their twofold character they correspond to God's dealing with people in such Law and Gospel.[29]

Before leaving the matter of contrition, it is important to note Luther's warning against demanding contrition or including it in the formula of absolution as if to convey the impression that the absolution hinges upon contrition.[30] Where the absolution hinges upon the degree of contrition and is accordingly pronounced conditionally, there reigns for Luther the *Fehlschlüssel*, the *clavis errans* (the erring key) of the pope "by which he has destroyed faith in

Christ and taken away all comfort and counsel from our conscience."[31]

Luther's high regard for the institution of confession does not result so much from the confessing aspect as such, but more from the absolution that is imparted to the anxious conscience and upon the comfort of the forgiveness of sins that is personally and individually imparted. It is this personal certainty of the heart that gives confession its significance and which should cause the Christian to make use of it.[32] The concreteness of penitence, understood from the standpoint of justification, requires that absolution stand at the very center—"absolution, which is the sacrament of penitence"—this is the sacramental and constitutive factor.[33] The absolution, to be sure, from the standpoint of content, does not differ from the preaching of the Gospel.[34] On the other hand, despising the absolution is tantamount to despising the Gospel.[35] In his sermon on the observance of St. Peter and St. Paul Day (1522) he asserts that the minister is commissioned by the church to exercise the Office of the Keys (Matt. 16:19; 18:18; John 20:21–23).[36] And in a sermon preached on the Nineteenth Sunday after Trinity Sunday of the same year he amplifies this thought by stating: "Therefore we have ordained pastors and priests in order that they might perform such services (baptizing, absolving, preaching, etc.) in our stead, and these should yield the power as our representatives."[37] Melanchthon describes this power of the pastor or bishop as *potestas ordinis* (power of the order) and the *potestas jurisdictionis* (power of jurisdiction), namely, the authority to excommunicate those who are guilty of public offenses or to absolve them if they turn from their evil ways and ask for such absolution.[38] Although Luther fought against such authority, or power, in his *Babylonian Captivity* (1520), claiming that confession could be made to and absolution received from any Christian brother,[39] one finds no such utterances after 1529. Moreover, although the keys are given by Christ to the entire church,[40] they are actually exercised *iuxta vocationem* (depending on one's calling),[41] and that in the sense of the public ministry.[42]

Of particular interest for present purposes are the formulas of absolution that developed in the centuries-long history of penance. Originally *absolutio* was the term used for a concluding blessing in any liturgy. In early canonical penance the emphasis was more on reconciliation of the penitent with the Christian community than on the remission and forgiveness that climaxed the process of penance. Emphasis on ecclesiastical forgiveness and the power of the keys in the Carolingian Reform caused *absolutio* to take on the meaning of pardon, or remission, indicating that the penance has been completed. The various forms of absolution from the eighth through the 15th centuries can generally be grouped and designated as follows. The terms optative (expressing wish or desire) and precative (Latin: *precatio*, prayer) imply prayer forms addressed to God. In the Gelasian Sacramentary (c. seventh century), a liturgical book containing some of the oldest penance rituals, expressions such as "so that the kindness of your pardon may release those accused," "may all iniquities be blotted out by your heavenly pardon," and "heal the wounds and forgive the sins" occur in the prayers for the reconciliation of penitents on Holy Thursday.[43] What is frequently designated as deprecative (seeking to avert disapproval by prayer) is a formula resembling "May the almighty Lord grant pardon, absolution, and remission of all your sins." Although adressed to the penitent, it is seemingly more supplicatory to God. The declarative formula ("I declare unto you the forgiveness of all your sins in the name of the Father, Son, and Holy Spirit") was gradually introduced around the year 1000, the result of an understanding of priestly absolution as the authoritative declaration to the individual that, in sorrow (*contritio*) on the part of the penitent, God has already forgiven sins. The deprecative formula, however, still remained in use, for Bonaventura (d. 1274) still attached sacramental significance to it. It was in the high scholastic period, under the leadership of Thomas Aquinas (d. 1274), that the indicative-operative, sometimes called effective, namely, "I forgive you (*Ego te absolvo*) all your sins in the name of the Father and of the Son and of the Holy Spirit," based on Matt. 16:19; 18:18; and John 20:21–23, came to the fore. Insisting that the expression *Ego te absolvo* ("I absolve you") has the same effective power as the baptismal formula, Aquinas demands its use.[44] It was frequently combined with one or more of the previous forms. The Synod of Nimes (1284), for instance, decided on the following combination: "May the almightly God grant pardon, absolution, and remission of all your sins. And I absolve you, by the authority of the Lord Jesus Christ and the blessed apostles Peter and Paul entrusted to me, of those sins which you have confessed. . . ." This combination, incidentally, is still reflected in the Roman Catholic rites of confession resulting from Vatican Council II (1962–65).[45]

Although Luther vehemently objected to the misuses and false theological premises connected with private confession in the Western Church of his time, he highly prized such confession in purified form, especially because of the absolution by which the comfort of the forgiveness of sins is personally and individually imparted to the penitent. Neither is it simply a proclamation or wish for forgiveness. It is the actual impartation and appropriation by faith of the forgiveness of sins in Christ. And the absolution of the pastor on earth is one with God's absolution in heaven.[46] "It is Christ who sits there, Christ who hears, Christ who answers and not a man."[47] As to the formula of absolution, Luther favored the indicative-operative (or effective), the form that he considered the most positive and comforting, the most suitable to the Gospel.[48] At times he combined the indicative-operative with the declarative.[49] In his earlier years he alluded to the declarative aspect.[50]

It is private, or individual, confession of which the Lutheran Confessions, or Symbols, exclusively speak and which they value highly in pastoral care, allowing it to be called a sacrament in the strict sense,[51] particularly in view of the theological importance of the indicative-operative (or effective) absolution: "I forgive you all your sins. . . ." It is this type of confession, in purified form, which Luther extolled in glowing terms[52] as he encouraged people to make frequent use of this salutary means.

The Missouri Synod

During the early years of its existence two controversies expecially stirred the Lutheran Church—Missouri Synod.[53] The one dealt with chiliasm and its related questions and the other with private confession and absolution.[54]

Articles appearing in *Der Lutheraner* in the early years indicate the prevailing attention given to confession and absolution.[55] In 1856 the subject was brought to the fore when the practice was questioned in Wisconsin. That same year the Northern District urged that private confession and absolution be retained, noting also that this practice was common in most of the congregations of the district. Among other things, this district declared that absolution pronounced by the pastor is effective (*kräftig und wirksam*); that individual sins need not be enumerated, but that absolution might be pronounced upon a "general" confession; and that Reformed influences had brought about the disuse of private confession. It bemoaned the fact that too many congregations incorrectly associated private confession with Roman Catholic auricular confession. It urged that the general confession, frequently employed after the sermon prior to the Holy Communion, should not be considered a genuinely Lutheran institution, since it did not arise in the most healthy period of the Lutheran Church. Finally, it enjoined pastors to remind their congregations of the salutary effect of private confession and absolution.[56]

In Trinity Church, Freistatt, Wisconsin, certain elements insisted on introducing general confession as a substitute for private confession. The controversy evoked a detailed reply from the leadership of the district, written by Ottomar Fuerbringer (1810–92) and Friedrich Lochner (1822–1902). This document, among other things, conceded that private confession was an adiaphoron, but argued that its retention and use in the Lutheran Church was in agreement with Luther and the Lutheran Symbols and as such had proved to be a salutary procedure. The two authors maintained that depriving a congregation of the blessings of private confession and absolution would bring harm to the congregation, to the Synod, to those outside of the Synod, and to posterity.[57]

At the synodical convention of 1860 an essay was read entitled "On the Intimite Connection of the Doctrine of Absolution with the Doctrine of Justification." The name of the author has not been preserved. The salient points discussed in this essay are

1. absolution, according to Luther, is the Gospel itself, whether it is proclaimed to many or to individuals;

2. private absolution is therefore not a power distinct and separate from the Gospel to forgive sins, but it is the preaching of the Gospel to the individual sinners;

3. the stewards and dispensers of absolution in the public ministry are the preachers of the Gospel. All Christians are involved in the dispensing of absolution, since the original possessor of the keys is the whole Church. It is the triune God, however, who forgives sins through the ministry of his servants;

4. absolution is not a judicial sentence. It is likewise not a bare proclamation or the confessor's wish in behalf of the penitent for the forgiveness of sin. It is an efficacious communication of pardon;

5. on the one hand, the effectiveness of the absolution does not depend on the penitent's contrition, confession, and satisfaction. On the other hand, it both demands faith and works and strengthens faith. Without faith it does not benefit the recipient, although the recipient's lack of faith does not invalidate the absolution (*Fehlschlüssel*);

6. the absolution is not the dispensing of an essentially different or of a better forgiveness than the preached Gospel in parts. Likewise, private absolution is not essential for receiving forgiveness, as if there could be no forgiveness without absolution. Nevertheless, absolution possesses its own distinct value and meets a real need, since it makes the individual more certain.[58]

C. F. W. Walther

Carl Ferdinand Wilhelm Walther (1811–87), the guiding hand during these troublesome times, whose theology has been defined as a "synthesis of Pietism and Orthodoxy,"[59] did not conceal his strong personal opinions regarding this issue. In his *American Lutheran Pastoral Theology* (*Americanisch-Lutherische Pastoraltheologie*) he cites Articles XI and XXIV of the Augsburg Confession and Article XXIV of the Apology to show that while the Sacred Scriptures do not command private confession, nevertheless, individual absolution ought not to be permitted to fall into disuse; furthermore, it would be ungodly and impious to abolish it from the church. While a pastor cannot make private confession an absolute condition or insist on its retention at all costs, he has the obligation, in an evangelical way, through instruction and admonition, to attempt at first to ensure that private confession be diligently used side by side with general confession and, where it is desirable, finally to restore private confession as the sole mode of confession. If private confession is already in use in his parish, the pastor is to preserve such practice. Under no circumstances should the pastor yield to the congregation that would not allow individual members to use private confession or absolution, for thus to abolish private absolution from the church would be impious.[60]

In Walther's view the practice of confession and absolution is closely associated with participation in Holy Communion. Where private confession is not the custom, there announcement for Communion is especially necessary (p. 150). Thus, whereas Luther and many of the 16th-century church orders merged an examination of the intending communicant's faith with private confession, Walther turns the announcement (*Beichtanmeldung*) into an examination of the penitent's faith. A major value of the practice of announcement is that it enables the pastor to explore the faith of those who intend to attend the Lord's table. This examination should elicit answers to questions like these: (1) if the penitent actually regards the pastor's word as God's Word; (2) if he knows the doctrines necessary for his salvation; (3) if he looks upon himself as a poor sinful creature; if he trusts alone in the merits of Christ and if consequently he has no serious intention toward evil and has been reconciled toward his neighbors; (4) if he believes in the mystery of the Holy Supper and therein seeks forgiveness, the strengthening of his faith, and godliness; and (5) if he really confesses that the Lutheran Church and its teachings, as the latter are set forth in Luther's Small Catechism, represent the true Christian Church and its teachings (p. 151). The pastor, however, should beware lest what should be a friendly conversation become a stiff and uncomfortable examination. It is best if the penitent is not made aware that he is being examined, since it is an indefensible procedure for the pastor to turn the announcement into a quest for secret sins or if he digs into family affairs (p. 151). The power of the keys, Walther says, has been given not for the investigation of secret sins, but for the healing of revealed sins (p. 161). It is not necessary that people be examined before every reception of the Holy Communion. Once a year or simply from time to time is sufficient (p. 152).

341

A deeper inquiry into Walther's theology of confession and absolution demonstrates that it has two foci: (1) the universal reconciliation of the world to God by Christ has been accomplished; (2) all that remains for men to do is to accept this reconciliation in faith.

In *The Proper Distinction Between Law and Gospel* he says that the Lutheran practice of absolution rests on the fact that

> by raising his Son Jesus Christ from the dead, God the Father confirmed and put the stamp of approval on the work of reconciliation and redemption which Christ finished on the cross. For by the resurrection of Christ he has, in the presence of heaven and earth, angels and men, declared: "As my Son has cried on the Cross 'It is finished!' so do I announce, It is finished indeed! You sinners are redeemed. Forgiveness of sins is prepared for everybody; it is ready; it must not first be acquired by you." By his command to preach the Gospel to every creature, Christ commanded at the same time to preach forgiveness of sins to all men, hence to bring to them the glad tidings: "all that is necessary for your salvation has been accomplished." When asking, What must we do to be saved? do but remember that all has been done. There is nothing more to do. You are only to believe all that has been done for you, and you will be relieved.[61]

Linking this preaching of forgiveness more closely to the individual application in absolution, he says,

> Christ did not only issue a general command to his apostles and their successors in office to preach the Gospel, hence the forgiveness of sin, but to minister to each individual who desires it this comfort: "You are reconciled to God." For if forgiveness of sins has been procured for all, it has been procured for each individual. If I may offer it to all, I may offer it to each individual. Not only *may* I do this, I am ordered to do it.[62]

Still equating absolution with the proclamation of the objective reconciliation in Christ Jesus, Walther continues,

> Now that forgiveness of sin has been procured as stated, not only has a minister a special commission to proclaim it, but every Christian, male or female, adult or child, is commissioned to do this. Even a child's absolution is just as certain as the absolution of St. Peter, yes, as the absolution of Christ would be, were he again to stand visibly before men and say: "Your sins are forgiven you."

There is no difference; for mark you! it is not a question of what man must do, but what has been done by Christ.[63]

And in a sermon on Mark 16:1–8 he says,

When Christ suffered and died he was being judged and sentenced to death by God in our place, but when God and Father raised him up again who was it that God was acquitting again in the person of Christ? Christ after all needed no acquittal for himself. For no one could charge him with a single sin. Tell me then, who was being justified in him? Who was being declared holy and innocent in him? It was we men. It was the whole world. When God said to Christ, "you shall live," that referred to us. His life is our life, his acquittal is our acquittal, his justification is our justification.[64]

Two paragraphs farther on he continues,

After all this, who is able to express fully what a high consolation lies in the resurrection of Christ? It is the absolution which has been spoken by God himself to all men, all sinners, in a word, to all the world—a most gloriously sealed absolution.[65]

In an article in *Der Lutheraner* entitled "How Great and Pernicious an Error Is That Which Denies to Preachers of the Gospel the Power to Forgive Sins on Earth," he insists that "to deny this power is to deny the completeness of Christ's redemption.[66] Furthermore, God has given the Gospel and the sacraments to his church to distribute to the world. The burden of the preacher's message is that Christ has already forgiven the sins of all: Therefore, you sinners, rejoice! You must not attempt to merit a salvation of your own; no, it has already taken place.[67]

Whereas the first great stress for Walther in the doctrine of absolution is the completed redemptive work of Christ, so the second is that to appropriate this redemption the individual has only to believe it. In a sermon preached on the Nineteenth Sunday after Trinity Sunday (1844), based on Matt. 9:1–8 and entitled "The Word of Jesus: Be Consoled, My Son, Your Sins Are Forgiven You," Walther speaks about the person who is not forgiven. He is still God's enemy, and God is his enemy.[68] Sin is like a sleep and a cloud. But when men are awakened from it, they cannot believe that God is gracious to them. They could be forgiven, but they have not yet accepted the gift (p. 595). In the second part of the sermon

Walther says, "What does it help me if Christ has not spoken that Word to me: Be consoled, my son, your sins are forgiven you" (p. 601). Within the context of this statement Walther employs the verb *accept* (*annehmen*) nine times (pp. 600ff.)

There is almost an identical pattern in a sermon from the year 1886 based on John 20:19–31 (pp. 302ff). Many, he says, who have faith cannot feel its power and they ask: What help does my faith give me? (p. 304). The main thrust of the sermon is in the title: "The Resurrection of Jesus Christ from the Dead Is the Key to the Mystery that in no Other Way than by Faith Are We Made Righteous and Holy before God." In this sermon the word "accept" (*annehmen*) occurs eight times. Only once does he mention that the apostles, by the power of Christ's resurrection, should dispense righteousness, life, and salvation through the preaching of the Gospel to all men (p. 306).

To return specifically to Walther's theology of absolution, his stress upon the identity of absolution with the individual proclamation of Christ's atonement is so complete that absolution takes on a declarative rather than an effective function. Thus he states,

> What does the Lutheran preacher do when he announces the forgiveness of sins and absolves? Nothing more than that he informs the people: This is the situation with you. Christ suffered as your Mediator and God now accepts you in faith.[69]

He admits, however, that the Lutheran minister does this by the command of Christ (p. 161). Again he says,

> At absolution we say nothing but what has happened. That is the precious truth that forgiveness of sins has been acquired. If we would truly believe in absolution, with what joy would we attend church whenever it is pronounced (p. 173).

Walther concedes that a confessional Lutheran, taking his stand on the Augsburg Confession, regards the absolution as an announcement in God's stead and by his command (p. 173). Nevertheless, he seems to place absolution as the simple announcement of Christ's atonement in a somewhat unrealistic light as far as the penitent is concerned. The problem of the penitent, who feels guilty and confesses his sin, is not one of ignorance but of wrath. The heaviness of his heart is not the result of a lack of information; it is the result of unbelief, unbelief that arises from so much and such valid evidence that God is displeased with him. Again, absolution does not merely inform a man about a change that has taken place once upon a time. Absolution is an effective Word that changes the present relationship of the penitent to God,[70] inasmuch as in the present act it is the action and the voice of the same God whose act in Christ was once and for all time.

In 1848 *Der Lutheraner*[71] carried an anonymous article reprinted from the *Harless'sche Zeitschrift*[72] entitled "Concerning the Power of the Keys, the Absolution and the Confession" (*Uber die Schlüsselgewalt, die Absolution und die Beichte*). Though this article was not written by Walther, he evidently gave it his approval by publishing it in *Der Lutheraner*. Readers certainly understood it thus. For that reason it is worthy of summary here.

Christ's redemption, the author argues, was accomplished for the forgiveness of sin. Christ wants this event not only to be known, but he also bestows it. What Jesus did visibly while here on earth he now continues to do through the gifts of his majesty which, as Lord of the church, he hands on to his disciples as servants. It is one thing to teach where and how one can acquire this forgiveness of sins. Actually to impart and to communicate this is an entirely different matter. The preaching of the Gospel goes forth to all men without distinction. The forgiveness of sins, however, is shared only with the contrite and, according to Christ himself who sits at the right hand of the Father, should be for them for participation through his disciples in the self-same power in which he himself imparted it when he sojourned on earth.[73]

As Christ was sent by the Father, so the disciples are his deputies who administer his power and through whom he communicates the Holy Spirit. When they forgive or retain sins, it is as powerful and real as if Christ himself spoke, for it is in Christ's name and stead that they speak. If one were to understand by "loosing" sins only the preaching of the Gospel, and by "binding" sins only the preaching of wrath, then the words of Christ would have a different meaning: to whomsoever you preach the Gospel, to them will it be preached; to whomsoever you announce the wrath of God, to them will it be announced.[74] The Lord has conferred the power of the keys on the teaching office (*Lehramt*). This power is the very heart of the care of souls.[75] The least perfect method of confession is general confession. Accordingly, private confession should be retained because of the absolution which is the Word of God by which the power of the keys looses us from sin.[76]

Note that this article presents a theology of absolution somewhat different from that of Walther. It is clear that some readers of *Der Lutheraner* sensed this. In a subsequent issue of *Der Lutheraner* Walther says that some have taken this article as if it should become a wedge for teaching that "the general preaching of the Gospel is no absolution, or that through private absolution something other or more is imparted than through the simple preaching.[77] Even though, he continues, we have not taken the article in that way, nevertheless, in order to protect the unity of doctrine, we expressly answer the aforementioned statement with a No. He quotes Johann Brenz (1499–1570), a staunch Lutheran theologian and friend of Luther, to demonstrate that there is no essential difference between the two. But immediately after this emphatic No Walther adds a significant footnote that indicates at least part of the antithesis in his mind:

> One must not think that thereby the Reformed and Methodistic doctrine is subscribed to, namely, that a man can only proclaim the forgiveness of sins but not impart it. On the contrary, it is affirmed that the preaching of the Gospel is no empty, powerless sound, no mere announcement alongside which the Holy Spirit works and leads to forgiveness, but that the preached Word is living and powerful and has a power of conferring forgiveness, whether now spoken to many or to the individual.[78]

Here Walther seems to reveal the tension which his theological position raises. On the one hand he wishes to maintain a reality of the here and now power of the Word; on the other hand, with the severe stress on the objective completeness, he tends to rob private absolution of present reality and efficacy. Although "Walther very correctly makes a more careful distinction between the sacred ministry and the 'royal priesthood' of the Christian community than some of his followers have done,"[79] nevertheless, he appears to minimize the power of the holy ministry to rule and sanctify.[80]

Note that in the rite for the Communion of the Sick in the first official agenda issued by the Missouri Synod[81] the rubrics direct that after the pastor has comforted the sick person with appropriate words from Scripture, he is to invite this person to make confession and thereafter receive the holy absolution and the Sacrament to the person's eternal life. The privacy of this confession is guarded by the rubric that directs everyone except the pastor to leave the room. A seriously ill person may make confession by responding to brief questions. The pastor may inquire whether there is anything that particularly oppresses the sick person's conscience. At his direction, the pastor may read the confession[82] with the sick person speaking it after him. Thereafter the pastor may ask the penitent whether this is his or her sincere confession. If so, the pastor pronounces the absolution in the indicative-operative form:

> Upon this your confession, I, by virtue of my office as a called and ordained servant of the Word, announce the grace of God unto you, and in the stead and by the command of my Lord Jesus Christ I forgive you all your sins in the name of the + Father and of the + Son and of the + Holy Ghost. Amen.[83]

Wilhelm Löhe

Closely associated with the Missouri Synod's beginnings was Wilhelm Löhe (1808–72), pastor in Neuendettelsau, Bavaria, notable preacher, catechist, counselor, and father-confessor. His interest in mission work in America prompted him to respond to F. C. D. Wyneken's (1810–76) call for help by sending workers to America and by establishing a theological school for the training of pastors at Fort Wayne, Indiana, the beginning of what was later to become Concordia Theological Seminary of Springfield, Illinois. Moreover, liturgical life of Lutheranism was greatly influenced by his *Agende* of 1844, prepared especially for the Lutheran immigrants from Bavaria who settled largely in Michigan.

In his *Simple Instruction in Confession* (1836) he describes the situation in Bavaria in his day: Private confession has been turned into a general service in which the pastor absolves everyone at one time; there is no difference between a preaching service and a confessional service except that the preacher has to prepare lists for the latter; the pastor absolves people with whom he is not acquainted; the contemporary procedure is a dead ceremony and gross abuse.[84] Löhe's deep pastoral concern prompted him to say, "The absolution is the heart of the cure of souls" (p. 189). Furthermore, "Without private confession and absolution one cannot effectively carry out the pastoral care of awakened sinners" (p. 182). Just as a person without a doctor cannot heal himself, so without the individual care of the pastor he cannot truly comfort himself (Matt. 9:36; John 21:15–17; Acts 20–28) (p. 167).

Löhe is content to permit both general and private confession to remain in use. He insists that if private confession alone were practiced, and if people would take the matter seriously, there would either be very few who would come or, if many, there would be numerous hypocrites among their number.[85]

Löhe's practice regarding confession is revealed in his letters: Confession of the lay people most often took place in the sacristy;[86] members of the various institutions in Neuendettelsau were often heard in the church, but most generally in the parsonage or prayer chapel of the deaconess home.[87]

Although private confession was a voluntary matter, Löhe demanded that announcement be made prior to it. Hardeland relates that on Fridays before confession Löhe stood in the choir of the church and took names and addresses of those who intended to make confession before Holy Communion. Those who for some reason or another had given offence were asked to remain in order that he might speak to them.[88]

Various members of Löhe's congregation complained to the consistory about his practice.[89] In a letter dated August 31, 1846, Löhe defended himself against such complaints. Among other things he said that the personal announcement before confession was a practice of long standing that customarily took place after vespers on Wednesdays and Fridays. Wives, children, or servants often made announcement for the men of their household;[90] after the hearing of private confession on Saturday, the confessional vespers (*Beichtvesper*) was held, after which followed the general absolution for those who had not made a private confession.[91]

In a letter of May 1, 1853, Löhe admitted that he at times permitted people to receive Holy Communion without their having made prior confession. Confession and absolution, he says, need not be inseparably united with the Holy Eucharist, since the sacrament itself contains an absolution.[92]

To the question as to how often a person should make confession and seek absolution Löhe replied that on the one hand it is wrong to assume, as some do, that absolution is never needed. Either such people have forsaken their sins or they have become more steeped in them. On the other hand, he pointed out, a Christian does not need to be absolved daily as though God's comfort and absolution lacked power. For God's absolution, rightly considered, is a saving power for yesterday, today, and tomorrow. In short, each person must individually determine for himself or herself the frequency with which he or she makes confession and seeks absolution. As a general rule, Christians should do so as often as their sins trouble them (pp. 187–188).

Löhe felt constrained to warn his people against the mere recitation of previously memorized formulas of confession. But among his close friends he admitted, "The worst private confession is better than the general confession." Gradually, however, he succeeded in teaching his people the constitutive elements of a good confession: confession of sins, confession of faith, desire for absolution, promise of amends. These, he said, the people gradually learned to their great gain (p. 214).

For Löhe, absolution is the sentence of acquittal from sin, from guilt, from everlasting punishment; with this is combined the bestowal of the divine blessing, the imparting of life and of everlasting salvation (p. 174). Whatever is absolved will not appear again for purposes of judgment (p. 184). Accordingly, the absolution is the "disclosure of justification" (*Offenbarung der Rechtfertigung*). On the other hand the retention is the "disclosure of God's judgment" (*Offenbarung des Göttlichen Gerichts*).

> The voice of the priest who binds on earth is God's voice—it has also a yes and amen from heaven; for the Lord says, "Whatever you bind on earth will be bound in heaven" (p. 190).

Löhe's view of the office of the ministry[93] permits no minimizing of the power of the keys. In his *Kirche und Amt* (Church and Ministry) of 1851 he speaks against the so-called delegation theory (*Übertragungslehre*):

> God gives the office. He does not first make the congregation to be the bearer and possessor of the office that the congregation then transfers to the individual ministers as if they then possessed

it in a secondary way. An office which the entire congregation and its members possess is and remains a contradiction.[94]

Under ordinary circumstances Löhe does not permit a layman to pronounce absolution. He encourages a person who has committed a grievous sin after baptism to go to his or her pastor, to whom God has given the keys of heaven and the power to forgive sins, and there seek relief.[95] In accordance with the Apology of the Augsburg Confession,[96] the function of this office in confession and absolution consists in the exercise of the special power of the keys in which a certain power of judgment or jurisdiction is ascribed to the confessor:

> Meanwhile confession is only a half-way measure when the key of binding is not employed the same as the key of loosing. Denial of the absolution and Holy Eucharist must lie in the hands of the individual pastor. This denial must rest upon fixed stipulation. The refusal of the individual case must be the business of the pastor, although he remains responsible to the church for his action.[97]

With Löhe, the power of the keys comes to the fore and the certainty and assurance of absolution receives renewed importance, elements that had almost become lost in Pietism. Paradoxically, however, although Pietism robbed the church of private confession, it also produced some competent and sincere father-confessors.[98] Löhe himself was spiritually oriented toward Pietism.[99] In Lausa-Radeberg, Pastor Roller, whom Richard Franke identifies as a pietist, regularly heard private confessions up to the year 1850.[100] Christoph Blumhardt exercised a salutary confessional practice in Möttlingen (1838–52) and Boll (1852–80).[101] Löhe and Blumhardt deserve particular credit for their efforts toward restoring private confession to the Lutheran Church in Germany.[102] In any case, the attempts to reintroduce private confession cannot simply be attributed to the so-called confessional-liturgical revival of the 19th century.[103]

Various factors contributed to the gradual decline of private confession and absolution in The Lutheran Church—Missouri Synod. It was difficult to revive a custom that had generally fallen into desuetude, especially when so many members of the Synod came from non-Lutheran or dubiously Lutheran backgrounds. Moreover, pietistic strains within the Synod, combined with the Puritanism in the

American environment, gradually tended to increase the pressure toward abrogating private confession in favor of group, or corporate confession.[104] Neither should a certain anti-Roman Catholic sentiment be dismissed. Also, a factor that may have abetted the trend is Walther's persistent equating private absolution with the mere pronouncement of objective reconciliation.

Some Contemporary Developments

General

Significantly, in every churchly renewal emphasis is invariably placed on repentance and its practical implementation in confession and absolution. In Europe, for instance, the churchly renewal following both World Wars is no exception. Particularly prominent in reviving private confession and absolution were the various contrafraternities that arose,[105] as well as organizations of university students and youth groups. The literature on this subject has been formidable indeed.

In America, too, the subject has not escaped the attention of various theological journals and the professional journals of psychiatry and psychology. The number of monographs and books on the subject,[106] together with the numerous conferences engaged in serious, responsible conversation,[107] attest to the interest in this area, so vital to the life of the church. This interest seems to focus not only on the broader aspects of sin and repentance as they relate to the ecclesial community, namely, to redemption, Baptism, the Eucharist, but also to a reexamination of the theology and practice of confession and absolution, especially individual confession and absolution.

Vatican Council II

The influence of Vatican II (1962–65) and its reforms in this area, the result of ten or more years of liturgical study and research,[108] should not be overlooked or minimized. From the single form of the sacrament of private penance, consisting basically of confession and juridical absolution as canonized and fixed by the councils of Lateran IV (1215) and Trent (1545–63) and promulgated for over three centuries, this sacrament may presently be administered in three different rites, or forms:

1. Rite of Reconciliation of Individual Penitents
2. Rite of Reconciliation of Several Penitents with Individual Confession and Absolution
3. Rite of Reconciliation with Several Penitents with General Confession and Absolution

Briefly summarized, in the first rite, priest and penitent greet each other and read an appropriate passage from Holy Scripture (optional). If necessary, the priest gives suitable counsel and thereafter proposes an act of penance.[109] Following the penitent's confession, the priest invokes the mercy of God the Father and grants absolution. Together they, by prayer or praise, acknowledge the gift of pardon before the penitent is dismissed.

The second rite—in reality a brief service—begins with a hymn or psalm, the priest's greeting and prayer, followed by Scripture readings[110] and a homily. Next comes a general confession spoken in unison followed by the Lord's Prayer. The penitents go to the priest designated to hear their individual confessions, each receives and accepts a fitting act of satisfaction and is absolved. Thereafter all penitents assemble for concluding prayers, blessing, and dismissal.

The third rite follows the pattern just previously described except that there are no individual confessions, and absolution is given by the priest to all as a group after they have said a general confession. Such group absolution is only lawful in the case of grave need, namely, cases involving danger of death or lack of sufficient confessors to hear individual confessions, so that penitents would go without sacramental grace for a long time. Again, the form ends with praise and thanksgiving, and the priest is enjoined to warn any individual who has received this absolution from grave sins to confess each such sin next time he or she goes to individual confession.

It is of particular interest to note that the same formula of absolution—comprised of a statement of God's love in Christ and the reconciliation of the world, and an optative absolution followed by the historical absolution—is used with the laying on of hands in all three rites. It reads,

God, the Father of mercies, through the death and resurrection of his son has reconciled the world to himself and sent the Holy Spirit among us for the forgiveness of sins; through the ministry of the Church may God give you pardon and peace, and I absolve you from your sins in the name of the Father, and of the Son, + and of the Holy Spirit.

Admittedly, the third rite gives first place to a considerably extended alternate form comprised of three paragraphs (referring to the work of Father, Son, and Holy Spirit respectively) with an optative absolution in each, followed with an amen by the penitential group. The whole is concluded with the sacramental "I absolve you. . . ." Captioned General Absolution, it reads,

God the Father does not wish the sinner to die but to turn back to him and live. He loved us first and sent his Son into the world to be its Savior. May he show you his merciful love and give you peace.

R: Amen

Our Lord Jesus Christ was given up to death for our sins, and rose again for our justification. He sent the Holy Spirit on his apostles and gave them power to forgive sins. Through the ministry entrusted to me may he deliver you from evil and fill you with his Holy Spirit.

R: Amen.

The Spirit, the Comforter, was given to us for the forgiveness of sins. In him we approach the Father. May he cleanse your hearts and clothe you in his glory, so that you may proclaim the mighty acts of God who has called you out of darkness into the splendor of his light.

R: Amen

And I absolve you from your sins in the name of Father, and of the Son, + and of the Holy Spirit.

R: Amen.

That neither this alternate form nor the previous one, pronounced by either priest or deacon, is considered valid for grave sins is evidenced by a rubric that enjoins the priest or deacon to warn any individual who has received this absolution from grave sins to confess each such sin next time he or she goes to individual confession.

Although the 1973 Rite of Penance in its various forms makes no mention of confessionals, the 1983 Code of Canon Law requires that they be available for those wishing to use them.[111]

New features of penance since Vatican II are the penitential celebrations, gatherings of God's people, both young and old, to hear his Word and meditate on it, to pray, and thus to be led to a deeper conversion of heart and renewal of life. Such gatherings may also serve as preparation for the sacrament of penance itself. The faithful, however, should be made aware that these celebrations are not the same as sacramental confession and absolution. Numerous liturgical materials are provided for such celebrations.[112]

The Rite: Individual Confession and Absolution

The phrase "consultation with the pastor" in rubric 1, page 310, in *Lutheran Worship*, should not be understood to imply an inseparable connection between pastoral counseling and individual confession and absolution. There are circumstances in which each action stands on its own. The focus in the former is the receiving of pastoral counsel; in the latter it is the absolution. Considering that it was Pietism—the overflow of Calvinism into the Lutheran Church, as someone has said—that supplanted private confession and absolution with pastoral counsel, the distinction is significant. This is not to deny an element of pastoral care in private confession, as, for instance, the "admonition and comfort" mentioned in rubric 5. Penitents undoubtedly expect some form of counsel. Moreover, the counseling element prevents the confession from becoming too formal. On the other hand, counseling without confession can often degenerate into a purely psychological procedure. Recall that Luther and the Lutheran symbols consider the comforting words of absolution the very heart of confession.[113]

The difficulty of distinguishing between pastoral counseling and individual confession intensifies the problem of the "confidential nature of a confession" refered to in rubric 1, the so-called seal of confession. Bo Giertz argues that one of the elements that makes private confession a sacramental act is the seal. He comments,

> Experience shows that in the same measure in which one begins to supplant private confession with private counsel, the respect for the seal of confession grows slack. . . . This was one of the most disastrous consequences of the dissolution of churchly forms by eighteenth century Pietism.[114]

No clergyman dare divulge what has been told him in confession, either to fellow pastors, to his wife, to a court, or to church authorities. Only when the seal of confession is preserved will Christians be willing to come to private confession.

In encouraging people to avail themselves of this salutary means of comfort, stipulated times for the hearing of individual confession should be posted as well as published in the service folders, church bulletins, newsletters, and schedules of worship, together with the designated place. Preparation for the high festivals would appear to be especially appropriate occasions for making confession, for instance, during Advent, Lent, and during the week of Pentecost. During the long post-Pentecost season the Nativity of St. John the Baptist (June 24) and again St. Michael and All Angels (September 29) might serve well. Not to be overlooked are times of great decision and crises in the Christian's life. Through instruction, pastoral counsel, and preaching the pastor will conscientiously prepare his people for making a good confession. Moreover, he himself should have a confessor and regularly practice private confession, not only because of its spiritual and mental benefits, but also to set a good example for his people. The Evangelical Brotherhood of St. Michael (*Michaelsbruderschaft*) goes so far as to warn its members against hearing private confession unless they have personally engaged in this practice.[115] Only ordained ministers should hear confession and absolve, for this is a function of the public ministry of the church and an important part of the care of souls entrusted to them. Appropriate vestments for the hearing of confession are alb (or surplice) and stole.

As to the most suitable place, much will depend on the facilities available and the circumstances. The church's sanctuary, at or near the altar, may prove most satisfactory, with the pastor and penitent either kneeling side by side at the communion rail or the pastor seated inside the rail at right angles to the kneeling penitent who faces the altar. In the concern that no one overhear the confession, penitents who await their turn should be seated at the rear of the nave. Here appropriate materials should be available to the penitents as an aid in preparing for the confession. Also the rite itself, either as contained in the hymnal or on a plasticized card, should be readily at hand. With respect to the former, the pastor should prepare what he considers to be necessary and helpful devotional aids, containing prayers, psalms, and hymn texts, including perhaps a form for the examination of conscience based on the Decalog, and possibly some verses from Ephesians 5–6 in Luther's Table of Duties.[116]

If what originally was intended and begun as a counseling session evolves into a private confession and a desire for absolution, the pastor should provide an appropriate transition, both verbally and perhaps spatially.

When the penitent arrives at the appointed place, the pastor greets him or her. Although this is not a time for pleasantries, it will be helpful if, by his brief opening words and actions, the pastor will attempt to establish a feeling of naturalness, calmness, and reverence, in contrast to a stern, rigorous, juridical approach. This will go a long way toward eliminating fear and nervousness on the part of the penitent. Marianka Fousek, a Lutheran teaching at Duke University, is perhaps correct when she writes,

> Luther's stress on justification tends to neglect the seriousness of sin, especially when we keep acknowledging our sinfulness only in vaguest generalities which cut no one to the quick and bring no shame on anyone. To be a "miserable sinner" is something a good Lutheran acknowledges quite cheerfully. To admit one's concrete sins to God alone, with one's own slanted perspective on them, is a much easier matter than owning up to the brother. . . . The discipline of hearing and making confession of specific sins on a regular basis is a wholesome medicine against taking the sinfulness of Christians, as well as grace, too glibly, and, on the other hand, medicine against forgetting what it means to be human.[117]

Beginning with the trinitarian invocation is a reminder of God's covenant with the penitent in Holy Baptism. The opening verses of Psalm 102 as well as the excerpt from Ps. 51:1–4a, said by the penitent and pastor, is a most fitting way to begin. The words of the latter, spoken by David, are unsurpassed as an expression of a heart overwhelmed by shame, humbled and broken by guilt, and yet saved from despair through faith in the mercy of God. With them the penitent honestly faces and openly confesses his sins to God.

The words of the penitent that follow, although perhaps sufficiently general in character, should be considered more as a guide than as actual words of confession. They are not expressly included to put words in the mouth of the penitent. It is to be regretted that the authors of so-called contemporary penitential services often become highly specific, frequently leading the faithful to mouth texts in the act of corporate confession in which they confess personal responsibility for all the world's social and even some spiritual ills. This should certainly not imply being "soft on sin." But such confessing appears, at least to this author, as inculcating a generalized guilt—the exact opposite of the intended penitential process—that is not only not alleviated by absolution but sometimes evokes serious negative psychological consequences. The statement of the penitent in individual confession that leads to the heart of the matter is "What troubles me particularly is that . . .," followed by the confessing of a specific sin or of those sins that trouble and grieve the conscience of the penitent.

When the penitent has contritely confessed and concretely dealt with a specific sin or sins, he or she now stands in the fellowship of sinners who live by the grace of God in the cross of Christ. The pastor may now offer any admonition he considers necessary in the circumstance; he can comfort the penitent with the aim of strengthening the bonds between the penitent and his or her neighbor and between the penitent and his or her God. In no case should the pastor engage in unnecessary questioning as though, as one pastor says, "sniffling around" for sins.[118] Together, the penitent and pastor speak verses 10–12 of Psalm 51.

Recognizing the statement in the Augsburg Confession that "in confession it is not necessary to enumerate all trespasses and sins, for this is impossible. Ps.19:12, 'Who can discern his errors?' ",[119] nevertheless, lest a penitent's conscience later be smitten by the thought of some unconfessed sin, the penitent may now pray the general confession.

Borrowing the question from Luther's Small Catechism that points up the importance of faith in this matter, the penitent is asked, "Do you believe that the word of Christ's forgiveness I speak to you is from the Lord himself?" Then follows the absolution, spoken by the pastor in the indicative-operative form, together with the laying on of his hand and the sign of the cross. Since the absolution is not considered to be simply a general declaration or an assurance that God is merciful to the repentant sinner, but rather an effective reconciliation and restoration of this particular person at this given time, the indicative-operative form is most appropriate. If pastor and penitent have been seated, it is less awkward if the pastor stands for this action.

With the weight now lifted from the penitent's heart, verses 4–5 from Psalm 30, spoken by the penitent and pastor, form a happy conclusion prior to the dismissal.

While it is true that Individual Confession and Absolution is a rite complete in itself and as such can stand on its own, when used in the congregation as frequently as there is desire for its comfort and peace of mind, it can well serve the Christian members as preparation for the common reception of the Holy Communion. Reconciled to God and the Church, the desire of the penitent to receive Christ's body and blood is a natural result.

Corporate Confession and Absolution

Historical Background

From the historical standpoint corporate confession "might well be considered as one step removed from individual confession and absolution."[120] Luther's principles were in general continued in the numerous church orders of the 16th century. Thus private confession, with but few exceptions, became the established practice. Following Luther's pronouncements, such confession was coupled with an examination of Christian doctrine and life prior to the penitents' attending Holy Communion.[121] But such a procedure was time consuming. As the number of penitents grew, pastors were frequently unable to cope with the situation, hence the custom arose of using prescribed formulas of confession. This facilitated hearing and absolving groups at one time. Here is a decided break with

Luther's practice. The personal element faded into the background; confession became a mechanical matter. It is quite understandable that at the close of the 17th century, some church leaders, particularly among the pietists, voiced strong objections to the prevailing practice, extolling instead the penitent's personal confession before God, and deeming the degree of contrition to be an essential element in the power of the absolution. Such voices, coupled with Rationalism and its minimizing the nature of sin, the use of general absolution by military chaplains, and a certain amount of anti-Roman Catholic sentiment caused the practice of private, or individual, confession to wane. By the end of the 18th century most provinces in Germany had introduced corporate, or group, confession. While some still retained private confession as an option,[122] there were others in which it was officially abolished altogether.[123] In corporate confession the absolution was either spoken to each penitent individually with the laying on of hands or, more customarily, over the entire group. Reflecting the theological climate of the time, the formulas of absolution often included various conditional statements that ascribed the effect of the absolution only to the truly penitent, or which included statements of retention. Furthermore, instead of the indicative-operative formula, the more weak declarative formula was used, a form that did not compel the penitents to believe, or tended at least to minimize, the actual effectiveness of the absolution. Various formulas often appearing in general confession, or *Offene Schuld*, about which more will be stated later, were transferred to corporate confession. In fact, the simple *Offene Schuld* was now often considered to be an adequate substitute.

Wherever corporate confession was introduced, it was customarily associated with Saturday vespers. This became a service of preparation. Although variations occurred from locality to locality, the service normally included a confessional address, general confession, absolution, and prayer.[124] The confessional address often took on a *de tempore* character. The confession at times was framed into a series of questions addressed to the congregation.[125] Absolution, particularly in the period of Rationalism, was largely in the form of a declaration or announcement.[126]

On the basis of the foregoing it perhaps appears as though corporate confession is a deteriorated form of confession, standing in stark contrast to private confession as exemplified by Luther and the Lutheran Symbols. Properly structured, this type can, however, serve a useful and salutary purpose in the life of the congregation. C. Mahrenholz says,

> Private confession and corporate confession complement each other and keep each other mutually healthy. Private confession helps us to take corporate confession seriously and to confess specific sins. Corporate confession encourages us also to beg forgiveness of unstipulated sins and to renounce all tormenting self-respect.[127]

Moreover, despite Wilhelm Löhe's pastoral concern for retaining private confession, he was content to permit both corporate and private confession to remain in use. He used the former to an advantage by pronouncing the absolution individually to each penitent. From this procedure he discovered that with a little encouragement his people began to take recourse to private confession and absolution.

Structural Considerations

From the liturgical standpoint, the forms for corporate confession and private confession must be distinguished. Corporate confession must have a set form; private confession may have a freer and more personal form. Furthermore, it appears proper that the character of private confession be reflected in corporate confession so that the latter does not appear as another form of *Offene Schuld*. The form should reflect that in this situation the pastor is dealing with a restricted group of Christians, not an unidentifiable mass. Again, although the actual confession of sins will necessarily be spoken by the penitents as a group, the absolution should preferably reflect the character of private absolution by the use of the indicative-operative form—the form that Luther considered the most comforting—and by being spoken and applied personally to each penitent. Moreover, as in private confession, the relationship of penitent versus confessor should preferably be maintained and reflected in both the rubrics and the form. The pastor leads the penitents in their confession; it is really not his confession. He absolves the penitents, not himself.

Service of Corporate Confession and Absolution

The general rubrics state, "This service [*Lutheran Worship*, pp. 308–309] is intended for use at confessional services apart from the Holy Communion,"[128] that is to say, as a separate service not directly connected to the Holy Communion, or the Divine Service. This reflects not only the trend in continental Lutheran practice in the 17th and 18th centuries but also the practice in the early history of the Synod. In those days it was customary to have the corporate confession, or the so-called confessional service, on Friday or Saturday evening prior to Communion Sunday.[129] Such an arrangement, it was felt, allowed more time for spiritual preparation and increased the meaning of both confession and the Lord's Supper. Moreover, this service envisions the presence of only those penitents who have specifically come to make confession and who are desirous of receiving the personal application and comfort of the indicative-operative absolution. Although this service may serve as preparation for the Divine Service and reception of Holy Communion (cf. the Exhortation in rubric 4), it is primarily intended to stand by itself, thus to relieve troubled consciences by the comfort and the personal application of the indicative-operative absolution and, in general, to increase the availability of such absolution while at the same time deepening the meaning of this important salutary act in the life of the congregation.[130] It is suggested that pastors consider establishing and announcing a schedule for this service, such as previously suggested for private confession and absolution.

Since the care of souls is specifically the responsibility of the pastor, it is inappropriate for anyone not ordained to preside at this service. Appropriate vestments for the pastor are alb (or surplice) and stole in the color of the day or season.

Preludial music, selected with care, should be of a quiet, meditative character. Preludes based on familiar chorales, reflecting and suggesting texts of repentance, confession, justification, and the Redeemer, are appropriate.

When the number of people is small, they should be requested to occupy the front pews or even previously provided chairs in the chancel. In instances where a small chapel is part of the church complex, this may prove to be the more fitting place to hold the service.

The Topical Index of Hymns and Spiritual Songs (LW pp. 978–984) will prove helpful in selecting the opening hymn for this service. First categories that come to mind are confession, forgiveness, and justification. In the first category, "As surely as I live, God said" (LW 235), which speaks of the power of the keys and absolution, is the hymn *par excellence*. In the second, "Today your mercy calls us" (LW 347) deserves consideration at times as well as "When in the hour of deepest need" (LW 428), usually looked upon as a cross-and-comfort hymn. In the third, the ever-popular "Drawn to the cross which you have blessed" (LW 356) will perhaps assert itself. Hymn categories should never be construed too strictly, for there is considerable overlapping of thought. Often an ideal hymn or stanza for a given purpose will suggest itself from an unimagined category.

As a reminder of Baptism, the pastor might invite the penitents to speak the Invocation with him and also to mark themselves with the sign of the cross, a practice that Luther encouraged to begin the Morning Prayer and the Evening prayer contained in his Small Catechism.[131]

Following the prayer in rubric 2 led by the pastor and concluded with the Amen by the penitents, Psalm 51 (LW, p. 329) is sung or said. Verse 10, "Create in me . . .," is suggested as the antiphon or refrain.[132] Other appropriate psalms are 32, 130, 139, and 143. As refrains or antiphons to these, an appropriate verse or portion of a verse from the psalm to be used or from another psalm or passage of Scripture may be selected to serve this purpose.

Depending on the circumstances, either a Confessional Address or the Exhortation, or both, may now follow. In the case of an address, the pastor may emphasize the gravity of sin, or the need to accept the responsibility for sin and its consequences. Primarily, however, he will direct his people to the unfailing mercy and the grace of God in Jesus Christ and the comforting words of the absolution. In connection with the latter, such Scripture passages as Matt. 16:19; 18:18; and John 20:20–23, reflecting the Office of the Keys, will be especially appropriate and useful.

Some form of exhortation seems appropriate, affording the pastor the opportunity to awaken the conscience and thus aid the penitents in their confession. If the historic Exhortation,[133] here in updated form, is used, it should be read quietly, distinctly, and unhurriedly.

The penitents should preferably kneel during the confession. If kneelers are not available and if the group is small, it may be convenient for the penitents to kneel at the altar rail. Barring these possibilities, the penitents may stand at their respective places.

The text of corporate confession here given is from the Saxony church order of 1581 (see p. 403). Wilhelm Löhe included it in his *Agende* of 1844,[134] and since its inclusion in the Synod's *Kirchen-Agende* of 1856, it has appeared in all its subsequent service books and hymnals.[135]

Following Luther's emphasis on faith in "How Plain People Are to be Taught to Confess" contained in the Small Catechism, the pastor addresses the penitents, "God be gracious to you and strengthen your faith," namely, your faith in the Lord's vicarious atonement, the faith that not only brought you to this occasion but also prompted you to confess your sins and plead for mercy and forgiveness.

Now comes the absolution. According to the Lutheran symbols, this is the very heartbeat of confession—"absolution, which is the sacrament of penitence"—this is the sacramental and constitutive factor.[136] God himself is the subject who acts in absolution:

> Our people are taught to esteem absolution highly because it is the voice of God and pronounced by God's command. The power of the keys is praised, and people are reminded of the great consolation it brings to terrified consciences, are told that God requires faith to believe such absolution as God's own voice heard from heaven, and are assured such faith truly obtains and receives the forgiveness of sins.[137]

Since the historical and theological thrust of this service is in the absolution imparted to the individual—the indicative-operative absolution, to Luther, the most comforting—the penitents should be invited to come forward and kneel near the altar or at the chancel rail, there individually to receive such absolution from the pastor. In the case of a larger group, the penitents may approach the altar in continuous fashion, filling the empty places when those who have received the laying on of the hand with the absolution have returned to their places.[138] Only as a last resort should recourse be taken by the pastor to absolve all penitents as a group.

The pastor's dismissal, based on 1 Thess. 5:23–24, followed by the congregation's Amen, brings the service to a reverential, yet joyful, close. Music at this point might disturb private prayer and meditation.

Unless this service has served as immediate preparation for the Divine Service (with Communion), the pastor would do well to be available for counseling.

General Confession/The Preparation

In the history of penance, what is frequently called general confession or preparation for the Divine Service is the result of two developments, namely, the *Confiteor* ("I confess") and the *Offene Schuld* (public, open, or general confession of sin [*Schuld*] in contrast to private confession).

The *Confiteor*

Earliest beginnings of the *Confiteor*, about the ninth century, are seen in the so-called entrance (Latin: *accessus*), or *Preparatio ad missam* (Preparation for the Mass), in which the priest privately recited certain prayers as he vested himself, thus preparing himself for his entrance. Gradually included as part of this process, first in the Gallican liturgy of the ninth century, were certain so-called apologies,[139] or personal confessions of the priest. With the increasing emphasis on private confession and absolution for the laity, such confession by the priest possibly developed as a counterpart. By the 11th century these apologies, perhaps derived from the Eastern Church, appeared frequently in various Western liturgies. Although at first spoken alone by the priest, the apology soon took on a dialog form between priest and deacon, or assistant, a practice originally to be found in the canonical hours, especially Prime and Compline. The actual text of the *Confiteor*, as gradually developed, was established and adopted by the Council of Ravenna in 1314 and finally authorized for the entire Western Church in the *Missale Romanum* of Pius V in 1570. In simple outline the *Confiteor* appears thus:

In nomine Patris: "In the name of the Father. . . ."

Introibo: "I will go in unto the altar of God. . . ."

Psalm 43: "Judge me, O God. . . ."

Introibo (repeated)

Adjutorum nostrum: "Our help is in the name . . . ."

Confiteor (in dialog form)

Misereatur: "May almighty God have mercy. . . ."

Indulgentiam: "May the almighty and merciful Lord grant us pardon. . . ."

Versiculus (little verse)

Domini, exaudi orationem meum: "Lord, hear my prayer. . . ."

Dominus vobiscum: "The Lord be with you. . . ."

Aufer a nobis: "Take away from us our iniquities. . . ."[140]

Offene Schuld

The *Confiteor*, as preparation for the clergy in pre-Reformation times, had its counterpart for the assembled congregation in the so-called *Offene Schuld*, a general confession (*confessio generalis*) followed by a general absolution (*absolutio generalis*). This form of confession, as part of the "sermon-liturgy" (*Predigtliturgie*) called the Prone (German: *Pronaus*; French: *prone*; Latin: *praeconium=praedicatio=proclamation=sermon*), existed as such as early as the 10th century.[141] In essence the Prone was a vernacular devotion in the midst of a Latin Mass, conducted by the priest from the pulpit, not in the altar space, as was the custom with the other parts of the Mass.[142] It is to be noted that in contrast to Rome, where the sermon disappeared in the Latin Mass, the Gallican rite, in use in the Frankish kingdom, invariably included a homily after the Gospel. Charlemagne's (c. 742–814) influence not only caused the sermon to be a regular part of the Sunday and festival services, his regulations also called for catechetical instruction, in the course of which the Apostles' Creed, the Lord's Prayer, and the Decalog were explained and thereafter recited in unison by the congregation. This explains the general contents of and the liturgical acts in the following outline of *Offene Schuld* from the 12th century:

Creed (congregation)

Confession (congregation)

Misereatur: "May almighty God have mercy. . . ." (priest in
  Latin)
Indulgentiam: "May the almighty God and merciful Lord grant
  us pardon. . . ." (priest in Latin)
Lord's Prayer (congregation)
Oratio pro ecclesia: Prayer of the Church (priest in German)[143]

As to the inclusion of a general confession, in contrast to the
then-ongoing, prevalent practice of private, or individual, confession for the laity, this was undoubtedly in anticipation of receiving
the Lord's Supper. The connection between the two is quite in evidence, thus for using the *Offene Schuld* as sort of a cleansing preparation for the Holy Communion.[144] On the other hand, using it when
there were no communicants appears to have been customary in
the late Middle Age, perhaps due to the desire of congregations
not only to confess their faith in the Creed but also to confess their
sins and thus receive the divine assurance of forgiveness.[145]

Luther and the Church Orders

In his liturgical reform of the Mass, Luther made no formal provision
for a preparation, neither for the pastor (*Preparatio ad missam*; German: *Stufengebet*) nor for the congregation (*Offene Schuld*), even
though he was well acquainted with both. Admittedly, the texts of
the former were not customarily included in the Mass books, since
they served only the priests.[146] As for the congregation's preparation,
in the *Formula Missae* (1523) Luther expressed the opinion, "Concerning the preparation for the Supper, we think that preparing
oneself by fasting and prayer is a matter of liberty."[147] Of special
importance to him is the Pax Domini (Peace of the Lord), which
he describes as

> a public absolution [by the priest] of the sins of the communicants,
> the true voice of the Gospel announcing the remission of sins, and
> therefore the one and most worthy preparation for the Lord's
> table, if faith holds to these words as coming from the mouth of
> Christ himself.[148]

History attests that the Lutheran Church has not drawn the same
conclusion regarding the Pax, but instead has kept various aspects
of pre-Reformation forms of preparation for the Divine Service.

Similarly, Luther's German Mass (*Deutsche Messe*) of 1526 eschews all historical forms of preparation. His acquaintance with the custom in *Offene Schuld* of making a general confession and reciting the Lord's Prayer leads him to suggest the use of a paraphrase of the Lord's Prayer, followed by an admonition, or exhortation, to communicants—both of his making—immediately after the sermon. These he construes theologically as proclamation of the joyful message of the forgiveness of Christ by the grace of God, not so much as confession. Concerning these he states,

> Whether such paraphrase and admonition should be read in the pulpit immediately after the sermon or at the altar, I would leave to everyone's judgment. It seems that the ancients did so in the pulpit, so that it is still the custom to read general prayers or to repeat the Lord's Prayer in the pulpit. But the admonition itself has since become a public confession. In this way, however, the Lord's Prayer together with a short exposition would be current among people, and the Lord would be remembered, even as he commanded at the Supper.[149]

The close association of the admonition with the Lord's Prayer paraphrase, the accent of which is evidently the Fifth Petition, confirms Luther's understanding of the latter as a preparation prayer. But he sees as the origin of *Offene Schuld* not the Lord's Prayer, but the admonition. And he appears concerned that this paraphrase and admonition become a constituent part of the service when he adds:

> I would, however, like to ask that this paraphrase or admonition follow a prescribed wording or be formulated in a definite manner for the sake of the common people. We cannot have one do it one way today, and another, another way tomorrow, and let everybody parade his talents and confuse the people so that they can neither learn nor retain anything.[150]

Thus the *Offene Schuld* (actually only the confession aspect of it), theologically—whether sacramental or non-sacramental—still left undecided,[151] is turned into an admonition and introduced into the liturgy. Practically speaking, Luther's proposal found little acceptance, neither in Saxony[152] nor in Wittenberg itself, where the priest's historical *Stufengebet* and the congregation's *Offene Schuld* continued to be used. Overarching these liturgical questions and reforms of Luther regarding formal rites of preparation, stands, however, the matter of private confession and absolution, which he prized so highly and concerning which he stated in his *Formula Missae*,

> Now concerning private confession before communion, I still think as I have held heretofore, namely, that it neither is necessary nor should be demanded. Nevertheless, it is useful and should not be despised.[153]

Concerned as they were about doctrinal purity, the Reformers still appreciated the spiritual values of both the *Confiteor* and *Offene Schuld*. And the numerous church orders of the 16th century exhibit both varied forms and usage. In some areas there are indications that when the Divine Service was in Latin, the pastor would use the customary *Confiteor* as a private (or in dialog) preparation prior to the service.[154] When, however, the service was in German, the pastor would lead the congregation in the customary *Offene Schuld* at the beginning of the service. This latter usage, incorporating certain elements of the *Confiteor*, becomes especially discernible as a principle in many church orders of this century.[155] These orders invariably use the optative—expressive of wish or desire—form of absolution, although a few contain the indicative formula, often coalescing with certain words of Scripture,[156] thus practically constituting a conditional absolution in the use of various expressions of retention. Use of the simple declaration of grace is also in evidence.

Structural Considerations

In evaluating this form of confession, both theologically and liturgically, certain principles, according to Mahrenholz, should be taken into consideration:

1. The core of general confession (*Offene Schuld*) lies in the confession of sins, not in the absolution as exemplified in the Office of the Keys. Therefore, such scriptural passages as Matthew 18 and John 20 should not come into play, but rather passages which speak of God's saving love for sinful men in Christ.

2. This form of confession in a public service is spoken by all and for all. The relationship between pastor and congregation is not

one of confessor versus penitent as in private confession. The pronouns employed will be such as to include the pastor.

3. In the practice of this confession there can evidently be no real absolution in the sense of the Office of the Keys. For one thing, there can be no individual consolation through absolution. For another, the pastor cannot absolve himself. Consequently, general confession cannot go beyond an optative plea or prayer for forgiveness in the first rather than the second person.[157]

Confession and Holy Communion

In discussing this subject it might be helpful to be reminded from history that confession and Holy Communion are two separate offices and that for a thousand years or more the church apparently had no formal confession of sins in its Sunday worship.[158] After all, Sunday was the joyous day commemorating the resurrection of Christ. Moreover, the early Christians thought of themselves as the holy and redeemed people, a community of priests and kings that had already obtained mercy. Christhard Mahrenholz, for instance, insists that neither on the basis of 1 Cor. 11:27–29 nor the Small Catechism can it be proved that confession is an indispensable presupposition for the reception of the Eucharist. He argues that confession, specifically absolution, is the exercise of the divinely ordained Office of the Keys (in the strict sense) and as such it stands as a function in its own right. Such separation, he asserts, is more in agreement with the practice of the early church.[159] Noting the distinction between the discipline to be exercised with regard to Holy Communion and the freedom and liberty in the use of confession and absolution helps clarify matters. In the practice of canonical penance, keeping gross sinners from participating in the Eucharist before completing their penance—and subsequently being publicly reconciled to the Christian community—was a disciplinary measure. Even the resolution *Omnis utriusque sexus*, passed by the Fourth Lateran Council in 1215, which imposed upon all Christians of either sex, having arrived at the year of discretion, the duty of confessing annually as well as receiving the Eucharist at Easter,[160] makes only an indirect connection between the two.[161] The purpose of this decree is not to impose the necessity of confessing to a priest; rather, it determines by positive law the time within which the obligation of receiving the Eucharist annually must be fulfilled.[162] It is succeeding councils, beginning already in the same century, that began to associate the two.[163]

Not the least of Luther's concerns was that private confession be a matter of Christian liberty, free from all coercion. Not a little convincing are his words in the *Formula Missae* (1523): "Now concerning private confession before Communion, I still think as I have held heretofore, namely, that it neither is necessary nor should be demanded. Nevertheless, it is useful and should not be despised."[164] Despite his urging that people make frequent use of this salutary means, which he praised in the most glowing terms,[165] fewer and fewer people came to confession, notwithstanding his sharp words against such negligence.[166] Moreover, in carrying out the Reformation in Wittenberg and beyond, the discipline of examining those who wished to commune was a necessary responsibility of the public ministry. Accordingly, on Maundy Thursday, 1523, in concern for specific knowledge and true faith on the part of recipients of the Eucharist,[167] Luther announced that each person should be examined regarding his faith and life before admission to the Lord's Table.[168] As to the frequency of such examination, he thinks "it enough for the applicants for Communion to be examined or explored once a year. Indeed, a man may be so understanding that he needs to be questioned only once in his lifetime or not at all."[169] The latter statement pertains to intelligent people. The simple and plain must be trained and treated differently.[170] Their examination soon came to include confession and absolution.[171] Unfortunately, Luther used the term confession for this procedure. This explains the statement in the Augsburg Confession (1530),

> Confession has not been abolished by the preachers on our side. The custom has been retained among us of not administering the sacrament to those who have not been *examined* and absolved.[172]

Granted that Luther never made confession and absolution a requirement for coming to the Lord's Table, his linking the free element of confession and absolution to the obligatory examination regarding doctrine and life resulted, however, in this type of confession becoming a preparation for the reception of Holy Communion. Nor did this conception change when, in the 18th century, private, or individual, confession gave way to general confession so current today. Luther's procedure—the so-called Wittenberg practice— furnished the means by which confession could be regulated in an ecclesiastical manner.[173]

Admittedly, "in a world where at times it would seem that the only requirement for Communion is the ability to open one's mouth,"[174] there arise circumstances that result in exclusion from the Lord's Table. When a Christian, for instance, sins so that he/she, according to the words of apostles Paul and John (1 Cor. 6:9ff.; Gal. 5:19–21; Eph. 5:5; Rev. 22:15) forfeits his/her membership in the kingdom of God and impenitently persists in such sin after repeated admonition, then this person must be excluded from the Christian community and consequently from the Lord's Table. Readmittance to both the Christian community and the Lord's Table calls for repentance, manifested in confession to and absolution from the pastor.

The aforementioned structure of private confession, as established in Wittenberg and its environs, soon became the generally established practice also in other areas of Lutheranism, a procedure that Melanchthon's "Instruction for Visitors" (1528),[175] Luther's two catechisms (1529), and the numerous church orders of the then many cities and states did much to disseminate.[176]

The foregoing developments constitute the background for the statement,

> Both Divine Service I and Divine Service II begin with Confession and Absolution or Confession and Declaration of Grace. While it is neither theologically nor liturgically necessary that this congregational act always precede the Holy Communion, custom and pastoral discernment may dictate the need for such a practice most of the time.[177]

Notes

1. For detailed developments regarding the Sacrament of Penance in the Western Church, two works remain classic: Paul F. Palmer, *Sacraments and Forgiveness* (Westminster, MD: Newman Press, 1959); and Bernard Poschmann, *Penance and the Annointing of the Sick*, trans. and rev. Francis Courtney (New York: Herder and Herder, 1964). Palmer's commentaries and interpretations, however, must be read cautiously. More recent works include: Herbert Vorgrimler, *Busse and Krankensalbung* (Freiburg: Herder and Herder, 1978), a work

that has replaced Poschmann in Herder's *Handbuch der Dogmengeschichte* series; Monica Hellwig, *Sign of Reconciliation and Conversion* (Wilmington: Glazier, 1982); James Dallen, *The Reconciling Community: The Rite of Penance* (New York: Pueblo, 1986); and Ladislas Orsy, *The Evolving Church and The Sacrament of Penance* (Denville, NJ: Dimension, 1978). Also deserving of attention is the post-Vatican II exhortation of Pope John Paul II, *Reconciliato et Paenitentia*, available in translation from the United States Catholic Conference, Washington, D.C.

2. Cf. R. C. H. Lenski, *The Interpretation of St. John's Gospel* (Columbus, OH: Lutheran Book Concern, 1942), pp. 1377–1388. There has been considerable debate as to whether the disciples had the power to grant forgiveness directly in Christ's name or in the name of the church. The biblical record as it stands allows both interpretations.

3. See Bida Rigaux, "Lier et delier. Les ministeres de reconciliation dans l' eglise des temps apostoliques," *Maison-Dieu* 117 (1974): 86–135.

4. The early identification of the incestuous person in 1 Corinthians with the reconciliation of the same in 2 Corinthians is borne out by Tertullian's *De Pudicitia*, written during his Montanist days, in which he devotes considerable space to prove the excommunicate in 1 Corinthians is not the one reconciled by Paul in 2 Corinthians, an indication that his catholic opponents put stress on their identity. *De Pudicitia* 13ff., *Patrologia: Patres Latini*, ed. J. P. Migne (Paris: n.p., 1874), II: 1003ff. This difference of opinion has continued down to the present. Plummer, for instance, does not identify the man in 2 Corinthians with the incestuous person in 1 Corinthians. Alfred Plummer, *A Critical and Exegetical Commentary on the Second Epistle of St. Paul to the Corinthians* (Edinburgh: T. & T. Clark [reprint, 1951]), pp. 58ff. On the other hand, Lenski implies that the same person is involved. R. C. H. Lenski, *The Interpretation of St. Paul's First and Second Epistle to the Corinthians* (Columbus, OH: Wartburg Press, 1946), pp. 886ff. Lea states that identifying this episode with the Western Church's concept of penance "is a typical instance of the facility with which men read into Scripture whatever they desire to find there." H. C. Lea, *History of Auricular Confession and Indulgences* (New York: Lea Bros., 1896), p. 5. Even so, to the early church fathers these texts retain their importance as evidence of ecclesiastical excommunication and forgiveness or reconciliation. Ivan Havener concludes that it was physical death and eventual salvation rather than temporary exclusion and eventual repentance in "A Curse for Salvation—1 Corinthians 5:1–5" in *Sin, Salvation and the Spirit*, ed. Daniel Durken (Collegeville, PA: Liturgical Press, 1979), pp. 334–344.

5. R. C. H. Lenski, *The Interpretation of the Epistles of St. Peter, St. John and St. Jude* (Columbus, OH: Wartburg Press, 1945), pp. 363ff.

6. This distinction is not to be indentified with mortal and venial sin of later theology.

7. Ethelbert Stauffer, *New Testament Theology*, trans. John Marsh (New York: The Macmillan Co., 1955), p. 142.

8. Although a Roman Catholic, Poschmann regards as unwarranted the use of 1 John 1:9 as scriptural proof for sacramental confession. Roman Catholic dogmatic theologians (e.g., Diekamp, Bartmann, Gierens, Schmaus), he states, also abandoned such interpretation. Poschmann, p. 18, n. 17.

9. John E. Huther states that "one to another" in the authorized version can only refer to the relation of the individual believers to each other. "Critical and Exegetical Handbook to the General Epistles of James, Peter, John, and Jude," *Meyer's Commentary on the New Testament*, trans. from the 3d. ed. of the German Paton J. Gloag, D. B. Greene, Clark H. Irwin; American edition Timothy Dwight (New York: Funk and Wagnalls, 1887), p. 159. Poschmann, p. 17, believes that James 5:16 indicates some kind of public confession.

10. The following are considered to be the most important penitentials: Penitential of Finnian (c. 525–550), Penitential of Cummean (c. 650), Penitential of Columban (c. 600), Penitential of Theodore (668–690), Penitential of Bede (8th century, erroneously ascribed to him), Penitential of Egbert (c. 750). This listing and respective dating is taken from the critical and minute study of John T. McNeill and Helene M. Gamer, *Medieval Handbooks of Penance* (New York: Columbia University Press, 1938), pp. 86ff. Additional scholars who have made important contributions in this area are F. W. H. Wasserschleben, *Die Bussordnungen der abendländischen Kirche* (Graz: Akademische Druck-U. Verlagsanstalt, 1851, [reprint, 1958]); Herman Josef Schmitz, *Die Bussbücher und die Bussdisciplin der Kirche*, 2 vols. (Graz: Akademische Druck-U. Verlagsanstalt, 1883 [reprint, 1958]); T. P. Oakley, *English Penitential Discipline and Anglo-Saxon Law in Their Joint Influence* (New York: Columbia University Press, 1923).

11. Cf. An Old Irish Table of Cummutations (8th century). As an example of the concentrated rigor of the *arrea*, this table prescribes the following for former laybrothers and laysisters: "sleeping in waters, sleeping on nettles, sleeping on nutshells, sleeping with a dead body in a grave." McNeill-Gamer, p. 144; pp. 142ff.; also Wasserschleben, pp. 139ff.

12. All references to the Council of Trent are from *Canons and Decrees of the Council of Trent*, trans. H. J. Schroeder (St. Louis: B. Herder Book Co., 1941).

13. WA 8: 311. Fischer agrees with Melanchthon's judgment. E. Fischer, *Zur Geschichte der evangelischen Beichte*, 2 vols. (Leipzig: Dieterisch'sche Verlags-Buchhandlung, 1902–1903), I: 1 (Introduction). Cf. also Oskar Planck, *Evangelisches Beichtbüchlein* (Stuttgart: F. S. Steinkopf Verlag, 1957), p. 23; Regin Prenter, *Spiritus Creator*, trans. John M. Jensen (Philadelphia: Muhlenberg Press, 1953), p. 151; Kliefoth goes so far as to state that the Reformation was basically a restoration of confession and absolution. Theodor Kliefoth, "Die Beichte und Absolution," *Liturgische Abhandlungen*, 8 vols. (Schwerin: Verlag der Stiller'schen Hof-Buchhandlung, 1856), II: 125.

14. Cf. WA 3: 284ff.

15. WA 2: 410; AE 31: 317.

16. Cf. WA 2: 721.

17. Ibid.

18. SA III, III, 36, BSLK, p. 446. All subsequent references in this chapter to the Lutheran Symbols in this chapter are taken from this work. The translations are normally taken from *The Book of Concord*, trans. and ed. Theodore G. Tappert in collaboration with Jaroslav Pelikan, Robert H. Fischer, and Arthur C. Piepkorn (Philadelphia: Fortress Press, 1959). Klein says that herein lies perhaps Luther's sharpest point of attack in his controversy with the medieval church's

teaching on confession. Laurentius Klein, *Evangelisch-Lutherische Beichte* (Paderborn: Verlag Bonifacius, 1961), p. 18.

19. Klein, p. 19.

20. WA 8: 181. The Fourth Lateran Council required the confession only of mortal sins. Perhaps Luther here implies that the penitent must recall and weigh all his sins before he decides which sins he should confess. Cf. Ibid., p. 278; WA 1: 576. But in another instance he says that it is necessary that all manifest mortal sins be confessed and bewailed (WA 1: 329), and this as preparation for the Eucharist. It is very difficult to determine in every case precisely what Luther means.

21. Palm Sunday Sermon (1524), WA 15: 489. The "general absolution" is undoubtedly the *Offene Schuld*, which will be treated later.

22. BSLK, p. 517, 20ff. New translation by Board for Parish Services, 1986.

23. Ibid., p. 519, 5ff.

24. Wolfgang Böhme, *Beichtlehre für Evangelische Christen* (Stuttgart; Evangelisches Verlagswerk, 1956), p. 31. He does this on the basis of Luther's own statement that the absolution is to be received as coming from God himself and that the penitent is not to doubt but firmly believe that by such absolution his sins are forgiven. BSLK, p. 517, 15ff.

25. BLSK, p. 519.

26. SA III, III, 14ff.; BSLK, p. 439.

27. SA III, III, 10–35; BSLK, pp. 438–446.

28. SA III, III, 1–8, BSLK, pp.436–438.

29. SA III, III, 1–9, BSLK, pp. 436–438.

30. *Pro veritate inquirenda*, WA 1: 632.

31. WA 30²: 453.

32. WA 15: 486. Similarly the Lutheran Symbols, or Confessions, consider the absolution to be the very heart of confession. Ernst Kinder, "Beichte und Absolution nach den lutherischen Bekenntnisschriften," *Theologische Literaturzeitung* 77 (September 1952): 544. Hence the frequent complaints on the part of the Reformers that the Western Church placed too much emphasis on either the act of confessing (cf. SA III, III, 20, BSLK, p. 441) and on the *satisfactio* (making satisfaction). Cf., for example, AC XXV, 5: "In former times the preachers who taught much about confession never mentioned a word concerning these necessary matters (faith in and comfort from the absolution) but only tormented consciences with long enumerations of sins, with satisfactions, with indulgences, with pilgrimages and the like." BSLK, p. 98.

33. Ap XIII, 4, BSLK, p. 292. Lack of agreement in the Lutheran Symbols regarding both the definition of the term sacrament and the fixed number of sacraments reflects the fact that the church "had not formulated an official, adequate, and comprehensive doctrine of the sacraments before the end of the Middle Ages." Arthur Carl Piepkorn, *What the Symbolical Books of the Lutheran Church Have to Say About Worship and the Sacraments* (St. Louis: Concordia Publishing House, 1952), p. 16. The Symbols generally recognize two sacraments as essential, namely, Holy Baptism and the Sacrament of the Altar (LC IV, 1; BSLK, p. 691; cf. also LC IV, 74; BSLK, pp. 705–706, where Penance is simply considered to be nothing else than Baptism).

34. Palm Sunday Sermon (1524), WA 15: 485. Cf. also WA 34¹: 308: "Absolution is nothing other than the preaching of the Gospel."

35. WA 29: 141.

36. WA 10³: 215ff.

37. Ibid., 395ff. Cf. also *De instituendis ministris ecclesiae* (About the Instituted Ministries of the Church), 1523, WA 12: 184.

38. Ap XXVIII, 13; BSLK, p. 400.

39. WA 6: 547.

40. SA III, VII, 1; BSLK, p. 452; Treatise on the Power and Primacy of the Pope 24, 68.

41. AC XXVIII, 8; BSLK, p. 273; AC XIV; BSLK, p. 69.

42. Ap XII, 103ff., 176; BSLK, p. 273, 290.

43. Cf. *Sacramentarium Gelasianum*, I, XV; *Liber Sacramentorum Romanae Aeclesiae Ordinis Anni Circuli*, ed. L. C. Mohlberg (Rome: Herder, 1960), pp. 17–18.

44. *Summa Theologica*, p. 3, q. 84, a. 3. *St. Thomas Aquinas' Summa Theologica*, trans. Fathers of the English Dominican Province (New York: Benzinger Bros., 1948), II: 2531. Although he admits that God alone authoritatively absolves from sin and remits sin, yet priests do both in a ministerial way, inasmuch as the words of the priest in this sacrament are instrumentally operative by divine power, as in the other sacraments. Since, however, the priest here acts as a minister, he adds what pertains to God's divine authority, namely, "I absolve you in the name of the Father, and of the Son, and of the Holy Spirit" or . . . "in virtue of Christ's passion" . . . or "by God's authority." Ibid., p. 2532. Cf. Joseph Jungmann, *Die lateinischen Bussriten in ihrer geschichtlichen Entwicklung* (Innsbruck: Fel. Rauch, 1932), pp. 259ff.

45. *Cf. The Rites of the Catholic Church as Revised by the Second Vatican Council*, study edition, English trans. the International Commission on English in the Liturgy (New York: Pueblo, 1976, 1983), pp. 383, 393, 398.

46. WA 12: 493; WA 15: 478.

47. WA, TR, 4: 5176. This conception of absolution is a revival of the similar view of the early church that it is Christ who alone forgives sins. Christhard Mahrenholz, "Begleitwort zu dem Ordnungen der Beichte," *Musicologica et Liturgica*, ed. Karl Ferdinand Mueller (Kassel: Bärenreiter Verlag, 1960), p. 488. One can thus speak of a "real presence" of Christ in absolution. Eric Roth, *Privatbeichte und Schlüsselgewalt in der Theologie der Reformation* (Gütersloh: C. Bertelsmann Verlag, 1952), p. 76. Cf. Arthur Carl Piepkorn, "Christ Today: His Presence in the Sacraments," *Lutheran World* (July 1963): 267–287.

48. Cf. Small Catechism, WA 21¹: 387; Lectures on Genesis, WA 1: 235.

49. *Resolutiones disputationem de indulgentiarum virtute* (1519), WA 1: 540, 595.

50. Thesis 38, WA 1: 235. Also sermon for the Nineteenth Sunday after Holy Trinity Sunday (1533), WA 52: 500.

51. Ap XIII, 4.

52. WA 8: 173, 170; cf. WA 6: 159–160; WA 15: 485; WA 8: 157.

53. This Synod was organized in 1847 at Chicago, with Carl Ferdinand Wilhelm Walther elected as its first president. He served in this capacity until 1850 and again from 1864–1878.

54. Carl S. Meyer, "Walther's Letter from Zurich, A defense of Missouri's Unity and Confessionalism," *Concordia Theological Monthly* XXXII/10 (October 1961): 644.

55. Significant is C. F. W. Walther's series of six articles in which he defends absolution against the objections of the Methodists. Entitled "Die heilige Absolution gerettet gegen die Lästerungen der Methodisten" (Holy Absolution rescued from the Slanders of the Methodists), the first article appeared in *Der Lutheraner* 2/15 (21 March 1846): 59–60; the last in *Der Lutheraner* 2/22 (27 June 1846): 85–88. Of interest is also the article, "Die christliche Freiheit, in Bezug auf die Privat- und Allgemeine Beichte und Absolution" (The Christian Freedom in relation to Private and General Confession and Absolution), *Der Lutheraner* 4/17 (18 April 1848): 129–131, by a certain J. N.

56. Missouri Synod, Northern District, *Proceedings*, 1856, pp. 11–17. In the congregation at Lebanon, Wisconsin, a controversy arose over the introduction of general confession alongside of private confession. Cf. Missouri Synod, Northern District, *Proceedings*, pp. 22–26. At the 1858 convention of the Northern District arguments were given for retaining private confession and absolution. The gradual waning of this practice is attributed to various forms of Enthusiasm which, among other things, denied the validity of the pastor's absolution. Ibid., pp. 26–34.

57. Cf. Missouri Synod, Northern District, *Proceedings*, 1859, pp. 24–31; also *Moving Frontiers,* ed. Carl S. Meyer (St. Louis: Concordia Publishing House, 1964), pp. 240–241.

58. Cf. Missouri Synod, *Proceedings,* 1860, pp. 34–58. See also the article by Carl Fricke, "Ist die Privatbeichte, Wie sie in der lutherischen Kirche geübt wird, ein Stück römischen Sauerteigs?" in *Der Lutheraner* XV (8 February 1859): 100–102. At the 1858 conventions of the Eastern and Western Districts private confession had been discussed and the districts had expressed agreement with the principles enunciated by the Northern and Central Districts. Cf. Missouri Synod, Western District, *Proceedings*, 1858, pp. 26–29; also Missouri Synod, Central District, *Proceedings*, 1858, p. 27, and Missouri Synod, Eastern District, *Proceedings*, 1858, pp. 18–22.

59. Arthur Carl Piepkorn, "Walther and the Lutheran Symbols," *Concordia Theological Monthly* XXXII/10 (October 1961): 609.

60. C. F. W. Walther, *Americanisch-Lutherische Pastoraltheologie*, 5th ed. (St. Louis: Concordia Publishing House, 1906), p. 155. This book is largely a reprint of articles that had appeared in *Lehre und Wehre*.

61. C. F. W. Walther, *The Proper Distinction Between Law and Gospel,* trans. W. H. T. Dau (St. Louis: Concordia Publishing House, 1928), p. 169. For the German original see C. F. W. Walther, *Die rechte Unterscheidung von Gesetz und Evangelium* (St. Louis: Concordia Publishing House, 1901), p. 159.

62. Walther, *The Proper Distinction,* pp. 169–180.

63. Ibid., p. 170.

64. C. F. W. Walther, *Americanisch-Lutherische Evangelien Postille, Predigten über die evangelischen Perikopen des Kirchenjahrs* (St. Louis: Concordia Publishing House, n.d.), p. 161.

65. Ibid.

66. C. F. W. Walther, "Wie gross und verderblich der Irrthum derjenigen sei den Predigern des Evangeliums die Macht absprechen, auf Erden Sünden zu vergeben," *Der Lutheraner* VI (19 March 1850): 115.

67. Ibid.

68. C. J. Otto Hanser, compiler, *Licht des Lebens, Ein Jahrgang von Evangelien Predigten von C. F. W. Walther* (St. Louis: Concordia Publishing House, 1905), p. 595.

69. Walther, *The Proper Distinction*, p. 172.

70. Ap XII, 41–42; BSLK, p. 259.

71. *Der Lutheraner* IV (11 Jan. 1848): 83–84; (8 Feb. 1848): 90–92; (22 Feb. 1848): 101–102; (7 March 1848): 106–107.

72. Gottlieb Christopher Adolph von Harless (1806–79), distinguished alike as a theologian, preacher, and administrator, was prominently associated with the confessional movement that affected the Lutheran Church in the 19th century.

73. *Der Lutheraner* IV (11 Jan. 1848): 84.

74. Ibid.

75. *Der Lutheraner* IV (22 Feb. 1848): 101.

76. Ibid., p. 102.

77. *Der Lutheraner* IV (4 April 1848): 125.

78. Ibid. Even though the very voice of the Gospel (*vera vox evangelii*) is sounded in both the absolution and in preaching, the confessional writings refrain from identifying absolution with the sermon. The two are different activities. Cf. Holsten Fagerberg, *A New Look at the Lutheran Confessions (1529–1537)* (St. Louis: Concordia, 1972), p. 98, n. 35.

79. Piepkorn, "Walther and the Lutheran Symbols," p. 619; see C. F. W. Walther, *Die Stimme unserer Kirche in der Frage von Kirche und Amt* (Erlangen: C. A. Blaesing, 1852), pp. 193–214; also Holsten Fagerberg, *Bekenntnis, Kirche und Amt in der deutschen konfessionellen Theologie des 19. Jahrhunderts* (Uppsala: Almqvist och Wiksells Boktrycheri, 1952), pp. 11, 112.

80. Ap XXVIII, 13; BSLK, 400 and AC XXVIII, BSLK, 120–133. Cf. also Arthur Carl Piepkorn, "The Sacred Ministry and Holy Ordination in the Sacred Scriptures and in the Symbols and Liturgy of the Church of the Augsburg Confession," *Una Sancta* XII (St. Michael's Day 1955): 3–11.

81. It was entitled *Kirchen-Agende für Evangelisch-Lutherischen Gemeinden ungeänderter Augsburgischer Confession*. See page 93 for the listing of its contents.

82. This is identical to the form on page 31 of the *Kirchen-Agende*.

83. *Kirchen-Agende*, p. 22.

84. GW III[1]: 180–181.

85. Ibid., 181. In his *Agende für Christliche Gemeinden lutherischen Behenntnisses* (1844), prepared for the use of pastors in North America, three forms of cor-

porate confession are included in the Communion Service. The first is that of Andreas Döber of Nürnberg (1525); the second that of Wittenberg (1559), Mecklenburg (1522), and Wolfgang (1570); and the third is from Austria (1571). Cf. GW VII, Part 1: 48–51.

86. GW V[2]: 740–741.

87. Ibid. These different locations, Löhe says, are necessary; otherwise the pastor would be confined to the unhealthy sacristy most of the time.

88. August Hardeland, *Geschichte der speziellen Seelsorge in der vorreformatorischen Kirche der Reformation* (Berlin: Reuther und Reichard, 1896), p. 518. Cf. also GW V[1]: 191.

89. Löhe himself says that when private confession was reintroduced by him, the church, to his astonishment, was filled with members who wanted to make such confession. Ibid., p. 190. Furthermore, reflecting the priority given to private confession on the part of his parishioners, he says that often several hundred made their private confession, whereas sometimes only a few came to general confession. GW III[1]: 214.

90. GW V[1]: 189.

91. Ibid., 190.

92. GW III[1]: 219.

93. He teaches that the office of binding and loosing given to the apostles is transferred to their successors. Ibid., 175. Kliefoth's view is similar. Cf. Theodor Kliefoth, *Acht Bücher von der Kirche* (Schwerin: Verlag der Stiller-schen Hof-Buchhandlung, 1854), p. 209. On Löhe's doctrine of the church and ministry see Siegfried Hebart, *Wilhelm Löhe's Lehre von der Kirche ihrem Amt und Regiment* (Neuendettelsau: Freimund Verlag, 1939).

94. *Kirche und Amt, Neue Aphorismen*, GW V[1]: 552.

95. Ibid., 580.

96. "A bishop has the power of the order (*potestatem ordinis*), namely, the ministry of the Word and the sacraments. He also has the power of jurisdiction (*potestatem jurisdictionis*), namely, the authority to excommunicate those who are guilty of public offences or to absolve them if they are converted and ask for absolution." Ap XXVIII, 13; BSLK, p. 400. The Augsburg Confession includes both of these powers under the term *potestas clavium* when it states, "Our teachers hold that according to the Gospel the power of keys or the power of bishops is a power or command of God to preach the Gospel, to remit and retain sins, and to administer the sacraments." AC XXVIII, 5; BSLK, p. 121. Alongside the power of the keys Luther recognizes another element in the Gospel which he calls "the mutual conversation and consolation of the brethern." SA III, IV; BSLK, p. 449.

97. GW V[1]: 175.

98. So, for instance, Oskar Planck quoting Hans Asmussen. Planck, *Evangelische Beichtbüchlein* (Stuttgart: J. F. Steinkopf Verlag, 1957), p. 33.

99. Klein, 117, n. 32.

100. Richard Franke, "Geschichte der evangelischen Privatbeichte in Sachsen," *Beiträge zur sächsischen Kirchengeschichte*, ed. Franz Dibelius and Theodor Brieger, 19 Heft (Leipzig: Johann Ambrosius Barth, 1906), p. 117.

101. For an excerpt of the original defense (*Verteidungsschrift*) of his practice see Christoph Blumhardt, *Bekenne einer dem anderen seine Sünde, ein Wort über Privatbeichte und Privatabsolution* (Elberfeld: Buchhandlung der Evang. Gesellschaft, 1889), pp. 18ff. and 152. For additional information cf. F. Seebase, *Johann Christoph Blumhardt, Sein Leben und Wirken mit einer Auswahl seiner Schriften* (Hamburg: Wittig, 1949), p. 76.

102. Planck, p. 34.

103. Klein, p. 217, n. 32. In this connection it is interesting to note Dieter Voll describing the Oxford Movement as "fundamentally the second phase of English Pietism." Dieter Voll, *Catholic Evangelicalism*, trans. Veronica Ruffer (London: Faith Press, 1963), p. 38.

104. Meyer, *Moving Frontiers*, p. 240.

105. For instance, the Confraternity of St. Michael (*Michaels bruderschaft*), the *Evangelisch-Ökumenische Johannisbruderschaft*, the *Evangelischer Humilitenorden*, the French Community of Taize, the *Christusbruderschaft in Selbitz*, the *Teologisk Oratorium* (Danish), the *Evangelische Franciskanerbruderschaft der Nachfolge Christi*, the *Ordo Crucis* (Norwegian), and the *Schwesternschaft des Gebetes*. For information on such communities as the Grandchamp Community, the Retreat of Pomeyrol, the *Marienschwestern* of Darmstadt, see Francois Biot, *The Rise of Protestant Monasticism*, trans. W. J. Kerrigan (Baltimore: Helicon Press, 1963), pp. 94–105. During World War II the *Bruderschaft des Finkenwalder Predigerseminars*, a group gathered about Dietrich Bonhoeffer, practiced private confession. Cf. Dietrich Bonhoeffer, *Gesammelte Schriften*, ed. Eberhard Bethge (Munich: Chr. Kaiser Verlag, 1959), II: 454.

106. James Dallen's *The Reconciling Community* contains an extensive and up-to-date bibliography. Another bibliographic listing worthy of attention is that in Joseph A. Favazza, *The Order of Penitents: Historical Roots and Pastoral Future* (Collegeville, MN: The Liturgical Press, 1988). Cf. Kurt N. Enger, "Private Confession in American Lutheranism, A Study of Doctrine, History, and Practice" (unpublished Th.D. dissertation; Princeton Theological Seminary, 1962); J. Gunstone, *The Liturgy of Penance* (London: Faith Press, 1966); W. Telfer, *The Forgiveness of Sins* (London: SCM, 1959); Thomas N. Tentler, *Sin and Confession on the Eve of the Reformation* (Princeton; Princeton University Press, 1977); Fred L. Precht, "Changing Theologies of Private and Public Confession and Absolution" (unpublished Th.D. diss.; Concordia Seminary, St. Louis, 1965).

107. One of the more recent of such conferences, the Eleventh Congress of the Societas Liturgica, was held in Brixen, Italy, August 17–22, 1987, on the theme "A Worshipping Church, Penitent and Reconciling." The principal papers presented there are contained in its official publication, *Studia Liturgica* 18/1 (1988). Focusing on the complex issues and offering fresh insights are the essays presented at the June 1986 conference hosted by the Notre Dame Center for Pastoral Liturgy and contained in *Reconciliation: The Continuing Agenda*, ed. Robert J. Kennedy (Collegeville, MN: The Liturgical Press, 1987).

108. Cf. James Dallen, "A Decade of Discussion on the Reform of Penance, 1963–1973: Theological Analysis and Critique" (unpublished S.T.D. dissertation; Catholic University of America, 1976).

109. While the integral parts of Roman Catholic penance are still contrition, confession, satisfaction, and absolution, Ladislas Orsy insists that satisfaction plays a small and insignificant role compared to that in early canonical and tariff penance. Cf. Orsy, pp. 143–144, n. 44.

110. "One specific area where we have learned from the Reformation confessions concerns the centrality of God's Word in any act of worship. This includes penance." So states Jesuit Robert F. Taft, "Penance in Contemporary Worship," *Studia Liturgica* 18/1 (1988): 14.

111. In the Middle Ages confessions were heard in the priest's home and then in the church, the priest seated before the altar and the penitent kneeling to one side. It was not until the 15th century that confessionals with a screen, separating the priest from the penitent, were introduced in some places and eventually placed in the side aisles, thus destroying the previous link of sacramental reconciliation with the ecclesial assembly. Charles Borromeo (1538–84), cardinal and archbishop of Milan, prominent at the Council of Trent, required confessionals in his diocese to prevent scandalous solicitation and accusation. The ritual of 1614 prescribed the screen; later decrees demanded it for hearing women's confessions. For a history of the confessional see Wilhelm Schlombs, *Die Entwicklung des Beichtstuhls in der katholischen Kirche* (Düsseldorf: L. Schwann, 1965).

112. For actual texts and other specifics of Roman Catholic penance here discussed cf. *The Rites of the Catholic Church*, pp. 357–465 passim. These pages include the Introduction (*Praenotanda*), an item that can be read to great benefit.

113. Kinder, "Beichte and Absolution," p. 545.

114. Bo Giertz, *Kristi Kyrka* (Stockholm: Svenska Kyrkans Diakonestyrelis Bokförlag, 1939), pp. 196–197.

115. Wilhelm Stählin, "Bruderschaft," *Kirche im Aufbau* (Kassel; Johannes Stauda Verlag, 1940), XI: 106. The *Michaelsbruderschaft*, which developed out of the *Berneuchner* movement, has worked to restore the spirit of Luther and the Lutheran Symbols in Germany. Their publishing center is the Johannes Stauda Verlag, Kassel, Germany, the publisher of the annual propitious *Jahrbuch für Liturgie und Hymnologie*.

116. For an interesting little guide in making confession see Jobst Schöne, *Ich bekenne, Eine Beichthilfe für evangelisch-lutherische Christen* (Ülzen: Feste-Burg Verlag, 1963). This could readily be translated.

117. Marianka Fousek, "Ecumenical Perspectives: Confession?" *Dialog: A Journal of Theology* V/4 (1966): 296.

118. Max Lackman, *Wie beichten Wir*, 2d ed. (Gütersloh: Evangelischer Verlag, 1950), p. 94.

119. AC XI, 2; BSLK, p. 66.

120. Cf. Notes on the Liturgy in *Lutheran Worship: Altar Book*, prepared by the Commission on Worship of The Lutheran Church—Missouri Synod (St. Louis: Concordia Publishing House, 1982), p. 33.

121. In the light of the *Formula Missae* (1523), developments now present this picture: (1) an examination in Christian doctrine, once a year, once a lifetime, or not at all, as circumstances direct, WA 12: 215; AE 53: 33; (2) an examination of the individual's life—whoever lives in open sins is not permitted at the Lord's Table; (3) private confession as such, something neither necessary

nor to be demanded, nevertheless, useful and not to be despised. Nothing is expressly stated concerning the connection among these three phases. In actual practice the first two were undoubtedly combined. This entire procedure is again enunciated by Luther in his Palm Sunday sermon of 1524. WA 15: 495ff. In 1526 Luther says that private confession is of value at least to simple and plain Christians. But as far as most people are concerned, they must be examined. WA 19: 520.

122. Prussia in 1781; Lauenberg in 1800; Hamburg in 1788; Bremen in 1791. Cf. Paul Graff, *Geschichte der Auflösung der alten gottesdienstlichen Formen in der evangelischen Kirche Deutchlands*, 2 vols. (Göttingen: Vandenhoeck & Rupprecht, 1939), I: 384.

123. The following is a brief overview of the official abrogation of private confession: Brunswick and Wolfenbüttel (1775); Landschut in Silesia (1782); Franfurt am Main (1783); Schweinfurt (1785); Halle in Saxony and Hildesheim (1786); Anhalt und Reuszsche Lande (1787); Quidlinburg (1788); Hessen-Kassel, Nürnberg, Mecklenburg (1790); Hannover (1791); Bremen (1792); Kleinschönau-Zittau (1793); Eutritzsch-Leipzig (1795). Cf. Klein, p. 207. See also Graff, II: 282–283. The numerous and varied obligations, usages, and formulas of absolution existing at this time make it difficult to demonstrate a common pattern. Cf. Kliefoth, "Die Beichte und Absolution," II: 477ff. and 486ff. On the other hand, diligent efforts to retain private confession were put forth in many areas. It continued in some areas as late as the 19th century and in exceptional cases even into the 20th. New confessionals were constructed in some Lutheran churches into the 20th century. Walter Uhsadel, *Evangelische Beichte in Vergangenheit und Gegenwart* (Gütersloh: Gerd Mohn, 1961), p. 31.

124. Graff, II: 284.

125. Not much can be said for the use of the question and answer form of confession contained in *The Lutheran Hymnal* (1941), p. 48, with its legalistic, hammer-blow effect of "Verily, you should confess," etc., following the penitent's affirmative answer to each question posed by the confessor, or pastor. This form, evidently included for the sake of variety, was borrowed from the Slovak *Agende, to jest Prace Cirkevni Knezi Cirkve Evangelicke Die Augspurskeho Vyzani Ceskoslovenske* (V Turcianskom Sv. Martine: tlacou knihtlaciarskeho spolku, 1922), pp. 152–153. It is also contained in *Cithara Sanctorum, Pisne Duchovini* (Tranoscius), 2d American ed. (Pittsburgh: Slavia Printing Company, 1928), pp. 27–28.

126. Graff, II: 286.

127. C. Mahrenholz, "Begleitwort zu den Ordnungen der Beichte," *Musicologica et Liturgica*, p. 500.

128. Notes on the Liturgy, *Lutheran Worship: Altar Book*, p. 33.

129. The influence of Pietism and Rationalism reduced such Communion Sundays to rather rare occasions; three to four times a year was deemed sufficient.

130. While confession and absolution has essentially been concerned with the reconciliation of the individual penitent to God and the church, consideration might be given—should the need arise—to adapting this service for the reconciliation of groups or individuals in the congregation who are at odds with one another. This, as Luther states, would be using the Gospel, "which

offers counsel and help against sin in more than one way . . . through the mutual conversation and consolation of the brethern, Matt. 18:20, 'Where two or three are gathered,' etc." (SA III, IV; BSLK, p. 449). In this circumstance it is suggested that the congregation's worship committee, which includes lay people, be involved in planning the service. Another hymn and appropriate Scripture readings might be added; the *Confiteor* form (the right column) in Compline (LW, p. 264) might be used in a reciprocal manner, each group confessing in turn, with the other group giving the optative absolution. Should more be demanded or desired in this process, the pastor might write a special confession, using this form as a model. For further help in dealing with and in the possible structuring of a rite for the reconciliation of groups see Dennis J. Woods, "Reconciliation of Groups," pp. 33–43, and Peter E. Fink and Dennis J. Woods, "Liturgy for the Reconciliation of Groups" in Peter E. Fink, ed., *Alternative Futures for Worship*, vol. 4, *Reconciliation* (Collegeville, MN: The Liturgical Press, 1987), pp. 147–165. Finally, should the reconciliation of two groups or individuals constitute the burden of this service, the pastor, at an appropriate place, should make the circumstances known to those assembled.

Incidentally, the type of *Confiteor* here alluded to became part of Prime and Compline as early as the 10th or 11th centuries. For the relationship between forgiveness and the canonical hours cf. V. Fiala, "Die Sündenvergebung und das lateinische Stundengebet," in *Liturgie et Remission des Peches*, pp. 97–114. This is a collection of 17 papers delivered during the "Twentieth Week of Liturgical Studies, Conferences of St. Serge" held in Paris in 1973. "Liturgy and the Forgiveness of Sins" was the theme of the conference.

131. For instructions in signing oneself see Notes on the Liturgy, *Lutheran Worship: Altar Book*, pp. 26–27.

132. Consult the notes on the Psalms in Notes on the Liturgy, ibid., p. 17.

133. This exhortation, ascribed to Veit Dietrich (1506–49), a colleague of Luther, one-time pastor in Nürnberg, appeared in a number of the better 16th-century church orders, where it often preceded the Words of Institution. The *Evangelical Lutheran Hymn-Book* (1912), predecessor to *The Lutheran Hymnal* (1941), included it as an option immediately before the Lord's Prayer and the Words of Institution in The Order of Morning Service, or the Communion. The latter hymnal included it only in the Confessional Service (p. 47). For the writing of this liturgical piece Dietrich may have taken his cue from Luther, who included an Admonition to Communicants in his German Mass (*Deutsche Messe*) of 1526. For the text of Luther's Admonition see Divine Service III in LW, pp. 197–198.

134. GW 7: 1.

135. In describing themselves as "miserable" (the translation of the German adjective *elender*), the penitents are making an objective statement of their sinful condition, not necessarily their feelings.

136. Ap XIII, 4; BSLK, p. 292.

137. AC XXV, 3ff.; BSLK, p. 98. Cf. also Ap XI, 2; BSLK, p. 249. Asmussen is of the opinion that focusing confession on "terrified consciences" contributed to the disuse of private confession and absolution in the Lutheran Church. In actual practice, he insists, confession must also be concerned with consciences that

are not terrified. Hans Asmussen, *Warum noch Lutherische Kirche?* (Stuttgart: Evangelisches Verlagswerk, 1949), p. 158.

138. Merseburg (1544) explicitly describes this ceremony as a visible expression of forgiveness to the penitent. Emil Sehling, ed., *Die evangelische Kirchenordnungen des XVI. Jahrhunderts*, vols. I–V (Leipzig: O. R. Reidand, 1902–13), vols. VI–XII (Tübingen: J. C. B. Mohr, 1955–63), II: 18. Schwarzburg (1587) makes a point of stating that absolution with the laying on of hands is to be pronounced individually to each person, and it forbids group absolutions. Sehling, II: 126.

139. Josef Jungmann, *Missarum Sollemnia*, 2 vols. (Wien: Herder. 1949), I: 100, n. 18, points out that this term carries the meaning similar to the English "to apologize." For a study of the eucharistic *apologiae* see Adrian Nocent, "Les Apologies dans la celebration eucharistique," in *Liturgie et Remmission des Peches*, pp. 179–196.

140. For a ready recourse to the full English texts see Luther D. Reed, *The Lutheran Liturgy*, rev. ed. (Philadelphia: Muhlenberg Press, 1959), pp. 693–696. The liturgical reforms of Vatican Council II (1962–65) turned the priest's *Preparatio ad missam* into a penitential act of the congregation containing various options in dialog between priest and people.

141. It is out of this environment and history that the various agendas of the Lutheran territorial churches in Germany include a *Predigtgottesdienst* (Preaching Service) in contrast to the *Hauptgottesdienst* (Chief Service), which includes both sermon and Holy Communion.

142. The early practice in the Missouri Synod of the pastor conducting the General Confession, General Prayer, and Lord's Prayer from the pulpit harks back to the custom in the Prone. Cf. *Kirchen-Agende* (1856), pp. 30–31.

143. Cf. Bernard Klaus, "Die Rüstgebete," *Leiturgia: Handbuch des Evangelischen Gottesdienstes*, ed. Karl Ferdinand Mueller and Walter Blankenburg (Kassel: Johannes Stauda Verlag, 1955), II: 534. This article gives an excellent overview of this subject. See also L. Veneser, "Bewertung der Generalabsolution im Lichte der Buszgeschichte," in *Studie moralia* 15 (1977): 469–482; and A. Heinz, "Die deutsche Sondertradition für einen Buszritus der Gemeinde in der Messe," in *Liturgisches Jahrbuch* 28(1978): 193–214.

144. Georg Rietschel, *Lehrbuch der Liturgik*, Zweite neubearbeitete Auflage von Paul Graff, 2 vols. (Göttingen: Vandenhoeck & Rupprecht, 1951), I: 318.

145. Eberhard Weismann, "Der Predigtgottesdienst und die verwandten Formen," *Leiturgia* III: 21.

146. Pastors in Wittenberg continued to use the customary Roman Confiteor for some time. Cf. L. Fendt, *Der lutherische Gottesdienst des 16. Jahrhunderts* (München: Reinhardt, 1923), p. 192.

147. WA 12: 216; AE 53: 34.

148. WA 12: 213; AE 53: 28–29.

149. WA 19: 96; AE 53: 80.

150. WA 19: 97; AE 53: 80.

151. Lack of clarity regarding especially the absolution in *Offene Schuld* precipitated a long struggle in Nürnberg that involved its city council, Andreas Osian-

der (1498–1552) and Johann Brenz (1499–1570), Luther and Melanchthon, and other members of the Wittenberg theological faculty. Cf. *Leiturgia* II: 553–555.

152. Cf. Visitation Articles of Saxony (1533): "Nach der predigt mag man die offen Schuldt auf der Canzel kurz und rein samt der absolution sprechen und Furbitt für all Stende und nott, und sonderlich die vorhanden und augen, und das Vater unser und vermanung zum hochwirdigen Sacrament," Aemelius L. Richter, ed., *Die evangelischen Kirchenordnungen des sechszehnten Jahrhunderts*, 2 vols. (Weimar: Landindustriecomptoir, 1846), I: 229. Similarly Celle (1545), Sehling, I: 297ff.; Herpf (1566), Sehling, II: 335; Meiningen (1566), Sehling, II: 340. Aschersleben (1575) stipulates that on ordinary Sundays a general confession and absolution is to be used after the sermon. On the eve of Christmas, Easter, and Pentecost, however, private confession is heard. Sehling, II: 476.

153. WA 12: 205–220; AE 53: 34.

154. Cf. Brandenburg-Nürnberg (1533), Sehling, XI: 186; Mark Brandenburg (1540, 1572), Sehling, III: 50, 96; Schleswig-Holstein (1542), Richter, I: 355; Pfalz-Neuberg (1543), Richter II: 27.

155. Cf. Nürnberg (1524), Sehling, XI: 39f.; Döber (1525), Sehling, XI: 51; Naumberg (1537), Sehling, II: 78; Mecklenburg (1540, 1552), Sehling, V: 175, Richter, II: 122.

156. Cf. Schwäbisch-Hall (1543): 1 Tim. 1:15; Schaumburg (1514): John 3:16.

157. Mahrenholz, p. 507.

158. This is not to overlook the statements in the Syrian *Didache* (c. 100): "In the church (*ekklesia*) you shall confess (*exomologese*) your sins, and you shall not betake yourself to prayer with an evil conscience" (IV,14); and "But on the Lord's Day assemble, break bread and give thanks, having confessed your sins in order that your sacrifice may be pure" (XIV,1). Cf. Hans Lietzmann, *Die Didache mit kritischen Apparat*, sechste Auflage (Berlin: Verlag Walter de Gruyter, 1962), pp. 8, 13. The fact that the *Didache* gives no formula for such a confession of sins or anything that resembles a *confiteor*, or preparation prayer, has evoked considerable discussion. Cf. Rietschel, *Lehrbuch der Liturgik*, p. 792; C. F. Vokes, *The Riddle of the Didache* (London: Society for Promoting Christian Knowledge, 1938), p. 205; R. C. Mortimer, *The Origins of Private Penance* (Oxford: Clarendon Press, 1939), p. 4, n. 7; G. Rauschen, *Eucharistie und Bussakrament in den ersten sechs Jahrhunderten der Kirche* (Freiburg im Breisgau: Herdersche Verlagshandlung, 1910), p. 215; Poschmann, *Penance and the Anointing of the Sick*, p. 17; Palmer, *Sacraments and Forgiveness*, p. 12.

159. Mahrenholz, pp. 515–516; cf. Rietschel-Graff, p. 793. It is interesting to note that also in the Reformed church voices have been raised in favor of this distinction. Cf. Julius Schweitzer, "The Elements of Liturgy," *Ways of Worship* (New York: Harper Brothers, 1951), p. 131.

160. *Concilium Lateranense* IV, Canon 21, Johannes Dominicus Mansi, ed., *Sacrorum conciliorum nova et amplissima collectio*, 31 vols. (Paris: Hubertus Welter, 1901–27), 22: 1008.

161. Admittedly the unofficial practice of *Offene Schuld* made a connection, limited in use to the Frankish kingdom of the Western Church.

162. Palmer, *Sacraments and Forgiveness*, p. 197.

163. Council of Trier (1227), Canon 3, Mansi, XXIII: 27ff.; Synod of Toulouse (1229), Mansi, XIII: 197; Synod of Münster (1279), Canon 13, Mansi, XXIV: 316; Synod of Canterbury (1236), Mansi, XXIII: 421; Synod of Lambeth (1282), Mansi, XXIV: 406. Concern for the penitent is also expressed in the Lateran Council's decree regarding the seal of confession. The priest who dares to reveal a sin "uncovered in the tribunal of penance is not only to be deposed from his priestly office but also to be shut up in a closed monastery to do perpetual penance." Canon 21, Mansi, XXII: 1010.

164. WA 12: 205; AE 53: 34. Cf. also WA 8: 170, 173; WA 6: 159–160; WA 15: 485; WA 8: 157.

165. Maundy Thursday sermon, WA 12: 493; Palm Sunday sermon (1524), WA 15: 187, 486; WA 17^1: 177 (1525); WA 30^3: 569 (1533); WA 8: 166.

166. Private absolution is the individual application of the Gospel. Refusal to make use of the private confession is tantamount to refusing to hear the Gospel, WA 15: 486; despising confession leads to the conclusion that "you are no Christian and that you ought not receive the sacrament." "Eine Kurze Vermahnung zu der Beicht," BSLK, p. 731; "When I urge you to go to confession, I am simply urging you to be a Christian," ibid., p. 732. In the Smalcald Articles (1537) Luther says, "Since absolution or the power of the keys, which was instituted by Christ in the Gospel, is a consolation and help against sin and a bad conscience, confession and absolution should by no means be allowed to fall into disuse in the church. SA III, VIII, 1; BSLK, p. 453.

167. WA 12: 479.

168. Ibid., 476–493.

169. *Formula Missae* (1523), WA 12: 215, 29ff.; AE 53: 33.

170. WA 26: 216, 20ff.

171. Klaus Harms, *Die gottesdienstliche Beichte als Abendmahls-vorbereitung in der evangelischen Kirche, ihre Geschichte und Gestalt* (Greifswald: Bamberg Verlag, 1930), pp. 46ff. Cf. Also Kurt Aland, "Die Privatbeichte im Luthertum von ihren Anfängen bis zu ihrer Auflösung," *Kirchengeschichtliche Entwürfe* (Gütersloh: Gerd Mohn, 1960), p. 466.

172. AC XXV, 1; BSLK, p. 97 (emphasis by author). The form of the confession in the Small Catechism, however, indicates that Luther is referring to private confession in the strict sense and not to the examination type (*Glaubensverhör*). Still, in the preface of this book he laments the general ignorance of both priests and people in spiritual matters, insisting that the refusal to learn the contents of the same should result in the exclusion from Holy Communion. BSLK, pp. 501–503.

173. The possibility must, however, be conceded that confession was not consistently coupled to Holy Communion and that it could be made without subsequent reception of the body and blood of Christ. On the other hand, one should not receive the same without prior confession. Examples of the former occur infrequently, as for instance, "wie und wie oft das [Beichten] geschieht, ehe er wille zum Sakrament gehen oder sonst." Brandenburg (1540), Sehling, III: 60.

174. Taft, *Studia Liturgica* 18/1 (1988): 15.

175. Sehling, I: 162; cf. also Constitution of the Consistorium at Wittenberg (1542), Sehling, I: 202, and Klein, p. 165.

176. Cf., for example, the order for Albertine Saxony (1539), Sehling, I: 268ff.
177. Notes on the Liturgy, p. 26.

11

Confirmation

Donald L. Deffner

Lutheran Worship: Altar Book states,

> Confirmation is a public rite of the Church that is preceeded by a period of instruction designed to help baptized Christians identify with the life and mission of the Christian community.

> Having been instructed in the Christian faith prior to admission to the Lord's Supper (1 Corinthians 11:28), the rite of Confirmation provides an opportunity for the individual Christian, relying on God's promise of Holy Baptism, to make a personal public confession of the faith and a lifelong pledge of fidelity to Christ.[1]

In practice, however, confirmation day has often become "graduation day." The confirmands may even line up on the chancel steps wearing gowns, just as in a graduation ceremony. Some may feel they now have their spiritual bags packed for the trip of life. Or a couple is heard to say that when their child is confirmed, they will stop attending church. A workman who has not been to church in years tells a pastor, "Oh, don't get me wrong. I remember my confirmation." He may "remember" it noetically, up in his head. But the sheer facts of memory have no effect in his daily life, which is absolutely devoid of worship, the sacraments, Bible reading, and prayer.

That man is typical of hundreds of thousands of people who have been confirmed in Lutheran churches, but who have fallen away from "the faith once delivered to the saints." At times we have lost up to 50 percent of our youth in the church within four years after confirmation.

How Came We Here?

To implement fully the *Altar Book* rubric noted above, a continual rethinking of what confirmation is all about is needed. Martin Luther is again of help here. When he discovered the religious ignorance of his day (many priests didn't even know the Lord's Prayer), he wrote the Small Catechism. It was for the father in the home to teach his children—not for the pastor to teach the youth as is thought today. There he stressed a proper understanding of Baptism. In his other writings he attacked the evils of confirmation as it was practised then. He called it "monkey business" (*Affenspiel*), "a fraud" (*Lügentand*), and "a humbug" (*Gaukelspiel*).[2] He was against anything that gave the impression that somehow confirmation "completes" Baptism.

That false view persists in this century. As recently as 1971 Lutheran theologian Frank Senn took such a position. In strong opposition to a Joint Commission study on confirmation authorized by three American Lutheran church bodies,[3] he defined confirmation in ritual terms, as a rite of the Christian Church which formally bestows the *charisma* of the Spirit upon the baptized through the process of laying on of hands, and that "confirmation is a necessary completion of baptism, and that baptism and confirmation together form a unitary sacrament of initiation into the body of Christ which is manifested in the Eucharist."[4]

In making this statement Senn reasserted the formula that Baptism plus confirmation equals admission to Holy Communion. Although Senn's position was not typical of the mainstream of Lutheran theologians' thinking, it demonstrated that the "completion" idea is still evident today.

Another noted Lutheran theologian used this illustration at a pan-Lutheran worship institute in the early 1970s. It was a view, he said, which he had taught "all his life": "When you were baptized a check was made out in your name to eternal life. On your confirmation day you cashed the check." But that unbiblical view of confirmation denigrates our *Baptism*, which is the time God bestowed his grace on us, and we received his gracious gift of eternal life. God's bank did not hold up the check and delay its cashing until our confirmation day. The Holy Scriptures assert: "You are all sons of God through faith in Christ Jesus, for all of you who were baptized into Christ have been clothed with Christ" (Gal. 3:26–27); "Baptism . . . now saves you" (1 Pet. 3:27); and "He saved us through the washing of rebirth" (Titus 3:5b).

In sum, erroneous ideas still persist at the present time with respect to the relation of Baptism to confirmation—as they did in Luther's day.

Historical Background

In medieval times confirmation was considered a complement of Baptism. It was viewed as giving the Christian the added gift of the Holy Spirit, and later as necessary for salvation. Luther rejected this, viewing any abridgment of Holy Baptism as blasphemous. Similarly the Augsburg Confession by implication rejected the Roman view. Arthur Repp, in his scholarly, hallmark study states,

> The Apology rejected it directly because it lacked God's express command and clear promise of grace. Veit Dietrich's (1506–49) German translation of Phillip Melanchthon's Treatise on the Power and Primacy of the Pope (1537) inserted one of Luther's invectives, "humbug," in rejecting this rite.[5]

Five main types of confirmation appeared in the Lutheran Church in subsequent centuries. They were (1) a catechetical (preparation for the Lord's Supper); (2) the hierarchical (surrender to Christ and a vow of obedience to the church); (3) the sacramental (combining Lutheran and Roman Catholic elements); (4) the pietistic (stressing a conversion experience with instruction secondary); and (5) the rationalistic (emphasis on the examination, instruction in civic duties, and rampant sentimentalism).[6] Repp concludes that there are only three essential elements in confirmation: (1) instruction in the Word, (2) the confession of faith, and (3) the intercession of the congregation in behalf of the catechumen.[7]

The question we must ask a generation later is whether there is still a tendency to exaggerate the importance of confirmation and whether instead the Christian's baptism and first communion are highlighted appropriately enough; for any overemphasis of confirmation is made at the expense of God's grace. The issue is whether our current practice of confirmation tends toward terminal instruction and still gives the impression that Baptism is being "completed" or "confirmed."[8]

In the 1960s, at the invitation of the Lutheran Church in America, the American Lutheran Church and The Lutheran Church—Missouri Synod agreed to participate in a joint study of the theology and practice of confirmation. In 1966 a Joint Commission undertook a survey, *Current Concepts and Practices of Confirmation in Lutheran Churches*. In December 1967 the Joint Commission completed a *Report for Study* and recommended to the presidents of the respective church bodies that they provide for authorization of a churchwide program of study to be carried out under the direction of the Boards of Parish Education in 1969.

In January 1969 the three church bodies separately initiated efforts to provide every pastor with a copy of *Confirmation and First Communion*. On the basis of reports received from 86,000 participants, the Joint Commission prepared *A Report on the Study of Confirmation and First Communion by Lutheran Congregations.*[9]

In its report to the Synod's 1971 convention, the Commission on Theology and Church Relations of the Synod, entrusted with the task of evaluating the *Report of the Joint Commission*, presented the following as significant arguments in that *Report*:

1. Baptism "gives the sinner a new relationship with the church. It makes him fully a member of the church (1 Cor. 12:13). It gives him the gift of the Holy Spirit (Titus 3:5). . . . It is therefore theologically indefensible to give a confirmation rite a meaning whereby it is elevated to a position in which it either complements or supplements the sacrament of Holy Baptism" (pp. 509–510).

2. "Further, the apostolic teaching of 1 Cor. 11:28 makes it incumbent upon the church to exercise its pastoral concern for its growing members to help them prepare for a meaningful participation in the Lord's Supper, each at his own level of development. . . . To receive Holy Communion without understanding would be to perform a meaningless act that would contribute nothing to the process of growth" (p. 510).

3. A definition of confirmation: "Confirmation is a pastoral and educational activity of the church which helps the baptized child through Word and Sacrament to identify more deeply with the Christian community and participate more fully in its mission" (p. 512).

   a. "This ministry comes to a close in middle adolescence, at about the time the young person turns toward adult interest, activities, and aspirations" (p. 512). Later the *Report* indicates that this stage is reached at grade 10.

b. "Participation in Holy Communion is thought of here as a part of confirmation ministry, a means of strengthening, rather than as a goal toward which the entire confirmation process points. In this way Holy Communion is an aid in the development of the child, rather than a privilege granted upon completion of a required course of study prescribed by the church" (p. 512–513). The *Report* argues that most persons are sociologically, educationally, and psychologically ready to receive the Lord's Supper at the fifth-grade level.[10]

Moreover, in response to the Joint Commission's *Report* the Commission on Theology and Church Relations noted the *Report's* sensitivity to "anything in the present rite of confirmation which appears to complement or supplement Holy Baptism (e.g., 'Upon these your voluntary professions and promises, I welcome you as members of the Evangelical Lutheran Church. . .') . . . [It also encouraged a reexamination of] the form for the rite of confirmation as found in the *Agenda*, with particular attention to any statements which appear to detract from the significance of Holy Baptism."[11]

The Commission on Theology and Church Relations stated that the Synod's present practice "has proved to be unifying and meaningful to the child and to the church," namely, "allowing for the child's spiritual maturation and readiness beyond the fifth-grade level with concentrated instruction in those years as better equipping the child to 'examine oneself.' " It expressed the concern that few children might avail themselves of opportunities for a period of intensified religious instruction if confirmation and first communion were separated, and, citing uniformity in practice as an objective of the Synod, it encouraged retention of its present emphasis on the values of combining confirmation and first communion.[12]

Synodical Resolution 2–47 urged congregations to study their present practice and view the recommendations of the Commission on Theology and Church Relations and the Joint Commission as "guides in the fulfillment of this responsibility."[13]

A tension, however, still remains between the substance of those conclusions and what is *historically Lutheran*. This is significant, particularly with respect to the need to commune children "of comparatively tender years" as Luther urged. Friedrich Bente notes,

> Luther was accustomed to direct his admonition to partake of the Lord's Supper diligently also to children, and that, too, to children of comparatively tender years. In his sermon of March 25, 1520, he says: "This exhortation ought not only to move us older ones, but also the young and the children. Therefore you parents ought to instruct and educate them in the doctrine of the Lord: the Decalog, the Creed, the Prayer, and the Sacraments. Such children ought also to be admitted to the Table that they may be partakers" [of the Lord's Supper]. (W.30,1,233.) In [Luther's] sermon of December 19, 1528, we read, "Hence, you parents and heads of families, invite your subordinates to this Sacrament; and we shall demand an account of you if you neglect it. If you will not go yourselves, let the young go; we are much concerned about them. When they come, we shall learn, by examining them, how you instruct them in the Word as prescribed. Hence, do come more frequently to the Sacrament, and also admonish your children to do so when they have reached the age of discretion. For in this way we want to learn who are Christians, and who not. If you will not do so, we shall speak to you on the subject. For even though you older people insist on going to the devil, we shall still inquire about your children. Necessity: because sin, the devil, and death are ever present. Benefit: because the remission of sins and the Holy Spirit are received." (121 f.) The tender age at which the young are held to partake of the Lord's Super appears from Bugenhagen's preface to the Danish edition of the Enchiridion of 1538, where he says "that after this confession is made, also the little children of about eight years or less should be admitted to the table of Him who says: "Suffer the little children to come unto Me." (433.)[14]

In parishes of the Evangelical Lutheran Church in America today this stance of Luther, Bugenhagen, and the other Reformers has been taken so seriously that many parishes now commune children earlier than they did a generation ago. In the Pacific Northwest some congregations offer first communion to children several years before age ten.

The practice has come about as a direct result of the study and recommendations of the Joint Commission cited earlier. Its dramatic effect in changing attitudes and practices of confirmation in many

Lutheran congregations is summarized by Douglas J. Adams in his doctoral study, "An Intergenerational Model for Confirmation Decision-Making in the Parish." There he cites the conclusions of 11 church leaders he interviewed from three Lutheran church bodies, each of which is a professional occupying a position involving the evaluation of national church life and trends. These are their conclusions:

> All respondents believed that the immediate impact of the report was a dramatic increase in the practice of fifth grade Communion. Before the report the practice was essentially nonexistent and by 1986 the percentage of congregations in the ALC and LCA communing in the fifth grade was approximately 55 percent, rising to about 70 percent for communion before the rite of Confirmation. The LCMS figures are approximately 20 percent and 25 percent respectively. The reason mentioned for such a sudden and pervasive change in tradition in the ALC and the LCA was the solid theological rationale developed by the Joint Commission combined with an effective nationally organized information dissemination program. The lack of such an official effort to endorse the concept on the part of the LCMS was one reason given by respondents to explain that church's lower percentages.[15]

The Lutheran Church—Missouri Synod may wish to reconsider its present practice both in light of the *ongoing* "confirmation complex" of apparent "graduation," and the historic Lutheran practice of communing those "of comparative tender years."

Further, we should ask whether the Sacrament of Baptism is given proper place in our people's thinking in contrast to confirmation. The frequency of the baptismal rite in a service may lead to a "just-another-baptism" type of thinking, and the worshiper may not vividly recall the blessings of his *own* baptism. *Confirmation Day* on the other hand may continue as a significant event in the minds of many people, coming as it does at the end of a period of intensive instruction and the hallowed moment of first communion. And the primary and sacramental significance of Baptism may be only tangential in the minds of people in a confirmation service.

The Key to Understanding *Confirmation:* Baptism

The Joint Commission affirmed that Baptism makes one fully a member of the church and that "it is therefore theologically indefensible to give a confirmation rite a meaning whereby it is elevated to a position in which it either complements or supplements the sacrament of Holy Baptism."[16]

The invocation at the beginning of the rite of confirmation, for example, is not only a reference to the Trinity. It is a recalling of the Father, Son, and Holy Spirit in whose holy name we were baptized. In Baptism, we were made members of the church, of the one holy, catholic, and apostolic church. There is only one kind of member in the church—a *baptized* member. (There is actually no such thing as an "inactive member.") Our baptismal covenant is unilateral. It is totally God at work in us (Phil. 2:13). We cannot even wiggle our little finger to come to God. "You did not choose me, but I chose you to go out and bear fruit" (John 15:16). "For it is by grace you have been saved, through faith—and this not from yourselves, it is the gift of God—not by works, so that no one can boast" (Eph. 2:8–9).

Accordingly no wording about the "renewal" of the baptismal vow appears in the confirmation rite in *Lutheran Worship.* Renewal is a fine word, but it gives a false impression if used in confirmation. We cannot renew that which is totally God's act. We cannot cooperate with God and somehow complete that which is totally *his* work in us. True, we are called to a life of good works (Matt. 5:16). But they are the fruit of the Holy Spirit's work in us (Galatians 5 and 6). Whatever good we do is not of our own doing. It is God at work in us. As Paul says, it is "Christ in me," a phrase he uses 32 times in the New Testament. Any "confirmation" then can only be understood in relation to a sound doctrine and practice of Holy Baptism.

But we have often lost the "breadth and length and height and depth" of our baptismal grace and its blessing. Rather, it should be living and active in our lives, for it is a dynamic, a power. Our daily affirmation of it should lead us up to Calvary, nail us to the cross, make us die with Christ, put us under cover of the earth, and bring us forth again into newness of life[17]—as we recall that "all of us who were baptized into Christ were baptized into his death . . . that, just

394

as Christ was raised from the dead through the glory of the Father, we too may live a new life" (Rom. 6:3–4).

Further, the contemplation of our Baptism may be a far more meaningful reminder of our salvation than some other theological concepts.[18] As Robert C. Schultz suggests,

> The pictures which Scripture uses to describe baptism are readily understandable and within the common framework of experience. It is the ship which saves us from being drowned in the flood. It is a washing. It is a being born again to life. . . . The latter should be particularly meaningful to a society in which adoption is as popular as it is today. Even the younger children can understand what it means to be an orphan; and they can appreciate the new life which the orphan receives when it is adopted.[19]

We need to learn anew the blessings of a baptism daily affirmed, and repeat the hymn,

> With one accord, O God, we pray;
> Grant us your Holy Spirit;
> Help us in our infirmity
> Through Jesus' blood and merit;
> Grant us to grow in grace each day
> By holy Baptism that we may
> Eternal life inherit. (LW 225, st. 2)

In sum, our preaching and teaching on the place of Baptism in people's lives must be emphasized more forcefully and practically. And any confirmation rite we use should be administered only in proper relation to this blessed Sacrament "that now saves" us (1 Pet. 3:21).

The Confirmation Rite

The Prospectus given the writers of this volume stated:

> As important as a mastery of details is, more important is the development of an attitude, understanding, a spirit with respect to corporate worship as a whole.

This is also crucial with respect to our understanding of the rite of confirmation in relation to Baptism. As noted, confirmation is only an episode, the stage along the way, a progress report in the Christian's walk of sanctification. However, many people over the years have attached far greater significance to the rite, including the misguided concept that at confirmation the individual is "joining the church." Accordingly we are dealing not only with what is intended in the rite of confirmation (*Lutheran Worship*, pp. 205–207), but what preconceived ideas people are bringing to the ceremony.

In the minister's address to the catechumens, the Great Commission is recalled, noting that our Lord commanded us both to baptize and to teach. The minister then says:

> **P** *You have been baptized and you have been taught the faith according to our Lord's bidding. The fulfillment of his bidding we now celebrate with thankful hearts.*

The focus here is celebration that the two parts of our Lord's mandate have been fulfilled: baptize and teach. This is not a private matter; it is acknowledged "in the presence of God and this congregation."

But care must be taken here that the impression not be conveyed that something was *not* fulfilled at the time of baptism in that grace was delayed *until this point*, that the "washing of regeneration" was incomplete until *this* rite of confirmation transpired.

Following the affirmation of the Apostles' Creed the confirmand is asked,

> **P** *Do you desire to be a member of the Evangelical Lutheran Church and of this congregation?*

Given the history of misunderstanding about when one becomes a member of the church, and people thinking for generations that they "joined the church" when they were confirmed, an explanation is in order.

The question must be understood against the background that at Baptism the child was made a member of Christ's church, the Una Sancta, or as previously mentioned, a member of the one holy, catholic, and apostolic church. While it is significant to note that no denominational loyalty is alluded to in the rite of Holy Baptism (*Lutheran Worship*, pp. 199–204)—something that would vitiate the unity of the body of Christ, a unity that Holy Baptism certainly attests—[20]when a child is baptized in a Lutheran Church it nevertheless becomes a baptized member of that congregation; both congregation and pastor assume a spiritual responsibility for that child. Rightly does Arthur Repp state, "Membership in a local congregation has meaning and validity in the sight of God only because it is derived from membership in the holy Christian church."[21] Previously in this rite of confirmation, it will be recalled, after confessing his or her faith in the words of the Apostles' Creed, expressing belief in the "holy Christian church," the confirmand was asked,

> **P** *Do you intend to remain steadfast in this confession and church [the Una Sancta], and to suffer all, even death, rather than fall away from it?*

Now, having been instructed in the Christian faith and having arrived at the age of discretion and an understanding of the covenant God made with him or her in Holy Baptism, the confirmand is asked, Do you desire to be a member of the Evangelical Lutheran Church and of this congregation? The emphasis here is on desire to *be*, not desire to *become*. The question calls for a personal commitment of membership in the Lutheran Church, evoking a sense of identification with the local congregation and an intentional and fuller participation in its worship and ministry. It is not to imply that one becomes a member of the Christian church by Baptism and a member of the Lutheran Church or of a local congregation by confirmation! Apparently the Synod's fathers construed the question thus, for the question is verbatim from *The Lutheran Agenda* (1948), predecessor to *Lutheran Worship: Agenda* (1984); it is also included in earlier editions of these official books,[22] even as far back as the *Kirchen-Agende* (1856), the first *Agende* produced and published by the Synod.

Admittedly, long held traditional thinking about *when* one becomes a member of the church is slow to die, especially when it is kept in sentimental, almost sacred memory: *my confirmation day.* As Von Schenk says, "It is easier to change a doctrine than a tradition."[23]

The point of practicing one's Christian life *in the church* is also of deep significance. One cannot go on being a Christian unlocatedly. Christianity is not a "solo trip." One is not a "theological butterfly," flitting here and there, but a member of a local parish.

Then, after the laying on of hands, the pastor says

P *[Name], God, the Father of our Lord Jesus Christ, give you his Holy Spirit, the Spirit of wisdom and knowledge, . . . of sanctification and the fear of God.*

We pray this again and again, and such wording need not imply that we are now calling for the Spirit for the first time. (Arthur C. Repp notes the medieval idea was that Baptism was intended for the forgiveness of sins and confirmation for the bestowal of the Holy Spirit).[24]

Finally, after the blessing the minister says,

P *Upon this your profession and promise I invite and welcome you, as members of the Evangelical Lutheran Church and this congregation.*

Here again the idea should not be transmitted that they are only *now becoming* members of the Body of Christ, and only *now* receiving the gift of grace God gave them long ago in Baptism. Nor should the words "upon this your profession" intimate that their *profession* makes the gifts possible. Careful instruction beforehand about Baptism, confirmation, and the meaning of *member* as well as clarification made in the sermon will hopefully obviate the possibility of any misunderstandings.

Confirmation day is a day of joy, to be sure, as confirmands confess their Christian faith in their own words before the congregation. And it is a time of celebration as they *affirm* another step along the way of their Christian walk, nurtured by God's holy Word and the sacraments.[25]

But the rite of confirmation is seen only in the light of a sound doctrine and practice of the Sacrament of Holy Baptism. *Every day*, as Luther said, the Old Adam is to be drowned again in the water of baptism and brought forth to newness of life (Rom. 6:3–4) with the precious forgiveness of sins which our Lord bought for us by his suffering and death on the cross. Thank God, "His mercies are new every morning" (Lam. 3:23).

God the Holy Spirit will *confirm* in us that growth in grace which we sinners are unable to effect, but which he has done *for us* through his blessed Son and bestowed on us in our Baptism.

Notes

1. *Lutheran Worship: Altar Book*, prepared by the Commission on Worship of The Lutheran Church—Missouri Synod (St. Louis: Concordia Publishing House, 1982), p. 33.

2. Arthur C. Repp, "Reconstructing Confirmation for Our Day," Proceedings of the Western District of The Lutheran Church—Missouri Synod, 1961, p. 27.

3. See "Recent Developments of Confirmation in the Lutheran Church in the United States," in Douglas J. Adams, "An Intergenerational Model for Confirmation Decision-Making in the Parish" (unpublished D.Min. diss., San Francisco Theological Seminary, San Anselmo, California, 1988), ch. 1.

4. Frank Senn, "Confirmation and First Communion: A Reappraisal," *Lutheran Quarterly* 23 (May 1971): 179.

5. Arthur C. Repp, *Confirmation in the Lutheran Church* (St. Louis: Concordia Publishing House, 1964), p. 16.

6. Ibid., p. 21.

7. Ibid., p. 58.

8. *Lutheran Worship*, prepared by the Commission on Worship of The Lutheran Church—Missouri Synod, 1982, still uses the term *Confirmation* for the rite, p. 205. The *Lutheran Book of Worship*, prepared by the Inter-Lutheran Commission on Worship (Minneapolis: Augsburg Publishing House, 1978), titles the rite *Affirmation of Baptism*, p. 198.

9. Missouri Synod, *Convention Workbook*, 1971, p. 42. The report submitted to the participating church bodies appeared as a reprint in this *Workbook* entitled *Report of the Joint Commission on the Theology and Practice of Confirmation*, pp. 510–515.

10. Ibid., p. 42. Adams states, "The report stressed that a new status be given to the youth in Confirmation and that they be recognized as full members of the church by virtue of baptism. This new status is significant in light of the common practice of many Lutheran churches that tend to relate to their confirmands as secondary members of the community of faith. One of the evidences of this secondary status is the traditional practice of excluding the youth from participation in the decision-making processes about the Confirmation ministry. In a great number of instances the Confirmation program of a congregation is determined solely by the adults of the church with the youth functioning as objects of ministry. The report of the Commission has called this orientation into question and suggested that congregations move from a 'ministry to' mindset to a 'ministry with' mindset in regard to Confirmation and youth involved. Because the Commission was formed to examine and discuss the issues in general terms, each congregation was to explore for itself how to employ the new theological/educational insights and involve the youth in more meaningful ways in the Confirmation process," ch. 1.

11. Ibid., p. 43.

12. Ibid.

13. Missouri Synod, *Proceedings*, 1971, p. 27.

14. Friedrich Bente, *Historical Introduction to the Book of Concord* (St. Louis: Concordia Publishing House, 1965), p. 82. References in parentheses in this long quotation are to WA.

15. Adams, ch. 1.

16. Missouri Synod *Workbook*, 1971, p. 510.

17. Robert K. Menzel, "Messengers of Peace," Preaching-Teaching-Reaching Mission to Ministers, Los Angeles, 1958, sec. 3, p. 3.

18. For example, *justification* in the New Testament means that although we are wholly guilty, by Christ's death and resurrection we are *vindicated* of the penalty for our sin. But in common speech today *justified* means I am guiltless. I am *justified* in going through a red light to take my critically ill wife to the hospital. I wasn't really guilty of breaking a law. This does *not* mean to imply that we eliminate the doctrine of justification in our teaching. But it must be carefully explicated.

19. Robert C. Schulz, "Justification in the 16th and 20th Centuries," The Cresset 20/10 (October 1957): 12–13. We might even have an occasional immersion in our baptismal rite, dramatically to remind us of the "drowning to sin" which is ours through faith in Christ, God's blessed Son.

20. This statement is corroborated by the fact that the Lutheran Church accepts as valid the baptism of other churches provided that such baptism in a given instance was administered according to God's command and promise. Analogously, pastors are not ordained to the ministry of The Lutheran Church—Missouri Synod; they are ordained by the Synod to the ministry of the one holy, catholic and apostolic church.

21. Repp, Confirmation in the Lutheran Church, p. 160.

22. Several early English editions asked the question of the group, "Do you desire to be members of the Evangelical Lutheran Church?"

23. Berthold von Schenk, "Confirmation and First Communion," Una Sancta 14/3 (Pentecost 1957): 3.

24. Repp, "Reconstructing Confirmation for Our Day," p. 27.

25. We affirm our faith in professing the Creed every Sunday in corporate worship. We have couples who reaffirm their marriage vow, or pledge, church officers and teachers who pledge anew their committment to their task each year. Why not have a number of such confirmation/affirmations throughout the Christian's life?

12

The Divine Service

THE PREPARATION: PART I

Charles J. Evanson

Lutheran Worship provides congregations with three forms of the Divine Service, derived from the familiar pattern of the Christian church, as having come particularly through Luther's Latin and German masses and other German and Northern European church orders.

Those who serve as presiding or assisting ministers will want background to the historic shape as well as suggestions for good practice. The suggestions are based on the Notes on the Liturgy in *Lutheran Worship: Altar Book* and grow out of the typical, historic practice of the Evangelical Lutheran Church. They provide a simple usage that will assist all in giving primary attention to the heart of worship, that together Christians may sit with Mary at Jesus' feet and both hear his Word and hearken to it.

Table 3

Comparison of Preparation Rites

DIVINE SERVICE I	DIVINE SERVICE II	DIVINE SERVICE III
Hymn of Invocation	Hymn of Invocation	[There is no preparatory rite in Divine Service III.]
Invocation	Invocation	
Admonition		
	NT Sentences	
OT Versicles		
	Silence	
Confession	Confession	

Absolution *or*   Absolution *or*
Declaration of   Declaration of
Grace   Grace

Hymn of Invocation

It is a choice of the local congregation whether or not a hymn of invocation is sung to begin the Divine Service. The service may begin with the Invocation. This option reflects the preparatory character of the confession of sins. The service proper then begins with the Introit of the Day, the appointed Psalm, or an Entrance Hymn. Moreover, there may be circumstances when the preparation is omitted altogether, as, for instance, when celebrating Holy Baptism immediately after an opening hymn.[1]

The Invocation and Sentences

The invocation of the name of the Father, Son, and Holy Spirit and the use of the sign of the holy cross, words first spoken and marked on us in Baptism, confess that the God upon whom we call is the God who calls his baptized people together by Word and Sacrament. We do not come before him as those who deserve to come because of what we have been or what we have done. We come because he has called us through the Holy Spirit, who calls, gathers, enlightens, and sanctifies the church. The Spirit keeps us in the true faith and unites us to Christ, covering us with his righteousness, innocence, and purity. While non-Christians may be present—and it is hoped that there are such—when we gather for corporate worship, the Divine Service is first and foremost an activity of a Christian congregation, members of which have been joined to their Lord by the work of the Holy Spirit in Baptism. It is by that word that they have been made the new creation, buried with Christ in his death for them and raised again to walk with him in newness of life (Rom. 6:3ff.).

The so-called Preparation in Divine Service I, sometimes called the Confiteor ("I confess"), combines the familiar patterns of The Order of Morning Service without Communion and The Order of Holy Communion as contained in *The Lutheran Hymnal* (1941), except that the texts have been updated. The versicles and their responses, comprised of Ps. 124:8 and Ps. 32:5b respectively, introduce the alternative forms of confession.

THE PREPARATION: PART II

Fred L. Precht

Confession and Absolution

In Divine Service I the first form (left column, pp. 136f.) is from the Saxony church order of 1581,[2] a form included in the *Kirchen-Agende* of 1856, the first official agenda of the Synod; it is followed by the indicative-operative absolution, historically considered sacramental. The second form (right column) is derived chiefly from Melanchthon's church order for Mecklenburg (1545),[3] as later adopted in Wittenberg (1559),[4] the form used in the Common Service of 1888. The expression "we are by nature sinful and unclean," based on Article II,1 of the Augsburg Confession, is unique to Lutheranism in its structuring of various preparatory rites. This confession is followed by the simple declaration of grace.

Interestingly, the *Evangelical Lutheran Hymn-Book* (1912), the first official English hymnal of the Synod, predecessor to *The Lutheran Hymnal* (1941), prescribed this second form of confession with its declaration of grace for The Order of Morning Service or the Communion. Thus it was used for both noncommunion and communion services. The first form ("O almighty God, merciful Father . . . .") found no place in the 1912 hymnal. In preparing and producing *The Lutheran Hymnal*, the Intersynodical Committee on Hymnology and Liturgics of the then Synodical Conference prescribed the first form with its indicative-operative absolution for the Order of Holy Communion, prescribing the Mecklenburg (1545, 1552) form with its simple declaration of grace for the service without Communion.

The preparation in Divine Service II is an altered version of the Brief Order for Confession and Forgiveness on page 77 in *Lutheran*

Book of Worship (1978). Essentially only the statement of 1 John 1:8–9, "If we say we have no sin . . .," the confession, and the declaration of grace is brought into *Lutheran Worship*, with some revisions. The statement of John becomes a versicle and response. The first sentence of the confession, ". . . we confess that we are in bondage to sin and cannot free ourselves," is supplanted by ". . . we confess that we are by nature sinful and unclean." Also inserted is the sentence "We justly deserve your present and eternal punishment." This notable form of confession is neither originally nor wholly the work of the Inter-Lutheran Commission on Worship that prepared *Lutheran Book of Worship*, for it closely resembles the form contained in the *Book of Common Prayer*, where it reads,

> Most merciful God, we confess that we have sinned against you in thought, word, and deed, by what we have done, and by what we have left undone. We have not loved you with our whole heart; we have not loved our neighbors as ourselves. We are truly sorry and we humbly repent. For the sake of your Son Jesus Christ, have mercy on us and forgive us; that we may delight in your will, and walk in your ways, to the glory of your Name. Amen.[5]

To the LBW declaration of grace the Commission on Worship added "May the Lord, who has begun this good work in us, bring it to completion in the day of our Lord Jesus Christ," a volitive statement based on Philippians 1:6.

What might be construed as a more important change by the Commission on Worship is the substitution of an indicative-operative absolution for the declarative form used in *Lutheran Book of Worship*. This declarative form at best should not imply the necessity of a called and ordained minister to pronounce it.

Note in both Divine Service I and Divine Service II the use of the second person pronoun in the indicative-operative absolution, spoken by the presiding minister, which reflects the relationship of confessor versus penitent. In the declaration of grace formula, however, the presiding minister includes himself.

Giving priority of place, so to speak, to the indicative-operative absolution in both Divine Service I and Divine Service II might suggest that the presiding minister use this formula in all services of Holy Communion—a usage contrary to that in the Common Service of 1888 and in the *Evangelical Lutheran Hymn-Book* (1912)—

reserving the declaration of grace for the noncommunion, sometimes called antecommunion, services. For a discussion of this matter the reader should consult chapter 10, General Confession/The Preparation (pp. 364–69).

> *Notes for ministers.* In order to emphasize its preparatory nature,the Preparation should be led by the presiding minister from a place outside the sanctuary, or altar area (in some churches defined by a chancel rail), from the lower level of the chancel, or from the nave level. The Invocation—the act of invoking the blessing of the triune God, in whose name the Christian congregation is gathered—is addressed to God, not to the congregation. The presiding minister will, therefore, position himself accordingly. The signing with the cross connected therewith is a personal signature, and it is appropriate that all join in this act as a remembrance of Holy Baptism and the call to repentance. Lutherans have commonly made this sign differently from Roman Catholics, specifically as to the direction of the last movement. With the palm of the right hand held flat with thumb and fingers together, first the forehead is touched ("My Lord Jesus Christ came down from heaven"), then the breast ("and was incarnate for me"), the right shoulder ("and was crucified for me"), and finally the left shoulder ("and entered into my heart"). Luther recommends the use of this sign in both the Small and the Large Catechism. A brief period of silence may follow the Preparation.

Ministers are reminded that the liturgical texts have been established by and are the property of the church, or denomination. Much thought has gone into them by members entrusted with that task; in many instances the wording represents centuries of Christian usage. Ministers should thus read the texts as they stand in the church's approved books. Adding to or editorializing the texts frequently reflects personal opinion—more homiletical than liturgical—that may better belong in the sermon or Bible class. Moreover, such editorializing disturbs the devotion of the worshipers who are following the texts that are before them.

This writer has observed the tendency on the part of some presiding ministers to add to the indicative-operative form of absolution, following "Holy Spirit" (LW, p. 137, left column; pp. 158, 178–179), a statement such as"As the Lord has forgiven you, forgive one another in the love of Jesus Christ." Although in itself a perfectly good, biblical injunction, this is nevertheless an ill-conceived procedure, specifically since it follows the assuring and comforting indicative-operative absolution; it approximates what might be considered a retention formula. No conditions should be attached to or reflected in this particular absolution formula.

In the past, the pastor who officiated at the Eucharist was often called the "celebrant." Recent understanding, however, of the corporate nature of both the church and its worship considers the congregation as the celebrant, and the priest or pastor as the presider, or presiding minister, not one who celebrates on behalf of or apart from the faithful. Thus, in neither *Lutheran Worship* (1982), *Lutheran Worship: Altar Book* (1982), *Lutheran Worship: Agenda* (1984), nor in *Lutheran Worship: Little Agenda* (1985) does the term celebrant appear.

Pastors are encouraged to teach their congregations the specific services of their choice that are provided in the hymnal for corporate worship so that the given service comes naturally to the worshipers, without their having to give much thought about the sequence. Lengthy explanations prior to the worship should not be the norm, nor should announcing every step of the way— whether to stand, sit or kneel, to sing this or that canticle—for this invariably hinders the flow and dynamic of the service and disrupts the devotion.

Creative worship is not the result of resorting to innovative experiments in the attempt to create a new and improved model that reflects the latest style or fads, a procedure that invariably results in a religious *program* for the approbation of the people. Rather, creative worship comes through using the vast array of options and possibilities for the so-called propers in the Divine Service— even some options for the ordinaries—and selecting appropriate hymns and attendant music—all manifesting and advancing the particular day's importance in the church year. To this end, *Proclaim: A Guide for Planning Liturgy and Music* (see blibiography) can be of inestimable value.

The Synod's so-called Special Emphasis Sundays are best observed by including a special prayer for the occasion in the Prayer of the Church, or The Prayers, and, if considered opportune, by reference in the sermon and/or service folder. To furnish congregations special liturgies for such occasions to supplant the church's customary Divine Service in Word and Sacrament is to ignore the fact that the Lord's Day worship is not to be so compromised as to wipe out the forward march of the church year with its propers in favor of promoting specific programs of the church or exploiting current issues.

THE SERVICE OF THE WORD

Charles J. Evanson

Table 4

Comparison of the Service of the Word

DIVINE SERVICE I	DIVINE SERVICE II	DIVINE SERVICE III
Introit of the Day	Introit of the Day	Introit of the Day
or Psalm	*or* Psalm	*or* Psalm
or Entrance Hymn	*or* Entrance Hymn	*or* Entrance Hymn
Threefold Kyrie	Kyrie (Ektenia)	Kyrie (Hymn)
Gloria in excelsis	Hymn of Praise	Gloria (Hymn)
Collect of the Day	Collect of the Day	Collect of the Day
Old Testament Reading	Old Testament Reading	
Gradual of the Season *or* Psalm	Gradual of the Season *or* Psalm	
Epistle	Epistle	Epistle
Verse *or* Alleluia	Verse	Gradual (Hymn)
Holy Gospel	Holy Gospel	Holy Gospel
Creed		Creed (Hymn)
Hymn of the Day	Hymn of the Day	
Sermon	Sermon	Sermon
	Creed	
	The Prayers	Prayer of the Church
Offering	Offering	Offering
Offertory	Offertory	
Prayer of the Church		

407

Introit

The service begins with the Introit of the Day, the appointed Psalm, or an Entrance Hymn. The Introit (from the Latin *introitus*, entrance) is a psalm or portion of a psalm, preceded and followed by an antiphon that summarizes the theme of the day. Originally the Introit was sung as the ministers entered the church and processed to the altar. The congregation sang the antiphon as a response to each verse of the psalm or to a group of verses. The Gloria Patri serves as a doxology at the end of the psalm verses. Except for Holy Week, it is the practice of the church always to include the Gloria Patri. When an entrance hymn replaces the Introit, it too should point the central theme and give time for the ministers to enter the chancel.

In the *Formula Missae* (1523) Luther has high praise for many of the introits, especially those appointed for Sundays and major festivals, but he suggests that it would be appropriate to sing the whole psalm from which each was taken.[6] *Lutheran Worship* provides for this by appointing a psalm to be used in place of the Introit of the Day. The antiphon from the Introit of the Day may be used with the whole psalm. While space limitations made it impossible to have all the psalms in the "Pew Edition," the complete Psalter, along with the tone appointed for each psalm, is provided in the *Altar Book*.

In most cases *Lutheran Worship* has a single introit for both the one-year and the three-year cycles of readings. When the dominant theme is sufficiently different, a second introit is provided for the three-year series.

Because it is intended that the congregation sing the introit or other psalms, the music is printed with the texts. The presider or a cantor may intone the introit or psalm with the congregation and choir responding in alternation, or the choir may intone it with the congregation alternating, or two groups of worshipers may sing in alternation.

Notes for ministers. During the singing of the Introit the presiding minister and assistants may go to their places in the chancel or to the altar. If they go to their places, they remain standing there until the conclusion of the collect. If they go to the altar, the presiding minister stands in the middle, flanked by the assisting ministers.

Kyrie

The Kyrie Eleison is the first prayer of the Service of the Word. It is the prayer of the gathered congregation. "Kyrie, eleison" is "Lord, have mercy," a prayer encountered frequently in the Scriptures, for example, the Canaanite woman (Matt. 15:22) and the Ten Lepers (Luke 17:13). The biblical and liturgical contexts do not support the thesis that this is a prayer of confession of sins.[7] It is instead a cry for mercy that our Lord and King hear us and help us in our necessities and troubles.

The Kyrie came into the Western mass from the Eastern Church, where it provides the invariable response of the congregation to the petitions introduced by the deacon (assisting minister). The people express their "amen" by praying "Kyrie, eleison!" after each bid. In the Eastern Church, this form of prayer is called "Ektenia" (also "Ektene"—earnest, insistent litany). It is a prayer of humble and fervent supplication, often in combination with deprecations and intercessions, forming a litany in which appropriate needs and wants are brought before the Lord. Such litanies are plentiful in the services of the Eastern Church. Especially significant are the Great Ektenia of Vespers and Grand Compline and the litanies found throughout the liturgy.[8]

Egeria's report of her visit to Jerusalem near the end of the fourth century is the first indication of the use of Ektenia in the Roman Church.[9] A contemporary report from Antioch tells of the same form in a prayer after the Gospel. The first appearance of such a litany in the West is apparently at Milan, where it was used between the Introit and the Collect of the Day. It probably was used in the same manner in Rome by the fifth or early sixth century. By the time of Gregory the Great (c. 540–604) the text "Kyrie, eleison" alone was used, without the supplications to which it had been a response. The use of the simple phrase appears to have been the practice on nonfestal occasions; the fuller form, with permission, was reserved for more solemn services.[10]

As early as 1545 the hymn, "Kyrie, Gott Vater in Ewigkeit," was used as the Kyrie. This is a versified setting of the chant tone of the Kyrie from the First Mass for solemn feasts, the "Kyrie Fons Bonitatis." This and some other hymns, such as Johann Spangenberg's "O Vater, allmächtiger Gott," appeared as hymns to be used for the Kyrie.[11] Divine Service I offers "Kyrie, God Father" (LW 209) as an alternative to the traditional threefold Kyrie. This hymn is also one option for the Kyrie in Divine Service III.

Gloria in Excelsis/Hymn of Praise

After the Kyrie, Divine Service I calls for the singing of the Gloria in Excelsis Deo ("Glory to God in the highest," the angelic hymn in Luke 2:14) and the earthly confirmation of the praise ("We praise you, we bless you"). The minister intones it and the congregation takes it up at the words "and on earth peace." On Sundays during the seasons of Advent and Lent the Gloria in Excelsis is omitted; Divine Service I suggests the singing of "Oh, come, oh, come, Emmanuel" (LW 1) at this place during Advent or "The royal banners forward go" (LW 2) during Lent. Divine Service II calls for the Hymn of Praise, which may be the Gloria in Excelsis or "This is the feast." Divine Service III gives two hymn options: "All glory be to God on high" (LW 215) or "All glory be to God alone" (LW 210). Neither hymn comes from the *Deutsche Messe*, after which Divine Service III is patterned, but both do paraphrase the Gloria and have melodies that are adaptations of plainsong tunes.

Like the Kyrie, the Gloria in Excelsis came into the eucharistic liturgy from the Eastern Church. When introduced into the West, it was first used as a song of thanksgiving. The earliest record of its inclusion in the Mass is found in the *Liber Pontificalis* (c. 530 A.D.).[12] Tradition has it that it was first used by the pope on Christmas Eve, since it is the hymn of the angels celebrating the incarnation. Its common use, however, was not permitted for another 600 years.[13] The Middle Ages witnessed a profusion of plainsong melodies, as well as textual elaborations and tropes. Some Lutheran liturgies of the 16th and 17th century prescribe the use of the Gloria, with the simple "et in terra pax" ("and on earth peace") on ordinary Sundays, reserving the rest of the piece for special occasions.[14]

Divine Service II offers as an alternative a modern hymn commemorating the resurrection, based on passages from the Book of Revelation (5:9–13; 19:4–9). This text first appeared in the Inter-Lutheran Commission on Worship's *Contemporary Worship 2* (1970).[15]

410

Notes for ministers. The congregation remains standing from the Introit through the Collect of the Day. For the Kyrie and Hymn of Praise the presiding and assisting ministers may remain at their places or at the altar.

Salutation and Collect of the Day

According to the earliest traditions, it was at this point that the presiding minister first spoke, the earlier parts of the service having been taken by others. The term *Collect* originally came from the Gallican liturgy, indicating that it was a collecting of the petitions of the congregation into one prayer. Jungmann notes that in the early Roman liturgy, "First the people were to pray, then the priest was to summarize their prayer in the oration. . . . The oration is always a prayer that the priest prays in the name of the people; he speaks for the congregation."[16]

The Collect is preceded by the salutation, "The Lord be with you," to which the people respond, "And with your spirit" or "And also with you." In ancient times, the salutation introduced not only the Collect, Preface, and Blessing—as it does today—but also the public announcement of the Gospel. The phrase is more than simply a greeting; it is indicative of the special relationship between the minister and the congregation. It has been called "The Little Ordination."[17] This is more than a fitting sentiment; it is part of the everyday speech of God's faithful people, as we find in Ruth 2:4, Luke 1:28, 2 Thessalonians 3:16, and elsewhere. The response parallels biblical usage in passages like Philemon 25 and Gal. 6:18.

The phrase, "Let us pray," is an invitation and admonition and should not be replaced by "We pray" or "God's people pray."

Notes for ministers. The presiding minister extends his hands in invitation for the salutation and the "Let us pray." If he has been facing away from the congregation, he turns to offer the salutation and turns again toward the altar for the prayer, extending his hands outward and upward in the traditional liturgical prayer gesture.

The traditional collects follow a classical pattern:

Address—   names the person of the Trinity to whom the prayer is particularly addressed.

Rationale—   notes the particular characteristic of God upon which this prayer is predicated.
Petition—   states the prayer, the blessing being asked.
Benefit—   gives the goal toward which the petition is directed.
Termination—   "who lives and reigns . . .," a doxology

Collect for Palm Sunday

[Address]   Almighty and everlasting God the Father,
[Rationale]   who sent your Son to take our nature upon him and to suffer death on the cross that all mankind should follow the example of his great humility,
[Petition]   mercifully grant that we may both follow the example of our Savior Jesus Christ in his patience
[Benefit]   and also have our portion in his resurrection;
[Termination]   through Jesus Christ, our Lord, who lives and reigns with you and the Holy Spirit, one God, now and forever.

In some cases the address is placed after the petition (as in three collects for the Sundays in Advent), and in other cases either the rationale or benefit, or both, may be omitted. The Collects in *Lutheran Worship* generally retain the classical pattern, creating a one-sentence prayer focused on a petition that flows from the rationale and into the statement of the benefit for which God's mercy and grace are being asked.

Readings

Three readings are provided for every Sunday and major festival: the Old Testament Reading (followed by the Gradual of the season or the appointed Psalm), the Epistle (followed by the Verse or Alleluia), and the Holy Gospel. For weekday services either the Old Testament Reading or the Epistle is dropped and only two readings are ordinarily used. The Gospel is always the last reading.

Two lectionaries are provided: an adaptation of the traditional lectionary of the Western Church, the *Comes* (One-Year Series), and an adaptation of the *Ordo Lectionem Missae* (Three-Year Series). These are discussed in chapter 5.

From the earliest times the Gospel has been given pride of place in the readings at the Divine Service. It is always read last. The congregation rises for it. More ceremony attends it. It is read by the presiding minister. Some of the Reformation church orders maintain the tradition of the salutation before the announcement of the Gospel of the Day and, in most cases, acclamations both precede and follow the reading.

Where three readings are used, the Gradual of the season or the appointed Psalm follows the Old Testament Reading and the Verse or Alleluia follows the Epistle. Where only two readings are used, the Verse may immediately follow or replace the Gradual or Psalm. (See also Notes on the Liturgy, *Lutheran Worship: Altar Book*, p. 30.)

> *Notes for ministers.* The readings may be announced and read from the altar or a lectern. If they are read from the altar, they may be read from the horns of the altar—the Old Testament and Epistle from the "liturgical"south and the Gospel from the "liturgical" north. (Liturgical directions assume that the chancel is at the east end of the church building and the nave is toward the west.) If an assisting minister reads the Old Testament Reading and the Epistle, the presiding minister should remain at his place at the altar during the readings. Readers are advised to use the prescribed wording to announce and to conclude the readings.
>
> A Gospel procession may be used at festival services, with crucifer and torchbearers accompanying the reader into the midst of the congregation as a reminder that the Gospel of our Lord Jesus Christ is to be taken into the world.
>
> In *Lutheran Worship* the services call for the presiding minister to announce and read the Gospel, symbolic of the work of the holy ministry of Word and Sacrament to proclaim the person and work of Christ to all. If the assisting minister is an ordained pastor, he may read the Gospel.

Creed

The Creed follows the Gospel in Divine Service I but in Divine Service II it comes after the Hymn of the Day and the Sermon. The proper Creed for Sunday and festival celebrations of Holy Communion is the Nicene Creed. This creed (*Symbolum Nicaeno-Constantinopolitanum*) took its traditional form—but without the "filioque" ("and the Son")—at the Council of Chalcedon in A.D. 451.

Lutheran Worship calls for the Apostles' Creed at nonfestival services. Some European Lutheran churches use the Apostles' Creed at the Eucharist; in the United States it has been customary to use it when there is no celebration of the Sacrament of the Altar. The Apostles' Creed is associated primarily with Holy Baptism and its daily remembrance, as Luther shows in his forms for Morning and Evening Prayer in the Small Catechism. The Nicene Creed is preferred at celebrations of the Sacrament even in cases where the Apostles' Creed has already been heard in the same service, as when Holy Baptism or Confirmation are administered. Since the Creed functions as a specific response to the proclamation of the Holy Gospel, it should occur at its normal place in the service. As a rule, no creed is used at weekday celebrations of Holy Communion, except when a major festival falls on a weekday.

The text of the creed in *Lutheran Worship* follows the Lutheran tradition of confessing belief "in one, holy, Christian and apostolic Church," adding a note that the original text reads "catholic." The original Greek reads *eis mian hagian katholikeen kai apostolokeen ekkleesian*. The Latin text in the *Book of Concord* follows the *Missale Romanum*: *et unam, sanctam, catholicam et apostolicam ecclesiam*, and the German reads, *und eine einige, heilige, christliche, apostolische Kirche*. No anti-Roman Catholic bias was or is indicated or intended by the use of *Christian* instead of *catholic*. The use of *christliche* (Christian) was the common and accepted practice among all German-speaking people before the Council of Trent (1545–63). Lutheran service books in practically all lands have followed the practice of translating *Christian*, and this continues to be the almost universal practice in Lutheranism. Even the most recent liturgical revisions of the Scandinavian churches continue to provide a vernacular substitute for the Latinate *catholic*, connoting the universality and oneness of the church. This accords with the meaning of *catholic*, which refers to the whole Christian faith drawn from the whole apostolic doctrine and the oneness and completeness of that faith and the church. It bears witness that the Holy Scripture is the final ground of all Christian truth.

Lutheran Worship provides for the occasional use of metrical paraphrases of the creeds (LW 213 for the Nicene Creed and LW 212 for the Apostles' Creed). "I believe in one God" (LW 4) provides the plainsong setting of Credo III from the *Liber Usualis*.

Notes for ministers. Since the recitation of the Creed is a solemn act of confession, the presiding minister leads it from the midst of the altar, not the lectern.

Hymn of the Day

The Hymn of the Day is the principal hymn of the Divine Service. In Lutheran corporate worship particular hymns have long been associated with particular Sundays and festivals of the church year (see chapter 17 on "Hymn of the Day"). *Lutheran Worship* includes a listing of hymns chosen to relate to the readings used in the service (see LW, pp. 976–78). Hymns are designated for both the one-year pericope system and the three-year system. Repeated use of these hymns will help the congregation to become familiar with a wide range of hymns reflecting the themes of the Sunday readings.

Notes for ministers. The longer hymns may be sung in sections, for example, part at the sermon, part at the distribution, etc., or in alternation. (See Notes on the Liturgy in *Lutheran Worship: Altar Book*, p. 34, where suggestions for alternating are given.)

Sermon

The Sermon is an integral part of the Service of the Word. It is not omitted, except in extraordinary circumstances, for the church is gathered around both pulpit and altar, Word and Sacrament. Through them believers receive from the Lord and, out of thankfulness, respond in word and act.

In his first word on public worship after leaving the protection of the Wartburg castle, Luther designates the omission and abuse of preaching as two of the three serious abuses that have crept into the churches. His 1523 letter to the congregation at Leisnig (Saxony) spells out these basic principles of evangelical reform:

First, God's Word has been silenced, and only reading and singing remain in the churches. This is the worst abuse. Second, when God's Word has been silenced such a host of un-Christian fables and lies, in legends, hymns, and sermons were introduced that it is horrible to see. Third, such divine service was performed as a work whereby God's grace and salvation might be won. As a result, faith disappeared. . . . Now in order to correct these abuses, know first of all that a Christian congregation should never gather together without the preaching of God's Word and prayer, no matter how briefly, as Psalm 102 says, "When the kings and the people assemble to serve the Lord, they shall declare the name and the praise of God." And Paul in 1 Corinthians 14 (26–31) says that when they come together, there should be prophesying, teaching, and admonition. Therefore, when God's Word is not preached, one had better neither sing nor read, or even come together.[18]

Luther does not restrict preaching to the sacramental service of the congregation; he also wants some interpretation of the Word to accompany its proclamation in Matins and Vespers. He goes on to recommend that Sunday morning preaching should be on the Gospel of the day, with preaching at Vespers on the Epistle or on some book of Scripture.[19]

The Gospel is the principal reading in each service, and will ordinarily serve as the foundation for the preaching when the congregation gathers on the Lord's Day. Traditionally, Sunday preaching in the Lutheran Church has been based upon the Sunday Gospel to a far greater degree than is the case in other churches using the pericopal system. This practice is based on the understanding that preaching in the chief service serves to interpret the Gospel and bring it into the present moment. The preacher "says what the Word says" to those whom the Word has gathered here and now, to hear it with open hearts and receive it into faithful hearts. The Old Testament serves as preparation and the Epistle for admonition and example.

The preacher will usually be a called and ordained minister of Word and Sacrament—one who has been called, set apart, and sent to his apostolic work according to the church's usual order. On occasions where the sermon is prepared and delivered by a student or candidate or some other properly designated person, his message shall have been examined and approved by a minister of the Word—most appropriately the pastor of the congregation or the dean of the chapel, the one who is responsible for the preaching and teaching of the Word among these people.

Notes to ministers. Before the sermon a short prayer asking for the blessing of God upon the preaching of his Word is fitting. Usually the preacher, kneeling at his place during the hymn, will offer that prayer silently. An ordained preacher may bless the hearers with the apostolic greeting or give the triune Invocation. Divine Service I suggests that the votum, "The peace of God, which passes all understanding, keep your hearts and minds in Christ Jesus" (Phil. 4:7), be spoken at the end of the sermon.

Offering and Offertory

The Offering and the Offertory follow the Sermon in Divine Service I. A different order is observed in Divine Service II, in which The Prayers come first and are followed by the Offering and Offertory. Divine Service III also has the Prayer of the Church before the Offering. Although this order differs from the Common Service tradition, it does employ a common pattern in German Lutheranism, which has intercessions after the Sermon and then continues with the offertory sentences and the gathering of offerings.

While the Offering symbolizes the "spiritual worship" (Rom. 12:1) of Christian lives offered in response to God, it also unites the faithful in an act of fellowship. Fellowship (*koinonia*) is a constitutive element in the worship and life of the apostolic congregation, as noted in Acts 2:42. Here Luke points to *fellowship* as an action of the congregation actively sharing. This concept can also extend to generosity and to gift, what has been given by the one for the benefit of the many. It is against the profaning of this fellowship that Paul speaks so strongly in 1 Corinthians 10. The gifts of fellowship that were shared included bread and wine, some of which was set apart for the celebration of the Sacrament. These gifts, representing the first fruits of creation and symbolic of the offering of the substance of bodily life, called the oblation, are offered as a sacrifice of thanksgiving to the Lord that by means of them he might accomplish his purpose to bless his people.

When Luther, in "An Order of Mass and Communion for the Church at Wittenberg" (the *Formula Missae* of 1523), speaks strong words against the Offertory, he is not speaking against the practice and use mentioned above. This is clear when he says, "After the Creed or after the Sermon let bread and wine be made ready for blessing in the customary manner."[20] His objection was to texts that talked of the sacrament as a propitiatory sacrifice.

> *Notes for ministers.* When the offerings have been gathered, they are received and may be presented at the altar to be placed on a credence table until the conclusion of the service. (In no case should the offerings be removed to be counted by worshipers who leave the Divine Service for that purpose.) Together with the offerings, the vessels containing bread (pyx or ciborium) and wine (cruet or flagon) may be brought by representatives of the congregation and placed on the altar to be made ready for the consecration and Communion. The altar and the vessels are prepared for the celebration of the Sacrament during the gathering of offerings and the singing of the offertory.

Prayer

Prayer is one of the marks of the congregation gathered in worship, according to Acts 2:42. Here the congregation, established and gathered by God according to his purpose, agrees together on earth that it may be done for them by the Father in heaven (Matt. 18:19), as prayers, supplications, and thanksgivings are offered for all in authority and all sorts of human need (1 Tim. 2:1–4). Although some of the Reformation church orders place this prayer in close connection with the readings, before the Sermon, the far more common practice has been to make the Prayer of the Church, or The Prayers, the point of connection between the Service of the Word and the Service of Holy Communion. The most ancient pattern of the church's intercessory prayer has been the form of the Ektenia or the Bidding Prayer (the latter still used on Good Friday), according to which an assisting minister publicly notes the matter for which prayer is to be offered, followed by a congregational response (as in the Ektenia) or by a specific collect (as in the Bidding Prayer).

Lutheran Worship employs the Ektenia form in Divine Services I and II. The rubrics list concerns for which prayer should be offered. The prayer in Divine Service I concludes with a remembrance of the person and work of Christ, a commemoration of the fulfillment of the kingdom of heaven toward which we look, and a doxology. The ending of The Prayers in Divine Service II reminds one of Jesus' final words on the cross ("Father, into your hands I commit my spirit" [Luke 23:46]), the psalmist's words ("I trust in God's unfailing love" [Ps. 52:8b]), and the apostle Paul's words ("Such confidence as this is ours through Christ before God" [2 Cor. 3:4]).

> *Notes for ministers.* The so-called Prayer of the Church, or The Prayers, should be carefully prepared in advance. The language is that of petition, intercession, and thanksgiving—concise and to the point. Worshipers are encouraged to make their prayer requests known to the pastor, either personally or by entering them in a special book provided in the narthex. If announcement of these requests is customary, this should be done after the introduction, "Let us pray for the whole people of God in Christ Jesus, and for all people according to their needs" (Divine Service II). Notice the twofold thrust: the church and the world. In Divine Service I this announcement is made after the introductory invitation, "In peace let us pray to the Lord" and the congregation's response, "Lord, have mercy." The Prayer of the Church may appropriately be led by an assisting minister and concluded by the presiding minister.

THE SERVICE OF THE SACRAMENT

The Father gives his Son; the Son freely submits himself to the Passion and cross; the Holy Spirit mediates the fruit of Christ's saving work through Word and Sacrament. The Service of the Word has proclaimed and interpreted the Gospel message so that faith may be awakened and strengthened in the speaking and hearing of the Word and that the congregation may both rejoice and offer prayer. Then, in the Service of Holy Communion God joins his act and deed to his Word; he gives us the body offered and the blood shed for the forgiveness of our sins and strength for Christian living.

Table 5

Comparison of the Service of the Sacrament

DIVINE SERVICE I	DIVINE SERVICE II	DIVINE SERVICE III
The Preface	The Preface	
Proper Preface	Proper Preface	
Sanctus	Sanctus	Admonition to Communicants
Thanksgiving	Thanksgiving	
Lord's Prayer	Lord's Prayer	Lord's Prayer
Words of Institution	Words of Institution	Words of Institution Sanctus
Peace	Peace	
Agnus Dei	Agnus Dei	
Distribution/Hymns	Communion/Hymns	Distribution/Hymns
Post-Communion Canticle	Post-Communion Canticle	
Versicle		
Post-Communion Collect	Prayer	Post-Communion Collect
Benedicamus		
Benediction	Blessing	Benediction
Silent Prayer		

Preface

The Preface dialog between presiding minister and congregation is very ancient and is almost universally used in both East and West; its absence from the *Deutsche Messe* is an exception to this pattern. The presider and the congregation committed to his care prepare themselves for the consecration. From early times the Preface assumed a set, invariable, and lengthy form in the liturgies of the Eastern Church. The insertion of sentences appropriate to the season or festival is of Western origin. The large number of Proper Prefaces was greatly reduced in the liturgical reforms of Pope Gregory the Great (590–604) and again in the reforms that followed the Reformation. The *Formula Missae* provided for the prefatory dialogue but no proper seasonal prefaces. Instead, Luther passed from the introductory words of the Preface to the Words of Institution:

> The bread and wine having been prepared, one may proceed as follows:

> The Lord be with you.
> *Response:* And with thy spirit.

> Lift up your hearts.
> *Response:* Let us lift them to the Lord.

> Let us give thanks unto the Lord our God.
> *Response:* It is meet and right.

> It is truly meet and right, just and salutary for us to give thanks to Thee always and everywhere, Holy Lord, Father Almighty, Eternal God, through Christ our Lord. . .

> Then:

> . . . Who the day before he suffered, took bread,. . . [21]

Later Lutheran church orders, however, generally called for appropriate Proper Prefaces without further specification.[22]

In Divine Services I and II the Proper Prefaces are based on the Latin prefaces of the pre-Tridentine period. Specifically, the Christmas, Passiontide, Easter, Ascension, Pentecost, Holy Trinity, Apostles and Evangelists, and weekday prefaces are of Latin origin; the Advent preface is of Lutheran origin, since the medieval Roman missal had no specific preface for this season—an indication of the relatively late acceptance of Advent into the church year—but used the Trinity preface for this occasion.[23] In American Lutheranism, it was apparently *The Lutheran Hymnal* (1941) that first included an Advent preface, a form evidently prepared by the Intersynodical Committee of the Synodical Conference that produced the book. Of the eight new prefaces in the Roman sacramentary of 1969, two are designated for Advent, reflecting the sacramentary's two-part division of the season.[24] The Epiphany, Lent, and All Saints prefaces in *Lutheran Worship* (1982) are of Lutheran origin; the one for All Saints was composed for *Lutheran Worship* (1982).

Sanctus and Benedictus

The Sanctus and Benedictus qui venit continue the Preface. The Sanctus is found in eucharistic liturgies from the time of Serapion (d. 360). The text climaxes with the quotation from Isaiah:

It is right and just to praise you,
to celebrate you, to glorify you,
the eternal Father of the only-begotten Son, Jesus Christ . . . .
For you are above every Principality,
Power, and Force and Domination,
above every name that is named,
in this age as in the age to come.
You are attended by thousands upon thousands
and myriads upon myriads
of Angels and Archangels,
of Thrones and Dominations,
of Principalities and Powers.
Beside you stand
the two august Seraphim, with six wings:
two to cover their face,
two to cover their feet,
two with which to fly.
They sing your holiness.
With theirs, accept also
our acclamations of your holiness:
Holy, holy, holy is the Lord of Sabaoth!
Heaven is filled, earth is filled with your wonderful glory.[25]

The liturgical text of the Sanctus is built on the opening verses of Isaiah 6, adding "God" to "Lord," "heaven" to the reference to earth, and the festal "Hosanna in the highest."

The Benedictus is Ps. 118:26, by which we greet the Lord who comes to us in his body and blood. This Scripture passage was retained in Lutheran liturgies but was omitted in Reformed churches, which rejected the doctrine of the bodily presence of Christ in consecrated bread and wine.

As late as the beginning of the 17th century, the Roman book of episcopal ceremonial placed the Benedictus after the consecration, emphasizing its relationship to the consecration. Similarly, Luther's Latin service put both Sanctus and Benedictus after the consecration with the elevation of the consecrated Sacrament at the

Benedictus. Luther does the same with the elevation in the German service, paraphrasing the Latin Sanctus in his German hymn "Isaiah, mighty seer" (LW 214).

Divine Service I provides a revised melody and setting of the Sanctus from the *Lutheran Hymnal*. Divine Service II, First and Second Settings, give modern settings prepared by Hillert and Nelson, respectively. "Holy, holy, holy is God" (LW 6) provides a melody based on a Sanctus from Mass XVII.[26]

> *Notes for ministers.* The ancient gesture of prayer, raised and outstretched hands, is appropriate during the seasonal Preface, the prayer that follows the Sanctus, and the Lord's Prayer.

Prayer of Thanksgiving

From the publication of the *Formula Missae* until recent times[27] Lutheran eucharistic rites have omitted the prayers (the Canon of the Mass) that followed the Sanctus and Benedictus in the Latin rite, leaving only the Lord's Prayer, the Words of Institution, the Pax Domini, and the private prayers of the presiding minister when receiving the Sacrament. There are almost no exceptions to this general rule.[28]

Luther notes in the *Formula* that the Mass most properly consists in our "using" the Gospel, that is, that we not only hear it with our ears but receive it and take it into faithful hearts, and in our communing at the table of the Lord. He sees the prayers of the canon as an idolatrous assertion of our power to please God on the basis of our cultic action. Fallen man offers his worship from that assertion; it stands as the basis for a multitude of cultic actions instituted and observed on the basis of the inspiration by Satan and our own opinion of self-rightouesness. In the "Admonition concerning the Sacrament of the Body and Blood of Our Lord" (1530), Luther affirms again that the Sacrament of the Altar is a gracious ordinance graciously instituted by God for our eternal welfare. The right *anamnesis* (act of remembering) is that we participate in the worship that God has established and blessed.

> Now if you want to engage in a marvelous, great worship to God and honor Christ's passion rightly, then remember and participate in the sacrament; in it, as you hear, there is a remembrance

of him, that is, he is praised and glorified. If you practice or assist in practicing this same remembrance with diligence, then you will assuredly forget about the self-chosen forms of worship, for, as has been said, you cannot praise and thank God too often or too much for his grace revealed in Christ.[29]

This stands behind Luther's reticence to produce new prayers that would replace the parts of the canon which turn the work of God into our work. The blessing in the Mass is in what Christ says and gives and not in an action by which we appropriate his sacrifice for ourselves and others. The proper remembrance is to have confidence in him and to do what he has said we are to do ("Take and eat" "Take and drink of it"), and not in the *anamnesis* we compose and speak. Thus, in Luther's liturgical works and in the majority of the church orders there is no continuation of the Great Thanksgiving of the Preface at the conclusion of the angelic hymn, the Sanctus.[30]

We have already noted that Luther's Latin Mass connects the Words of Institution to the Preface; and in the German Mass, the Words of Christ follow a paraphrase of the Lord's Prayer and the admonition to the communicants. It became customary in many of the church orders that such an exhortation follow the Sanctus, after the model Luther provided. The "Admonition to Communicants" in Divine Service III is a translation of the exhortation in the *Deutsche Messe*:

> I exhort you in Christ that you give attention to the Testament of Christ in true faith, and above all take to heart the words with which Christ presents his body and blood to us for forgiveness; that you take note of and give thanks for the boundless love that he showed us when he saved us from the wrath of God, sin, death, and hell by his blood: and that you then externally receive the bread and wine, that is, his body and blood, as a guarantee and pledge. Let us then in his name, according to his command, and with his own words administer and receive the Testament.[31]

Luther's "Abomination of the Secret Mass" (1525) provides a detailed critique of the Canon of the Mass, prayer by prayer. Christ has shed his blood for us and suffered death on our behalf, and in the sacrament he gives us the fruit of his sacrifice. But that sacrifice is not honored when sinful people undertake by their own works to do what only Christ can do or by means of their worship apply the work of Christ to themselves.

> That, I say, is our gospel, that Christ has made us righteous and holy through that sacrifice and has redeemed us from sin, death, and the devil and has brought us into his heavenly kingdom. We have to grasp this and hold it fast through faith alone. We have preached this and reiterated it so often that everyone can know it well and can conclude from it that all our own works undertaken to expiate sin and escape from death are necessarily blasphemous. They deny God and insult the sacrifice that Christ has made and disgrace his blood, because they try thereby to do what only Christ's blood can do.[32]

Lutheran Worship does not provide a specific prayer of *anamnesis* or an *epiclesis* (invocation of the Holy Spirit on the elements) in the Divine Services. It includes instead brief thanksgivings and prayers for beneficial reception. They occur before the Lord's Prayer and Words of Christ in Divine Services I and II. The prayer in Divine Service I is adapted from the prayer in the Swedish *Kyrko-Handboken* of 1942.[33] The prayer in Divine Service II is loosely based on the prayer in *Agende I* of the United Evangelical Lutheran Church of Germany (VELKD).[34] *Lutheran Worship* distinguishes between the thanksgiving prayer and the Words of Institution.

Lord's Prayer

The Lord's Prayer and Words of Institution are traditionally bound together in Lutheran communion rites. Some Lutheran liturgies follow the pattern established in the *Formula Missae*, where the Lord's Prayer follows the Words of Christ; others follow the pattern of the *Deutsche Messe*, in which the Lord's Prayer, or a paraphrase, precedes the consecration.

The use of the Lord's Prayer before the consecration emphasizes its significance as the "Prayer of the Faithful," the children of the heavenly Father whom he tenderly invites to call upon him as beloved children approach their dear father. Here, as we pray the family prayer of the Church of Christ, we are reminded who we are and in what relationship to God we come before him; we exercise our right of access as the general priesthood of believers into which we have been called and baptized. The Lord's Prayer is the concise summary of the Gospel and of all for which we can and could pray. From at least the third century, Christians have also confessed a special connection between the Fourth Petition ("Give us this day our daily bread") and the bread now to be set apart for God's purpose by and according to his own Word and blessing. It is bread above all other bread, bread that feeds us as the children of God. Where the Lord's Prayer follows the Words of Institution (the consecration), the way is left open for the interpretation of the Lord's Prayer as the prayer that accomplishes the consecration, as though it were our act of prayer and invocation that effected the sacramental presence. Such was clearly not the interpretation of Luther; the majority of Lutheran liturgical orders follows the pattern set in the German Mass and so does each form of the Divine Service in *Lutheran Worship*.

In many places the Lord's Prayer may be still accompanied by the tolling of a tower bell.[35] This is a survival of the practice of ringing a small, handheld bell at the consecration.[36]

Words of Institution

The Words of Institution are designated as the "Consecration" in the Lutheran liturgical tradition. Luther illustrates the Lutheran understanding in "The Private Mass and the Consecration of Priests" (1533):

> For, God be praised, in our churches we can show a Christian a true Christian mass according to the ordinance and institution of Christ, as well as according to the true intention of Christ and the church. There our pastor, bishop, or minister in the pastoral office, rightly and honorably and publicly called, having been previously consecrated, anointed, and born in baptism as a priest of Christ, without regard to the private chrism, goes before the altar. Publicly and plainly he sings what Christ has ordained and instituted in the Lord's Supper. He takes the bread and wine, gives thanks, distributes and gives them to the rest of us who are there and want to receive them, on the strength of the words of Christ: "This is my body, this is my blood. Do this," etc. Particularly we who want to receive the sacrament kneel beside, behind, and around him, man, woman, young, old, master, servant, wife, maid, par-

ents, and children, even as God brings us together there, all of us true, holy priests, sanctified by Christ's blood, anointed by the Holy Spirit, and consecrated in baptism. On the basis of this our inborn, hereditary priestly honor and attire we are present, have, as Revelation 4 [4] pictures it, our golden crowns on our heads, harps and golden censers in our hands; and we let our pastor say what Christ has ordained, not for himself as though it were for his person, but he is the mouth for all of us and we all speak the word with him from the heart and in faith, directed to the Lamb of God who is present for us and among us, and who according to his ordinance nourishes us with his body and blood. This is our mass, and it is the true mass which is not lacking among us.[37]

Central in the church's celebration of the Lord's Supper is the Word and promise of the Lord who has instituted it, so that everything is done on the basis of his Word. We do not deal "effectively" with God, but God is dealing with us in a most merciful, loving, and effectual manner.

Here we surely have the intention of Christ and of the church. Here we do not have to be concerned whether the pastor is speaking the words secretly or whether he also is effecting conversion or whether he, too, believes, for we hear the words of institution publicly and say them along with him in our hearts. And the institution of Christ (not our action or the chrism) effects a change or gives us the body and blood of Christ. If the pastor does not believe or doubts, we do believe. If he blunders in speaking the words or becomes confused and forgets whether he has spoken the words, we indeed are there, listen to them, cling to them, and are sure that they have been spoken. For this reason we cannot be deceived, and because the ordinance and true faith are present, it must be certain that we are receiving the true body and blood of Christ. God be praised and thanked, that I have lived to see the true Christian mass and the pure Christian usage of the holy sacrament.[38]

The Words of Institution are not merely the obligatory recital of a historical narrative concerning the original institution and the first Supper in the upper room. They are words of consecration—not that by means of these words we consecrate bread and wine, but that Christ speaks them by and through us to do and give now what he did and gave then.

No man's word or work, be it the merit or the speaking of the minister, be it the eating and drinking or the faith of the communicants, can effect the true presence of the body and blood of Christ in the Supper. This is to be ascribed only to the almighty power of God and the Word, institution, and ordinance of our Lord Jesus Christ. For the truthful and almighty words of Jesus Christ which he spoke in the first institution were not only efficacious in the first Supper but they still retain their validity and efficacious power in all places where the Supper is observed according to Christ's institution and where his words are used, and the body and blood of Christ are truly present, distributed, and received by the virtue and potency of the same words which Christ spoke in the first Supper. For wherever we observe his institution and speak his words over the bread and cup and distribute the blessed bread and distribute the blessed cup, Christ himself is still active through the spoken words by the virtue of the first institution, which he wants to be repeated.[39]

The consecrated bread and wine, the body and blood of our Lord, may be elevated after the Words of Christ have been spoken over each, or at the Peace, which follows. The elevation itself is not essentially associated with the doctrine of the Sacrifice of the Mass. Luther originally retained the elevation for the sake of the weak;[40] in later life he came to see that this action, exhibiting and illustrating Christ's words, "This is my body given for you," could help incite the Christian people to faith.[41] When in 1542 the elevation was discontinued at Wittenberg, Luther chose not to oppose the pastor and thereby create dissension.[42] Where the elevation is used, its significance must be clearly explained.

Notes for ministers. To assist the distinction between prayer to God (thanksgiving) and words from God (Words of Institution), the presiding minister discontinues any prayer gesture (outstretched arms or folded hands) during the Words of Institution. The Words of Institution should be chanted or said with particular distinctiveness and reverence. At the words "took bread" the presiding minister takes the vessel in his hands and then replaces it on the altar. Other vessels with bread for consecration are touched. The sign of the cross may be made over all the bread to be consecrated at the words "this is my body." Similarly, he takes the chalice in his hands and replaces it on the altar at the words "took the cup," and other vessels with wine to be consecrated are touched. The sign of the cross may be made over all the wine to be consecrated at the words "this is my blood." Or, the paten and later the chalice may be held in his hands while he says the appropriate Words of Institution over each vessel.

The Peace

In the *Missale Romanum* (1570) the order of prayers and actions after the Sanctus were as follows:

> *Te igitur:* offering of the bread and wine; prayer for the Church.
> *Memento & Communicantes:* remembrance of the living and the dead.
> *Hanc igitur:* prayer that the sacrifice be accepted and elements consecrated.
> *Qui pridie:* the Words of Institution.
> *Unde et memores:* remembrance of the death and resurrection of Christ.
> *Supra quae propitio:* offering of the sacrifice of Christ's body and blood.
> *Memento:* remembrance of the departed.
> *Nobis quoque peccatoribus:* remembrance of the living.
> *Pater Noster & Embolism:* the Lord's Prayer followed by the breaking of the bread.
> *Pax Domini:* the body and blood of Christ mingled as a portion of the bread is dropped into the chalice.[43]

As we have noted, Luther retained the position of the Lord's Prayer after the consecration in his Latin service of 1523, along with the customary admonition ("Taught by your saving precepts and guided by your Word, we are bold to pray. . . ."). He directed that the Embolism and the accompanying ceremonial actions be dropped, including the mingling of the elements in the chalice at the Pax.[44]

> But immediately after the Lord's Prayer shall be said, "The peace of the Lord," etc., which is, so to speak, a public absolution of the sins of the communicants, the true voice of the gospel announcing remission of sins, and therefore the one and most worthy preparation for the Lord's Table, if faith holds to these words as coming from the mouth of Christ Himself.[45]

Augustine (354–430) had long before declared in a similar vein that the Kiss of Peace (Pax) was a good preparation for Communion when he defended its placement just before the distribution.[46] Originally placed at the conclusion of the Service of the Word, the Peace was inserted before the Communion to demonstrate the Fifth Petition of the Lord's Prayer just prayed: we forgive one another as we have ourselves been forgiven by God.

> *Notes for ministers.* It is appropriate that when the presiding minister has spoken or sung the Peace, he shares it with the ministers and servers who are assisting at the altar, and the people present share the word and blessing they have received with their immediate neighbors, saying, "Peace be with you," or "The Peace of the Lord be with you."

Agnus Dei

The Agnus Dei was first introduced into the service by Pope Sergius I (d. 701) to cover the action of breaking the bread into as many pieces as were needed for the Communion. Originally it was sung for as long as required. By the 12th century the use of smaller hosts had been introduced and the original use of the Agnus Dei no longer obtained. The hymn was not dropped, but the pattern was set as a threefold repetition, the first two verses ending with the prayer, "Have mercy," and the last with "Grant us peace." The wording of the body of the hymn is taken from the Words of John the Baptist in John 1:29, except that "sin" (*peccatum*) is used in place of "sins"(*peccata*).

The Agnus Dei serves as a hymn of adoration to the Savior Christ who is present for us in his body and blood. It is for this reason that the hymn did not survive in the liturgies of Reformed churches, which refused to affirm the real presence of the body and blood of Christ in the sacramental elements. Its present use outside the Roman and Lutheran communions represents a recent addition. The Divine Services in *Lutheran Worship* call for it at every celebration of Holy Communion; Divine Service III provides for its use as the first communion hymn.

The communing of the ministers and congregation begins during the Agnus Dei or as the Agnus Dei concludes.

For most of Christian history the presiding minister has communed himself rather than receiving it from an assisting minister or neglecting his own need to commune.[47] This practice continued during the Reformation. The warning against self-communion in the Smalcald Articles does not refer to the presiding minister's communing himself together with the people in the public service, but is directed against the practice by which priests would commune themselves as a devotional act privately and apart from the congregation.[48]

Personal prayer at Communion is most appropriate, but the earliest sacramentaries contain no particular prayers. In fact, the sacramentaries characteristically end their treatment of the Mass at the Agnus Dei, apparently with the understanding that the service will be concluded as quickly as possible after that. At the time of the Reformation, the Roman Missal provided two prayers, "Domine Jesu Christe, fili Dei vivi" and "Perceptio corporis tui" for the use of the presiding minister before his reception.[49] Luther approved of their continued use, if only they be changed from the singular to the plural, so that they would become the prayer of all.[50] In addition, three adapted Scripture verses came to be associated with the reception of the Sacrament in the course of time:

1. Before Communion: I will receive the Bread of Heaven, and call upon the name of the Lord (*Panem coelestem,* based on Ps. 116:17)

2. Before receiving the body of Christ: Lord, I do not deserve to have you come under my roof. But speak the Word, and my soul shall be healed (*Domine, non sum dignus,* Matt. 8:8, with "soul" for "servant")

3. Before receiving the blood of Christ: How can I repay the Lord for all his goodness to me? I will lift up the cup of salvation and call on the name of the Lord. I call to the Lord, who is worthy of praise, and I am saved from my enemies (*Quid retribuam,* Ps. 116:12–13; 18:3).[51] Their use is seen first in Germany and then elsewhere until they were incorporated into the Roman Missal. They have continued in numerous Lutheran services since the Reformation.

Notes for ministers. At Communion the presiding minister speaks the distribution formula to himself as pastor to communicant, and responds "Amen." After a short thanksgiving, he communes the ministers who assist him in the distribution. One or more assisting ministers, chosen and instructed for this purpose, may assist in the distribution of the Sacrament by administering the blood of Christ. The presiding minister himself always administers the body of Christ, because the administration of the Lord's body indicates admission to the Sacrament. The presiding minister bears responsibility both for the celebration and for the administration of the sacrament, and he is to exercise pastoral judgment in admitting communicants to the table. This responsibility may not be borne by vicars, field workers, or other lay persons.

Alternative distribution formulae are provided in the Divine Services. Both state clearly the nature of the gift and blessing here provided. Other formulae should not be used as a substitute for these powerful words, nor ought the practice of addressing the communicants by name be followed.

The body of Christ may be placed directly on the tongue or in the hand of the communicants. It is helpful to the minister if communicants are instructed to guide the chalice to their mouths. Communion by chalice is the church's standard practice. While it is recognized that there may be situations and circumstances that make some other mode of reception expedient, for example, intinction or the use of small cups for each individual communicant, congregations should not resolve to displace the use of the chalice or bind the communicants to some other practice.

Communion hymns sung by the congregation as well as choral and instrumental music are proper and useful during the distribution. Suitable music includes music directly related to the institution or use of the Sacrament and its blessings, or the theme of the readings of the day or season. It is appropriate that there be periods of silence during the distribution.

Post-Communion Canticle

The singing of a communion verse is an ancient practice that antedates even the use of the Introit and the Offertory. Anciently Psalm 145 and Psalm 34, together with appropriate antiphons, were sung during the communing of the people, until the signal was given that all had communed. At that point the singing closed with the Gloria Patri. By the tenth century, the psalms themselves were often dropped and only the antiphons retained, leading finally to the practice in the Roman rite of including a proper antiphonal verse, the "Communion," for each mass. At the same time, in some places the Agnus Dei was used as the communion hymn of the people, and the verse was reserved for use only after all had communed.[52]

The practice of the Greek liturgy was to sing the Nunc Dimittis as a final hymn in the service. This practice was taken up also in some places in the West.[53]

In the *Formula Missae* Luther provided for the singing of the communion verse, followed by a collect.[54] In addition to the Nunc Dimittis, Divine Service II provides an alternative post-communion canticle, "Thank the Lord and sing his praise," prepared by the Inter-Lutheran Commission on Worship.[55] "Thank the Lord" is appropriate for use at all times except Lent and the Sundays and festivals falling in the Lenten season.

Post-Communion Collect

The Post-Communion Collect combines thanksgiving with a prayer that the gifts here given by the Lord may accomplish his purposes in his people.

As early as the *Apostolic Constitutions* (c. A.D. 380), provision is made for such a prayer after Communion.[56] Eastern rites provide a short litany at this point. In time the Roman liturgy came to provide short, succinct post-communion collects proper to each service. In Luther's Latin service no provision is made for any prayers in addition to the two noted above. In the German Mass Luther provides a collect incorporating thoughts—not exactly original with him—that eventually resulted in a collect common to a great number of Lutheran liturgies, a prayer for the twofold outgoing fruit of beneficial Communion, namely, in faith toward God and love toward neighbor.[57] This is the first of the two collects provided in Divine Services I and II. The second collect is derived from the 13th-century Sarum (Salisbury, England) rite, where it was a prayer of the priest's devotion in the mass as he held the body of Christ in his hands. Now a prayer of the congregation, it is an updated version of that which appeared as a post-communion collect in *The Lutheran Hymnal.*

> *Notes for ministers.* In addition to the two post-communion collects provided (set to chant in Divine Service I), the Collect for Maundy Thursday, *Lutheran Worship,* p. 44, composed by Thomas Aquinas (1225–74) for the Feast of the Body of Christ, may occasionally be used.

The Dismissal

In the Middle Ages there was no final blessing; the Mass ended simply with the customary salutation ("The Lord be with you") and its usual response, followed by the announcement, "Go; it is the dismissal" (*Ite, missa est*). The people responded, "Thanks be to God" (*Deo gratias*). If the presiding minister was a bishop, he might give a blessing to the people as he departed, as was customary at Rome. In the tenth century, the Gallic custom of dismissing the congregation with the words "Bless we the Lord" (*Benedicamus Domino*) began to appear in Roman liturgies in place of *Ite, missa est*. Both formulae are used in the 11th century, depending on the season of the church year. This century also saw the introduction of "A Prayer over the People," given in optative form: "May the Almighty God, the Father, and the Son, and the Holy Spirit, bless you."[58] This is a prayer, not properly a benediction.

In the *Deutsche Messe* only the Aaronic blessing is given, in the form of a blessing rather than a prayer. Virtually all Lutheran liturgies have followed the usage of the *Deutsche Messe*, with the Swedish liturgy adding after it the invocation, "In the name of the Father, and of the Son, and of the Holy Spirit."[59] The people respond with "Amen" or, in some cases, with a triple "Amen."

> *Notes for ministers.* The service ends with the blessing, without a closing hymn. The Lord's Word of benediction to his people concludes the liturgy. If local custom favors a musical response in addition to the Amen, the singing of the Doxology or a short hymn stanza is to be preferred to singing a hymn. In announcing portions of hymns or printing them in the worship folder, it is well to distinguish between *stanza* and *verse*. According to Webster, *verse* is "a line of metrical writing"; *stanza* is a "division of a poem consisting of a series of lines . . . in a usually recurring pattern of

meter and rhyme." The use of *verse* for *stanza* is thus contrary to good usage.

SUMMARY

Evangelical Lutheran worship is liturgical worship. We call it Divine, because it is God's service, in which he is giver, host, butler, and server. Christ is our "liturgist," who "has a permanent priesthood. Therefore he is able to save completely those who come to God through him, because he always lives to intercede for them" (Heb. 7:24–25).

That Lutheran worship is liturgical says nothing about the degree or extent of its ritualism or ceremonialism. It does bear witness that we are a people who desire to receive faithfully God's blessings in Word and Sacrament according to the pattern he has set. Such worship is not understood to be missionary, evangelistic, or catechetical activity directed toward those who are outside the church. Rather, the church's missionary, evangelistic, and catechetical activity flows from the preaching and hearing of the Word of God and the faithful receiving of the Lord's body and blood. What comes forth from the Lord also returns to him, as candidates are brought to the font and confirmands are led to the altar, thus, in turn, to worship the Triune God in Word and Sacrament. Rightly does David Truemper assert: "An understanding of the church based on the CA VII [*Confessio Augustana* VII] leads to the conviction that we do not worship in order to gain converts but rather we evangelize in order to gain worshipers."[60]

For all this, the church humbly and reverently thanks God and it confesses, "You have done it all; you have built your church. We have trusted in you and we are not put to shame in our hope."

Notes

1. Cf. Notes to Holy Baptism in *Lutheran Worship: Agenda*, prepared by the Commission on Worship of The Lutheran Church—Missouri Synod (St.Louis: Concordia Publishing House, 1984), pp. 98–99; also Notes on the Liturgy in *Lutheran Worship: Altar Book*, prepared by the Commission on Worship of The Lutheran Church—Missouri Synod (St. Louis: Concordia Publishing

House, 1982), p. 32. For a brief historical background of preparatory rites see chapter 10.

2. Emil Sehling, ed., *Die evangelischen Kirchenordnungen des XVI. Jahrhunderts*, vols. I–V (Leipzig: O. R. Reisland, 1902–1913), vols. VI–XV (Tübingen: J. C. B. Mohr, 1955–1977), I¹: 557.

3. Ibid., V: 151. This form appeared also in Mecklenburg (1552); ibid., V: 198.

4. Aemilius Richter, ed., *Die evangelischen Kirchenordnungen XVI. Jahrhunderts*, 2 vols. (Weimar: Landindustriecomptoir, 1946), II: 222.

5. *The Book of Common Prayer* (New York: The Church Hymnal Corporation and Seabury Press, 1979), p. 360. Marion Hatchett says that it is "based on a form proposed by a British ecumenical organization, the Joint Liturgical Group." Cf. Marion J. Hatchett, *Commentary on the American Prayer Book* (New York: Seabury Press, 1980), p. 343.

6. AE 53: 22f.

7. Peter Brunner, *Worship in the Name of Jesus*, trans. by M. H. Bertram (St. Louis: Concordia Publishing House, 1968), p. 208.

8. See, for example, "The Great Ektenia" in the Divine Liturgy of St. John Chrysostom, *Service Book of the Holy Eastern Orthodox Catholic and Apostolic Church*, 3d ed. (Brooklyn, NY: Syrian Antiochian Orthodox Diocese, 1960), p. 92.

9. John Wilkinson, *Egeria's Travels to the Holy Land* (Jerusalem: Ariel Publishing House, 1981), p. 57.

10. Hatchett, p. 320.

11. Eduard Emil Koch, *Geschichte des Kirchenlieds und Kirchengesangs der christlichen, insbesondere der deutschen evangelischen Kirche*, 3d ed.(Stuttgart: Chr. Belser'schen Verlagshandlung, 1866), I: 375.

12. Josef A. Jungmann, *The Early Liturgy to the Time of Gregory the Great*, trans. Francis A. Brunner (Notre Dame: University of Notre Dame Press, 1959), p. 295.

13. Cheslyn Jones, Geoffrey Wainwright, and Edward Yarnold, eds., *The Study of Liturgy* (New York: Oxford University Press, 1978), p. 183.

14. Ludwig Schoeberlein, *Schatz des liturgischen Chor- und Gemeindegesangs nebst den Altarweisen in der deutschen evangelischen Kirche* 3 vols. (Göttingen: Vandenhoeck & Ruprecht's Verlag, 1865), I:142.

15. Inter-Lutheran Commission on Worship, *Contemporary Worship 2: Services, The Holy Communion* (Minneapolis: Augsburg Publishing House, et al., 1970), p. 5.

16. Jungmann, p. 293.

17. See Luther D. Reed, *The Lutheran Liturgy*, rev. ed. (Philadelphia: Muhlenberg Press, 1959), p. 278.

18. AE 53: 11.

19. Ibid., pp. 12f.

20. Ibid., p. 26.

21. Ibid., p. 27.

22. For example, Braunschweig in 1528. See Sehling, VI¹: 441.

23. *Liber Usualis Missae et Officii* (New York: J. Fischer & Bros., 1947), p. 7.

24. See Raymond Avery, "A Preview of the New Prefaces," *Worship* 42/9 (December 1968): 587–598.

25. Quoted in Lucien Deiss, *Springtime of the Liturgy*, trans. Matthew J. O'Connell (Collegeville: The Liturgical Press, 1979), pp. 193f.

26. Cf. Schoeberlein, I: 338 and *Liber Usualis*, p. 66.

27. The debate over whether to have or not have a Eucharistic Prayer in the Divine Service was often a heated one. The reader is alerted to a sampling of the literature. Regarding historical documents: Gregory Dix, *The Shape of the Liturgy* (Westminster, Dacre Press, 1945), an influential interpretation; R. C. D. Jasper and G. J. Cuming, *Prayers of the Eucharist: Early and Reformed*, 2d ed. (New York: Oxford University Press, 1980), which gives primary texts in translation; Frank C. Senn, ed., *New Eucharistic Prayers: An Ecumenical Study of their Development and Structure* (New York: Paulist Press, 1987), which provides an analysis of recent creations. In support of its inclusion: Eugene Brand, "Luther's Liturgical Surgery: Twentieth Century Diagnosis of the Patient," in *Interpreting Luther's Legacy: Essays in Honor of Edward C. Fendt*, ed. Fred W. Meuser and Stanley D. Schneider (Minneapolis: Augsburg Publishing House, 1969); Frank Senn, "Martin Luther's Revision of the Eucharistic Canon in the Formula Missae of 1523," *Concordia Theological Monthly* 44 (1973): 101–118; Horace D. Hummel, "The 'Great Thanksgiving' in the 'Lutheran Book of Worship,'" *Christian News* 12/4 (January 22, 1979). Against its inclusion: Oliver K. Olson, "Contemporary Trends in Liturgy Viewed from the Perspective of Classical Lutheran Theology," *The Lutheran Quarterly* 26/2 (1974): 110–157, which points to significant issues; Armand J. Boehme, "Sing a New Song: The Doctrine of Justification and the *Lutheran Book of Worship* Sacramental Liturgies," *Concordia Theological Quarterly* 43/2 (1979): 96–119, which offers extensive references; Bryan Spinks, *Luther's Liturgical Criteria and His Reform of The Canon of The Mass* (Nottingham: Grove Books, 1982), but also his "Berakah, Anaphoral Theory and Luther," *Lutheran Quarterly* III/3 (Autumn 1989): 267–280.

28. The Pfalz-Neuberg church order of 1543 has this prayer: "Lord Jesus Christ, eternal, true Son of the living God,. . . we bring before your divine majesty these your own gifts of bread and wine, and pray that of the same, your divine grace, goodness and power, you would sanctify, bless, and make this bread to be your body and this wine your blood, and would grant that all those who eat and drink of them eternal life." Sehling XIII: 73. The "RedBook" of King John III of Sweden, *Liturgia Svecanae Ecclesiae, Catholicae & Orthodoxae Conformis*, facsimile ed. (Malmö: Malmö Ljustrycksanstadt, 1953), pp. XLI verso ff.

29. AE 38: 106.

30. For a carefully argued defense of Luther's liturgical work see Spinks, *Luther's Liturgical Criteria*.

31. WA 19: 96, translation by the Commission on Worship. Cf. AE 53: 79–80.

32. AE 36: 313.

33. *Svenska Kyrko-Handboken . . . 1942* (Stockholm: Svenska Kyrkans Diakonistyrelses Bokförlag, 1956), p. 35.

34. *Agende für evangelisch-lutherische Kirchen und Gemeinden*, vol. 1, 2d ed. (Berlin: Lutherisches Verlagshaus, 1963), pp. 216f.

35. Walter Reindell, "Die Glocken der Kirche," *Leiturgia: Handbuch des evange-lischen Gottesdienstes*, vol. 4, *Die Musik des evangelischen Gottesdienstes* (Kassel: Johannes Stauda-Verlag, 1961), pp. 873ff.

36. See Bard Thompson, *Liturgies of the Western Church* (Cleveland: World Publishing Company, 1961) pp. 72–75.

37. AE 38: 208f.

38. Ibid., p. 209.

39. FC SD VII, 74–75.

40. AE 53: 28.

41. Brief Confession Concerning the Holy Sacrament, 1544, AE 38: 314.

42. Table Talk Recorded by Caspar Heydenreich, 1542–43, AE 54: 461f.

43. Thompson, pp. 72–79. With few exceptions (alterations, abbreviations, occasional sequence, inclusion of four eucharistic prayers), this outline pertains today in *The Sacramentary* (1969), typical edition of which was authorized by the decree *Celebrationis Eucharisticae*, issued by the Sacred Congregation for Divine Worship, March 26, 1970. Variously referred to as the Roman Missal, *Missale Romanum*, Missal of Paul VI, it is the book that contains the texts for the Mass.

44. AE 53: 28.

45. Ibid., pp. 28f.

46. Dix, p. 109.

47. For helpful insights regarding this matter see Toivo Harjumpaa, "The Pastor's Communion," *Concordia Theological Quarterly* 52/2–3 (April–July 1988): 149–167. This article is an updated version of *Una Sancta Study Document 1* (1964). C. F. W. Walther, first president of the Missouri Synod, did not object to the pastor communing himself. In fact, he saw this necessary in certain isolated congregations. See C. F. W. Walther, *Americanisch-Lutherische Pastoraltheologie*, 4th ed. (St. Louis: Concordia Publishing House, 1897), pp. 197–200. Admitting that a lone pastor in the service can legitimately commune himself, John Fritz, however, suggests that the congregation choose a layman to distribute to him. John H. C. Fritz, *Pastoral Theology: A Handbook of Scriptural Principles* (St. Louis: Concordia Publishing House, 1932), p. 146. This appears to be a then-novel suggestion in the Synod's history. The procedure should evidently be resorted to only in special situations, for, ordinarily, he maintains, "pastors . . . have ample opportunity to receive the Sacrament when Conference and synods are held or by calling in a brother to minister for that purpose."

48. SA II, 8.

49. Thompson, p. 80.

50. AE 53: 29.

51. See Thompson, pp. 80–83.

52. Hatchett, p. 387.

53. Reed, p. 379.

54. AE 53: 29.

55. *Contemporary Worship 2*, p. 19.

56. Hatchett, p. 392.

57. AE 53: 29, 84.

58. Reed, pp. 385f.

59. AE 53: 30, 84; *Svenska Kyrko-Handboken*, p. 41.

60. David G. Truemper, "Evangelism: Liturgy *versus* Church Growth," *Lutheran Forum* 24/1 (Lent, February 1991): 32.

13

Daily Prayer

John T. Pless

Historical Background

Prayer in Jesus' name begins by listening to the voice of the Good Shepherd as he speaks to us from his Word, the Holy Scriptures. On the basis of that Word, the believer voices his petitions, intercessions, and thanksgivings. Kenneth Korby writes,

> As human beings learn to talk by listening to others around them, so liturgical prayer must be learned by listening to the "Our Father," to the Word addressed to us, and to the company of the family of God among whom we live. Where that lively and life-giving Word is received in the heart of faith, the prayer that is "conversation with God" happens.[1]

In his Word, the Father invites us to pray with all "freedom and confidence" (Eph. 3:12). The prayer forms of the daily office, litanies, and collects are not merely the vehicles of the Christian's prayer; they are also instructors that cement the believer to the Word of the Lord and tutor the faithful in that conversation with God, which is prayer. The Evangelical Lutheran Church is a grateful recipient of these ancient forms, which have their roots in the Scriptures.

The history of the early formation of the daily office is by no means clear. The New Testament is replete with injunctions to pray (Luke 18:1; 21:36; Rom. 12:12; Eph. 6:18; Col. 4:2; 1 Thess. 5:17; 1 Pet. 4:7). The early church was undoubtedly influenced by the Old Testament practice of fixed times for prayer (Ps. 34:1; 55:17; 65:8; 119:62, 164; Dan. 6:10) as is exemplified by Peter and John going up to the temple "at the time of prayer—at three in the afternoon" (Acts 3:1). Although more recent scholarship[2] has corrected and modified many of his findings, the statement of C. W. Dugmore is undoubtedly right that the early Christian custom of specific times for prayer each day is "the legacy of the synagogue."[3] The historical evidence does not allow for a firm answer to the question of how long Christians continued to attend Jewish synagogues, taking part in daily services of prayer. The *Didache* (c. 150) enjoins early Christians "day and night" to "remember him who preaches God's word to you, and honor him as the Lord, for where his lordship is spoken of, there is the Lord. Seek daily contact with the saints to be refreshed by their discourses."[4] The *Didache* continues to instruct the faithful that they are not to fast on the days on which the hypocrites (Jews) fast. Neither are they to pray with the hypocrites; rather they are to pray the Lord's Prayer "as commanded by the Lord in the Gospel. . . . Say this prayer three times a day."[5] The pattern for Jewish daily prayer provided the form, if not the content, for the daily prayers of the early church.

By the time of Hippolytus (d. 235), morning and evening prayer were normative. Hippolytus instructs Christians to pray at each of the three divisions of the Roman day (9:00 in the morning—*terce*; noon—*sext*; and 3:00 in the afternoon—*none*) in addition to the morning and evening prayers. It seems that these prescribed times for prayer were chiefly occasions for personal prayer and meditation. Cyprian, the third-century Bishop of Carthage, attached symbolic significance to each hour of prayer. Prayer at the break of day was observed in celebration of our Lord's rising from the grave. At the third hour the believer was to call to mind the descent of the Holy Spirit and the condemnation of the Savior. The prayer at noon was to commemorate the crucifixion. The ninth hour was to be observed as the hour when Christ washed away the sin of mankind by his blood. The final prayer in the evening was in praise of Christ who brought light into the darkness of the world. These prayers at the divisions of the day, along with morning and evening prayer, served as the basis for the establishment of a regular pattern of prayer.

Historians of liturgy have recently come to recognize that two different patterns of daily prayer developed at the same time in the church of the fourth century.[6] The so-called monastic office evolved out of the prayer life of monastic communities. At first, the liturgical life of the monasteries was normed by the church's liturgy. Yet for the most part the early monastic communities were isolated from the life of the local church. As Grisbrooke states, "The monks largely cut themselves off from the common worship of the church because they cut themselves off from its common life in the world, in order to give themselves to constant prayer." [7] The aim of the monastic life was contemplation and prayer. Thus, the liturgical forms of prayer that developed within monasticism focused on the maintenance of a regular and ordered life of prayer and praise. The central ingredient in the monastic office was the recital of the Psalter (*recitatio continua*) over a set period of time. In some places the monks participated by shift in the recitation and prayers. In most places various portions of the Psalter were assigned to each office.

Using Ps. 119:164, "Seven times a day I praise you for your righteous laws," as a biblical warrant for the practice, the monastic communities adopted prayer offices attached to the divisions of the day, adding to them two lesser offices, Prime and Compline. This resulted in the development of the following plan for the monastic communities of the West: Matins (night office); Lauds (at dawn); Prime (beginning of the day); Terce (9 a.m.); Sext (noon); None (3 p.m.); Vespers (close of day); Compline (before bed). The first two were combined into one, thus conforming to the psalmist's "seven times a day." Exact times of observance varied, depending on the purpose or occupation of the monastic community and the season of the year. Prescribed in the canon (rule) of Saint Benedict (c. 530), these prayer times became known as the *canonical hours.*

The cathedral office is the title given to the church's public services of Scripture reading, praise, and prayer. After the recognition of Christianity under Constantine, the daily services of the church became more common and took on a more fixed pattern. As the Spanish pilgrim lady, Egeria, testifies in her accounts of Vespers and Lauds in Jerusalem in the late fourth century, both clergy and laity attended these services.[8] Yet, the cathedral office, almost from its inception, was influenced by the monastic forms. Grisbrooke concludes, "Ultimately the monastic round and structure of the office conquered nearly everywhere."[9]

The history of daily prayer in the West during the Middle Ages is complex. The number of psalms used in the prayer offices varied from place to place. To the basic core of psalms with antiphons,

Scripture readings, responsories, and prayers, a number of elements were added. During the ninth century hymns began to find a place in the office even though there was strong opposition in some quarters to the inclusion of "nonscriptural" compositions in the services. It was not until the end of the 12th century that hymns were admitted into the daily office in Rome. Additional offices were created to supplement the orders of daily prayer. The Office of the Dead and the Office of the Blessed Virgin were regularly used with the daily office. Readings from the church fathers and other hagiographical writings eventually found a place within the daily office.

By the 16th century the daily office was, for the most part, the domain of the clergy. Luther simplified the daily office and returned it to the congregation. In his "Concerning the Order of Public Worship" (1523), Luther calls for the retention of the daily services:

> And though these daily services might not be attended by the whole congregation, the priests and pupils, and especially those who, one hopes, will become good preachers and pastors, should be present. And one should admonish them to do this willingly, not reluctantly or by constraint, or for the sake of reward, temporal or eternal, but alone to the glory of God and the neighbor's good."[10]

Luther's key concern is that the Word of God be made central in these services. In 1523 he complained,

> Three serious abuses have crept into the service. First, God's Word has been silenced, and only reading and singing remain in the churches. This is the worst abuse. Second, when God's Word had been silenced such a host of un-Christian fables and lies, in legends, hymns, and sermons were introduced that it is horrible to see. Third, such divine service was performed as a work whereby God's grace and salvation might be won. As a result, faith disappeared and everyone pressed to enter the priesthood, convents, and monasteries, and to build churches and endow them.[11]

"When God's Word is not preached," says Luther, "one had better neither sing nor read, or even come together."[12] Luther preserved Matins and Vespers as proper vehicles for the reading and proclamation of the Divine Word, calling forth praise and prayer of the Christian congregation.

Even though many of the *Kirchenordnungen* [13] (church orders) did retain Matins and Vespers, the office fell into disuse in most of the churches in Germany by the early part of the 17th century.[14] In certain Lutheran territories, Matins and Vespers did survive as late as the opening years of the 18th century.[15] In the 19th century Theodor Kliefoth in northern Germany and Wilhelm Löhe in Bavaria provided orders for Matins and Vespers for use in Lutheran congregations, schools, and deaconess communities.[16] Matins and Vespers were introduced to English-speaking Lutherans by way of the Common Service of 1888.

Matins

Matins (LW, pp. 208–23), which means "of the morning," is the name given to an ancient prayer office originally attached to the office of Lauds and conducted at the break of day. Eventually Matins was to become an office distinct from Lauds. Along with Vespers, Luther retained Matins as a daily office of preaching, praise, and prayer.

As the Christian congregation prays Matins, it receives the new day as a gift from God's hand with praise, thanksgiving, and intercession. God's Word is read and proclaimed. Thus the opening of the day is "consecrated by the word of God and prayer" (1 Tim. 4:5). The petitions of Matins seek God's blessing, protection, and guidance as the Christian prepares for the duties of the day.

The rubrics of *Lutheran Worship* indicate that Matins may begin with a hymn or invocation of the Holy Spirit.[17] The versicles have been part of the office of Matins since the sixth century. The first versicle is taken from Ps. 51:15. Here the believer calls on God to open the lips, for it is only then that praise and prayer takes place. The second versicle is from Ps. 70:1 where the psalmist calls on the name of the Lord for deliverance from his enemies. The use of this versicle represents the survival of a fragment of the ancient monastic custom of monks chanting the whole of Psalm 70 as they walked from their sleeping quarters to the chapel. The versicles conclude with the Gloria Patri and an ascription of praise. The practice of concluding each psalm with the Gloria Patri was in place in Gaul at the end of the fourth century, although trinitarian doxologies appear before the fourth century. These doxological forms were not fixed; therefore it was possible for Arians to shape them according to their own unorthodox understanding of the Trinity. Thus, the text of the Gloria Patri was fixed, becoming a test of orthodox faith.

Lutheran Worship provides three ascriptions of praise. The first is "Praise to you, O Christ, Alleluia." This ascription is appropriately used throughout the church year with the exception of Advent and Lent. The second ascription, "Praise to you, O Christ, King who comes to save us," is designated for Advent. "Praise to you, O Christ, Lamb of our salvation" is the ascription for Lent.

The Invitatory introduces and concludes the Venite and, in that sense, becomes an antiphon to this psalm of adoration. The Common Invitatory, "Blessed be God, the Father, the Son, and the Holy Spirit," is never inappropriate. Proper or seasonal invitatories are provided in *Lutheran Worship: Altar Book*.[18] The proper invitatories are brief statements that capsulize the theme of the day or season. Invitatories for the Time of the Church are drawn from Luther's Explanation to the Third Article of the Apostles' Creed in the Small Catechism and thus focus on the work of the Holy Spirit who calls, gathers, enlightens, and sanctifies his people. The Invitatory consists of two parts: statement and response. The statement, which is chanted by the leader, may vary according to the church year (note pp. 42–43 of *Lutheran Worship: Altar Book*), but the congregation's response, "Oh, come, let us worship him," remains invariable.

The Venite (Ps. 95:1–7a) is the chief psalm in Matins. In the Rule of St. Benedict (c. 480–c. 543) it is prescribed for use in the Nocturns, a forerunner of Matins. By way of the Roman and Sarum breviaries, it found its way into Lutheran and Anglican usage.

The principal hymn of Matins is the Office Hymn. Hymns appeared as a fixed part of the daily office in the Rule of Saint Benedict, although it was not until the 12th century that such hymns found a permanent place in Roman usage. The office hymn reflects the character of the daily office in that it is a hymn of praise and petition.[19] Traditionally, the final stanza of the office hymn is a trinitarian doxology.

After the office hymn, one or more Psalms are sung or said. The early church eagerly embraced the Psalter, "the hymn book of Israel" (see Eph. 5:19; Col. 3:16). The Psalms were the basic substance of the earliest forms of the daily office, with the whole of the Psalter being divided among the various offices.[20] Luther recognized the value of the church's use of the Psalms. In his treatise, "Concerning the Order of Public Worship" (1523), Luther urged that the congregation "unite in giving thanks to God, in praising him, and in praying for the fruits of the Word, etc. For this, the Psalms should be used and some good responsories and antiphons."[21] This practice is continued in *Lutheran Worship's* Matins.[22]

Each psalm may be framed with an appropriate antiphon. The antiphon is a brief sentence, usually a text from Scripture that points to the thematic emphasis of the psalm. Seasonal antiphons are provided on pages 122–25 of *Lutheran Worship: Altar Book.* The actual text of the psalm is concluded with the Gloria Patri. If an antiphon is used, it follows the Gloria Patri.

The rubrics of *Lutheran Worship* call for one or two readings from Holy Scripture. If Matins is used as a church service on Sundays and festivals, the appointed readings for the day are used. When Matins is prayed daily, either privately or corporately, the readings may be drawn from the table, Readings for Daily Prayer, page 133 in *Lutheran Worship: Altar Book.* This lectionary, derived from the Church of Sweden, follows the ancient practice of presenting consecutive readings (*lectio continua*) from various books of the Bible.

The readings are followed by the versicle "O Lord, have mercy on us"/"Thanks be to God" or the appropriate responsory. In the versicle, the Christian congregation joins the leper (Luke 17:11–19) in imploring our Lord for mercy and giving thanks that through the Word of God the promised mercy is bestowed.

Of the Responsory, Luther D. Reed writes,

> The responsory is an ancient and characteristic chant form originally sung after each lesson at Matins. With the development of the Divine Office, the responsory assumed a unique liturgical pattern which combined verses and responses from Scriptures appropriate to the feast or season. The name may have been derived from the arrangement of the text or from the method of its musical rendition.[23]

The medieval practice was to sing a responsory after each reading from Scripture. Unlike the Anglican liturgical reformers, the

Lutheran reformers retained a number of the "pure" responsories for use after the last Scripture reading in Matins and Vespers.

The Responsory is made up of a Scripture verse and a refrain that remains constant throughout the responsory. The first part of the third pairing in the common responsory and the responsory for Easter and its season is the Gloria Patri (first part). The responsory for Lent omits the Gloria Patri altogether. The common responsory is composed of texts from Ps. 119:89; Ps. 26:8 (refrain); and Luke 11:28. Texts from 1 John 2:1; Rom. 8:32 (refrain); and Ps. 32:1 make up the responsory for Lent. The responsory for Easter and its season is constructed with sentences from Ps. 96:2; Ps. 29:1–2 with alleluias (refrain); and 1 Cor. 15:20.

The Sermon follows the Responsory. If no sermon is to be preached (which may be the case when Matins is used as the daily prayer of a congregration, seminary, or college community), it is appropriate that a brief exposition accompany the Readings. The advice of Olof Herrlin is to the point:

> It [the daily office] keeps the flame of prayer alive in the church all week long, prayer that is nourished by God's word and which is, essentially, a praying of the word which nourishes the personal, intimate act of worship. It fosters familiarity with the word; it is an assertion of the word, which by no means makes preaching superfluous, but rather provides a new sensitivity to preaching, and imparts increased creativity to it.[24]

If an offering is to be included in the service, it is received after the sermon.

The canticles for use at Matins are the Te Deum and the Benedictus. The Te Deum is a Latin hymn to the Father and the Son in rhythmical prose. A tradition that dates back to the ninth century assigns authorship of this hymn to St. Ambrose and St. Augustine upon the occasion of Augustine's baptism. Dom Morin's studies have concluded that the Te Deum is the composition of Niceta, Bishop of Romesiana in Dacia, and a contemporary of Saint Jerome. This conclusion is generally accepted in modern liturgical scholarship,[25] although some argue that the Te Deum was derived from a text of a Paschal Vigil.[26] At any rate, the Te Deum has remained an integral part of Matins since the time of Saint Benedict.

In Luther's estimation, the Te Deum deserved to be ranked with the Nicene and Athanasian Creeds as one of "the three symbols or creeds of the Christian Faith."[27] In 1529, Luther provided a hymnic paraphrase of the Te Deum entitled "Lord God, Thy Praise We Sing," recommending it as a "vernacular song [that] I should like us to have."[28]

The use of the Te Deum is appropriate at Matins on all Sundays and festivals except during Advent and Lent. The rubrics of *Lutheran Worship* specify that "the Te Deum may be sung to an alternate setting (see Canticles and Chants, No. 8)."[29] An additional alternative is the hymn, "Holy God, we praise your name" (LW 171).

The Benedictus is the song of thanksgiving spoken by Zechariah at the birth of his son, John the Baptist (Luke 1:68–79). This canticle follows the form of the Jewish *berakah* in praising God for the fulfillment of his messianic promises given "by the mouth of his holy prophets, who have been since the world began." The Benedictus was first used at Lauds and eventually incorporated into Matins. Two forms of the Benedictus are given in *Lutheran Worship*. The shorter form is appropriately used on weekdays and during Lent. The longer form is especially appropriate during Advent, as it provides a definite focus on the work of the forerunner who, as the prophet of the Most High, "will go before the Lord to prepare his ways; to give knowledge of salvation to his people in the forgiveness of their sins, through the tender mercy of our God."

Two options are provided for the Prayers in Matins according to the rubrics of *Lutheran Worship*. The sequence of the threefold Kyrie, Lord's Prayer, Salutation or Versicle, Collects, Benedicamus, and Blessing may conclude the service. Responsive Prayer 1 (p. 270) may be used in place of the above-mentioned sequence.

Sometimes called "the lesser litany," the Kyrie echoes the cry of David for divine mercy in Psalm 51:1. Luther D. Reed notes,

> Scriptural parallels to this liturgical invocation are Is. 33:2; Matt. 15:22, 20:30; and Luke 16:24, though they were probably not its source. In every case we find here the cry of those in need and distress imploring divine mercy and help. In the ancient breviary offices the Kyrie at this place expanded into lengthy litany forms of prayer and intercession. As used here [in Matins] the Kyrie is a prelude to the supplications which follow, just as the Gloria at

the end of the opening versicle in the office is a prelude to praise.[30]

The Lord's Prayer is the prayer from which all other Christian prayers flow, and it thus precedes the collects. The Lord's Prayer is separated from them by the Salutation.

Hermann Sasse notes that the Salutation expresses the connection of the prayer of the Christian congregation with Christ himself:

"The Lord be with you": this introductory salutation of the bishop expresses the wish to the congregation that the Lord Christ may now pray with it and make its prayer his own. The Head of this Body prays together with the Body. The response "and with thy spirit" expresses the wish of the congregation to the minister who leads the prayer that the Lord may pray together with him, make his prayer His own, so that the prayer rises up before God's throne "through Jesus Christ our Lord." Despite the fact that the Salutation with its *parallelismus membrorum* may well go back to Jewish sources, in the church that has all received a new meaning because of its strict Christological relationship.[31]

When a lay person leads Matins, it is appropriate that the versicle ("O Lord, hear my prayer."/"And let my cry come to you") be used in place of the Salutation.

The Collect of the Day is the first collect to be prayed and should be prayed at all services during the week. Additional collects may be added according to the needs of the congregation. *Lutheran Worship* provides three concluding collects. The first is based on the Third Commandment and invokes the Holy Spirit to prepare the hearts of God's people "to hear and keep" the Word, thus "rightly sanctifying" the holy day. This collect would be most appropriate for Saturday Matins. The second is a prayer of thanksgiving for God's mercies and a petition for the Holy Spirit "that we may heartily acknowledge" God's merciful goodness. The third concluding collect is the Collect for Grace, the traditional collect at Matins. The final collect always ends with the full termination, which generally reads, "through Jesus Christ, your Son, our Lord, who lives and reigns with you and the Holy Spirit, one God, now and forever."[32]

In the pre-Reformation orders for daily prayer, the Benedicamus concluded the service. The Benedicamus calls on the congregation to give thanks to God. Reed sees the roots of the Benedicamus in the doxologies that conclude the first four divisions of the Psalter (Ps. 41:13; 72:18; 89:52; 106:48) and in 1 Cor. 15:57 where the apostle gives thanks for grace received.

Two forms of the Blessing are provided. Both are drawn from 2 Cor. 13:14. The first form is used when the officiant is an ordained minister. If the service is led by someone other than an ordained minister, the second form is used.

Vespers

Vespers (LW, pp. 224–35), meaning "evening" (from the Latin *vespera*), was originally known as *lucernarium,* as candles or lamps were lit in the course of its liturgy. Vespers was originally part of the night office, but by the time of Saint Benedict, it was transferred to the early evening or late afternoon. In structure, Vespers is very similar to Matins as both services provide for the praise of God in psalmody, hymns, and canticles, the opportunity for the reading and proclamation of God's Word, and space for the prayers of the faithful.

Like Matins, Vespers may begin with a hymn of invocation of the Holy Spirit. The versicles and ascriptions of praise in Vespers are identical to those in Matins. There is no parallel in Vespers to the Venite of Matins. The rubrics for Vespers direct that one or more psalms are sung or said, each concluding with the Gloria Patri. *Lutheran Worship: Altar Book* suggests that Psalms 23, 110, 111, and 114 be used on Sundays and major festivals, while Psalms 6, 38, 46, 51, 105, 116, 117, 118, 126, 130, 135, 136, 138, 139, 141, 142, 143, and 146 be used on other days. When Vespers is prayed on a Sunday or festival, the Psalm appointed for that day (see LW, pp. 10–123) should be prayed. The Psalm appointed for Sunday may be used at Vespers throughout the week. As in Matins, "each Psalm may be framed by an appropriate antiphon."[33]

The psalmody is followed by one or two Readings, the Versicle ("O Lord, have mercy on us."/"Thanks be to God.") or a responsory. The responsories for Vespers are similar to those provided for Matins.

The Office Hymn in Vespers serves the same function as it does in Matins: it reflects the time of day or the particular season of the church year.[34] The sermon and offering may follow the office hymn.

A versicle from Ps. 141:2 introduces the Canticle, reminiscent of the time when Psalm 141 in its entirety was a prominent part of the service as both the *Apostolic Constitutions*[35] (c. 380) and Ambrose of Milan (c. 339–397) confirm. In fact, Ambrose refers to the evening office as "the evening sacrifice."[36]

Two canticles are provided. The Magnificat (see Luke 1:46–55) is the hymn of the virgin Mary in response to Gabriel's announcement that she is to be the mother of the Savior. The Magnificat has been used in Vespers since at least the sixth century. Luther prefaced his rather extensive commentary on the Magnificat with these words:

> Now, in all of Scripture I do not know anything that serves such a purpose so well as this sacred hymn of the most blessed Mother of God, which ought indeed to be learned and kept in mind by all who would rule well and be helpful lords. In it she really sings sweetly about the fear of God, what sort of Lord He is, and especially what His dealings are with those of low and high degree. Let someone else listen to his love singing a worldly ditty; this pure virgin well deserves to be heard by prince and lord, as she sings him her sacred, chaste, and salutary song. It is a fine custom, too, that this canticle is sung in all churches daily at vespers, and in special and appropriate settings that set it apart from other chants.[37]

Not only did Luther urge the retention of the Magnificat in Vespers, in 1533 he provided a chant setting of this canticle for use in the congregations of Saxony.[38]

The Nunc Dimittis is the second canticle provided for Vespers in *Lutheran Worship*. Like the Magnificat, this is also from the Gospel According to Saint Luke (2:29–32). As early as the fourth century, the Nunc Dimittis was included in the evening prayers of the church.[39] Apparently it was originally used as a canticle in the *Lucernarium*. Eventually it came to be used in the Roman office of Compline. In the Reformation, the number of daily offices was reduced. It appears that elements of Compline were included in Vespers. Thus Löhe notes that "the Lutheran Matins follows essentially upon the Roman Matins, and the Lutheran Vespers upon the

Roman Vespers, only that besides the Te Deum in Matins, there is the Benedictus which has been taken from Lauds, and besides the Magnificat in Vespers there is the Nunc dimittis which has been taken from Compline."[40] The Notes on the Liturgy in *Lutheran Worship: Altar Book* suggest that "the Magnificat, historically speaking, is the more appropriate [for use in Vespers]. The Nunc Dimittis is better reserved for Prayer at the Close of the Day."[41]

As in Matins, there are two options for the Prayers in Vespers. The Kyrie, Our Father, Salutation or Versicle, Collects, Benedicamus, and Blessing may conclude the service, or Responsive Prayer 2 (p. 273 in LW) may be used at this point.

Four collects are provided in the service. The Collect at Vespers ("Direct us, O Lord") has as its source the Gregorian Sacramentary, where it occurs as a collect to be prayed on the Saturday before the Lenten ordination and at the end of the service of ordination itself. This collect is also used as the final prayer of the Mass in the Sarum Missal and as a post-communion collect in the *Book of Common Prayer*. This collect is most fitting for Vespers as it implores God to direct the activities of his people by his most gracious favor "that in all our works begun, continued, and ended" in him, his name may be glorified and by his mercy we may be brought to eternal salvation. The Collect in Late Afternoon is addressed to the "Lord, our dwelling place and our peace, who has pity on our weakness." This collect petitions God to "put far from us all worry and fearfulness that . . . we may, when night shall come, commit ourselves, our work, and all we love into your gracious keeping receiving from you the gift of quiet sleep." Thus, this collect anticipates the ending of the day in Christ's name. The third collect ("O Lord God, the life of all the living") is appointed for use in the evening as it invokes the Lord God who is "the life of the living, the light of the faithful," to grant his people a peaceful and quiet night that they may be "endued in the new day with the guidance of your Holy Spirit and enabled to render thanks to you." The final collect is the Collect for Peace, traditionally the final collect of Vespers. This collect, from the Gelasian Sacramentary, dates back to the fifth century. Reed notes, "As we use this collect in Vespers it also looks backward over the experiences of the day, and, catching up the tone of the Nunc Dimittis ere it dies away, prolongs it in this petition for that peace which the world cannot give."[42]

Morning Prayer

Morning Prayer in *Lutheran Worship* (pp. 236–49) is a slightly revised form of the order by the same name in *Lutheran Book of Worship*. The service begins with a versicle (Ps. 51:15) and the Gloria Patri. The Alleluia follows the Gloria. The Venite is introduced and concluded with the Invitatory ("Give glory to God, our light and our life."/"Oh, come, let us worship him"). Seasonal invitatories may replace the common invitatory during Advent, Christmas, Epiphany, Lent, and Easter (see LW, pp. 288–90). The Invitatory and Venite are omitted during Holy Week. The rubrics of *Lutheran Worship* suggest that another canticle or, on weekdays, "a hymn that reflects the theme of resurrection, light, or morning" may replace the Venite.[43] Appropriate hymns as substitutes for the Venite would include

Christ Is Arisen 124
Awake, My Heart, with Gladness 128
The Day of Resurrection 133
This Joyful Eastertide 140
Come, You Faithful, Raise the Strain 141
That Easter Day with Joy Was Bright 147
O God of God, O Light of Light 83
Arise and Shine in Splendor 85
Awake, My Soul, and with the Sun 478
O Holy, Blessed Trinity 479
Christ, Whose Glory Fills the Skies 480
O Splendor of the Father's Light 481
May God Embrace Us with His Grace 288

Alternate canticles would include

Holy, Holy, Holy 6
All You Works of the Lord 9
Christians, to the Paschal Victim (for Easter and its season) 10

As the Benedictus, Magnificat, and Te Deum have fixed positions in other parts of the daily office, they should never be used as substitutes for the Venite.

Additional psalms should be sung or said after the Venite as the Venite invites the congregation to come into God's presence with thanksgiving and "make a joyful noise to him with songs of praise." Thus, the Venite actually serves as the introduction to this central portion of Morning Prayer. Each psalm is concluded with the Gloria Patri. Silence for reflection may follow the psalmody.

The psalmody and the Readings are bridged by the Hymn. This is the chief hymn or office hymn in Morning Prayer and as such it should reflect the particular season of the church year or the theme of morning, resurrection, or light. For a listing of the suggested office hymns see Appendix 1.

A period of silence may follow each reading. If this option is exercised, the congregation may need some instruction as to the proper use of this portion of the liturgy, lest it become a break in the service. The period of silence is provided in order that the worshipers may prayerfully ponder the Word of God that has been read; thus the time of silence should be more than a mere pause. After the silence following the final reading, the officiant, or leader, and congregation speak responsively the versicle drawn from Heb. 1:1–2a.

The Gospel Canticle for Morning Prayer is the translation of the Benedictus in the International Consultation on English Texts. The rubrics in *Lutheran Worship* note, "If the Paschal Blessing is not used at the end of the service, the canticle 'You are God, we praise you,' page 246, or 'We praise you, O God,' page 214, may replace this canticle."[44] An antiphon may be sung before and after the Benedictus. Seasonal antiphons for use with the Benedictus are provided on pages 122–25 of *Lutheran Worship: Altar Book*.

Perhaps the most significant antiphons for use with the Benedictus and Magnificat are the "O Antiphons" (see *Lutheran Worship* pp. 288–89 and pp. 122–23 of *Lutheran Worship: Altar Book* for the texts of these ancient antiphons) appointed for use in Morning and Evening Prayer in the days preceding Christmas (December 17–23). The authorship and time of composition of the "O Antiphons" is unknown, although they were in use in the eighth century in Rome. Each of the seven antiphons, beginning with the vocative "O," invokes God, using a particular messianic title.[45] The great hymn of Advent, "Oh, come, oh, come, Emmanuel" (LW 31) is based on these venerable antiphons.

In *Lutheran Worship,* Morning Prayer may conclude in various ways. A series of collects beginning with the Collect of the Day and concluding with the Collect for Grace (adapted), which is then followed by the Lord's Prayer, Benedicamus, and Blessing brings the service to completion. The Litany, the classic Western form (p. 279), or Responsive Prayer 1 (p. 270) may take the place of the above-mentioned sequence. When The Litany is used, the service would be concluded with the Collect for Grace, Benedicamus, and the Blessing (pp. 242–243).

The rubrics in *Lutheran Worship,* taking their cue from *Lutheran Book of Worship,* follow the rather recent Anglican practice of placing the sermon at the end of the service. After the Benedicamus, Offering, and Hymn, the Sermon is preached. Unfortunately, this arrangement separates the sermon from the Readings. One of three prayers then follows the Sermon. The first prayer ("Almighty God, grant to your Church") is from page 14 of *The Lutheran Hymnal.* The second ("Lord God, you have called") is by Eric Milner-White.[46] The third prayer ("Lord, we thank you") is from the former Evangelical Lutheran Church's *Lutheran Hymnary.*[47] The trinitarian Blessing concludes the service.

Finally, the Paschal Blessing may be used on Sundays (except during Lent) and throughout the 50 days of Easter to conclude Morning Prayer. If there is no sermon, it follows immediately after the Benedicamus; if there is a sermon, it follows the concluding prayer. The Paschal Blessing may be conducted from the baptismal font, thus to emphasize the connection between our Lord's resurrection and our baptism into his death. This connection makes its use appropriate also in family devotions to observe baptismal anniversaries.

Bangert notes that "the Paschal Blessing is really a liturgical gloss on the Benedicamus,"[48] appearing to have its roots in the resurrection vigil conducted each Sunday in Jerusalem.[49] It is introduced by a sentence from Gal. 3:27 ("All of you who were baptized into Christ have been clothed with Christ"), to which the congregation responds by chanting "Alleluia." The Easter Gospel from Luke 24:1–7 is chanted by the officiant. The Te Deum is the congregation's song of praise to the risen Savior. A collect that connects the Lord's redemptive death and glorious resurrection with the believer's deliverance from the power of death through Baptism follows the Te Deum. The service is concluded with the Blessing.

Evening Prayer

Evening Prayer in *Lutheran Worship* (pp. 250–62) is a slightly revised form of the order by the same name in *Lutheran Book of Worship*. Evening Prayer begins with the Service of Light, a form of the ancient *Lucernarium*. For pious Jews of the first century, the beginning and end of the Sabbath was marked with a ceremony of lamplighting accompanied by the benediction, "Blessed are you, O Lord our God, King of the Universe, who creates the light of fire."[50] It is uncertain as to how this ceremony is related to the development of the *Lucernarium*. The time of evening prayer is referred to as the "lamplighting psalm." Paul Bradshaw points out that "there is no evidence that anything more is intended by this than a reference to the time of day at which the psalm was sung."[51] By the time of Gregory of Nyssa (c. 330–c. 395) the *Lucernarium* had been incorporated into the cathedral vespers of the Eastern Church.[52]

The Service of Light in Evening Prayer in *Lutheran Worship* begins with sentences that focus on Jesus Christ, the Light of the world (John 8:12; 1:5) and the Emmaus disciples' request that the risen Lord remain with them (Luke 24:29). Seasonal versicles (see *Lutheran Worship* p. 290 and pp. 122–25 of *Lutheran Worship: Altar Book*) may be substituted for the sentences during Advent, Christmas, Epiphany, Lent, and Easter. The Service of Light is omitted during Holy Week, when the Office begins with Psalm 141. As the sentences are chanted, a large lighted candle may be carried into the darkened church. The candle is set in its place in front of the congregation and thus serves as the focal point of the service, signifying that Jesus Christ, the Light of the world, is present to enlighten his faithful people through his Word, which "is a lamp to my feet and a light for my path" (Ps. 119:105).

The sentences serve as an introduction to the hymn, "Joyous light of glory" (*phos hilaron*). Basil the Great (d. 379) notes that this hymn was to be received as a revered song of praise, even though he did not know who wrote it:

It seemed fitting to our fathers not to receive the gift of the evening light in silence, but to give thanks immediately upon its appearance. We cannot say who was the father of the words of thanksgiving for the light. But the people utter the ancient formula, and those that say "We praise you Father, Son, and Holy Spirit of God" were never thought impious by anyone.[53]

The hymn remained an integral part of the Byzantine Vespers.

As the "Joyous light of glory" is sung, the candles on and near the altar may be lighted with a flame from the large candle. On occasion, "O gladsome Light" (LW 486), a metrical paraphrase of the *phos hilaron,* may replace the "Joyous light of glory."

The Service of Light is concluded with the thanksgiving, a form adapted from the Roman Catholic *Morning Praise and Evensong.*[54] Pfatteicher notes that "it is cast in the form of the Jewish *Berekah* which thanks God for his goodness."[55] Two alternate forms of the thanksgiving are provided in *Lutheran Worship: Altar Book* (p. 125). The first alternate ("We praise and thank you, O God, for you are without beginning") is from the *Apostolic Constitutions* (c. 380); the second, from the *Apostolic Traditions* of Hippolytus (c. 215).[56]

The writings of John Chrysostom (c. 347–407) demonstrate that Psalm 141 was in use in Evening Prayer in the fourth century. *The Apostolic Costitutions* from the same period confirms the testimony given by Chrysostom as it directs the faithful to "assemble yourselves together every day, morning and evening, singing psalms and praying in the Lord's house, in the morning saying the 62d (63d) psalm and in the evening the 140th (141st)."[57] It is not surprising, therefore, that this psalm or portions thereof found a place in the evening office in many sectors of the ancient church.

In *Lutheran Worship* selected verses of Psalm 140 (141)—verses 2, 1, 3, 4, 8—are woven together into a song invoking God's deliverance and protection. Verse 2, paraphrased as "Let my prayer rise before you as incense; the lifting up of my hands as the evening sacrifice," serves as the antiphon. Between the psalm and the psalm prayer, a time of silence is kept for meditation. The psalm prayer extends the theme of the antiphon, associating the incense with "our repentant prayer" and imploring God to let his "loving kindness descend on us that with purified minds we may sing" his praises with "the church on earth and the whole heavenly host." Additional psalms may follow the psalm prayer.

As in Morning Prayer, the Hymn serves as a bridge between the psalmody and the Readings. This hymn is the office hymn and as such it should reflect the evening theme or the emphasis of the season of the church year. See Appendix 2 for suggested office hymns.

The office hymn is followed by one or two Readings. Silence for meditation may follow each reading. The versicle from Heb. 1:1–2a is spoken responsively.

The Gospel Canticle for Evening Prayer is the Magnificat. In Evening Prayer, the translation of the Magnificat by the International Consultation on English Texts is used. Seasonal antiphons (see pp. 122–25 of *Lutheran Worship: Altar Book*) may be used to introduce and conclude the Gospel Canticle. "My soul now magnifies the Lord" (LW 211), a metrical paraphrase of the Magnificat, may be used in place of the Gospel Canticle.

The Litany appointed for Evening Prayer has its roots in the evening office used in Jerusalem. Egeria, the Spanish pilgrim, provides this description of the fourth-century service:

> Hymns and antiphons are recited. When they have finished them according to their custom, the bishop rises and stands in front of the screen and one of the deacons makes commemoration of individuals according to the custom, and when the deacon says the names of individuals, a large group of boys respond, *Kyrie eleison,* or as we say, "Lord have mercy." Their voices are very loud. When the deacon has finished all that he has to say, the bishop first recites a prayer and prays for all.[58]

The Litany achieved a permanent place in the liturgy of the Eastern church by way of the Liturgy of Saint John Chrysostom. The text in Evening Prayer is a conflation based largely on the Liturgy of Chrysostom.[59] It is at once all-inclusive and quite specific as the praying congregation makes petitions to God for the whole world, the church throughout the world, those who serve in church and world, and the local congregation. Christian names of the district president, as well as the president of the Synod, may be used in the fifth bid. The litany is not without a note of thanksgiving as the eleventh bid invites the congregation to give thanks to the Lord for the faithful who are now at rest. A period of silence is kept before the final bid, wherein the whole life of the Christian is commended to Christ. As the litany commences with the invitation, "In peace let us pray to the Lord," so it is fitting that the litany concludes with the Collect for Peace.

After the Collect for Peace, the Our Father is introduced with the petition "Lord, remember us in your kingdom, and teach us to pray." This introductory petition is a conflation of Luke 23:41 and 11:1. It is especially appropriate during Advent and Lent to use the classic Litany (LW, p. 279) in place of the Eastern Litany, Collect for Peace, and Our Father, since the classic Western Litany is more penitential in content.

When there is no sermon, the service concludes with the Benedicamus and the trinitarian Blessing. If a sermon is to be preached, the following order would be used after the Benedicamus:

> Offering
> Hymn
> Sermon
> Prayer
> Trinitarian Blessing

Compline

Prayer at the Close of the Day (LW, pp. 263–69), or, as it has been known since the fourth century, Compline (from the Latin *completorium*), is the final prayer office of the day. Compline had its genesis in the monasteries of the fourth century; it was the order of night prayers said by the monks in their dormitories just before retiring for the evening. There is evidence to suggest that the original form of Compline was constructed by Saint Basil (c. 330–79). It was Benedict of Nursia (c. 540) who gave Compline its liturgical form in the West. In his Rule, Benedict writes,

> Let Compline be limited to the saying of three psalms, which are to be straightforwardly said without antiphons, after which let there be the hymn of that hour, a lesson, a versicle, the Kyrie, and a blessing to conclude. . . . Let the same psalms be repeated everyday at Compline which are Psalms 4, 91, and 134.[60]

In time, various additions were made to Compline, including the Lord's Prayer, the Ave Maria, the Apostles' Creed, Confession and Absolution, antiphons for the psalms, collects, and the Nunc Dimittis.

In *Lutheran Worship* Compline is introduced with the sentence, "The Lord grant us a quiet night and peace at the last," a sentence that draws a parallel between a quiet night of sleep and a peaceful death. The remainder of the sentences are from Ps. 92:1–2. These sentences bring the day to completion with their emphasis on the heralding of God's love in the morning and the declaration of his truth at the ending of the day.

A hymn appropriate for a night service is to be sung after the sentences. The placement of this hymn in the structure of Compline is parallel to the Venite in Morning Prayer and the "Joyous light of glory" in Evening Prayer. Appropriate hymns are

All Praise to Thee, My God, This Night 484
Now Rest Beneath Night's Shadow 485
O Gladsome Light, O Grace 486
O Trinity, O Blessed Light 487
Before the Ending of the Day 489
God, Who Made the Earth and Heaven 492

The hymn used at this point in Compline should be dominated by the motif of praise to God for his blessings at the end of the day.

Compline contains two forms for the Confession of sin. Both are introduced with the invitation, "Let us confess our sin in the presence of God and of one another." The invitation to confession is followed by a period of silence for self-examination. The first form consists of a brief prayer of general confession, spoken by the congregation, and a declaration of forgiveness, spoken by the officiant. The second is the reciprocal form of confession between officiant, or leader, and congregation, thereafter between congregation and officiant—the form historically associated with Compline.

In addition to the three fixed psalms (4, 91, and 134) of Compline according to Benedict's Rule, *Lutheran Worship* lists Psalms 34 and 136 as also appropriate. Each psalm is concluded with the Gloria Patri.

Compline is a devotional office at the end of the day; it is not a preaching office. Its structure, therefore, does not include lengthy readings from Holy Scripture. Instead, a Brief Reading (sometimes called the "Little Chapter") from Jer. 14:9; Matt. 11:28–30; John 14:27;

Rom. 8:38–39; or 1 Peter 5:6–9a is read. The reading from Jer. 14:9 is the reading traditionally associated with Compline. The brief reading is followed by the Responsory drawn from Ps. 31:5.

The Hymn that follows the responsory is the chief hymn of the service and, as such, it should reflect the time of day, or perhaps the season of the church year. In addition to the evening hymns (484–92) contained in *Lutheran Worship,* the following may be appropriately used as the chief hymn of Compline.

Advent
O Lord of Light, Who Made the Stars 17
O Savior, Rend the Heavens Wide 32

Christmas
We Praise, O Christ, Your Holy Name 35
O Savior of Our Fallen Race 45
On Christmas Night All Christians Sing 65

Epiphany
From God the Father, Virgin-Born 74
O God of God, O Light of Light 83

Lent
Jesus, Refuge of the Weary 90
Grant, Lord Jesus, That My Healing 95

Easter
Abide with Us, Our Savior 287
Lord Jesus Christ, Will You Not Stay 344

Pentecost
Come, Gracious Spirit, Heavenly Dove 161

Sentences from Ps. 17:1, 8, 15 are sung responsively. The use of these can be traced to their place in the office of Compline in the medieval Sarum and Roman service books.

The order of Compline in *Lutheran Worship* contains six evening prayers. The first ("Be present, merciful God") is an adapted form of a prayer in the *Book of Common Prayer* (1979). The second ("O Lord, support us") has as its source a sermon by John Henry Newman (1801–90). An unknown editor fashioned the concluding words of Newman's sermon into a prayer that made its way into the *Book of Common Prayer* in 1928. The third prayer ("Be our light in the darkness") is a Gelasian collect that was part of the office of Vespers in the Sarum Breviary. The fourth prayer ("Visit our

461

dwellings") is the traditional prayer at Compline. The fifth prayer ("Eternal God, the hours of both day and night") is based on a prayer in the *Authorized Services* of the Episcopal Church. And the final prayer ("Gracious Lord, we give you thanks") is by Edward Roe.[61] The Our Father is prayed after one or more of the above-mentioned prayers.

The Nunc Dimittis is the canticle historically associated with Compline. Pfatteicher writes that Prayer at the Close of the Day concludes "with the singing of the Song of Simeon as the departure song of the people of God. With this song and the Gloria Patri their praise is concluded for the day."[62] The Nunc Dimittis is framed with the antiphon, "Guide us waking, O Lord, and guard us sleeping that awake we may watch with Christ and asleep we may rest in peace," an antiphon that aptly summarizes the whole of the office. "In peace and joy I now depart" (LW 185) may occasionally be used as a substitute for the Nunc Dimittis. The service is concluded with the trinitarian Blessing.

Responsive Prayer 1

Responsive Prayer 1 (LW, pp. 270–72) is subtitled *Suffrages* (from the Latin *suffragia,* meaning prayer seeking God's support and assistance). Responsive Prayer 1 is for use in the morning. It may be used alone as an office of morning prayer, or it may be used in place of the prayers in Matins and Morning Prayer. When Responsive Prayer 1 is used as a separate office, it may be prefaced with a psalm or hymn and a reading from Scripture.

Responsive Prayer 1 begins with a versicle that is an adapted form of the *Trisagion* (thrice holy), a prominent feature of Greek liturgies. The versicle serves as an introduction to the Our Father. The Apostles' Creed follows the Our Father. When Responsive Prayer 1 is used as the prayers in Matins or Morning Prayer, the Creed may be omitted.

A litany of versicles and responses, called the *preces feriales,* was part of the daily offices of prayer as early as the time of Cyprian (c. 200–258). The *preces* were preserved in Lutheran orders of Matins and Vespers at the time of the Reformation. The *preces* in

Responsive Prayer 1 represent selected psalm verses (Ps. 88:13; 51:12; 71:8; 145:2; 103:1, 5).

The salutation precedes the Collect of the Day. Additional collects may follow the Collect of the Day. The final prayer in Responsive Prayer 1 is an updated version of Luther's morning prayer in the Small Catechism.

The Benedicamus and the Blessing conclude the service.

Responsive Prayer 2

Responsive Prayer 2 (LW, pp. 273–75) is for use at times other than the morning. It may also be used as the *Itinerarium,* the prayer office before travel. Responsive Prayer 2 may be used in place of the prayers in Vespers or the litany in Evening Prayer. It may also serve as a separate prayer office.

The structure of Responsive Prayer 2 is identical to that of Responsive Prayer 1. In Responsive Prayer 1, the *preces* praise God while calling him to sustain and bless. The *preces* in Responsive Prayer 2 petition God on behalf of the church and the world, using such portions of Scripture (with one exception) as Ps. 85:7; 132:9; Lev. 26:6; Ps. 67:2; 9:18; and 51:10. The exception is the fourth set, consisting of statements derived from the prayer For Peace Among the Nations in the *Book of Common Prayer* (1979), page 816. Responsive Prayer 2 provides four concluding prayers. When Responsive Prayer 2 is prayed for Noon, the prayer "Gracious Jesus, our Lord and God," is used, a prayer that recalls our Lord's suffering on the cross and implores him for mercy "now and at the hour of our death." The Prayer for the Afternoon is taken from the *Book of Common Prayer* (1979). In the midst of the activities of the day, the praying congregation asks God "so to guide and govern us" by Word and Spirit "that in all the cares and occupations of our life we may not forget" him. The prayer for the Evening is from Luther's Small Catechism. It is a prayer for forgiveness, mercy, and protection. The Prayer Before Travel is from the *Lutheran Book of Worship.* This prayer, recalling God's protection and guidance given to Abraham and Sarah, the children of Israel, and the Wise Men, implores him to keep those set out to travel in safety and joy. Like Responsive

Prayer 1, Responsive Prayer 2 concludes with the Benedicamus and the Blessing.

The Bidding Prayer

The Bidding Prayer (LW, pp. 276–78) represents an ancient form of corporate prayer that grows out of the Apostle's directive "that requests, prayers, intercession and thanksgiving be made for everyone—for kings and all those in authority, that we may live peaceful and quiet lives in all godliness and holiness" (1 Tim. 2:1–2). The early Roman liturgy included intercessions known as the Prayer of the Faithful. By the time of Gregory the Great (c. 540–604), this prayer was omitted from the regular eucharistic liturgy and retained only in the service of Good Friday, immediately after the reading of the Passion according to St. John. This prayer came to be known as the Bidding Prayer ("bid" from the Anglo-Saxon word meaning "to pray"). Reed suggests that the text of the Bidding Prayer in the Roman liturgy probably dates from the time of Leo the Great in the fifth century.[63] At the time of the Reformation, many church orders retained the Bidding Prayer, editing it to conform to scriptural teachings.

In *Lutheran Worship* the Bidding Prayer finds its primary use in the liturgies of Good Friday.[64] This practice follows the historical usage of the Western church as noted above. An assisting minister leads the Bidding Prayer by reading the bids, while the presiding minister reads the actual intercession. A time of silence may be kept between each bid and prayer.

The Bidding Prayer is composed of eight bids and prayers, making intercessions for both church and world:

1. The whole church
2. Ministers of the Word and the whole people of God
3. Catechumens
4. Those in secular authority
5. Deliverance from disease, famine, and bondage; health to the sick; safety for those who travel
6. For unbelievers
7. Our enemies
8. For the fruits of the earth

The Bidding Prayer culminates in the praying of the Our Father as the prayer which embraces all that our Lord invites his church to include in its prayer.

The Litany

The Litany (LW, pp. 279–87) is a treasured form of congregational prayer in the Church of the Augsburg Confession. Luther D. Reed notes,

> Luther regarded the Litany as "next to the holy Lord's Prayer the very best that has come to earth!" Lucas Lossius, the church musician and friend of Melanchthon, spoke of it as "*explicatio orationis dominicae,*" or "exposition of the Lord's Prayer." Wilhelm Löhe, the 19th-century liturgical scholar, says that the Litany is a glorious creation of ancient times whose power lies in the incessant stroke upon stroke of intonation and response. "Beginning with adoration, confessing Christ in its heart, it ends in the lovely Agnus . . . how evangelical, how entirely agreeable to our church and its temper."[65]

The name *litany* is derived from the Greek *litaneia,* meaning "prayer, supplication, or entreaty." It appears that litanies were first used in Antioch in the fourth century. Their use apparently spread from Antioch to Constantinople, where they enjoyed great popularity. In the Eastern church, the Litany was expanded to include additional petitions and was commonly used as a preparatory part of the Mass, sometimes in connection with a procession.

From Constantinople the Litany was transported to Rome, where Pope Gelasius (d. 496) inserted it between the entrance chant and the Collect of the Day, thus using it as a replacement for the intercessions after the sermon. The oldest extant text of the Western Litany is known as *Deprecatio Gelasii,* a Latin litany of the fifth century, which has many similarities in structure and content with Byzantine litanies. E. C. Radcliff believes that it was this litany, which Pope Gelasius decreed to be sung "on behalf of churches throughout the world," that determined the shape of later Roman litanies.[66]

Luther loved the Litany and retained it for use in the evangelical congregations of Germany, desiring that it be used in the church rather than in processions, as superstitions had attached themselves to these processions. In 1528, as the Turks neared Vienna, Luther wrote a tract entitled, "On War Against the Turks," in which he urged Christians to pray against the infidels. He commented, "This might help if at Matins and Vespers, or after the sermon, we had the Litany sung or read in the churches, especially by the young folk."[67]

In 1529 Luther revised the Litany of All Saints (the so-called Great Litany), providing both a German and Latin text. His redaction of this Litany purged it of unbiblical prayers to the saints and provided it with an enlarged element of intercessory prayer by the inclusion of 25 additional petitions. Piepkorn notes the absence of intercessions for fellow-Christians in medieval litanies,[68] a deficiency that Luther's revision of the classic Litany corrected. His revised Litany enjoyed influence beyond the Lutheran Church, since it was used by Thomas Cranmer (1489–1556) as a key source in the preparation of the Litany for the *Book of Common Prayer* (1549).

The Litany as it appears in *Lutheran Worship* begins with the threefold Kyrie. The direct plea, "O Christ, hear us," bridges the Kyrie to the invocation of the Holy Trinity, as it is only through Christ that sinners may approach God (see 1 Tim. 2:5).

The body of the Litany is composed of deprecations, obsecrations, supplications, and intercessions. The deprecations (from the Latin *deprecari,* meaning "to avert by prayer") are a set of five petitions imploring God to grant deliverance from sin, error, evil, crafts and assaults of the devil, sudden and evil death, pestilence, famine, war, bloodshed, sedition, rebellion, lightning, tempest, calamity by fire and water, and everlasting death. To these petitions, the congregation responds, "Good Lord, deliver us."

The obsecrations (from the Latin *obsecrare,* meaning "to ask on religious grounds") center the prayer in Christ. The foundation for the requests of the praying congregation is the obedient humiliation and victorious exaltation of the Savior. "Help us, good Lord" is the congregation's reply to the obsecrations.

The supplications are prayers for ourselves. They are short and to the point: "In all time of our tribulation, in all time of prosperity; in the hour of death; and in the day of judgment: Help us, good Lord." Although the supplications are brief, they embrace all that

Christians should be asking for themselves: God's help in all of life and in death.

The intercessions, which make up the largest portion of The Litany, are prefaced with a line that confesses the sinner's dependence on God: "We poor sinners implore you . . . to hear us, O Lord." The intercessions are prayers on behalf of others: the whole Christian church and its pastors, those who have erred and fallen, the weak-hearted and the distressed, those in authority, peace and concord for all people, those in danger or tribulation, travelers, women with child, mothers with infants, orphans, widows, the sick, young children, those in bondage, and our enemies. The congregation responds to each set of intercessions with "We implore you to hear us, good Lord."

The prayer, "Lord Jesus Christ, Son of God . . . we implore you to hear us," links the intercessions with the Agnus Dei. The placement of the Agnus Dei at this point in the Litany bears witness to the fact that the crucified Lamb of God is the sinner's only source of mercy and peace. The Kyrie, which was sung at the beginning of the Litany, is repeated. The Lord's Prayer is chanted by the congregation.

The Litany is concluded with one of the litany collects accompanied by a versicle. These collects are all from Luther's revision of the Litany[69] and they aptly summarize human need and divine mercy.

The Litany may be used as a separate service, augmented with psalms and a Scripture reading. The structure of such a service may take the following shape:

Psalm(s)
Scripture Reading
Litany
Collect of the Day
Blessing

In Advent and Lent, the Litany may be used in place of the Introit (Psalm or Entrance Hymn), Kyrie, and Hymn of Praise in the Divine Service. The Litany may be used in the place of the Prayers in Matins and Vespers. "When so used in Matins, it is concluded with one of the collects therein given. When so used in Vespers, it is concluded with the Collect for Peace."[70] If the Litany is used in

Morning Prayer, it follows the Gospel Canticle; thereafter Morning Prayer will conclude with the Collect for Grace, the Benedicamus, and the Blessing. When used in Evening Prayer, the Litany simply replaces the Eastern Litany, the Collect for Peace, and the Our Father given in the text of Evening Prayer.

Notes

1. Kenneth Korby, "Prayer: Pre-Reformation to the Present," in *Christians at Prayer,* ed. John Gallen (Notre Dame: University of Notre Dame Press, 1977), p. 115. Also see Charles McClean, "Matins and Vespers in the Life of the Church," *Church Music* 75-2 (1975): 1–9.

2. For a review of recent scholarship on the relationship of early Christian prayer to its Jewish antecedents see Paul F. Bradshaw, *Daily Prayer in the Early Church* (New York: Oxford University Press, 1982), pp. 1–46, and Robert Taft, *The Liturgy of the Hours in East and West* (Collegeville, MN: The Liturgical Press, 1986), pp. 3–12.

3. C. W. Dugmore, *The Influence of the Synagogue Upon the Divine Office* (Westminster: The Faith Press Ltd., 1964), p. 47.

4. J. Barry Colman, *Readings in Church History,* vol. I, *From Pentecost to the Protestant Revolt* (New York: Newman Press, 1960), p. 26.

5. Ibid., p. 27.

6. See W. Jardine Grisbrooke, "The Formative Period: Cathedral and Monastic Offices," in *The Study of Liturgy,* ed. Cheslyn Jones, Geoffrey Wainwright, and Edward Yarnold (New York: Oxford University Press, 1978), pp. 358ff., for a discussion of these two types of the daily office.

7. Ibid., p. 359.

8. Philip Pfatteicher, "Disciplined Daily Prayer in the Western Church," *Una Sancta* XXIII (Pentecost 1966): 27.

9. W. Jardine Grisbrooke, "Cathedral Office," in *Westminster Dictionary of Worship,* ed. J. G. Davies (Philadelphia: Westminster Press, 1972), p. 125.

10. AE 53: 13.

11. Ibid., p. 16.

12. Ibid. For a discussion of the daily office in the churches of the Reformation see D. H. Tripp, "The Office in the Lutheran, Reformed, and Free Churches," in *The Study of Liturgy,* pp. 396–402.

13. Tripp, p. 396.

14. Werner Elert, *The Structure of Lutheranism,* trans. Walter Hansen (St. Louis: Concordia Publishing House, 1962), p. 335.

15. Günther Stiller, *Johann Sebastian Bach and Liturgical Life in Germany,* trans. Herbert J. A. Bouman, Daniel Poellot, and Hilton C. Oswald (St. Louis: Concordia Publishing House, 1984), pp. 111–12.

16. Wilhelm Löhe, *Agende für Christliche Gemeinden des Lutherischen Bekenntnisses,* vol. VI of *Gesammelte Werke* (Neuendettelsau: Freimund, 1953), p. 89.

17. Suggested hymns of invocation of the Holy Spirit are LW 154, 155, 156, 157/158, 160, 161, 162, 164, 165, 166, 167, 169, 197, 198, 201, 202, 206, 210, 215, 225, 255, 288, 314, 319, 321, 328, 336, 339, 373, 385, 389, 432, 437, 446, 448, 479, 480, and 482.

18. *Lutheran Worship: Altar Book,* prepared by the Commission on Worship of The Lutheran Church—Missouri Synod (St. Louis: Concordia Publishing House, 1982), pp. 42–43.

19. See Victor Gebauer, "Office Hymn," in *Key Words in Church Music,* ed. Carl Schalk (St. Louis: Concordia Publishing House, 1978), pp. 270–271. Also see Herbert F. Lindemann, "Contemporizing the Office Hymn," *Church Music* 75–2 (1975): 21–23.

20. Massey Shepherd, *The Psalms in Christian Worship: A Practical Guide* (Minneapolis: Augsburg Publishing House, 1976), p. 58.

21. AE 53: 12. For a very helpful discussion of the use and eventual decline of the Psalter in the daily services of the Lutheran Church see Lowell C. Green, "The Use of the Psalms in the Liturgical Hours," *Church Music* 76–1 (1976): 28–36.

22. See the Table of Psalms for Daily Prayer in *Lutheran Worship: Altar Book,* p. 127.

23. Luther D. Reed, *The Lutheran Liturgy,* rev. ed. (Philadelphia: Fortress Press, 1959), p. 401.

24. Olof Herrlin, *Divine Service: Liturgy in Perspective,* trans. Gene J. Lund (Philadelphia: Fortress Press, 1966), p. 30.

25. W. K. Lowther Clarke, *Liturgy and Worship* (London: Society for the Promotion of Christian Knowledge, 1932), p. 273.

26. F. L. Cross, ed., *The Oxford Dictionary of the Christian Church* (New York: Oxford University Press, 1983), p. 1343.

27. AE 34: 199.

28. AE 53: 39.

29. LW, p. 214.

30. Reed, p. 421.

31. Hermann Sasse, "Ecclesia Orans," *Quartalschrift* 48 (April 1951): 89.

32. Reed, p. 426.

33. *Lutheran Worship: Altar Book,* p. 13.

34. See Gebauer, "Office Hymn," in *Key Words in Church Music,* p. 270.

35. Taft, p. 45.

36. Bradshaw, p. 112.

37. AE 21: 298.

38. AE 53: 176.

39. Paul Grime, "The Use of the Nunc Dimittis in the Liturgy of the Eucharist" (unpublished Master's thesis, Concordia Theological Seminary, Fort Wayne, IN, 1986), 5.

40. Cited in Grime, p. 11.

41. *Lutheran Worship: Altar Book,* p. 13.

42. Reed, p. 447

43. *Lutheran Worship: Altar Book,* p. 14.
44. LW, p. 239.
45. Adrian Nocent, *The Liturgical Year,* vol. 1, *Advent, Christmas, Epiphany,* trans. Matthew O'Connell (Collegeville: The Liturgical Press, 1977), pp. 162–68.
46. Philip Pfatteicher and Carlos R. Messerli, *Manual on the Liturgy: Lutheran Book of Worship* (Minneapolis: Augsburg Publishing House, 1979), p. 286.
47. Ibid.
48. Mark Bangert, "Daily Prayer of the Church," *Currents in Theology and Mission* 4/3 (June 1977): 181.
49. Note the description given by Egeria cited in Taft, pp. 51–52.
50. Bradshaw, p. 22.
51. Ibid., p. 75. Also see Taft, p. 26.
52. Taft, p. 37.
53. Ibid., p. 38.
54. Pfatteicher, *Manual on the Liturgy,* p. 279.
55. Ibid.
56. Ibid. Also see Taft, p. 26.
57. Bradshaw, p. 75.
58. Ibid.
59. Pfatteicher, *Manual on the Liturgy,* p. 285.
60. Marion Hatchett, *Commentary on the American Prayer Book* (Minneapolis: Seabury Press, 1980), p. 144.
61. Pfatteicher, *Manual on the Liturgy,* p. 289.
62. Ibid.
63. Reed, p. 652.
64. *Lutheran Worship: Agenda,* prepared by the Commission on Worship of The Lutheran Church—Missouri Synod (St. Louis: Concordia Publishing House, 1984), pp. 49, 65.
65. Reed, p. 623.
66. Ibid., p. 626.
67. AE 53: 153.
68. Arthur Carl Piepkorn, "Let Us Pray for our Fellow-Pilgrims," *Response* VII (Epiphany 1966): 135.
69. For the sources of these collects see Reed, pp. 633–34.
70. *Lutheran Worship: Altar Book,* p. 16.

14

The Psalms
in *Lutheran Worship*

THE PSALMS AND THEIR USE

David Held

The Psalms in History

It is most appropriate that an abundance of psalmody is present in *Lutheran Worship*. Psalmody has been an important ingredient of worship from the Old Testament times to the present, not only as a textual component of worship but also as a musical element. Because of this, the compilers of *Lutheran Worship* made it possible for the psalms not only to be read but also to be sung in corporate worship.

It is abundantly clear that during Old Testament times, psalms were used in temple worship. Performance practices associated with the singing of the Psalms included the following: (1) at times the psalms were sung by a choir of Levites; (2) instruments were often used to accompany or alternate with the singing of the psalms; and (3) occasionally the people responded with refrains such as "He is good; his love endures forever."[1] Questions pertaining to the use of psalmody in synagogue worship have perplexed scholars. While the psalms eventually were employed in synagogue worship, the question is whether or not they were a part of such worship prior to the beginning of Christian worship.[2] Several references to psalm singing in the New Testament (Eph. 5:19; Col. 3:16) indicate that undoubtedly the psalms were included in the worship of early Christians. Moreover, the inclusion of psalmody in early Christian orders of worship is borne out by Tertullian, Athanasius, and Augustine.[3]

During the Middle Ages, as the Roman Mass developed, psalmody became important. Psalm texts were used in the Introits, Graduals, Alleluias/Tracts, the Offertory, and the Communion. In addition, the psalms were a regular part of the Divine Offices.

Luther had a great admiration for the psalms. In the preface to a psalter appearing in 1545 at Neuburg-on-the-Donau he wrote,

> It is proper for every Christian who would pray and be devout to let the Psalter be his book. And no doubt it would be well if every Christian used it so diligently and became so well acquainted with it as to know it by heart, word for word, and constantly to have it on his tongue whenever called on to say or to do something.[4]

The use of psalmody in the Introit and Gradual was continued by Luther in his revision of the Roman Mass, the *Formula Missae* of 1523. He also included provision for using a psalm in the German language in his *Deutsche Messe* of 1526.

Ironically, it was Calvin (1509–64) who, though opposed to the use of much music in worship, provided an impetus for the development of metrical psalmody. Calvin's insistence on using only scripturally based texts resulted in the writing of metrical psalm paraphrases, texts that were set to music by composers of the day. The first important complete psalter resulting from Calvin's decrees was the French Psalter, published in 1562, also known as the Genevan Psalter, or the Huguenot Psalter. Clement Marot (c. 1495–1544) and Theodore de Bèze (1519–1605) were responsible for the texts, while the tunes were the editorial and compositional work of Louis Bourgeois. Of this Psalter 225 editions were printed during its first century of existence; it was translated into at least 20 languages or dialects.[5]

In that same year an English psalter, the Sternhold and Hopkins Psalter (also known as the Day Psalter or the Old Version) appeared. The Scottish Psalter was published in 1564. Additional English psalters made their appearance during the 16th and 17th centuries. An important step in the development of English metrical psalmody was the contribution of Isaac Watts (1674–1748). He paraphrased more freely the texts of the psalms, a procedure demonstrated in his *The Psalms of David Imitated in the Language of the New Testament.*[6]

The first complete metrical psalters by Lutheran writers appeared during the 16th century, when poets such as Georg Major (1502–74), Nicolaus Selnecker (c. 1528–92), and others prepared metrical German psalm texts. German musicians who were active in providing melodies for these metrical psalm texts were Lucas Lossius (1508–82), Seth Calvisius (1556–1615), and Johann Hermann Schein (1586–1630). Heinrich Schütz (1585–1672) wrote musical settings for the metrical psalm texts edited by Cornelius Becker (1561–1604), texts he created to offset the influence of Ambrosius Lobwasser (1515–85), Lutheran theologian, poet, professor at Königsberg University, who had made a German psalter based on the Reformed French Psalter of 1562.[7]

Some of these psalters found their way to the Americas. The French Psalter was used by the Huguenot expeditions (1562–65) in Florida. A Dutch translation of it was brought by the Pilgrims when they settled at Plymouth in Massachusetts. The first psalter published in the colonies was the Bay Psalm Book, which appeared in 1640.[8]

The Psalms in *Lutheran Worship*

Since psalmody played such a prominent role in the unfolding of worship practices, it is not surprising that metrical psalmody is a significant resource in *Lutheran Worship*. Of the 32 psalm paraphrases found in the hymn section (p. 1004), 17 of Isaac Watts's texts and 8 tunes of Louis Bourgeois are included. Reference to the *Lutheran Worship* index, Composers and Sources of Hymns and Spiritual Songs, will demonstrate the inclusion of psalm texts or psalter tunes from at least eight psalters (pp. 988–91).

Psalmody is included in the following services in *Lutheran Worship:*

Divine Service I
    Introit
    Psalm of the Day
    Gradual
    Verse
    "Create in me"

Divine Service II
  Introit
  Psalm of the Day
  Gradual
  Verse

Divine Service III
  Psalm of the Day
  Introit

Matins
  Venite (Ps. 95)
  Psalm(s)

Vespers
  Psalm(s)

Morning Prayer
  Venite (Ps. 95)
  Psalm(s)

Evening Prayer
  "Let my prayer rise" (Ps. 141)
  Psalm(s)

Compline
  Psalm(s)

In addition, psalm verses are contained in both Responsive Prayer 1 and 2 (pp. 270–75). There is an opportunity for the use of psalms in the Daily Devotion for Family or Individual Use (pp. 293–94). Finally, in the Daily Lectionary, all psalms are to be read twice during the course of a year (pp. 295–99).

In the "Pew Edition" of *Lutheran Worship* 60 psalms are included, psalms chosen to meet the worship needs of the Divine Services and minor services. The complete Psalter is contained in *Lutheran Worship: Altar Book,*[9] the text and verse divisions from *The Holy Bible: New International Version.*

A listing of psalm appointments for each of the Sundays and festivals in the church year is included in the Propers of the Day in the "Pew Edition" of *Lutheran Worship* (pp. 10–123) and in the Psalm Index in the *Altar Book* (pp. 578–80). Suggested psalms to be used in Daily Prayer services are listed in both the "Pew Edition" (p. 292) and in the *Altar Book* (pp. 126–27). A Table of Psalms for Daily Prayer, in which the psalms are arranged in a seasonal table (except those appointed on calendar days from December 24 to January 6), is included in the *Altar Book* (p. 127). This table should be of special value to those wishing to use the psalms in daily, private use. Seasonal antiphon texts for psalms used in Morning Prayer and Evening Prayer are included in the section, Propers for Morning Prayer and Evening Prayer ("Pew Edition," pp. 288–91). These antiphons are pointed for use with the psalm tones in *Lutheran Worship* (pp. 367–68).

This wealth of psalmody in *Lutheran Worship,* coupled with various rubrics encouraging its use, is reflective of contemporary liturgical reforms that accord a certain primacy of the Psalter for praise and prayer in Christian worship. One is reminded of Dietrich Bonhoeffer's (1906–45) assertion regarding the christological, thus liturgical, character of the psalms:

> If we want to read and to pray the prayers of the Bible and especially the Psalms, therefore, we must not ask first what they have to do with us, but what they have to do with Jesus Christ. We must ask how we can understand the Psalms as God's Word, and then we shall be able to pray them. . . . Thus if the Bible also contains a prayerbook, we learn from this that not only that Word which he has to say to us belongs to the Word of God, but also that word which he wants to hear from us, because it is the word of his beloved Son. This is pure grace, that God tells us how we can speak with him and have fellowship with him. We can do it by praying in the name of Jesus Christ. The Psalms are given to us to this end, that we may learn to pray them in the name of Jesus Christ.[10]

Methods of Presenting the Psalms

Since the Psalter is a book of liturgical poetry for singing or corporate reading, several traditional methods of reciting or singing the psalms have been suggested by the compilers of *Lutheran Worship.*

1. Direct recitation. The whole psalm or a portion of the psalm is chanted or read in unison.

2. Antiphonal recitation. This is a verse-by-verse alternation between groups of singers or readers.

3. Responsorial recitation. The verses of a psalm are sung by a solo voice or choir with the congregation singing a refrain or antiphon after each verse or group of verses.

4. Responsive reading. This is a verse-by-verse alternation between a pastor/leader and the congregation. This method is usually limited to a spoken manner of presentation.[11]

Since psalmody has a strong historical association with chanting, the psalms, both in the "Pew Edition" and in the *Altar Book,* are pointed for chanting. To this end, simple chant tones, or psalm tunes, are provided (see below), and congregations are encouraged to chant these liturgical pieces. While learning to sing or chant them without accompaniment is the desideratum, appropriate organ accompaniments for the tones are provided.[12] Instruments, such as handbells, may also be used to provide accompaniment.

In order to avoid monotony, variety in presenting the psalms is desirable. Fortunately, several systems of singing the psalms are available for use by cantors, choirs, and congregations. Paul Thomas has compiled a three-year cycle of psalm settings in which a four-part choral refrain is joined with psalm verse set to the psalm tones of the Gregorian system. The psalm verse may be sung by a choir or cantor.[13] Roger Petrich has prepared a set of psalm antiphons that may be coordinated with the psalm tones contained in the *Lutheran Book of Worship.*[14] Charles Frischmann has edited a three-year cycle of psalm settings that employs a short choral or congregational refrain coupled with psalm verses set to one of four psalm tones. These may be sung by cantor or choir.[15] French priest Joseph Gelineau has translated the psalms and composed music to be sung with these new texts. The tunes have a folk-like, yet ancient sound and they carry the psalms in a number of ways, most often with the psalm verse sung by a cantor or choir and the antiphon or refrain by the congregation.[16] Music directors may find information about these and other psalm collections in *Proclaim.*[17]

In addition, there are numerous choral settings of individual psalms or portions of psalms, for example, "Psalm 23" by Heinz Werner Zimmermann. A valuable index to such settings is given under the psalm citation for each of the Sundays and festivals listed in *Proclaim.*

Choral settings of Verses (brief scriptural passages [with alleluias, except during Lent] sung after the Epistle in welcoming the reading of the Gospel) have become increasingly available in recent years. Concordia, Augsburg Fortress, and Morning Star publishing houses have issued collections (including Offertories) for the small parish choir.[18] While no musical settings of the new Introits and Graduals contained in *Lutheran Worship* have yet appeared, music directors in the meantime may wish to use older settings whenever appropriate and feasible.[19]

THE MUSICAL CARRIAGE
FOR THE PSALMS

Paul G. Bunjes

The ten simple tones designated A to K in *Lutheran Worship* (pp. 367–68), which carry the texts of the Psalms, Introits, and Graduals, are hewn from the generative forces of the church modes that have served the church well for centuries, from the early Middle Ages to modern times.

The Minor Class of Modes

There are five psalm tones of the minor class in *Lutheran Worship:* three Aeolian, one Dorian, and one Phrygian. These are based on minor tonic triads (the Aeolian tones designated *C* and *E* in the key of *g*: g/bb/d; the Aeolian tone *D* in the key of *a:* a/c/e; the Dorian tone *A* in the key of *d:* d/f/a; the Phrygian tone *B* in the key of *f♯*: f♯/a/c♯. In each of the five melodic courses, the tonic and minor mediant (third step) elements occur in the melody. To differentiate the modes in each class, the characterizing elements (see below) appear in the melodies also.

The Aeolian Model and Its Adjustments

The yardstick for the minor class is tone *C*, which is in the pure or natural Aeolian form, whose approach to the tonic is upward through a whole step (subtonic). Tone *D* (modified Aeolian) introduces an adjustment to a high seventh degree (g♯ in the key of *a:* the "harmonic" format of the Aeolian) to produce an upward approach to its home tone through a half step (leading tone) that gives the mode a shade of tonal character. Tone *E* (modified Aeolian) engages the high sixth step in conjunction with the high seventh (e♮ with f♯ in the key of *a:* the "melodic" format of the Aeolian). The purpose of this historic adjustment is to erase the vocally uncomfortable interval of the augmented second (sesqui-tone of one and one-half steps) between the natural sixth and high seventh degrees. Tones *C, D,* and *E* derive their key signatures from the "pure" Aeolian mode, and, in order to delineate the mode effectively, their melodic courses embrace, respectively, the subtonic (tone *C*), the high seventh degree (tone *D*), and the high sixth and seventh degrees (tone *E*).

The Dorian and Phrygian

Minor triads underlie also tones *A* and *B:* the Dorian and Phrygian modes. These are constructed of alphabets, each of which contains one tone that is foreign to the Aeolian yardstick. Since these ingredients give the modes distinctive character, they are known as "characteristic tones," which, for each mode, are an "all-time" feature. The Dorian exhibits a high sixth degree; the Phrygian, a low second degree. So that the mode comes into effect in the melody, these characteristic tones appear therein: in the Dorian mode in *d,* the tone *b;* in the Phrygian mode in *f♯,* the note *g*. Both modes also approach their home tones by a whole step upward through the subtonic.

The Major Class of Modes

The major class of modes is comprised of the Ionian (in *Lutheran Worship,* tones *H, J,* and *K*), the Lydian (tone *F*), and the Mixolydian (tone *G*). They are all based on major tonic triads of which at

478

least the tonic and major mediant members occur in the melodies (the Ionian tone *H* in the key of *D:* d/f♯/a; tone *J* in the key of *C:* c/e/g; tone *K* in the key of *A:* a/c♯/e. The Lydian tone *F* in the key of *E♭:* e♭/g/b♭; the Mixolydian tone *G* in the key of *E:* b/g♯/b).

The Ionian Model and Its Adjustments

The Ionian is the yardstick by which the other modes in the major class are measured. Tone *H* exemplifies the straight Ionian model in its pure form; the approach to its home tone is upward through a half-step (leading tone, implied in this example). Tone *J* encapsulates the historic practice of the "convoluted third" (i.e., shrinking a major third to a minor third as the melody turns in on itself). See example 1.

Example 1. The unadulterated major third at 1 shrinks to a minor third at 2.

Tone *K* (in *Lutheran Worship*) engages the historic practice of the "returning tone" (i.e., shrinking a major second to a minor second when the melody returns to a tone it has just left). See example 2.

Example 2. The unadulterated major second at 1 shrinks to a minor second at 2.

The Lydian and Mixolydian

Two more major modes serve as the building blocks for tones *F* and *G* in *Lutheran Worship:* the Lydian and the Mixolydian. Each of these contains one tone that is foreign to the pure Ionian "yardstick." These "characteristic tones" are a high fourth degree in the Lydian (*a* in the key of *E♭*), and a low seventh degree in the Mixolydian (*d* in the key of *E*). In each of these melodic courses the characteristic tone helps materially to delineate the mode. Beyond that, the Lydian bears a leading tone, while the Mixolydian shows a subtonic in the upward approach to the final; both appear in their melodic courses.

In sum, for the modality to come into full effect and to provide a broad-based vehicle, the psalm tones in *Lutheran Worship* must, and do, exhibit in their terse melodic courses a large majority of the distinguishing features: the tonic, the mediant, the characteristic tone, the adjusted tones, the approach to the final, or home-tone, and, where applicable, modifications sanctioned by long, historic practice.

Melodic Shape and Disposition

All 10 psalm tones contained in *Lutheran Worship* exhibit a similar shape in their melodic construction; various terms used to identify the parts are exhibited in example 3 below.

Example 3. Tone G (VII E: Mixolydian)

The recitation proceeds on a fixed plane (note *a*; note *f♯*) until the near-end of the half-verse (hemistiche) is approached, whereupon it flows into a melodic contour (cadence) of which one occurs in the "middle" of the verse (medial cadence), and another at the end (terminal cadence).

The Cadence Ictuses

Each cadence has a musical and rhythmic existence of its own, defined by the innate disposition of its ictuses ("bounces"), of which there are two in each half-verse. See example 4.

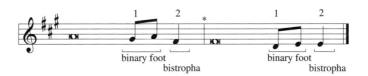

Example 4. Tone G (VII E: Mixolydian)

The penultimate ictus occurs at 1 and signals a binary foot of two eighth notes; the ultimate ictus ocurs at 2 and signals a bistropha (two eighth notes fused into a quarter value). The penultimate ictus may signal a ternary foot if the underlaid text accent shifts the ictus to the left, thereby detaching one eighth note from the recitation and adding it to the cadence contour. See example 5.

Example 5. Tone G (VII E: Mixolydian)

The penultimate ictus seeks an accented syllable, or an equivalent one, in the underlaid text; that is, one that is less unaccented than its immediate fellows.

Assignment of Cadence Syllables

Every one of the cadences can, and may, carry two, three, or four syllables of text. However, in each case the underlayment, or pointing, is so contrived that an accented syllable of the text (or its equivalent) falls on the penultimate ictus, whereas the ultimate ictus will accept an accented or unaccented syllable of text.

The former condition reveals a requisite congruence between the ictus of the music and the accent of the text, whereas the latter does not. This point of view concerning the relationship of ictus and accent is a critical factor in the effort to secure a sensible and sensitive underlayment of the text. Most abuses that have corrupted the pointing of the psalms and psalmodic forms have been caused

481

by a lack of discernment in this regard, as shall be demonstrated subsequently.

In a cadence of two syllables, the two notes of the penultimate ictus are fused (i.e., slurred) to carry the first syllable, while the ultimate ictus carries the final syllable, be it accented or not (Case A). See example 6.

In a cadence of three syllables, the two notes of the penultimate ictus are kept discrete, each one carrying one syllable, while the ultimate ictus accepts either an accented or unaccented final syllable (Case B). See example 6.

In a cadence of four syllables, the penultimate ictus shifts to the left, which, in effect, detaches one note from the recitation and adds it to the cadence, in order to produce a ternary foot able to carry three syllables, while the final syllable of the half-verse falls on the ultimate ictus, be it accented or not (Case C). See example 6.

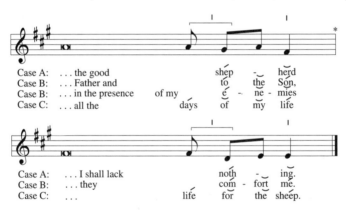

Example 6. Tone G (VII E: Mixolydian)

It should be observed that the shifted ictus is not notated in the page presentation of the psalm tones; a slight stress on the accented syllable preceding the entry into the cadence will organize the rhythm effectively.

Pointing the Text to the Tone

The practice of "pointing" the Psalms, the Introits, and the Graduals, plus a few additional psalmodic forms, is a simple signal system that indicates which syllable of the text in the half-verse is the first one to leave the recitation and enter the melodic contour of the cadence. The purpose of such a simple system is to obviate the space-consuming and expensive necessity of underlaying the text in a full score. It should immediately be noted, however, that this signal, whatever it may be, is not necessarily a mark of accent in the text or of ictus in the musical line; it just alerts the singer to move away from the plane of the recitation. To be sure, oftentimes, if not most of the time, an accent in the text or an ictus in the music coincides with the location of this signal, but not always; in fact, it is just such a simplistic point of view (which does not differentiate among accent, ictus, and point-signal) that has opened the door to corruptive influences that have tended to debase the chanting of psalms, introits, graduals, and the like into aberrations which have plagued the church for more than a century and condemned it to chant with a high degree of insensitivity to the prosodic dispositions of the texts.

The Anglican Thump

The most glaring and pervasive aberration in psalm singing in our time is what is generally known as the "Anglican thump," already decried by Winfred Douglas, Canon of Denver. This unfortunate feature embraces a condition of text underlayment that can only be described as a "post-tune dribble." See example 7.

they are jubilant   in   your   righteousness.
Anglican thump

Example 7. Ps. 89:16b (Anglican thump pointing)

The "thump" or "dribble" is caused by "text left over at the end of the tune" as in the following secular excerpt, slightly adapted, as adduced by Canon Douglas in similar form. See example 8.

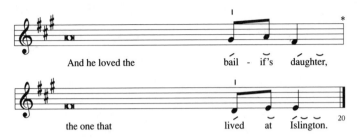

And he loved the bail - if's daughter,

the one that lived at Islington. 20

Example 8. Anglican thump pointing

This method of pointing (which rigidly forces the text accent to coincide with the musical ictus of the tune in every instance) is analogous to a reciprocal condition of "tune left over at the end of the text." See example 9.

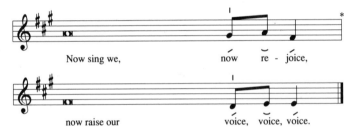

Now sing we, now re - joice,

now raise our voice, voice, voice.

Example 9.

The Solesmes Solution

In *Lutheran Worship* a determined effort was made to expunge this musical and poetic *faux pas* in the pointing of the Psalms, Introits, and Graduals, and to embrace the logical and sensible principles of the Solesmes method delineated earlier (where accent, ictus, and point-signal are kept discrete from each other). In example 10, the "Anglican thump," or "post-tune dribble," does not materialize.

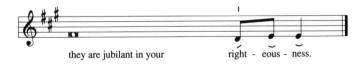

they are jubilant in your right - eous - ness.

Example 10. Ps. 89:16b. Solesmes pointing

Further, there is no "left-over text at the end of the tune" as in the secular example cited above. See example 11.

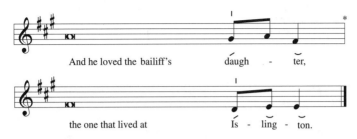

Example 11. Solesmes pointing

Conversely, there is no "left-over tune at the end of the text." See example 12.

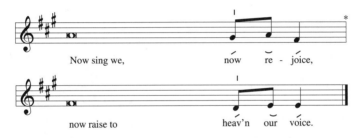

Example 12. Solesmes pointing

Although both methods are equally easy to perform, the greater sensitivity and logic of the second method over the first becomes abundantly clear by singing Psalm 23 from *Lutheran Book of Worship* (1978), which espouses the "Anglican thump" method, followed by the same psalm in *Lutheran Worship* (1982), which exemplifies the Solesmes method. It is unfortunate that a large body of Christian worshipers is being compelled to "thump" its way through the Psalter for the next generation or two.

The Point-Signals

In *Lutheran Worship* two point-signals are employed: the vertical mark (') which indicates that the cadence of three notes engages three syllables (Case A in Example 6), and the horizontal mark (-)

above the word, which indicates that the cadence of three notes engages two syllables, the first of which fuses two notes of the penultimate ictus (Case B). The cadence of four text syllables is not notationally identified (Case C).

Notes

1. Massey Shepherd, *The Psalms in Christian Worship* (Minneapolis: Augsburg Publishing House, 1976), pp. 19–20. For a definitive and scholarly work see John A. Lamb, *The Psalms in Christian Worship* (London: Faith Press, 1962).

2. James McKinnon, "On the Question of Psalmody in the Ancient Synagogue," *Early Music History 6,* ed. Ian Fenlon (Cambridge: Cambridge University Press, 1986), pp. 165ff.

3. Shepherd, pp. 37–38.

4. Ewald Plass, *What Luther Says,* 3 vols. (St. Louis: Concordia Publishing House, 1959), II: 1000.

5. James Davidson, *A Dictionary of Protestant Church Music* (Metuchen, New Jersey: Scarecrow Press, 1975), pp. 256–59.

6. Ibid., pp. 259–65.

7. Lowell Green, "The Use of Psalms in the Liturgical Hours," *Church Music* 76–1 (1976): 32.

8. Davidson, pp. 265–68.

9. *Lutheran Worship: Altar Book,* prepared by the Commission on Worship of The Lutheran Church—Missouri Synod (Concordia Publishing House, 1982), pp. 387–513.

10. Dietrich Bonhoeffer, *Psalms: The Prayer Book of the Bible,* trans. James H. Burtness (Minneapolis: Augsburg Publishing House, 1970), pp. 14–15.

11. *Lutheran Worship: Altar Book,* p. 17.

12. *Lutheran Worship: Accompaniment for the Liturgy* (St. Louis: Concordia Publishing House, 1982), pp. 148–150. For ready use, these accompaniments are also reproduced on a handy plasticized card that comes inserted in the volume. John Folkening, *Handbells in the Liturgical Service* (Concordia Publishing House, 1984) has accompaniments.

13. Paul Thomas, *The Psalms for the Church Year,* 12 vols. (St. Louis: Concordia Publishing House, 1982). This collection contains psalm settings for each of the Sundays of the three-year cycle selected for use in *Lutheran Book of Worship.*

14. Roger Petrich, *Psalm Antiphons for the Church Year* (Philadelphia: Fortress Press, 1979), pp. 3–5. The psalm citations are those contained in *Lutheran Book of Worship.*

15. Charles Frischmann, ed., *The Psalmody for the Day,* 3 vols. (Philadelphia: Fortress Press, 1974–75).

16. Joseph Gelineau, *The Grail/Gelineau Psalter,* ed. J. Robert Carroll (Chicago: GIA Publications, 1972). For more information on the Gelineau settings see

"Singing the Psalms and the Propers: An Interview with Father Gelineau," in *Church Music* 69–1 (1969): 27–31.

17. Barry Bobb and Hans Boehringer, *Proclaim: A Guide for Planning Liturgy and Music,* 12 vols. (St. Louis: Concordia Publishing House, 1985–88).

18. Ibid., Series C, Part 1, p. 13.482.

19. Ibid., pp. 11–12.

20. Charles Winfred Douglas, *Church Music in History and Practice,* rev. ed. (New York: Charles Schribner's Sons, 1962), p. 112.

15

The Hymns in *Lutheran Worship*

HYMN WRITING AND TRANSLATING

Jaroslav J. Vajda

The recently published (1984) *Dictionary of American Hymnology,* compiled under the direction of Leonard Ellinwood, lists 1,500,000 (one-and-a-half million!) first lines from some 4,700 hymnals published in America alone. Add to that number the thousands of hymns that have been written in languages other than English and which did not get translated into American hymnals, and the total number of hymns is staggering. One would think that every needed hymn has been written and that the church could stop publishing new hymnals, as one Mennonite church has done: It has simply been reprinting its German hymnal for the past three centuries, with no thought or intention of revising, updating, or increasing the number of hymns in their repertory.

And yet, new editions of hymnals continue to be published, and worship commissions continue to gather new hymns for new hymnals and supplements. *Lutheran Worship* is an example of the never-ending process.

Hymns are being composed because the church seems to feel a need for them. Some of those presently occupying space in older hymnals are not being used, as demonstrated by surveys conducted by both the Inter-Lutheran Commission on Worship and the Commission on Worship of The Lutheran Church—Missouri Synod. Hymns that had not been used even once in two years by half of the congregations of the participating bodies were excluded from the new listing. The space thus made available was quickly filled by hundreds of eager candidates. Evidently, hymn writing had been going on while the old hymnals were being used.

Who Writes the Hymns?

Who was writing hymns? Who continues to write hymns? Judging from a cursory review of authors of extant hymns, most of the hymn writers have been either clergy or someone closely and actively connected with the worshiping church, such as teachers, musicians, lay leaders, and religious poets. In general, the clergy represent the largest percentage of hymn writers.

It is not hard to guess why. They are the most deeply involved with the preparation and conduct of worship. They know which hymns are needed and how often they are used. They know which hymns are theologically sound and consistent. They deal with people's spiritual needs on a daily basis; they must apply the Law and Gospel to the spiritual lives of those under their care. They must handle life-and-death issues; they follow the course of a person's life from birth to death, from baptism to burial. They must see and present life in perspective, setting the place of God's people in history, in time and eternity. All of life has a spiritual and immortal dimension for them, and in their preaching and counseling they must keep in balance the temporal and the eternal. Every aspect of human life has a connection with the divine; every creature illustrates a spiritual truth.

This kind of experience and relationship comes about only with the passing of time; hence one should expect hymn writers usually to be middle-aged or older, having confronted and tested those features of physical and spiritual life they take note of in their religious verse. One can almost draw a spiritual profile of psalm and hymn writers from their literary efforts. Whereas a novelist draws upon imagination and need not live out the experiences and ecstasies of his fictional characters, the authentic hymn comes out of one's own experience of God's judgment and mercy or that of those whom one serves in such circumstances. Any references to areas beyond those actually experienced or witnessed must be derived from the Scriptures, which are the testimony of the One who existed before Abraham was and who views the universe from an everlasting throne.

Although anyone can string words together and rhyme them and produce what looks like a poem, the poem's authenticity comes from something inside and outside the writer. And the verse rings true or hollow depending on whether the user of the hymn can sing it honestly and hear in it an echo of one's own life, history, and the Scriptures. Whatever in the hymn is contrived or used for effect or merely for the requirements of poetry, counterfeits and exploits the true purpose of the hymn.

Next, and as important as the previous elements, is the gift and practice of good poetry. Certainly God does not despise the sincere jingle composed to his glory by a child. But let that remain what it is, a mere finger exercise and not a work of art coming out of the crucible of experience, study, suffering, and hard work, honing a God-given talent as a musician or an architect would his craft.

The hymn writer should be skilled in composing acceptable and, preferably, memorable verse. The hymn as poetry should meet the requirements of good poetry: rhythm, imagery, unity, emotion, and originality. The words and lines must not only inspire music but should be suited to musical rendition, for a hymn is often remembered more because of its tune than for its text. There are a number of books on poetry and its exercise that propound principles that should be second nature to the hymn writer, so that he or she satisfies the criteria of a good hymn without exposing the skeleton or blueprint of the finished work. Since originality has not been exhausted in past centuries and previous hymnals, there is always room for further exploration on the frontiers of this craft. So the classical hymn writers composed songs that were truly new for their age and opened new dimensions for petition and praise.

So much hymn writing is imitative and derivative, down to the religious cliches pimpling the features of songs that are "new" only because they were recently written. Hymn writers and hymnal committees must continually ask themselves, What is new about this text, this melody? Has something better been written on the same subject, for the same occasion? How is this hymn different, more effective, more expressive, closer to the language and style of today's worshiper?

And, since hymns are songs without music, it is to the advantage of the hymn writer and the prospective composer if the writer of the text has some knowledge and understanding of music, its rhythms, accents, and singability. Again, some of the best hymn writers of the past and present have had some musical training. A text written by such a person almost sings itself into a composer's heart and suggests by its mood and phrasing a suitable melody. On the other hand, if the best text is saddled with an unattractive or prosaic tune, it will wither and die unsung.

Still another characteristic of a strong and memorable hymn is a keen sense of awareness of God's majesty, grace, and glory, and the capturing of such awareness in words and phrases that paint pictures or trigger the memory of significant and deeply moving experiences. At the end of a humdrum or trying week, an inspiring hymn can lift drooping spirits and strengthen weak knees with words or phrases that open eyes to vistas that bring life into perspective and balance once again. Every one of us treasures certain lines and verses that place a motto on the walls of our private prayer closet, our workplace, our sickroom, our family room, and finally, our dying chamber. Many a Christian, launching out on the glorious eternal adventure, leaves this world with the precious words of a hymn that seemed to have been provided by the Holy Spirit for just that person and that occasion. How blessed to be able to call up such a fitting Nunc Dimittis, and how equally blessed to have been inspired to write it!

Why Write Hymns?

If the church were to stop producing new hymnals, hymns would still continue to be written. They would be composed spontaneously to express what cannot be voiced except in that form. Saint Paul, contemplating the wondrous workings of God in history and in his life, bursts forth in songs of praise and doxologies. The very word *Alleluia* is a song that says in four syllables what every hymn exults. Anyone with a gift of poetry who is moved by the glory of God will break into lofty and emotional language, just as musicians and artists express their adoration and wonder in their art forms. The glorious compositions of Bach and the works of Michelangelo and Lucas Cranach are just several of thousands of artists who have been inspired by the majesty and grace of God.

It would be a pity and a sign of atrophy if the church's song were to become silent, or a generation appear that would have no hymns to voice. The most prolific hymn writers produced songs for the church when it was most vigorous, when it was in conflict or distress, when it challenged the status quo, when its Easter theme shattered the rigor mortis of a moribund faith. There have been barren periods in the history of hymnody, generations when the song was bland if not altogether silent—times when the church wallowed in sentimental privatism, when it closed its eyes to the state of warfare going on since Pentecost, when it exchanged its prophetic role for the favors of the oppressors of spiritual freedom, or when it sought escape from reality in a soporiphic ecstasy like that of a drug addict.

The potential hymn writer reacts to scriptural inspiration and to the conditions in the church regardless of whether his or her song is heard by anyone but God. Singers must sing, even if the church does not hear their song during their lifetime, only to discover it in a later generation. Not all hymns are written on assignment. They are less likely to be stilted and contrived if they are not. This does not mean that they are necessarily formless or that they disregard poetic principles, but they are more likely to capture the spirit of spontaneity that many commissioned hymns lack.

Such private hymns may also suffer oblivion when they remain tuneless, for a hymn is not complete until it is provided with the wings or wheels of music. So the psalms, for all their beauty and power, are hymns to be sung, and it was for that reason that they have been versified or set to chants, and why so many Psalters fill the archives of hymnody. So, unless appropriate and attractive melodies are provided for hymn texts, they stand to remain unused in public or private worship. This fate, however, should not deter the religious poet from writing hymns. The primary reason for doing so is to make a sincere personal statement to God in response to his Word and will.

Most hymns in use by the church in the past and in our day, however, were composed for specific occasions, as elements of a liturgical service, or to commemorate some event. The liturgy suggests hymns of invocation, Kyries, Credos, and Glorias, baptismal and communion hymns, and, in Lutheran practice, the Hymn of the Day which is tied to the theme of the day. Hymn writers supply the repertory for a church year's usage for the Sundays of the church calendar, holidays, Matins and Vespers, weddings and funerals. An average-size hymnal requires at least 500 hymns to serve these purposes with adequate variety.

Although thousands of hymns are available for these various needs, there are still gaps that have developed as the church has moved into new eras and situations. Congregations and hymnals should make room for fresh and contemporary hymnic resources that speak the old truths in today's language and apply the age-old Gospel to modern problems. Hymns composed for a rural, European society feel strange and out of place in an industrialized and computerized space age, with its problems of world hunger, mass dislocations of populations, unemployment and nuclear threat, to mention just a few. The confessional church of the late 20th century cannot rely on its historic background for doctrinal references in the hymns, diluted as it is by the absorption of new members from other denominations. The worshiping family is fast losing the character and shape it had as lately as the 1950s. As broken families reach the 50 percent proportion, even in Christian congregations, the traditional family hymns, assuming the presence of both parents and several children, cannot be sung honestly by a distressingly growing portion of the worshiping community. The discontinuation or absence of confession of sins lays a greater burden on hymns of repentance, which have lost their popularity but not their necessity. The rapid blurring of the line dividing church and state, the increasing reliance on government and civil laws to determine moral decisions for society, the plague of addictions of all kinds, the despoiling of nature, the cheapening and wanton destruction of life, hedonism and the idolization of celebrities, the competition for the hour of worship—all demand a scripturally sparked response by religious poets who can write the psalms of today with all their passion and profundity.

Not all occasional or situational hymns are or need to be contrived. They can be opportunities for expressing thoughts the hymn writer has gathered, applied to a particular situation or event. Then, too, the occasional hymn need not be so specific that it is restricted to a once-in-a-lifetime use, for example, the dedication of a particular church. In such a case, one can write a hymn based on a scriptural truth that has universal application as well as being suited for a special occasion.

Changing patterns bring changing needs. A study of present-day worship services in today's society will expose a number of imbalances. Very few morning or evening hymns are sung in most denominations or family circles, and it is regrettable that so many fine morning hymns will eventually go out of circulation. However, the space they occupy can be assigned to themes that have been neglected in previous or present editions. The same is beginning to be true of general hymns of praise, of which there are more than a congregation needs for a varied church-year repertory.

Hymn writers go on creating because the range of glory is inexhaustible, and the Christian's life is an endless series of discoveries. Beyond the mountains already scaled is another and another. There are still subjects to serve as themes for petition and praise. New witnesses and new voices deserve to be heard.

Among other reasons one may give for the writing of hymns is the following: If it were not for good hymns, even fewer Christians would come under the influence of good poetry, which is the highest level of human speech. Generally, despite its latent power and ability to uplift the human spirit and to lead it into a contemplation of the majesty of God and his mighty works, good poetry is ignored and even scorned by the general public; popular taste runs toward the banal and shallow. Many people, including too many Christians, are stuck at a certain level of literary quality and religious poetry; and never in a whole lifetime do they rise above the elevation of foothills of great mountain ranges, their vistas limited to the range of their own emotions and a sentimental view of the church and the world. Were it not for the psalms with their uncompromising literary quality, their acquaintance with good poetry would be poor indeed.

The psalms and the literary quality of the Scriptures save us from banality and provide us with models and standards for religious poetry. Though not intended as literary paradigms, the Scriptures testify to God's choice of the highest standards for religious poetry. The church does its constituents a disservice by perpetuating mediocrity or even banality in its hymnody. There is no need to talk down or sing down to God's people. The biblical level of literature is the highest one can find, and it is accessible even to the unlettered and illiterate, who can memorize its lofty and profound verses and be lifted close to the vision of glory we will one day fully comprehend and appreciate.

The general public is impoverished enough without having its worship materials cramp and freeze it culturally in an undernourished state poetically and musically. So little of one's lifetime is spent in the glorious presence of God, so little time is devoted to the reading of fine literature, so little exposure to great music, art, and architecture; what a tragedy then, if that meager hour on Sunday is not quality time in every respect, the best that can be offered to our God who has no delight in cheapness and slovenliness.

Quality hymn writing usually has been the result of a desire to improve what is available and to raise the standards of worship. Although beginners can and should offer God the best they are capable of giving, the worship service should not remain at the level of an amateur night, or a lazy rehash of old favorites that do not stretch the talents God gives in such amazing variety. Luther opened the floodgates to good hymnody with his modest collection of eight hymns, setting a standard for future collections; and Isaac Watts would never have turned the tide and character of the hymnody of his day had he not been dissatisfied with the doggerel to which the English church's hymnody had deteriorated, and had he not set out to compose more than 600 hymns. Were it not for these two hymn writers' attempts to elevate the church's hymnic repertory, we would not have today such treasures as "A mighty fortress" (LW 297, 298), "Our God, our help in ages past" (LW 180), "Joy to the world" (LW 53), "When I survey the wondrous cross" (LW 114, 115), "From all that dwell below the skies" (LW 440), and dozens of other classics that even the least cultured and educated can get a taste of quality and lend lips and heart to the voicing of some of the best worship offerings ever created. The church's hymnal should be a standard of excellence rather than a collection of the mediocre and inferior.

New editions and supplements of established hymnals also provide opportunities for the expansion of the genre beyond the four-line, common, short, and long meter forms. Within the past quarter century, unrhymed hymns have made their way into the hymnals and hearts of today's worshipers. Strict rhymes have been worn almost threadbare by this time, so that one way of breaking out of the bondage of tradition is to go more frequently to assonance or unrhymed lines. Some Scripture songs avoid the problem altogether by simply setting repeated Bible verses to a rhythmic musical setting, or, as in one case, to create an entire song or chant, repeating the word *Alleluia*. Of course, one must then decide whether such a song qualifies as a hymn or is really a musical response, like the word *Amen*.

So for a number of valid reasons hymns should continue to be written today and tomorrow. And there are also quite a few reasons why hymns should be translated.

Why Translate Hymns?

A large and important part of our hymnic heritage comes to us by way of translation, beginning with the hymnic portions of Scripture, then continuing through the Greek and Latin hymnody of the early Christian era, and during Reformation times chiefly via the German, and then in smaller portions from Scandinavian, Slavic, and other sources. The more ecumenical the hymnic repertory, the larger the proportion of translated hymns. Accordingly, the more translated hymns, the richer the hymnody.

Just as each age and generation has a contribution to make to the song of the church, so each worshiping Christian nation has a contribution to make to the body of hymnody. A quick examination of the provenance of the contents of any hymnal will reveal the broadness or narrowness of its worship resources. As individuals differ in their experiences and observations of life, so also national church bodies offer a testimony to their times and circumstances. By our hymns we establish a kinship with the saints of the past and ties with those living in our time around the globe.

Apart from the symbolic expression of the Una Sancta that the translation of hymns from all ages and nations (and denominations) gives, significant treasures are to be acquired and shared by translating great hymns and songs. What a gap there would be in our

496

(Lutheran) hymnals without the translations from the Latin by John Mason Neale, the masterful English recreations of German hymnody by Catherine Winkworth, and the smaller number of translations that have become familiar and dear to so many worshiping communities today, such as "Oh, come, all ye faithful" (LW 41), "Built on the Rock" (LW 291), and "How great thou art" (LW 519), to mention just a few.

Hymnody transferred from other languages and times has an advantage over the contemporary hymn, having been tested by circumstances and the passage of time. A hymn that has been in constant use for two, three, or more centuries has a record that is hard to establish in modern hymnody. Who is duplicating hymns today of such universal appeal and application as "A mighty fortress," "Praise to the Lord," "Now thank we all our God," and other durable chorales? Hymnals that choose to ignore these age-old treasures impoverish their congregations and rob contemporary hymn writers of models and thematic substance. What would the major holidays be without the sturdy, profound, and lofty hymns: "Of the Father's love begotten," "From heaven above," "Oh, come, Oh, come, Emmanuel," "O sons and daughters of the King," "Christ the Lord is risen today," "Jesus Christ is risen today," "Come, you faithful, raise the strain," "Come, Holy Ghost, God and Lord," and so on? What hymns of equal stature have been written in the past half century? While waiting and working for a larger contemporary hymnody, the church must continue to be inspired and nourished by the classics of the past which are ours by translation.

The art of translating is unique and different from original hymn writing. One can be a good translator without being able to write comparable original hymns. In original writing, one must choose a theme and a fitting poetic form, and then hope that a fine tune will be written for the text. In translating hymns, these three essentials are already in existence. Furthermore, they have stood the test of time and usage. The translator, however, must possess and practice two skills: he or she must be able to write authentic poetry and have a knowledge of music. The translator need not know the original language, although it would be tremendously helpful to understand the nuances of the original, for example, the special characteristics of Paul Gerhardt's great texts, his synonymous doublets and plays on words. These can seldom be translated literally into another language, but they do challenge the translator to be creative in producing something similar in meaning and effect.

In the end, the translator will be creating a new hymn that should seem to have been written in the translated language. A study of great hymn writers in other languages reveals how masterful they were in translating from languages not their own, but which they themselves understood well enough to write in them. One such writer was Jiri Tranovsky (1591–1637), who was as facile in Latin and German as he was in Czech and Slovak, and many of his translations from the Latin and German are superior in hymnic quality to the original. The 90 translations he made for his classic collection of 414 hymns prove his indebtedness to the ecumenical hymnody of the church, to his German and Bohemian church fathers, and to the hymnological expression of theological orthodoxy in worship resources.

One cannot overemphasize the requirement of poetic skill in the translator's own language. So many translations, especially of the chorales, sound wooden and contrived in English, with inversions and clumsy constructions, and a woeful lack of imagery, frequently ending up as versified dogmatics and embarrassing verse at that. Some drab translations have been responsible for alienating contemporary worshipers and causing them to reject what might have been good texts, had they been handled skillfully and creatively.

Translation need not be literal. Many a good old hymn would survive if expressed in contemporary idiom and imagery. Such translations should honestly be called paraphrases, to credit the original theme and meter, and to indicate the liberties taken to present the original in contemporary English. Here the use of assonance or the dropping of rhyme might be excusable. In fact, one would be creating a new hymn on the basis of subject and form suggested by the original.

Nor should contemporary foreign hymnody be ignored in favor of what is old and tested. Hymns are being written by Christians in other languages which could enrich current American and English hymnals, so long as they are compatible with our taste in music; for it is the musical setting that first captures our attention. In doing so, however, care must be taken to transfer the idiom along with the contents of the hymn or song. Religious folk song texts should be translated into a comparable English folk idiom, the more formally structured hymn likewise. Perhaps easiest are those that are being written in free verse in the original, which should not make them less eligible for consideration than formal hymns.

Conclusion

Hymnody is alive and blooming in many parts of the Christian church. It deserves to be encouraged and tried. Some of it may endure, some may serve only a momentary need, as did hundreds in the past. New forms should be tried, new settings given an opportunity. Some may strike fire, others may be snuffed out on first exposure. But the church's poets and musicians will continue to create new songs to the glory of God and their fellow pilgrims; and all offerings, sincerely and humbly presented to God, are accepted by him with pleasure as the grateful gifts of his beloved children. But let them, like all sacrifices, be the best we can offer.

RENEWAL OF HYMNS
FOR *LUTHERAN WORSHIP*

F. Samuel Janzow

Lutheran hymnody, like Lutheran liturgy, was born and its essential character formed in the Reformation struggle to renew, strengthen, and keep Christians in the fullness in Christ's saving grace and truth as proclaimed by the Holy Spirit in the Scriptures.

Deliberately, by means of the example and impulse of his own hymns of robust, Spirit-filled Gospel proclamation, Luther called congregational hymn singing back from its long and almost total banishment.[1] Ever since then the church has raised its voice in hymns of praise bearing witness to the truths of the Gospel of grace.

Fed by many a tributary stream of Christian experience, poetic ability, and musical talent, the river of the church's song has flowed in generational wave upon wave to the present day. Carried upon the latest of these waves in the second half of the 20th century, there came also the hymn collection in *Lutheran Worship* (1982).

In 1965 The Lutheran Church—Missouri Synod decided to produce a new hymnal to replace *The Lutheran Hymnal* of 1941. It invited other Lutheran synods to join in the venture and help make the new hymnal one which all might use. This action did not imply any turning away from the Scripture-based theology in which the hymns of *The Lutheran Hymnal* were embedded, but rather a desire that Lutherans of North America might bear witness to God's truths with one mind and spirit and voice. A not inconsiderable motive for this action was also the wish to improve the language of hymns where it had become obsolescent or archaic. Moreover, musicians may also have wanted an improvement over some musical aspects of *The Lutheran Hymnal*. But who among them would have faulted that hymnal for its numerous chorale tunes?

Hymnology's most eminent recent British authority, Erik Routley, declared concerning "the music of the Lutheran hymns of 1524–1750,"

> It is easily the largest body of fine music in the whole literature of hymns. Going through the classic chorales as they appear in TLH one is constantly impressed by the sheer weight of excellence that they represent—and the tunes in this book are only a small fraction of the tunes which were available for selection. . . . No other category of tunes comes near the chorales for sustained high quality combined with rich variety and sheer weight of numbers.[2]

This estimate came three years after The Lutheran Church—Missouri Synod took the first step that led finally to the making of *Lutheran Worship*. But the Synod's church musicians who urged the production of a new hymnal had needed no superlatives from overseas to stimulate an appreciation of the Lutheran heritage of fine hymn tunes. Their call for a successor to *The Lutheran Hymnal* was not on the ground that its chorale tunes had outlived their usefulness. They may well have wished, however, for a fuller and more balanced use of the church's hymn-tune resources. Some fine melodies in this hymnal were much overused. One of its tunes is used for eight different texts; five other tunes for seven different hymns apiece; each of five further tunes for six hymn texts apiece; each of nine more tunes for five texts apiece; and eighteen tunes for four texts apiece. Yet, as Routley points out, only a fraction of the Lutheran heritage chorale tunes appears in *The Lutheran Hymnal.*

Lutheran Worship avoids such neglect of the church's musical heritage. It introduces to the Synod's constituency fresh melodies from both their own and other church music traditions. The new melodies provide a bracing challenge and a promise of ultimate rich rewards for congregations that will take them in. And in contrast to the *The Lutheran Hymnal,* the distribution of tunes among the texts in *Lutheran Worship* is much more balanced. While 11 tunes in *The Lutheran Hymnal* serve more than five texts each, no tune in *Lutheran Worship* is used that often. And whereas 27 tunes in *The Lutheran Hymnal* are used either four or five times each, this is true of only eight tunes in *Lutheran Worship.* Thus the music in the hymn corpus of *Lutheran Worship* has been notably upgraded from that in *The Lutheran Hymnal.*

This early comment on the music rather than the texts of hymns in *Lutheran Worship* serves a purpose. It helps clarify the concept of the Christian hymn by suggesting that only when a tune is joined to a hymn text does that text attain its majority and become a hymn in the full sense. As a house unoccupied is not yet a home, so a set of stanzas incapable of being sung for lack of a tune is not quite yet a hymn; it is only the literary text for one still in the making.

However, the text is always primary in a Christian hymn. It is the hymn's soul and body. The soul of a hymn is its text's scripturally generated and controlled matter, substance, meaning. Its body, the instrument or vehicle for the expression of its spirit and meaning, is language. For language gives external form and utterance both to the mental and emotional aspects of the text's meaning and spirit.

The music of a hymn is related to the emotional (often poetically expressed) elements of the hymn text; it uses patterns of sound for symbolizing and evoking emotional states. Music is akin to poetry. "Through poetry and music the worshipper is able to give expression to ideas and feelings that burst the bounds of ordinary speech."[3] Ordinary speech may shuffle along, walk briskly toward a goal, march in a parade to the beat of a drum, even run a great race. But only poetry lets the feeling heart in its utterances rise and soar, and only music sets it singing as it soars.

Thus music supports and enhances that mood or emotional tone which is always present wherever God's words and human responses to them intersect. A Christian hymn is a place of mingling echoes—echoes of the voice of God speaking the Word and of the responses of the listening human heart. This mingling is charged with the emotion inherent in the situation. The language of the text may or may not make such emotion explicit, but it often tries to do so, or at least to suggest it, through the heightened form of expression we call poetry. In either case music supports and enhances the emotion. From the mystery of its hills and caves, its heights and its depths, music sends back reverberations of the tones and moods of the hymn texts' voices, divine and human, and amplifies them.

Appropriate in this connection are some paragraphs from a notable article by Oliver C. Rupprecht published the year after the appearance of *Lutheran Worship* in 1982. His purpose in these paragraphs is to supply examples of the correspondence between the mood of a hymn's text and that of its melody. His examples come from hymns published both in *Lutheran Worship* and in *The Lutheran Hymnal,* but in different text versions of the same hymn. His references list first the hymn's number in the former, then its number in the latter. To get the point he makes about a hymn's tune and text it will be necessary for the reader to know and to sing each hymn. Singing the hymn is the only way to hear what Rupprecht is saying.

There is another reason, a hidden agenda, in presenting the Rupprecht paragraphs at just this point. It is to offer readers the challenge and the opportunity to discover independently the kind of language "renewals" that were made in the hymn in *The Lutheran Hymnal* for inclusion in *Lutheran Worship.* Here Rupprecht's listing of corresponding LW and TLH hymn texts becomes a godsend. For it happens that almost every kind of text alteration made for *Lutheran Worship* is represented in the pairs of hymn versions Rupprecht points to. The satisfaction of personal accomplishment can be guaranteed to any reader who takes Rupprecht's guided tour and at each stage pauses to compare and contrast the LW and TLH hymn texts. The sleuthing for the alterations made from TLH to LW text could itself be fun. But the sense of achievement comes after the legwork is all finished and one can finally make an informed and fair estimate of the overall effect of the alterations.

What to look for on the tour? One may notice such things as these: single words or phrases in *Lutheran Worship* updated from the *The Lutheran Hymnal* version; rhyme changes made necessary by such updating, or the updating of a rhyming word (e.g., a change from *thee* to *be*) making necessary a complete sentence revision; the remodelling of whole sentences, even complete hymns; an entirely fresh translation. If eating is the proof of a pudding, the careful reading and comparison of the versions and hearty singing of the hymns is a person's testing of a hymn's language and singability. A bonus would be the discovery of the cook's rationale or, in the case of hymns, that of the updaters or translators.

To come now to the challenge and the opportunity. Rupprecht writes,

> The thoughtful and discriminating reader will note the mood of carefree confidence distinguishing 423[LW]–523[TLH]; . . . the exultation in 306–619; the thrill of rejoicing in 355–377; the soothing assurance, but also the firmness of 420–518; the mood of serene and unquestioning confidence in 422–521; the determination and defiance in 439–25; the deep reverence in 431–458; the deeply penitential mood of 230–329, whose cry "from depths of woe" is skillfully—and scripturally— restrained and controlled by strength of confidence in divine mercy; a similarly picturesque portrayal of the repentant mood in 233–326, where the lament is transformed by intervening elements of bright hope: the sudden interposition of eight successive chords in the variety of major keys; the serene tranquility and peacefulness of 485–554.

> Hymn 287–53 is especially suitable for children. The tune is one of beautiful, almost delicate, simplicity. The artless, unaffected naturalness and easy effortless progression from note to note conceals from the superficial observer the skill with which it expresses the quiet trust of the Christian whose spirit rests in God. It is, nonetheless, a masterpiece in miniature, a *multum in parvo.*

> In addition there is the majesty of utterance in hymns like 214–249, 213–251B, and 298–262. Hymn 288–500 is a marvelous combination of grandeur and gentleness—an ideal source of

assurance invigorating the faith and replenishing the hope of missionaries, or other isolated persons, who stand lonely in their field of labor. By its slow, steady rhythm, hymn 155–231 achieves an almost cathedral-like effect of grandeur and solemnity, the rise and fall of the melodic line emphasizing the fervor of the petition.

Occasionally, two or more of the three basic elements (melodic line, harmonic structure, rhythmic pattern) combine and converge to establish a mood, or bring about a change. Hymn 25–75 has a joyous rhythm, but any tendency toward superficiality of mood (perhaps even a suggestion of a waltz tempo) is interrupted and broken three times by a change in the rhythm, and the worshiper is immediately restrained in his enthusiasm and reminded that his joy should be of a kind with which, as H.C. Colles, music critic of *The London Times* said, he would like to "come before His presence." Hymn 339–296 has no change in the rhythmic flow, but the sudden interposition of a minor chord in the fifth line achieves the same effect as that obtained in 25–75.[4]

Readers who have completed the above tour as suggested may want to take a breather, and it may or may not occur to some to paraphrase the opening line of Gerard Manley Hopkins' poem "God's Grandeur" and say, "Church music's charged with the grandeur of God." It is at any rate true that wherever the harmonies of the Gospel of grace are interlaced with the Christian church's best melodies, people of God have cause to rejoice in what Martin Luther called God's greatest gifts: theology and, next to theology as its helpmate, music.

Both they who use and they who prepare for use those earthly vessels, the hymns fashioned out of an amalgam of music and language, would love to have them be flawless to the glory of God and the perfect delight of the church. Hence, from generation to generation and from hymnal to hymnal, there is a ceaseless striving for the improvement and increased usefulness of hymns. Yet both the music and the hymn texts are often, again in words from Hopkins' poem, bleared and smudged—ironically by the very toil which aimed at their perfection.

Happily, however, the church throughout its history has felt free to correct whatever flaws had been built into a hymn at its inception, or developed over time through the corrosion of language elements used in the hymn. A Christian love able to cover multitudes of sins knows also how to find the kindness to correct the blemished parts of a hymn writer's gifts to the church.

We who enjoy the use of hymnic treasures inherited from the church's past have reason to be thankful for this. Charles Wesley's great Christmas hymn "Hark! The herald angels sing" (LW 49) would not today be a favorite had it remained as Wesley wrote it. The original opening line was, "Hark! How all the welkin rings." The hymn had no refrain. Not one stanza ended with the joyous couplet,

> Hark! The herald angels sing,
> "Glory to the new-born king!"

The first stanza, for example, had the ending,

> Universal nature say,
> "Christ the Lord is born today!"[5]

We can similarly be grateful to the compilers of *The Lutheran Hymnal* for making an alteration in Augustus M. Toplady's "Rock of Ages, cleft for me." They replaced "When my eye-strings break in death" with the line familiar to us, "When my eyelids close in death."[6]

Changes in hymns are bound to cause initial discomfort and even some irritation when, for example, a singer fails to make it around the bend when unexpectedly coming to a new turn of phrase. Many a person may stub the epiglottis on a new word. Nevertheless, congregations most often have a liveliness in the bones and a loveliness of spirit that fortunately enables them to take changes in the externals of hymns in stride.

The best example of a church's readiness to accept great numbers of changes in its hymnody is *The Lutheran Hymnal* itself. Check the information printed above every TLH hymn text. A text changed in any way from its original version will be marked "alt." if one or many words of the original wording were altered; "ab." if the original was abridged by one stanza being omitted; "cento" if the hymn was shortened by omission of more than one stanza; "tr." if the text differs from the original by virtue of translation; and "ad." if the hymn was adapted to a new flow of thought differing somehow from that in the original.

The most important of these categories of hymn changes are the adaptations (TLH has five), the translations (TLH has 352, 88 from languages other than German), and the alterations, namely, internal changes of the wording of the English hymn text used, whether that was a translation into English or not. (TLH has 241 texts marked "alt."; these may overlap with ad. and tr. texts. The ab. and cento texts number 207.) These numbers provide persuasive evidence of how freely and how frequently a church re-tailors hymns to fit its needs at a given time.

Good people will differ, of course, as to what constitutes a need for making changes in hymns. Some may even argue that both aesthetic sense and ethical obligation require that a hymn text be kept intact in its original form for all time.[7]

Arguments for the allowability of hymn text alterations were offered by a featured lecturer at a meeting of the Hymn Society of Great Britain and Ireland in Cheltenham, England, July 1982. The speaker declared that the principle which in general literature required the inviolability of an author's text does not apply to hymns. For hymns are gifts offered to the church for the purpose of serving in the best way possible the needs of corporate worship.

The Cheltenham lecturer offered specific pastoral arguments for updating the language of hymns: When the language of a hymn remains static though the language of ordinary use has changed, the hymn must to some degree fail to communicate. When antiquated forms of speech are used in worship, they create a gap between religion and everyday life. Private "religious" language is an offense. For mission work to be effective—and hymns are certainly involved in mission work—contemporary language is mandatory. Hymns are, among other things, a teaching instrument, and teaching must be done in the language of the learner. Family worship needs hymns that use language forms not familiar to some family members.

Henry L. Lettermann, a member of the Synod's Commission on Worship when the updating of hymns for *Lutheran Worship* was in progress, stresses some of these same arguments, especially that the separation of the language of worship from the language used by the worshiper in everyday life promotes "an unhealthful separation of religion and worship from life." He does, however, concede that "This is probably not true for people of mature age whose many meaningful spiritual experiences are (for them) inseparable from the hallowed forms of language, but I would propose that it is progressively more true for most of us as time passes and as language inevitably continues to change."[8]

Convinced that "worship materials have a profound influence on the life and faith that the church professes" and that in forms of worship "one finds the living embodiment of the creeds and confessions of the church," Lettermann declares that "therefore one 'tampers' with the forms of worship with great fear and trembling. Each generation must approach this ongoing evolution of its forms of worship with reverential orthodoxy, with theological acuity, with piety, and with prayer. And for perhaps many, any change in language hallowed by long use and meaningful experience will seem a kind of reductionism. (The other side of this is that new language might also invigorate, enliven, perhaps even supply new insight.)"[9]

Motivated by the kind of spirit here expressed, the Synod's Commission on Worship saw it as part of its task to contemporize, as much as possible and desirable, the language of hymns to be included in *Lutheran Worship*. The Inter-Lutheran Commission on Worship had already accomplished much of this work in the case of TLH hymns which it had included in its *Lutheran Book of Worship*. Through Concordia Publishing House these already updated hymns were available to the Synod's commission. Numerous other TLH hymns were chosen by the commission for inclusion in *Lutheran Worship* on the basis of a survey of all Synod's congregations as to which TLH hymns they were using and how often. The commission's Hymn Text and Music Committee updated these where necessary and as directed to do so by the commission.

There are thus 384 hymns in *Lutheran Worship* that are also in *The Lutheran Hymnal*,[10] almost all of which have in varying degree had their language updated. It should be noted that certain hymns, if extensively recast or retranslated, will not be easily recognizable as being a TLH hymn in a new form.

Sixty-eight of the hymns in *Lutheran Worship* are from the *Worship Supplement* (1969), a book of liturgical materials and hymns used extensively within Synod until *Lutheran Worship* appeared. One of these new hymns is "Immortal, invisible, God only wise" (LW 451) by Walter Chalmers Smith (1824–1908). Henry L. Lettermann updated this hymn from *Worship Supplement* for *Lutheran Worship*, and in 1982 he recorded exactly why and how he made the complex alterations, which, as readers will be glad to learn, transformed its original, but since then out-dated, 19th-century language into a noble 20th-century counterpart. The beautifully crafted account of the transformation was published in *Lutheran Education*[11] and is "must" reading for anyone who wishes to understand precisely how a labor of love carried out by a master of the art can renew a lovely hymn's radiance to the modern equivalent of what it must have been before changes in the English language partly obscured it. The relevant major portion of the Lettermann article is therefore placed into the appendix of this book.

If alterations in hymns are desirable in order to contemporize the language in the interest of clearer communication, these become essential when hymns contain words, images, or sentiments that have become acutely embarrassing. A word may, for example, have taken on a connotation that tends to contaminate even the most wholesome or even solemn contexts. Or it may be that culture and attitudinal changes in society have branded a once accepted phrasing or imagery as offensive and intolerable.

This happened to some striking imagery in Luther's great Easter hymn "Christ lag in Todesbanden" ("Christ Jesus lay in death's strong bands," LW 123). Luther wished to make as vivid as possible the divine fervent love that brought Christ to his agony on the cross. Therefore he made an analogy between that suffering and the roasting of a lamb for the Passover: *Hier ist das recht Gotteslamm, davon Gott hat geboten, das ist dort an des Kreuzes Stamm in heiszer Lieb' gebraten.* The problem for modern sensibility posed by the final prepositional phrase is splendidly solved in the modern German version in the *Evangelisches Kirchengesangbuch: Stammausgabe* (1950), hymn 76. It removes the offending *gebraten* (the roasting imagery) and in the process changes the approximate rhyme (*geboten/gebraten*) to a perfect rhyme (*leben/gegeben*): *Hie ist das recht Gotteslamm davon wir sollen leben, das ist an des Kreuzes Stamm in heiszer Lieb gegeben.* A literal English translation of Luther's original final prepositional phrase would be intolerable. Therefore the *Evangelisches Kirkengesangbuch* alters it to read "given in fervent love." Richard Massie's translation (LW 123, st. 3) omits both the original imagery and the *heisze Lieb* phrasing; he simply has "Whom God so freely gave us."

The eminent authority on 18th-century English literature George Sherburn declares the poet William Cowper to be "notable as a writer of great hymns." But he faults Cowper for being guilty of "the frequent fault of hymn writers," namely, "their incongruous mixture of secular metaphor with biblical symbolism." Sherburn continues, "Cowper is not an outrageous offender here except in 'There is a fountain filled with blood.' "[12]

The hymn that opens with this line is rightly loved for its strong assurance to penitents that "the blood of Jesus, his [God's] Son, purifies us from every sin" (1 John 1:7). The fountain image appears repeatedly in Scripture. Here in his hymn Cowper uses it to make vivid the great good news that "where sin increased, grace increased all the more" (Rom. 5:20). But his imagination elaborated on that image by undoubtedly drawing on his memory of some such fountain as tourists go to see in London or Rome; water from the Thames or the Tiber pours from many pipes into huge basins where chimney sweeps, by the half dozen, could simultaneously be submerged. The picture of so great a basin being filled in the manner stated in Cowper's opening lines has seemed offensively inappropriate to persons of active imagination. The Commission on Worship decided to spare the sensibilities of any who might be deflected by the baroque implications of the imagery from the contemplation of the hymn's saving meaning. Consequently it used as the hymn's first stanza an early wording of it:

> There stands a fountain where for sin
> Immanuel was slain,
> And sinners who are washed therein
> Are cleansed from every stain. (LW 506)

Another example of a popular hymn needing alteration on grounds other than obsolescent or archaic language elements was "From Greenland's icy mountains" (LW 322). Written by Reginald Heber (1783–1826) on request and used the following morning for a service in aid of foreign mission work, this hymn has been perceived by many as unfortunately marring its own high missionary fervor by an implied imperial and cultural sense of superiority toward natives of non-Western lands where "only man is vile." The reaction of the Synod's Commission on Worship was not to banish the entire hymn (LBW [1978] solution) but to have a revision made that would somehow show awareness of the massive moral, spiritual, and social ills that Christians of any land can observe and that call to them to share the "lamp of life" globally, nationally, and, yes, locally. Hence the stanza,

> Our own lands's fairest breezes
> Bear sound of steeple bells,
> All nature's beauty pleases,
> Yet man builds countless hells.
> In vain with lavish kindness
> The gifts of God are strown;
> Throngs turn from him in blindness
> To false gods of their own.

No person singing the line, "Yet man builds countless hells," need feel guilty of mouthing the chauvinistic heresy. "Man" is here a generic term meaning humans, and no woman need feel excluded by the term. Nor need the lack of specificity be regretted in the term "hells," as to the social and other ills produced by human sinfulness. The natural idolatries of the human heart are portable and provide unlimited material for the building of living hells that defy individual hymnic enumeration and full description.

Hymns sometimes attempt to list specific national and societal consequences of human sin in the interest of generating social concern. But an inclusive term having power of suggestion may do a much better pastoral job by allowing singers to fill it with specifics out of their individual observation, experience, and need. This, for example, is what the broad concepts in the petitions of the Lord's Prayer allow the worshiper to do. Thus, that prayer never becomes dated though prayed every day of the year. Despite constant use it stays new.

The hymns in *Lutheran Worship* that represent the most complete change from their originals are of course the translated hymns. Translation thoroughly alters at least the poetic quality a hymn may have had in the original, and usually changes much more than that.

Verse patterns can often be duplicated in translation with comparative ease. But these are a matter of external form created by combinations of meter and rhyme and they do not in themselves create poetry. The one-third of the Bible that is written in Hebrew poetry is devoid of meter and rhyme. Its poetic quality is not dependent on the verse patterns of modern poetry.

Poetry is a heightened form of language in which expression and evocative emotional voltage is increased above the ordinary levels of speech meant to inform or to persuade. It uses a variety of means for doing this effectively so that the words may move the heart. Among such means are visual and other kinds of imagery; figurative language (e.g., metaphor, personification, metonomy); and musical devices (e.g., the recurrence of vowel or consonental sounds in association with word meanings). The complexity of such language devices as these interlaced with the intended sense of the words defies duplication in another language. The best that can be hoped for is some degree of approximation of some of the poetic intent of the original.[13]

Luther, though not the father of the evangelical hymn or of congregational singing, did invent for congregational singing the translation of Hebrew psalms into German poetic verse.[14] Because he originated the psalm-hymn for right pastoral reasons, he did not try for close correspondence between his hymns and their originals: he either paraphrased the psalm or he totally recast it. And he always gave the psalm a contemporary applicability, to a sometimes remarkable degree. He related the living, abiding ancient truths to the realities of life in his modern post-medieval age.

Had he not done this, we would not still be singing his "From depths of woe I cry to you," Psalm 130 (LW 230), his "May God embrace us with his grace," Psalm 67 (LW 288), or his "A mighty fortress is our God," Psalm 46 (LW 297, 298). One may be confident that the Chief Shepherd takes delight in an under-shepherd's free rephrasing of his Spirit's inspired words to suit the language, imagery, and contemporary application of hymns to the needs of his people.

Luther's practice in translating psalms has much in common with the theory or translation of literary texts that dominated the field until a little over a century ago. According to that theory the translator's goal in translating a poem was not cloning but re-creation. The translator's task was to render contemporary the poetic expression of a former time. Renewal was "the heart of his labor.

This is why literary translators are, to the acute distress of scholars, so often careless of the literal words of their originals, and so attentive to the spirit (by which is often meant the meaning to its own)."[15]

The excellent literary and poetic quality of so many hymns in *Lutheran Worship* that were translated in England from Greek and Latin, especially those of John Mason Neale (1818–66), is surely to be credited less to their classical scholarship than to their freedom from today's restrictive academic theory of literary translation; not to be overlooked, of course, are their literary training and individual talents. If Neale contributed the most translations and the most poetic ones from the classical languages, then Catherine Winkworth contributed the greatest number (41) faithfully translated from German Lutheran hymnody.

These and all the translators of hymns represented in *The Lutheran Hymnal* of 1941 had preserved the "hallowed" obsolescent and archaic pronouns (and their attendant archaic verb forms) associated with the King James Bible. In addition to having that same preference for antique language, the early 20th-century translators who contributed to that hymnal were doubtless handicapped also by the new restrictive translation theory which the academic world had begun to apply to poetic literary texts. Be the reason what it may, Erik Routley declared, "I find that nearly all the hymns which seem to be great in this book [TLH] are in fact German: and nearly all these have been more or less marred by translation."[16]

Hymn translators of more recent decades represented in *Lutheran Worship* have tended to avoid not only the 19th-century forms of language but also the fetish of scientific accuracy in their translations of poetic hymn texts. This might be interpreted as being in keeping with the spirit in which Luther recreated the psalms he loved into hymns that would best serve the people.

The method Luther used when turning Hebrew psalms into German hymns has not been applied often enough to the recasting of the great Lutheran hymns into English. It is probably a safe guess, however, that Jaroslav Vajda when translating Slovak hymns into English used his fine poetic gifts to recreate rather than to attempt photocopying them (see LW 132 and 183). But one would need a knowledge of the Slovak language to verify this. A winsome example of translating a psalm into contemporary Christian feeling and language is Henry L. Lettermann's "The Lord's my shepherd leading me," Psalm 23 (LW 417). Here is no trace of the stiff inflexibility often present in the metrical psalms that dominated hymn writing in England until Isaac Watts opened a great new channel for English hymn writing with his own massive outpouring of texts.

Generally speaking, the recent hymn translations contributed to *Lutheran Worship* demonstrate a striving for contemporary language, imagery, metaphor, and applicability. The Inter- Lutheran Commission on Worship had begun the process of looking for new translations of that sort for *Lutheran Book of Worship,* and the Synod's Commission on Worship continued the process and expanded it. The effort by that commission in this regard can be seen, for example, in its inclusion of a number of new translations of Luther hymns which it found available in an earlier project of Concordia Publishing House.[17] It may be of interest to know that Luther is represented in the *Service Book and Hymnal* (1958) by seven hymns; in *The Lutheran Hymnal* (1941) by 19 hymns; in *Lutheran Book of Worship* (1978) by 17 hymns; and in *Lutheran Worship* (1982) by 23 hymns. The appreciation for Luther's hymns continues to rise.

Like the Luther hymns, all hymns in *Lutheran Worship* are in that book because they represent what Carl Schalk has called "a usable tradition of church music." They are there not to satisfy hymn loyalties within a variety of ethnic cultures and music traditions. The Lutheran Church—Missouri Synod is more homogeneous than to require a distribution of hymnic favors according to some quota system. Nor does it see itself as a curator for a museum of the arts and sciences of hymn making across the cultures and down the centuries. Rather, its Commission on Worship sought hymns that fit the triangular framework of the "catholic, . . . confessional, . . . pastoral."[18]

Luther reasserted that trinity in his hymns better than anyone. And every Christian hymnbook should do the same. Its hymn corpus should be catholic, limiting itself to teachings derived from the sentiments in harmony with the church's only source and norm of Christian truth, Holy Scripture. It should be confessional, making those distinctions between and placing those emphases upon the individual truths in the same manner and for the same saving purpose as does the inscriptured Word. It should be pastoral, embodying the spirit of the Chief Shepherd's caring for people and supplying their various spiritual needs. Such is the sense in which a Christian hymn corpus designed for corporate worship should be catholic, confessional, and pastoral. It is this that *Lutheran Worship* wants to be.

Its pastoral, caring spirit is evident even in the rubrics it supplies with certain long hymns that it divides into two separate hymns placed on facing pages. The suggestions for various ways of using such a divided hymn are examples of creative planning in order to add refreshing variety to congregational hymn singing. By acting on these suggestions, worship planners, choirs, and people will discover the joy of singing to the Lord a new song in the very act of singing one that is old—but sung in a new way. This creation of variety can be learned from the Creator himself. Within the invariable pattern of sunrise and sunset he provides a continuous kaleidoscope of changing colors. Options and variety are part of the happy renewal of hymns and hymn singing offered in *Lutheran Worship*.

As in the case of "Rupprecht's tour," which readers were invited to take, so also the possibilities offered in the hymn rubrics cannot be enjoyed unless the rubric suggestions are followed and the options tested. To whet one's appetite for the challenge, it will be enough to visualize what the rubrics say can be done, for example, with "From heaven above to earth I come" (LW 37 and 38), "Upon the cross extended" (LW 120 and 121), and the communion hymn "Jesus Christ, our blessed Savior" (LW 236 and 237); also what might be done with "On Christmas night all Christians sing" (LW 65), "The royal banners forward go" (LW 104), "O sons and daughters of the King" (LW 130), and "May God the Father of our Lord" (LW 84).

The two hymns on Law and Gospel by Matthias Loy (1828–1915) deserve special mention for their summary of the two chief doctrines the church must ever proclaim, also in its hymnody. Placed on facing pages, they are "The Law of God is good and wise" (LW 329) and "The Gospel shows the Father's grace" (LW 330). This placement displays their fine and deliberate parallelism of form. Not only that. It demonstrates also the sharp contrast, point by point, between the substance of the Law and that of the Gospel. Loy's artistry and theological acuity are here splendidly used for clear teaching on the nature and purpose of the apparently contradictory but tightly interrelated divine truths designed for the rescue of mankind. Devoid of poetic expression, the hymns are nevertheless charged with the embedded emotion involved in forthright truths about the holiness and grace of God. Placement on opposite pages permits the stanzas to be sung in alternation. Sung this way they exemplify the art of orderly, clear, step by step teaching, aided by the rhetorical devices of comparison and contrast. Presenting, as they do, the two primary doctrines of the divine truth, they represent the steady, living heartbeat of the Bible.

Renewal of a body of hymns offers numberless possibilities and opportunities for new vitality and variety in congregational singing. Finding and using them to blessed effect over the long haul of the years can invigorate the ministries of worship planners and choirs and pastors and people. An ongoing challenge! One that calls for the spirit of John Bunyan's Pilgrim. That pilgrim's progress inspired the fitting words of encouragement and reponse in the hymn below. Those responsible for a congregation's hymn singing may find them to be a welcome *vade mecum*.

All who would valiant be
'Gainst all disaster,
Let them in constancy
Follow the master.
There's no discouragement
Shall make them once relent
Their first avowed intent
To be true pilgrims.

Since, Lord, you will defend
Us with your Spirit,
We know we at the end
Shall life inherit.
Then fancies flee away!
We'll fear not what they say,
We'll labor night and day
To be true pilgrims. (LW 383, 384)

THE SELECTION OF HYMNS

Alfred E. Fremder

Erik Routley, one of the leading authorities in the 20th century on the music of the church, particularly hymnody, began one of his last books, *Christian Hymns Observed,* with the startling statement: "Hymns are delightful and dangerous things."[19] He was well aware of the "dangerous" fact that the music of the hymn—the hymn tune—may often overshadow textual considerations in determining the acceptability or popularity of a hymn. A listening congregation is often keenly aware of some doctrinal deviation or some questionable interpretation in a sermon, but when this same congregation sings a hymn, especially a hymn with a well-loved tune, it may often be less critical and less aware of a deficiency in the text. It may come to accept in a hymn what it would not accept in a sermon, perverse as that may seem.

Routley, in comparing the relationship of text (poetry) and music, assesses the influence of each upon the other:

> The music carries the poetry into the mind and experience; and if the poetry is too weighty for the music to get it moving, it won't move; while if the music is so eloquent as to drown the sound of the words, the words, no matter what nonsense they may talk, will go clear past the critical faculty into the affections.[20]

The Hymn Text and Music Committee for *Lutheran Worship* (1982), appointed by The Lutheran Church—Missouri Synod Commission on Worship in 1978, was well aware of the close relationship between the text of a hymn and its accompanying music; it fully realized the necessity of striking a proper balance between the two. Accordingly, although its initial study centered on the Report and Recommendations of the Special Hymnal Review Committee,[21] the Hymn Text and Music Committee felt constrained at the outset to adopt precise criteria for the selection of hymns (text and music) in the interest of conscientious and faithful service to the Lord and his church.

Although literary and musical considerations were deemed important in the selection of hymns, the foremost considerations in the proposed criteria were theological. In his highly regarded book, *The Lutheran Liturgy,* Luther Reed also stresses the prime importance of correct theology:

> In addition to having a high and holy objective, worship must be pure in content and form. And there is no greater impurity than heresy. Impure doctrine may be taught in sermons, in phrases in the liturgy or the hymnal and even by improper ceremonial and decoration. Because of this, the historic liturgical churches have seen to it that in the preparation of their liturgies and hymnals able scholars have weighed every sentence, studied every phrase, and considered the finest points of capitalization and punctuation in the effort to secure not only all possible literary grace but a clear and consistent expression of doctrinal truth as well.[22]

After considerable discussion and revision, the Hymn Text and Music Committee adopted the following criteria.

Table 6

Criteria for Selection of Hymns

WORSHIP AND THEOLOGY

1. God-ward and God-centered.
2. Evangelical, congregational, doxological.
3. Theologically sound.
4. Conveying the Word; keeping the Word in circulation (Luther).
5. Truthful and clear in interpreting the Word.
6. Expressive of the spirit of Christian worship; "unto edifying."
7. Both ecumenical and confessional.
8. In keeping with the tenor of Lutheran liturgical worship, but possibly related also to wholesome Christian folkcharacter.
9. Didactic and hortatory texts coupled with expressions of thankfulness and grace (Col. 3:16; Eph. 5:19).
10. Devoid of ambiguity, exaggerations, unfortunate anthropomorphisms, and sentimentality.
11. References to Bible passages checked carefully and corrected.

TEXTUAL CONSIDERATIONS

1. Language dignified and simple, not obsolete, pompous, ephemeral, vulgar.

2. Poetry good, not doggerel.

3. Since ordinarily objective texts are better suited for congregational and corporate use, hymns with objective texts should ordinarily be preferred; however, not all instances of subjectivity need be excluded provided that the thoughts and sentiments can be shared by average Christian people.

4. Translations as true to the denotative and connotative values of the original as possible.

5. Composite translations to be avoided whenever possible.

6. Standard texts and translations to be altered to conform as much as possible to modern usage.

7. Added Amens to be omitted on all hymns.

8. Alleluia instead of Hallelujah.

9. Spellings American, not British.

10. Liturgical principles of capitalization to be followed.

11. In dating texts and translations, follow the best sources available.

12. Provide hymn texts for all days listed in the calendar.

13. Include as many noteworthy hymns by noteworthy hymnographers as possible.

14. Observe notable practices and tendencies in present-day Lutheran hymnals, but not to the exclusion of good practices and tendencies found in other Christian hymnals.

15. Try earnestly to include hymns of the twentieth century.

16. Take care that the texts are well-fitted to their tunes.

MUSICAL CONSIDERATIONS

1. Apart from the support of its text, each hymn tune should be music which is intrinsically good and well-suited for use in a Lutheran service of worship.

2. The hymn tunes should not suggest what is foreign to the text.

3. The melodic line and the tessitura should be convenient for congregational use and in a key which best serves the spirit of the hymn.

4. The rhythm should serve and not dominate; it should not suggest what is unrelated to Christian worship.

5. Emotion should be under control and not suggest sentimentalism.

6. Hymn tunes may be beautiful but not "pretty"; their beauty is not to be an end in itself.

7. Since the hymnal is intended chiefly for corporate worship, its hymn tunes should be virile and masculine rather than suave and catchy.

8. While some hymn tunes will present more difficulties than others, all should be well adapted to reasonable learning abilities and efforts of worshipers.

9. Hymn tunes should be so harmonized that they will create no special problems (e.g. pedalling) for organists of average ability.

10. Following the practice of noteworthy present day hymnals of America and England (EpH, SBH, HCS, SoP, CP, EH), time signatures shall be omitted.

11. The use of measure bars shall be reduced to a minimum.

12. Suggestions of tempo shall be omitted.

13. Taking the limitations of many organists into consideration, keys having three or more sharps and four or more flats should ordinarily be avoided.

14. Modal hymns should be harmonized modally.

15. Since the harmonizations of many English hymn tunes are standard and may be found in most good hymnals in which the English language is used, we should return to these harmonizations.[23]

Briefly to distill this rather long list of criteria might help even the novice better to understand what makes a hymn "good": theologically, a good hymn is scriptural, rightly dividing the Word of truth, not confusing Law and Gospel; a good hymn is clear, saying clearly what it means to say; and a good hymn focuses on God. In a perceptive article appearing in *Christianity Today,* E. Margaret Clarkson comments,

> Good hymns adore the eternal Godhead for what he is, worshiping him for his holiness, wisdom, power, justice, goodness, mercy, and truth. They praise him for his mighty acts—for creation, preservation, redemption; for guidance, provision, protection; for the hope of glory. They offer petition suitable to their theme. Good hymns are free from introspection; they focus on God, not man. When man enters the picture it is to acknowledge the darkness of his sinful nature in the light of such a God, to seek his mercy, and to marvel and rejoice in his redeeming grace.[24]

Musically, a good hymn tune is singable and fits the mood of the text; it does not wander hit or miss, but has good direction and drive. Remember, "It is the words that decide the worth of a hymn. The music is merely the setting against which the words will be experienced, the purpose of which is to strengthen and enhance the message of the words. The best hymn tunes are those that best illustrate their text."[25]

Poetically, there are many technical niceties that make up a good hymn text. Again, E. Margaret Clarkson summarizes some important principles in this regard.

> *Good hymns have words of beauty, dignity, reverence, and simplicity.* Whether lofty exultations or simple declarations of trust, good hymns are chaste, precise, and lovely in their utterance. Their language is clear and concise. Such hymns are never glib or pat or extravagant or sentimental; they are always true. They speak beautifully, feelingly, compellingly, and with restraint of the things of God, and they do not transgress the limits of good taste.
>
> Good hymns are adult in word and tone. They do not insult our intelligence by requiring us to sing immortal truths in childish or unsuitable modes of expression. They contain nothing to bewilder or embarrass an unbeliever, but will speak to him of a deep, sincere, vital experience of God. While their figures of speech will have meaning for the contemporary worshiper, they will be in keeping with the worth-ship of God.[26]

All of these concerns were certainly paramount for the Hymn Text and Music Committee in considering the selection of hymns for *Lutheran Worship.* In regard to its initial concern, however, that of consulting the Report of the Special Hymnal Review Committee, the Hymn Text and Music Committee generally followed the recommendations of this report. A few exceptions were made in the interest of filling the need for the inclusion of hymn texts in particular categories. When it was thought desirable or necessary, appropriate revisions in a given hymn were made.

An example is "O God, whose will is life and good," a hymn designed to focus on God's blessing in medical situations, an almost non-existent topic in previous Lutheran hymnals. Compare stanzas 3 and 4 of the original text with the *Lutheran Worship* revision.

Original version	*Lutheran Worship*
Stanza 3	
By healing of the sick and blind,	By healing of the sick and blind,
Christ's mercy they proclaim,	Christ's power they proclaim;
Make known the great physician's mind,	It is the great physician's mind
Affirm the Savior's name.	Still heals the bruised and lame.
Stanza 4	
Before them set your gracious will,	Assert to them your grace and will,
That they, with heart and soul,	And teach them, heart and soul,
To you may consecrate their skill	To consecrate to you their skill,
And make the suff'rer whole.	Who makes the suff'rer whole.
(LBW 435)	(LW 396)

Another example of a hymn chosen to fill a particular need is "When seed falls on good soil" (LW 338). For the important pericopal selection, the Parable of the Sower, in the past there had been a scarcity of hymns that dwelt on this specific theme. To include this hymn it was considered necessary to revise the second stanza to convey the thought that it is God who prepares the soil, man's heart, for the fruitful reception of the seed, the means of grace. Luther's explanation of the Third Article of the Apostles' Creed makes this abundantly clear in the words, "I believe that I cannot by my own reason or strength believe in Jesus Christ my Lord, or come to Him; but the Holy Ghost has called me by the Gospel, enlightened me with His gifts, sanctified and kept me in the true faith."[27] Scripture itself clearly states this in Eph. 2:8–9: "For it is by grace you have been saved, through faith—and this is not from yourselves, it is the gift of God—not by works, so that no one can boast." And in Phil. 2:13, "It is God who works in you to will and to act according to his good purpose."

Compare stanza 2, then, with the revised version in *Lutheran Worship*.

Original version	*Lutheran Worship*
God's Word in Christ is seed;	God's Word in Christ is seed,
Good soil its urgent need;	Good soil its urgent need;
For it must find in humankind	And it would work in humankind
The fertile soil in heart and mind.	The fertile soil in heart and mind.
Good soil! A human field!	Good soil, a human field,
A hundredfold to yield.	A hundredfold to yield.
(LBW 236)	(LW 338)

One of the more popular 18th-century Olney Hymns, "Amazing Grace," which is new to Lutheran hymnals, was requested by many people for inclusion in *Lutheran Worship*. This hymn by John Newton has a stanza that uses the word "fear" with two different meanings, one that is in accord with Luther's catechism explanations of the Ten Commandments, namely, "We should *fear* and love God," which goes hand in hand with the term "God-fearing" as aplied to Christians motivated by the Gospel; the other which is the abject trembling fear of God that is tied to the Law and can be removed only by the free and full forgiveness of sins in Christ, that is, the message of the Gospel.

Accordingly, this stanza was dropped, stanza 4 of the original six-stanza hymn took its place, and an altered form of the original stanza 5 was added as stanza 4.

Deleted stanza 2	*Added stanza 4*
'Twas grace that taught my heart to fear,	Yes, when this flesh and heart shall fail
And grace my fears relieved;	And mortal life shall cease,
How precious did that grace appear	Amazing grace shall then prevail

The hour I first believed!   In heaven's joy and peace.
(LBW 448)   (LW 509)

The inclusion of another hymn text, "Earth and all stars" (LW 438), was in doubt because of unscientific phrases such as "loud rushing planets," "loud blowing snowstorm." The almost hypnotic repetition of the word "loud" seemed at times rather incongruous. The idea, however, of everyone and everything praising God for the great things he has done is certainly not inconsistent with Scripture. Compare Psalms 148–150, for example, as well as also a much earlier hymn, "Oh, that I had a thousand voices" (LW 448), with its unique phrases:

Stanza 3
You forest leaves so green and tender
That dance for joy in summer air,
You meadow grasses, bright and slender,
You flow'rs so fragrant and so fair,
You live to show God's praise alone,
Join me to make his glory known. (LW 448)

The Hymn Text and Music Committee finally decided to request the author, Herbert F. Brokering, to append an additional stanza that would summarize the basic thought. The result is stanza 7:

Children of God,
Dying and rising,
Sing to the Lord a new song!
Heaven and earth,
Hosts everlasting,
Sing to the Lord a new song! *Refrain* (LW 438)

The above examples are representative of the careful scrutiny and evaluation carried on by the Hymn Text and Music Committee of the Commission on Worship in its deliberations. Obviously, in regard to hymn texts, adherence to Scripture was considered paramount. In any of the texts under consideration, if some phrases or stanzas were clearly false, there would be no problem in evaluating properly and then correcting or deleting.

Problems in evaluating could arise because of puzzling or ambiguous statements, poetic inferences that are meaningless to the average person, poetic rapture, and certain subjective lines of thought not conducive to the edifying of the saints (1 Cor. 14:12,

26). Any of these problems or a combination of them might be sufficient reason to exclude, or at least revise, certain texts.

For example, a change of two words in one of the great Charles Wesley hymns was made in the interest of clarification, not because of false doctrine. Charles Wesley certainly held the scriptural teaching of the unlimited atonement, namely, that Christ died for all, thus opposing the Calvinist teaching that Christ died to save only the "elect." And yet, in his majestic Advent hymn the opening two lines read: "Lo! He comes with clouds descending, Once for favored sinners slain" (WS 702). By "favored sinners" Wesley undoubtedly meant *all* sinners, for all sinners were favored by God in sending his Son to reconcile the *world* to himself, for Christ died for *all* (2 Cor. 5:19, 15). *Lutheran Worship* altered Wesley's text to read, "Lo, he comes with clouds descending, Once for ev'ry sinner slain" (LW 15). This change was thus not made to correct the original Wesley text, but merely to clarify it as a pastoral concern for some who might misunderstand the original.

Pastoral concern was also a factor in selecting some hymns which had scripturally based texts coupled with somewhat inferior music. While a high standard of musical judgment was desirable, there were instances when this judgment would clash with the preferences of many members of the Synod who had grown up with and lived with certain hymns which provided rich spiritual comfort textually, and whose music, though less than the best, was tightly bonded to the text. In such cases pastoral concern prevailed over musical judgment.

Provenance of the Hymn Corpus

When The Lutheran Church—Missouri Synod in its 1979 convention adopted *Lutheran Worship* as an official hymnal of the Synod, it did so with the knowledge that the Special Hymnal Review Committee (SHRC) had recommended that the *Lutheran Book of Worship* be adopted with revisions and that the synodically appointed Commission on Worship and its adjunct committees had prepared *Lutheran Worship*, "based on the evaluation and recommendations of the SHRC, as well as numerous suggestions from the membership of the Synod."[28] This resolution contained a listing of 515 hymns proposed for inclusion in the new hymnal. Resolution 3–01 was adopted "after it had been stated by way of information that . . . suggestions for the addition of hymns could still be received and considered by the commission."[29]

After the Synod's convention the Commission on Worship received over 1,700 letters and numerous telephone calls with various hymn suggestions from *The Lutheran Hymnal* for inclusion in *Lutheran Worship*. The following four hymns received the highest number of votes: "Onward, Christian soldiers" (LW 518), "From Greenland's icy mountains" (LW 322), "Nearer, my God to thee" (LW 514), and "Jesus, Savior, pilot me" (LW 513). Initially, the Hymn Text and Music Committee accepted 35 hymns from these many suggestions. In order to make room for even more hymns from *The Lutheran Hymnal,* the committee decided to delete some strictly new, unfamiliar *Lutheran Book of Worship* hymns that were in the originally proposed hymn corpus. Also consulted was a 1975 survey of the Synod's congregations in regard to usage of hymns in *The Lutheran Hymnal.* This procedure expanded the hymn corpus from 515 to 604 hymns, which now included 425 hymns from *The Lutheran Hymnal.*

Concordia Publishing House, shortly thereafter, informed the Commission on Worship that 100 pages of material would have to be culled in order to keep the number of pages in *Lutheran Worship* down to 1,000, a manageable number. Thus, even though some material from the liturgical section was removed, this still required the removal of close to 100 hymns. Again, unfamiliar hymns were the primary target. Some hymns from *The Lutheran Hymnal,* which had enjoyed very little usage, were then removed.

Of the 509 hymns that remained, 380, or 75 percent, were from *The Lutheran Hymnal,* and 129, or 25 percent, were from other sources, including 51 from *Worship Supplement,* a 1969 publication of the Commission on Worship, plus 12 "new" hymns. Actually, the total of 68 *Worship Supplement* hymns found in *Lutheran Worship* included 17 hymns that are also in *The Lutheran Hymnal.*

The Commission on Worship of the Wisconsin Evangelical Lutheran Synod, in its study guide which looked forward to the preparation of its own hymnal, prepared the following chart.

Table 7

The Hymn Corpus in *Lutheran Worship*[30]

Church Year	12–195	(Nos. 1–11 are canticles)
184 hymns		Texts from TLH: 127
35 percent		Other texts: 57
		New tunes in this section: 59

Divine Service	196–269	
74 hymns		Texts from TLH: 64
15 percent		Texts from other sources: 10
		New tunes in this section: 12

Christian Church	270–344	
75 hymns		Texts from TLH: 57
15 percent		Texts from other sources: 18
		New tunes in this section: 18

Christian Life	345–477	
133 hymns		Texts from TLH:101
26 percent		Texts from other sources: 32
		New tunes in this section: 27

Times & Seasons	478–502	
25 hymns		Texts from TLH: 18
5 percent		Other sources: 7
		New tunes in this section: 8

Spiritual Songs	503–520	
18 hymns		Texts from TLH: 13
4 percent		Other sources: 5
		New tunes in this section: 6

This study also included a breakdown of the 364 melodies, or tunes, used in *Lutheran Worship*.

Table 8

Sources of the Hymn Tunes Used
in *Lutheran Worship*[31]

English	33
American	29
German	23
Latin	10
French	7
Scandinavian	6
Irish	6
Welsh	4
Slavic	3
Dutch	2
Gaelic	1
	125

English
Irish
Welsh   } 45
Gaelic   } 74 (59 percent)

American   29

German
Dutch
Scandinavian } 34   (27 percent)
Slavic

Latin
French   } 17   (14 percent)

Summary:

Anglo-American	59 percent
North European	27 percent
Latin-French	14 percent

The same study commends *Lutheran Worship's*

> careful choice of the best of hymnody from the various periods
> and denominations of western Christianity . . . . As it reaches into
> the repertory of contemporary hymnody, it avoids cheap and sen-
> timental expressions and includes the best that has been written in
> America and elsewhere.[32]

Comment is also made on the music of the hymns:

> Considerable interest should be generated among worshipers by
> the greater variety of melodies in LW. While they are not easier
> to sing, frequent use will make them an enjoyable addition to wor-
> ship. The keyboard accompaniments in LW are different from
> those in TLH. While they are different, they add a conservative
> measure of richness that is considered to be refreshing. They also
> display excellence in musical craftsmanship.[33]

Another reviewer comments particularly on the ecumenical
hymnody found in *Lutheran Worship* as well as the emphasis on the
Lutheran chorale:

> In general, the hymns included in the book show a healthy appre-
> ciation of ecumenical hymnody, adding to the commission's desire
> to make the book a witness to Lutheranism's role as part of the
> Church catholic. . . . As one would expect of the successor to TLH,
> Lutheran hymnody, especially the chorales of the beloved German
> Lutheran hymnwriters and composers, is very amply represented
> . . . . The Church Year portion of the hymnal, as is usually the case
> in Lutheran hymnals, is quite strong both theologically and musi-
> cally. The hymns chosen include many of the best hymns in the
> Christian tradition. . . .
>
> LW offers much beauty and depth to the worship life of the
> Lutheran Church. While having as its goal the faithful transmission
> of the Church's historic faith, it still shows creativity and a good
> sense of the contemporary state of the Church. It is the symbol
> of a largely ethnic Church broadening to include the backgrounds
> and heritages of the people who now compose its members. In
> this it has fared well, even while it has moved cautiously. The
> choice of hymns which seeks to be representative of all periods of
> Church history and the enlargement of the musical repertoire lend
> a greater sense of ecumenicity to this hymnal than to its prede-
> cessor, TLH.[34]

Even *The Lutheran Hymnal,* strange as it may seem to some, was not lacking in ecumenical resource. E. Theo. DeLaney, a former executive secretary of the Synod's Commission on Worship, prepared a list in 1977 of religious affiliations represented in that hymnal.

Table 9

Religious Affiliations of Hymns in *The Lutheran Hymnal*[5]

Anglicans (including Episcopalians)	149
Baptists	11
Congregationalists	11
Eastern Orthodox	5
Methodists	5
Moravians	12
Pre-Reformation Catholic	17
Presbyterians	23
Prussian Union	1
Reformed	19
Roman Catholics	13
Swedenborgians	2
Unitarians	7
Religious affiliations unknown	27
Lutherans (of all times and kinds)	215

A book on hymnody prepared by two eminent scholars of the Southern Baptist tradition comments on the tendency of 20th-century hymnals to assimilate the best of hymnody from various traditions:

> Remarkable progress has characterized American hymnody in the twentieth century. Strict denominational lines have given way to a merging of many traditions, as hymnal committees have drawn on the resources of a common heritage for congregational singing. A common core of hymnody has emerged as each new publication has borrowed freely from previous hymnals of other faiths. Editorial standards have steadily risen, resulting in hymnals far superior to those of the previous century. . . .

During recent decades, more well-edited hymnals have been published than in any other period of American hymnody. To make a critical comparative study of these hymnals would be unrealistic and inappropriate. A denominational hymnal is prepared, not for competition or comparison with hymnals of other denominational groups, but solely as a collection of hymns for congregational use in churches of that denomination. While a common core of hymnody is increasingly evident, there remain major distinctive characteristics of the denominational groups themselves. These characteristics, having to do with differences in forms of worship, hymnological heritage, and cultural and economic backgrounds of the people, are inevitable factors in hymnal compilation.[36]

A factor not mentioned above but which was basic in the preparation of *Lutheran Worship* is the confessional, or doctrinal, agreement with Scripture. Even though a number of hymns that appear in *Lutheran Worship* come from other traditions or denominations, the scriptural integrity of the hymns selected was the paramount factor. For example, "At the name of Jesus" (LW 178) was written by Caroline M. Noel, the daughter of an Anglican clergyman. A powerful paraphrase of Phil. 2:5–11, it is coupled to one of the finest 20th-century hymn tunes, the work of Ralph Vaughan Williams, thus also from a tradition other than Lutheran. *Lutheran Worship* follows the lead of *The Lutheran Hymnal* in adopting for Lutheran usage great hymns from the various periods and denominations of western Christianity, a characteristic of *Lutheran Worship,* which is commended in the previously mentioned report of the Wisconsin Evangelical Lutheran Synod. This ecumenical selection, however, was not done at the expense of the chorales of the Lutheran tradition.

Contemporary Lutheran poets and composers are also represented in *Lutheran Worship.* There are original hymn texts and translations by Martin H. Franzmann, F. Samuel Janzow, Henry L. Lettermann, and Jaroslav J. Vajda, as well as two excellent translations by Oliver C. Rupprecht of German hymns that are new to English Lutheran hymnals, namely, "Today in triumph Christ arose" (LW 136) and "Jesus has come and brings pleasure eternal" (LW 78). Among Lutheran composers represented by original hymn tunes are Barry L. Bobb, Henry V. Gerike, Richard W. Hillert, Friedrich O.

Reuter, Bruce Backer, Carl F. Schalk, Ralph Schultz, Bernard Schumacher, and Heinz Werner Zimmermann.

The introduction in *Lutheran Worship* summarizes well the provenance of the hymn corpus contained therein:

> The hymns in *Lutheran Worship* draw on the vast treasury of Christian hymnody old and new, with words that speak God's Law and Gospel and express our faith's response and with music that nourishes both memory and heart.[37]

Spiritual Songs

The term "spiritual songs" is derived from the mention of "psalms, hymns and spiritual songs" in Col. 3:16, where the meaning of the last term is not clearly defined. The word "songs" as used here and in Eph. 5:19 is coupled with the word "spiritual," thus giving it the meaning of sacred, although the Greek word is a generic term signifying any type of song, secular or sacred. Because there are no examples given in these two passages of Scripture, the precise meaning of the term cannot be determined. The meaning—sacred songs of whatever type, accompanied or unaccompanied—will have to suffice.

The Lutheran Hymnal used the term to designate a section of hymns following the hymn corpus proper. Under this heading many of the weak, less-esteemed (by hymnologists, theologians, musicians) "hymns" were placed. This was considered a favorable solution to the vexing problem of quality versus popular demand. The Hymn Text and Music Committee decided to follow the same usage of this term as did *The Lutheran Hymnal*.

Although the hymns placed under this category generally could be thought of as being not as strong hymnologically as the hymns preceding this section, these "popular" spiritual songs fulfill a real spiritual need for use in family and private devotions as well as on special occasions. When the need—for whatever reasons—arises, so-called spiritual songs are a legitimate resource also for the Divine Services.

The last hymn in this section, namely, hymn 520—not really a spiritual song—is placed here because, as its dual title ("Rejoice, rejoice this happy morn" and "He is arisen! Glorious word!") indicates, one stanza is for Christmas Day use and the other for Easter Day. The reason for this is the long-standing custom of Norwegian Lutherans to stand and sing the appropriate stanza after the sermon introduction of the pastor on both Christmas and Easter festival days. It was difficult to find a different location in the hymnal for these two stanzas without repeating the hymn tune itself. Space was thus a determining factor for placing this hymn at the end of this section.

Admittedly the use of the term *Spiritual Songs* as a title for the category following the main body of hymns is subject to some criticism. An article in *The Hymn,* which reviewed *Lutheran Worship,* comments critically on this distinction:

> LW follows TLH in reserving certain hymns for the category of "spiritual songs." These are often among the favorites of many Christians, but they have limited liturgical value and, perhaps, lack the depth of the hymns located earlier in the book. One questions whether such a classification is of value. Does it not become highly subjective when one has to judge which hymns are "in" the book proper and which are "out?" The answer is obvious when one compares those so listed in TLH that have "made it" into the hymnal proper of LW.[38]

It is true that subjective judgments are involved in the selection of hymns for the *Spiritual Songs* section. It is also true that these judgments will vary from person to person and from committee to committee, as is evident from the differences in the judgments made for *The Lutheran Hymnal* and now for *Lutheran Worship.* One must bear in mind that these subjective judgments are similar to some extent to the other judgments of acceptability or unacceptability of certain hymns, of the inclusion or exclusion of various hymns in the preparation of *Lutheran Worship.* The Hymn Text and Music Committee along with the Commission on Worship made these judgments not to please their own tastes, but with the intent that God alone be glorified and that God's people be edified and strengthened in the true faith by the hymns included in *Lutheran Worship.*

Notes

1. Millar Patrick, *The Story of the Church's Song,* rev. James Rawlings Sydnor (Richmond, VA: John Knox Press, 1962), p. 71.

2. Erik Routley, "*The Lutheran Hymnal, 1941:* A Report to the Inter-Lutheran Commission on Worship," MS copy in The Lutheran Church—Missouri Synod Commission on worship files, 1968, p. 2.

3. Reuben G. Pirner, "The Nature and Function of the Hymn in Christian Worship," *Church Music* 66–1 (1966): 5.

4. Oliver C. Rupprecht, "The Modern Struggle for Standards in Religious Music: A Theological-Musical Appraisal Viewing the Work of Luther, Bach, and Mendelssohn," *Concordia Journal* 9/4 (July 1983): 134–35.

5. Fred L. Precht, *Lutheran Worship: Hymnal Companion* (St. Louis: Concordia Publishing House, 1992, pp. 59–61.

6. W. G. Polack, *The Handbook to The Lutheran Hymnal* (St. Louis: Concordia Publishing House, 1942), p. 269.

7. A suggestion of this kind appeared, for example, among the eloquent and witty comments by Richard Neuhaus in the *Forum Letter* 16/5 (September 1987): 3. Under the title "The Mischievous Alts" Neuhaus chastizes *Lutheran Book of Worship* (1978) for the procedure by which "lyrics are fiddled with to rid them of thees and thous, others in order to excise alleged sexism and similar voguish sins. . . . The procedure raises ethical questions about doing violence to other people's poetry and attributing to them words they never wrote."

8. Henry Lettermann, "Make It New": *Lutheran Worship,* 1982," *Lutheran Education* 117/3 (January–February 1982): 158–59. Prime targets for updating efforts are of course the now archaic pronoun forms which for devout readers appear to be hallowed by their use throughout the King James version of the Bible. In the time of Shakespeare, Queen Elizabeth, and her successor James I, the pronouns thou, thee, thy, and thine were not archaic, not poetic, not reverential. In fact they were the common everyday pronouns used in ordinary speech, the same as the singular pronoun forms you, your, and yours are used today in English and as *du, dein, dir,* and *dich* are used in German. The fact that thou and thee, etc., were the common and so-called familiar forms of daily speech was precisely the reason why the KJV translators used them in reference to prince or peasant, king or servant, God or man. They did exactly what Luther did when using the *du* and *dich* throughout his translation, and never the polite forms *Sie* and *Ihr.* It's the everyday language of ordinary people they were after, Luther and King James' men. If one wishes to follow the example of the KJV and of Luther's Bible, one can but stand and do no other than use today's plain and simple everyday pronouns also in reference to God, who tenderly invites us "to believe that he is our true Father, and that we are his true children." What little child asking father to pass a slice of bread would ordinarily say, "Please, sir" or "Would your highness please"?

9. Lettermann, p. 159.

10. This number of hymns, some would say, is sufficient to serve a congregation's needs. In Germany the *Evangelisches Kirchengesangbuch: Stammausgabe* (1950) contains only ten more hymns, namely 394. And Erik Routley,

having stated that 50 percent of the hymns in the hymnbook he had to use were irrelevant to his people's needs, declared, "that leaves 350 hymns—which is plenty for any congregation." From "An Interview with Erik Routley," *Church Music*, 66–1 (1966): 35.

11. Lettermann, pp. 157–164.

12. George Sherburn, "The Restoration and the Eighteenth Century (1660–1789)," *A Literary History of England*, ed. Albert C. Baugh (New York and London: Appleton-Century-Crofts, Inc., 1948), p. 1099.

13. Cf. Werner Winter, "Impossibilities of Translation," in *The Craft and Context of Translation: A Critical Symposium*, ed. William Arrowsmith and Roger Shattuck, Anchor Books Edition (1964, reprint; Garden City, New York: Doubleday & Company, 1961), p. 104, where Winter writes: "As one moves up the scale [from the direct, denotative meaning and form of scientific prose, through novels of the poetic kind and poetry free of form, to 'the most difficult of all, poetry in rigid form'], the number of instances in which one has to give up all hope of duplicating the original increases; at the same time, of course, the number of opportunities for the translator-poet increases."

14. Markus Jenny, "Kirchenlied, Gesangbuch und Kirchenmusik," *Martin Luther und die Reformation in Deutschland: Ausstellung zum 500. Geburtstag Martin Luthers Veranstaltet vom Germanischen Nationalmuseum Nürnberg in Zusammenarbeit mit dem Verein für Reformations Geschichte* (Frankfurt am Main: Insel Verlag, 1983), p. 293, col. 1. Jenny describes it as a shallow observation to say that Luther was the father of the Protestant hymn (*evangelischen Kirchenliedes*) and creator of the Protestant hymnbook, though he influenced the development of both immeasurably. But he is the originator of the transformation of psalms into hymns: "Biblische Psalmen zu Liedern umzuformen, hat vor ihm keiner unternommen, und alle seit 1524 entstehenden Psalmlieder anderer sind endgueltig auf den von Wittenberg ausgehenden Anstosz hin geschaffen worden." Luther also created the first hymnal in the modern sense of the term: "Ein deutsches Kirchengesangbuch im heutigen Sinn hat es nicht gegeben, ehe Luther 1529 das Wittenberger Gesangbuch schuf."

15. William Arrowsmith and Roger Shattuck, eds., in the introduction to *The Craft and Context of Translation: A Critical Symposium*, p. xviii. (See note 13 for the bibliographical information.)

16. Routley, p. 46.

17. F. Samuel Janzow, Paul Bunjes, Richard Hillert, and Carl Schalk, *The Hymns of Martin Luther*, 6 vols. (St. Louis: Concordia Publishing House, 1978–82). Persons who comment on my hymn contributions chosen for *Lutheran Worship* frequently suppose that Concordia Publishing House paid for their use. But no payments for such or similar work for the Synod were ever desired or expected or offered. Whatever fee payments this publisher receives from those to whom it grants permission to reprint these materials it has copyrighted will help support the work of the Synod.

18. Insofar as these goals were realized in the hymn section of *Lutheran Worship*, the book can be seen as closely fitting the framework of basic concerns Carl Schalk had suggested for "a usable tradition of Lutheran church music." In an editorial article on the search for such a tradition he reasserted "three basic emphases":

Lutheran worship and church music is *catholic,* emphasizing in its forms and expressions its oneness with the entire community of Christians throughout the world.

Lutheran worship and church music is *confessional,* emphasizing those unique characteristics which identify Lutheranism as a confessing movement within Christianity.

Lutheran worship and church music is *pastoral,* concerned with meeting the needs of people in particular circumstances.

19. Erik Routley, *Christian Hymns Observed: When in Our Music God is Glorified* (Princeton: Prestige Publications, 1982), p. 1.

20. Ibid.

21. The Special Hymnal Review Committee was appointed by President J. A. 0. Preus at the direction of the 1977 synodical convention to review the contents of the proposed *Lutheran Book of Worship,* prepared by the churches participating in the Inter-Lutheran Commission on Worship (Minneapolis: Augsburg Publishing House, 1978), and to submit its recommendations to the congregations of the Synod.

22. Luther D. Reed, *The Lutheran Liturgy,* rev. ed. (Philadelphia: Muhlenberg Press, 1959), p. 11.

23. Minutes of the Hymn Text and Music Committee of the Commission on Worship of The Lutheran Church—Missouri Synod, January 4, 1979.

24. E. Margaret Clarkson, "What Makes a Hymn 'Good'?" in *Christianity Today* XXIV/12 (27 June 1980): 22.

25. Ibid.

26. Ibid., p. 23.

27. Martin Luther, *Luther's Small Catechism,* rev. ed. (St. Louis: Concordia Publishing House, 1986), p. 15.

28. Missouri Synod, *Proceedings,* 1979, p. 113.

29. Ibid., p. 117.

30. *Guidelines,* submitted by the Commission on Worship of the Wisconsin Evangelical Lutheran Synod, 1982, p. 20.

31. Ibid., p. 21.

32. Ibid., p. 24.

33. Ibid.

34. Theodore W. Asta, review of *Lutheran Worship* in *The Hymn* 34/3 (July 1983): 181–185, the official magazine of The Hymn Society of America, New York.

35. E. Theo. DeLaney, "Response to Judicius," in *Concordia Theological Quarterly* 41/1 (January 1977): 14.

36. William J. Reynolds and Milburn Price, *A Survey of Christian Hymnody* (Carol Stream, IL: Hope Publishing Company, 1987), p. 107.

37. LW, p. 7.

38. Asta, p. 183.

16

The Music
of *Lutheran Worship*

Paul G. Bunjes

Liturgical Chant

In preparing the liturgical settings for the pastor and congregation in
Lutheran Worship, the problem of prose rhythm and its reflection
in the musical score had to be thoroughly readdressed by those who
were charged with producing the manuscripts for publication. The
editors and arrangers had to examine and sort out the several directions of earlier attempts, appraise them, and hopefully adjust and
refine them to a uniform and viable representation in symbolic notation that would simplify and effectively convey the forces that gen-
erate the prose rhythm of the text and then reflect them in the
notated music with a high degree of fidelity. Determined efforts
were also expended to bring the musical page presentation more
in line with accepted international, as opposed to provincial, practice. The latter had surfaced to some extent in earlier attempts.

The two generic methods of notation (unstemmed and stemmed
notes) appearing in earlier essays were thankfully adapted as a useful and uncomplicated way to differentiate between the pastor's
chant and that of the congregation. Beyond that, further refinements
were applied in the detailed page notation of each genus.

In order to present clearly the whole system as eventually realized in *Lutheran Worship*, it is perhaps best to pursue three
avenues: the pastor's chant; the congregation's chant; and bar lines
in liturgical chant.

The Pastor's Chant

The basic single rhythmic unit in the pastor's chant is the *punctum* (•), a black note without a stem. All the puncta in a chant melody are nominally of equal duration, and serve, therefore, as the prime propulsive force on the one hand, and as the true measuring stick of the time lapse, on the other. Two additional symbols are used to indicate combinations of puncta: one is the *bistropha* (••), a symbol that indicates two puncta fused and occupying twice the time value of the single punctum; and the *feathered white note, or reciting note* (◖), which represents multiple puncta whose number is delineated by the syllables of the underlaid text. These notational elements can be illustrated in the following way:

Make haste, O God, to de - liv - er me;

Excerpt from introductory sentences, LW, p. 224

These several notational elements are organized into various groups so that the musical score can reflect the prosodic disposition of the virtually exclusive prose rhythm of the text it must carry.

The organizational unit is the *ictus,* of which there are, in essence, only two sizes: the *short ictus,* which embraces two puncta (••) or their equivalent, the *bistropha* (••); and the *long ictus,* which comprises three puncta (•••) or their equivalents (• •• or •• •). In *Lutheran Worship* the ictus is signaled by a vertical stroke (') placed over the initial punctum of the two-note or three-note group to indicate a pulse at the moment the ictus is assumed. The various ictus dispositions can be illustrated in the following way:

Ictus of: 2 units   3   2

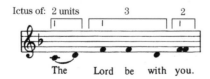

The   Lord be   with you.

Excerpt from Preface, LW, p. 170

The summation of a series of ictuses produces the rhythmic line, that is, the x-axis for the chant. The series often contains short and

537

long ictuses intermixed, and their artful deployment creates a rhythmic framework that can be fully sensitive to the prosodic disposition of the underlaid text. Because of this shuttling between long and short, and the various time lapses that the ictuses produce in the rhythmic line, the pulses will be variously spaced as in the following example:

Excerpt from Common Preface, LW, p. 146

In the foregoing it is to be noted that the punctum is the unit of measure. The short ictus equals two puncta, the long ictus comprises three. The ictuses along the feathered white note, or reciting note, are delineated by the underlaid text and are ordinarily not marked except here for purposes of illustration.

The Congregation's Chant

The liturgical music of the congregation divides itself into two categories. One is liturgical *chant*; the other, liturgical *song*. Liturgical *chant* is the freely flowing melodic line that carries the prose text without reference to a beat, meter, or measure. A certain portion of the liturgical text is carried by this method. Examples of such chant are: "Lord, now let your servant" (LW, pp. 152f.); "Glory be to the Father" (LW, pp. 208f.); the Responsories (LW, pp. 211ff. and 226ff.); the Benedictus (LW, pp. 217ff.); the Magnificat (LW, pp. 228ff.); the Nunc Dimittis (LW, pp. 230f.); "Blessed be the Lord" (LW, pp. 239ff.); "Joyous light of glory" (LW, pp. 251f.); "My soul proclaims" (LW, pp. 255ff.); "Into your hands" (LW, p. 265); "Lord, now you let your servant" (LW, pp. 268f.); chant melodies for the psalms and propers (LW, pp. 367f.).

Liturgical *song* clothes the prose text as well, but the carrying melodies are laced into a rhythmic harness where the beat and measure (identified by either a bar line or an implied one) are the generative and propulsive rhythmic force. Many settings of the liturgical texts in *Lutheran Worship* are clothed in this manner.

Since stemmed and beamed notes are more familiar to the worshiper in the pew, the notational elements for congregational chant look different from those for the pastor's chant, but they function similarly. The basic rhythmic unit is the eighth note (♪), either flagged or beamed. All the eighth notes are nominally of equal duration and provide the basic propulsion, serving as a rule of measure for the time lapse. Two additional symbols find application. The first is the quarter note (♩), which equals two units fused to produce twice the time value. The second is the feathered white note, or reciting note, which serves the same purposes and functions as in the pastor's chant. The following illustrates the notational elements of the congregation's chant:

And with your spir - it.

Excerpt from Salutation, LW, p. 139

These basic notational elements are organized into groups in such a way that the rhythm of the text is sensitively reflected in the musical score. As in the pastor's chant, the ictus serves as the organizing element. Two sizes prevail: the short ictus of two notes, and the long ictus of three. In *Lutheran Worship* the ictus comprises the group of notes connected by one beam. The initial note of such a group carries the pulse, as in the following example:

We lift them to the Lord.

Excerpt from Preface, LW, p. 170

Sometimes four eighth notes are combined under one beam to represent two short ictuses and, consequently, to carry two pulses.

Excerpt from Te Deum, Canticles and Chants, No. 8

The harnessing of the notational elements in an ictic layout produces the rhythmic line in which there occur both short and long ictuses. Consequently the pulses are unevenly distributed and the ictuses occupy variant time spans, as illustrated in the following example:

Excerpt from Magnificat, LW, p. 255, alt.

In the foregoing examples the reciting notes (a' and b') are notated in the more usual form of a feathered white note. Moreover, it is to be noted that the eighth note is the unit of measure. The short ictus comprises two eighths, the long ictus, three. The ictuses along the feathered white note are defined by the underlaid text.

Bar Lines in Liturgical Chant

The complement of bar lines in liturgical chant is somewhat greater than that used for metered music and serves quite different purposes. Instead of marking off measures as in a metered setting, the bar lines serve largely as musical punctuation. The following five types are evident:

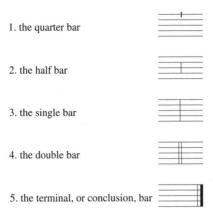

1. the quarter bar

2. the half bar

3. the single bar

4. the double bar

5. the terminal, or conclusion, bar

The *quarter* bar marks a place in the chant where it is convenient to catch a short or quick breath (analogous to a comma). The
half bar suggests a more generous breath (analagous to a semi-
colon). The *single* bar serves several purposes. It marks the separation of the forephrase and afterphrase in dialog chant and in psalm
tones. This is illustrated here and also later in the Salutation and its
response.

Excerpt from Post-Communion Canticle, LW, p. 152

As illustrated below, the single bar is often used just to separate phrases of equal or unequal length without regard to their internal rhythmic structure.

Excerpt from Gospel Canticle, LW, p. 239

The *double* bar also serves several purposes. It closes the afterphrase in dialog chants, as illustrated below:

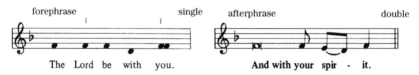

The Salutation, LW, p. 139

The *double* bar is also used to separate performance media—single voice to vocal group, or the opposite, as illustrated below:

Excerpt from Common Responsory, LW, p. 226

At times the double bar serves to separate a refrain from the body of a chant, or to divide the sections if a chant falls into several discrete parts.

The *terminal,* or conclusion, bar signals the ultimate close of a chant.

In sum, bar lines of various kinds in liturgical music serve largely purposes of punctuation, not of rhythmic measurement.

Liturgical Song

Another *genre* of musical expression might, for lack of a commonly accepted term, be called "liturgical song." This genre exhibits discrete properties from those of liturgical chant, and is employed in *Lutheran Worship* for a goodly portion of the liturgical texts that appear in musical settings in the forepart of the hymnal.

Liturgical Chant versus Liturgical Song

First of all, it would appear to be prudent to set the concepts of liturgical chant and liturgical song in juxtaposition and explore their basic and critical differences as they emerge in the pertinent musical settings of *Lutheran Worship.*

Liturgical chant is the freely flowing melodic line that carries the prose text without reference to a beat, meter, or measure. The unit of rhythmic measurement is the punctum. Small groups of these, in turn, organize themselves, through the compelling influence of the underlaid prose text, into short or long ictuses which are signaled by ictus marks (') or beams (♩♩ or ♩♩♩) in the notation. The only other note value that finds application in liturgical chant is a bistropha. All other divisions or extensions are avoided. A rhythmic grid constructed of bar lines to delineate uniform or diverse measures finds no application because the melodic lines are *not* measured in the notation; rather, the bar lines serve to punctuate the musical carriage, so as to reflect the actual or implied grouping of the words and thoughts of the text.

Liturgical song, on the other hand, employs the *beat* as the unit of rhythmic measurement which, in turn, is organized in several different ways either to produce a rhythmic grid to organize the rhythmic flow of the melodies, or to omit the development of such a grid, in which case the flow of the rhythm relies on the propulsive force of the beat alone. In liturgical song, in contradistinction to liturgical chant, a much larger variety of note values is marshalled from geometric divisions of the whole note (𝅝). Among such are the sixteenth (𝅘𝅥𝅯), the eighth (𝅘𝅥𝅮), the dotted eighth (𝅘𝅥𝅮.), the quarter (𝅘𝅥), the dotted quarter (𝅘𝅥.), the half (𝅗𝅥), the dotted half (𝅗𝅥.), and the whole (𝅝) note.

In the subjoined discussion, three dispositions of the rhythmic notation for liturgical song will be presented in turn, with illustrative examples from *Lutheran Worship,* under the following headings:

Songs Cast in Consistent Measures

Songs Cast in Inconsistent Measures

Songs Cast in No Measures

Songs Cast in Consistent Measures

In melodies that represent "songs cast in consistent measures" (i.e., the first species of liturgical song), the unit beat is defined most frequently by the simple quarter note, occasionally by the simple half note, and very seldom by the compound three-eighth note. In general, the measures are of a uniform rhythmic disposition (say, for example, two or four beats); but there may very well occur an occasional elongated measure exhibiting three or six simple beats and circumscribing within it the contents of one-and-one-half measures, without materially destroying the concept of "consistent measures." A representative example of such a liturgical song in *Lutheran Worship* is "This is the feast of victory for our God" from Divine Service II (First Setting):

blood set us free to be peo - ple of God.

In line with the general practice in *Lutheran Worship,* the meters of measured melodies are not designated because they can easily be surmised. In the quoted excerpt, the meter, if designated, would probably be 2/2 for twelve of the measures and 3/2 for two, or, expressed more tersely: 2 in 12, 3 in 2 (i.e., 2 beats in 12 measures, 3 beats in 2).

The bar lines inscribe a rhythmic grid on the score and serve to assort the beats into generally consistent groups, as well as to signal rhythmically significant downbeats. In short, the rhythmic flow of the melody is organized and controlled by two factors: the simple beat on the one hand, and the measure on the other.

Other examples of liturgical song in *Lutheran Worship* that reflect the just-described disposition of the rhythmic notation are

LW, p. 168, "Let the vineyards be fruitful": 4 in 12, 5 in 2
LW, p. 173, "Thank the Lord": 4 in 6, 3 in 2
LW, p. 180, "Glory to God": 4 in 36, 6 in 2
LW, p. 182, "This is the feast": 2 in 56
LW, p. 184, "Alleluia": 2 in 6, 3 in 1
LW, p. 184, "Return to the Lord": 4 in 6
LW, p. 187, "Let the vineyards be fruitful": 3 in 16
LW, p. 188, "What shall I render": 4 in 23, 6 in 1
LW, p. 189, "Holy, holy, holy": 4 in 15, 6 in 2
LW, p. 191, "Lamb of God": 4 in 23
LW, p. 192, "Thank the Lord": 2 in 17
LW, p. 214, "We praise you": 4 in 39, 3 in 2.

Songs Cast in Inconsistent Measures

The *genre* of liturgical songs in *Lutheran Worship* exhibits also melodies that contain a greater variety of measures than discussed above, where the great majority of measures are either rigidly consistent throughout the melodic course or employ at most two meters, one engaging a substantial majority of the measures, the other, a select one or two.

A number of the "songs cast in inconsistent measures" (i.e., the second species of liturgical song) exhibit, at times, three identifiable meters, sometimes four; occasionally five. These melodies may properly be looked upon as possessing a greater rhythmic diversity during their courses; hence, the suggested appellation. A representative example of this second species is "Lord, now you let your servant go in peace" from Divine Service II (First Setting):

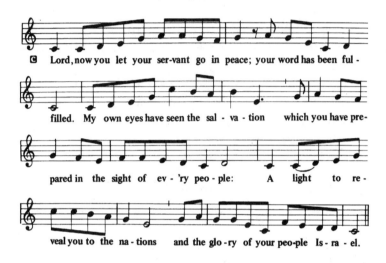

Lord, now you let your ser-vant go in peace; your word has been ful-filled. My own eyes have seen the sal - va - tion which you have pre-pared in the sight of ev - 'ry peo - ple: A light to re-veal you to the na - tions and the glo-ry of your peo-ple Is - ra - el.

The "Glory be to the Father" has, for the present discussion, been detached from the "Lord, now you let your servant" because it represents a third species of liturgical song to be discussed below.

The diversity of beats in the measures comprising this song lines up as 5–7–4–3–4–5–5–4–4–2. Schematically summarized as before, we have 4 in 4, 5 in 3, 3 in 1, 7 in 1, 2 in 1. It is obviously a liturgical "song cast in inconsistent measures."

In this second species of the *genre* of liturgical song the beat is pre-eminent and controls the rhythmic flow of the melody. The variously spaced bar lines do *not,* and are not intended to, serve effectively in organizing the beats, but rather in signaling or pointing up significant downbeats in the course of the melody.

Other examples of liturgical song in *Lutheran Worship* that embody the just-described layout of the rhythmic notation are

LW, p. 169, "What shall I render": 4 in 12, 3 in 4, 5 in 2, 3 in 1
LW, p. 170, "Holy, holy, holy": 4 in 9, 3 in 3, 6 in 2
LW, p. 172, "Lamb of God": 4 in 6, 5 in 3, 2 in 1

Songs Cast in No Measures

A third species of the genre of liturgical song is found in generous quantity in *Lutheran Worship*. Since the bar line in this species does not concern itself with any real assortment in the organization of the rhythmic flow, the species may appropriately be called "songs cast in no measures." Herein, the bar lines serve as punctuation only, in order to separate the text phrases from each other, together with their musical carriages.

The apparent purpose of this *modus operandi* is to divorce, as much as possible, the free prose rhythm of the text from the rather rigid and largely inflexible machinery of rhythm delineation encountered in metered music; the striving is toward flexibility, so that the rhythm of the underlaid text can develop more freely and sensitively.

The bar lines appear simply at the ends of the phrases, and the rhythmic flow is controlled exclusively by the beat without assistance from "measures" of any kind. The number of beats from one phrase to another changes rather constantly, depending entirely on the text content. Significant downbeats are not signaled at all, but reliance is placed upon the text to identify such prime accents. A representative example of this species is "Oh, come, let us sing to the Lord" from Morning Prayer:

In this excerpt the bar lines are simply placed at the end of each text-phrase and serve no rhythmic organizational purpose, nor do they point up hidden downbeats; on the contrary, they indicate the end of a text-phrase and show where a breath might appropriately be taken. The rhythmic flow of the melody is controlled entirely by the propulsive force of the beat alone. Between the bars, in the excerpt cited (and in its continuation), the number of beats varies indiscriminately: 7–10–9–9–(5–7–7–9–6–7–7–8–5–8–5–5–8–8–6). Other examples of liturgical song in *Lutheran Worship* that exhibit no measures (with the number of beats between bar lines shown) are

LW, p. 148, "Holy, holy, holy": 12–6–8–10–8

LW, p. 151, "O Christ, the Lamb of God" (strophic): 12–12–12–5

LW, p. 160, "Glory to God": 8–6–6–7–4–6–4–7–4–6–4–5–6–5–4

LW, p. 164, "Alleluia": 9–8–7

LW, p. 165, "Return to the Lord" (this example is indicative of two *modi operandi*: the first two text-phrases are cast in the third species; the last phrase is reminiscent of the second species, where a bar line has been introduced to point up a significant downbeat)

LW, pp. 175 and 194, "Create in me": 6–8–6–8–7–9

LW, p. 246, "You are God": 5–6–5–5–7–10–4–4–10–10–8–8–7–9–7–4–4–8–5–8–8–8–7–9–10–10–5–6–5–6

LW, p. 253, "Let my prayer" (this melody contains four vignettes reminiscent of liturgical chant in the form of elongated beats, each exhibiting 1 1/2 values; they will be counted here as single beats): 7–10–7–6–7–10–5–5–17–5–5–4–11–12–7–10

The Hymn Tunes

This discussion addresses the more complex rhythmic and metric organizations that underlie the body of hymn tunes in *Lutheran Worship* (1982) and to a similar extent in *Lutheran Book of Worship* (1978).

As a point of departure, the arrangers and editors of these hymnals sought to liberate the tunes from the often awkward and inconvenient restraints of the bar lines used so rigidly to demarcate the measures in earlier hymnals. The purpose of this adopted policy was to encourage a freer and more flexible flow of the music in the rhythmic landscape of many hymns. Such a viewpoint opened the door to intrinsically three *modi operandi:*

1. Retain the pre-existing metric grid for many tunes that appeared to be simply comfortable with it
2. Reduce the number of bar lines or reassort them, where the more comprehensive measure units would enhance the rhythmic sweep of the tunes
3. Abandon the metric grid entirely where bar lines, instead of clarifying the meters in a simple and straightforward way, would tend to rigidify and torture the score

To be sure, the largest number of tunes clearly exhibit generally uniform meters; therefore, the metric grids into which they had been cast have been retained. On the other hand, a goodly number of tunes, or melodies, inherited from the vast legacy of the church's history, as well as contributions from contemporary composers, resist such uniform grids; they seek a more unfettered disposition. Their melodic courses embrace a number of implied meters, and the melodies wander somewhat randomly from one to another. Among such, bar lines are not used to delineate the various meters, but rather to mark off the phrases from each other. Still other tunes resist orderly organization either actually or implied; in such cases measures are not defined, and bar lines in single or fractional form (quarter bars, half bars) serve another purpose.

In view of this considerable variety of actual and implied meters that prevail in the hymnic repertoire, the use of meter signatures was avoided in general: for the uniformly metrical tunes the signature can easily be surmised; for those that exhibit a disposition of mixed meters, signatures are a burden on the notation, and tend to complicate the score; for those tunes in which meters are indefinite or not readily applicable, signatures would be of little or no help—here the pulses of the unit beat are sufficient to propel the rhythm without the added burden of a restless metric scheme. Accordingly, the rhythmic disposition and the page-presentation of the hymn tunes in *Lutheran Worship* fall into four discrete categories:

1. metrically consistent
2. metrically inconsistent
3. metrically indefinite
4. metrically resistant

Metrically Consistent Tunes

Format A is the first of two in this category, which employs a simple beat, either a quarter note or a half note. The tune is scored in visible measures (delineated by single bar lines) which are equal in content. Among these tunes the *de facto* meters are 2/4, 3/4s (=simple), 4/4; also 2/2, 3/2. Examples are

> LW 53 Joy to the World: 2/4
> LW 171 Holy God, We Praise Your Name: 3/4
> LW 258 God of the Prophets: 4/4
> LW 30 Once He Came in Blessing: 2/2
> LW 149 A Hymn of Glory Let Us Sing: 3/2

Format B uses a compound beat for which the unit is either a 3/8 note (♩.) or a 3/4 note (𝅗𝅥.). Again, the score exhibits visible measures (defined by single bar lines) that are of uniform content. For this rhythmic disposition the *de facto* meters are 6/8 (2 beats) and 6/4c (=compound; 2 beats). Examples are

> LW 47 Now Sing We, Now Rejoice: 6/8
> LW 252 Lord, When You Came as Welcome Guest: 6/4c

Metrically Inconsistent Tunes

Format C, the first one in this category, exhibits a simple beat for which the unit is a quarter note or a half note. Bar lines are used to separate the measures which, however, are unequal in content. This inequality is caused by increments or decrements of one or two unit beats. The *de facto* meters in this format are 2/4, 3/4s (=simple), 4/4, 5/4, and 6/4s (=simple); also 2/2, 3/2, 4/2, and 5/2. The 6/4s (=6 unit beats of quarter notes) is not to be confused with 6/4c (2 unit beats of 3/4 notes); it is, in this context, simply a "stretch" of the 4/4 measure by an additional half-measure. Examples of these *de facto* meters, where the measures display some degree of unequal content, are

> LW 69 Let Our Gladness Have No End: 4/4 + 2/4
> LW 71 From Shepherding of Stars: 2/4 + 3/4 + 4/4
> LW 167 Creator Spirit, by Whose Aid: 4/4 + 6/4s
> LW 76 O Chief of Cities, Bethlehem: 5/4 + 6/4s
> LW 91 My Song Is Love Unknown: 2/2 + 3/2

LW 140 This Joyful Eastertide: 2/2 + 3/2 + 4/2
LW 206 God Himself Is Present: 4/2 + 5/2

Example 1 illustrates how these meters are dispersed in one tune.

Example 1: Ride On, Ride On in Majesty (LW 105)

Format D employs a compound beat distributed over scored unequal measures. The format occurs rather seldom, and the unit beat is a 3/4 note. The vagrant measures are caused by increments or decrements of one beat which lengthen or shorten the prevailing measures. The *de facto* measures are 6/4c (2 beats), 9/4 (3 beats), and 3/4c (1 beat). Examples of this inconsistent metric disposition are

LW 97 Alas! And Did My Savior Bleed: 6/4c + 3/4c
LW 65 On Christmas Night All Christians Sing: 6/4c + 9/4c

Example 2 illustrates how two meters are deployed in one melody in this format:

Example 2: Awake, My Heart, with Gladness (LW 128)

Formats C and *D,* in a number of instances, are intermingled, so that the scored measures contain not only various numbers of beats but also various species of the same. Unit beats emerge in half note (♩) and 3/4 note (♩.) symbols. The tunes are scored in visible, dissimilar measures, oftentimes, but not always, equal in duration but unequal in content. The *de facto* meters are 6/4c + 3/2; 6/4c + 3/2 + 9/4c. Examples of these conditions are

> LW 201 Lord Jesus Christ, Be Present Now: 6/4c + 3/2
> LW 130 O Sons and Daughters of the King: 6/4c + 3/2 + 9/4c

Example 3 demonstrates not only how the simple and compound meters intermingle, but also how the insertion of the meter signature in the correct places overcomplicates the score and tends to discourage the freely forward-flowing course of the melody.

Example 3: Now Let Us Come Before Him (LW 184)

Metrically Indefinite Tunes

Format E, the initial one in this category, is based on the simple beat, where the unit is either a quarter note (♩) or a half note (♩). A metric grid is absent from the score. Implied meters encompass 2/4, 3/4s (=simple), 4/4, 5/4, 6/4s; 1/2, 2/2, 3/2, 4/2, 5/2, and 6/2. Occasional modifications occur at *ad libitum* finals where decrements of one beat appear from time to time. A relatively substantial number of melodies in *Lutheran Worship* are scored as metrically indefinite. Examples are

> LW 123 Christ Jesus Lay in Death's Strong Bands: 2/4 + 3/4s + 4/4
> LW 37 From Heaven Above to Earth I Come: 4/4 + 6/4s
> LW 33 Let the Earth Now Praise the Lord: 4/4

LW 124 Christ Is Arisen: 1/2 + 2/2
LW 248 Lord Jesus Christ, Life-Giving Bread: 2/2
LW 177 Wake, Awake, For Night Is Flying: 2/2 + 3/2
LW 134 With High Delight: 2/2 + 3/2 + 4/2
LW 43   From East to West: 3/2 + 4/2 + 5/2
LW 160 O Holy Spirit, Enter In: 3/2 + 4/2 + 6/2
LW 126 At the Lamb's High Feast We Sing: 4/2
LW 154 Come, Holy Ghost, God and Lord: 5/2 + 6/2

Example 4 shows one way of realizing the implied meters of 2/2 and 3/2 within this format.

Example 4: Lord of the Church, We Humbly Pray (LW 261)

Format F occurs very seldom in *Lutheran Worship,* but it does occur. Its unit compound beat is the 3/4 note. The tunes run their courses without a metric grid, and the implied meter is 6/4c. Example 5 shows a melody without defined measures, but whose implied meter is 6/4c throughout.

Example 5: Make Songs of Joy (LW 132)

Formats E and *F* in combination are of somewhat more frequent occurrence. Here the simple beats are intermingled with the compound, without the additional encumbrance of bar lines and recurring meter signatures. The underlying unit beats comprise the quarter note, the half note, and the 3/4 note. Implied meters appear to be 3/4s, 5/4; 2/2, 3/2, 4/2; 6/4c. Examples of various combinations are

LW 28 Comfort, Comfort These My People: 2/2 + 3/2 + 6/4c
LW 109 Jesus, I Will Ponder Now: 2/2 + 4/2 + 6/4c
LW 257 Let Me Be Yours Forever: 3/4 + 6/4c

Example 6 illustrates a layout with three implied meters: two simple and one compound.

Example 6: "Comfort, Comfort," Says the Voice (LW 21)

Metrically Resistant Tunes

Format G, the first one in this category, shelters all of the plainsong tunes in which measures and beats play no role. The rhythm is pulsed by the ictus which appears either in short form or in long form. In many instances the two species of ictus are distributed over a single melody. Bar lines (in single or fractional form as quarter bars or half bars) are used to demarcate phrases from each other. They have no actual or implied metric implications; such interpretations would only serve to ossify the inherent plasticity of these melodies. A plainsong tune, rhythmically constructed of short ictuses exclusively, is "Oh, come, oh, come, Emmanuel" (LW 31). Example 7 illustrates the combination of 13 short and 7 long ictuses in one melody.

Example 7: Come, Holy Ghost, Our Souls Inspire (LW 158)

Format H gathers together those tunes that do not fit comfortably into any of the formats described earlier. They display no scored metric grid, and the unit beat is either a quarter note ($\quarternote$) or a half note ($\halfnote$). Somewhat implied but unclear metric organizations containing diverse elements can be forced upon the melodies, but such are usually neither convincing nor satisfactory. The absence of bar lines liberates the melodies from the confining restraints of such fetters and lets them move forward freely, pulsed only by the subtly propulsive force of the beat. Examples are

LW 144 Triumphant from the Grave: unit beat is probably a half note
LW 223 To Jordan Came the Christ: unit beat seems to be a half note
LW 213 We All Believe: unit beat, more than likely, the quarter note
LW 214 Isaiah, Mighty Seer: unit beat appears to be a quarter note
LW 209 Kyrie, God Father: unit beat seems to be a quarter note

A good illustrative model for this format is subjoined in example 8.

Example 8: To God the Holy Spirit Let Us Pray (LW 155)

17

Planning Corporate Worship

GENERAL CONSIDERATIONS

David Held

Lutherans are fortunate to have their worship practices rooted in the historic rite of the Western Church. Their system and style of church services reflect centuries of the Western Church's developments in worship. Operating under the general umbrella of the church year, each service has its theme shaped by the propers (Introit, Collect, Readings, Gradual, and Verse) assigned to that service. The discipline imposed by this system ensures worshipers that the major teachings of Christianity will be shared with them throughout the course of a year.

> The propers . . . are the insurance that worship will dwell on each point of the Gospel, keeping them in balance and insuring full coverage. They keep the prayers, praise, and preaching of the church from the subjective whim of the preacher or musician by keeping both under a discipline imposed by common agreement of the whole church.[1]

Because the church year and the propers have such an important influence on the shape and conduct of the worship service, it is imperative that advance worship planning occur. Halter and Schalk have made a poignant observation regarding the current worship scene:

> The public worship of God's people is only rarely what we know it can or should be. A lack of understanding on the part of pastors, church musicians, and laity alike as to what Lutheran worship really is or might be is all too common.[2]

And Van Loon's observation can hardly be gainsaid: "Meaningful worship usually results when good planning has been done."[3]

The scenario described by Halter and Schalk may be avoided if congregational leaders work at developing a strategy of education for all involved in worship and a procedure for planning worship in a regular and orderly manner.

In a typical congregation the most likely place for people to come in contact with Word and Sacrament is in a worship service. It is imperative that the time worshipers spend in church for a given service reflect more than a last-minute concern on the part of the worship leaders. For congregations, pastors, organists, choir directors, choirs, altar guilds, lectors, cantors, ushers, and all lay leaders involved in the worship to function at optimum level, it is necessary that planning not only take place but that it also occur far enough in advance so adequate preparation may be realized.

The planning of worship may take place with a standing worship committee or an ad hoc group. Since worship involves people in their response to God's initiative in Christ Jesus, the committee should include some lay members of the congregation. Also included should be the pastor(s), the organist(s), and choir director(s).

Before the group begins to function, it is essential that it become thoroughly familiar with the history and principles of corporate worship. The worship planning committee should understand the church year, the orders of service available, the use of worship space, and the history of worship. Part of its meeting time can be used to develop deeper understandings of these topics. Background information is vital, lest the group fall into the trap of relying only on the personal likes and dislikes of committee members.

Service planning will occupy much of the worship committee's time. Before planning a service, the group will need to determine the major thrust of the day by studying the appointed readings and other propers. Hymns may then be chosen that reflect the day's theme; chief among these hymns will be the Hymn of the Day. The committee will also need to decide which Divine Service and music setting will be used. With this basic information, the next steps in service planning can occur: (1) the pastor may decide upon the text and topic for his sermon; (2) the organist may choose the prelude, voluntary, postlude, hymn introductions, and hymn settings to be used in the service; (3) the choir director may make decisions regarding the choice of verse setting, psalm setting, possible choral settings of hymns to be used antiphonally with the congregation, and attendant choral music that may be used throughout the service. Further decisions may then be reached concerning any processions, the development of art work, and the use of any traditional customs and ceremonies associated with the day.

As the time of the service nears, the committee must be certain that the service plans are communicated to all who are involved in leading the service. In addition to members of the worship committee, the altar guild members, ushers, custodians, and acolytes must know their particular responsibilities for the day.

Many materials are available to assist a worship committee in its functioning. Two major publications, invaluable to a committee's day-to-day worship planning, are the *Proclaim* series published by Concordia Publishing House and the *Worship Blueprints* volumes published by Augsburg Publishing House. In addition to general and seasonal aids, *Proclaim* contains a wealth of information. Listed under each service are a summary of the day's theme, a listing of readings for the day coordinated with related choral compositions (when available) for each reading, a listing of choral settings for the Psalm of the Day, hymn suggestions for the service, and a listing of choral settings of the Hymn of the Day.[4] The *Worship Blueprints* series contains many suggestions for worship possibilities in services. Included are seasonal emphases, weekly themes, suggestions for choice of services, ideas for prayers, methods of presenting the Scripture readings, ideas for visuals, hymn selections, and choral selections.[5] Both series should be consulted.

The worship committee also will need to consider long range projects. This might include an evaluation of the building's acoustics. A reverberant sound is vital to the development of a concept of corporateness in worship. Worshipers need to feel they are part of a group, not isolated individuals who happen to be in the company of an assembly.

The organization and appearance of the worship folder will contribute much to the ease with which a congregaion can move through a service. A major irritant for a worshiper is not knowing what is happening in a service. The committee should also examine the worship folder to see how it may best contribute to a congregation's understanding of the day's corporate worship.

The scope and condition of the congregation's musical instruments is properly the worship committee's responsibility. To lead an assembly, the organ must be adequate. The committee should determine whether the instrument can adequately lead the congregational singing. The organ must be in good repair and be tuned regularly. Additional instruments of concern to the committee might include pianos, handbells, tympani, and wind instruments.

The committee may also wish to evaluate the current worship education program—activities of the day school or weekday school, the Sunday school, the Vacation Bible school, Bible classes, and workshops on worship.

Items indirectly related to worship may be examined by the worship committee and referred to the congregational committees responsible for them—for example, the available parking space, undoubtedly under the purview of the Board of Trustees, or the condition of the worship furnishings, the appearance of the church interior, the regulation of temperature and ventilation in the building, and the schedule of worship services.

If the worship committee considers all factors affecting worship, a congregation can become the beneficiary of centuries of experience. Involving people in the planning and in the conduct of worship will increase participation and ownership in the worship life of the church.

THE HYMN OF THE DAY

Edward Klammer

The Hymn of the Day is the name given to the chief hymn in the Divine Service for every Sunday and festival, the hymn that responds most intimately to the dominant theme of the day, usually contained in the Gospel. It is variously referred to as the *de tem-*

pore (of the time) hymn, since it fits the season and the specific day in the church year; as the gradual hymn, because it was originally sung between the Epistle and the Gospel in place of the historic Gradual; and as the Hymn of the Week, since the original intention was that the hymn be used also at church meetings during the week, in Bible classes, confirmation instruction, at the opening and closing devotions in Christian day schools, and home devotions.

History of the Plan

The Hymn of the Day is a product of the Reformation. When Martin Luther reformed the service in his *Formula Missae* (1523), the evangelical Latin Mass intended for cathedrals, city churches, convents, and monasteries, he retained the Gregorian gradual in its original form as a solo song of the cantor. However, in his *Deutsche Messe* (German Mass) of 1526, designed for smaller congregations in the villages, he gave this gradual back to the people in the form of the congregational hymn. Many of the church orders of the Reformation era followed Luther's example. Thus it came about that already in the 16th century a fixed order of a *de tempore* or gradual hymn for every Sunday and festival of the church year was established. The hymns were mainly chosen to fit the Gospel for the day according to the Old Standard pericopic series.

With the substitution of a congregational hymn for the ancient gradual-psalm, the Reformers created something entirely new. The congregational hymn was elevated to the same rank as the Psalm in the Mass. While in the Mass the gradual-psalm was intended mainly as adoring meditation, the Hymn of the Day in the Lutheran service has a more complex character. It certainly is intended as meditative adoration, but more than that. Just as the intrinsic character of all genuine church music is doxological proclamation, or sung adoration, so also the "singing and saying" of melody and text of the Hymn of the Day is the good news of the Gospel proclaimed in song, and that by the congregation!

The Hymn of the Day plan was in general use in the Lutheran Church until well into the 18th century. When the old Lutheran understanding of the Divine Service was lost during the ages of

Pietism and Rationalism, this plan also went into decline and by the end of the 18th century was practically forgotten. During the 19th century liturgical and hymnological scholars like Freiherr Rochus von Liliencron, Ludwig Schoeberlein, Friedrich Riegel, and Salomon Kümmerle tried to reintroduce the plan; however, the time was not ripe. It remained for scholars of our day like Christhard Mahrenholz, Wilhelm Thomas, Konrad Ameln, and others responsible for the preparation of the *Evangelisches Kirchengesangbuch: Stammausgabe* (1950) and the official liturgical books of the Evangelical Church in Germany to reintroduce the plan in the 20th century. Similar plans are in use in Holland, Switzerland, and the Scandinavian countries. Credit must be given the Reverend Ralph Gehrke for introducing the Hymn of the Week plan to American Lutheranism and promoting its use in the Divine Service.[6]

The eight volumes in the Hymn of the Day series (see p. 563) contain choral settings for all the hymns in the Hymn of the Day listing in *Lutheran Worship* (pp. 976–978), and for the asterisked hymns in the listing, Hymns for the Church Year (pp. 929–931), in *Lutheran Book of Worship,* for the three-year series and one-year lectionaries.

According to the rubrics in *Lutheran Worship* the Hymn of the Day is sung before the sermon in Divine Service I and Divine Service II, First and Second Settings, and in place of the Gradual in Divine Service III. According to the rubrics in *Lutheran Book of Worship* the Hymn of the Day is preferably sung after the sermon but may be sung before the sermon.

Antiphonal Hymn Singing

A fundamental rhythm takes place in every Christian worship service—the rhythm of proclamation and response, the rhythm of *arsis* and *thesis.* God speaks to us; we respond in praise. Luther enunciated this principle in the sermon he preached at the dedication of the chapel at Torgau Castle when he stated, "[In this chapel] nothing else . . . happens, than that our Lord himself speaks to us through his Holy Word, and we in turn answer through prayer and praise in song (*Lobgesang*)." Just as in the synagogue service each Scripture reading was followed by a psalm, so in the service of the early

561

church the gradual psalm followed the first reading, the Alleluia and psalm verses followed the second reading, and—beginning probably as early as the sixth century—the Creed—as a sacrifice of praise, similar to a psalm—followed the reading of the Gospel.

From earliest days psalms were sung antiphonally in the church, that is, two parts of the congregation or two choirs, often facing each other, sang alternate verses of a psalm, thus encouraging one another by the reciprocal, lively rhythm of alternate tension and relaxation. Similarly in the Reformation era, hymns were sung antiphonally by the unison-singing congregation and a "partner." This partner was either a unison choir (the schola), a choir singing in harmony (the figural choir), the organ playing an organ chorale (such as the settings in Scheidt's *Das Görlitzer Tabulaturbuch*), or a brass ensemble. Thus the congregation was usually busy every other stanza. When it was not singing, its partner could bring into play the entire treasure of church music in order to unfold and interpret the melody (the *cantus firmus*) and thus interpret the content of the hymn for the congregation. In this way genuine artistic music became an organic part of the Divine Service; the congregation was drawn into the music-making of choir and organ, even as choir and organ by their subjection to the *cantus firmus* of the congregation's hymn showed that they understood that they were not called to lord it over the congregation independently but rather to serve it in its worship. The same applies to antiphonal singing of hymns today.

This plan gives a definite task to the organ and instrumental music. And, so far as the choir is concerned, it can have no more beautiful task than that given it by antiphonal singing, because the choir functions not only as the congregation's "rival," interpreting the Word of God contained in hymns for the congregation, but the choir is also the congregation's partner, its precentor, leader, and teacher, singing out the melodies, and in this way contributing much more to the hymn education of the congregation than even the best organ playing can do. By alternate listening and singing, the congregation can learn these fine hymns much more easily; its attention is focused on the content of the hymn; it can sing all stanzas of such great chorales as "Dear Christians, one and all, rejoice" (LW 353, LBW 299) without destroying the magnificent unity of its thought. Moreover, such antiphonal singing will lead the choir *away from* the mistaken ideal of "beautifying the service" with added selections and will lead it toward the great ideal of performing a genuine service to the congregation as a liturgical group that is ready and happy to help the congregation toward all the blessings of genuine worship.

Choral Settings and Their Use

The following volumes of Choral Settings for the Hymn of the Day are available:

Volume I: Advent 1–Christmas 2, No. 97-5809
Volume II: Epiphany–Epiphany 4, No. 97-5810
Volume III: Epiphany 5–Transfiguration, No. 97-5834
Volume IV: Ash Wednesday–Good Friday, No. 97-5835
Volume V: Easter Eve–The Day of Pentecost, No. 97-5836
Volume VI: Trinity to Pentecost 9, No. 97-5864
Volume VII: Pentecost 10–Pentecost 20, No. 97-5865
Volume VIII: Pentecost 21–Lesser Festivals, No. 97-5866[7]

The settings of chorales and hymns in these books are primarily intended for the singing of alternate stanzas of the Hymn of the Day in harmony by a mixed choir. (Other choirs—SAB, SSA, male, unison, or children's choirs—may sing alternate stanzas in unison accompanied by the settings in these books.) If a hymn has three stanzas, the choir will as a rule sing stanza two; if there are four stanzas, the choir sings one and three, or only stanza three; if there are five stanzas, the choir sings two and four; if there are six stanzas, the choir sings one, three, and five, and so on. As a general rule the congregation should always sing the first and last stanzas. The choir should also sing the first and last stanzas in unison with the congregation.

One method of singing "Savior of the nations, come" (LW 13, LBW 28), the Hymn of the Day for the First Sunday in Advent, is given as a suggestion:

Organ Introduction: Georg F. Kauffmann (Concordia Hymn
    Prelude Series, vol. 2, p. 8)
Stanza 1: Congregation
Stanza 2: Choir (setting by Vulpius)
Stanza 3: Congregation

Stanza 4: Choir (setting by Kubeck) or Organ alone (the Scheidt setting in *Das Görlitzer Tabulaturbuch,* 1650)
Stanza 5: Congregation
Stanza 6: Choir (setting by Vulpius)
Stanza 7: Congregation and choir
Stanza 8: Congregation and choir

The settings may also be played by brass, strings, or woodwind instruments, or single instruments (trumpet, flute, oboe, clarinet, or violin) may double the melody of the stanzas sung by the congregation or choir. (Instrumental parts are not provided in the Choral Settings for the Hymn of the Day volumes.)

It is most important that the tempo of all the stanzas of a hymn, whether sung by the congregation or choir, played on the organ or by a brass ensemble or other instruments, remain the same throughout the hymn.

Since some choirs might find it difficult to learn a new setting of the Hymn of the Day every week, they can begin by learning one new setting every month, or every six weeks. On the Sundays in-between, the choir should sing alternate stanzas of the Hymn of the Day in unison, either accompanied or unaccompanied. By following this practice year after year, the choir will eventually learn all the settings for the entire three-year series.

Where it is not possible to sing the Hymn of the Day in alternation with the congregation, the settings may be used as chorale motets or anthems on the respective Sundays and festivals.

Teaching the Hymn of the Day to the Congregation

Many of the hymns in the Hymn of the Day listing are already familiar to congregations. However, there are some that perhaps have never been sung in some congregations and must, therefore, be taught to the congregation. The choirs, particularly the adult church choir, should act as the congregation's precentor and lead in the teaching of new hymns.

These hymns should be taught by the choirmaster at every opportunity, especially at meetings of the various organizations (but in small doses!). They should be taught the children in the Christian day school; the children's choirs so that they can participate in the alternatim singing of the congregation; also the children in Sunday school, released-time school, confirmation classes, women's and men's groups as well as the youth in general, as difficult as the latter may prove to be. All teaching should be done by the human voice, rather than by the use of a piano or organ. Once these hymns are learned and the Hymn of the Day becomes an established practice, every Sunday and festival the congregation's singing will improve and be alive like never before. In the absense of the choir in a given service, the Hymn of the Day may still be sung in alternation, for example: Epistle-side of the congregaion over against the Gospel-side; men—women; or organ—congregation. Should this be impossible for various reasons, the Hymn of the Day settings may be used as chorale motets on the respective Sundays and festivals.

Notes

1. Eugene L. Brand, "The Liturgical Life of the Church," in *A Handbook of Church Music,* ed. Carl Halter and Carl Schalk (St. Louis: Concordia Publishing House, 1978), p. 27.
2. Halter and Schalk, "Music in Lutheran Worship: An Affirmation," Introduction to *Handbook,* p. 13.
3. Ralph Van Loon, *Parish Worship Handbook* (Philadelphia: Parish Life Press, 1979), p. 5. See also Mandus Egge, *How to Involve People in Planning and Leading Worship* (Minneapolis: Augsburg Publishing House, 1976); and Hugo Gehrke, *Worshiping God with Joy: A Planning Guide for the Worship Committee* (St. Louis: Concordia Publishing House, 1979).
4. Barry Bobb and Hans Boehringer, *Proclaim: A Guide for Planning Liturgy and Music,* 12 vols. (St. Louis: Concordia Publishing House, 1985–88). Materials herein are related to both *Lutheran Worship* and *Lutheran Book of Worship.*
5. Karen Wahlhof, ed., *Worship Blueprints* (Minneapolis: Augsburg Publishing House, 1979). Materials in this series correspond with *Lutheran Book of Worship.*
6. Ralph Gehrke's rather definitive article, "The Hymn-of-the-Week Plan," in the *Theologische Quartalschrift* 56/4 (October 1959): 274–294, was shortly followed by his *Planning the Service: A Workbook for Pastors, Organists, and Choirmasters.* (St. Louis: Concordia Publishing House, 1961), a work that was extensively used by pastors and worship committees. A more recent contribution to this subject is Carl Schalk, *The Hymn of the Day and Its Use in Lutheran Worship,* Church Music Pamphlet Series, ed. Carl Schalk (St. Louis: Concordia Publishing House, 1983).
7. Paul Thomas, *Choral Settings for the Hymn of the Day* (St. Louis: Concordia Publishing House, 1984). These volumes contain mixed choir settings by a variety of composers for all the Hymns of the Day for every Sunday and festival plus the articles, History of the Plan, Antiphonal Hymn Singing, and How to Use the Settings in This Book.

APPENDIX 1

Duties of the Assisting Minister(s) in *Lutheran Worship*

DIVINE SERVICE I

Gloria in Excelsis
    Introductory sentence: "Glory be to God on high"
Old Testament Reading
Epistle
Prayer of the Church
Distribution of the Cup
Versicle and Post-Communion Collect
Benedicamus

DIVINE SERVICE II

Kyrie
Hymn of Praise
First Setting
    Introductory sentence: "Glory to God in the highest"
Second Setting
    Introductory sentence: "Glory to God in the highest"
                or
        "This is the feast of victory for our God"
Old Testament Reading
Epistle
The Prayers (concluded by the presiding minister)
Distribution of the Cup
Post-Communion Prayer

APPENDIX 2

Suggested Office Hymns for Matins or Morning Prayer

Advent	The Advent of Our God 12
	Savior of the Nations, Come 13
	On Jordan's Bank the Baptist's Cry 14
	Hark! A Thrilling Voice Is Sounding 18
Christmas	Of the Father's Love Begotten 36
	From East to West 43
	Let All Together Praise Our God 44
	O Savior of Our Fallen Race 45
Epiphany	The Only Son from Heaven 71
	From God the Father, Virgin-Born 74
	O Chief of Cities, Bethlehem 76
	The People That in Darkness Sat 77
	Within the Father's House 80
	When Christ's Appearing Was Made Known 81
Transfiguration	Oh, Wondrous Type! Oh, Vision Fair 87
Lent	Sing, My Tongue 117
Holy Week	The Royal Banners Forward Go 104
	Sing, My Tongue 117
Easter	At the Lamb's High Feast We Sing 126
	Jesus Christ Is Risen Today 127
	Now All the Vault of Heaven Resounds 131
	Make Songs of Joy 132
	The Day of Resurrection 133
	Today in Triumph Christ Arose 136
	Lo, Judah's Lion Wins the Strife 146

	That Easter Day with Joy Was Bright 147
Ascension	A Hymn of Glory Let Us Sing 149
	O Christ, Our Hope 151
Pentecost	Creator Spirit, Heavenly Dove 156
	Come, Holy Ghost, Our Souls Inspire 157, 158
	Creator Spirit, by Whose Aid 167
Trinity	Father Most Holy 175
	Father, We Praise You 482
Minor Festivals	By All Your Saints in Warfare 193, 194
	For All Your Saints 195
General	O Splendor of the Father's Light 481
	Father, We Praise You 482

APPENDIX 3

Suggested Office Hymns
for Vespers
or Evening Prayer

Advent	Savior of the Nations, Come 13
	On Jordan's Bank the Baptist's Cry 14
	O Lord of Light, Who Made the Stars 17
Christmas	Of the Father's Love Begotten 36
	Let All Together Praise Our God 44
	O Savior of Our Fallen Race 45
Epiphany	The Only Son from Heaven 72
	From God the Father, Virgin-Born 74
	O Chief of Cities, Bethlehem 76
	The People That in Darkness Sat 77
	Within the Father's House 80
	When Christ's Appearing Was Made Known 81
Transfiguration	Oh, Wondrous Type! Oh, Vision Fair 87
Lent	Sing, My Tongue 117
Holy Week	The Royal Banners Forward Go 104
	Sing, My Tongue 117
Easter	At the Lamb's High Feast We Sing 126
	Jesus Christ Is Risen Today 127
	Now All the Vault of Heaven Resounds 131
	Make Songs of Joy 132
	Today in Triumph Christ Arose 136
	Lo, Judah's Lion Wins the Strife 146
Ascension	A Hymn of Glory Let Us Sing 149
	O Christ, Our Hope 151
Pentecost	Creator Spirit, Heavenly Dove 156

Matins Compared

The Lutheran Hymnal (p. 32)	*Lutheran Worship* (p. 208)
Hymn of Invocation	Hymn of Invocation
Versicles with Hallelujah	Versicles with Ascription of Praise
Invitatory	Invitatory
V: Oh, come, let us worship the Lord:	L: Blessed be God, the Father, the Son, and Holy Spirit.
R: For He is our Maker.	C: Oh, come, let us worship him (or a Seasonal Invitatory from *LW: Altar Book*, pp. 42–43)
The Venite	The Venite
The Hymn	Office Hymn
Psalmody	Psalms
Lection	Readings
Response	Response
V: But Thou, O Lord, have mercy upon us.	L: O Lord, have mercy on us.
R: Thanks be to Thee, O Lord.	C: Thanks be to God.
(A Responsory may be said or chanted.)	(or a Responsory, Common or Seasonal)
Sermon	Sermon
Offering	Offering
Canticle	Canticle
(Te Deum, Benedictus, or other Canticle)	(Te Deum, Benedictus, Benedictus with additional verses for Advent)
Prayers	Prayers
(or Suffrages or Litany)	(or Responsive Prayer 1 or Litany)
Kyrie	Kyrie
Lord's Prayer	Lord's Prayer
Salutation	Salutation or Versicle
Collect of the Day	Collect of the Day

Other Collects	Other Collects
Collect for Grace	One of three collects, one of which is the Collect for Grace
Benedicamus	Benedicamus
Benediction	Blessing
Silent Prayer	Silent Prayer

Vespers Compared

The Lutheran Hymnal (p. 41)	*Lutheran Worship* (p. 224)
Hymn of Invocation or another Hymn	Hymn of Invocation
Versicles with Hallelujah	Versicles with Ascription of Praise
One or more Psalms with	One or more Psalms with
Gloria Patri	Gloria Patri
Lection	One or two Readings
Response	Response
V: But Thou, O Lord, have mercy upon us.	L: O Lord, have mercy on us.
R: Thanks be to Thee, O Lord.	C: Thanks be to God.
(or a Responsory)	(or a Responsory, Common or Seasonal)
Hymn may be sung	Office Hymn
Sermon	Sermon
Offering	Offering
The Hymn	
Versicle (common or special)	Versicle
Canticle	Canticle
(Magnificat or Nunc Dimittis)	(Magnificat or Nunc Dimittis)
Prayers	Prayers
(or Suffrages, Litany, or other prayers)	(or Responsive Prayer 2)
Kyrie	Kyrie
Lord's Prayer	Lord's Prayer
Salutation	Salutation or Versicle
Collect for the Day	Collect of the Day
Other Collects	Other Collects
Collect for Peace	One of three Collects, one of which is the Collect for Peace
Benedicamus	Benedicamus
Benediction	Blessing (two forms)

" 'Make It New'
Lutheran Worship 1982"
(excerpt)

Henry L. Lettermann

I chose as my example [of hymn text revision] a hymn from *Worship Supplement* which is included in an updated version in LW [see "Immortal, invisible, God only wise," LW 451], CPH, 1982. No question of translation is involved here; the text is English of the 19th century by Walter Chalmers Smith (1824–1908), though the language seems of an earlier vintage. The hymn is notable for its stateliness and dignity, especially in combination with its Welsh tune, and for these qualities I love it dearly, though I would guess that in many Missouri Synod congregations the hymn is unknown.

Pronouns

Some of the updating is quite unexceptional, even routine. One expects simple changes in pronouns on the basis of the bias of the Commission in favor of modern pronouns. One may mourn the loss: "thy great name we praise" may seem more impressive than "*your* great name we praise," but what is lost (if it is) in dignity, is gained in intimacy, is gained in a more personal relationship. The "rulest" in stanza 2, line 2 is solved simply by the addition of another pronoun, "thou rulest in might" becoming "you rule in your might."

Riming

Stanza three is a much greater problem. Not only are the verb forms "givest/livest" archaic, but they are involved in the internal riming which is the norm of the whole hymn. One might simply insert an emphatic, as in "To all life you give, yes—to both great and small—/In all life you live, yes, the true Life of all." The updater here takes a greater risk and involves himself in more far-reaching problems. Paraphrasing "To all life thou givest" (note the meaning without the hymnic inversion of word order is "You give life to all"), he hazards "All life you *engender.*" The inversion is still present, yet the possibility of misunderstanding is, to my mind, considerably lessened. The word "engender" is abstract (a disadvantage) and relatively uncommon (a possible advantage), but consorts agreeably with and echoes words like "immortal, invisible" and "inaccessible" from stanza one. The consequence of this change, however, of course, is the necessity of finding a riming word for line two which will adequately paraphrase "In all life thou livest." The updater proposes "To all life befriender"; the inversion echoes the previous inversion and here may actually be an aid to immediate understanding. "Befriender" may seem faintly archaic to some, though *The American Heritage Dictionary of the English Language* does not restrictively label "befriend" in any way, and the noun patterning adding *er* is ancient and honorable in English. On the positive side, if one's life is befriended by God, it seems to me that the line has gained significantly in emotional warmth.

Combinations

Lines 3 and 4 of stanza 3 also present a major problem in that the riming word in line 4 is the pronoun "thee" ("naught changes thee"). The imagery is effective: "We blossom and flourish as leaves on the tree/And wither and perish—but naught changes thee." ("Changes" in WS sounds in this context like a modern alteration, and one's suspicions are confirmed if one examines the LBW text. Stanza 3, line 4 in LBW uses "changeth" and stanza 4, line 4 uses "hideth." In addition, stanza 4, line 1 in LBW reads "Thou reignest in glory, thou dwellest in light." Without having researched the problem, I would guess the LBW text to be the more authentic, and in these details WS already begins an updating process. Hymnologists are noted for tinkering; they changeth anything they think will improve a text for the specific audience they have in mind.) In the updated version the blossoming and flourishing are kept with the riming contrast in withering and perishing, but "naught changes thee" becomes "you never change." There is a shift in emphasis here: "naught changes thee" has the greater power and dignity, though it also has the archaic freight of "naught" and "thee." "You never change," viewed hostilely, may sound like the faint echo of a domestic altercation. Having chosen "change" as the terminal word, the updater is forced to a re-writing of the end of line 3. The "as leaves on the tree" imagery is sacrificed for "We blossom and flourish, in rich[n]ess and range," which has alliteration to recommend itself for what it loses in concreteness, and one could argue that these new nouns have poetic suggestion in connection with life, and are not out of harmony with the tone of the whole. Another "trick" used by the updater is to introduce the unlikely word first ("range"), which makes the riming word ("change") sound more "right," rather than vice versa.

Coinage?

Finally, there are the alterations in stanza 4. We must hurry on. We note that in lines 1 and 2 the updater is somewhat lame in riming "your glory" with "adore you," although "glory/adore thee," though closer in sound, are not an exact rime in the original either. Line 2 introduces "unveiling," which appears to be the updater's coinage. This may be a completely gratuitous interposition of an unnecessary obstacle. On the other hand, it may be ignored. The meaning, even with the coined word, presents no difficulty. The "thee" rime at the end of the stanza is a more crucial problem, as is the archaic "Tis" at the beginning of the line. The updater's solution here is "oh, lead us to see/The light of your splendor, your love's majesty!" In terms of its meaning, "majesty" is a happy choice; unfortunately, the accents of the word fall in somewhat of a disarray. (I have not, to this point, made any issue of how the accents of the text fit the accents of the music; much less the subtler but also telling issue of how the tone of the text matches the tone of the music. The success of the original is adequate evidence.) At any rate, the accents of the word "majesty" fall in the wrong places in relation to the tune, and supply the only instance in the whole text of a terminal riming word which is not a single, strong, monosyllabic word. Ah, but the meaning seems so right!

Compromise

Any melding of words to music involves compromises, of course. Whether the compromises of the updater here vitiate the effect of the original by his adherence to his updating principle, or whether the strengthening effect of updating overrides some of the smaller details, is obviously open to argument, and probably will be decided by the taste of the person, who should consider all the nuances of the problem. For myself, I am inclined to award the updater at least a "B." (But then, I know who the updater is, and I can claim no objectivity in this.)

LW's Purpose

Literally thousands of instances of changes in language like this appear in LW (hymnic and liturgical), that deserve this detailed kind of analysis. My personal experience is that a "good" update (or a good new translation) will seem so right, that after a singing or two, the old version passes out of memory. If LW's updating is successful, it will become the new standard of the church, and it will re-invigorate the church's worship life. I believe that it has that potential! Only time, of course, will tell. *Lutheran Education* 117/3 (January/February 1982): 160–64.

Bibliography

Adams, Douglas J. "An Intergenerational Model for Confirmation Decision-Making in the Parish." D.Min. diss., San Francisco Theological Seminary, San Anselmo, California, 1988.

Agenda, to jest Prace Cirkevni Knezi Cirkve Evangelicke Die Augspurskeho Vyzani Ceskoslovenske. V Trucianskom Sv. Martine: tlacou knihtlaciarskeho spolku, 1922.

Agende fur evangelisch-lutherische Kirchen und Gemeinden. Berlin: Lutherisches Verlagshaus. 1963.

Aland, Kurt. "Die Privatbeichte in Luthertum von ihren Anfangen bis zu ihrer Auflosung." In *Kirchengeschichtliche Entwurfe,* 452-519. Gutersloh: Gerd Mohn, 1960.

Andrews, James E., and Burgess, Joseph A., eds. *An Invitation to Action.* Philadelphia: Fortress Press, 1984.

Aprocryphal Old Testament, The. Ed. H. F. D. Sparks. Oxford: Oxford University Press, 1984.

Aquinas, Thomas. *St. Thomas Aquinas' Summa Theologica.* 4 vols. Trans. Fathers of the English Dominican Province. New York: Benzinger Bros., 1948.

Arrowsmith, William, and Shattuck, Roger, eds. *The Craft and Context of Translation: A Critical Symposium.* Reprinted. Garden City, N.Y.: Doubleday, 1964.

Asmussen, Hans. *Warum noch Lutherische Kirche?* Stuttgart: Evangelisches Verlagswerk, 1949.

Bass, George M. *The Renewal of Liturgical Preaching.* Minneapolis: Augsburg Publishing House, 1967.

Baugh, Albert C., ed. A *Literary History of England.* New York and London: Appelton-Century-Crofts, 1948.

Bekenntnisschriften der evangelisch-lutherischen Kirche, Die. 4th ed. Gottingen: Vandenhoeck & Ruprecht, 1959.

Bente, Friedrich. *Historical Introduction to the Book of Concord.* St. Louis: Concordia Publishing House, 1965.

BIBLIOGRAPHY

Berger, Reupert, and Hjollerweger, Hans. *Celebrating the Easter Vigil.* Trans. Matthew J. O'Connell. New York: Pueblo Publishing Company, 1983.

Bethune-Baker, James Franklin. *An Introduction to the Early History of Christian Doctrine to the Time of the Council of Chalcedon.* London: Methuen, 1903.

Biot, Francois. *The Rise of Protestant Monasticism.* Trans. W. J. Kerrigan. Baltimore: Helicon Press,

Blankenbuehler, L. "The Christian Hymn: A Glorious Treasure." Ogden, Iowa: Ogden Reporter Print, 1940.

Blum, Heinz. *Martin Luther Creative Translator.* St. Louis: Concordia Publishing House, 1965.

Blumhardt, Christoph. *Bekenne einer dem anderen seine Sunde, ein Wort uber Privatbeichte und Privatabsolution.* Elberfeld: Buchhandlung der Evang. Gesellschaft, 1889.

Böhme, Wolfgang. *Beichtlehre für evangelische Christen.* Stuttgart: Evangelisches Verlagswerk, 1956.

Boehringer, Hans, and Bobb, Barry, eds. *Proclaim: A Guide for Planning Liturgy and Music.* 12 vols. St. Louis: Concordia Publishing House, 1985-88.

Book of Common Prayer, The. New York: Church Hymnal Corporation, 1979.

Book of Concord: The Confessions of the Evangelical Lutheran Church, The. Trans. and ed. Theodore G. Tappert in collaboration with Jaroslav Pelikan, Robert H. Fischer and Arthur C. Piepkorn. Philadelphia: Fortress Press, 1959.

Bonhoeffer, Dietrich. *Gesammelte Schriften.* 2 vols. Ed. Eberhard Bethge. Munich: Chr. Kaiser Verlag, 1959.

_____. *Psalms: The Prayerbook of the Bible.* Minneapolis: Augsburg Publishing House, 1970.

Bosch, Paul. *Church Year Guide.* Minneapolis: Augsburg Publishing House, 1987.

Bouyer, Louis. *Liturgy and Architecture.* Notre Dame: University of Notre Dame Press, 1967.

_____. *Rite and Man: Natural Sacredness and Christian Liturgy.* Notre Dame: University of Notre Dame Press, 1963.

Bradshaw, Paul F. *Daily Prayer in the Early Church.* New York: Oxford University Press, 1982.

Brand, Eugene L. *The Rite Thing.* Minneapolis: Augsburg Publishing House, 1970.

Brown, Edgar S., Jr., ed. *Liturgical Reconaissance*. Papers presented at the Inter-Lutheran Consultation on Worship, February 10–11, 1966, Chicago, Illinois. Philadelphia: Fortress Press, 1968.

Bruggink, Donald J., and Droppers, Carl H. *Christ and Architecture*. Grand Rapids: William B. Eerdmans, 1965.

Brunner, Peter. *Worship in the Name of Jesus*. Trans. M. H. Bertram. St. Louis: Concordia Publishing House, 1968.

Canons and Decrees of the Council of Trent. Trans. H. J. Schroeder. St. Louis: B. Herder Book Co., 1941.

Casel, Odo. *The Mystery of Christian Worship*. Ed. Burkhard Neunheuser. London: Darton, Longman and Todd, 1962.

Church Liturgy for Evangelical Lutheran Congregations of the Unaltered Augsburg Confession. St. Louis: Concordia Publishing House, 1881.

Cithara Sanctorum, Pisne Duchovini (Tranoscius). 2d American ed. Pittsburgh: Slavia Printing Company, 1928.

Clarke, William Kemp Lowther, and Harris, Charles, eds. *Liturgy and Worship: A Companion to the Prayer Books of the Anglican Communion*. London: Society for the Promotion of Christian Knowledge; New York: Macmillan, 1932.

Colman, J. Barry. *From Pentecost to the Protestant Revolt. Vol. 1. Readings in Church History*. New York: Newman Press, 1960.

Commission on Theology and Church Relations. *The Theology and Practice of the Lord's Supper*. St. Louis: The Lutheran Church—Missouri Synod, 1983.

———. *Women in the Church: Scriptural Principles and Ecclesial Practice*. St. Louis: The Lutheran Church—Missouri Synod, 1985.

Concordia Triglotta: Die symbolischen Bücher der evangelisch-lutherischen Kirche. St. Louis: Concordia Publishing House, 1921.

Constitution on the Sacred Liturgy of the Second Vatican Council and the Motu Proprio of Pope Paul VI, The. Glen Rock, N.J.: Paulist Press, 1964.

Contemporary Worship 2: Services, The Holy Communion. Prepared by the Inter-Lutheran Commission on Worship. Minneapolis: Augsburg Publishing House; Philadelphia: Board of Publication of the Lutheran Church in America; St. Louis: Concordia Publishing House, 1970.

Contemporary Worship 6: The Church Year Calendar and Lectionary. Prepared by the Inter-Lutheran Commission on Worship. Minneapolis: Augsburg Publishing House; Philadelphia: Board of Publication of the Lutheran Church in America; St. Louis: Concordia Publishing House, 1973.

Convention Proceedings of The Lutheran Church—Missouri Synod.

Convention Workbooks of The Lutheran Church—Missouri Synod.

BIBLIOGRAPHY

Cooke, Bernard. *Ministry to Word and Sacraments: History and Theology.* Philadelphia: Fortress Press, 1976.

Cross, F. L. *The Oxford Dictionary of the Christian Church.* 2d ed. London: Oxford University Press, 1974.

Dallen, James. "A Decade of Discussion on the Reform of Penance, 1963-1973: Theological Analysis and Critique." S.T.D. diss., Catholic University of America, 1976.

_____. *The Reconciling Community: The Rite of Penance.* New York: Pueblo, 1986.

Davidson, James. *A Dictionary of Protestant Church Music.* Metuchen, New Jersey: Scarecrow Press, 1975.

Davies, J. Gordon, ed. *The Westminster Dictionary of Worship.* Philadelphia: Westminster Press, 1972.

_____. *The New Westminster Dictionary of Liturgy and Worship.* Philadelphia: Westminster Press, 1986.

Deiss, Lucien. *Springtime of the Liturgy.* Trans. Matthew J. O'Connell. Collegeville: The Liturgical Press, 1979.

Deutsches Gesangbuch fur die Evangelish-Lutherische Kirche in den Vereinigten Staaten. Philadelphia: L. A. Wollenweber, 1849.

Dix, Gregory. *The Shape of the Liturgy.* Westminster: Dacre Press, 1945.

Douglas, Mary Tew. *Natural Symbols: Explorations in Cosmology.* New York: Pantheon, 1970.

Drummond, Andrew L. *German Protestantism Since Luther.* London: Epworth Press, 1951.

Dugmore, Clifford William. *The Influence of the Synagogue Upon the Divine Office.* Rev. ed. Westminster: Faith Press, 1964.

Durken, Daniel, ed. *Sin, Salvation and the Spirit.* Collegeville, Minn.: Liturgical Press, 1979.

Edwards, O. C. *Elements of Homiletic.* New York: Pueblo Publishing House, 1984.

Egge, Mandus A., ed. *Worship: Good News in Action.* Minneapolis: Augsburg Publishing House, 1973.

Elert, Werner. *Eucharist and Church Fellowship in the First Four Centuries.* Trans. N. E. Nagel. St. Louis: Concordia Publishing House, 1966.

_____. *The Structure of Lutheranism.* Trans. Walter A. Hansen. St. Louis: Concordia Publishing House, 1962.

Eller, Vernard. *In Place of Sacraments.* Grand Rapids: Eerdmans, 1972.

Empereur, James. *Worship: Exploring the Sacred.* Washington, D.C.: Pastoral Press, 1987.

Enchiridion Symbolorum: Definitionum et Declarationum de Rebus Fidei et Morum. Ed. Henricus Benzinger and Adolfus Schonmetzer. 33d ed. Rome: Herder, 1965.

Enger, Kurt. N. "Private Confession in American Lutheranism, A Study of Doctrine, History, and Practice." Th.D. diss., Princeton Theological Seminary, 1962.

Ergang, Robert. *The Myth of the All-Destructive Fury of the Thirty Years' War.* Pocono Pines, Penn.: The Craftsmen, 1956.

Evangelical Lutheran Hymn-Book [1912]. Edition of 1930. St. Louis: Concordia Publishing House, 1930.

Evangelisches Kirchengesangbuch. Stammausgabe. Kassel: Barenreiter-Verlag, [1950].

Evangelisch-Lutherisches Choralbuch fur Kirche und Haus, Sammlung der gebräuchlichsten Choräle der lutherischen Kirche ausgezogen und unverändert abgedruckt aus "Kern des deutschen Kirchengesangs von Dr. F. Layriz." St. Louis: L. Volkening, 1863.

Fagerberg, Holsten. *Bekenntnis, Kirche und Amt in der deutschen konfessionellen Theologie des 19. Jahrhunderts.* Uppsala: Almqvist och Wiksells Boktrycheri, 1952.

_____. *A New Look at the Lutheran Confessions* (1529-1537). St. Louis: Concordia Publishing House, 1972.

Fenlon, Ian, ed. *Early Music History.* Vol. 6. Cambridge: Cambridge University Press, 1986.

Fendt, Leonhard. *Der lutherische Gottesdienst des 16. Jahrhunderts: Sein Werden und Sein Wachsen.* Munich: Reinhardt, 1923.

Ferguson, Marilyn. *The Aquarian Conspiracy: Personal and Social Transformation in the 1980s.* Los Angeles: J. P. Tarcher, 1980.

Fiala, V. "Die Sündenvergebung und das lateinische Stundengebet." In *Liturgie et Remission des Peches,* 97–114. Conferences Saint-Serge, XXᵉ Semaine d'Etudes Liturgiques. Rome: Edizioni Liturgiche, 1975.

Fink, Peter E., ed. *Alternative Futures for Worship,* Vol. 4, *Reconciliation.* Collegeville, Minn.: The Liturgical Press, 1987.

Fischer, E. *Zur Geschichte der evangelischen Beichte.* 2 vols. Leipzig: Dieterisch'sch Verlags-Buchhandlung, 1902–1903.

Franz, Adolph. *Die Messe im deutschen Mittelalter.* Darmstadt: Wissenschaftliche Buchgesellschaft, 1963.

Franzmann, Martin H. *Follow Me: Discipleship According to Saint Matthew.* St. Louis: Concordia Publishing House, 1961.

Frischmann, Charles, ed. *The Psalmody for the Day.* 3 vols. Philadelphia: Fortress Press, 1974–1975.

BIBLIOGRAPHY

Fritz, John H. C. *Pastoral Theology: A Handbook of Scriptural Principles*. St. Louis: Concordia Publishing House, 1932.

Gallen, John, ed. *Christians at Prayer*. Notre Dame: University of Notre Dame Press, 1977.

Gehrke, Ralph. *Planning the Service: A Workbook for Pastors, Organists, and Choirmasters*. St. Louis: Concordia Publishing House, 1961.

Gerhard, Johann. *Ausführliche schriftmäszige Erklärung der beiden Artikel von der heiligen Taufe und dem heiligen Abendmahl*. Jena: Tobias Steinmann, 1610; Berlin: Gustav Schlawitz, 1868.

Giertz, Bo. *Kristi Kyrka*. Stockholm: Svenska Kyrkans Diakonestyrelis Bokforlag, 1939.

Gelineau, Joseph. *The Grail/Gelineau Psalter*. Ed. J. Robert Carroll. Chicago: G.I.A. Publications, 1972.

Gotsch, Herbert. "The Organ in the Lutheran Service of the 16th Century." *Church Music* 67/1: 7–12.

Graff, Paul. *Geschichte der Auflösung der alten gottendiestlichen Formen in der evangelischen Kirche Deutschlands*. 2d rev. ed. 2 vols. Göttingen: Vandenhoeck und Ruprecht, 1939.

Green, Lowell C. "The Use of Psalms in the Liturgical Hours." *Church Music* 76/1: 28–36.

Grime, Paul. "The Use of the Nunc Dimittis in the Liturgy of the Eucharist. S.T.M. diss., Concordia Theological Seminary, Fort Wayne, Ind., 1986.

Guidelines. Submitted by the Commission on Worship of the Wisconsin Evangelical Lutheran Synod, 1982.

Gunstone, J. *The Liturgy of Penance*. London: Faith Press, 1966.

Halter, Carl, and Schalk, Carl, eds. *A Handbook of Church Music*. St. Louis: Concordia Publishing House, 1978.

Hanser, C. J. Otto, compiler. *Licht des Lebens, Ein Jahrgang von Evangelien Predigten von C. F. W. Walther*. St. Louis: Concordia Publishing House, 1905.

Hardeland, August. *Geschichte der speziellen Seelsorge in der vorreformatorischen Kirche der Reformation*. Berlin: Reuther und Reichard, 1896.

Harms, Klaus. *Die gottesdienstliche Beichte als Abendmahlsvorbereitung in der evangelischen Kirche, ihre Geschichte und Gestalt*. Greifswald: Bamberg Verlag, 1930.

Hatchett, Marion. *Commentary on the American Prayer Book*. New York: Seabury Press, 1980.

Hebart, Siegfried. *Wilhelm Löhe's Lehre von der Kirche ihrem Amt und Regiment*. Neuendettelsau: Freimund Verlag, 1939.

Hedegard, David. *Seder R. Amram Gaon*, Part I. Lund: A. B. Ph. Lindstedts Universitets-bokhandel, 1951.

Heiler, Friedrich. *Die Ostkirchen*. Munich and Basel: Ernst Reinhardt Verlag, 1971.

Hellwig, Monica. *Sign of Reconciliation and Conversion*. Wilmington: Glazier, 1982.

Herrlin, Olof. *Divine Service: Liturgy in Perspective*. Trans. Gene L. Lund. Philadelphia: Fortress Press, 1966.

Heydt, Johann Daniel von der. *Geschichte der evangelischen Kirchenmusik in Deutschland*. Berlin: Trowitzsch & Sohn, 1926.

Hitchcock, James. *Recovery of the Sacred*. New York: Seabury Press, 1974.

Hoelter, H. F., ed. *Choralbuch*. Eine Sammlung der gangbarsten Choräle der evang.-lutherischen Kirche, meist nach Dr. Fr. Layriz, nebst den wichtigsten Sätzen. St. Louis: Lutherischer Concordia-Verlag, 1886.

Hoon, Paul W. *The Integrity of Worship*. Nashville: Abingdon Press, 1971.

_____. *The Three Days: Parish Prayer in the Paschal Triduum*. Chicago: Liturgical Training Publications, 1981.

Huffmann, Walter C., and Stauffer, S. Anita. *Where We Worship*. St. Louis: Concordia Publishing House, 1987.

Jacobs, Henry Eyster. *A History of the Evangelical Lutheran Church in the United States*. New York: Christian Literature Co., 1893.

Jagger, P. J. *Christian Initiation, 1552-1969*. London: Society for the Promotion of Christian Knowledge, 1970.

Janzow, F. Samuel; Bunjes, Paul; Hillert, Richard; and Schalk, Carl. *The Hymns of Martin Luther*. St. Louis: Concordia Publishing House, 1978–82.

Jasper, R. C. D., and Cuming, G. J., eds. *Prayers of the Eucharist: Early and Reformed*. 3d rev. ed. New York: Pueblo Publishing Co., 1987.

Jenny, Markus. "Kirchenlied, Gesangbuch und Kirchenmusik." *In Martin Luther und die Reformation in Deutschland: Ausstellung zum 500. Geburtstag Martin Luthers Veranstaltet vom Germanischen Nationalmueseum Nuernberg in Zusammenarbeit mit dem Verein für Reformations-geschichte*, p. 293. Frankfurt am Main: Insel Verlag, 1983.

Jeremias, Joachim. *The Eucharistic Words of Jesus*. Trans. Norman Perrin. New York: Charles Scribner's Sons, 1966.

_____. *The Lord's Prayer*. Trans. John Reumann. Philadelphia: Fortress Press, 1964.

_____. *The Origins of Infant Baptism*. Trans. Dorothea M. Barton. London: SCM Press, 1963.

John Paul II, Pope. *Reconciliato et Paenitentia*. Washington, D.C.: United States Catholic Conference.

Jones, Cheslyn; Wainwright, Geoffrey; and Yarnold, Edward, eds. *The Study of Liturgy*. New York: Oxford University Press, 1978.

BIBLIOGRAPHY

Jungmann, Joseph A. *The Early Liturgy to the Time of Gregory the Great*, trans. Francis A. Brunner. Notre Dame: Notre Dame University Press, 1959.

_____. *Die lateinischen Bussriten in ihrer geschichtlichen Entwicklung*. Innsbruck: Fel. Rauch, 1932.

_____. *The Mass of the Roman Rite*. Trans. Francis A. Brunner. 2 vols. New York: Benziger Brothers, 1951, 1955.

_____. *The Mass*. Collegeville, Minn.: Liturgical Press, 1976.

_____. *Missarum Sollemnia*. 2 vols. Wien: Herder, 1949.

Kalb, Friedrich. *Theology of Worship in 17th Century Lutheranism*. Trans. Henry P. A. Hamann. St. Louis: Concordia Publishing House, 1965.

Kavanagh, Aidan. *Elements of Rite: A Handbook of Liturgical Style*. New York: Pueblo Publishing Co., 1982.

_____. *The Shape of Baptism: The Rite of Christian Initiation*. New York: Pueblo Publishing Co., 1978.

Kelly, J. N. D. *Early Christian Creeds*. 3d ed. London: Longman, 1972.

Kirchen-Agende für Evangelisch-Lutherische Gemeinden ungeänderter Augsburgischer Confession. Zusammengestellt aus den alten rechtgläubigen Sächsischen Kirchenagenden und herausgegeben von der Allgemeinen deutschen Evangel.-Lutherischen Synode von Missouri, Ohio und anderen Staaten. St. Louis: Druckerei der Deutschen Ev.-Luth. Synode v. Missouri, 0. u. a. St., 1856.

Kirchenbuch für den evangelischen Gottesdienst der Königlich Sächsischen Lande. Dresden: in der Königlichen Hofbuchdruckerei, 1812.

Kirchengesangbuch für evangelisch-lutherische Gemeinden ungeänderter Augsburgischer Confession, darin des seligen D. Martin Luthers und andere geistreichen Lehrer gebräuchlichste Kirchen-Lieder enthalten sind. New York: Gedruckt für die Herausgeber bei H. Ludwig. In Verlag der deutschen evang. luth. Gemeinde A.C. in St. Louis, Mo., 1847.

Klausner, Theodor. *A Short History of the Western Liturgy*. Trans. John Halliburton. New York: Oxford University Press, 1969.

Klein, Laurentius. *Evangelisch-Lutherische Beichte*. Paderborn: Verlag Bonifacius, 1961.

Kliefoth, Theodor F. D. *Liturgische Abhandlungen*. [Acht Bücher von der Kirche.] Schwerin: Verlag der Stillerschen Hof-Buchhandlung, 1854–1861.

Klos, Frank W. *Confirmation and First Communion*. Minneapolis: Augsburg Publishing House; Philadelphia: Board of Publication of the Lutheran Church in America; St. Louis: Concordia Publishing House, 1968.

Koch, Eduard Emil. *Geschichte des Kirchenlieds und Kirchengesangs der christlichen, insbesondere der deutschen evangelischen Kirche.* 3d ed. 8 vols. Stuttgart: Chr. Belser'chen Verlagshandlung, 1866–71.

Koenker, Ernst. *Worship in Word and Sacrament.* St. Louis: Concordia Publishing House, 1959.

Krauth, C. P. *The Conservative Reformation and Its Theology.* Minneapolis: Augsburg Publishing House, 1963.

Krodel, Gottfried G. "The Great Thanksgiving of the Inter-Lutheran Commission on Worship: It is the Christians' Supper and Not the Lord's Supper." *The Cresset: Occasional Paper 1.* Valparaiso, Ind: Valparaiso University Press, 1977.

Lackmann, Max. *Wie beichten Wir?* 2d ed. Güütersloh: Evangelischer Verlag, 1950.

Lamb, John Alexander. *The Psalms in Christian Worship.* London: Faith Press, 1962.

Lang, Paul H. D. *What an Altar Guild Should Know.* St. Louis: Concordia Publishing House, 1964.

Layriz, Friedrich. *CXVII geistliche Melodien meist aus dem 16. und 17. Jahr. in ihren ursprünglichen Rhythmen zweistimmig gesetzt.* Erlangen: Theodor Bläsing, 1839.

———. *Geistlich Melodien meist aus dem 16. und 17. Jahr. in ihren ursprünglichen Tönen und Rhythmen zum Gebrauche für Schule und Haus zweistimmig gesetzt.* Erstes Hundert. 2d rev. ed. Erlangen: Theodor Bläsing, 1848. Zweites hundert. 2d ed. Erlangen: Theodor Bläsing, 1850.

———. *Kern des deutschen Kirchengesangs.* Eine Sammlung von CC. Chorälen, meist aus dem 16. und 17. Jahrhundert in ihren ursprünglichen Tönen und Rhythmen mit alterthümlicher Harmonie, vierstimmig zum Gebrauch in Kirche und Haus. 4 vols. Nördlingen: C. H. Beck'sche Buchhandlung, 1844–1855.

Lea, H. C. *History of Auricular Confession and Indulgences.* New York: Lea Bros., 1896.

Leaver, Robin A., ed. *Latimer Studies 16: Language and Liturgy.* Oxford: Latimer House, 1984.

Lenski, R. C. H. *The Interpretation of the Epistles of St. Peter, St. John and St. Jude.* Columbus, Ohio: Wartburg Press, 1945.

———. *The Interpretation of St. John's Gospel.* Columbus, Ohio: Lutheran Book Concern, 1942.

———. *The Interpretation of St. Paul's First and Second Epistle to the Corinthians.* Columbus, Ohio: Wartburg Press, 1946.

BIBLIOGRAPHY

Letts, Harold C., ed. *The Lutheran Heritage, Christian Social Responsibility.* Philadelphia: Muhlenberg Press, 1957.

Leube, Hans. *Die Reformideen in der deutschen lutherischen Kirche zur Zeit der Orthodoxie.* Leipzig: Verlag von Dörfling und Francke, 1924.

Lewis, C. S. *Letters to Malcolm: Chiefly on Prayer.* New York: Harcourt, Brace, and World, 1964.

Liber Sacramentorum Romanae Aeclesiae Ordinis Anni Circuli. Ed. L. C. Mohlberg. Rome: Herder, 1960.

Liber Usualis Missae Et Officii. New York: J. Fischer & Bro., 1947.

Lietzmann, Hans. *Die Didache mit kritischen Apparat.* 6th ed. Berlin: Verlag Walter de Gruyter, 1962.

Lindberg, Carter. *The Third Reformation?* Philadelphia: Fortress Press, 1983.

Lindemann, Herbert. *New Mood in Lutheran Worship.* Minneapolis: Augsburg Publishing House, 1971.

Liturgical Homilies of Narsai, The. Trans. R. H. Connolly. Cambridge: Cambridge University Press, 1909.

Liturgy and Agenda. Abr. ed. St. Louis: Concordia Publishing House, 1918.

Löhe, Wilhelm. *Agende für christliche Gemeinden des Lutherischen Bekenntnisses.* Nördlingen: C. H. Beck'sche Buchhandlung, 1853.

_____. *Gesammelte Werke.* 7 vols. Ed. Klaus Ganzert. Neuendettelsau: Freimund Verlag, 1951–1985.

_____. *Three Books about the Church.* Trans. and ed. James Schaaf. Philadelphia: Fortress Press, 1969.

Luther, Martin. *Dr. Martin Luther's Small Catechism.* Rev. ed. St. Louis: Concordia Publishing House, 1989.

_____. *Martin Luther's Werke.* Kritische Gesamtausgabe. Ed. J. K. F. Knaake, G. Kaverau, et al. Weimar: Herman Bohlau, 1883–.

_____. *Luther's Works.* American Edition. 55 vols. St. Louis: Concordia Publishing House; Philadelphia: Fortress Press, 1955–1986.

Lutheran Book of Worship. Prepared by the churches participating in the Inter-Lutheran Commission on Worship. Minneapolis: Augsburg Publishing House; Philadelphia: Board of Publication, Lutheran Church in America, 1978.

Lutheran Hymnal, The. Authorized by the Synods constituting The Evangelical Lutheran Synodical Conference of North America. St. Louis: Concordia Publishing House, 1941.

Lutheran Worship. Prepared by the Commission on Worship of The Lutheran Church—Missouri Synod. St. Louis: Concordia Publishing House, 1982.

Lutheran Worship: Accompaniment for the Liturgy. St. Louis: Concordia Publishing House, 1982.

Lutheran Worship: Agenda. Prepared by the Commission on Worship of The Lutheran Church—Missouri Synod. St. Louis: Concordia Publishing House, 1984.

Lutheran Worship: Altar Book. Prepared by the Commission on Worship of The Lutheran Church—Missouri Synod. St. Louis: Concordia Publishing House, 1982.

Lutheran Worship: Little Agenda. Prepared by the Commission on Worship of The Lutheran Church—Missouri Synod. St. Louis: Concordia Publishing House, 1985.

Mahrenholz, Christhard. *Kompendium der Liturgik.* Kassel: Johannes Stauda Verlag, 1963.

Marquart, Kurt E.; Stephenson, John R.; and Teigen, Bjarne W., eds. A *Lively Legacy: Essays in Honor of Robert Preus.* Fort Wayne: Concordia Theological Seminary, 1985.

Martimort, Aimé Georges, ed. *The Church at Prayer: An Introduction to the Liturgy.* Vol. II: *The Eucharist* and vol. IV: *Liturgy and Time.* New ed. Trans. Matthew J. O'Connell. Collegeville: Liturgical Press, 1986.

McNeill, John T., and Gamer, Helene M. *Medieval Handbooks of Penance.* New York: Columbia University Press, 1938.

Mehrstimmiges Choralbuch zu dem "Kirchengesangbuch für Evangelisch-Lutherische Gemeinden Ungeänderter Augsburgischer Confession." Edited by Karl Brauer. St. Louis: Concordia Publishing House, 1888.

Menzel, Robert K. "Messengers of Peace." Mimeographed. Preaching-Teaching-Reaching Mission to Ministers, Los Angeles, 1958.

Meuser, Fred W., and Schneider, Stanley D., eds. *Interpreting Luther's Legacy.* Minneapolis: Augsburg Publishing House, 1969.

Meyer, Carl S., ed. *Moving Frontiers: Readings in the History of The Lutheran Church—Missouri Synod.* St. Louis: Concordia Publishling House, 1964.

Meyer's Commentary on the New Testament. Trans. from the 3d ed. Paton J. Gloag, D. B. Greene, Clark H. Irwing. American ed. Timothy Dwight. New York: Funk and Wagnalls, 1887.

Migne, J. P., ed. *Patrologia: Patres Latini.* Paris: n.p., 1874.

Mishnah, The. Ed. H. Danby. London: Oxford University Press, 1933.

Mortimer, R. C. *The Origins of Private Penance.* Oxford: Clarendon Press, 1939.

Müller, Karl Ferdinand, and Blankenburg, Walter, eds. *Leiturgia: Handbuch des evangelischen Gottesdienstes.* 4 vols. Kassel: Johannes Stauda Verlag, 1952–1961.

BIBLIOGRAPHY

_____, ed. *Musicologica et Liturgica*. Kassel: Barenreiter Verlag, 1960.

Nicum, J. *Geschichte des evangelisch-lutherischen Ministeriums vom Staate New York und angrenzenden Staaten und Laendern*. Verlag des New York-Ministeriums, 1888.

Nocent, Adrian. *The Liturgical Year*. 4 vols. Trans. Matthew J. O'Connell. Collegeville, Minn.: The Liturgical Press, 1977.

O'Connell, J. B. *Church Building and Furnishing: The Church's Way*. Notre Dame: University of Notre Dame Press, 1955.

Oakley, T. P. *English Penitential Discipline and Anglo-Saxon Law in Their Joint Influence*. New York: Columbia University Press, 1923.

Ohl, J. F. "The Liturgical Deterioration of the Seventeenth and Eighteenth Centuries." In *Memoirs of the Lutheran Liturgical Association*. Ed. Luther D. Reed. 7 vols. in 1. Pittsburg: The Association, 1906.

Orsy, Ladislas. *The Evolving Church and The Sacrament of Penance*. Denville, N.J.: Dimension Books, 1978.

Oxford Universal Dictionary. 3d ed., rev. Oxford: Oxford University Press, 1955.

Palmer, Paul F., ed. *Sacraments and Forgiveness*. Westminster, Md.: Newman Press, 1959.

Patrick, Millar. *The Story of the Church's Song*. Rev. by James Rawlings Sydnor. Richmond, Va.: John Knox Press, 1962.

Pelikan, Jaroslav. *The Vindication of Tradition*. New Haven and London: Yale University Press, 1984.

Periodicals

Beiträge zur sächsischen Kirchengeschichte.

Christian News.

Christian Century.

Christianity Today.

Church Music.

Concordia Journal.

Concordia Theological Monthly.

Concordia Theological Quarterly.

Cresset, The.

Currents in Theology and Mission.

Dialog: A Journal of Theology.

Forum Letter.

Irish Theological Quarterly, The.

Journal of Ecumenical Studies.

Lehre und Wehre.

Liturgy.

Lutheran Education.

Lutheran Quarterly, The.

Lutheran Witness, The.

Lutheran World.

Lutheran Worship Notes.

Lutheraner, Der.

Hymn, The.

Maison-Dieu.

Monatschrit für Gottesdienst und kirchliche Kunst.

Musik und Kirche.

Partners.

Quartalschrift.

Response.

Studia Liturgica.

Theologische Literaturzeitung.

Theologische Quartalschrift.

Una Sancta.

Worship.

Petrich, Roger. *Psalm Antiphons for the Church Year.* Philadelphia: Fortress Press, 1979.

Pfatteicher, Philip, and Messerli, Carlos R. *Manual on the Liturgy: Lutheran Book of Worship.* Minneapolis: Augsburg Publishing House, 1979.

Pieper, Francis. *Christian Dogmatics.* 3 vols. St. Louis: Concordia Publishing House, 1951.

Piepkorn, Arthur Carl. *The Survival of the Historic Vestments in the Lutheran Church after 1555.* St. Louis: Concordia Seminary, 1956.

_____. *What the Symbolical Books of the Lutheran Church Have to Say About Worship and the Sacraments.* St. Louis: Concordia Publishing House, 1952.

Planck, Oskar. *Evangelisches Beichtbüchlein.* Stuttgart: F. S. Steinkopf Verlag, 1957.

Plass, Ewald M. *What Luther Says: An Anthology.* 3 vols. St. Louis: Concordia Publishing House, 1959.

Plummer, Alfred. *A Critical and Exegetical Commentary on the Second Epistle of St. Paul to the Corinthians.* Edinburgh: T. & T. Clark [reprint, 1951].

BIBLIOGRAPHY

Polack, W. G. *Handbook to the Lutheran Hymnal.* St. Louis: Concordia Publishing House, 1942.

Porter, H. Boone, Jr. *The Biblical and Liturgical Meaning of Sunday: The Day of Light.* Washington, D.C.: Pastoral Press, 1987.

Poschmann, Bernard. *Penance and the Anointing of the Sick.* Trans. and rev. Francis Courtney. New York: Herder and Herder, 1964.

Precht, Fred L. "Changing Theologies of Private and Public Confession and Absolution." Th.D. diss., Concordia Seminary, St. Louis, 1965.

_____. *Handbook to Lutheran Worship.* St. Louis: Concordia Publishing House, 1992.

Prenter, Regin. *Spiritus Creator.* Trans. John M. Jensen. Philadelphia: Muhlenberg Press, 1953.

Preus, Robert, and Rosin, Wilbert, ed. *A Contemporary Look at the Formula of Concord.* St. Louis: Concordia Publishing House, 1978.

Rauschen, G. *Eucharistie und Bussakrament in den ersten sechs Jahrhunderten der Kirche.* Freiburg im Breisgau: Herdersche Verlagshandlung, 1910.

Reed, Luther D. *The Lutheran Liturgy.* Rev. ed. Philadelphia: Muhlenberg Press, 1959.

_____. *Worship.* Philadelphia: Muhlenberg Press, 1959.

Reich, Philipp. *Das Wochenlied.* Kassel und Basel: Barenreiter-Verlag, 1952.

Religion in Geschichte und Gegenwart, Die. Ed. Kurt Galling. 3d ed. 3 vols. Tuebingen: J. C. B. Mohr, 1957–1965.

Rendtorff, Franz M. *Die Geschichte des christlichen Gottesdienstes unter dem Geschichtspunct der liturgischen Erbfolge.* Giessen: Töpelmann, 1914.

Report and Recommendations of the Special Hymnal Review Committee (May 1978). The Lutheran Church—Missouri Synod, 500 North Broadway St. Louis, Mo.

Repp, Arthur C. *Confirmation in the Lutheran Church.* St. Louis: Concordia Publishing House, 1964.

Reynolds, William J., and Price, Milburn. *A Survey of Christian Hymnody.* Carol Stream, Ill.: Hope Publishing Company, 1987.

Richardson, C., ed. *Library of Christian Classics.* 24 vols. Philadelphia: Westminster Press, 1953–1966.

Richter, Aemelius L., ed. *Die evangelischen Kirchenordnungen des sechszehnten Jahrhunderts.* 2 vols. Weimar: Landindustriecomptoir, 1846.

Rietschel, Georg. *Lehrbuch der Liturgik.* 2 vols. Berlin: Reuther and Reichard, 1900, 1909. 2d ed. Paul Graff. Göttingen: Vandenhoeck und Rupprecht, 1951.

Rigaux, Bida. "Lier et delier. Les ministeres de reconciliation dans l' eglise des temps apostoliques." *Maison-Dieu* 117 (1974): 86–135.

Rites of the Catholic Church as Revised by the Second Vatican Council, The. Study ed. English trans. the International Commission on English in the Liturgy. New York: Pueblo, 1976, 1983.

Rordorf, Willi. *The Eucharist of the Early Christians.* New York: Pueblo Publishing Co., 1978.

_____. *Sunday: The History of the Day of Rest and Worship in the Earliest Centuries of the Christian Church.* Philadelphia: Westminster Press, 1968.

Roth, Eric. *Privatbeichte und Schlüssel-gewalt in der Theologie der Reformation.* Gütersloh: C. Bertelsmann Verlag, 1952.

Routley, Erik. *Christian Hymns Observed: When in Our Music God is Glorified.* Princeton: Prestige Publications, 1982.

_____. "*The Lutheran Hymnal,* 1941: A Report to the Inter-Lutheran Commission on Worship." Mimeographed. 1968.

Sacrorum Conciliorum Nova et Amplissima Collectio. 53 vols. in 57. Paris: Hubertus Welter, 1901–27.

St. Louis. Commission on Worship. Minutes of the Inter-Lutheran Commission on Worship.

St. Louis. Commission on Worship. Minutes of the Commission on Worship of The Lutheran Church—Missouri Synod.

St. Louis. Concordia Historical Institute. Transcript of minutes of Trinity Congregation, St. Louis, Mo.

Sasse, Hermann. *This is My Body.* Minneapolis: Augsburg Publishing House, 1959.

_____. *We Confess Jesus Christ.* Trans. Norman E. Nagel. St. Louis: Concordia Publishing House, 1984.

_____. *We Confess the Church.* St. Louis: Concordia Publishing House, 1986.

_____. *We Confess the Sacraments.* Trans. Norman Nagel. St. Louis: Concordia Publishing House, 1985.

Schalk, Carl. *The Hymn of the Day and Its Use in Lutheran Worship.* Church Music Pamphlet Series. St. Louis: Concordia Publishing House, 1983.

_____, ed. *Key Words in Church Music.* St. Louis: Concordia Publishing House, 1978.

_____. *The Pastor and the Church Musician: Thoughts on Aspects of a Common Ministry.* Church Music Pamphlet Series. St. Louis: Concordia Publishing House, 1984.

_____. *The Roots of Hymnody in The Lutheran Church—Missouri Synod.* Church Music Pamphlet Series. St. Louis: Concordia Publishing House, 1965.

Schlink, Edmund. *The Doctrine of Baptism.* Trans. Herbert J. A. Bouman. St. Louis: Concordia Publishing House, 1972.

Schlombs, Wilhelm. *Die Entwicklung des Beichtstuhls in der katholischen Kirche.* Düsseldorf: L. Schwann, 1965.

Schmitz, Herman Josef. *Die Bussbücher und die Bussdisciplin der Kirche.* 2 vols. Graz: Akademische Druck-U. Verlagsanstalt, 1883 [reprint, 1958].

Schoeberlein, Wilhelm. *Schatz des liturgischen Chor- und Gemeindegesangs nebst den Altarweisen in der deutschen evangelischen Kirche.* 3 vols. Göttingen: Vandenhoeck & Ruprecht's Verlag, 1865–1872.

Schöne, Jobst. *Ich bekenne: Eine Beichthilfe für evangelische-lutherische Christen.* Ülzen: Feste-Burg Verlag, 1963.

Schweitzer, Julius. *Ways of Worship.* New York: Harper Brothers, 1951.

Searle, Mark, ed. *Sunday Morning: A Time for Worship.* Collegeville, Minn.: The Liturgical Press, 1982.

Seasoltz, R. Kevin. *New Liturgy, New Laws.* Collegeville: Liturgical Press, 1980.

Seebase, F. *Johann Christoph Blumhardt, Sein Leben und Wirken mit einer Auswahl seiner Schriften.* Hamburg: Wittig, 1949.

Sehling, Emil, ed. *Die evangelischen Kirchenordnungen des XVI. Jahrunderts.* 15 vols. Vols. I–V, Leipzig: 0. R. Reisland, 1902–1913; vols. VI–XV, Tubingen: J. C. B. Mohr, 1955–1977.

Senn, Frank C. *Christian Worship and Its Cultural Setting.* Philadelphia: Fortress Press, 1983.

_____. *The Pastor As Worship Leader: A Manual for Corporate Worship.* Minneapolis: Augsburg Publishing House, 1977.

Service Book of the Holy Eastern Orthodox Catholic and Apostolic Church. 3d ed. Brooklyn, N.Y.: Syrian Antiochian Orthodox Diocese, 1960.

Shaughnessy, James D., ed. *The Roots of Ritual.* Grand Rapids, Mich.: Eerdman's, 1973.

Shepherd, Massey H., Jr., ed. *The Liturgical Renewal of the Church.* New York: Oxford University Press, 1960.

_____. *The Psalms in Christian Worship.* Minneapolis: Augsburg Publishing House, 1976.

Simcoe, Mary Ann, ed. *The Liturgy Documents: A Parish Resource.* Rev. ed. Chicago: Liturgy Training Publications, 1985.

Snyder, H. A., and Runyon, D. V. *Foresight: 10 Major Trends That Will Dramatically Affect the Future of Christians and the Church.* New York: Nelson, 1986.

Sovik, E. A. *Architecture for Worship.* Minneapolis: Augsburg Publishing House, 1973.

Spener, Philip Jacob. *Pia Desideria.* Trans. and ed. Theodore G. Tappert. Philadelphia: Fortress Press, 1964.

_____. *Theologische Bedencken.* 4 vols. Halle: Verlegung des Waysenhauses, 1712–1717.

Spinks, Bryan. *Luther's Liturgical Criteria and His Reform of the Canon of the Mass.* Bramcote, Notts.: Grove Books, 1982.

Spitz, Lewis, and Lohff, Wenzel, eds. *Discord, Dialogue, and Concord.* Philadelphia: Fortress Press, 1977.

Stahlin, Wilhelm. "Bruderschaft." *In Kirche im Aufbau,* Vol. 9. Kassel: Johannes Stauda Verlag, 1940.

Stauffer, Ethelbert. *New Testament Theology.* Trans. John Marsh. New York: Macmillan, 1955.

Steffens, D. H. *Doctor Carl Ferdinand Wilhelm Walther.* Philadelphia: Lutheran Publication Society, 1917.

Steinberg, S. H. "The Thirty Years War: A New Interpretation." In *The Making of Modern Europe.* Ed. Herman Ausubel. New York: Macmillan, 1951.

Stiller, Guenther. *Johann Sebastian Bach and the Liturgical Life in Leipzig.* Trans. Herbert J. A. Bouman, Daniel Poellot, and Hilton C. Oswald. St. Louis: Concordia Publishing House, 1984.

Svenska Kyrko-Handboken. . .1942. Stockholm: Svenska Kyrkans Diakonistyrelsses Bokförlag, 1956.

Taft, Robert F. *The Great Entrance.* Rome: Institutum Studiorum Orientalium, 1975.

_____. *The Liturgy of the Hours in East and West.* Collegeville, Minn.: The Liturgical Press, 1986.

Teigen, Bjarne Wollan. *The Lord's Supper in the Theology of Martin Chemnitz.* Brewster, Mass.: Trinity Lutheran Press, 1986.

Telfer, W. *The Forgiveness of Sins.* London: S.C.M., 1959.

Tentler, Thomas N. *Sin and Confession on the Eve of the Reformation.* Princeton: Princeton University Press, 1977.

Thomas, Paul, ed. *Choral Settings for the Hymn of the Day.* St. Louis: Concordia Publishing House, 1984.

_____. *The Psalms for the Church Year.* 12 vols. St. Louis: Concordia Publishing House, 1982.

BIBLIOGRAPHY

Thompson, Bard. *Liturgies of the Western Church*. Cleveland: World Publishing Company, 1961.

Turner, Victor W. *The Ritual Process*. Ithaca: Cornell University Press, 1969.

Uhsadel, Walter. *Evangelische Beichte in Vergangenheit und Gegenwart*. Gütersloh: Gerd Mohn, 1961.

Van Gennep, A. *The Rites of Passage*. Chicago: University of Chicago Press, 1960.

Van Loon, Ralph. *Parish Worship Handbook*. Philadelphia: Parish Life Press, 1979.

Vokes, C. F. *The Riddle of the Didache*. London: Society for Promoting Christian Knowledge, 1938.

Voll, Dieter. *Catholic Evangelicalism*. Trans. Veronica Ruffer. London: Faith Press, 1963.

Vööbus, Arthur. *Liturgical Traditions in the Didache*. Stockholm: Estonian Theological Society in Exile, 1968.

Vorgrimler, Herbert. *Busse und Krankensalbung*. Freiburg: Herder und Herder, 1978.

Wagner, C. Peter. *What Are We Missing?* Carol Stream, Ill.: Creation House, 1973.

Walhof, Karen, ed. *Worship Blueprints*. Minneapolis: Augsburg Publishing House, 1979–.

Walther, Carl Ferdinand Wilhelm. *Americanisch-Lutherische Evangelien Postille, Predigten über die evangelischen Perikopen des Kirchenjahrs*. St. Louis: Concordia Publishing House, n.d.

_____. *Americanisch-Lutherische Pastoraltheologie*. 4th ed. St. Louis: Concordia Publishing House, 1897.

_____. *The Proper Distinction Between Law and Gospel*. Trans. W. H. T. Dau. St. Louis: Concordia Publishing House, [1928].

_____. *Die rechte Unterscheidung von Gesetz und Evangelium*. St. Louis: Concordia Publishing House, 1901.

_____. *Die Stimme unserer Kirche in der Frage von Kirche und Amt*. Erlangen: C. A. Blaesing, 1852.

Wasserschleben, F. W. H. *Die Bussordnungen der abendlandischen Kirche*. Graz: Akademische Druck-U. Verlagsanstalt, 1851 [reprint, 1958].

Webb, Geoffrey. *The Liturgical Altar*. Westminister, Md.: Newman Press, 1949.

Webber, Robert, and Bloesch, Donald, eds. *The Orthodox Evangelicals*. New York: Thomas Nelson, 1978.

Wedgwood, C. V. *The Thirty Years' War*. Garden City: Doubleday, 1961.

Western District of The Lutheran Church—Missouri Synod. *Proceedings,* 1961.

White, James F. *Introduction to Christian Worship.* Nashville: Abingdon Press, 1980.

_____. *Protestant Worship and Church Architecture.* New York: Oxford University Press, 1964.

Wilkinson, John. *Egeria's Travels to the Holy Land.* Jerusalem: Ariel Publishing House, 1981.

Wisloff, Carl. *The Gift of Communion.* Trans. Joseph Shaw. Minneapolis: Augsburg Publishing House, 1964.

Worship Supplement. Authorized by the Commission on Worship, The Lutheran Church—Missouri Synod and Synod of Evangelical Lutheran Churches. St. Louis: Concordia Publishing House, 1969.

[Zwingli] *Huldyrich Zwingli: Writings.* Trans. H. W. Pipkin. 2 vols. Allison Park, Pennsylvania: Pickwick, 1984.

Index

Note: Some topics and people who are mentioned pervasively in this volume are not cited each time they appear. Instead, they are usually cited in connection with a particular topic (e.g., Luther in connection with absolution). Also, certain items (e.g., the various parts of the Divine Service; LW; TLH; etc.) are as a rule indexed only when they are actually discussed in their own right, and not every time they appear in the volume.

SUBJECT INDEX

INDEX

INDEX

601

INDEX

INDEX

INDEX

SCRIPTURE INDEX

637

LUTHERAN CONFESSIONS